Juvenile Delinquency

Juvenile Delinquency

EIGHTH EDITION

Clemens Bartollas
University of Northern Iowa

Frank Schmalleger
Emeritus, University of North Carolina at Pembroke

Prentice Hall
Boston Columbus Indianapolis New York San Francisco Upper Saddle River
Amsterdam Cape Town Dubai London Madrid Milan Munich Paris Montreal Toronto
Delhi Mexico City Sao Paulo Sydney Hong Kong Seoul Singapore Taipei Tokyo

Editorial Director: Vernon Anthony
Acquisitions Editor: Eric Krassow
Development Editor: Elisa Rogers
Editorial Assistant: Lynda Cramer
Director of Marketing: David Gesell
Marketing Manager: Adam Kloza
Senior Marketing Coordinator: Alicia Wozniak
Marketing Assistant: Les Roberts
Senior Managing Editor: JoEllen Gohr
Project Manager: Jessica H. Sykes
Senior Operations Supervisor: Pat Tonneman
Senior Art Director: Diane Ernsberger
Text and Cover Designer: Ilze Lemesis
Manager, Visual Research: Beth Brenzel
Photo Researcher: Truitt and Marshall

Manager, Rights and Permissions: Zina Arabia
Image Permission Coordinator: Cynthia Vincenti
Manager, Cover Visual Research & Permissions: Karen Sanatar
Cover Art: ARTLIFE
Media Editor: Michelle Churma
Lead Media Project Manager: Karen Bretz
Full-Service Project Management: Janet Bolton
Composition: S4Carlisle Publishing Services
Printer/Binder: Edwards Brothers
Cover Printer: Lehigh-Phoenix Color/Hagerstown
Text Font: Sabon LT Std

Library of Congress Cataloging-in-Publication Data
Bartollas, Clemens.
    Juvenile delinquency / Clemens Bartollas, Frank Schmalleger.—8th ed.
        p. cm.
    Includes bibliographical references and index.
    ISBN-13: 978-0-13-505261-7
    ISBN-10: 0-13-505261-0
    1. Juvenile delinquency—United States.   2. Juvenile justice, Administration of—United States.   3. Juvenile delinquency—United States—Prevention.
4. Juvenile delinquents—Rehabilitation—United States.   I. Schmalleger, Frank.   II. Title.
    HV9104.B345 2011
    364.360973—dc22

                                                                    2010001272

10   9   8   7   6   5   4   3   2   1

Prentice Hall
is an imprint of

www.pearsonhighered.com

ISBN-10:   0-13-505261-0
ISBN-13: 978-0-13-505261-7

Brief Contents

Contents

Preface

What Is New in This Edition?

Overall, the eighth edition has a number of features that make it different from previous editions:

- As authors, we have made a particular attempt to make this edition more accessible and student-friendly. We have summarized materials and studies; as a result, it is about 15% smaller than previous editions. At the same time, we expanded our use of summary statements, line art, and tables. At the end of each chapter, there are three new learning vehicles for students: Review Questions, Discussion Questions, and Group Exercises.

- Most chapters build on the theme of delinquency across the life course, which is one of the most important theoretical developments in delinquency studies in the past 20 years.

- Most chapters contain integrated materials on delinquency and social policy where a vital question is posed: What can be done about the delinquency issues raised in this chapter?

- Data have been updated throughout the text, including juvenile court statistics, data on the co-occurrence of substance abuse behaviors in youth, juvenile offense data, and statistics from the *Monitoring the Future* study. Statistical updates from the Federal Bureau of Investigation, the Bureau of Justice Statistics, and the Office of Juvenile Justice and Delinquency Prevention have also been incorporated into the text.

- The number and types of boxes have been reduced, resulting in a streamlined text that is easier to comprehend.

- A number of new Exhibit boxes throughout the text highlight the changing nature of delinquency in America and the juvenile justice system's response.

Chapter 1

This chapter now has a section on youth culture and a discussion titled "Promise of Positive Youth Development (PYD)," an alternative approach to working with troubled youths. Chapter 1 also includes new information on the co-occurrence of substance abuse behaviors in youth.

Chapter 2

Validity and reliability of data are considered for each type of measurement of official and unofficial youth crime. There is also more concern about comparing the findings of the various types of measurement data. The section on Delinquency across the Life Course extends the dimensions of youth crime to include youth crime and adult criminality and length of criminal career along with age of onset, escalation of offenses, specialization of offenses, and chronic offenders. Data on delinquency offenses have been updated using new information from the FBI and the Bureau of Justice Statistics, along with new federal juvenile court statistics.

Chapter 3

The chapter on different individual causes of delinquency presents more contemporary findings on biological and psychological causes, and cognitive theory is now discussed. There is also the attempt to provide more contemporary longitudinal findings of delinquent behavior. In addition, there is a section on the importance of theory as well as a social policy section examining what Positive Youth Development (PYD) offers to policy makers as well as to those who study delinquency.

Chapter 4

Two needed additions to this chapter are updating Shaw and McKay with findings from social ecology and adding institutional anomie theory developed by Steven Messner and Richard Rosenfeld.

Chapter 6

There is a new major section to this chapter on restorative justice and peacemaking.

Chapter 7

There is an expanded discussion of gender differences between males and females and how they affect delinquency. A new section on female delinquency is now included in the chapter.

Chapter 9

There is more extensive coverage of bullying in this chapter than previously. A revised list of indicators of school crime and safety from the U.S. Departments of Education and Justice is provided.

Chapter 10

Several sections of this chapter, including the one on urban gangs, have been reorganized.

Chapter 11

National data on adolescent drug use has been updated throughout, and the most recent results from the Monitoring the Future study are presented.

Chapter 12

This chapter focuses on prevention and includes a new section on the victimization of children.

Chapter 13

This chapter (as the previous one) has been greatly reorganized. In the section titled "Trends for the Future," it now also includes the discussion of such topics as the expanding use of restorative justice, the increased use of technology, and the greater use of evidence-based practice principles and approaches in juvenile justice.

Chapter 15

This chapter now includes a section on graduated sanctions as well as a proposal for juvenile courts of excellence. Although the material on the death penalty and juveniles has been removed because of the 2005 U.S. Supreme Court decision *Roper* v. *Simmons*, a new concern is the sentencing of 13- and 14-year-olds to life without parole.

In late 2006, the nation's police chiefs, mayors, and other government officials met in Washington, D.C., to participate in a National Violent Crime Summit. Although violent crime had been dropping for almost a decade, officials at the meeting talked about new FBI statistics that may presage the end of that decline and a resurgence in some forms of violence—especially violent crime by juveniles. The central topic of concern was "a growing trend of teenagers shooting robbery victims even if they surrender their valuables."* Cincinnati Police Chief Thomas Streicher gave voice to what many others already knew: "There's almost a different code on the streets, that it's not a robbery unless you shoot somebody."

Juvenile delinquency—crimes committed by young people—constitutes, by recent estimates, nearly one-third of the property crimes and one-sixth of all crimes against

---

*Richard Willing, "Violent Crime on the Rise, Summit Participants Say," *USA Today*, August 31, 2006, p. 5A.

persons in the United States. Not only does the relatively high incidence of juvenile crime make the study of juvenile delinquency vital to any understanding of American society today, but special kinds of violent offenses—such as gang killings tied to perceived slights or imagined signs of disrespect—are on the upswing. Los Angeles Police Chief William Bratton, one of the attendees at the Washington summit, told meeting participants, "Crime is coming back, and it has a new and troubling element—a youthful population that is largely disassociated from the mainstream of America."

Clemens Bartollas and Frank Schmalleger, who were classmates and friends at The Ohio State University during their Ph.D. studies, have joined together to coauthor this eighth edition of Bartollas's well-known text, *Juvenile Delinquency*. The authors believe that students and instructors alike will find the following features especially helpful in understanding delinquency today and in preparing society to deal with it:

- *Strong sociological focus throughout the text*. The root causes of delinquency, along with the environments in which it either flourishes or is discouraged—including family, school, peers, and community—receive major emphasis. Each chapter includes a theme of delinquency across the life course, which is one of the most promising and exciting perspectives in the study of delinquency. This theme helps students understand how delinquent behavior originates and then either continues and evolves into adult criminality or terminates.

   Each chapter also addresses social policy and what can be done about the particular problem of delinquency that is the focus in that chapter.
- *Special attention to desistance, which dovetails with the examination of behavior across the life course*. Some individuals persist in antisocial behavior throughout life, whereas others make the decision to end their involvement in antisocial behavior and become law-abiding citizens. This book helps to identify what young people in given circumstances are likely to do.
- *Emphasis on the important roles that gender, race, social class, and place of residence play in the formative adolescent years*. Specifically, Chapter 7 examines gender and delinquency while race and ethnicity receive attention in Chapter 13.
- *Discussion of gangs and gang activity*. Gangs, an increasingly important aspect of juvenile offending, are given special coverage, with significant discussion of groups such as Mara Salvatrucha, or MS-13.
- *Substantial policy-oriented analyses*. In the midst of national soul-searching about what to do with serious and repeat juvenile offenders, nearly every chapter of this text offers policy recommendations on prevention and suggests possible treatment interventions.

Organization of the Text

This text is divided into four parts: The Nature and Extent of Delinquency, The Causes of Delinquency, The Environmental Influences on and the Prevention of Delinquency, and The Juvenile Justice System.

- Part 1 explores how delinquent behavior affects the larger society and reports on the measurement of the nature and extent of delinquency by examining the available statistical tools.
- Part 2 looks at four types of explanations for delinquent behavior: (1) individual causes, ranging from free will to biological and psychological positivism; (2) social structural factors; (3) social process factors; and (4) social interaction theories.
- Part 3 examines the relationship between delinquency and gender; problems in the family, such as child neglect and abuse; experiences in the school; peer and gang delinquency; and drug abuse. It also looks at the issue of preventing delinquency and some programs aimed at delinquency prevention.
- Part 4 includes an overview of the juvenile justice process, police–juvenile relations, the juvenile court, and juvenile corrections.

Special Features

This text contains a number of special features that students should find especially helpful in understanding juvenile delinquency, including its causes, consequences, deterrence, prevention, and treatment:

- **Themes and boxes.** This book builds on three exciting themes: social context of delinquency, delinquency across the life course, and delinquency and social policy. Two types of boxes are also used in this text, including Juvenile Law boxes and individually titled exhibits.
- **Marginal glossary terms and a comprehensive end-of-book glossary.** Key terms and their definitions are found throughout the book in the margins, and a comprehensive end-of-book glossary makes it easy for students to learn the terminology used by professionals who work with delinquents. The glossary incorporates selected terms adapted from the FBI's *Uniform Crime Reporting Handbook*, the *Juvenile Court Statistics* report series, and the Census of Juveniles in Residential Placement. The National Center for Juvenile Justice's *State Juvenile Justice Profiles* was also influential in determining the content of selected definitions.
- **Web features.** An outstanding assortment of Web-based resources complements the text; they are found in the margins or at the end of chapters for ease of access. Included here are MyCrimeKit features such as *Library Extras* and *Web Extras*. Library Extras consist of documents found on the Web that are available as supplements to the discussions in the text. Library Extras documents include publications from the Office of Juvenile Justice and Delinquency Prevention (OJJDP), the National Institute of Justice (NIJ), the federal office of Community Oriented Policing Services (COPS), and the National Institute on Drug Abuse (NIDA), as well as articles from some of the field's most notable journals. Web Extras consist of websites of special relevance to the study of juvenile delinquency and include sites such as the Office of Juvenile Justice and Delinquency Prevention, the Child Trends Databank, the Child Welfare Information Gateway of the U.S. Department of Health and Human Services, the National Youth Gang Center, the American Bar Association, the National Library of Medicine, and the Centers for Disease Control and Prevention.

Supplements

A carefully designed supplements package supports the aims of *Juvenile Delinquency* and provides both instructors and students with a wealth of support materials to ensure success in teaching and in learning.

Instructor Resources

- **Instructor's Manual and Test Bank.** Each chapter in the Instructor's Manual contains lecture outlines, teaching tips, and student activities. Each chapter in the Test Bank includes a multitude of different types of questions as well as an answer key.
- **TestGen EQ Computerized Testing Program.** This computerized version of the Test Bank is available with Tamarack's easy-to-use TestGen software, which lets you prepare both print and online tests. It provides full editing capability for Windows and Macintosh.
- **Blackboard and WebCT Test Item Files.** Both of these popular online learning platforms are available for use with the text.
- **PowerPoint Lecture Presentations.** This complete set of PowerPoint presentations contains approximately 20 slides per chapter, specific to the text, to reinforce the text's central ideas.

To access supplementary materials online, instructors need to request an instructor access code. Go to www.pearsonhighered.com/irc, where you can register for an instructor access code. Within 48 hours after registering, you will receive a confirming e-mail, including an instructor access code. Once you have received your code, go to the site and log on for full instructions on downloading the materials you wish to use.

Student Resources

- **MyCrimeKit—www.mycrimekit.com.** This interactive and instructive multimedia resource can be used either as a supplement to the traditional lecture course or as a stand-alone online course. MyCrimeKit features multimedia, practice quizzes, web quests, key-term flashcards, career information, and access to the Cybrary. Geared to meet the teaching and learning needs of every professor and student, MyCrimeKit is a valuable tool for any classroom setting.

A Special Supplement: *Voices of Delinquency*

Voices of Delinquency contains 26 real-life stories that range from those told by children who quickly turned their delinquent behavior around during their adolescent years and then lived exemplary lives as adults to those related by delinquents who committed serious crimes such as murder and who are now serving life in prison (one of these stories comes from an individual who is presently on death row). These fascinating and sometimes very sad stories reveal how the theoretical explanations in this textbook apply to the actual life experiences of delinquents. This supplement is available on MyCrimeKit, and particular stories are referred to throughout the text.

Acknowledgments

Many individuals have made invaluable contributions to this text. Foremost, we would like to thank our wives, Linda Dippolid Bartollas and Harmonie Star-Schmalleger. At the University of Northern Iowa, we would like to express our appreciation to Wayne Fauchier and Gloria Hadachek, who in various ways helped to keep the manuscript moving. Thanks to the following reviewers: Felix Brooks Jr., Western Michigan University; Julia Glover Hall, Drexel University; Jeri Kirby, West Virginia University; Jiletta Kubena, Sam Houston State University; David Levine, Florida Atlantic University; Ruth X. Liu, San Diego State University; David Musick, University of Northern Colorado; John Paitakes, Seton Hall University; Beverly Quist, Mohawk Valley Community College; and Jennifer L. Schulenberg, Sam Houston State University.

Clemens Bartollas, Ph.D., is Professor of Sociology at the University of Northern Iowa. He holds a B.A. from Davis and Elkins College, a B.D. from Princeton Theological Seminary, an S.T.M. from San Francisco Theological Seminary, and a Ph.D. in sociology, with a special emphasis in criminology, from The Ohio State University. Dr. Bartollas taught at Pembroke State University from 1973 to 1975, at Sangamon State University from 1975 to 1980, and at the University of Northern Iowa from 1981 to the present. He has received a number of honors at the University of Northern Iowa, including Distinguished Scholar, the Donald McKay Research Award, and the Regents' Award for Faculty Excellence.

Dr. Bartollas, like his coauthor, is also the author of numerous articles and more than 30 books, including previous editions of *Juvenile Delinquency* (Allyn & Bacon, 2006), *Juvenile Justice in America* (with Stuart J. Miller; Prentice Hall, 2011), and *Women and the Criminal Justice System* (with Katherine Stuart van Wormer; Prentice Hall, 2011).

Frank Schmalleger, Ph.D., is Distinguished Professor Emeritus at the University of North Carolina at Pembroke. He holds an undergraduate degree from the University of Notre Dame and both the master's (1970) and doctoral (1974) degrees, with special emphasis in sociology, from The Ohio State University. From 1976 to 1994, he taught criminology and criminal justice courses at the University of North Carolina at Pembroke; for the last 16 of those years, he chaired the university's Department of Sociology, Social Work, and Criminal Justice. The university named him Distinguished Professor in 1991.

Dr. Schmalleger has taught in the online graduate program of the New School for Social Research, helping to build the world's first electronic classrooms in support of distance learning through computer telecommunications. As an adjunct professor with Webster University in St. Louis, Missouri, Dr. Schmalleger helped develop the university's graduate programs in administration of justice as well as security administration and loss prevention and taught courses in those curricula for more than a decade. A strong advocate of Web-based instruction, Dr. Schmalleger is also the creator of numerous award-winning websites.

Dr. Schmalleger is the author of numerous articles and more than 30 books, including the widely used *Criminal Justice Today* (Prentice Hall, 2011), *Criminal Justice: A Brief Introduction* (Prentice Hall, 2010), *Criminology Today* (Prentice Hall, 2009), *Criminology: A Brief Introduction* (Prentice Hall, 2011), *Criminal Law Today* (Prentice Hall, 2010), and *Corrections in the Twenty-First Century* (with John Smykla; McGraw-Hill, 2010). He is also founding editor of the journal *Criminal Justice Studies* and has served as imprint adviser for Greenwood Publishing Group's criminal justice reference series. Visit the author's website at www.schmalleger.com.

Juvenile Delinquency

The Nature and Extent of Delinquency

The study of juvenile delinquency is vitally important today, just as it was in the 1930s when sociologist Clifford R. Shaw first began using case studies to explore this exciting field. Later, Henry D. McKay, with colleagues at the University of Chicago, helped Shaw develop what became known as the Chicago Area Projects. In the Area Projects, which thrived throughout Chicago for 50 years, local neighborhoods took responsibility for the problems of youths, including juvenile crime.

Contemporary studies examine delinquency from the same three perspectives that brought focus to the work of Shaw and McKay, and in this text, we use specific headings in each chapter to denote these three perspectives. The first perspective—social context of delinquency—reminds us that the study of delinquency is about the environments of delinquents, young people who frequently have disruptive home lives, struggle through school, become involved with troubled peers, and make poor decisions along the way. The second perspective—delinquency across the life course—focuses on such factors as what the extent and scope of delinquency is over the span of adolescents' lives. Finally, we magnify our approach to delinquency through the lens of the social policy perspective—delinquency and social policy—which is concerned with how we can prevent and control delinquent behavior.

Our first chapter examines delinquency within the larger framework of adolescence. In this chapter, both delinquent and status offenses are defined, and attention is given to how the behavior of status offenders differs from that of delinquents. The chapter then turns to how delinquents have been perceived and handled in the United States, from colonial times to the present.

Our second chapter analyzes the measurement of delinquent behavior. Chapter 2 also expands on the concept of delinquency across the life course—one of the central themes of this text.

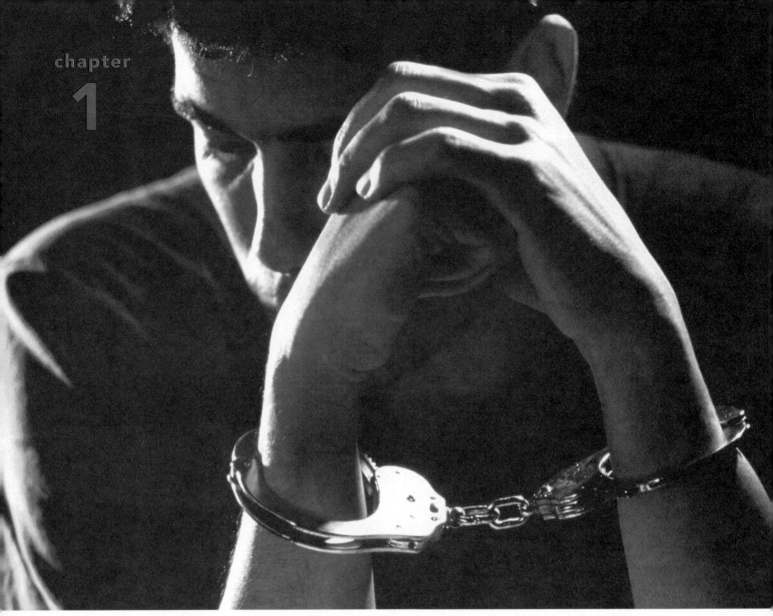

Adolescence and Delinquency

CHAPTER OBJECTIVES

After reading this chapter, you should be able to answer the following questions:

- Who are those adolescents most likely to become delinquent?
- Are adolescents treated the same now as in the past?
- What problem behaviors characterize adolescence?
- What group receives the benefits of the least restrictive approach?
- What is a status offense?
- How have delinquents been handled throughout history?
- What are the major themes of this text?

The future promise of any nation can be directly measured by the present prospects of its youth.

—President John F. Kennedy,
February 14, 1963

Introduction

Four boys who were students at Winslow Township High School in New Jersey were arrested in April 2006 and foiled in a plot that was reminiscent of the April 1999 shootings at Columbine High School in Colorado.

Teased for wearing "Goth" clothing, the Winslow boys had compiled a hit list of 25 students, teachers, and other community members. But unlike in the Columbine massacre, none of the boys actually procured firearms and no one was hurt.

The plotters, ages 14 to 16 at the time, were initially charged as terrorists under the PATRIOT Act, the federal antiterrorism law enacted after the attacks of September 11, 2001. But eventually all four were found guilty of one charge, conspiracy to possess a firearm for an unlawful purpose.

Edwin DeLeon, age 15 at the time of the plot and said to be its mastermind, and his accomplice Peter Cunningham, age 16 at the time, were sentenced to six years and five years in prison, respectively. The two other accomplices, ages 14 and 15, were expected to serve up to three years in a juvenile detention facility.

"I regret ever thinking of this idea," DeLeon said at his sentencing. "I didn't mean for it to get out of hand like it did. I'm sorry to those people I hurt and whose families I put in worry." The plot shook the school. One girl who never missed classes "became too scared to go to school for several days afterward," a Winslow resident said.

The cases "send a strong message to anyone considering entering into such a plot that the matter will be dealt with seriously," said acting Camden County Prosecutor James P. Lynch.[1]

In this illustration, a serious incident appears to have been prevented. Communities, however, are increasingly finding themselves having to react to juvenile offenses that might have been prevented by effective proactive measures. People are most concerned about violent crime. The victims of violent juveniles are often those youths' parents, peers, or teachers—the people the violent youths perceive to be the causes of their problems. Consequently, even though homicides committed by juveniles are near a year low, they still garner a lot of media attention. A few recent news bites, for example, include the following: A 15-year-old Boy Scout was charged with killing his parents and two younger brothers; he shot them while they slept.[2] In Georgia, a 17-year-old boy was charged with killing his mother, a local sheriff's deputy, and his two small sisters, one of whom (4 years old) was the daughter of rapper juvenile Anthony Tyrone Terrell Jr.[3] The best friend of a Chicago vocational student was charged with involuntary manslaughter; he was playing with a gun, which fired and killed his friend. This was the third student in this vocational high school who was violently killed in the last two months.[4] A 9-year-old girl was accused of stabbing her 11-year-old friend to death in a tussle over a ball.[5]

The focus of this book is **juvenile delinquency**. The juvenile court codes in every state define what constitutes delinquency and the conditions under which the state can legitimately intervene in a juvenile's life. To bring the subject of delinquency into clearer focus, this chapter places it in the broader context of adolescence and the narrow context of those adolescents who are youths at risk. High-risk children can be further divided into delinquents and status offenders, which is what is discussed next. The chapter then examines how juvenile delinquents have been handled from the past to the present and concludes with presenting three themes that will be examined throughout the text.

Adolescence is a term that refers to the life interval between childhood and adulthood. In fact, prior to the 1930s, the concept of adolescence or teenager did not exist.

juvenile delinquency An act committed by a minor that violates the penal code of the government with authority over the area in which the act occurs.

adolescence The life interval between childhood and adulthood; usually the period between the ages of 12 and 18 years.

The term has been used in the last few decades to mark a new stage of human growth and development, but there is no agreed-on way to pinpoint this period chronologically or to restrict it within physiological boundaries; for purposes of discussion in this chapter, however, adolescence is considered to be the years between ages 12 and 18 years. Within this transitional period, youngsters experience many biological changes and develop new attitudes, values, and skills that they will carry into their young adult years.

Delinquency and other problem behaviors increase during the adolescent years for several reasons. These years bring increasing freedom from parental scrutiny, and with this freedom come more opportunities to be involved in socially unacceptable behavior. Teenagers develop new, often expensive tastes for such things as sound systems, clothing, automobiles, and alcohol, yet legitimate means for satisfying these desires are often not available. The lengthening of adolescence in U.S. culture has further expanded the crises and struggles of this life period, thereby increasing the chance of problems with the law, at school, and in the home. In addition, there is often a mismatch between adolescents' needs and the opportunities provided them by their social environment.[6] Finally, in some cases, the unmet needs and frustrations of early childhood fester into socially unacceptable behavior in later years.

Changing Treatment of Adolescents

Adolescence, as a term describing a particular stage of human growth and development, evolved out of the modern notion of childhood. The concept of childhood, as reflected in today's child-centered culture, is a relatively recent phenomenon.[7] Much of recorded history reveals abuse and indifference to be the fate of many children. Lloyd de Mause, an American social thinker known for his work in the field of psychohistory, depicted childhood historically as a time when children were "killed, abandoned, beaten, terrorized, and sexually abused"; he prefaced this statement by saying, "The history of childhood is a nightmare from which we have only recently begun to awaken."[8]

The end of child labor was one of the watersheds in the development of modern adolescence. Throughout history, children have worked, but until the Industrial Revolution their work was usually done within or around the house, often outdoors. As work moved from the home to the factory, children were considered a source of cheap labor. It was not unusual for them to work in the worst of conditions for 16 hours a day, six days a week.[9] Until the child labor laws were actually enforced, children as young as ages 4 and 5 worked in mines, mills, and factories. But with advancing technology and mechanization, children and adolescents were no longer needed in the labor market, and by 1914, every state but one had passed laws prohibiting the employment in industry of children under a certain age, generally 14.

Another important stage in the development of modern adolescence was compulsory public schooling. As Chapter 9 discusses, nineteenth-century U.S. schools were violent and chaotic places in which teachers attempted to maintain control over unmotivated and unruly children, sometimes using brutal disciplinary methods. The Progressive education movement arose partly because of the dissatisfaction of some elements of society with the schools. The influence of John Dewey and other Progressive educators encouraged individualism and personal growth in the classroom. Compulsory education laws also evolved from early-twentieth-century social and religious views, which held that adolescents should be kept in school because they needed guidance and control.

A further stage in the development of modern adolescence was the development in the twentieth century of the belief that raising children had less to do with conquering their spirits than with training and socializing them (see Library Extra 1.1). Parents in the United States, especially since the 1940s, have emphasized a helping relationship, attempting to meet their children's expanding needs in a democratic and supportive environment. An additional stage in this development took place in the 1960s and 1970s when special legal protections for juveniles were granted, highlighting the perception of adolescents as needing special attention, guidance, and

Library Extra 1.1

National Institute of Justice (NIJ) publication: *A Century of Juvenile Justice*

A young girl watches as people receive monthly food handouts distributed by the Imperial Valley Food Bank on March 13, 2009, in El Centro, California. Poverty increases the risk of illness and delinquency among children and decreases the likelihood that they will receive quality education or find suitable employment later in life. ▶ **What other risk factors increase with lower income levels?**

support. Psychologist Erik H. Erikson has observed, "Childhood is the model of all oppression and enslavement, a kind of inner colonization, which forces grown-ups to accept inner repression and self-restriction."[10] A chief reason for the repression of childhood, according to Erikson and others, is the lack of rights given to young people. The children's rights movement, which encompasses a spectrum of approaches, became popular in the 1970s as a means to compensate for young people's lack of rights. Consensus also increased on what components are thought necessary for an adolescent to achieve responsible adulthood:

- Search for self-identity.
- Search for a personal set of values.
- Acquisition of competencies necessary for adulthood, such as problem solving and decision making.
- Acquisition of skills necessary for social interaction.
- Attainment of emotional independence from parents.
- Ability to negotiate between the need for personal achievement and the need for peer acceptance.
- Need to experiment with a wide variety of behaviors, attitudes, and activities.[11]

In sum, the concept of adolescence centers on a set of beliefs that emerged during the late nineteenth and twentieth centuries. These beliefs have had the result of removing young people from the employment world and the mainstream of society. This process of lengthening childhood and delaying adult responsibilities was strongly influenced not only by humanitarian considerations but also by major economic, social, and political forces in society.

Youth Culture

A youth culture, which has emerged in recent decades in the United States and other nations, can be defined as the unique beliefs, behaviors, and symbols that represent young people in society; how, when, what, where, and whom they interact with is part of this culture. A primary feature of youth culture is the incorporation of trends or fads.[12] A youth culture has distinctive clothing styles, hairstyles, behaviors, footwear, and interests. Vehicles such as cars, motor scooters, motorcycles, skateboards, and surf boards, as well as video games, have played central roles in the development of youth culture. As will be discussed in future chapters, the features of youth cultures vary by class, gender, race, and ethnicity.

Body piercing—often multiple piercings for both males and females in literally every part of the body, including the tongue, eyebrows, lips, cheeks, navel, genitals, and breasts—and tattooing are widely found among some youth cultures today. Ritual scarification and 3D-art implants are popular, and so are stretching and cutting of the genitals, scrotal implants, transdermal implants, tooth art, and facial sculpture.[13]

Adolescents have always been connected to their peers, but they are now connected at all times of the day, texting in class or in the middle of the night. In addition to constant communication, adolescents are also joining online groups or communities, posting numerous self-portraits, creating their own Facebook or MySpace layouts. The groups, or subcultures, that adolescents join include youth gangs or street gangs and social or informal groups in school. Another subculture is hip-hop, which is made up of rapping, urban art/tagging (graffiti), and break dancing.[14]

Youths at Risk

The population of children in the United States is increasing and becoming more racially and ethnically diverse. In 2007, there were approximately 73.9 million children, ages newborn to 17 years, in the United States. There were approximately equal numbers of children in each age group: 0–5 (25 million), 6–11 (24 million), and 12–17 (25 million) years of age.[15] This represented 25% of the population, which was down from a peak of 36% at the end of the baby boom in 1964.[16] The population of **juveniles**, according to the U.S. census Bureau estimate, will increase 14% between 2000 and 2025; by 2050 the juvenile population will be 36% larger than it was in 2000.[17]

juvenile A youth at or below the upper age of juvenile court jurisdiction in a particular state.

The juvenile population is also becoming more racially and ethnically diverse. In 2003, 60% of this nation's children were white, 16% were African-American, and 4% were Asian. The proportion of Hispanic children has increased faster than the other racial and ethnic groups; it grew from 9% of the population of children in 1980 to 19% in 2004.[18]

Of the 25 million adolescents (ages 12 through 17 years) in the United States, approximately one in four was at high risk of engaging in multiple problem behaviors. These behaviors, particularly committing delinquent acts and abusing drugs and alcohol, quickly bring adolescents to the attention of the juvenile justice system. Another 6 million youngsters, making up 25%, practice risky behavior but to a lesser degree and, consequently, are less likely to experience negative consequences.[19]

Noted youth researcher Nanette J. Davis said that this population of children, increasing in number and diversity, is experiencing a crisis that ranges from "the personal to the global, from the specific to the general, and from the material to the symbolic levels."[20] She added that an important feature of this crisis is that much of it is invisible. Invisible crises lurk beneath the surface of many adults' everyday lives, and they may choose not to see them, yet youths caught in crises are involved in such "structural" arrangements as the discrimination and humiliation of racism, the hazards and deprivations of poverty, the culture of violence, and the ever-present temptation of drugs and alcohol. The consequences of these crises are burgeoning youth gangs, rising homelessness among young persons, dropout rates of 50% in inner-city schools, widespread experimentation with various forms of dangerous drugs, and increasing numbers of youths sentenced to adult prisons.[21]

Davis rejected the notion that it is the youths who are the problem. Instead, she argued that the sources of the problems are within society. She hypothesized that American institutions are contributing in major ways to this youth crisis, suggesting that U.S. cultural arrangements "have made life more difficult, often impossible, much less welcoming, and certainly far less nurturing for those growing up today."[22]

The Children's Defense Fund (CDF) has argued for the past 30 years that children, especially poor and minority children and children with disabilities, are in grave crisis. This nonprofit organization seeks to educate the nation about the needs of children and to encourage preventive investment before youngsters become sick, get into trouble, drop out of school, or suffer family breakdown.[23] See Exhibit 1.1, which shows how poverty is related to the crises of so many children in our society.

In *The State of America's Children 2008*, the CDF further charged that "children in America lag behind almost all industrialized nations on key child indicators. The United States has the unwanted distinction of being worst among industrialized nations in relative child poverty, in the gap between rich and poor, in teen birth rates, and in child gun violence, and first in the number of incarcerated persons."[24] The CDF contended that it is morally and economically indefensible that the plight of African-American children is what it is in the United States:

- African-American children are more likely than white children to be sick because they are more inclined to be poor. They are more likely than white children to lack a regular source of health care, to have unmet or delayed medical care, and to have had no dental visits in the past two years. Infant mortality rates are more than twice as high for African-American infants as for white infants.
- African-American and Latino children are about three times as likely to be poor as white children. These poor children face a losing struggle with poverty throughout childhood. African-American families are more than twice as likely as whites to live in overcrowded housing. African-American fathers are twice as likely as white fathers to be unemployed.
- An African-American preschool child is three times as inclined as a white child to depend solely on a mother's earnings.
- An African-American mother is more likely to go out to work sooner, to work longer hours, and to make less money than a white mother. An African-American child is seven times more likely than a white child to be on welfare.
- An African-American child is only half as likely as a white child to grow up with parents who graduated from college.
- One out of every three African-American children attends a school with 90% enrollment of minorities. An African-American child is more than twice as likely as a white child to be suspended, expelled, and given corporal punishment. An African-American child is more likely than a white child to drop out of school, more than twice as likely to be behind a grade level or to be labeled mentally retarded, but only one-half as likely to be labeled gifted. Whites are almost three and a half times more inclined than African-Americans to take advanced placement exams. The longer an African-American child is in school, the further he or she falls behind.
- An African-American youth is twice as likely as a white youth to be unemployed. An African-American college graduate has a greater chance of being unemployed than a white high school graduate.[25]

High-Risk Behaviors

Researchers have identified several important insights into adolescence and problem behaviors (see Web Extra 1.1, Web Extra 1.2, and Library Extra 1.2). Those adolescents who have the most negative or problem-oriented factors in their lives are defined as "high risk." First, high-risk youths often experience multiple difficulties: They are frequently socialized in economically stressed families and communities, more often than not have histories of physical abuse and sexual victimization, typically have educational and vocational skill deficits, and are prone to become involved in alcohol and other drug abuse and forms of delinquency.[26] The more of these problem behaviors that are present, the more likely it is that a youth will become involved in socially undesirable behaviors (see Figure 1.2).[27] Second, adolescent problem behaviors—especially delinquent acts such as being involved in drug and alcohol abuse, failing in or dropping out of school, and having unprotected sex—are interrelated, or linked; that is, an involvement in one problem behavior is generally indicative of some

Web Extra 1.1
Office of Juvenile Justice and Delinquency Prevention (OJJDP) website

Web Extra 1.2
Youth Risk Behavior Surveillance System (YRBSS) website (part of the Centers for Disease Control and Prevention)

mycrimekit

Library Extra 1.2
OJJDP publication: *Juvenile Offenders and Victims: 2006 National Report, Chapter 1*

> > > **EXHIBIT 1.1** < < <

Welfare of U.S. Children, 2008

The Children's Defense Fund's research publication, *The State of America's Children 2008*, tells us the following:

- Every 33 seconds a baby is born into poverty, and 1 in 6 children in America is poor.
- About 1 in 13 children in the United States—5.8 million—lives in extreme poverty. Young children are more likely than school-age children to live in extreme poverty.
- Nearly a million children are abused or neglected in America.
- In 33 states and the District of Columbia, the annual cost of center-based child care for a preschooler is more than the annual tuition at a 4-year public college.
- Only about one-half to two-thirds of children eligible for Head Start are enrolled, and only about 3% of eligible infants and young children are enrolled in Early Head Start.
- Currently, 8.9 million children are uninsured.
- Approximately 7 out of 10 public school 8th-graders cannot read or do math at grade level.
- An African-American boy born in 2001 has a 1 in 3 chance, a Latino boy a 1 in 6 chance, and a white boy a 1 in 17 chance of going to prison in his lifetime.

WHY POVERTY MATTERS!

Poor children lag behind their peers in many ways beyond income: They are less healthy, trail in emotional and intellectual development, and do not perform as well in school. The challenges that poor children face accumulate and interact, casting long shadows throughout their lives. Every year that we keep children in poverty costs our nation half a trillion dollars in lost productivity, poorer health, and increased crime.

WHY HEALTH CARE MATTERS!

People who are uninsured are sicker and die sooner. The United States is the wealthiest nation in the world, yet children's health status in our country as measured by selected indicators is among the worst in the industrialized world (see Figure 1.1).

WHY EDUCATION MATTERS!

Attainment of a high school diploma is the single most effective preventive strategy against adult poverty, yet the United States has the sixth-lowest high school graduation rate in 30 industrialized market economies.

WHY ABUSE AND NEGLECT OF CHILDREN MATTER!

The annual total direct and indirect costs of child maltreatment are estimated to be nearly $104 billion. Children left with no permanent family connections or a connection with a caring adult have no one to whom they can turn for social, emotional, or financial support and face numerous barriers as they struggle to become self-sufficient adults.

WHY CRIME MATTERS!

States spend about three times as much money per prisoner as per public school pupil. Unless we focus our efforts on early intervention and prevention rather than punishment, we are robbing thousands of youths each year of their future and our country of vital human resources.

> ▶ Why is the issue of poverty so closely related to the general problem of youth crisis and the particular problem of juvenile delinquency? Why did the poor do better in the 1990s than they have in the early years of the twenty-first century? What do you believe society needs to do about the issue of poor children who seem to be getting poorer?

Source: Children's Defense Fund, *State of America's Children 2008* (Washington, D.C.: CDF, 2008). Reprinted with permission from the Children's Defense Fund.

FIGURE 1.1 Child Poverty Rates, 1959–2007

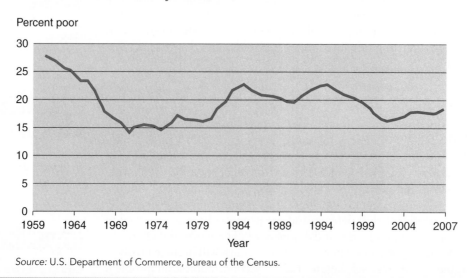

Source: U.S. Department of Commerce, Bureau of the Census.

FIGURE 1.2 Youths at Risk and Delinquency

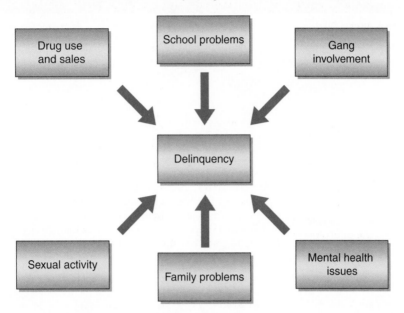

participation in other socially undesirable behaviors.[28] Third, high-risk youths tend to become involved in behaviors that contribute to unintentional injury and violence; some of these behaviors include carrying a weapon, driving when they have been drinking, riding with someone else who has been drinking, and rarely or never wearing a seat belt when driving or riding with someone else.[29]

The Program of Research on the Causes and Correlates of Delinquency (Causes and Correlates Program, which is described in more detail in Chapter 2) comprises three coordinated longitudinal projects: the Denver Youth Survey, the Pittsburgh Youth Study, and the Rochester Youth Development Study. These three projects examined the co-occurrence or overlap of delinquent behavior with drug use, problems in school, and mental health problems. Across all three study sites, the prevalence of persistent problem behaviors was usually consistent: 20–30% of males were serious delinquents, 7–22% had school problems, 14–17% used drugs, and 7–14% had mental health problems.[30]

Another study analyzed the prevalence and overlap of substance-related behaviors among youths. The central finding of this study is that given one substance-related behavior, other substance-related behaviors became much more likely. For example, among youths who reported drinking alcohol (23% of all youths ages 12–17), the level of marijuana use was 32% and the level of drug selling was 23%.[31] Table 1.1 conveys that higher levels of problem behaviors and delinquency appeared among substance users across age groups.

An alternative position is that a common factor may underlie all problem behaviors. The pursuit of this general tendency is generating considerable excitement among those interested in adolescent research.[32] John E. Donovan and Richard Jessor suggested that a common factor of "unconventionality" underlies all of these behaviors. This factor of unconventionality is measured by lower religiosity, tolerance of deviance, approval of drug abuse, peer approval of deviant behavior, more liberal views, and poor school performance.[33]

Travis Hirschi explained the relationship between drug abuse and delinquency by suggesting that the two are not merely influenced by the same factors but "are manifestations of the same thing"; this "thing" is criminality, which Hirschi defines as "the tendency or propensity of the individual to seek short-term, immediate pleasure," which provides "money without work, sex without courtship, revenge without court delays."[34] In their 1990 publication *A General Theory of Crime,* Michael R. Gottfredson and Travis Hirschi defined lack of self-control as the common factor underlying problem behaviors.[35] See Library Extra 1.3 for more information on risk factors for delinquency.

Library Extra 1.3

OJJDP publication: *Risk Factors for Delinquency: An Overview*

TABLE 1.1 Substance Abuse, by Age

Behavior	Drank Alcohol (30 days)		Used Marijuana (30 days)		Sold Drugs (ever)	
	No	Yes	No	Yes	No	Yes
Youths Ages 12–14						
Suspension from school	18%	31%	19%	46%	19%	55%
Vandalize property	13	37	14	50	14	56
Major theft	2	11	2	20	2	27
Attack/assault	8	28	9	36	9	53
Belong to a gang	1	7	1	16	1	18
Carry handgun	4	12	4	20	4	25
Arrested	2	8	3	15	2	22
Youths Ages 15–17						
Suspension from school	27%	38%	27%	52%	27%	63%
Vandalize property	10	23	11	33	11	40
Major theft	3	10	4	17	3	23
Attack/assault	8	21	10	29	9	37
Belong to a gang	1	5	1	9	1	12
Carry handgun	4	10	5	15	5	18
Arrested	5	12	5	21	5	26

Note: The time frame for "Suspension from school" was ever; for the other items, it was the past 12 months. The value in the "Yes" column differs significantly (*p*<.05) from the value in the "No" column for all column pairs within substance behavior and age groups.

Source: Carl McCurley and Howard N. Snyder, *Co-Occurrence of Substance Use Behaviors in Youth* (Washington, D.C.: Office of Juvenile Justice and Delinquency Prevention, 2008), p. 3.

Yet researchers tend to be dubious about accepting this generality of deviance hypothesis. Helene Raskin White suggested that several factors challenge the acceptability of a total generality of deviance hypothesis.[36] She stated that "the low correlations among problem behaviors indicate that the majority of the variance in one behavior is not shared with the others."[37] According to White, "Various problem behaviors follow different developmental paths; for example, delinquency peaks between ages 15 and 17 and then declines, whereas polydrug use increases through adolescence into young adulthood."[38] White's longitudinal study of males and females also revealed that the constellation of problems varied by gender and that the associations among problem behaviors over time were unstable.[39] Moreover, White reported that the "data indicate that problem behaviors do not cluster together in one homogeneous group of adolescents and the degree of overlap among problems is often low."[40] Finally, she claimed that "there are several independent influences on each behavior."[41]

Delinquency is one of the problem behaviors with which all but low-risk adolescents become involved from time to time (see Chapter 2). *Delinquency* is a legal term initially used in 1899 when Illinois passed the first law on juvenile delinquent behavior. The age at which an

Teenage boys smoking hashish. According to the Program of Research on the Causes and Correlates of Delinquency, drug use and other problem behaviors correlate with other forms of delinquency. ▶ What factors are likely to account for the relationship?

individual is considered a minor varies among states, but it is 16 or 17 years and younger in most states.

Some evidence indicates that delinquency in U.S. society is changing. Beginning in the late 1980s and extending even throughout the 1990s, adolescents participated widely in street gangs, some of which provided a base for trafficking narcotics; had rising rates of murder from 1989 through 1993; were more likely to own and use firearms than ever before; and were becoming increasingly involved in various forms of hate crimes. These trends continued throughout the first decade of the twenty-first century.

Yet the average American delinquent is far more likely to shoplift, commit petty theft, use marijuana, violate liquor laws, or destroy property than to commit a violent or serious crime. In 2007, juveniles between the ages of 10 and 17 years were arrested for 319,225 property crimes, compared with 73,427 arrests for violent crimes. In other words, juveniles were arrested for committing four and one-half times more property crimes than violent crimes.[42]

Besides committing the same crimes as adults, juveniles also are arrested for truancy, incorrigibility, curfew violations, and runaway behavior. Such offenses are called **status offenses** because they would not be defined as criminal if adults committed them. (Status offenses are discussed in more detail below.) The legal separation between status offenders and delinquents is important because of the large number of arrests each year for acts such as being truant, disobeying parents, and running away from home. The Federal Bureau of Investigation (FBI) *Crime in the United States 2007 (CUS 2007)* data (see Chapter 2) reveal that three times as many youths were arrested for status offenses as for violent crimes. This ratio between status offenses and violent crimes would be even greater if truancy and incorrigibility were included, two of the most common status offenses.

status offense A nondelinquent/noncriminal offense; an offense that is illegal for underage persons but not for adults. Status offenses include curfew violations, incorrigibility, running away, truancy, and underage drinking.

Promise of Positive Youth Development (PYD)

A different way of thinking about youth development can be found in **Positive Youth Development (PYD)**, a relatively new perspective that represents an alternative to the deficit-based approaches that dominated policy and practice throughout much of the twentieth century. The typical way of seeing adolescence is to see it as a period of turmoil and risk; when it is seen this way, the task of researchers is to identify and fix problems affecting individual youths, especially those identified as high risk. In challenging the deficit-based perspective, some researchers and practitioners have pointed out that most youths, even in the midst of multiple risk factors, manage to thrive. The term *resilience* has been used to describe the qualities that support healthy adolescent development in the face of adversity. Adolescent development began to be seen as a process sparked by the interactions that youths have with adults across such social environments as families, schools, workplaces, neighborhoods, and communities. Adolescents, in turn, are seen not as objects to be acted upon but rather as self-directed, independent individuals who may deserve special care but at the same time merit the dignity and autonomy accorded other members of the community. PYD suggests that youths can develop and flourish when they are connected to the right mix of opportunities, relationships, and social assets.[43] In addition to presenting the traditional model of juvenile justice, this text will also discuss, when applicable, PYD and the resilience of youths.

Positive Youth Development (PYD) A comprehensive way of thinking about adolescence that challenges the traditional deficit-based perspective by pointing out that youths can sometimes thrive even in the presence of multiple risk factors.

Juvenile Court Codes and Definitions of Delinquency

Juvenile court codes, which exist in every state, specify the conditions under which states can legitimately intervene in a juvenile's life. State juvenile codes, as part of the *parens patriae* philosophy of the juvenile court, were enacted to eliminate the arbitrary nature of juvenile justice beyond the rights afforded juveniles by the U.S. Constitution and to deal with youths more leniently because they were seen as not fully responsible

Juvenile Law 1.1

Definitions of Delinquency

- Violates any law or ordinance
- Violates juvenile court order
- Associates with criminal or immoral persons
- Engages in any calling, occupation, or exhibition punishable by law
- Frequents taverns or uses alcohol
- Wanders the streets in the nighttime
- Grows up in idleness or breaks curfew
- Enters or visits a house of ill repute
- Is habitually truant
- Is habitually disobedient or refuses to obey reasonable and proper (lawful) orders of parents, guardians, or custodians
- Engages in incorrigibility or is ungovernable
- Absents himself or herself from home without permission

- Persists in violating rules and regulations of school
- Endangers welfare, morals, and/or health of self or others
- Uses vile, obscene, or vulgar language (in a public place)
- Smokes cigarettes (around a public place)
- Engages in dissolute or immoral life or conduct
- Wanders about railroad yards or tracks
- Jumps a train or enters a train without authority
- Loiters or sleeps in alleys
- Begs or receives alms (or is in the street for that purpose)

▲ These definitions are taken from various state codes. Which of these definitions is most surprising to you? Are these definitions especially favorable or unfavorable to any particular economic, racial, or ethnic group? Explain your response.

for their behavior. The *In re Poff* (1955) decision aptly expresses the logic of this argument:

> The original Juvenile Court Act enacted in the District of Columbia was devised to afford the juvenile protections in addition to those he already possessed under the Federal Constitution. Before this legislative enactment, the juvenile was subject to the same punishment for an offense as an adult. It follows logically that in the absence of such legislation the juvenile would be entitled to the same constitutional guarantees and safeguards as an adult. If this is true, then the only possible reason for the Juvenile Court Act was to afford the juvenile safeguards in addition to those he already possessed. The legislative intent was to enlarge and not diminish those protections.[44]

Juvenile court codes usually specify that the court has jurisdiction in relation to three categories of juvenile behavior: delinquency, dependency, and neglect. First, the courts may intervene when a youth has been accused of committing an act that would be a misdemeanor or felony if committed by an adult. Second, the courts may intervene when a juvenile commits certain status offenses. Third, the courts may intervene in cases involving dependency and neglect; for example, if a court determines that a child is being deprived of needed support and supervision, it may decide to remove the child from the home for his or her own protection.

An examination of the various juvenile court codes, or statutes, shows the diverse definitions of delinquent behavior that have developed. Some statutes define a "delinquent youth" as a young person who has committed a crime or violated probation; others define a "delinquent child" in terms of such behaviors as "associating with immoral or vicious persons" (West Virginia) or "engaging in indecent or immoral conduct" (Connecticut).[45] A particular juvenile, then, could be considered a delinquent under some juvenile codes and not under others. The Juvenile Law 1.1 box lists behaviors that have been defined as delinquent.

Some controversy surrounds the issue of how long juveniles should remain under the jurisdiction of the juvenile court. The age at which a youthful offender is no longer treated as a juvenile ranges from 16 to 18 years. In 37 states and the District of Columbia, persons under 18 years of age charged with a law violation are considered juveniles. In 10 states, the upper limit of juvenile court jurisdiction is 16 years, and in 3 states, the upper limit is 15 years. (See Figure 1.3 for the upper age of juvenile court jurisdiction.)[46]

What Is a Status Offender?

status offender A juvenile who commits a minor act that is considered illegal only because he or she is underage.

In various jurisdictions, **status offenders** are known as minors in need of supervision (MINS), children in need of supervision (CHINS), juveniles in need of supervision (JINS), children in need of assistance (CHINA), persons in need of supervision (PINS),

FIGURE 1.3 Upper Age Limit for Defendants in Juvenile Court, 2004

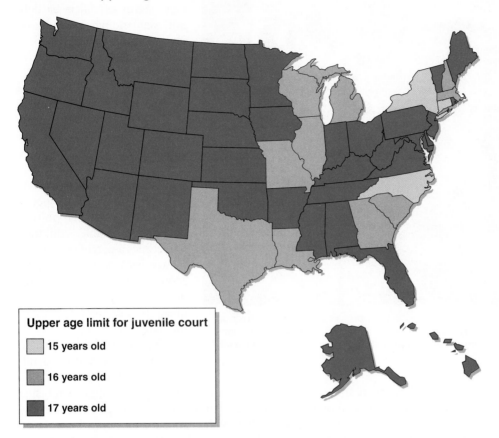

Upper age limit for juvenile court

☐ 15 years old

☐ 16 years old

■ 17 years old

Source: Howard N. Snyder and Melissa Sickmund, *Juvenile Offenders and Victims: 2006 National Report* (Washington, D.C.: Office of Juvenile Justice and Delinquency Prevention, March 2006), p. 103.

children in need of protection and services (CHIPS), or members of families in need of supervision (FINS). They also may be termed *predelinquent, incorrigible, beyond control, ungovernable,* or *wayward.* What these terms and acronyms have in common is that they view the status offender as being in need of supervision or assistance.

There are three important questions about status offenders: Why do they behave the way they do? How do status offenders differ in offense behavior from delinquents? Should the juvenile court have jurisdiction over status offenders?

Explanations for Status Offense Behavior

In an effort to determine and explain the behavior of status offenders, the authors interviewed status offenders, probation officers, juvenile judges, teachers in public schools, and institutional staff. Interviewees shared a number of insights, including descriptions of how they view the problems they are having, what the nature of parental conflicts is, and the difficulties they have in school. Those who work with this population also had a number of observations. One caveat should be mentioned: These observations are generalizations and may not apply to all offenders.[47]

Generally speaking, status offenders, many of whom come from single-parent homes, place the blame for their problems on parental figures in the home and believe that fulfilling their need for a warm, accepting, and loving relationship with their parents is not possible. They want to be loved by a parent who may not have the capacity to provide that love. Although their needs for sustenance and shelter may have been met, some have been physically or sexually abused; at the least, they feel rejected and neglected. They become resentful and angry with their parents, who may have problems in expressing physical affection, setting reasonable and consistent limits, and showing acceptance to their children. Many of these parents were abused as children, have limited parenting skills, or evince immature behaviors themselves.

Status offenses involve acts that are illegal only because of a person's age, such as smoking, drinking, or running away from home. Very few youths who commit only status offenses come in contact with the juvenile justice system. ▶ Should status offenders be treated more harshly?

The parents, in turn, often view status offenders as defiant, demanding, and obnoxious. Parents usually believe that they have no control over their children, who will not accept restrictions or limitations on their behavior, and a power struggle results. The struggle often climaxes in verbal altercations, and physical violence can erupt when the child strikes or pushes the parent. As a result, parents call the police to intervene with their abusive or unmanageable children. Sometimes a parent asks police to act because the youngster stays out very late, associates with older youths or delinquent friends, or responds to the parent with rage.

School officials and teachers tend to view status offenders, some of whom have had conflicts with teachers since kindergarten, as resistant to authority. Besides refusing to accept the limits placed on their behavior, status offenders also tend to be disruptive, disrespectful, belligerent, emotionally withdrawn or explosive, and unfocused or unconcerned. Many are psychologically tested and are found to be hyperactive or to have attention deficit disorder. They are then prescribed varying doses of medication, typically imipramine or Ritalin, to help them focus and control their emotional difficulties.

While acknowledging these psychological explanations, some theorists argue that society's response to status offenders, especially female status offenders, is a major contributing factor in defining who has this legal status. Society believes that young males should behave in a certain way, typically granting leniency for the right of "boys to be boys." Society's expectations for young females, however, are still based on the notion that "Sugar and spice and everything nice, that's what little girls are made of." University of Hawaii Women's Studies Professor Meda Chesney-Lind and Lisa J. Pasko found during their examination of the judicial handling of female status offenders that the juvenile justice system discriminates against girls because of the fear of sexual activity.[48] According to Chesney-Lind and Pasko, a double standard exists between male and female adolescents because society believes it must protect adolescent girls from the potential consequences of sexual activity. The labeling of female adolescents continues when they are victims of violence and sexual abuse at home. If they run away from these abusive environments, they are regarded as runaways and processed as status offenders. Their cycle of victimization continues as they are forced to engage in panhandling, petty theft, and sometimes prostitution to survive.[49]

Law-Breaking Behaviors of Status Offenders and Delinquents

Several conclusions can be drawn from a number of studies on the behavior of status offenders:

- Those who commit only status offenses represent a relatively small proportion of all youths who come in contact with the juvenile justice system. Most adolescents who are brought to court for status offense behavior are mixed offenders who have, at one time or another, been involved in misdemeanors and felonies as well as status offenses.[50]

■ Status offenders vary by the seriousness of their behavior. One study identified three groups: the "heavies," who are predominantly serious delinquent offenders; the "lightweights," who commit misdemeanors as well as status offenses; and the "conforming youths," who occasionally become involved in status offenses. The meaning of "status offenses," according to this study, differs for each group. For heavies, a status offense is likely to be an incidental event; for lightweights, the pattern is one of minor and intermittent delinquent acts as well as status offenses.

Conforming youths are likely to restrict themselves to multiple status offenses, perhaps as an outburst of rebellion against adult authority.[51]

■ Researchers have generally agreed, however, that the majority of status offenders do differ in offense behavior from delinquents.[52]

■ Status offenders are principally between the ages of 13 and 16 years, equally distributed between males and females, and more likely to be white than non-white.[53]

■ Little evidence exists of escalation in offense behavior; that is, those juveniles who begin their careers engaging in status offenses are not likely to graduate into more serious crime.[54] In a longitudinal study that followed more than 2,000 adolescent males, the researchers found little evidence of escalation; indeed, about two-thirds remained status offenders or never committed another offense.[55]

■ There appears to be significant differences between male and female status offenders. One study found that male status offenders' behavior was much more likely to escalate than that of females.[56]

■ Some evidence exists that those referred to the court for violations of liquor laws, truancy, and curfew are much more likely to commit more serious offenses than are runaways and incorrigibles.[57]

■ There is strong support for the fact that status offenders are less prone to recidivism than are delinquent offenders.[58]

In sum, the studies generally conclude that status offenders differ in offense behavior from delinquents, that most status offenders are not likely to escalate to more serious behavior, that the behavior of female and male status offenders is frequently different, and that status offenders are less prone to recidivism than are delinquents. Yet many status offenders are also mixed offenders who commit delinquent offenses along with status offenses.[59] See Web Extra 1.3 for research on indicators of youths' well-being.

Social Control and the Status Offender

The handling of status offenders, one of the most controversial issues in juvenile justice, has focused on two questions: Should status offenders be institutionalized with delinquents? Should the juvenile court retain jurisdiction over status offenders?

Deinstitutionalization of Status Offenders In the 1970s, the policy of confining status offenders with delinquents came under increased criticism. One disturbing finding was that before their dispositional hearing, status offenders were more likely to be detained or treated more harshly than delinquents.[60] Studies of juvenile institutionalization also show that status offenders stayed longer in training schools than did delinquents, were vulnerable to victimization in these settings, and found institutionalization with delinquents to be a destructive experience.[61]

The **Deinstitutionalization of Status Offenders (DSO) Project**, established by the **Juvenile Justice and Delinquency Prevention (JJDP) Act of 1974**, has been successful in

mycrimekit

Web Extra 1.3
Child Trends Databank (with the latest national trends and research on over 100 key indicators of child and youth well-being)

Deinstitutionalization of Status Offenders (DSO) Project A project that evaluated the effects of deinstitutionalization of status offenders in eight states and prompted a national evaluation.

Juvenile Justice and Delinquency Prevention (JJDP) Act of 1974 A federal law that established a juvenile justice office within the then-existing Law Enforcement Assistance Administration to provide funds for the prevention and control of youth crime.

encouraging states to amend laws, policies, and practices that led to secure confinement of juveniles who committed no criminal act. This act gave the juvenile justice system the impetus to no longer confine status offenders in secure detention facilities or secure correctional facilities with delinquents and also limited the placement of juveniles in adult jail facilities.[62] The DSO's core protection of the JJDP Act is premised on the belief that juveniles who exhibit problematic behavior but who have not violated the law are more properly served by social services, mental health, and community agencies and may actually be damaged by placement in secure detention or correctional institutions.[63] Following the adoption of the JJDP Act and its DSO requirement, the Office of Juvenile Justice and Delinquency Prevention (OJJDP) recorded approximately 171,581 violations of the DSO requirement; according to OJJDP's 2006 compliance monitoring reports, the number of DSO violations had dropped to 6,234.[64]

However, the 1980 reauthorization of the JJDP Act incorporated the valid court order (VCO) exception permitting states that have enacted appropriate statutes to securely detain youths who have committed a status offense and subsequently have violated a court order regarding disposition of this offense. This exception continues to be a topic of considerable discussion among juvenile justice professionals.[65]

Juvenile Court's Jurisdiction over Status Offenders   Another volatile issue is whether the juvenile court should continue to have jurisdiction over status offenders. Critics argue that the status offender statutes' lack of clarity often makes these laws blatantly discriminatory, especially in regard to gender. It is further argued that governmental bodies have no legitimate interest, or right to intercede, in many of the behaviors categorized as status offenses. Other critics contend that the juvenile court's intervention promotes rather than inhibits status offense behaviors. Many insist that status offenders represent a special class that must be treated differently from delinquents.[66]

Several states, including Maine, New York, and Washington, have decriminalized status offenses, thus removing them from the juvenile court's jurisdiction. However, the status offense legislation in Maine and Washington was partly repealed to give the juvenile courts a degree of jurisdiction, especially over abandoned, runaway, or seriously endangered children.[67]

The most broad-based movement to strip the juvenile court of jurisdiction over status offenders has taken place in New York State, heralded by the passage of the 1985 PINS Adjustment Services Act. A central goal of this legislation was to displace the family court as the institution of first choice for minor family-related matters. The PINS legislation also constructed an innovative system of its own that operates as formally as the family court. Children whose families are receptive are referred to the Designated Assessment Service (DAS), which in turn refers these youths to a community-based agency for long-term services. As long as youths are responsive to the rehabilitative programs designed for them, legal proceedings are suspended.[68]

Two boys play in the village stocks at St. Mary's Parish church in Cheshire, England. Throughout much of history, children were treated the same as adults for purposes of the law, and those who committed crimes were severely punished. ▶ **Why are children treated differently today?**

According to Barry Feld, one of the nation's leading scholars of juvenile justice and Centennial Professor of Law at the University of Minnesota Law School, juvenile court judges frequently challenge the movement to strip courts of jurisdiction over status offenders (which is called "divestiture"), charging that status offenders will have no one to provide for or protect them if they are removed from the court's jurisdiction. This argument is reinforced every time a status offender is victimized or commits a serious crime.[69]

The fact is that juvenile court personnel do have jurisdiction over the status offender because they have the option of labeling youngsters downward as dependent or neglected youths, upward as delinquent youths, or laterally as needing private mental health facilities.[70] Thus, even in states that strongly support deinstitutionalization, the juvenile court still can institutionalize status offenders by redefining them as being delinquent or as needing mental health services. A truant may be charged with a minor delinquent offense and be institutionalized in a private facility, or a court may require school attendance as a condition of probation and then define further truancy as a delinquent offense.[71] This permits the "invisible" institutionalization of status offenders in either private or public institutions.

Handling of Juvenile Delinquents

The philosopher George Santayana reminded us that "those who cannot remember the past are condemned to repeat it."[72] Many contemporary sociological interpretations of delinquency lack a sense of history. Such approaches have serious shortcomings because the history of how law-violating juveniles have been dealt with is important in understanding how delinquent youths are handled today.

The history of societal responses to juvenile delinquency in the United States can be divided into seven periods: (1) colonial period, (2) houses of refuge, (3) juvenile courts, (4) juvenile rights, (5) reform agenda, (6) social control and juvenile crime, and (7) contemporary delinquency and U.S. society.

Review Historical Treatment of Children and Juvenile Justice System

Colonial Period (1636–1823)

The history of juvenile justice in the United States actually began in the colonial period. The colonists saw the family as the source and primary means of social control of children. In colonial times the law was uncomplicated, and the family was the cornerstone of the community.[73] Town fathers, magistrates, sheriffs, and watchmen were the only law enforcement officials, and the only penal institutions were jails for prisoners awaiting trial or punishment.

Juvenile lawbreakers did not face a battery of police, probation, or parole officers, nor would the juvenile justice system try to rehabilitate them; instead, young offenders were sent back to their families for punishment. If they were still recalcitrant after harsh whippings and other forms of discipline, they could be returned to community officials for more punishment, such as public whippings, dunkings, or the stocks, and in more serious cases, expulsion from the community or even the use of capital punishment.

Houses of Refuge (1824–1898)

In the nineteenth century, reformers became disillusioned with the family and looked for a substitute that would provide an orderly, disciplined environment similar tothat of the "ideal" Puritan family.[74] **Houses of refuge** were proposed as the solution; there, discipline was to be administered firmly and harshly. These facilities were intended to protect wayward children from "weak and criminal parents," "the manifold temptations of the streets," and "the peculiar weakness of [the children's] moral nature."[75] Houses of refuge reflected a new direction in juvenile justice, for no longer were parents and family the first line of control for children; the family's authority had been superseded by that of the state, and wayward children were placed in facilities presumably better equipped to reform them.

Houses of refuge flourished for the first half of the nineteenth century; but by the middle of the century, reformers were beginning to suspect that these juvenile

house of refuge An institution that was designed by eighteenth- and nineteenth-century reformers to provide an orderly, disciplined environment similar to that of the "ideal" Puritan family.

institutions were not as effective as had been hoped. Some had grown unwieldy in size, and discipline, care, and order had disappeared from most. Reformers also were aware that many youths were being confined in institutions—jails and prisons—that were filthy, dangerous, degrading, and ill equipped to manage juveniles effectively. A change was in order, and reformers proposed the juvenile court as a way to provide for more humane care of law-violating youths.

Juvenile Courts (1899–1966)

First created in Cook County, Illinois, the juvenile court came into existence to handle all illegal behaviors among people under a certain age. This new court for children was based on the legal concept of *parens patriae*, a medieval English doctrine which sanctioned the right of the Crown to intervene in natural family relations whenever a child's welfare was threatened. The concept was explained by the committee of the Chicago Bar Association that created the new court:

> The fundamental idea of the juvenile court law is that the state must step in and exercise guardianship over a child found under such adverse social or individual conditions as to encourage the development of crime. The juvenile court law proposes a plan whereby he may be treated, not as a criminal, or legally charged with crime, but as a ward of the state, to receive practically the care, custody, and discipline that are accorded the neglected and dependent child, and which, as the act states, "shall approximate as nearly as may be that which should be given by its parents."[76]

Proponents of the juvenile court promised that it would be flexible enough to give individual attention to the specific problems of wayward children. These reformers believed that once the causes of deviance were identified accurately, specific problems could be treated and cured; thus, juveniles would be kept out of jails and prisons, thereby avoiding corruption by adult criminals.

The juvenile court period did not see radical change in the philosophy of juvenile justice, because the family continued to be subservient to the state and children still could be institutionalized. What differed was the viewpoint that children were not altogether responsible for their behavior. They were seen as victims of a variety of factors, including poverty, the ills of city life, and inadequate families, schools, and neighborhoods. No longer regarded as criminals, youthful violators were defined as children in need of care, protection, moral guidance, and discipline. Accordingly, the juvenile court was established as another official agency to aid in controlling wayward children. Juvenile delinquents would continue to be under the control of the state until they were either rehabilitated or too old to remain under the jurisdiction of juvenile authorities.

Society extended its control over the young in several other ways. Police departments established juvenile bureaus. The notion of treating juveniles for their specific problems was evidenced by the implementation in the first part of the twentieth century of both probation and parole (aftercare) agencies. Commitment to a training or industrial school, a carryover from the nineteenth century, was reserved for those whose needs became secondary to the protection of society.

Juvenile Rights (1967–1975)

Mounting criticism of the juvenile court culminated in the 1960s when the court was widely accused of dispensing capricious and arbitrary justice. The U.S. Supreme Court responded to this criticism with a series of decisions that changed the course of juvenile justice: *Kent* v. *United States*, 1966; *In re Gault*, 1967; *In re Winship*, 1970; *McKeiver* v. *Pennsylvania*, 1971; and *Breed* v. *Jones*, 1975.[77] (See Chapter 15 for discussion of these cases.) The *In re Gault* decision, a landmark case, stated that juveniles have the right to due process safeguards in proceedings in which a finding of delinquency could lead to confinement; that juveniles have rights to notice of charges, counsel, confrontation, and cross-examination; and that juveniles are

parens patriae A medieval English doctrine that sanctioned the right of the Crown to intervene in natural family relations whenever a child's welfare was threatened. The philosophy of the juvenile court is based on this legal concept.

FIGURE 1.4 Seven Historical Eras of Societal Response to Juvenile Delinquency

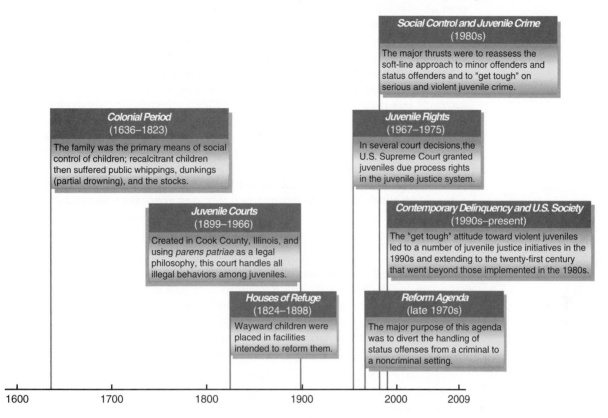

Social Control and Juvenile Crime
(1980s)
The major thrusts were to reassess the soft-line approach to minor offenders and status offenders and to "get tough" on serious and violent juvenile crime.

Colonial Period
(1636–1823)
The family was the primary means of social control of children; recalcitrant children then suffered public whippings, dunkings (partial drowning), and the stocks.

Juvenile Rights
(1967–1975)
In several court decisions, the U.S. Supreme Court granted juveniles due process rights in the juvenile justice system.

Juvenile Courts
(1899–1966)
Created in Cook County, Illinois, and using *parens patriae* as a legal philosophy, this court handles all illegal behaviors among juveniles.

Contemporary Delinquency and U.S. Society
(1990s–present)
The "get tough" attitude toward violent juveniles led to a number of juvenile justice initiatives in the 1990s and extending to the twenty-first century that went beyond those implemented in the 1980s.

Houses of Refuge
(1824–1898)
Wayward children were placed in facilities intended to reform them.

Reform Agenda
(late 1970s)
The major purpose of this agenda was to divert the handling of status offenses from a criminal to a noncriminal setting.

1600   1700   1800   1900   2000   2009

privileged against self-incrimination. The intent of the Court decisions was to ensure that children would have due process rights in the juvenile justice system.[78]

Reformers also believed that inconsiderate treatment by the police, five-minute hearings in juvenile courts, and degrading and sometimes brutal treatment in training schools fostered rather than reduced juvenile crime. Lower-level federal courts responded to the curbstone justice dispensed by police and the repressive justice administered in training schools by handing down numerous decisions that brought more due process rights to juveniles at the time they were arrested and taken into custody and more humane conditions during their time of confinement.

Community-based programs received an enthusiastic response in the late 1960s and early 1970s as more and more states began a process of deinstitutionalization under which only hard-core delinquents were sent to long-term training schools. Enthusiasm for community-based corrections was so widespread in the early 1970s that many observers believed that training schools would soon become extinct.

The children's rights movement also gathered momentum during the 1960s. Interest groups began to examine children's special needs, and in the 1970s, the rights of children were litigated in the courts. That decade also saw progress in the areas of custody in divorce cases, guardianship for foster children, protection of privacy rights, independent access to medical care, and legislation on child abuse. See Figure 1.4 for a list of the seven historical eras reflecting society's varied responses to juvenile delinquency.

Reform Agenda (Late 1970s)

The reform agenda of the middle to late 1970s emphasized reducing the use of juvenile correctional institutions, diverting minor offenders and status offenders from the juvenile justice system, and reforming the juvenile justice system. The major purpose of the reform agenda was to divert the handling of status offenses from a criminal to a noncriminal setting. Status offenders were accorded such an emphasis because of the mandate of the federal JJDP Act of 1974 (discussed earlier). The principal objectives of this act were to promote the deinstitutionalization of status offenders as dependent, neglected, and abused children; to encourage the elimination of the practice of jailing juveniles; and to encourage the development of "community-based alternatives to juvenile detention and correctional facilities."[79]

However, noted gang researchers Ira M. Schwartz, Lloyd Ohlin, and others argue that proponents of this liberal agenda blundered by paying too little attention to the problem of serious juvenile crime. At a time when public concern about serious juvenile crime was running high, the federal government was emphasizing a very different agenda.[80] Less than 10% of the nearly $120 million in discretionary funds given out by the OJJDP between 1975 and 1980, for example, targeted the population of violent and serious juvenile offenders.[81] At that time, Ohlin predicted that the failure to address violent youth crime and repeat offenders would prove to be "the Achilles' heel of the reform process."[82] The failure of the reformers of the 1970s to provide meaningful programs and policies aimed at youthful offenders who committed serious crimes contributed to the wave of "get tough" legislation that was to later sweep across the United States.[83]

Social Control and Juvenile Crime (1980s)

By the 1980s, the public had been alerted by the media to the chilling realities of youth crime and wanted something done to curb the serious problem of juvenile delinquency (see Web Extra 1.4). Ronald Reagan was in the White House, and the hard-liners' formerly muted criticisms suddenly became public policy. The new federal agenda attacked the JJDP Act as being "anti-family" and called for cracking down on juvenile law violators. Alfred S. Regnery, administrator in the OJJDP, communicated this new federal perspective in a speech delivered on December 2, 1984:

> In essence, we have changed the outlook of the office from emphasizing the lesser offender and the nonoffender to one emphasizing the serious juvenile offender. We have placed less emphasis on juvenile crime as a social problem and more emphasis on crime as a justice problem. In essence, the office now reflects the general philosophy of President Reagan and his administration rather than that of President Carter and his administration.[84]

In 1984, the National Advisory Committee (NAC) for Juvenile Justice and Delinquency Prevention said that "the time has come for a major departure from the existing philosophy and activity of the federal government in the juvenile justice field."[85] The NAC recommended that the "federal effort in the area of juvenile delinquency should focus primarily on the serious, violent, or chronic offender."[86] The committee also recommended that federal initiatives be limited to research, to carefully designed and evaluated demonstration projects, to "dissemination of information," and to "training and technical assistance."[87] It rejected basic components of the JJDP Act, such as the continued provision of grants to accomplish deinstitutionalization of status offenders and the removal of juveniles from jail.[88]

Several factors led to this reassessment of the soft-line, or least restrictive, approach to minor offenders and status offenders: Young people seemed to be out of control, drug and alcohol abuse were viewed as serious problems, teenage pregnancy had reached epidemic proportions, and teenage suicide was increasing at an alarming rate.[89] Additionally, the spirit of the times was about "getting tough." Nationwide, politicians assured their constituencies that the answer to youth problems was to crack down at all levels. Furthermore, "tough love" and other such movements evidenced a growing acceptance of the notion that parents must be stricter with their children. Finally, the Reagan administration made a concerted effort to show that the soft-line approach had had disastrous consequences in children's lives; government-sponsored studies, for example, showed that increasing numbers of middle-class runaway girls ended up as prostitutes.

The major thrusts of the Reagan administration's crime-control policies for juveniles, then, were to "get tough" on serious and violent juvenile crime and to undermine the reform efforts of the 1970s. This federal mandate encouraged the development of five trends: (1) preventive detention, (2) transfer of violent juveniles to adult court, (3) mandatory and determinate sentencing for violent juveniles, (4) increased confinement of juveniles, and (5) enforcement of the death penalty for juveniles who commit brutal murders.[90] These trends are described and evaluated later in this text.

mycrimekit™

Web Extra 1.4
U.S. Department of Health and Human Services (HHS) Child Welfare Information Gateway

Even though the federal government and the public favored a more punishment-oriented response to juvenile delinquency, the juvenile court continued throughout the 1980s to have three approaches to juvenile lawbreakers (see Figure 1.5). On one end of the spectrum, the court applied the *parens patriae* doctrine to status offenders and minor offenders; as in the past, these youths were presumed to need treatment rather than punishment, because their offenses were seen as caused by internal psychological or biological conditions or by sociological factors in their environment. On the other end of the spectrum, juveniles who committed serious crimes or continued to break the law were presumed to deserve punishment rather than treatment on the grounds that such youngsters possessed free will and knew what they were doing; that is, the court viewed serious delinquents' crimes as purposeful activities resulting from rational decisions in which youths weighed the pros and cons and performed the acts that promised the greatest potential gains.[91] Their behavior was seen as being bad rather than sick and as arising from a rational decision-making process. In other words, youths in this group were to be treated by the juvenile justice system more like adults than juveniles.

Between these two groups fell youths who saw crime as a form of play and committed delinquent acts because they enjoyed the thrill of getting away with illegal behavior or because they wanted to relieve their boredom. Although criminologists usually conclude that the crimes these juveniles commit represent purposeful activity, the courts in the 1980s did not consider the youths in this middle group to be as bad as the serious delinquents, reasoning that even though these youths might be exercising free will, their behavior was mischievous rather than delinquent. The juvenile court today commonly continues to excuse such mischievous behavior.

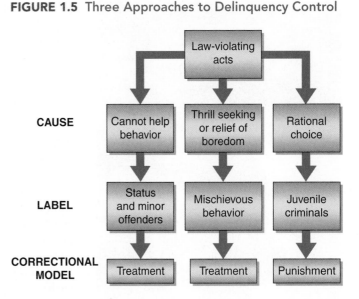

FIGURE 1.5 Three Approaches to Delinquency Control

Contemporary Delinquency and U.S. Society (1990s–Present)

Several interrelated social trends emerged in the 1980s, influenced delinquency in U.S. society in rather dramatic ways in the 1990s, and continue to the present. In the mid-1980s, crack cocaine became widely available in urban areas. There was soon a large demand for this drug—some even referred to it as a crack epidemic—and this led to the recruitment of young people into the market to sell crack. By 1988–1989, the crack epidemic became a major impetus for the development and spread of drug-trafficking street gangs across the nation. Indeed, by the end of the decade, street gangs were found in nearly every city and in many smaller communities across the United States. One of the consequences of this illegal marketplace was that young people used guns to protect themselves from being robbed of the "valuable goods" they were carrying. Significantly, by the early 1990s, the use of guns had spread from individuals involved in drug transactions to larger numbers of young people, and the availability and use of guns, the spread of the drug market, and the skyrocketing growth of street gangs all contributed to a dramatic rise in murder rates among young people.[92] Finally, beginning in the 1980s and continuing through the 1990s, young people became increasingly involved in various forms of hate crimes.

This changing nature of delinquency, as well as increased media coverage of violent juveniles who carried weapons and were typically involved in gangs, began to harden public attitudes toward juvenile delinquents. The resulting "get tough" attitude toward the violent juvenile led to a number of juvenile justice initiatives in the 1990s that went beyond those implemented in the 1980s. The urgency with which states responded is seen in the fact that in the 1990s, nearly every state

Anthony and Susan Provenzino (shown here) were convicted of violating a parental responsibility ordinance when their 16-year-old son was charged with breaking and entering and possession of marijuana. Such laws make parents liable for the actions of their dependent children. ▶ **Do you agree with the idea of holding parents responsible for the behavior of their underage children?**

enacted legislation changing the way juvenile delinquents were handled.[93] This legislation led to nine state initiatives in juvenile justice that continue in force today: (1) curfews, (2) parental responsibility laws, (3) combating of street gangs, (4) movement toward graduated sanctions, (5) juvenile boot camps, (6) youths and guns, (7) juvenile proceedings and records, (8) juvenile transfers to criminal court, and (9) expanded sentencing authority.

Curfews   Curfews have reemerged as a popular means to control delinquent behavior. Most curfews restrict minors to their homes between 11 P.M. and 6 A.M., with some jurisdictions allowing later hours on weekends and during the summer months. States with curfew ordinances include Minnesota, Ohio, and Tennessee.[94] One survey found that of the 200 largest cities in the United States, 60% enacted a new curfew statute or revised an existing law between 1990 and 1995. By 1995, more than three-quarters of these cities had a curfew ordinance in effect.[95] Juvenile arrests for curfew and loitering violations increased 113% between 1990 and 1999. In 1999, 28% of curfew arrests involved juveniles under age 15 years, and 30% involved females.[96] The constitutionality of juvenile curfews has been litigated in several states, but the current trend is for courts to uphold juvenile curfews as long as the language of the curfew reveals a compelling government interest for use of the curfew and the ordinance makes exceptions for legitimate activities.[97] The research findings of the use of curfews have been mixed. In one study, 400 police agencies were surveyed and reported that they had found curfews to be an effective tool, especially against offenses such as vandalism and nighttime burglaries.[98] However, another study, conducted in California, found that curfews did not decrease juvenile crime and may, in fact, have increased it.[99]

Parental Responsibility Laws   In 1995, Susan and Anthony Provenzino of St. Clair Shores, Michigan, were each fined $100 and ordered to pay an additional $1,000 in court fees because they were convicted of violating the local parental accountability ordinance. This case brought national attention to a growing trend at both local and state levels: the effort to combat youth crime by making parents criminally responsible for the delinquent behavior of their children. Of course, parents have been civilly responsible for their children's actions for a long time, but what is new is the body of law that now makes parents criminally liable for their children's actions.[100] More than 40 jurisdictions have mandated some type of parental responsibility provision above and beyond parents' civil liability for their children's actions.[101] Recent legislation places limits on recovery, with an average of $2,500. Some states, such as Colorado, Louisiana, and Texas, require that parents as well as children participate in counseling and community service activities. Parents may also be held civilly liable for the damages caused by their children. In a few jurisdictions, parents have been held criminally liable for the unlawful acts of their children—some have even been ordered to serve time in jail because of the truancy of their children.

Combating of Street Gangs   In the middle and late 1990s, some communities developed gang prevention and control strategies incorporating grassroots community involvement and providing services to gang youths. More typically, however, approaches to gang control involved repressive methods. The word *combating* aptly portrays antigang measures such as harsher penalties for gang leaders convicted of drug dealing; increased penalties for gang-related violence, such as drive-by shootings; and enhanced penalties for any criminal act committed by a gang member.[102]

Movement toward Graduated Sanctions   Through graduated, or accountability-based, sanctions, states are endeavoring to ensure that youths who are adjudicated delinquent receive an appropriate disposition by the juvenile court. Underlying the philosophy of graduated sanctions is "the notion of providing swift and appropriate punishment to youthful offenders based on the gravity of their offense and an assessment of the potential risk for reoffending, coupled with appropriate treatment to reduce the risk of reoffending."[103]

Juvenile Boot Camps First started in Georgia in 1983, adult boot camps soon spread across the United States, with more than 70 adult boot camp programs now operating in 30 states. It did not take long for the prevailing "get tough" climate to prompt the use of boot camps in juvenile justice as well. As of 1999, 10 states had implemented about 50 boot camps for juveniles, which housed a total of about 4,500 juvenile offenders.[104] In recent years, however, juvenile boot camps (as will be discussed in Chapter 16) have come under intense criticism for brutal treatment of youths, and several have been closed.

Youths and Guns In the midst of a continuing debate over gun control in the United States, there is consensus about the need to maintain and strengthen current laws restricting the possession, storage, licensing, and transfer of guns to juveniles and to enact new laws regarding juveniles who bring guns to school.[105] School shootings in recent years have added urgency to the public's desire to get guns out of the hands of juveniles. The recent laws on keeping guns out of the hands of juveniles have been credited as one of the reasons for the decline of juvenile violence in recent years (see Chapter 2).

Juvenile Proceedings and Records Not only is the public concerned about juvenile crime, but government agencies, school officials, and victims also want more information about juvenile offenders. An increasing number of states are responding to this need by broadening access to juvenile records, allowing public access to and victim participation in juvenile proceedings, altering expungement laws for juvenile records, and fingerprinting and photographing youthful offenders.[106] (This important juvenile justice policy is more extensively discussed in Chapter 14.)

Juvenile Transfers to Criminal Court In the 1990s, many states expanded the legislation passed in the 1980s allowing for prosecution of juveniles in adult court. This trend has increased to permit transfer of younger offenders for a larger number of offenses. The three mechanisms used to transfer juvenile offenders to adult court are judicial waiver, statutory exclusion, and direct file. The extensiveness of this movement of juvenile transfer is evident in the fact that in 1995, 17 states expanded or amended their waiver sanctions.[107] A reduction in the use of juvenile transfers now seems to be taking place (see Chapter 15).

Expanded Sentencing Authority Several states have created blended sentencing structures for cases involving repeat and serious juvenile delinquents. A mechanism for holding juveniles accountable for their offenses, this expanded sentencing authority allows criminal and juvenile courts to impose either juvenile or adult sentences—or at times both.[108]

In sum, a review of history reveals that juveniles constitute the only age group required to obey special laws, that juveniles usually receive less punishment than adults who commit the same offenses, that contemporary juveniles are viewed (accurately or not) as committing more frequent and more serious offenses than juveniles in the past, and that juvenile justice policies are consistently blamed for the high rates of juvenile crime because the public views these policies as either too lenient or too harsh.[109]

Themes in the Study of Delinquency

Before concluding this introductory chapter, it is important to discuss the three themes that flow through this text. The first theme focuses on the *social context of delinquency*, looking at the environment in which youngsters grow up and by which they are influenced; an appreciation for social context provides one critical component in understanding delinquent behavior. The second theme, *delinquency across the life course*, examines risk factors that contribute to delinquent behavior and how such behavior affects subsequent life experiences. *Delinquency and social policy* forms our third theme, one that asks what can be done to improve the quality of young people's lives and one that provides ideas for effectively preventing and controlling youth crime.

Social Context of Delinquency

A focus on social context harks back to the 1930s Chicago School of Sociology and has a long history in American scholarship.[110] In his writings, Andrew Abbott, a contemporary professor of sociology at the University of Chicago, notes the Chicago school's emphasis on context in understanding social life when he said:

> [According to the Chicago school], one cannot understand social life without understanding the arrangements of particular social actors in particular social times and places.
> No social fact makes any sense abstracted from its context in social (and often geographic) space and social time.[111]

Applying the notion of social context to the study of juvenile delinquency helps us to understand that definitions of delinquency, the portrayal of delinquent events, the reform and punishment of delinquents, and policy decisions about delinquency all take place within a social setting shaped by historical, legal, sociocultural, economic, and political contexts.

The *historical context* defines how juvenile delinquents were handled in the past and influences how they are perceived and handled in the present. A study of history also enables us to perceive previous cycles of juvenile justice and to understand the emergence and the eventual decline of the philosophies undergirding these cycles.[112]

The *legal context* establishes the definition of delinquent behavior and status offense behavior. It is within this context that the roles and jurisdictions of the juvenile courts are determined. This context also determines the legal basis of juvenile court decisions and the constitutional procedure for dealing with youths in trouble.

The *sociocultural context* shapes the relationship between the delinquent and societal institutions, including the family, the school, and the church or synagogue. Sociocultural research investigates the extent to which peer groups, neighborhoods, urbanization, and industrialization contribute to delinquent behavior. Sociocultural forces also shape society's norms and values, including its attitudes toward youth crime.

The *economic context* sets the conditions under which delinquents live and determines the extent to which economic factors contribute to delinquent behavior. This context cannot be ignored in U.S. society because so many attitudes and behaviors are influenced by success goals and the means people employ to achieve them. The economic context gains in importance in fiscally hard times, as high unemployment and tight budgets affect all institutions (including those for youths) in society.

Finally, the *political context* influences local and national policy decisions that deal with youth crime. It is in this context that decisions are made to toughen or soften the approach to juvenile crime. Political factors have a direct impact on juvenile justice agencies; the mood of reform may begin in the wider society, but it is in the political context that the philosophy of reform is designed and the procedures for reform are implemented.

Some studies of delinquency use contextual analysis to understand how much the interrelationships of various contexts affect the interpretation and handling of delinquency. Interest in doing contextual analysis in examinations of delinquency increased during the 1980s and 1990s. We will describe some of these studies later in this text.

developmental life-course (DLC) theory A framework suggesting that four key factors determine the shape of the life course: location in time and place, linked lives, human agency, and timing of lives.

Delinquency across the Life Course

Developmental life-course (DLC) theory, a relatively new but extremely promising theoretical orientation, represents a major change in how we think about and study lives.[113] Until recently, sociological research largely neglected life histories and individual life trajectories. However, the many publications of Glen H. Elder Jr. and his colleagues have done much to stimulate the use of life-course theory as an appropriate research base in the study of individuals and groups.[114] Drawing on the increased numbers of longitudinal studies that examine the lives of young children and that follow these cohorts sometimes for decades, many researchers are using the life-course perspective in the study of delinquent behavior.[115]

DLC theory is concerned with three main issues in the study of delinquency: (1) development of offending and antisocial behavior, (2) protective factors and risk of offending at different ages, and (3) effects of life events on the course of each individual's development. DLC theory attempts to integrate knowledge about individual, family, school, neighborhood, peer, community, and situational influences on offending and integrates key elements of earlier theories of delinquency, such as strain, control, differential association, and social learning.[116]

The increased study of the life course in both sociology and delinquency studies has been accompanied by a dramatic resurgence of interest in **human agency**, which recognizes the important fact that juveniles, like people everywhere, are influenced by social opportunities and structural constraints and that they make choices and decisions based on the alternatives that they perceive. Life-course theory relates individuals to a broad social context, and it recognizes that within the constraints of their social world, individuals purposely plan and make choices from among the options they believe are available to them, and those decisions largely determine their life course.[117]

> **human agency** The active role juveniles take in their lives; the fact that juveniles are not merely subject to social and structural constraints but also make choices and decisions based on the alternatives that they see before them.

Janet Giele and Glen Elder identified four key factors that determine the shape of the life course: (1) location in time and place (cultural background), (2) linked lives (social integration), (3) human agency (individual goal orientation), and (4) timing of lives (strategic adaptation). First, individual location affects personal experience and therefore can be understood as being socially and individually patterned in ways that carry through time. Second, all levels of social action (cultural, social, institutional, psychological, and sociobiological) interact and mutually influence one another—not only as parts of the individual's whole but also as the result of contact with other individuals sharing similar experiences. Some individuals will show discontinuity and disruption, whereas others will show a harmonious interweaving of individual attainments with social and cultural expectations. Third, in order to meet their needs, individuals make decisions and organize their lives around goals: to be economically secure, to find satisfaction, to avoid pain. Fourth, to accomplish their goals, individuals both respond to the timing of external events and undertake actions and engage in events and behavior in order to use the available resources.[118] As diagrammed in Figure 1.6, the first three elements come together through the funnel of the fourth—timing.

On November 16, 2005, John H. Laub delivered the Sutherland Award Address at the Annual Meeting of the American Society of Criminology in Toronto, Ontario. In his speech, Laub identified the five principles of what he, along with collaborator Robert Sampson, called "Life-Course Criminology." Laub asserted "that these [principles] can provide the basis of a paradigm on the causes and dynamics of crime for the field. In turn, this body of knowledge can be referred to as the core, that is, the soul of criminology"[119]:

> The first principle, then, is that *crime is more likely to occur when an individual's ties to society are attenuated.*

FIGURE 1.6 Four Key Elements of the Life-Course Paradigm

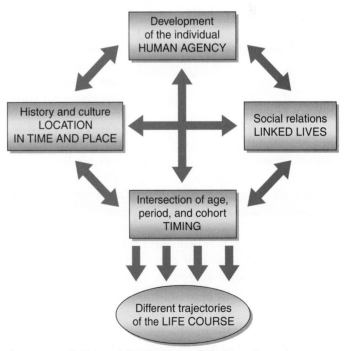

Source: Janet Z. Giele and Glen H. Elder Jr., "Life Course Research: Development of a Field," in *Methods of Life Course Research: Qualitative and Quantitative Approaches,* edited by Janet Z. Giele and Glen H. Elder Jr., p. 9. Copyright © 1998 by Sage Publications. Reprinted by permission of Sage Publications, Inc.

Voices of Delinquency

Twenty-six stories written by former delinquents can be accessed on the MyCrimeKit website that supports this book under the *Voices of Delinquency* tab. The *Voices of Delinquency* resource is helpful in understanding delinquency across the life course as well as the influence of theory and environment on delinquents. Where appropriate, various *Voices of Delinquency* stories are cited throughout this book.

mycrimekit™

Web Extra 1.5

OJJDP PowerPoint presentation: "Juvenile Population Characteristics"

FIGURE 1.7 Relationship between Research, Theory, and Social Policy

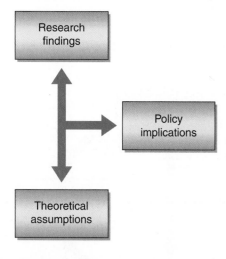

The second principle is that *delinquency and other forms of antisocial behavior in childhood are strongly related to troublesome adult behaviors including crime as well as other problem behaviors in a variety of life domains.*

The third principle is that *social ties embedded in adult transitions explain variation in crime unaccounted for by childhood propensities. The adult life course matters.*

The fourth principle is that *human agency is vitally important to understanding patterns of stability and change in criminal behavior over the life course. Individuals, whether criminal actors or not, make choices and are active participants in the construction of their lives.*

The fifth principle is that *a dual policy focus emphasizing prevention and reform should be the central feature of criminal justice practices* (italics in the original).[120]

Delinquency and Social Policy

There is much to be discouraged about in the approach to handling juveniles in general and of law-violating juveniles in particular in this society (see Web Extra 1.5). Far too many children are involved in delinquent behaviors and go on to adult crime. The Children's Defense Fund's *State of America's Children 2008* is quick to remind us of the cost of letting vast numbers of young people grow up without realizing their potential. To stay on the path to successful adulthood, it states, it is necessary to champion policies and programs that lift children out of poverty, protect them from abuse and neglect, and ensure their access to health care, quality education, and a moral and spiritual foundation. What this requires also is healthy communities, constructive peer relationships, after-school and summer programs, and positive role models.[121] The pressing and exciting challenge for all of us is to design policy recommendations that provide helpful directions for dealing more effectively with adolescents in general and with delinquents in particular.

The two basic tools of science are research and theory; each helps to guide and direct the other. Research identifies appropriate methods to collect data, helps to identify variables to be studied, tests variables for their impact on the subject under study, analyzes related variables, and suggests new directions for theory. Theory points the way to new research, helps derive new variables, builds interconnections among variables, interprets old and new ideas, builds systems of thought, and leads the way to new social and theoretical conclusions. Research collects and theory analyzes; research discovers and theory explains; research disproves and theory reorders.[122] Policy recommendations will be taken more seriously by policy makers if they are based on research findings that are inextricably bound to sound theory. See Figure 1.7 for the relationship between research, theory, and social policy.

Chapter Summary

This chapter has placed delinquent behavior within the wider context of adolescent problem behaviors and has emphasized the following points:

- Those adolescents most likely to become delinquents are high-risk youths who are involved in multiple problem behaviors.

- Characteristic problem behaviors include school failure and dropout, teenage pregnancy and fatherhood, and drug use and other forms of delinquency.

- About one in every four adolescents is at high risk of engaging in multiple problem behaviors.

- The history of responses to juvenile misbehavior displays a pattern in which society has taken authority away from the family and given it to juvenile authorities while simultaneously growing dissatisfied with the official handling of juvenile crime.

- The legal context for dealing with delinquency stems from the early philosophy of *parens patriae* and provides for the juvenile court to become a substitute parent for wayward children. Historically, the task of the juvenile court has been to reconcile the best interests of the child with the adequate protection of society.

- Although they sometimes commit the same crimes as adults, juveniles may also be apprehended for status offenses, behaviors that would not be defined as criminal if adults engaged in them.

- Although the public is child centered, there is a growing concern about serious juvenile crime, and a "get tough" attitude has come to characterize recent public awareness.

- Policy makers are presently focused on serious and repeat juvenile criminals, and both the public and legislators want to make certain that these offenders are held accountable.

- One of our book's themes, social context of delinquency, focuses on the environments in which young people find themselves and considers how these contexts influence the likelihood of delinquent behavior.

- Another theme of this text is delinquency across the life course, also called life-course theory, life-course criminology, or life-course perspective, which examines the extent and causes of delinquency as well as the methods to control it.

- A third text theme is delinquency and social policy, which looks at the process of proposing and enacting means by which youngsters in our society can realize their potential and lead productive and satisfying lives while ensuring safety and security for all.

Key Terms

adolescence, p. 3
Deinstitutionalization of Status Offenders (DSO) Project, p. 15
developmental life-course (DLC) theory, p. 24
house of refuge, p. 17

human agency, p. 25
juvenile, p. 6
juvenile delinquency, p. 3
Juvenile Justice and Delinquency Prevention (JJDP) Act of 1974, p. 15

parens patriae, p. 18
Positive Youth Development (PYD), p. 11
status offender, p. 12
status offense, p. 11

Review Questions

1. How has the role of the family changed throughout the history of juvenile justice in the United States?
2. What is the concept of *parens patriae*? Why is it important in the history of juvenile delinquency?
3. What are the three categories in which the juvenile court has jurisdiction over youth?
4. What are some of the factors that made juvenile delinquents a serious problem in U.S. society?
5. How have the juvenile justice initiatives of the 1990s affected the way delinquents are handled?

Discussion Questions

1. What is meant by the phrase "the lengthening of adolescence"? What elements of U.S. culture have contributed to this phenomenon?
2. Do you agree with Gottfredson and Hirschi's contention that lack of self-control is the common factor underlying problem behavior? What other causative factors compel adolescents to adopt such behaviors?
3. As we begin the twenty-first century, many American youths are significantly more mature than young people were at the beginning of the twentieth century. Therefore, should the age at which an offender is considered a minor be reduced? If so, what age would be appropriate today?
4. Is involvement in status offenses a progressive behavior that inevitably leads to delinquency and then criminality? What factors might dissuade a status offender from continued problem behavior? What factors might propel a status offender into more severe offenses?
5. Do you agree with the notion that juvenile offenses are a response by young people to being victimized by such life factors as poverty, broken families, and poor schools and neighborhoods? If such victimization can be used to defend criminal behavior in juveniles, why shouldn't it be used to defend criminal behavior in adults? For youths, at what point does victimization become outweighed by the requirements to accept responsibility for their decisions and actions?
6. Do you agree with or oppose parental responsibility laws? Explain your position. How do you feel about curfews in a community?

Group Exercises

1. Divide the class into two groups. Have the first group research child labor laws in the 50 U.S. states; have the second group research labor laws in the 30 most populous countries. Have each group present its findings.

2. Ask volunteers to relate personal "turning point" experiences that diverted them from delinquency and to describe the factors that helped them make the choices they made. How are their experiences related to those found in the *Voices of Delinquency* of those youngsters who turned their lives around?

3. Poll the class to determine how many hold the conservative view that using a "get tough" approach to crime control is most effective and how many hold the more liberal view that solving social problems such as poverty and joblessness will reduce crime. Allow the students to debate/discuss their respective viewpoints.

4. Divide the class into two groups, the first consisting of those who believe status offenses result from normal youthful exuberance, irresponsibility, immaturity, and a tendency to challenge authority or test limits and the second consisting of those who believe such behavior is indicative of a tendency toward criminality. Ask members of each group to explain their reasoning, and allow the groups to debate/discuss the issue.

mycrimekit™

Go to mycrimekit.com to explore the following study tools and resources specific to this chapter:

- **Practice Quiz:** Practice with multiple-choice, true/false, short-answer, and essay questions.

- **WebQuests:** Do web activities about child and family statistics and their relevance to juvenile crime and delinquency.

- **Flashcards:** Use 13 flashcards to test your knowledge of the chapter's key terms.

Measurement and Nature of Delinquency

Most juvenile crime does not come to the attention of the juvenile justice system.

—Juvenile Offenders and Victims: 2006 National Report

CHAPTER OBJECTIVES

After reading this chapter, you should be able to answer the following questions:

- What do official and unofficial statistics tell us about the extent of juvenile delinquency?
- Is juvenile violent crime increasing in the United States?
- How do such social factors as gender, racial/ethnic background, and social class relate to delinquency?
- What other dimensions of offending appear to be important in delinquent behavior?
- Why do the majority of juvenile offenders desist from delinquent activity by the end of their adolescent years?

Introduction

New Jersey's child protection agency stopped monitoring a New Brunswick boy 8 months before he beat a toddler to death, but state officials said the agency acted appropriately.

The boy, whose name was withheld, was age 10 when he lured 3-year-old Amir Beeks of Woodbridge, New Jersey, from a public library on March 26, 2003. The boy admitted to beating the toddler with a baseball bat in a plastic playhouse and depositing him in a nearby culvert, still alive; the child died the next day. In December 2003, the boy was sentenced to 18 years in the custody of the New Jersey Juvenile Justice Commission.

When the killing came to light, it turned out that the Division of Youth and Family Services (DYFS) had closed a case on the assailant in July 2002. Then-Governor James E. McGreevey asked the division to explain the decision—the second time within a year that the governor had called the agency to account. But the division was exonerated because "it appears that DYFS followed all of its policies and procedures," a spokesman for McGreevey said.

Details of the governor's decision were not made public, but an unnamed state source told the Associated Press that the division determined that the boy's behavior and grades were improving and that the state agency for the blind had vouched that his father could take care of him.

The boy's mother, who was blind, died several years before of brain cancer, leaving him with his father, who was also blind. Neighbors said the boy had few friends, vandalized their cars, and threw rocks at other children. During sentencing, Amir's stepmother accused the boy and his father of not showing remorse.[1]

The boy was sentenced to spend 18 years in New Jersey's juvenile justice system. He will be under detention or parole supervision for 24 years, until he is 35 years old.

Uniform Crime Reporting (UCR) Program The Federal Bureau of Investigation's program for compiling annual data about crimes committed in the United States.

cohort studies Research that usually includes all individuals who were born in a specific year in a particular city or country and follows them through part or all of their lives.

prevalence of delinquency The percentage of the juvenile population who are involved in delinquent behavior.

cohort A generational group as defined in demographics, in statistics, or for the purpose of social research.

incidence of delinquency The frequency with which delinquent behavior takes place.

Video Uniform Crime Report

Sensational crimes like the murder of little Amir Beeks have fueled public concern over juvenile crime. Some of the questions that we will address in the pages that follow include: Is juvenile crime more serious today than it was in the past? Is it increasing or decreasing? What do we know about violent and chronic delinquents? Is a major juvenile crime wave about to engulf our society? Are there more juvenile "monsters" now than there were before, or have the media merely sensationalized the violent acts of a few?

To determine answers to these questions, it will be necessary to examine the extent of delinquent behavior, the social factors related to delinquency, the dimensions of delinquent behavior, and the various ways that are used today to measure delinquency. **Uniform Crime Reporting (UCR) Program** data, juvenile court statistics, **cohort studies**, self-report studies, and victimization surveys are the major sources of data that researchers use to measure the extent and nature of delinquent behavior. Knowledge of both the prevalence and the incidence of delinquency is necessary if we are to understand the extent of youth crime. The term **prevalence of delinquency** has to do with the proportion of members of a **cohort** or specific age category who have committed delinquent acts by a certain age[2]; **incidence of delinquency** refers to the frequency of offending or to the number of delinquent events.

Measurements of Delinquency

Uniform Crime Reports

New York, Massachusetts, and Maine were the first states to collect crime statistics, but for the most part, record keeping by states and localities during the early years of U.S. history was haphazard or nonexistent. Federal record keeping was authorized in 1870 when Congress created the Department of Justice. Initially, the states and local police establishments largely ignored the task of record keeping (either because of indifference or because of fear of federal control), but this tendency began to reverse in the early part of the twentieth century when the International Association of Chiefs of Police formed a Committee on Uniform Crime Reports. In 1930, the attorney general designated the Federal Bureau of Investigation (FBI) to serve as the national clearinghouse for data collected by the UCR Program. Beginning with the 2005 data set (posted in 2006), the UCR Program no longer publishes a printed copy of annual crime data. Instead, it is electronically posted to the FBI's website under the title *Crime in the United States (CUS) XXXX*, where *XXXX* indicates the year represented by the data.

An examination of the *CUS 2008* indicates that juveniles are arrested for the same kinds of offenses as adults, as well as for status offenses (see Chapter 1). For example, although both adults and juveniles are arrested for such serious offenses as aggravated assault and murder and for such less serious offenses as simple assault and carrying weapons, only juveniles can be taken into custody for running away, violating curfew, or being truant from school.

The crimes for which the FBI collects information are divided into two classes: Part I and Part II offenses. Part I offenses, also known as **index offenses**, are subdivided further into crimes against the person, such as murder, rape, robbery, and aggravated assault, and crimes against property, such as burglary, larceny, auto theft, and arson. Juveniles who are arrested for violent Part I offenses are more likely to be held for trial as adults, whereas those who are arrested for less serious offenses usually are processed by juvenile authorities. The exceptions to this general rule are those juveniles who have lengthy records of crime, including violent offenses, and those who are held over for trial in adult court because they are believed to be a threat to society.

> **index offense** The most serious type of offense reported in the FBI's Uniform Crime Reporting Program, including murder and nonnegligent manslaughter, forcible rape, robbery, aggravated assault, burglary, larceny-theft, motor vehicle theft, and arson.

Each month, police departments across the United States report to the FBI the number of offenses that come to their attention and the number of offenses that the police are able to clear by arrest. **Clearance by arrest** indicates that a person was arrested because he or she confessed to an offense or was implicated by witnesses or by other criminal evidence. These monthly reports are summarized in year-end reports, which constitute our major official source of information about crimes in the United States. The data are subdivided into many different statistical categories, including the backgrounds of alleged offenders and the types of crimes for which they are arrested.

> **clearance by arrest** The solution of a crime by arrest of a perpetrator who has confessed or who has been implicated by witnesses or evidence. Clearances can also occur by exceptional means, as when a suspected perpetrator dies prior to arrest.

In response to law enforcement's need for more flexible in-depth data, the UCR Program formulated the National Incident-Based Reporting System (NIBRS), which presents comprehensive and detailed information about crime incidents. One advantage of NIBRS is that, unlike the UCR Program, it reports all offenses committed during a crime event, not just the most serious offense. Although more law enforcement agencies are participating, the data still are not pervasive enough to make generalizations about crimes in the United States.

In evaluating the measurement of the extent and nature of delinquency in this chapter, one of the important considerations is the **validity** and **reliability** of the data sources. *CUS 2008* data pose numerous problems. In terms of validity, one of the most serious complaints is that the police can report only crimes that come to their attention. Many crimes are hidden or are not reported to the police; therefore, the UCR Program vastly underestimates the actual amount of crime in the United States. Some critics also charge that because the police arrest only juveniles who commit serious property and personal crimes and ignore most of the other offenses committed by young people, these statistics tell us more about official police policy and practice than about the amount of youth crime. Moreover, youthful offenders may be easier to detect in the act of committing a crime than older offenders, with a resulting inflation of the rates for youths. Finally, there is the reliability issue: Do local police departments often manipulate the statistics that are reported to the FBI? The intent may be to make the problem appear worse or better, depending on the reporting agency's agenda.

> **validity** The extent to which a research instrument measures what it says it measures.
>
> **reliability** The extent to which a questionnaire or interview yields the same answers from the same juveniles when they are questioned two or more times.

A mother, distraught over the arrest of her 13-year-old son, pleads with police officers not to take her son away. ▶ **What types of offenses are likely to be committed by juveniles?**

Crime by Age Groups

The UCR Program examines the extent of juvenile crime; compares youth crime to adult crime; considers gender and racial variations in youth crime; and presents urban, suburban, and rural differences in youth crime. Following are the chief findings of the *CUS 2008* data as they relate to juveniles[3]:

1. Youth crime is widespread in U.S. society. For example, the *CUS 2008* data revealed 2,111,200 juveniles under age 18 were arrested in that year. While juveniles between the ages of 10 and 17 constituted about 25% of the U.S. population, youths in this age group were arrested for 16% of the violent crimes and 26% of property crimes.
2. The percentages of total arrests involving juveniles are highest in curfew breaking, disorderly conduct, liquor-law violations, drug-abuse violations, vandalism, larceny-theft, and runaways.
3. Juveniles are arrested for serious property offenses as well as violent offenses. As Figure 2.1 indicates, juveniles were arrested for 27% of all burglaries, 27% of robberies, 26% of weapon offenses, 10% of murders, and 13% of aggravated assaults in 2008.
4. Juvenile murder rates increased substantially between 1987 and 1993. In the peak year of 1993, there were about 3,800 juvenile arrests for murder; between 1993 and 2003, however, juvenile arrests for murder declined, with the number of arrests in 2008 (1,280) averaging a little over one-fourth of the 1993 figure.
5. The 633,360 juvenile females arrested in 2008 represented 30% of all juvenile arrests that year.
6. Juveniles were involved in 10.6% of all drug arrests in 2008. Juvenile males were arrested for 153,000 drug-abuse violations; juvenile females were arrested for 27,000 drug-abuse violations.

Youth Crime Trends

The FBI's *CUS 2008* data provide one indicator of the rise and fall of youth crime. According to these official statistics, between 1971 and 2008 the percentage of arrests for major offenses involving juveniles under the age of 18 declined from 45% to 15.4%; in those years, the percentage of violent arrests declined from 22% to 15.3%, and the percentage of property crimes declined from 51% to 26%.[4]

The most pressing question concerning youth crime is where youth crime trends are headed. Back in the mid-1990s, Alfred Blumstein explained that the crime rate would skyrocket with the introduction of crack cocaine and the recruitment of young people into the market to sell crack.[5] He argued that a long-term decline in the rates of homicide by youths depended on both getting guns out of the hands of the young and addressing the fact that an increasing number of youths are being socialized in high-risk settings.[6] John DiIulio added that with the increased growth in the adolescent population, society must be ready for a new and more vicious group of predatory street criminals than the nation has ever known.[7] In the 1990s, Alfred Blumstein, James Allen Fox, and John J. DiIulio Jr. predicted an upward trend in violent youth crime.[8]

In the midst of these predictions of a violent juvenile crime wave, Franklin E. Zimring as well as Philip J. Cook and John Laub represented dissenting voices. In 1996, Zimring argued that "using demographic statistics to project how many kids are going to commit homicide [has] extremely limited utility."[9] He added that "the overall incidence of homicide, which is variable and cyclical, is still a much better predictor of future violence than assumptions based on demographic shifts."[10]

Cook and Laub's 1998 explanation for why youth gun violence had peaked in 1993 and had rapidly declined since then represented another dissenting voice.[11] They proposed that a change in context could help explain the reduced rate of juvenile homicides between 1993 and 1997, and this changing context, especially a more limited availability of guns, would continue to depress rather than escalate youth homicide in the immediate future.[12]

In recent years, the early support for a violent juvenile crime wave, especially from such recognized scholars as Blumstein, Fox, and DiIulio, has given way to the realization that youth homicide rates have been declining since 1993 and that the reduced use of handguns by minority youths in large cities has been a chief contributor to this decline. However, the decades-long decrease in juvenile crime now may be at an end—partly because of the upsurge in the number of young people in the United States.

FIGURE 2.1 Juvenile Arrests

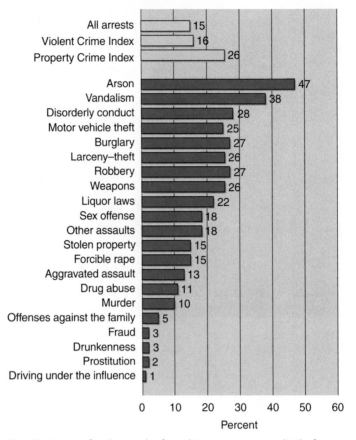

Note: Running away from home and curfew violations are not presented in this figure because, by definition, only juveniles can be arrested for these offenses.

Source: Data from *Crime in the United States 2008* (http://www.fbi.gov/ucr/cius2008/index.html).

Review How Crimes Are Measured

Juvenile Court Statistics

Most information about the number of children appearing before the juvenile court each year comes from the publication *Juvenile Court Statistics*. In 1926, the Juvenile Court Statistics Project was inaugurated by the Children's Bureau of the Department of Labor. One of the most important objectives of compiling **juvenile court statistics** was "to furnish an index of the general nature and extent of the problems brought before the juvenile court."[13]

The reporting procedures, content, and project objectives of the annual reports of juvenile court statistics have been modified since the project was implemented. Initial reports included analyses of trends in delinquency based on factors such as gender, race, home conditions, reason for referral, place of detention care, and disposition; in 1952, the amount of information requested from jurisdictions was limited to a summary account of delinquency, dependency, neglect, traffic cases, and cases involving special proceedings. In 1967, responsibility for *Juvenile Court Statistics* was shifted from the Department of

juvenile court statistics The data about youths who appear before the juvenile court, compiled annually by the National Center for Juvenile Justice.

A handgun is being purchased in a back alley. Studies show that violent crimes committed by juveniles are directly linked to the availability of handguns. ▶ **How might the availability of handguns be better controlled?**

Health, Education, and Welfare to the Law Enforcement Assistance Administration (LEAA), and under a grant awarded by LEAA in 1975, the National Center for Juvenile Justice was given the responsibility of maintaining the series.

The data found in the publication *Juvenile Court Statistics*, like the *Crime in the United States* data, have some serious limitations. Their validity is compromised by the usual time lag between gathering and publishing these statistics and by the fact that the cases reported make up only a small percentage of the total number of juvenile offenses. The data collected by the National Institute of Juvenile Justice and Delinquency Prevention also represent only an estimate of juvenile crimes that come to the attention of the juvenile court. Still, these national statistics, as well as statistics of local juvenile courts, provide a means by which researchers can examine the characteristics of referred juveniles and the emerging trends in juvenile justice.

The number of children appearing before the juvenile court significantly increased from 1960 until the early 1980s, when it began to level off. It then started to rise again and continued to rise until the late 1980s, when it began to level off again. In 2005, juvenile courts in the United States handled an estimated 1,667,900 delinquency cases: 35% of these cases were property cases, 25% were person offenses, 28% were public-order offenses, and 12% were drug offenses (see Figure 2.2). The largest percentage of person offenses consisted of simple assaults, followed by aggravated assaults and then robberies; larceny-theft made up the largest number of property offenses, followed by vandalism and burglary, and obstruction of justice, and disorderly conduct comprised the largest percentages of public-order offenses.[14]

The publication *Juvenile Court Statistics 2005* describes what happens to the cases brought into the system. For example, 56% of the delinquency cases were petitioned; that is, these youths came into the juvenile court as a result of the filing of a petition or complaint requesting the court to declare the youths as delinquent or dependent or to transfer the youths to an adult court. In terms of nonpetitioned delinquency cases, 44% of the total were informally handled cases in which authorized court personnel screened the cases prior to the filing of a formal petition and decided not to prosecute the offenders.[15] See Figure 2.3, which shows the typical case processing of 1,000 delinquency cases in juvenile court in 2005.

Comparison of Self-Reports and Official Statistics

self-report study A study of juvenile crime based on surveys in which youths report on their own delinquent acts.

hidden delinquency Any unobserved or unreported delinquency.

In the late 1950s and 1960s, the use of delinquency studies that relied on official statistics on incarcerated populations declined, whereas self-report surveys using community or school samples rapidly increased.[16] Like other forms of measurements, **self-report studies** have shortcomings, but criminologists generally consider them to be helpful tools in efforts to measure and understand delinquent behavior. The main justifications for self-report surveys are that a large proportion of youthful offenders are never arrested and that a large amount of **hidden delinquency** is not contained in official arrest statistics.

New national interview data that became available in the 1980s and 1990s have led to improved self-report studies. The National Youth Survey (NYS) involves a probability sample of seven birth cohorts in a panel design. The sample of 1,725 adolescents ages 11 to 17 years old was selected to be a representative sample of U.S. youths born in the years 1959 to 1965. This youth panel has been interviewed nine times: in the calendar years 1977–1981 (waves 1 to 5), in 1984 (wave 6), in 1987 (wave 7), in 1990 (wave 8), and in 1993 (wave 9).[17]

Another study, the 1997 National Longitudinal Survey of Youth, consists of a nationally representative sample of 9,000 youths who were between the ages of 12 and 16 at year-end 1996. The survey, which asked youths to report whether they had engaged in a variety of deviant and delinquent behaviors, has the strength of being able to assess which delinquent behaviors cluster together. Analysis of the first round revealed connections between drug use or sale and other problem behaviors, such as belonging to a gang, consuming alcohol, and carrying a handgun. Round six of this sample became available in 2003.[18]

The logic of self-report studies is based on the fundamental assumption of survey research: "If you want to know something, ask."[19] Researchers have gone to juveniles themselves and asked them to admit to any illegal acts they have committed. However, self-report studies have been criticized for three reasons: Their research designs have often been deficient, resulting in the drawing of false inferences; the varied nature of social settings in which the studies have been undertaken makes it difficult for investigators to test hypotheses; and the studies' validity and reliability are questionable.[20]

Validity and Reliability of Self-Report Studies

The most serious questions about self-report studies relate to their validity and their reliability. In terms of validity, how can researchers be certain that juveniles are telling the truth when they fill out self-report questionnaires? James F. Short Jr. and F. Ivan Nye argued that items can be built into questionnaires to "catch the random respondent, the over-conformist, and the individual who is out to impress the researcher with his devilishness, the truth notwithstanding."[21] Yet Michael J. Hindelang and his colleagues contended that self-report studies are likely to underestimate the illegal behavior of seriously delinquent youths, because any juvenile who has committed frequent offenses is less likely to answer questions truthfully than is the youth who is less delinquent.[22] Stephen A. Cernkovich and his colleagues, who surveyed both a youth sample in the community and an institutional sample, added that "institutionalized youth are not only more delinquent than the 'average kid' in the general youth population, but also considerably more delinquent than the *most delinquent* youth identified in the typical self-report survey."[23]

Reliability gauges the consistency of a questionnaire or an interview, that is, the degree to which administration of a questionnaire or an interview will elicit the same answers from the same juveniles when they are questioned two or more times. After analyzing the reliability of self-report studies, Hindelang and colleagues concluded that "reliability measures are impressive, and the majority of studies produce validity coefficients in the moderate to strong range."[24]

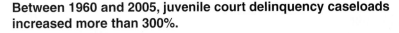

FIGURE 2.2 Delinquency Cases in Juvenile Courts

Between 1960 and 2005, juvenile court delinquency caseloads increased more than 300%.

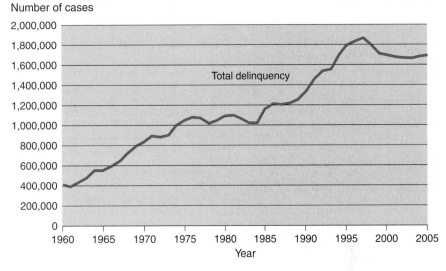

Between 1985 and 2005, delinquency caseloads involving person, drug, and public-order offenses more than doubled; in contrast, the property offense caseload decreased 15%.

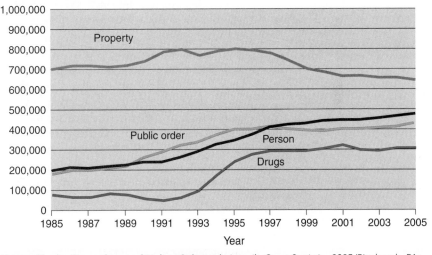

Source: Charles Puzzanchera and Melissa Sickmund, *Juvenile Court Statistics 2005* (Pittsburgh, PA: National Center for Juvenile Justice 2008), p. 6. Reprinted by permission.

FIGURE 2.3 Delinquency Cases Processed in Juvenile Courts

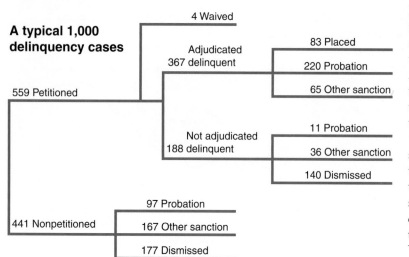

Source: Charles Puzzanchera and Melissa Sickmund, *Juvenile Court Statistics 2005* (Pittsburgh, PA: National Center for Juvenile Justice and Office of Justice Programs, 2008), p. 6. Reprinted by permission.

Findings of Self-Report Studies

In the 1940s, Austin L. Porterfield conducted the first study of hidden delinquency, asking several hundred college students whether they had ever engaged in delinquent acts.[25] Although all of the students reported that they had engaged in delinquent acts, few of them had been brought to police or court attention. But it was Short and Nye in the late 1950s who pioneered the first self-report study of a delinquent population.[26] After their first study of a training school population, they conducted a self-report study that surveyed members of three Washington communities, students in three Midwestern towns, and delinquents in training schools in Washington State.[27] In their findings from these two studies, as well as in other published papers, Short and Nye concluded that delinquency was widespread throughout the adolescent population, that the seriousness and frequency of delinquent behavior were major factors determining the actions taken against juvenile lawbreakers, and that no relationship could be found between delinquency and social class.[28]

Self-report studies also commonly agree that almost every youth commits some act of delinquency. In 1987, David H. Huizinga and Delbert S. Elliott, using information from the NYS, the UCR Program, and other sources, concluded that only 24% of juveniles who committed offenses for which they could have been arrested were in fact arrested.[29] Franklyn W. Dunford and Delbert S. Elliott's 1984 analysis of self-report data from a national youth panel wave and seven birth cohorts of youths ages 11 to 17 years old also had found that arrest data reflected only a small fraction of the delinquent activity occurring in U.S. society.[30] Of course, offenders who commit violent or predatory crimes are more likely than minor offenders to be arrested and referred to juvenile court, yet Dunford and Elliott found that of 242 self-reported career offenders, 207 (86%) had no record of arrest during a three-year period when they were involved in frequent and serious delinquent offenses.[31] (Exhibit 2.1 provides an example of a self-report questionnaire.)

> > > **EXHIBIT 2.1** < < <

Example of a Self-Report Questionnaire

Please indicate how frequently in the past twelve months you did each of the following (circle the best answer).

Stole something of little value	Never	Once	2–5 Times	6–10 Times	Over 10 Times
Stole something worth more than $100	Never	Once	2–5 Times	6–10 Times	Over 10 Times
Broke into a place to do something illegal	Never	Once	2–5 Times	6–10 Times	Over 10 Times
Beat up or hurt someone on purpose	Never	Once	2–5 Times	6–10 Times	Over 10 Times
Carried a gun or a knife	Never	Once	2–5 Times	6–10 Times	Over 10 Times
Took a car without the owner's permission	Never	Once	2–5 Times	6–10 Times	Over 10 Times
Took money by threatening someone with a weapon	Never	Once	2–5 Times	6–10 Times	Over 10 Times
Smoked marijuana	Never	Once	2–5 Times	6–10 Times	Over 10 Times
Used cocaine	Never	Once	2–5 Times	6–10 Times	Over 10 Times

> > >   **EXHIBIT 2.2**   < <

Highlights from the Denver, Pittsburgh, and Rochester Youth Surveys

DENVER

The Denver longitudinal self-report study followed 1,527 boys and girls from high-risk neighborhoods in Denver who were 7, 9, 11, 13, and 15 years old in 1987. In exploring the changes in the nature of delinquency and drug use from the 1970s to the 1990s, the Denver study's findings were as follows:

- Overall, there was little change in the prevalence rates of delinquency, including serious delinquency and serious violence. However, the prevalence rate of gang fights among males doubled (from 8% to 16%).
- The level of injury from violent offenses increased substantially.
- The prevalence of drug use decreased substantially: alcohol, from 80% to 50%; marijuana, from 41% to 18%; and other drug use, from 19% to 4%.
- The relationship between drug use and delinquency changed, in that a smaller percentage (from 48% to 17%) of serious delinquents were using hard drugs other than marijuana and a greater percentage (from 27% to 48%) of hard drug users were serious offenders.
- More than half (53%) of the youths in the study ages 11 through 15 in 1987 were arrested over the next five years.

PITTSBURGH

The Pittsburgh study, a longitudinal study of 1,517 inner-city boys, followed three samples of boys for more than a decade to advance knowledge about how and why boys become involved in delinquency and other problem behaviors. Its chief findings were as follows:

- There were no differences between African-American and white boys at age 6, but differences gradually developed, with the prevalence of serious delinquency at age 16 reaching 27% for African-American boys and 19% for white boys.
- As prevalence increased, so did the average frequency of serious offending, which rose more rapidly for African-American boys than for white boys.
- The onset of offending among boys involved in serious delinquency occurred by age 15, when 51% of African-American boys and 28% of white boys had committed serious delinquent acts.
- The boys generally developed disruptive and delinquent behavior in an orderly, progressive fashion, with less serious

problem behaviors preceding more serious problem behaviors.
- The researchers identified three groups of developmental pathways.

ROCHESTER

The Rochester study, a longitudinal survey of 1,000 urban adolescents, investigated the causes and consequences of adolescent delinquency and drug use by following a sample of high-risk urban adolescents from their early teenage years through their early adult years. Its chief findings were as follows:

- Attachment and involvement were both significantly related to delinquency. Children who were more attached to and involved with their parents were less involved in delinquency.
- The relationship between family process factors and delinquency was bidirectional—poor parenting increased the probability of delinquent behavior, and delinquent behavior further weakened the relationship between parent and child.
- The impact of family variables appeared to fade as adolescents became older and more independent from their parents. Weak school commitment and poor school performance were associated with increased involvement in delinquency and drug use.
- Association with delinquent peers was strongly and consistently related to delinquency, in part because peers provided positive reinforcement for delinquency. There was a strong relationship between gang membership and delinquent behavior, particularly serious and violent delinquency.

▶ **What do the findings of these three studies have in common? How do they differ?**

Sources: Katharine Browning, Terence P. Thornberry, and Pamela K. Porter, "Highlights of Findings from the Rochester Youth Development Study," *OJJDP Fact Sheet* (Washington, D.C.: Office of Juvenile Justice and Delinquency Prevention, 1999); Katharine Browning and Rolf Loeber, "Highlights from the Pittsburgh Youth Study," *OJJDP Fact Sheet* (Washington, D.C.: Office of Juvenile Justice and Delinquency Prevention, 1999); and Katharine Browning and David Huizinga, "Highlights from the Denver Youth Survey," *OJJDP Fact Sheet* (Washington, D.C.: Office of Juvenile Justice and Delinquency Prevention, 1999).

Self-report studies conducted in the early 1990s in several locations, as part of the Program of Research on the Causes and Correlates of Delinquency, showed that a surprisingly large proportion of juveniles committed violent acts.[32] By the time they were tenth- or eleventh-graders, 54% of the Denver (Colorado) juveniles and 58% of the Rochester (New York) youths reported that they had been involved in a violent crime at some time in their lives; chronic violent offenders, constituting 14% of the sample in Denver and 15% in Rochester, accounted for 82% of the violent offenses in Denver and 75% of the violent offenses in Rochester. According to these self-report studies, a large proportion of those who became involved in violent behavior at an early age later became chronic violent offenders. In Denver, chronic violent offenders reported a total of 4,134 violent crimes, an average of 33.6 per person, and in Rochester, chronic violent offenders reported 5,164 violent acts, an average of 51.7 per person.[33] See Exhibit 2.2 for more extensive findings from these longitudinal self-report studies.

David S. Kirk, in using official and self-report arrest data on a sample from the Project on Human Development in Chicago Neighborhoods, examined whether the life course of adolescent crime appears differently across self-report and official crime data and found that a sizable number of juveniles self-report being arrested without having a corresponding official arrest record while a sizable proportion of those juveniles with an official arrest record failed to self-report that they had been arrested. Yet despite significant differences across the two arrest measures on many criminal career dimensions, parent–child conflict, effects of family supervision, and neighborhood disadvantage operated similarly across these two types.[34]

Andre B. Rosay and colleagues' examination of the validity of self-reported drug use found that African-American offenders provide less accurate self-reports than white offenders because they are more likely to underreport crack/cocaine use than white offenders, but at the same time, an African-American offender who tests positive is not more likely to underreport crack cocaine use than a white offender who tests positive.[35]

The desire to uncover the true rate of delinquency and the recognition that official statistics on juvenile delinquency have serious limitations have led to a growing reliance on the use of self-report studies. Taken together, these studies appear to reveal the following:

1. Considerable undetected delinquency takes place, and police apprehension is low—probably less than 10%.
2. Juveniles in both the middle and lower classes are involved in considerable illegal behavior.
3. Not all hidden delinquency involves minor offenses; a significant number of serious crimes are committed each year by juveniles who elude apprehension by the police.
4. Socioeconomically lower-class youths appear to commit more frequent delinquent acts, especially in their early years, and are more likely to be chronic offenders than are youths in the socioeconomic middle class.
5. African-Americans are more likely than whites to be arrested, convicted, and institutionalized, even though both groups commit offenses of similar seriousness.
6. Females commit more delinquent acts than official statistics indicate, but males still appear to commit more delinquent acts and to perpetrate more serious crimes than do females.
7. Alcohol and marijuana are the most widely used drugs among adolescents, but other drug use has decreased in recent years.

Youth Crime Trends

The use of national samples enables self-report studies to shed more light on youth crime trends. For example, the *Monitoring the Future* study, an annual national survey of high school seniors conducted by the University of Michigan's Institute for Social Research, tracked large samples over 22 years (1975–1996). The study showed that some offenses increased during this period but that others did not. Overall crime trends, especially in the population of 17- to 23-year-olds, failed to indicate any increased tendency toward criminality.[36]

Self-report studies have been particularly useful in helping researchers estimate the prevalence and incidence of drug use among adolescents in the United States, revealing how drug use among adolescents reached epidemic proportions in the late 1960s and into the 1970s, appeared to peak sometime around 1979, and decreased into the 1990s and early years of the twenty-first century. In the Centers for Disease Control and Prevention survey, the percentage of students who reported marijuana use was 47.2% in 1999, 42.4% in 2001, and 40.2% in 2003.[37] (See Chapter 11 for a more extensive discussion of drug use among adolescents.)

victimization study An ongoing survey of crime victims in the United States conducted by the Bureau of Justice Statistics to determine the extent of crime.

Victimization Studies

In 1972, the Census Bureau began conducting **victimization studies** to determine as accurately as possible the extent of crime in the United States. New data were needed because the UCR Program measured only the number of arrests that police made, not the actual numbers of crimes committed. The volume of "hidden crime" has long been known to be substantial, and it exists because people often simply fail to report victimizations to the police. The National Crime Victimization Survey (NCVS) was created to address this issue and to give policy makers a better idea of just how much crime actually occurs.

Initially the NCVS involved three different procedures. The largest component of the program was the National Crime Panel, which oversaw the interviewing of a national sample of approximately 125,000 people in 60,000 households every six months for up to three and one-half years, and data from these individuals were used to estimate the national frequency of the crimes found in the FBI's Crime Index (except for murder, which is almost always reported to or discovered by the police). The Census Bureau also interviewed the owners, managers, and clerks of 42,000 businesses selected randomly to provide an estimate of business robbery and burglary rates. This portion of the survey ended in 1976. Finally, the Census Bureau conducted victimization surveys in 26 major cities. Housing units in the central area of each city were randomly selected, and each member in the household age 12 or older was questioned about his or her experiences (if any) as a victim of crime.[38]

The Bureau of Justice Statistics (BJS) took over the responsibility for conducting crime victimization surveys in the 1990s, and the NCVS was completely redesigned in 1993. The redesign came about following criticisms that the survey seemed unable to effectively gather information about certain crimes such as sexual assault and domestic violence. Moreover, by 1993, the survey's designers realized that public attitudes toward victims had changed and that those changes permitted more direct questioning about sexual assaults. In addition, enhanced survey methodology improved the ability of those being interviewed to recall events. As a result of the redesign, victims quickly began reporting more types of criminal incidents, including undetected victimizations, to interviewers. Under the redesigned survey, for example, victims are now more likely to report aggravated and simple assault, nonrape sexual assault, and unwanted or coerced sexual contact that involves a threat or an attempt to harm.[39]

The 2006 NCVS was administered to a random sample of 134,000 residents in 77,200 households throughout the United States. It collected data from household residents 12 years of age or older, and the data were used to assess the prevalence of all crimes—whether or not they had been reported to the police.[40]

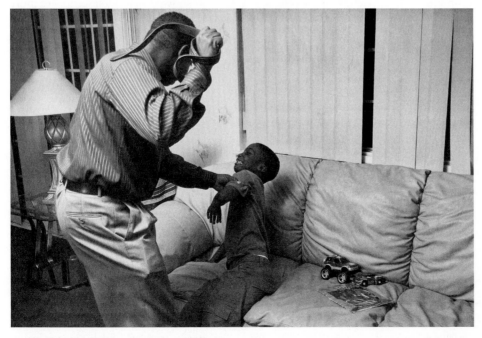

A child being beaten. Children are at risk for many kinds of violent victimization, some at the hands of their peers and some at the hands of their caregivers. ▶ **Why do juveniles experience such high rates of violent victimization?**

FIGURE 2.4 Violent Crime Rates 1973–2008

Adjusted victimization rate per 1,000 persons age 12 or older

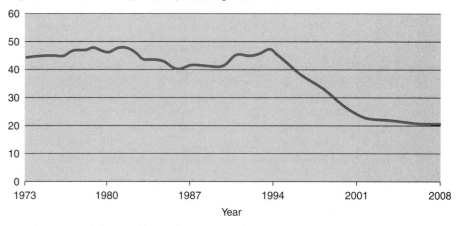

Note: Violent crimes include rape, robbery, and aggravated and simple assault. Property crimes include burglary, theft, and motor vehicle theft. The National Crime Victimization Survey redesign was implemented in 1993. The data before 1993 are adjusted to make them consistent with later years.

Source: Bureau of Justice Statistics, *Criminal Victimization, 2008* (Washington, D.C.: Bureau of Justice Statistics, 2009).

Findings from the 2006 NCVS showed that persons 12 years or older suffered over 25 million criminal victimizations per year, of which nearly 19 million were property crimes, 6 million were violent crimes, and approximately 14 million were crimes of theft.[41] Overall, the number of victimizations discovered was much higher than the number of offenses reported to the police. See Figure 2.4 for changes in reported property and violent crime victimization rates since 1973.

Data from the NCVS showed that juveniles are highly overrepresented in comparison to other age groups in the population of those victimized. Juveniles between the ages of 16 and 19 experience the highest victimization rate of any age group for all violent crimes, and youths between ages 12 and 15 have the next highest rate, with rates dropping with the victim's increasing age. Data also showed that adolescents are more likely than adults to commit violent crimes against peers and to report knowing their assailants. Crimes against adolescents are also less likely to be reported to the police than are crimes against adults.[42]

Within the adolescent population, males are more likely than females to become victims of most violent crimes, but females are much more likely to be victims of rape and sexual assault (see Figure 2.5). The survey also revealed that African-Americans are several times more likely than whites to be victims of violence overall—including rape, sexual assault, aggravated assault, and robbery. Finally, the NCVS showed that persons ages 16 to 19 experienced overall violence, rape, sexual assault, and assault at rates at least slightly higher than rates for individuals in other age categories.[43]

Although victimization surveys have not been used as widely in analyzing delinquency as have the Uniform Crime Reports, *Juvenile Court Statistics,* cohort

FIGURE 2.5 Sexual Assault Victimization Rates by Age and Sex

Victims (per 1,000 total sexual assault victims)

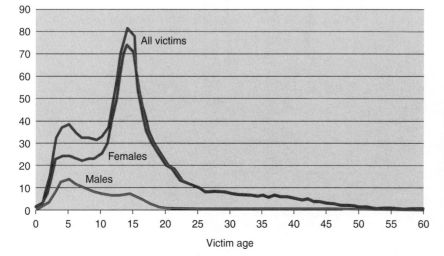

Source: Office of Juvenile Justice and Delinquency Prevention, *Juvenile Offenders and Victims: 2006 National Report* (Washington, D.C.: OJJDP, 2006), p. 31.

studies, and self-report studies, they add significantly to what is known about crime in the United States. Following are some of the principal findings of victimization surveys:

1. Much more crime is committed than is recorded, and the discrepancy between the number of people who say they have been victimized and the number of crimes known to the police varies with the type of offense.
2. The rank order of serious offenses reported by victims, with the exception of vehicle theft, is identical to that of the Uniform Crime Reports.
3. The probability of being victimized varies with the kind of crime and with where people live. The centers of cities are more probable sites of violent crimes.
4. Juveniles are more likely to commit crimes, especially property offenses, than any other age group; juveniles also are more likely to be victimized than any other age group (see Web Extra 2.1).
5. African-Americans are overrepresented both as perpetrators and as victims of serious personal crimes. Official arrest data indicate that a somewhat greater proportion of African-American offenders are involved in forcible rape, aggravated assault, and simple assault than the victimization data indicate.[44]

Web Extra 2.1
OJJDP PowerPoint presentation:
"Juvenile Victims"

The NCVS data have similar problems with validity and reliability as the self-report studies. Individuals may define their victimization differently, and if they are asked more than once, they may give different answers to interviewees' questions. Another problem with the validity of NCVS data is that victimizations of people under age 12 are not included. The Uniform Crime Reports have a category of arrests for those age 10, but the NCVS does not.

Contributions of Data Sources and the Extent of Delinquency

The UCR Program has contributed important findings about the extent of youth crime in the United States:

- Youth crime is widespread in U.S. society.
- Juveniles are arrested for property as well as violent crimes.
- Juvenile arrests for homicide have declined sharply in recent years, but in 2008 there was a rise in juvenile murders.
- Juvenile males commit much more frequent and serious youth crimes than do juvenile females.
- Urban youths commit more frequent and more serious offenses than do suburban or rural youths.

The publication *Juvenile Court Statistics* focuses on what happens to a juvenile when he or she is referred to the juvenile court:

- The number of cases referred to the juvenile court has dramatically increased in the past 50 years.
- This is true for all offense categories.
- Nearly 60% of the youths referred to juvenile court were petitioned; that is, these youths came to juvenile court as a result of the filing of a petition or complaint requesting the court to declare them as delinquent or dependent.

Self-report surveys tell us the following:

- Most youths are involved in delinquent behavior, and almost 90% of delinquent acts are undetected or ignored.
- Girls commit more delinquent acts than are recorded in official accounts of delinquency, but boys still appear to commit more serious crimes than girls do.

Victimization surveys add this information:

- There are nearly four times as many victims each year as the Uniform Crime Reports statistics show.
- Juveniles are more likely than adults to become victims.

Social Factors Related to Delinquency

The first half of this chapter has examined the extent of delinquency in the United States; the second half will focus on the nature of youth crime, another important topic in understanding delinquency. An examination of gender, racial and ethnic relations, and social class reveals much about the social factors affecting delinquency in U.S. society. The importance of gender in delinquency is examined in Chapter 7, the relationship of social class and delinquency is considered in Chapter 4, and the disproportionate handling of racial and ethnic groups is a major juvenile justice concern addressed in Chapters 13–15. Here, we'll focus on the measurement of these social factors.

Gender and Delinquency

Official arrest statistics show that adolescent males are involved in more frequent and more serious delinquent acts than are adolescent females. *CUS 2008* data documented that male–female arrest ratios were five to one for drug violations, more than five to one for violent crimes, and more than three to one for property crimes. The gender ratios were much closer for some offenses, averaging about two to one for larceny-theft and embezzlement. The overall ratio between adolescent male and female arrests in 2008 was about three to one (females accounted for almost 30% of the total arrests).[45] See Figure 2.6 for trends in arrest rates by gender.

Adolescent males are far more likely to be arrested for possession of stolen property, vandalism, weapons offenses, and assaults; in contrast, adolescent females are more likely to be arrested for running away from home and prostitution (arrests for running away from home account for nearly one-fifth of all female arrests).[46] Longitudinal research adds that males are arrested for more serious charges than are females. In Cohort II of the Philadelphia study, the ratio for male–female arrests was almost 9 to 1 for index crimes and 14 to 1 for violent offenses.[47] Furthermore, males are more likely than females to begin their careers at an early age and to extend their delinquent careers into their adult lives.[48]

Self-report studies indicate, however, that female delinquency is more prevalent and more similar to male delinquency than official arrest statistics suggest.[49] For example, in the early 1990s, David C. Rowe, Alexander T. Vazsonyi, and Daniel J. Flannery found that the correlates of delinquency were similar for both adolescent males and females; in examining whether such variables as impulsivity, rebelliousness, and deceitfulness could explain the gender differences in delinquency, they found that the mean differences in delinquent behavior between boys and girls arise largely because boys are exposed more to criminogenic factors than girls.[50]

Hee-Soon Juon and colleagues, following a sample of African-American children from first grade to age 32, found that females who were often punished as first-graders were more likely to have later arrests for serious crimes and that males who were from mother-only families were at higher risk of having serious criminal arrests compared to those youths from two-parent families.[51]

Victimization data reveal that adolescent females are more likely to be victims than are adolescent males and that their victimization is shaped by their gender, race, and social class.[52] Meda Chesney-Lind and Lisa Pasko have argued that many adolescent females become victimized by "multiple marginality," in that their gender, race, and class place them at the economic periphery of society.[53] (See Chapter 7 for a more extensive development of this thesis.) Gender differences in child abuse are particularly

FIGURE 2.6 Arrest Trends by Gender

Arrest trends by gender, males/females ages 10–17 (per 100,000)

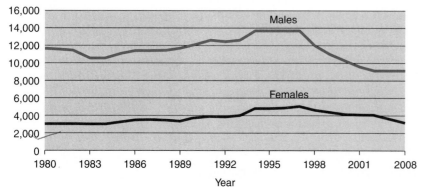

Source: Howard Snyder, *Juvenile Arrests 2008* (Washington, D.C.: Office of Juvenile Justice and Delinquency Prevention, Bureau of Justice Statistics, 2009).

A homeless girl on the sidewalk in the Soho District of Manhattan holds a sign that reads: "Traveling, Broke, Hungry." Self-reports seem to show that female delinquency is more prevalent and more similar to male delinquency than official statistics suggest. ▶ **What kinds of delinquency are most likely to characterize girls?**

pronounced: Data from the federal Child Welfare Information Gateway (formerly the National Clearinghouse on Child Abuse and Neglect) showed that the rate of sexual abuse is significantly higher for girls (1.7 per 1,000) than for boys (0.4 per 1,000).[54]

In sum, official arrest statistics and self-report studies all reveal that adolescent males are involved in more frequent and more serious delinquency than are adolescent females, but self-report studies have found that female delinquency is more similar to male delinquency than official arrest statistics indicate (see Web Extra 2.2). Victimization data add that adolescent females are victimized more often than adolescent males, and this victimization is influenced by their gender, race, and class.

my crime kit

Web Extra 2.2
OJJDP PowerPoint presentation: "Juvenile Offenders"

Racial/Ethnic Background and Delinquency

Studies based on official statistics have reported that African-Americans are overrepresented in arrest, conviction, and incarceration relative to their population base. In contrast, most studies using self-report measures have found that African-Americans are more likely to be adjudicated delinquent but are not significantly worse than whites in their prevalence or frequency of offending.[55] See Figure 2.7 for arrest rates by race.

Two national studies published in the 1970s found that whites and African-Americans reported involvement in 17 delinquent behaviors with similar frequencies, but when the seriousness of delinquency was tallied, investigators found that the seriousness of self-reported delinquency was slightly greater for African-American males than for white males.[56] Furthermore, Suzanne S. Ageton and Delbert S. Elliott analyzing the

FIGURE 2.7 Juvenile Arrest Rates for All Crimes by Race, 1980–2008

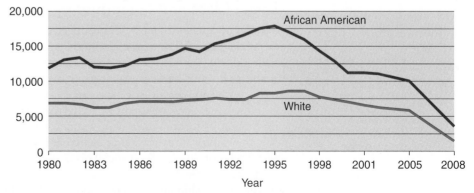

Juvenile arrest rates, ages 10–17 (per 100,000)

Source: FBI, *Crime in the United States 2008* (www.fbi.gov/ucr/08cius/index.html).

Library Extra 2.1

OJJDP publication:
Disproportionate Minority Confinement: Year 2002 Update

ratio of African-Americans to whites for the total number of offenses, found that it was nearly two to one and concluded that this difference was due primarily to the greater involvement of African-Americans in serious property offenses, especially the involvement of a large number of multiple (or chronic) African-American offenders[57] (see Library Extra 2.1).

Thomas L. McNulty and Paul E. Bellair, using data from the National Longitudinal Survey of Adolescent Health, compared involvement in serious violence for African-Americans, Asians, Hispanics, Native Americans, and whites. The results from this analysis, published in 2003, indicated that African-American, Hispanic, and Native American adolescents were involved in significantly higher levels—and Asians in significantly lower levels—of serious violence than were whites, and the researchers explained the statistical differences between whites and minority groups by variations in community disadvantage (for African-Americans), situational variables (for Asians), involvement in gangs (Hispanics), and social bonds (for Native Americans).[58]

Alex R. Piquero and Robert W. Brame's 2008 study, which used both official records and self-report data on samples of serious youthful offenders in Philadelphia and Phoenix to reach a better understanding of the relationship between race and criminal activity, determined that racial differences of the kind usually seen in the delinquency literature were not evident in their sample of serious offenders.[59] Richard B. Felson and colleagues' 2008 article used the National Longitudinal Study of Adolescent Health and found that African-American adolescents do have higher rates of violence, especially armed violence, but they do not have higher rates of serious or minor property or drug crime.[60]

A 2005 article by University of Miami professor Joanne M. Kaufman also called for research that considers the importance of community context. Using the Add Health data collected at the University of North Carolina, Kaufman found that both macro- and micro-contexts are important in understanding why African-Americans and Latinos tend to be overrepresented as violent offenders and that the combination of neighborhood context, social class, and social psychological processes can explain most of the relationship between race and violence as well as ethnicity and violence.[61]

Furthermore, female victimization rates are influenced by race. African-American females, regardless of age, are more likely than white females to be victimized by violent crime; in fact, the victimization rate for violent offenses of 12- to 15-year-old African-American females is equal to the rate for white males. For crimes of theft, adolescent white females report more property victimization than either African-American adolescent males or females and are victimized at a rate nearly equivalent to that of adolescent white males.[62]

In sum, official statistics and self-report data produce conflicting data. Official statistics reported that African-Americans tend to be overrepresented in rates of arrest, conviction, and incarceration, but self-report studies have found that African-Americans are not significantly worse than whites in their prevalence or frequency of offending. There does appear to be some evidence that African-Americans and some other minorities are involved in more serious and violent forms of delinquency than are whites, but this may be influenced by neighborhood context and social class (see Library Extra 2.2).

Library Extra 2.2

OJJDP publication: *Statistical Briefing Book (SBB)*

Social Class and Delinquency

Decades of debate still have not produced consensus on the true relationship between social class and delinquency. Common sense tells us if a child comes from a neighborhood where crime prevails, from a poverty-stricken family in which the parent is unable to provide basic needs, or from an environment where friends are involved in and arrested for delinquent acts, there is not much hope that the child will avoid delinquent activity. Consistent with this reasoning, we know that juvenile arrest rates are highest in economically deprived and socially disorganized communities. However, the empirical reality is that available research data still do not consistently support a relationship between social class and delinquency.

Charles Tittle, Wayne Villemez, and Douglas Smith's review of 35 studies examining the relationship between class and crime concluded that very little support existed

> > > **EXHIBIT 2.3** < <

Social Class and Delinquency

The middle-class youth whose interview appears below was never arrested or referred to juvenile court, even though she was involved in both status offenses and delinquent behaviors. This interview originally took place in 1995, and some information was updated in 2003:

> I was a real mess as a teenager. I got into the party crowd in high school. My mother is a doctor, and I ran around with lawyers' and doctors' kids. We were looked upon as rich kids. But I had such low self-esteem at the time that I would do just about anything to make friends.
>
> Fourteen was a big turning point for me. I had my first beer [and] my first cigarette, had sex for the first time, and started to do drugs. I would sleep with guys just to make myself feel like I was liked. We would get high before school or skip classes and get high. It started out with marijuana, but by my junior year I started to do acid. We drank a lot. We got drunk every weekend and sometimes during the week. A lot of people I hung out with did cocaine, but I pretty much stayed away from it.
>
> I never got into the crime thing. I think the reason for this was I was a good student. I went to a Catholic school,

made good grades, and didn't have to put any effort into it. I did run away from home my junior year and stayed with an abusive boyfriend for a week. I almost got kicked out of school for that.

> I came from the classic dysfunctional family. My father is an alcoholic. He controlled every aspect of my life. My father is incapable of loving anyone but himself. The turning point for me was when my parents divorced my senior year in high school.
>
> I got rid of my abusive boyfriend. I started to grow up and realize that I am not totally worthless. Now, I am a senior in college. It has been two years since I've done drugs. I have a boyfriend who loves me and wants to marry me. I've learned so much by everything I've been through. It makes me appreciate what I have and what I am now.
>
> I am now working with kids a lot like I was. The only difference is that I never got involved with the system, and these kids have been arrested, referred to the juvenile court, and sent to this residential facility.

Source: Author interview.

for the contention that delinquency is basically a lower-class phenomenon.[63] Critics also charge that self-report studies overload their questionnaires with trivial offenses, so when middle- and upper-class youths record their participation in such offenses as swearing or violating curfew, they are found to be as delinquent as lower-class youths.[64]

Elliott and Huizinga applied a new self-report measure deemed to be more representative of the full range of official acts for which juveniles could be arrested to a national probability sample of adolescents. These researchers reported class differences in the number of youth crimes in society (prevalence) and in the frequency of delinquent acts for serious offenses (incidence), and their study also revealed class differences in the incidence of nonserious offenses; class differences, according to these researchers, were more pervasive and stronger according to an incidence (as opposed to a prevalence) measure.[65]

Margaret Farnworth and her colleagues, in examining the first four waves of data from the Rochester Youth Development Study, found that the "strongest and most consistent class-crime associations are found between measures of continuing underclass status and sustained involvement in street crimes."[66] Their 1994 article also explored the possibility that "inadequate measurement may explain past findings indicating no relationship between class and delinquency."[67]

Bradley R. Wright and his colleagues, in research published in 1999, found that socioeconomic status has both a negative and a positive indirect effect on delinquency but that these negative and positive effects coexist and cancel each other out. As a result, these investigators concluded that there are many causal links between socioeconomic status and delinquency but little overall correlation.[68]

There are those who argue that membership in certain social classes influences the reporting of delinquent behavior and that middle-class youngsters, especially those who are white and whose parents possess substantial financial resources or hold valued social positions, are more likely to be diverted from formal handling by the justice system than are lower-class youths.

In sum, research traditionally has been unable to find a relationship between social class and delinquency. It may be that lower-class youngsters vary not in the frequency of delinquent acts from middle- and upper-class youngsters but in the types of delinquent behaviors. It may also be that the delinquent acts of adolescents from lower-class backgrounds are more frequent and serious than those committed by youths from upper-class backgrounds.

Delinquency across the Life Course: Age of Onset and Desistance

One question we might ask is whether delinquency ends with adolescence or if offending behavior tends to continue throughout life. For some individuals, delinquency is strictly confined to their adolescent years; one story that illustrates this is "I Was a Chosen Child" in the *Voices of Delinquency*. Other individuals, however, make a transition from delinquency during adolescence to crime during their adult years (see Parts III and IV of *Voices of Delinquency*).

Developmental life-course criminology is particularly concerned with documenting and explaining within-individual changes in offending across the life course. This paradigm has greatly advanced knowledge about the measurement of criminal career features such as (1) age of onset, (2) continuation or persistence, (3) escalation of offenses, (4) specialization of offenses, (5) tendency toward chronic offending, (6) length of criminal career, and (7) **desistance** or termination of offending. One of the reasons that developmental life-course criminology became important during the 1990s was the enormous volume of longitudinal research on offending that was published during this decade.[69,70]

Age of Onset

Several studies have found that the **age of onset** is one of the best predictors of the length and intensity of delinquent careers.[71] Alfred Blumstein, David P. Farrington, and Soumyo Moitra showed that one of the factors predicting those who became chronic offenders was offending at an early age.[72] Farrington also found that those who were first convicted at the earliest ages (10 to 12 years old) offended consistently at a higher rate and for a longer period than did those first convicted at later ages.[73]

The Causes and Correlates program yielded important insights into the initiation of juvenile careers. In the Rochester study, for example, 39% of the youths who initiated the commission of violent offenses at age 9 or younger became chronic violent offenders during their adolescent years, and of those who began committing violent offenses between ages 10 and 12, 30% became violent offenders.[74] The Denver findings were even more striking: Of those who began committing violent behavior at age 9 or younger, 62% became chronic violent offenders.[75]

Farrington and colleagues found from the Seattle Social Development Project data that an early age of onset predicted a high rate of offending in both self-reports and court referrals. There was significant continuity of offending in both court referrals and self-reports, but continuity was greater in court referrals; the concentration of offending, as well as the importance of chronic offenders, was greater in self-reports.[76]

Kevin W. Altucker and colleagues, examining the differences between early- and late-start youthful offenders in a sample of previously incarcerated youths in Oregon's juvenile justice system, determined that youths with foster care experience were four times more likely to be early-start offenders than those without foster care experience and that those youths who had family members convicted of a felony were two times more likely to be early-start delinquents than those with no family felons.[77] (See Library Extra 2.3 and Library Extra 2.4 for information on juvenile offenders and victims.)

Escalation of Offenses

The findings on **escalation of offenses**, or the increase in the frequency and severity of an individual's delinquent offenses, are more mixed than those on age of onset. Official studies of delinquency have generally found that the incidence of arrest accelerates

Bullying behavior takes place on a Texas playground. Some studies have found that the age of onset is one of the best predictors of the length and intensity of delinquent careers. ▶ **How might the findings of those studies help in delinquency prevention efforts?**

at age 13 and peaks at about age 17, but this pattern is not so clearly evident in self-report studies.

Rolf Loeber and colleagues' longitudinal study on the development of antisocial and prosocial behavior in 1,517 adolescent males in Pittsburgh found numerous correlates of escalation in offending among the three samples. The across-age effects were low educational achievement and low school motivation; the age-specific effects were physical aggression, untrustworthiness, unaccountability, truancy, negative attitude toward school, school suspension, positive attitude toward problem behavior, single parenthood, and negative caretaker–child relations.[78] Using data from two community samples of boys, Loeber and colleagues identified three developmental pathways to a delinquent career:

1. An early "authority conflict" pathway, which consists of a sequence of stubborn behavior, defiance, and authority avoidance
2. A "covert" pathway, which consists of minor covert behaviors, property offenses, and moderate to serious forms of delinquent behavior
3. An "overt" pathway, which consists of fighting, aggression, and violence[79]

They concluded that these pathways are interconnected; that is, youths may embark on two or three paths simultaneously. An implication of this research is that the youths' problem behaviors may escalate as youths become involved in more than one developmental pathway. See Figure 2.8 for a diagrammatic representation of these three pathways to boys' disruptive behavior and delinquency.[80]

Terrie Moffitt differentiated the small group of early-onset persistent offenders from the much larger category of "adolescence-limited" delinquent males, contending that these two groups differ both in age-related profiles of offending and in patterns of early risk. For persistent offenders, risks center on individual vulnerabilities that were evident early in childhood; in contrast, later-onset adolescence-limited groups are characterized by more marginal levels of psychosocial and individual risks, and their adolescent difficulties are perceived to be prompted by experiencing frustration associated with an adolescent maturity gap and by copying the behavior of deviant peers.[81] (See Chapter 3 for more discussion of Moffitt's theory.)

In 2007 Alex Piquero and colleagues, using data from the Baltimore portion of the National Collaborative Perinatal Project, tested Moffitt's hypothesis that life-course-persistent offenders will be at high risk in midlife for poor physical and mental

FIGURE 2.8 Pathways to Boys' Disruptive Behavior and Delinquency

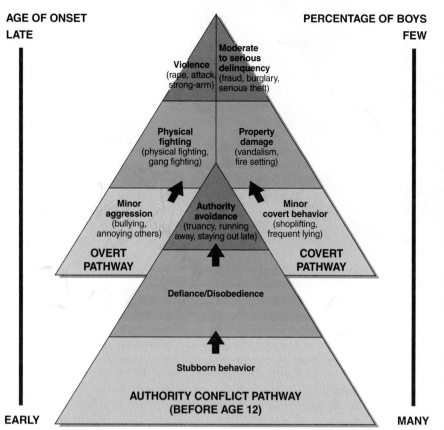

Source: Barbara Tatem Kelley, Rolf Loeber, Kate Keenan, and Mary DeLamatre, *Developmental Pathways in Boys' Disruptive and Delinquent Behavior* (Washington, D.C.: Office of Juvenile Justice and Delinquency Prevention, 1997), p. 9.

specialization The repeated involvement of a juvenile in one type of delinquency during the course of his or her offending.

Library Extra 2.5

Bureau of Justice Statistics (BJS) publication: *Juvenile Victimization and Offending*

chronic youthful offender
A juvenile who engages repeatedly in delinquent behavior. The Philadelphia cohort studies defined chronic offenders as youths who had committed five or more delinquent offenses. Other studies use this term to refer to a youth involved in serious and repetitive offenses.

health, early disease morbidity, and cardiovascular disease. This study found that compared to adolescence-limited offenders, life-course-persistent offenders are more likely to experience adverse physical and mental health outcomes, and they explained these findings by saying that life-course-persistent offenders are more likely than their counterparts to be involved in the type of antisocial lifestyles that increase the chances of adverse health outcomes.[82]

Specialization of Offenses

The findings on **specialization**, or repeated involvement in one type of offense, have generally reached a greater consensus than those on escalation. The majority of early studies found little or no specialization among delinquent populations, but several recent studies have found some evidence of specialization.

Paul Mazerolle and his colleagues, in using data from the second Philadelphia Birth Cohort study, examined the interaction between gender and age at onset of offending and asked how these factors relate to specialization. They determined that offenders who initiated offending earlier in the life course demonstrated more versatility in their offending patterns and that delinquents who began offending at a later age tended to be more specialized. Early-onset females tended more toward offending diversity than early-onset males, whereas among late-onset groups, males tended more toward offending diversity than females.[83]

Glenn Deanne, David Armstrong, and Richard Felson used data from the National Longitudinal Study of Adolescent Health in their 2005 examination of delinquency and violence and dispelled the belief that there is a great deal of versatility in offending; instead, they found that violent offenders are more likely to engage in additional violent offenses and that nonviolent offenders are more likely to continue nonviolent offense patterns.[84]

D. Wayne Osgood and Christopher J. Schreck, using 2007 data from three studies, further concluded that there are substantial levels of specialization in violence, that specialization remains considerably stable over time, and that the consistent relationships of specialization are partly explained by gender, parental education, and risk seeking[85] (see Library Extra 2.5).

Chronic Offending

Chronic offending is drawing increased attention for several reasons. Some believe that **chronic youthful offenders** constitute a majority of the active offenders, and the finding that a small number of chronic juvenile offenders account for a disproportionate share of all crimes also helps to account for this increased attention. To understand chronic youthful offenders, researchers examine their social background and criminal history and analyze potential predictors of chronic offending.

Seen here are members of a Chicago street gang. A small number of chronic youthful offenders account for a disproportionate share of all juvenile offenses. ▶ **What kinds of prevention programs might successfully target chronic offenders?**

Social Background The vast majority of chronic offenders are identified by most cohort studies as coming from the ever-growing minority underclass that finds itself permanently trapped. These youths are marginal to the social order and perceive crime as representing the best option they have. With no stake in the system, they are not easily amenable to measures designed to rehabilitate them by making them employable or to deter them from delinquent or criminal conduct. Contributing to the hopelessness among minority males is the realization that they are several times more likely to be victims of homicides than any other demographic group and that they finish last in nearly every socioeconomic category, from the high school dropout rate to unemployment.

Criminal History Criminal careers, long a concern of adult studies in criminology, have recently received attention among delinquency researchers. The cohort studies consistently report that chronic offenders are more frequently involved in violence than are other juvenile offenders and that they are more likely than other youthful offenders to use crack cocaine or other hard-core drugs or to traffick drugs to other juveniles at school and in the neighborhood.[86] Furthermore, they generally assume leadership roles in drug-trafficking gangs and are more likely to continue their gang involvement as they become adults. Finally, they frequently are involved in gang assaults and drive-by shootings.[87] (See Web Extra 2.3.)

Predictors of Chronic Offending One of the most important but controversial issues is whether chronic juvenile offending can be predicted. Several important studies have come up with predictors of chronic offending with delinquent populations.

Blumstein and colleagues identified three population groups in their study: a group of "innocents" never involved with law enforcement, a group of "amateurs" with a relatively low recidivism probability, and a group of "persisters" with a relatively high recidivism probability. They also discovered seven factors that distinguished the persisters (or chronics) from other convicted offenders: (1) conviction for crime before age 13, (2) low family income, (3) "troublesome" rating by teachers and peers at ages 8 to 10, (4) poor public school performance by age 10, (5) psychomotor clumsiness, (6) low nonverbal IQ, and (7) convicted sibling.[88]

Farrington and Hawkins's examination of the Cambridge Study in Delinquent Development found that persistence in crime between 21 and 32 years of age was

mycrimekit

Web Extra 2.3
OJJDP PowerPoint presentation: "Law Enforcement and Juvenile Crime"

predicted "by low paternal involvement with the boy in leisure activities, a low degree of commitment to school and low verbal IQ at ages eight to ten years," as well as by heavy drinking and unemployment during the adolescent years.[89] Kimberly L. Kempf's analysis of Cohort II (Philadelphia study) found that "delinquents who became adult offenders by the age of twenty-six were somewhat more likely than other delinquents to have had more seriously offensive adolescent careers."[90]

Somewhat alarming is the popular assumption that childhood factors, some of which are crime related, can be used to predict chronic delinquency and adult criminality and that intervention is justified based on these predicted factors. Peter Greenwood—and Paul Tracy, Marvin Wolfgang, and Robert Figlio as well as Alfred Blumstein, David Farrington, and Soumyo Moitra—claimed that a group of chronic offenders who are responsible for a disproportionate share of crime can be identified.[91] Greenwood argued that he has developed a calculus that can predict who adult chronic offenders will be and can produce estimates of crime reduction that would be achieved through their imprisonment[92]; however, this selective incapacitation policy has been soundly dismissed by a host of other researchers.[93]

Lila Kazemian and David P. Farrington's 2006 longitudinal study of a sample of British males and their fathers examined residual career length (average remaining number of years in criminal careers until the last offense) and residual number of offenses (average remaining number of offenses in criminal careers), concluding that official records make it difficult to accurately predict criminal career outcomes.[94]

Youth Crimes and Adult Criminality

The influence that youth crimes have on continuing adult criminality has generated considerable research. Katherine S. Ratcliff and Lee N. Robins, using data on a cohort of 233 African-American males who grew up in St. Louis, studied the relationship between childhood and adult criminal behavior and reached these conclusions: (1) Serious antisocial behavior in adults rarely takes place without high levels of childhood antisocial behavior—70% of highly antisocial adults were highly antisocial children; (2) only about half of very antisocial children become antisocial adults; and (3) the number of antisocial behaviors in childhood is the best indicator of severe antisocial behavior in adults.[95] Nadine Lanctot and colleagues' 2007 study, which examined the consequences of both delinquent behavior and institutionalization of youthful offenders on the quality of adult functioning and well-being, revealed that having been institutionalized as a juvenile seriously compromised multiple life domains in adulthood, especially for females and that institutionalization was strongly predictive of premature, unstable, precarious, and unsatisfied conditions in multiple life domains but was much less predictive of behavior outcomes.[96]

Michael Gottfredson and Travis Hirschi's *A General Theory of Crime* concluded that competent research regularly shows that the best predictor of crime is prior criminal behavior.[97] James Q. Wilson and Richard Herrnstein also observed that "the offender offends not just because of immediate needs and circumstances but also because of enduring personal characteristics, some of whose traces can be found in his behavior from early childhood on."[98] Both of these works draw on a vast literature that shows a positive association between delinquency as well as adult criminality and such factors as poor parental supervision, parental rejection, parental criminality, delinquent sibling, and low IQ.[99]

Daniel S. Nagin and Raymond Paternoster, in examining the relationship between delinquency and adult criminality, suggested two interpretations of this relationship. The first is that "prior participation has a genuine behavioral impact on the individual. Prior participation may, for example, reduce inhibitions against engaging in delinquent activity."[100] Nagin and Paternoster referred to such an effect as "state dependence." Another explanation is that individuals have different propensities to delinquency and that each person's innate "propensity is persistent over time"; this second explanation is similar to the findings of Gottfredson and Hirschi and of Wilson and Herrnstein.[101] Nagin and Paternoster, in using a three-wave panel set, found that the positive association between past and future delinquency is due to a state-dependent influence.[102]

Sampson and Laub sought to explain both the continuity of delinquency into adult criminality and noncriminality (that is, a change) in adulthood for those who were delinquent as children using a basic threefold thesis:

1. Structural context mediated by informal family and school social control explains delinquency in childhood and adolescence.
2. In turn, there is continuity in antisocial behavior from childhood through adulthood in a variety of life domains.
3. Informal social bonds in adulthood to family and employment explain changes in criminality over the life span despite early childhood propensities.[103]

Using life-history data drawn from the Gluecks' longitudinal study, Sampson and Laub found that although adult crime is connected to childhood behavior, both incremental and abrupt changes still take place through changes in adult social bonds, and the emergence of strong bonds to work and family among adults deflects early established behavior trajectories. Sampson and Laub also posited that the events that trigger the formation of strong adult bonds to work and family commonly occur by chance or luck.[104]

Length of Criminal Careers

The length of criminal career has been relatively neglected in empirical research until recently. Brian Francis and colleagues examined criminal career length using data from six different birth cohorts between 1953 and 1978 (totaling 58,000 males and females from England and Wales) and came up with four key findings: (1) It is possible to estimate career length from variables available at the first court conviction, (2) the risk of desistance remains constant during a 20- to 25-year period if the offender does not immediately stop after the first conviction, (3) the most significant variable is the age at first conviction, and (4) gender differences and birth cohorts are of further importance.[105]

Piquero and colleagues examined the career lengths of a sample of California Division of Juvenile Justice (DJJ) parolees released in the 1970s and followed them through early adulthood. They determined that the average career length of these serious offenders was 17.3 years, with white parolees having shorter careers than non-white parolees (16.7 versus 17.7 years); this study further revealed that age of onset, low cognitive abilities, and disadvantaged childhood environment significantly affected length of their careers.[106]

Michael E. Ezell, who also used a random sample of offenders released from the CYA in 1981–1982 who were followed into their thirties, examined the career length for five categories of offenses—serious, violent, serious violent, drug, and property—and found five results:

1. The overall mean career length for this sample was roughly 17 years.
2. The distribution of overall career lengths varied from a low of 0.01 year to a high of 34 years.
3. Violent careers tended to be slightly longer than property careers.
4. The mean residual career lengths (time remaining in career) peaked early in the life course and then strongly declined with age.
5. Several control variables, particularly age at first criminal arrest and ethnic/racial differences (African-American offenders in the sample had the longest careers on average), were found to significantly affect the mean career length.[107]

In sum, this section addresses some key issues important in evaluating developmental life-course theory. They include why delinquents start offending, how onset sequences are explained, why there is continuity in offending from adolescence to adulthood, why early onset predicts a long criminal career, whether there is versatility in offending, what the main factors are in predicting chronic offenders, and what we

Voices of Delinquency

Read the story "My Father Was an Alcoholic," and identify this person's onset, escalation, specialization, and continuance into adult crime. Given the factors that made up his delinquency and adult criminality, are you surprised that he is on death row today?

TABLE 2.1 Dimensions of Delinquent Behavior

Dimension of Behavior	Finding	Consensus
Age of onset	It is the best predictor of length and continuity of delinquent behavior	Strong
Escalation of offenses	Official studies have generally found that the incidence of arrest accelerates at age 13 and peaks at about age 17	Mixed
Specialization	The majority of studies have found little or no specialization	Fairly strong
Chronic offender	A small group of offenders commit the most serious offenses	Strong
Youth crimes and adult criminality	Some childhood factors have been identified as contributing to the continuity of criminality	Very mixed
Lengths of criminal careers	Careers tend to be longer for violent offenders, for those with early convictions, and for minority offenders	More studies needed to determine outcomes

mycrimekit™

Library Extra 2.6

OJJDP publication: *Juvenile Offenders and Victims: 2006 National Report* (Chapter 5)

know about lengths of criminal careers[108] (see Library Extra 2.6). The studies revealed greater consensus on some of these dimensions of delinquent behavior than on others, but together, they do represent a helpful understanding of the nature of delinquent behavior. (See Table 2.1 for a summary of these dimensions of delinquent behavior.)

Delinquency and Social Policy: Guns and Youth Violence

One of the most important issues facing juvenile delinquency at the present time is the continued reduction of youth violence. The national epidemic of youth violence began in the mid-1980s, peaked in the 1990s, and then remained relatively stable until 2005 (see Figure 2.9). There is common agreement that this outburst of youth violence was as deadly as it was because more guns were carried and used than ever before. Homicide death rates of males 13 to 17 years old tripled, primarily because of gun assaults.[109]

The studies also reported the following findings:

- Youths who carried guns were more likely to live in communities that had a high prevalence of gun ownership.
- Youths who lived in communities with high rates of violence were more likely to carry guns than were those who lived in communities with low rates of violence.
- Youths who carried guns were significantly more likely to engage in serious assaults and robberies than were those who did not carry guns.
- Youths who sold large amounts of drugs at every age were more likely to carry guns than were those who did not sell drugs.
- Youths who were dealing large quantities of drugs and money that could be stolen were more likely to carry guns because they believed that gun carrying was necessary to protect themselves and their investment.
- Youths who were heavy drug users were also more likely to carry guns because they believed that buying drugs from armed dealers made it necessary for them to be armed themselves.
- Youths who were members of gangs had a higher probability of carrying a hidden gun than those who were not members of gangs.
- Youths who were chronic offenders and were involved in gangs played some part in most youth homicides, both as offenders and as victims.[110]

The police have played a major role in the decline of gun use by juveniles. Their efforts have resulted in a reduction of firearm violence in Atlanta, Boston, Detroit, Indianapolis, Los Angeles, and St. Louis. The Boston Gun Project has been one of the most successful projects; the two main elements of its Operation Ceasefire were a direct law enforcement attack on illicit firearms traffickers supplying juveniles with guns and an attempt to generate a strong deterrent to gang violence. Youth homicides decreased dramatically following the first gang intervention in May 1996 and have remained low to the present.[111]

The Office of Juvenile Justice and Delinquency Prevention (OJJDP) implemented the Partnership to Reduce Juvenile Gun Violence Program to focus on gun violence and juveniles. Gun ownership, possession, and carrying have led to violence in drug transactions, schools, and gangs. After examining 400 gun violence programs throughout the United States, it was decided that implementation of the following seven strategies would be required if the program is to achieve its goals:

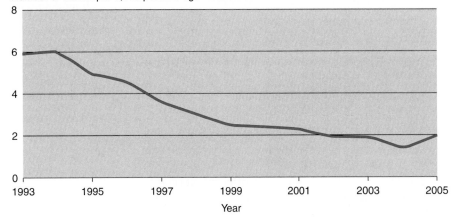

FIGURE 2.9 Nonfatal Firearm-Related Violent Victimization Rate, 1993–2005

Source: Bureau of Justice Statistics, *Nonfatal Firearm Crime Rates,* (Washington, D.C.: U.S. Government Printing Office, 2007).

1. A firearms suppression strategy that reduces youths' access to illegal guns and prevents illegal gun trafficking by developing special law enforcement units, using community allies to report illegal gun trafficking, targeting gang members, prosecuting those who possess illegal guns, and imposing sanctions on those who are involved in gun violence.

2. A juvenile justice strategy that applies appropriate alternative sanctions and interventions to respond to the needs of juvenile gun offenders.

3. A communications strategy that unites law enforcement with neighborhoods, includes community policing, and initiates community supervision to educate at-risk and court-involved youths on the legal consequences of gun violence.

4. A positive opportunities strategy that provides young people with beneficial programs such as academic tutoring, mentoring, job training and placement, and after-school activities.

5. An education strategy that teaches at-risk youths how to resolve conflicts and resist peer pressure to carry or possess guns.

6. A public information strategy that engages broadcast and print media to communicate the dangers and consequences of gun violence to juveniles, families, and residents.

7. A community mobilization strategy that encourages neighborhood residents and youths to improve the community.[112]

With an increasing number of high-risk juveniles in the next several decades, the control of youths and guns will likely be a critical factor in determining whether and/or how much youth violence increases in the United States.

Chapter Summary

Official and unofficial statistics reveal much of significance about youth crime in U.S. society today:

- Juveniles under the age of 18 commit a disproportionate number of property and violent offenses.

- Juveniles today are committing more violent crimes than their counterparts did in the past, but juvenile rates of homicide have been decreasing since 1994.

- Juveniles are carrying far more guns than in the past. The good news is that law enforcement efforts in large urban areas in the middle to late 1990s have had some success in reducing juveniles' use of guns. Most youths are involved in delinquent behavior at some point, but more than 90% of delinquent acts go unreported.

- Lower-class youths are involved in more frequent and more serious offenses than are middle-class youths, and long-lasting serious youth crime is primarily found among the lower classes.

- Nonwhites commit more frequent and more serious offenses than do whites.

- Males commit more frequent and more serious offenses than do females.

- Urban youths commit more frequent and more serious offenses than do suburban or rural youths.

- The dimensions of delinquency that can affect delinquency across the life course have been examined, and the most significant of these dimensions are age of onset, escalation of offenses, specialization of offenders, specialization of offenders, and

tendency toward chronic offending that continues into adulthood.

- Young people who begin offending early tend to have long delinquent careers.

- Evidence exists that at least some youthful offenders progress to increasingly serious forms of delinquency.

- A small group of youthful offenders, primarily lower-class minority males, commit half or more of all serious offenses in urban areas.

- Some youthful offenders go on to become career offenders.

- The easy availability of handguns has contributed to a growing trend in youth violence in this country.

Key Terms

age of onset, p. 46
chronic youthful offender, p. 48
clearance by arrest, p. 31
cohort, p. 30
cohort study, p. 30
desistance, p. 46
escalation of offenses, p. 46

hidden delinquency, p. 34
incidence of delinquency, p. 30
index offense, p. 31
juvenile court statistics, p. 33
prevalence of delinquency, p. 30
reliability, p. 31

self-report study, p. 34
specialization, p. 48
Uniform Crime Reporting (UCR)
  Program, p. 30
validity, p. 31
victimization study, p. 38

Review Questions

1. What do the data from the FBI publication *Crime in the United States* show about official delinquency in U.S. society?
2. What do official juvenile court statistics reveal about juvenile delinquency in the United States?
3. Are self-reports and official statistics consistent in their findings about delinquency?

4. What do victimization surveys contribute to our understanding of the extent of youth crime in U.S. society?
5. What is a cohort study? Why are cohort studies important in understanding delinquency behavior?
6. What is the relationship between life-course criminology and the dimensions of delinquent behavior?

Discussion Questions

1. Do you think improved decisions and investigation procedures have impacted the public's perception of juvenile crime rates and severity?
2. Do you think the media's wider scope of inquiry and faster communication capabilities have impacted the public's perception of juvenile crime rates and severity?
3. What factors in society have contributed to the seemingly greater willingness of youths to use guns to resolve conflicts and their apparently reduced concern for the consequences of doing so?

4. Do you think respondents are more or less truthful on self-report studies? Explain your position.
5. The youthful chronic offender is a concern to the public and its policy makers. What do you think can be done to reduce the numbers of chronic offenders who commit a disproportionate number of serious and violent delinquent acts?
6. Why are the dimensions of delinquent behavior important in understanding delinquency in U.S. society?
7. What factors make the experience of being victimized increase the likelihood of becoming an offender?

Group Exercises

1. Appoint two teams to research the Uniform Crime Reports and *CUS* juvenile crime data for the past 25 years. Have one team report the data for your state and the other report the data for the nation. Have the class discuss factors that might explain any variation between state and national trends.

2. Designate two teams. Have Team 1 research juvenile arrest, conviction, and incarceration data for your state's five lowest-risk, highest-income communities, and have Team 2 research the same data for the five highest-risk, lowest-income communities. Ask the teams to make a joint presentation; then have the class discuss the findings.

3. Assign three students to report on the data and resources available at the Juvenile Justice and Delinquency Prevention website at www.ojjdp.ncjrs.org.

4. Have students collect clippings from newspapers and articles from the Web regarding juvenile justice issues. A useful website for juvenile justice–specific events is www.usatoday.com.

mycrimekit

Go to mycrimekit.com to explore the following study tools and resources specific to this chapter:

- **Practice Quiz:** Practice with multiple-choice, true/false, short-answer, and essay questions.

- **WebQuests:** Do web activities using the OJJDP Power-Point presentation.

- **Flashcards:** Use 18 flashcards to test your knowledge of the chapter's key terms.

part 2

The Causes of Delinquency

Chapter 3
Individual Causes of
Delinquency 57

Chapter 4
Social Structural Causes
of Delinquency 84

Chapter 5
Social Process Theories
of Delinquency 105

Chapter 6
Social Interactionist
Theories of
Delinquency 126

The four chapters in this section raise important questions about why some young people commit delinquent acts but others don't. Chapter 3 discusses explanations for delinquency that focus on causes at the individual level, including personal decision making involving rational choices made at the individual level. The chapter also examines the claims made by some that delinquents are propelled into illegal behavior by biological features or psychological drives or by other personal traits. Within the context of these claims, we will also examine the psychological development of adolescents and look at how that development impacts the choices and decisions that they make.

In Chapter 4, we turn our attention to sociological explanations for delinquency. Sociological explanations fault individual-level perspectives for failing to account for the underlying social and cultural conditions that give rise to delinquency. Social structural approaches claim that forces such as social disorganization, cultural deviance, strain, and status frustration are so powerful that they induce young people—especially those from the lower classes—to become involved in delinquency. Social process approaches, discussed in Chapter 5, detail the influence that the social environment exerts over delinquent acts. In this chapter, differential association, drift theory, and social control theory provide theoretical mechanisms for the translation of environmental factors into individual motivation.

Chapter 6, Social Interactionist Theories of Delinquency, looks at the role that social groups, economic organizations, and social institutions have in producing delinquent behavior. The three major social interactionist perspectives discussed in that chapter are labeling theory, symbolic interactionist theory, and conflict theory. As we will learn, social interaction occurs within individualized contexts that can vary widely but that usually involve the family, the school, peers and other groups, and official actors in the justice system and in the government.

Individual Causes of Delinquency

America's best hope for reducing crime is to reduce juvenile delinquency and youth crime.

—President's Commission on Law Enforcement and Administration of Justice, 1967

CHAPTER OBJECTIVES

After reading this chapter, you should be able to answer the following questions:

- What role does free will have in the classical school's understanding of criminal or delinquent behavior?

- What are the main forms of positivism? How does each form explain delinquent behavior?

- How does rational choice theory differ from positivism?

- Which types of delinquency are more likely to be brought about by biological factors?

- Which types of delinquents are more likely to be held responsible for their actions?

Introduction

In 2009, researchers at Shippensburg University in Pennsylvania released results of a study showing that unpopular first names are frequently associated with juvenile delinquency for children of all races.[1] The researchers concluded that unpopular names are probably not the direct cause of crime but are instead correlated with socioeconomic factors that increase the tendency toward juvenile delinquency, such as a disadvantaged home environment, low income, place of residence, and acquisition of cultural values supportive of delinquency. At the same time, it is possible to imagine that some people are unconsciously influenced by the need to live up to their name. The study's authors reviewed other literature that showed that job applicants with certain first names were more likely to receive calls back from potential employers, even when their skills and other qualifying attributes were similar to those of other job candidates. The authors suggested that juveniles with unpopular names may be treated differently by their peers, making it more difficult for them to form positive relationships and that they may turn to crime or delinquency when their names result in a negative employment bias. Finally, as noted by the study authors, their findings have "potential implications for identifying . . . who may engage in disruptive behavior or relapse into criminal behavior."[2]

In this chapter we offer some possible explanations for delinquent behavior. In contrast to the unconscious influence exerted by unpopular first names, described in this chapter's opening story, some authors suggest that much delinquency is caused not by factors beyond the offender's control but by a conscious thought process that considers the costs and benefits of particular behavior and with some degree of planning and foresight reasons whether the behavior is desirable or not.[3]

On the other hand, if something as simple as a first name can impact people's behavior, then they might not be able to make fully conscious choices. This kind of deterministic view—that delinquents cannot stop themselves from committing socially unacceptable behavior because of some overpowering influences—builds on a perspective known as **positivism**, a major theoretical position in criminology.

A third explanation discussed in this chapter highlights the significance of developmental theories. A developmental approach suggests that while some young people have the opportunity to learn how to act legally and morally, others do not. In such cases, the effects of life circumstances and a lack of moral development can place adolescents on a trajectory with tragic consequences.

positivism The view that just as laws operate in the medical, biological, and physical sciences, laws govern human behavior and these laws can be understood and used.

Classical School and Delinquency

The association between criminal behavior and the rationality of crime has roots in the eighteenth-century classical school of criminology. This school's founders were Charles de Secondat, Baron de Montesquieu; Cesare Bonesana, Marquis of Beccaria; and Jeremy Bentham. These thinkers viewed humans as rational creatures who are willing to surrender enough liberty to the state so that society can establish rules and sanctions for the preservation of the social order[4]:

■ *Montesquieu.* The debate on the classical school was begun by its advocate, the French aristocrat Montesquieu, who was primarily concerned with government's proper role in the punishment of criminals. In his 1747 book, *On the Spirit of the Laws,* he argued that "the severity of punishment is fitter for despotic governments whose principle is terror, than for a monarchy or a republic whose strength is honor and virtue. In moderate governments the love of one's country, shame and the fear of blame, are restraining motives, capable of preventing a great multitude of crimes."[5] Montesquieu added that under a moderate and lenient government, "the greatest punishment of a bad action is conviction. The civil laws have therefore a softer way of correcting, and do not require so much force and severity."[6] His book was a literary success; 22 editions were published in less than two years. But many readers of this time, used to the ghastly punishments inflicted in England and France, considered Montesquieu's ideas of moderation of punishment nothing less than sedition.

- *Beccaria.* In 1764, Cesare Bonesana, Marquis of Beccaria, an Italian who was then only 26 years old and just out of law school, published a slim volume titled *On Crimes and Punishments.* This essay, which appeared anonymously because Beccaria feared reprisals if its authorship were known, was read avidly and translated into all the languages of Europe.[7] Beccaria based the legitimacy of criminal sanctions on the **social contract.** The authority for making laws rested with the legislator, who should have only one view in sight: "the greatest happiness of the greatest number." Beccaria saw punishment as a necessary evil and suggested that "it should be public, immediate, and necessary; the least possible in the case given; proportioned to the crime; and determined by the laws."[8] He then defined the purpose and consequences of punishment as being "to deter persons from the commission of crime and not to provide social revenge. Not severity, but certainty and swiftness in punishment best secure this result."[9]

High school students in Mission Viejo, California, fill out applications at a community college recruiting fair. Rational choice approaches to explaining delinquency claim that juvenile offenders are active, rational decision makers who respond to the incentives and deterrents they encounter. ▶ **What implications might rational choice theory have for delinquency prevention and control?**

- *Bentham.* In 1780, the Englishman Jeremy Bentham published *An Introduction to the Principles of Morals and Legislation,* which further developed the philosophy of the classical school. Believing that a rational person would do what was necessary to achieve the most pleasure and the least pain, Bentham contended that punishment would deter criminal behavior, provided it was made appropriate to the crime. He stated that punishment has four objectives: (1) to prevent all offenses if possible; (2) to persuade a person who has decided to offend to commit a less rather than a more serious offense; (3) "to dispose [a person who has resolved on a particular offense] to do no more mischief than is necessary to his purpose"; and (4) to prevent crime at as cheap a cost to society as possible.[10]

The following are the basic theoretical constructs of the classical school of criminology:

- Human beings were looked on as rational creatures who, being free to choose their actions, could be held responsible for their behavior. This doctrine of **free will** was substituted for the widely accepted concept of theological determinism, which saw humans as predestined to certain actions.
- Punishment was justified because of its practical usefulness, or utility. No longer was punishment acceptable for purposes of vengeful retaliation or as expiation on the basis of superstitious theories of guilt and repayment. According to **utilitarianism,** the aim of punishment was the protection of society, and the dominant theme was deterrence.
- The classical school saw the human being as a creature governed by a **felicific calculus**—an orientation toward obtaining a favorable balance of pleasure and pain.
- There should be a rational scale of punishment that would be painful enough to deter the criminal from further offenses and to prevent others from following his or her example of crime.

social contract An unstated or explicit agreement between a people and their government as to the rights and obligations of each.

free will The ability to make rational choices among possible actions and to select one over the others.

utilitarianism A doctrine that holds that the useful is the good and that the aim of social or political action should be the greatest good for the greatest number.

felicific calculus A method for determining the sum total of pleasure and pain produced by an act; also the assumption that human beings strive to obtain a favorable balance of pleasure and pain.

Review The Classical School of Thought in Criminology

- Sanctions should be proclaimed in advance of their use; these sanctions should be proportionate to the offense and should outweigh the rewards of crime.
- Equal justice should be offered to everyone.
- Individuals should be judged by the law solely for their acts, not for their beliefs.

According to the principles of the classical school, then, juveniles who commit serious crimes or continue to break the law are presumed to deserve punishment rather than treatment, because they possess free will and know what they are doing. Proponents of the classical school view delinquency as purposeful activity resulting from rational decisions in which offenders weigh the pros and cons and perform the acts that promise the greatest potential gains.[11]

Rationality of Crime

Library Extra 3.1
Rational Choice Theory

In the 1970s and 1980s, workers in a variety of academic disciplines, including the sociology of deviance, criminology, economics, and cognitive psychology, began to view crime as the outcome of rational choices and decisions[12] (see Library Extra 3.1). The ecological tradition in criminology and the economic theory of markets, especially, have applied the notion of rational choice to crime. Ecological researchers have inferred from the distribution of particular crimes that offenders make rational choices. For example, findings from several studies have revealed that homes on the borderline of affluent districts are at most risk of burglary.[13]

Economic analysis of criminal behavior argues that criminals, like noncriminals, are active, rational decision makers who respond to incentives and deterrents. In economic models of criminal decision making, crime is assumed to involve rational calculation and is viewed essentially as an economic transaction or a question of occupational choice.[14]

Rational Choice Theory

Rational choice theory, borrowed primarily from the utility model in economics, is one of the hottest topics today in criminology, sociology, political science, and law.[15] It is based on the assumption that the delinquent or the criminal chooses to violate the law and has free will. Rational choice theory in its pure form can be seen, at least in part, as an extension of the deterrence doctrine found in the classical school, which includes incentives as well as disincentives and focuses on individuals' rational calculations of payoffs and costs before delinquent and criminal acts are committed.[16] Raymond Paternoster presented what he labeled a "deterrence/rational choice model" to examine a youth's decision to participate in, continue with, or desist from delinquent acts. Rational choice, according to Paternoster, recognizes that there are "choice-structuring" variables and that choices do not require complete information or rational analytic methods.[17]

Routine Activities Approach

routine activities approach The contention that crime rate trends and cycles are related to the nature of everyday patterns of social interaction that characterize the society in which they occur.

Another approach to the rationality of crime is the **routine activities approach**. Lawrence E. Cohen and Marcus Felson, guided by ecological concepts and the presumed rationality of offenders, developed a routine activities approach for analyzing crime rate trends and cycles. This approach links the dramatic increase in crime rates since 1960 to changes in the routine activity structure of U.S. society and to a corresponding increase in target suitability and a decrease in the presence of "guardians" such as neighbors, friends, and family. The decline of the daytime presence of adult caretakers in homes and neighborhoods is partly the result of a trend toward increased female participation in the labor force. Cohen and Felson believed that the volume and distribution of predatory crime are related to the interaction of three variables relating to the routine activities of U.S. life: the availability of suitable targets, the absence of capable guardians, and the presence of motivated offenders.[18]

Steven F. Messner and Kenneth Tardiff used the routine activities approach to help interpret patterns of homicides in Manhattan and found that the approach did indeed provide a useful framework for interpreting the social ecology involved in urban homicides. They found that people's lifestyles affected patterns of victimization; for example, people who were victimized by strangers tended to go out more often, whereas those who preferred to stay at home were more likely to be victimized by someone they knew.[19]

D. Wayne Osgood and colleagues, in analyzing within-individual changes in routine activities and deviance across five waves of data from a national sample, extended routine activities approach's situational analysis of crime to a broad range of deviant behaviors.[20] They found that "unstructured socializing with peers in the absence of authority figures presents opportunities for deviance. In the presence of peers," they added, "deviant acts will be easier and more rewarding; the absence of authority figures reduces the potential for social control responses to deviance; and the lack of structure leaves time available for deviant behavior."[21]

Let us now evaluate how much choice delinquents have in violating the law. Some youthful offenders clearly engage in delinquent behavior because of the low cost or risk of such behavior. Much of delinquency can be interpreted as a form of problem-solving behavior in response to the pressures of adolescence. Finding themselves struggling with issues of perceived control, seeking positive evaluation of self, and facing the negative impact of others who punish, sanction, or reject them, delinquents address these problems by deriving short-term pleasures from delinquent involvements.[22] Conversely, offenders also may decide on rational grounds that the risks of continued delinquent behavior are not justified by the rewards. Even more to the point, most persistent offenders appear to desist from crime as they reach their late teens or early twenties, claiming that continued criminality is incompatible with the demands of holding a full-time job or settling down to marriage and a family.[23] Desistance from crime, or maturing out of crime, is a process of deciding that the benefits of crime are less than the advantages of ceasing to commit crime.

Confined in a Los Angeles County correctional facility, this youth contemplates his future.
▶ **What might he be thinking?**

Yet there are important qualifications in assuming too much rationality in delinquent behavior. Rationality theory is based on the notion that delinquent behavior is planned—at least to some degree. Planning has to do both with formulating a scheme or a procedure for doing something before doing it or having an intention of acting and with assessing the possible alternative courses of actions available, choosing a particular course, and constructing a complex set of acts to achieve the intended results. But many studies of delinquency have reported that most delinquent behavior is not planned; spur-of-the-moment decision making most frequently characterizes juvenile wrongdoing.[24]

The concept of rationality also assumes that individuals have free will and are not controlled by their emotions, but many youngsters do not appear to have such control. Youths who are mentally ill or who engage in obsessive-compulsive acts, such as compulsive arsonists, kleptomaniacs, or sex offenders, seem to be held in bondage by their emotions. Furthermore, in examining the actual process of rational choice, it is apparent that there are degrees of freedom for all juveniles and that juveniles' rationality is contextually oriented. The notion of degrees of freedom suggests, then, that delinquents "are neither wholly free nor completely constrained but fall somewhere between."[25] The contextual nature of rationality further suggests that in most situations delinquents do have some control over their acts but that in some situations they may have little or no control.

Robert Agnew's examination of hard and soft determinism led him to conclude that freedom of choice varies from one individual to another. It is dependent on factors—such as biological, psychological, or social nature—that exist previous to the choice process itself. For example, one individual may be forced to choose between two different alternatives, but another may have six different alternatives; the latter, Agnew suggests, has more freedom of choice.[26]

Positivism and Delinquency

This section examines perspectives such as biological and psychological positivism to see how they might enhance our understanding of why delinquent behavior occurs. Instead of viewing delinquency as a logical selection from among an available set of alternative behaviors, as rational choice theorists do, this section suggests that delinquents are affected by biological or psychological factors that impair their decision-making abilities.

According to many philosophers of natural law, human behavior is merely one facet of a universe that is part of a natural order, but human beings can study behavior and discover how natural laws operate. Two positions diverge at this point: One view states that because a natural order with its own laws exists, changing human behavior is impossible; the other view is that the laws that govern human behavior can be understood and used and that the causes of human behavior, once discovered, can be modified to eliminate or ameliorate many of society's problems. This second position is the one most scientists accept. This concept, as it applies to juvenile justice, is called *positivism*.

Positivism became the dominant philosophical perspective of juvenile justice at the time the juvenile court was established in the last year of the nineteenth century. During the **Progressive era** (the period from about 1890 to 1920), the wave of optimism that swept through U.S. society led to the acceptance of positivism. The doctrines of the emerging social sciences assured reformers that through positivism their problems could be solved. The initial step was to gather all the facts of the case; equipped with these data, reformers were then expected to analyze the issues in scientific fashion and discover the right solutions.[27]

Armed with these principles, reformers set out to deal with the problem of delinquency, confident that they knew how to find its cause. Progressives looked first to environmental factors, pinpointing poverty as the major cause of delinquency. Some progressives were attracted also to the doctrine of eugenics and believed that biological

Voices of Delinquency

Read "The Thinker." This is the story of a 15-year-old who, with his brother, committed a vicious murder. How much rationality do you believe affected his brief life of crime? To what extent did his life of abuse, family disruption, and peers affect his rational choice?

Video Positivism

Progressive era The period from around 1890 to 1920, when a wave of optimism swept through American society and led to the acceptance of positivism.

limitations drove youthful offenders to delinquency. But eventually the psychological origins of delinquency came to be more widely accepted than either the environmental or biological origins.[28]

The positivist approach to youth crime is based on three basic assumptions.[29] First, the character and personal backgrounds of individuals explain delinquent behavior. Positivism, relegating the law and its administration to a secondary role, looks for the cause of deviancy in the actor.

Second, the existence of **determinism** is a critical assumption of positivism. Delinquency, like any other phenomenon, is seen as determined by prior causes—it does not just happen. Because of this deterministic position, positivism rejects the view that the individual exercises freedom, possesses reason, and is capable of choice.

Third, the delinquent is seen as fundamentally different from the nondelinquent, so the task is to identify the factors that have made the delinquent a different kind of person. In attempting to explain this difference, positivism has concluded that wayward youths are driven into crime by something in their physical makeup, by aberrant psychological impulses, or by the meanness and harshness of their social environment.[30]

> **determinism** A philosophical position that suggests that individuals are driven into delinquent or criminal behavior by biological or psychological traits that are beyond their control.

Early Theories of Biological Positivism

The belief in a biological explanation for criminality has a long history. For example, the study of physiognomy, which attempts to discern inner qualities through outward appearance, was developed by the ancient Greeks. Indeed, a physiognomist charged that Socrates' face reflected a brutal nature.[31] The attention given to **biological positivism** in the United States may be divided into two periods. The first period was characterized by the nature–nurture debate during the latter part of the nineteenth century and the early twentieth century, and Cesare Lombroso's theory of physical anomalies, genealogical studies, and theories of human somatotypes (body types) represent early approaches relating crime and delinquency to biological factors:

> **biological positivism** The belief that juveniles' biological characteristics and limitations drive them to delinquent behavior.

- *Lombroso and biological positivism.* Frequently regarded as the founder of biological positivism, Lombroso is best known for his theory of the atavistic criminal. According to Lombroso, the **born criminal** was atavistic, someone who reverts to an earlier evolutionary form or level; in other words, the characteristics of primitive men periodically reappeared in certain individuals.[32]
- *Genealogical studies and delinquency.* Henry Goddard's finding that at least half of all juvenile delinquents were mentally defective sparked intense debate for more than a decade.[33] But the findings of John Edwin Sutherland discouraged future investigations of the correlation between intelligence and delinquency.[34] Sutherland, evaluating IQ studies of delinquents and criminals, concluded that the lower IQs of offenders were related more to testing methods and scoring than to the offenders' actual mental abilities.[35]
- *Body type theory.* Ernst Kretscher, a German, first developed the theory that there are two body types: the schizothyme and the cyclothyme. Schizothymes are strong and muscular, and according to Kretscher, they are more likely to be delinquent than are cyclothymes, who are soft-skinned and lack muscle.[36] William Sheldon,[37] Sheldon Glueck and Eleanor Glueck,[38] and Juan B. Cortes and Florence M. Gatti also supported body type theory. Cortes and Gatti even drew on body type theory to develop a biopsychosocial theory of delinquency.[39]

> **born criminal** An individual who is atavistic, who reverts to an earlier evolutionary level and is unable to conform his or her behavior to the requirements of modern society; thus, an individual who is innately criminal.

Contemporary Biological Positivism: Sociobiology

Central to the second period of biological positivism was **sociobiology**, which stresses the interaction between the biological factors within an individual and the influence of the particular environment. Supporters of this form of biological

> **sociobiology** An expression of biological positivism that stresses the interaction between biological factors within an individual and the influence of the person's particular environment; also the systematic study of the biological basis of all social behavior.

The infamous Kray twins; English gangsters Ronald and Reginald Kray—who committed many crimes during the 1960s throughout the United Kingdom. They are shown with Francis Shae, at her wedding to Reggie. Genealogical studies seem to say that a predilection for various types of behavior, including delinquency, might have at least a partial genetic basis. ▶ What implications might such theories have for controlling delinquency?

Library Extra 3.2

DNA and Behavior: Is Our Fate in Our Genes?

positivism claim that what produces delinquent behavior, like other behaviors, is a combination of genetic traits and social conditions. Recent advances in experimental behavior genetics, human population genetics, the biochemistry of the nervous system, experimental and clinical endocrinology and neurophysiology, and other related areas have led to more sophisticated knowledge of the way in which the environment and human genetics interact to affect the growth, development, and functioning of the human organism.[40]

Sociological research has examined the influence of environment and genetics through twin and adoption studies and has also addressed intelligence; neuropsychological factors, including brain functioning and temperament as well as learning disabilities; and biochemical factors in delinquency. Let's look at each of these areas of investigation.

Twin and Adoption Studies

The role of genetic influences on behavior has been suggested by numerous twin and adoption studies.[41] These studies were supported early on by research done in Denmark and other European countries, but more recently they have found support among researchers in the United States (see Library Extra 3.2).

Twin Studies   The comparison of identical twins (monozygotic [MN]) with same-sex nonidentical (or fraternal) twins (dizygotic [DZ]) provides the most comprehensive data for exploring genetic influences on human variation. Identical twins develop from a single fertilized egg that divides into two embryos; hence, their genes are the same. Fraternal twins develop from two separate eggs that were both fertilized during the act of conception, so about half their genes are the same. Early in the twentieth century, researchers reasoned that by studying twins, they could accurately determine hereditary influences on behavior by comparing concordance rates of behavior (rates of agreement in behavior outcomes among pairs of individuals) of identical and fraternal twins. If heredity influenced behavior more than environment, identical twins should have higher concordance rates than fraternal twins.[42] A number of twin studies have found support for genetic contributions to criminal behavior:

- Karl O. Christiansen and S. A. Mednick reported on a sample of 3,586 twin pairs from Denmark between 1870 and 1920. The subset used by these researchers included almost all the twins born between 1881 and 1910 in a certain region of Denmark. Criminal justice statistics turned up 926 offenses for the 7,172 twins, coming from 799 twin pairs. Although the concordance rates (i.e., frequency of both twins showing the same trait) in this study were lower than in earlier surveys, they were still significant and indicated a genetic contribution to criminal behavior.[43]
- Thomas Bouchard Jr. examined three large data sets to assess the heritability of five basic personality traits: extroversion, neuroticism, agreeableness, conscientiousness, and openness.[44] He concluded, "The similarity we see in the personality between biological relatives is almost entirely genetic in origin."[45]
- Robert Plomin, Michael Owen, and Peter McGuffin summarized the findings on medical disorders, behavioral disorders, and various abilities in identical and nonidentical twins. They concluded that a strong genetic component appears to be present with a wide range of disorders and abilities but that a wide variation in the importance of genetics also seems to be evident among the disorders and abilities considered.[46]

- M. J. H. Rietveld and colleagues' 2003 study of 3,853 twin pairs found that shared environment, which is usually conceived of as family environment, had little effect on a child's level of overactivity.[47] This study of twins, drawn from the Netherlands Twin Registry, suggests that attention problems are due more to genetic factors than to environmental influences. The study adds weight to the literature supporting a significant role for genetic factors as determinants of human behavior.[48]
- The Minnesota Twin Family Study of twins raised apart from each other found that identical (MZ) twin children have similar brain wave patterns, become more similar in terms of abilities (arithmetic scores and vocabularies), and tend to die at about the same age. Fraternal twins become less similar in terms of abilities as they age, fraternal twins do not show as much similarity in brain wave patterns, and they are likely to die at different ages.[49]

Adoption Studies   The largest systematic adoption study of criminality examined all nonfamilial adoptions in Denmark from 1924 to 1947, a sample which included 14,427 male and female adoptees and their biological and adoptive parents. After exclusions—because criminal records or other kinds of demographic information were missing—the analysis involved no fewer than 10,000 parents in the four parental categories (i.e., biological/adoptive, mother/father) and more than 13,000 adoptees. The parents were counted as criminal if either the mother or father had a criminal conviction. Of adopted boys who had neither adoptive nor biological criminal parents, 13.5% had at least one conviction. The percentage rose slightly to 14.7 if adoptive (but not biological) parents were criminal; if biological (but not adoptive) parents were criminal, 20% of the boys had at least one conviction. Boys with both adoptive and biological criminal parents had the highest proportion: 24.5% Christiansen concluded that criminality of the biological parents is more important than that of the adoptive parents, a finding that suggests genetic transmission of some factor or factors associated with crime.[50]

In sum, the evidence from these and other studies of twins and adoptees is impressive. However, the twin method does have a number of weaknesses. The differences in MZ and DZ twin similarities tell us about genetic involvement only to the extent that the MZ–DZ difference is not related to environmental differences; also, the small number of twin pairs makes adequate statistical comparisons difficult. Further, it is not always easy to determine if twins are monozygotic or dizygotic. Finally, official definitions of crime and delinquency, with all their limitations, are exclusively used.[51]

Intelligence

With the growing acceptance of sociobiology in the 1960s and 1970s, researchers again turned their attention to intelligence as a possible factor in delinquent behavior. A number of studies have been done:

- D. J. West and D. P. Farrington, in conducting a longitudinal study of 411 English boys, found that those who later became criminals typically had lower IQs than those who did not. The authors concluded that intelligence is a meaningful predictive factor for future delinquency.[52]
- Lis Kirkegaard-Sorensen and Sarnoff A. Mednick also conducted a longitudinal study on the value of adolescent intelligence test scores for the prediction of later criminality. They found that adolescents who later committed criminal acts had lower intelligence test scores than their more law-abiding peers.[53]
- Robert A. Gordon, in comparing delinquency prevalence rates and delinquency incidence rates, concluded that minority juvenile males had higher arrest rates and court appearance rates than white males or females regardless of any specific geographic location, rural or urban. He proposed that differences in IQ might provide the strongest explanation of these persistent differences in unlawful behavior.[54] In another paper, Gordon stated that "[lower] IQ was always more successful in accounting for the black–white differences [in crime] than income, education, or occupational status."[55]

Some research suggests that temperament, including tendencies toward aggression, has a biological basis. ▶ What implications might such theories have for controlling or preventing delinquency?

Library Extra 3.3
Problem Behaviors in Maltreated Children and Youth: Influential Child, Peer, and Caregiver Characteristics

autonomic nervous system The system of nerves that govern reflexes, glands, the iris of the eye, and activities of interior organs that are not subject to voluntary control.

Library Extra 3.4
OJJDP Research Overview: *Juvenile Firesetting*

■ Travis Hirschi and Michael Hindelang reexamined three research studies—Hirschi's 1969 data from California, Marvin Wolfgang and associates' Philadelphia data, and Joseph Weis's data from the state of Washington—and found that "the weight of evidence is that IQ is more important than race and social class" for predicting delinquency.[56] These researchers also rejected the contention that IQ tests are race and class biased in that they favor middle-class whites and are therefore invalid means of comparing lower- and middle-class youths. They concluded that low IQ affects school performance, resulting in an increased likelihood of delinquent behavior.[57]

■ James Q. Wilson and Richard J. Herrnstein further contended that there is an inverse relationship between intelligence and certain types of adult criminality.[58]

Sociologists thought that the IQ issue was dead in the mid-1930s when research consistently challenged the relationship between IQ and delinquency, but later studies resurrected the issue. Unquestionably, whatever the correlation between IQ and delinquency, the association is strengthened by other environmental factors, such as school performance.[59] (See Library Extra 3.3 for a discussion of the effects of maltreatment on children's behavior.)

Neuropsychological Factors

Some neuropsychological factors appear to be more directly related to delinquent behavior than others, and some have received wider attention than others in various studies:

■ Studies by Hans Eysenck on the **autonomic nervous system** have their origins in the earlier attempts to understand the relationship between constitutional factors and delinquency. But his sociobiological theory goes one step further by noting the interactions of both biological and environmental factors. Eysenck contended that some children are more difficult to condition morally than others because of the inherited sensitivity of their autonomic nervous system. He argued that individuals range from those in whom it is easy to excite conditioned reflexes and whose reflexes are difficult to inhibit to those whose reflexes are difficult to condition and easy to extinguish (see Library Extra 3.4). Yet the moral conditioning of the child also depends on the quality of the conditioning the child receives within the family.[60]

■ Diana H. Fishbein and Robert W. Thatcher argued that electroencephalographic (EEG) abnormalities have been significantly correlated with individuals who are at risk for antisocial and aggressive behavior.[61] Fishbein and Thatcher reported that computerized EEG equipment can now measure the adequacy of neural processing and contend that an examination of EEG measures provides the hope of early detection and intervention for children with abnormal EEGs before behavioral problems develop. The dynamic interaction among physiology, biochemistry, environment, and behavior, then, can be identified by factors that have negative effects on brain development and functioning.[62]

■ Numerous studies have found that violent criminal offenders may have neuropsychological impairments.[63] An underlying contention of these studies, according to Elizabeth Kandel and Sarnoff A. Mednick, is that developmental deficits, in turn, may "predispose affected children to aggressive or violent behavior."[64] There is some evidence that pregnancy and birth complications may result in fetal brain damage, predisposing a child to impulsive and aggressive behavior.[65] For example, Kandel and Mednick's study of a Danish birth cohort found that "delivery events predicted adult violent offending, especially in high-risk subjects and recidivistically violent offenders."[66]

Brain Functioning and Temperament   A child's temperament is hard to define but can more easily be identified by the behaviors associated with it. Activity and emotionality are two of these behaviors. The term *activity* in this context refers to gross motor movements, such as moving the arms and legs, crawling, or walking. Children who exhibit an inordinate amount of movement compared with peers are sometimes labeled "hyperactive" or are said to have **attention deficit hyperactivity disorder (ADHD)**. **Emotionality** ranges from very little reaction to intense emotional reactions that are out of control.

The hyperactive child remains a temperamental mystery. This child's three behaviors are inattention (the child is easily distracted and does not want to listen), impulsivity (he or she shifts quickly from one activity to another), and excessive motor activity (he or she cannot sit still, runs about, is talkative and noisy). Educators note that ADHD children have difficulty staying on task, sustaining academic achievement in the school setting, remaining cognitively organized, and maintaining control over their behavior.[67]

ADHD is the most common neurobehavioral disorder of children, with the condition affecting between 5% and 10% of the children in the United States.[68] A 1999 study indicated that two-thirds of children with ADHD have at least one other condition, such as depression, anxiety, or learning disabilities.[69] There is also evidence that ADHD children have other problem behaviors, in addition to those in school, and that these problem behaviors increase the likelihood that such youngsters will become involved in delinquent acts and perhaps even go on to adult crime.[70] Exhibit 3.1 covers ADHD in detail.

attention deficit hyperactivity disorder (ADHD)   A cognitive disorder of childhood that can include inattention, distractibility, excessive activity, restlessness, noisiness, impulsiveness, and so on.

emotionality   An aspect of temperament. It can range from a near absence of emotional response to intense, out-of-control emotional reactions.

Learning Disability (LD)   Some evidence points to a link between having a **learning disability (LD)** and being involved in delinquent behavior. Research on LDs had its origin in 1948 when scientists labeled an organic disorder in children a "hyperkinetic impulse."[71] An LD is different from other types of disabilities because it does not disfigure or leave visible signs that would invite others to be understanding or offer support. It is a disorder that affects people's "ability . . . either [to] interpret what they see and hear or to link information from different parts of the brain. These limitations can show up in many ways—as specific difficulties with spoken and written language, coordination, self-control, or attention. Such difficulties extend to schoolwork and can impede learning to read or write or to do math."[72]

An LD can be a lifelong condition that affects many parts of an individual's life: school or work, family life, daily routines, and even friendships and play. Some people have many overlapping LDs, while others may have a single isolated learning problem that has little impact on other areas of their lives. LDs can be divided into three broad categories:

learning disability (LD)   A disorder in one or more of the basic psychological processes involved in understanding or using spoken or written language.

1. Developmental speech and language disorders
2. Academic skills disorders
3. Other (a catchall category including certain coordination disorders and learning handicaps not covered by the other classifications)[73]

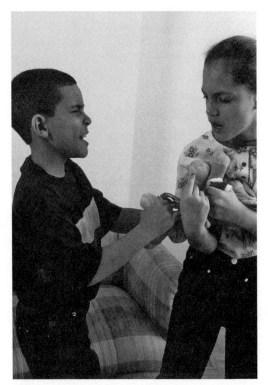

The most common types of LDs are dyslexia, aphasia, and hyperkinesis. Dyslexia is expressed in reading problems, particularly the inability to interpret written symbols. Aphasia consists of speech difficulties, often resulting from both auditory and visual deficiencies. Hyperkinesis, frequently equated with hyperactivity, is excessive muscular movement.[74] The dominant explanations for the cause of an LD lie in organic or neurological disorders, including birth injury or anything contributing to premature birth, infant or childhood disease, head injury, or lack of proper health care or nutrition.[75]

Fighting is characteristic of children who have ADHD. ▶ What is likely to happen to such children as they grow up?

EXHIBIT 3.1

Attention Deficit Hyperactivity Disorder (ADHD)

- Lacks attention to details or makes careless mistakes.
- Fails to sustain attention.
- Does not seem to listen.
- Has difficulty following through on instructions.
- Lacks organizational skills.
- Does not care for tasks that requires continuous mental effort.
- Misplaces things.
- Can be easily distracted.
- Tends to be forgetful.

AD/HD Predominantly Hyperactive-Impulsive Type: (AD/HD-HI)

- Squirms in chair or fidgets with hands or feet.
- Remaining seated is a problem.
- Climbs or runs about excessively.
- Finds it difficult to quietly engage in activities.
- Is hyper active in his movements.
- Seems to talk excessively.
- Has difficulty not blurting out answers before questions are completed.
- Struggles to take turns or wait on others.
- Frequently interrupts or intrudes upon the rights of others.

The possibility of a link between LDs and delinquency has been the subject of considerable debate, but the research findings are mixed.[76] Although the link between LDs and delinquency is questionable, the fact is that youngsters with LDs frequently do fail in school, and officials of the justice system seem to be influenced by this evidence of school failure to process them through the juvenile justice system.

Biochemical Factors

orthomolecular imbalance
A chemical imbalance in the body, resulting from poor nutrition, allergies, and exposure to lead and certain other substances, which is said to lead to delinquency.

Research has shown that some delinquent behavior can be attributed to an **orthomolecular imbalance** in the body or to brain toxicity. (The term *orthomolecular* refers to "correct chemical balances in the body.") Biochemists suggest that when normal functioning is affected by diet, pollutants, and/or genetic deficiencies such as allergies, abnormal deficits or excesses in molecular brain concentrations of certain substances can lead to various mental and behavioral problems, including delinquency.[77]

For example, there has been some interest in recent years in investigating the relationship between inadequate diet and delinquent behavior. S. Schoenthaler and I. Bier have conducted several tests in which they have consistently found a significant association between adolescents' diets and aggressive or delinquent behavior.[78]

Additionally, several studies have found that the presence of lead in a person's system can lead to increased delinquent behavior. Lead in extreme amounts can be fatal, but in smaller amounts it will cause negative behavior.[79] For example, Paul Stretesky and Michael Lynch examined lead concentrations in air across the United States and found that the areas with the highest amounts of lead reported the highest level of homicidal behaviors.[80]

In sum, there is some support for the idea that chemical imbalances in the body, resulting from faulty nutrition, allergies, and lead, are related to delinquent behavior (see Library Extra 3.5); at best, however, the link is very weak. Although faulty diet and vitamin deficiencies may affect how a juvenile feels, it does not necessarily follow that the adolescent will become involved in delinquent behavior.

Psychological Positivism

Some theories claim that juveniles commit delinquent acts because they have some underlying emotional problems or disturbances. According to these theories, juveniles may not have received adequate nurturing at home, and with that emotional

Library Extra 3.5
Greater Boston Physicians for Social Responsibility: *In Harm's Way: Toxic Threats to Child Development*

> > **EXHIBIT 3.2** < <

Henry's Story

One of the themes in this text is the social context of delinquency, that is, the influence of both the physical environment and other people on juveniles and their behavior. The following extract is taken from Bruce Bower's "Violent Developments: Disruptive Kids Grow into Their Behavior":

> Henry was headed for serious trouble. The 15-year-old provoked an endless series of fights at school and frequently bullied girls. Teachers regularly suspended him for his classroom disruptions. Older students taunted Henry in the hallways by calling him a sexual pervert or jeered him for having been held back in kindergarten. At home, his father browbeat and denigrated the boy, while his mother cried and muttered about how sick Henry had become.
>
> Henry liked violent video games. He downloaded information from a website on how to make pipe bombs and drew pictures of gory deaths of people who mistreated him. The boy openly expressed jealousy of the attention lavished on the youths in Columbine, Colo., who in 1999 fatally shot 12 of their classmates and a teacher and then committed suicide.
>
> In 2001, Henry's life took a fortunate turn. At his high school principal's insistence, he and his parents sought psychotherapy from Stuart W. Twemlow of the Menninger Clinic in Houston. In individual and family sessions, psychiatrist Twemlow zeroed in on the boy's fury at his parents and his tendency at school to view himself as a passive victim who needed to strike back at evil tormenters.
>
> Henry's feelings of rage abated as he grasped that his father struggled with his own deep-seated problems. Henry began taking martial arts training, as suggested by Twemlow, and attending a new school that had a healthier social environment. His grades improved. He started dating.
>
> Henry's story highlights a theme that is attracting scientific attention: Like all children, chronic troublemakers and hell-raisers respond to a shifting mix of social and biological influences as they grow. Some developmental roads are relentlessly toward brutality and tragedy. Others, like Henry's, plunge into a dark place before heading into the light of adjustment.
>
> Developmentally minded researchers are now beginning to map out violence-prone paths in hopes of creating better family and school interventions. New evidence indicates that a gene variant inherited by some people influences brain development in ways that foster impulsive violence, but only in combination with environmental hardships. Other studies explore how family and peer interactions build on a child's makeup to promote delinquency. Separate work examines ways to counteract the malign effect of bullying rituals and other types of coercion in schools.
>
> "Violence is such a complicated issue," Twemlow says. "There's always a set of preconditions to violent behavior and never just one cause."

SIGNATURE BRAINS

Andreas Meyer-Lindenberg says that he knows what a genetic risk for impulsive violence looks like in the brain. Ironically, he and his colleagues at the National Institute of Mental Health in Bethesda, Md., traced a portrait of rash aggression in the brains of placid people free of emotional problems, brain disorders, substance abuse, and arrest records.

Meyer-Lindenberg, a neuroscientist, directed studies of 142 white adults who had inherited one of two common versions of a gene that triggers production of an enzyme called monoamine oxidase A (MAOA). That enzyme controls the supply of an important brain chemical. One of the gene variants yields weak MAOA activity in the brain, resulting in elevated concentrations of serotonin. Too much of that chemical messenger upsets the regulations of emotions and impulses.

The other gene variant sparks intense MAOA activity, leading to serotonin concentrations at the low end of the normal range.

Several teams have already reported that children who endure severe abuse and also possess the weak-MAOA gene variant commit violent and delinquent acts later in life far more often than do abused kids who carry the strong-MAOA gene variant.

Source: Bruce Bower, "Violent Developments: Disruptive Kids Grow into Their Behavior," *Science News*, May 27, 2006. Reprinted with permission of *Science News*.

---

deprivation, they find it difficult to function in social contexts, such as school, sports, or community activities. They may also feel depressed, angry, or alienated, and this influenced their becoming involved in drugs and alcohol, property crimes, or even violent crimes. Psychologists view these emotional behaviors, which exist across gender, race/ethnicity, and class, as ultimately more important than social factors in explaining delinquency. Thus, psychological positivism differs from both classical and contemporary biological positivism because its focus is more on the emotional makeup of the personality than on the biological nature of the individual. At first, psychoanalytic (Freudian) theory was widely used with delinquents, but more recently other behavioral and humanistic schools of psychology have been applied to the problem of youth crime.

Psychoanalytic Explanations

Sigmund Freud, in developing **psychoanalytic theory**, contributed three insights that have shaped the handling of juvenile delinquents: (1) The personality is made up of three components; (2) every normal child passes through three psychosexual

psychoanalytic theory A theory based on Sigmund Freud's insights, which have helped to shape the handling of juvenile delinquents. They include these axioms: (1) The personality is made up of three components— id, ego, and superego; (2) a normal child passes through three psychosexual stages of development— oral, anal, and phallic; and (3) a person's personality traits are developed in early childhood.

stages of development; and (3) a person's personality traits are developed in early childhood.

Freud's theory of the personality involves the id, the ego, and the superego. The id has to do with a person's raw instincts and primitive drives; it wants immediate gratification of its needs and therefore tends to be primitive and savage. The ego and superego, the other two components, have the express purpose of controlling the primitive drives of the id; the ego mediates between the id and the superego and is important in the socialization of the child, and the superego, or the conscience, internalizes the rules of society. Thus, as a child develops, he or she learns to distinguish socially acceptable behavior from socially unacceptable behavior.[81]

Freud identified the oral, anal, and phallic stages as the life stages that shape personality development. The oral stage is experienced by the newborn infant, and pleasure is experienced in this stage through eating, sucking, and chewing. In the anal stage, which takes place between one and three years of age, urinary and bowel movements replace sucking as the basic source of pleasure for the child. During the phallic stage, which takes place in a normal child between the ages of three and six, the child receives pleasure from the genitals. Each stage brings increased social demands on the child and affects the way in which he or she deals with basic innate drives. The sexual and aggressive drives, in particular, create tensions that a child must learn to resolve in socially acceptable ways.[82]

Library Extra 3.6

The Juvenile Psychopath: Fads, Fictions, and Facts

Freud also argued that by the time the child reaches age five, all the essential ingredients of a child's adult personality are determined (see Library Extra 3.6). What a child has experienced emotionally by the age of five affects that child for the rest of his or her life. Emotional traumas experienced in childhood are likely to cause lifelong psychological problems.[83] Delinquency across the life course, according to this position, is continually affected by what a person has experienced as a young child.

Freud's followers have identified four ways in which emotional problems that develop in childhood might lead to delinquent behavior[84]:

1. Delinquent behavior is related to neurotic development in the personality. Freud established a relationship between desire and behavior; that is, everything is integrated in the subconscious drives of the organism. A youth may feel guilty about a socially unacceptable desire and, as a result, seek out self-defeating behaviors.
2. Freudians attribute delinquent behavior to a defective superego. A person who fails to develop a normally functioning superego can be unable to feel guilt, to learn from experience, or to feel affection toward others.[85] Such individuals, sometimes called sociopathic or psychopathic, may constantly express aggressive and antisocial behavior toward others.
3. Violent delinquent behavior sometimes can result if a child with an overdeveloped superego represses all negative emotional feelings throughout childhood to the degree that these repressed feelings explode in a violent act in adolescence. So-called model adolescents occasionally become involved in violent crimes toward parents and neighbors, sometimes horribly mutilating their victims.[86]
4. Delinquent involvements can be related to a search for compensatory gratification. According to Freud, individuals who are deprived at an early age of development later seek the gratification they missed. An adolescent may become an alcoholic to satisfy an oral craving or may become sadistic because of poor toilet training received during the anal period.

Many workers have taken the insights of psychoanalysis and applied them to the situations of delinquents. William Healy focused on mental conflicts that originated in unsatisfactory family relationships. He pioneered the establishment of psychiatric child guidance clinics in several U.S. cities under the auspices of the Commonwealth Fund Program for the Prevention of Delinquency.[87] August Aichhorn thought that delinquents had considerable hatred toward their parents because of the conflictual nature of the family relationship and that they transferred this hatred to other authority figures; he believed that institutionalized delinquents, exposed to the love and acceptance of a therapeutic relationship, would learn to trust one adult figure and, in turn, to respond more appropriately to other adults.[88] Kate Friedlander focused on the development of antisocial characteristics in the personality, such as selfishness, impulsiveness, and irresponsibility, which she defined as the results of disturbed ego development in early childhood. According to Friedlander, delinquency is an alternative way to fulfill desires the youth is unwilling to express directly.[89]

Sensation Seeking and Delinquency

Sensation seeking is a much different approach to psychological positivism. Derived from optimal arousal theory, sensation seeking can be defined as "an individual's need for varied, novel and complex sensations and experiences and the willingness to take physical and social risks for the sake of such experiences."[90] Ideas about sensation seeking assume that organisms are driven or motivated to obtain an optimal level of arousal.[91] Could this desire for excitement be a factor in delinquency?

Several observers have noted that delinquency is an enjoyable activity.[92] Researchers in the 1980s and 1990s gave frequent attention to the relationship between sensation seeking and crime. Helene Raskin White, Erich W. Labouvie, and Marsha E. Bates found that both male and female delinquents have higher rates of sensation seeking and lower rates of inhibited behavior than nondelinquents.[93] Walter R. Gove found from his study of inmates in a medium-security prison that inmates most frequently cited sensation seeking as an important motive for the crimes of shoplifting, burglary, robbery, assault, and rape.[94]

Jack Katz's controversial book *Seduction of Crime* conjectured that when individuals commit a crime, they become involved in "an emotional process—seductions and compulsions that have special dynamics" and that it is this "magical" and "transformative" experience that makes crime "sensible," even "sensually compelling"; for example, Katz stated that for many adolescents, shoplifting and vandalism offer "the attractions of a thrilling melodrama," because "quite apart from what is taken, they may regard 'getting away with it' as a thrilling demonstration of personal competence, especially if it is accomplished under the eyes of adults."[95]

Katz argued that instead of approaching criminal or delinquent behavior from the traditional focus on background factors, we need to give more consideration to the foreground or situational factors that directly precipitate antisocial acts and reflect crimes' sensuality. According to Katz, offenders' immediate social environment and experiences encourage them to construct crimes as sensually compelling.[96]

Reinforcement Theory

James Q. Wilson and Richard Herrnstein's *Crime and Human Nature* combined biosocial factors and psychological research with rational choice theory to redevelop reinforcement theory.[97] Wilson and Herrnstein considered potential causes of crime and of noncrime within the context of **reinforcement theory**, the theory that behavior is governed by its consequent rewards and punishments, as reflected in the history of the individual.

reinforcement theory A perspective that holds that behavior is governed by its consequences, especially rewards and punishments that follow from it.

The rewards of crime, according to Wilson and Herrnstein, are found in the form of material gain, revenge against an enemy, peer approval, and sexual gratification. The consequences of crime include pangs of conscience, disapproval of peers, revenge by the victim, and, most important, possibility of punishment. The rewards of crime tend to be more immediate, whereas the rewards of noncrime generally are realized in the future. Wilson and Herrnstein showed how gender, age, intelligence, families, schools, communities, labor markets, mass media, and drugs, as well as variations across time, culture, and race, greatly influence the propensity to become involved in criminal behavior, especially violent offenses.[98]

Wilson and Herrnstein's theory has serious flaws. Most importantly, according to Edgar Z. Friedenberg, is that the theory shows a disdain for the social context in which crime occurs. What Wilson and Herrnstein do, in effect, is factor society out of their consideration of crime. Instead of examining criminal behavior as part of complex social mechanisms and attempting to understand the connection, they typically reason that no conclusion is possible from the available data and therefore that no programs for reducing criminality among groups perceived as major sources of crime are worth their costs.[99]

Personality and Crime

trait-based personality model
A theory that attributes delinquent behavior to an individual's basic inborn characteristics.

A **trait-based personality model** offers another set of perspectives on the sources of criminal behavior.[100] Traits are essential personal characteristics of individuals that are relevant to a wide variety of behavioral domains, including delinquency and criminality.[101] There are a number of researchers who have made contributions in this area:

■ Sheldon Glueck and Eleanor Glueck's study *Unraveling Juvenile Delinquency* examined a sample of 500 juvenile offenders and 500 nonoffenders in an effort to discover significant distinctions in the personality traits of the two groups. They found that the delinquents were more defiant, ambivalent about authority, extroverted, fearful of failure, resentful, hostile, suspicious, and defensive than the nondelinquents.[102]

■ J. J. Conger and W. C. Miller, in a longitudinal study of male delinquents using all the boys entering the tenth grade in Denver, Colorado, public schools in 1956, found that by the age of 15, delinquents could be differentiated from nondelinquents either by the standard personality tests or by teacher evaluations. Delinquents, on the average, were characterized as emotionally unstable, impulsive, suspicious, hostile, given to petty expressions of irritation, egocentric, and typically more unhappy, worried, and dissatisfied than their nondelinquent counterparts.[103]

■ Avshalom Caspi and his colleagues examined the personality traits of youthful offenders in New Zealand and Pittsburgh and found that "greater delinquency participation was associated with a personality configuration characterized by high Negative Emotionality and weak Constraint."[104] They concluded that "negative emotions may be translated more readily into antisocial acts when Negative Emotionality (the tendency to experience aversive affective states) is accompanied by weak Constraint (difficulty in impulse control)."[105]

■ Joshua D. Miller and Donald Lynam's meta-analysis of the basic models of personality identified certain traits that are more characteristic of antisocial personalities: hostility, self-centeredness, spitefulness, jealousy, and indifference to others. Antisocial individuals also typically lack ambition, perseverance, and motivation; hold nontraditional and unconventional values and beliefs (e.g., are low in conscientiousness); and have difficulty controlling their impulses.[106]

psychopath An individual with a personality disorder, or a hard-core juvenile delinquent/adult criminal; also called a *sociopath*.

Web Extra 3.1
Society for Research in Psychopathology

The Psychopath

Hard-core juvenile delinquents are sometimes diagnosed as **psychopaths** (also called *sociopaths*). According to DSM-IV, these individuals are usually diagnosed with a conduct disorder (see Web Extra 3.1). The claim is made that the psychopath or sociopath is the unwanted, rejected child who grows up but remains an undomesticated "child" and never develops trust in or loyalty to other adults.[107] Hervey Cleckley gave an early description of this type of personality, listing 16 characteristics he had noted in his practice.[108] More recently, Robert D. Hare and colleagues developed a new checklist for those with antisocial personality with a conduct disorder. Among the most significant items on the list are the following:

1. Conning and manipulativeness
2. Lack of remorse or guilt
3. Callousness and lack of empathy
4. Lack of realistic long-term goals
5. Impulsivity
6. Failure to accept responsibility for their actions[109]

The continuity between childhood symptoms of emotional problems and adult psychopathic behavior emerged in L. N. Robins's 30-year follow-up of 526 white children who were patients in a St. Louis, Missouri, guidance clinic in the 1920s.[110] Excluding cases involving organic brain damage, schizophrenia, mental retardation, or symptoms appearing only after heavy drug or alcohol use, she found that the adult sociopath is almost invariably an antisocial child grown up. In fact, she found no case of adult sociopathy without antisocial behavior before the age of 18; more than 50% of the sociopathic males showed an onset of symptoms before the age of 8.[111]

Linda Mealey argued that there are two kinds of sociopaths: primary sociopaths and secondary sociopaths. *Primary sociopaths* have inherited traits that predispose them to illegal behavior; that is, they have a genotype that predisposes them to antisocial behavior. *Secondary sociopaths,* in contrast, are constitutionally normal but are influenced by such environmental factors as poor parenting. Thus, she argued that one type of sociopathic behavior has a genetic basis and the other is environmentally induced.[112] See Web Extra 3.2 for information on treatment for antisocial personality disorder.

Some interest has been expressed in measuring the relationship between psychopathy and violent behavior among juveniles. At least four instruments have been designed to assess psychopathic features among juveniles: the Psychopathy Checklist, Youth Version (PCL:YV); two versions of the Antisocial Processes Screening Device (APSD); and a Psychopathy Content scale on the Millon Adolescent Clinical Inventory (MACI). Daniel C. Murrie and colleagues found that the PCL:YV scores were significantly correlated with the severity of prior violence, violent offense history, and institutional violence.[113] Raymond R. Corrado and colleagues' study also revealed that the PCL:YV significantly predicted violent and general recidivism among male adolescent offenders, but this latter study indicated that this instrument showed behavioral psychopathic symptoms more clearly than it did interpersonal or affective traits.[114]

How frequently are psychopaths found among delinquents? One study of prison inmates found that only 15–25% met the criteria for psychopathy.[115] Based on working with inmates for several years in a maximum-security juvenile institution, one of the authors would agree that those numbers seem reasonable for delinquents who commit serious personal and property offenses. Yet the numbers are much higher, perhaps 30–40%, for those institutionalized delinquents who have some psychopathic characteristics. These psychopathic characteristics, such as the inability to feel shame, result in so many of these youths being classified with conduct disorders when they are admitted to an institution.[116] Delinquents in the community would appear to have considerably lower rates of psychopathy, and this is probably even more true with status offenders.

Cognitive Theory

Another psychological approach that has been applied to delinquent behavior is **cognitive theory**, a theory indebted to Jean Piaget, a Swiss psychologist who proposed that children's reasoning processes develop in an orderly fashion. His theory asserts that children construct their cognitive abilities through self-motivated action in the

Web Extra 3.2

National Library of Medicine: *Antisocial Personality Disorder*

Voices of Delinquency

Read "Forgotten Children." This is an account of an offender who has been diagnosed as having a conduct disorder or psychopathic tendencies. How does the subject explain why he became a violent person? From your reading of this story, do you believe that he is psychopathic?

cognitive theory A perspective on human development that says children develop cognitive abilities through interaction with the physical and social worlds.

world, and he proposed that children develop through four main periods: (1) sensori-motor period (years 0–2), (2) preoperational period (years 2–7), (3) concrete operational period (years 7–11), and (4) formal operational period (years 11–adulthood). This final period is when adults can use abstract and logical thinking.[117]

Lawrence Kohlberg later adapted cognitive theory to moral development in children's decision making, using three levels and six stages. He interviewed 72 white boys in Chicago about the dilemma of Heinz, asking the boys whether a fictional and financially strapped person named Heinz did right or wrong in stealing a drug for his dying wife. Kohlberg found that young children assumed they had no choice but to obey the rules handed down by authorities. Accordingly, Heinz was wrong to steal the drug, a child typically says in Stage 1, "because it is bad to steal" or "because it is against the law to steal." However, once children become aware that more than one way exists of doing things, they move to making moral decisions from a position of self-interest (Stage 2). Improving individual relationships becomes the main concern in Stage 3, whereas by Stage 6, a person works for a moral society—for justice—to the point of disobeying unjust laws.[118] Kohlberg's levels and stages of moral reasoning are as follows:

Level I: Preconventional Morality

Stage 1. Individuals make moral decisions on the basis of what is best for themselves, without regard for the feelings or needs of others. In terms of punishment, avoidance and obedience, they obey rules only if established by more powerful individuals.
Stage 2. Individuals begin to recognize that others also have needs, but they continue to define right and wrong primarily in terms of consequences to themselves.

Level II: Conventional Morality

Stage 3. Individuals make moral decisions on the basis of what actions will please others, especially authority figures. They now consider others' intentions in determining innocence or guilt.
Stage 4. Individuals look to society as a whole for guidelines concerning what is right or wrong. They believe rules to be inflexible and believe that it is their "duty" to follow them.

Level III: Postconventional Morality

Stage 5. Individuals recognize that rules represent an agreement among many people about appropriate behavior and that rules are flexible and can be changed if they no longer meet society's needs.
Stage 6. Individuals adhere to a small number of abstract universal principles that transcend specific concrete rules. They answer to an inner conscience and may break rules that violate their own ethical principles.[119]

Kohlberg later extended his studies to a population of criminals and found that they were significantly lower in moral judgment than noncriminals. The majority of criminals were classified in Stages 1 and 2 while the majority of nonoffenders could be placed in Stages 3 and 4.[120] In later studies of delinquents, he found that they were "stuck" in a state of moral immaturity and usually could be placed in any of the first three stages. Many hard-core delinquents, he further found, would be placed at the punishment stage (Stage 1), because they only believe something is right or wrong because it hurts if you do what society thinks is wrong.[121]

Aaron T. Beck, who has become a major spokesperson for cognitive theory, has also examined offenders and found that offenders' sense of personal vulnerability is seen in their hypersensitivity to specific kinds of social confrontations, including domination or disparagement. These individuals react by fighting back or by attacking a weaker adversary. Whether juveniles or adults, violent offenders see themselves

TABLE 3.1 Summary of Biological, Sociobiological, and Psychological Theories of Delinquency

Theory	Proponents	Causes of Crime Identified	Supporting Research
Atavistic (or born) criminal	Lombroso	The atavistic criminal is a reversion to an earlier evolutionary form.	Weak
Genealogical studies	Dugdale, Goddard	Criminal tendencies are inherited.	Weak
Body type	Sheldon, Glueck and Glueck, Cortes, Gatti	Mesomorphic body type correlates with criminality.	Weak
Genetic factors	Christiansen and Mednick	Twin and adoption studies show a genetic influence on criminal tendencies.	Moderately strong
Intelligence	Hirschi and Hindelang	IQ is a meaningful factor in criminal behavior when combined with environmental factors.	Moderately strong
Autonomic nervous system	Eysenck	Insensitivity of the autonomic nervous system, as well as faulty conditioning by parents, may cause delinquent behavior.	Weak
Psychoanalytic theory	Freud	Unconscious motivations resulting from early childhood experiences lead to criminality.	Weak
Psychopathic or sociopathic personality	Cleckley	Inner emptiness as well as biological limitations causes criminal tendencies.	Moderately strong
Reinforcement theory	Wilson and Herrnstein	Several key constitutional and psychological factors cause crime.	Weak
Cognitive theory	Piaget, Kohlberg, and Beck	Lack of reasoning and moral development result in delinquent behavior.	Moderately strong

as victims and others as victimizers. Offenders' thinking is shaped by such rigid beliefs as authorities are controlling and punitive; spouses are deceitful, rejecting, and manipulative; outsiders are self-serving, hostile, and treacherous; and nobody can be trusted.[122]

In sum, psychologists present an abundance of qualitative evidence that delinquents are psychologically different, but it is difficult to substantiate on paper-and-pencil tests that personality differences actually exist between delinquents and nondelinquents.[123] What appears to be a reasonable position is that most delinquents have psychological traits within the normal adolescent range but that some delinquents do have acute emotional deficits. Table 3.1 summarizes the biological, sociobiological, and psychological theories of delinquency.

Developmental Theories of Delinquency

The effort to understand why individuals commit unlawful behavior began in earnest in the eighteenth century with the classical school of criminology. It continued throughout the twentieth century, where positivism took various forms: biological, psychological, and sociological. The twentieth century also saw renewed interest in the rational nature of criminal and delinquent behaviors. In the closing decades of the twentieth century, developmental (longitudinal) studies of delinquency—in which measurements of study subjects and groups were made over time—were undertaken in Canada, England, New Zealand, and the United States.[124]

These developmental studies found that delinquency has a beginning, continues for some youths into adulthood, and ends for most at some point during their lives. Developmental studies uncovered multiple dimensions to delinquency and underscored the importance of an integrative approach to understanding human behavior. Multi-causal understandings of delinquency recognize the role played by society, individual psychology, and biology (neurology and genetics), as well as the social pressures and opportunities facing young people. Still, developmental perspectives usually acknowledge that the adolescent retains human agency, or the ability to make decisions, at least to some degree. Thus, the final piece in understanding individual-level causes of delinquent behavior is recognition of the interrelationships among neurological, psychological, and sociological factors across the life course.

This section, which concludes this chapter, presents three well-known longitudinal studies of offending: (1) the New Zealand Developmental Study of Terrie E. Moffitt and colleagues, (2) the Montreal Longitudinal Experimental Study of Richard E. Tremblay and colleagues, and (3) the Cambridge Study in Delinquent Development led by David P. Farrington. The Rochester Youth Development Study, the Denver Youth Survey, the Pittsburgh Youth Study, and the Seattle Social Development Project are other important longitudinal studies of delinquent behavior that are described elsewhere in this text. The three studies discussed here, like most longitudinal studies in the field of delinquency, concerned themselves with accurately predicting antisocial behavior.

Moffitt's Trajectories of Offending

Terrie E. Moffitt, Donald R. Lynam, and Phil A. Silva, in their examination of the neuropsychological status of several hundred New Zealander males between the ages of 13 and 18 years, found that poor neuropsychological scores "were associated with early onset of delinquency [but were] unrelated to delinquency that began in adolescence."[125] Moffitt's developmental theory views the emergence of delinquency as proceeding along two developmental paths:

1. Children develop a lifelong tendency toward delinquency and crime at an age as early as 3 years, according to one path. They may begin to bite and hit at age 4, shoplift and be truant at age 10, sell drugs and steal cars at age 16, rob and rape at age 22, and commit fraud and child abuse at age 30.[126] These "life-course-persistent" (LCP) offenders, according to Moffitt, are likely to continue to engage in illegal activity throughout their lives, regardless of the social conditions and personal situations they experience. During childhood, they may also exhibit such neuropsychological problems as attention deficit disorders or hyperactivity and learning problems in school.[127]

2. Moffitt also identified a path wherein the delinquents start offending during their adolescent years and then begin to desist from delinquent behavior around their eighteenth birthday. Moffitt refers to these youthful offenders as "adolescent-limited" (AL) delinquents, and it is this limited form of delinquency that characterizes most children who become involved in illegal activity.

The early and persistent problems that characterize members of the LCP group are not found in the AL delinquents, yet the frequency of offending and even the violence of offending among members of the AL group during their adolescent years may be as high as in LCP delinquents. Moffitt noted that AL antisocial behavior is learned from peers and sustained through peer-based rewards and reinforcements. AL delinquents continue in delinquent acts as long as such behaviors appear profitable or rewarding to them, but they will abandon those forms of behavior when prosocial activities become more rewarding.[128]

Tremblay's Trajectories of Offending

The Montreal Longitudinal Experimental Study (MLES) began in 1984. Its original aim was to study the development of antisocial behavior from kindergarten to high school with a major focus on the role of parent–child interactions. The study initially assessed all kindergarten boys in 53 schools located in poor socioeconomic areas in Montreal in an effort to identify the most disruptive boys. The study also examined parent–child social interactions of a subset of approximately 80 of these boys throughout their high school years. The study authors believed that disruptive kindergarten boys from low socioeconomic environments in large urban areas would be more at risk of frequent and serious delinquent behavior later in life compared to population samples of other young males and females. It was hoped that comparisons of the two groups would provide cues to the causes of delinquency in the high-risk group and that the results would also provide indicators of effective preventive interventions using parent–child interactions.[129]

Mother and teacher ratings and self-reported delinquency were the main instruments used to assess behavioral problems under the MLES. Behavior ratings were obtained annually from mothers and from classroom peers at ages 10, 11, and 12 years. A psychiatric interview was conducted with the boys and their mothers when the boys were 15 years old; direct observations of social interactions were made at home, at school, and in laboratory situations from ages 7 to 15 years; and psychophysiological and neuropsychological tests, as well as various biological assessments, were used with boys in the study group until they reached the age of 20 years.[130]

The study produced the following key findings:

- Higher levels of disruptive behavior during kindergarten effectively predicted higher levels of delinquency before entry into high school.
- Physical aggression during kindergarten is the best behavioral predictor of later delinquency.
- No significant group of boys started to show chronic problems of physical aggression, opposition, or hyperactivity after their kindergarten year.
- Hyperactivity and anxiety significantly predicted the age of onset of smoking cigarettes, drinking to excess, and using drugs up to 15 years of age. Boys who had a high score on hyperactivity and a low score on anxiety were more likely to use substances at an early age.
- Boys exhibiting high levels of aggression and fighting between 5 and 12 years of age had generally lower heart rates at 11 and 12 years of age than other boys, controlling for pubertal status, body size, and level of family adversity.
- Family poverty predicted academic failure at age 16 years. Family poverty also predicted delinquency, but only more serious forms of adolescent antisocial behavior.
- Not being in an age-appropriate classroom at age 16 years was associated with delinquency.
- Less parental monitoring was associated with an increased risk of self-reported extreme delinquency.
- Deviant friends led to more delinquency, irrespective of boys' disruptiveness.
- Assessment of the boys up to 17 years of age revealed that parent training interventions had long-term beneficial influences on many boys' development.[131]

Realizing that the potential for later antisocial behavior could be identified as early as kindergarten, Tremblay and his colleagues decided to investigate the earliest age of delinquency onset with new longitudinal studies beginning as early as pregnancy. The initial results indicated "that children initiate oppositional behavior, taking things away from others, and physical aggression as soon as they have the motor coordination and the opportunity to do so."[132]

Cambridge Study in Delinquent Development

This Cambridge study is a 40-year longitudinal survey that followed the development of antisocial behavior in 411 South London boys who were mostly born in 1953. The study was begun in 1961, with Donald West as its director during the first 20 years; for the last 20 years, David P. Farrington served as director.[133] The study aimed to measure as many factors as possible that might contribute to the development of delinquency.

Participants in the study were interviewed from ages 8 to 46 years. They were also periodically interviewed and tested in their schools, in their homes, and at the researchers' offices. Interviews with parents were also conducted by psychiatric social workers about once a year until each boy was in his last year of compulsory education. In addition, teachers completed questionnaires, and a variety of other behavioral and health information was collected.[134]

The study's chief findings were as follows:

- About 40% of the males in the study group were convicted of criminal offenses up to age 40 years, compared to a national prevalence of convictions for same-age males born in England and Wales of 31%.
- The prevalence of offending increased up to age 17 years and then decreased.
- The peak age of increase in the prevalence of offending was 14 years.
- Up to age 40 years, the mean age of first conviction was 18.6, and the mean age of last conviction was 25.7. Hence, criminal careers lasted an average of 7.1 years.
- Persistence in offending was seen in the significant continuity of offending that took place from one age range to another.
- Little specialization was evident in offending.
- Most juvenile and young adult offenses resulting in convictions were committed with others, but the incidence of co-offending declined steadily with age.
- The most important risk factors of later offending were (1) antisocial behavior during childhood, including troublesomeness, dishonesty, and aggressiveness; (2) hyperactivity-impulsivity; (3) low intelligence; (4) poor school achievement; (5) family criminality; (6) family poverty; and (7) poor parenting.[135]

The Cambridge study shows that delinquent acts that lead to convictions are components of a larger syndrome of relatively persistent antisocial behavior. Farrington observed a high degree of delinquent continuity between ages 18 and 32 years and proposed that behavioral stability can be found mostly in the individual rather than in the environment. Study authors noted "that there are individual differences between people in some general underlying theoretical construct which might be termed 'antisocial tendency,' which is relatively stable from childhood to adulthood."[136] See Table 3.2 for a summary of these developmental theories.

TABLE 3.2 Comparison of Three Developmental Studies

	Moffitt	Cambridge	Tremblay-Montreal
Sample	Followed 100 males and females from ages 3 to 29	Males born between 1951 and 1954	Followed Montreal children from birth
Delinquent Population	Two groups: Adolescence-Limited path (AL) and Life-Course-Persistent Path (LCP)	About one-third of the cohort	Potential for delinquency could be identified as early as kindergarten
Gender	Persistent Path is extremely rare with females	Only boys in study	Only boys in study
Race	N/A	N/A	N/A
Chronic Offenders	N/A	6 percent; 23 boys of the 396 had 6 or more convictions	N/A
Patterns of Delinquent Behavior	AL may be as high as LCP during adolescence, but LCP continue into adult behavior.	Early discrimination and treatment of persistent delinquency can help prevent adult criminality.	Higher levels of disruptive behavior during kindergarten predicts higher levels of delinquency before high school.

Importance of Theory

The last chapter pointed out that theory and research are intertwined and that they need to be the foundation for policy recommendations to deal with juvenile delinquency in the United States. Researchers have spent considerable time and effort trying to understand the causes and correlates of delinquency.[137] The question is: What is the value of studying theories of delinquent behavior? Perhaps the answer to this question can be found in the *Voices of Delinquency* that supplements this text.

With nearly every story, questions can be raised: How did this person's family background influence the course of his or her behavior? How did success or failure in school influence subsequent behaviors? How was he or she affected by the environment? Why did he or she become involved in a youth gang? Why did this person become a drug user? What influenced this person to stop taking drugs or becoming involved in other illegal behaviors?

More specifically, the student can inquire: Which theory found in Chapters 3–7 of this text seems to apply closely to the choices that this person made? If more than one theory is required to explain behavior, what theories would you use? If none of the theories found in these chapters seem to apply to a particular story, what theoretical constructs are needed to understand this behavior?

Delinquency theory, it will be found, is helpful in understanding why youngsters do what they do (see Figure 3.1). With this understanding comes the ability to provide guidance and direction for those who work with delinquent youths. With this understanding, parents can also have insight regarding how to provide nurturance and acceptance to their children. Finally, with this understanding, researchers are able to design studies that will further the knowledge of delinquent behavior.

FIGURE 3.1 Importance of Theory

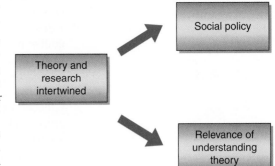

Delinquency across the Life Course: Desistance from Crime

An important consideration of life-course criminology is the matter of **desistance** from crime. One of the problems of establishing desistance is the difficulty of distinguishing between a gap in a delinquent career and true termination. There are bound to be crime-free intervals in the course of delinquent careers. To explain changes in offending over time, or desistance, theorists have proposed several explanations, which we'll consider by category:

desistance The termination of a delinquent career or behavior.

- *Maturation and aging account for desistance.* The maturation process appears to be involved in desistance, as youths or adults become aware either of the desirability of pursuing a conventional lifestyle or of the undesirability of continuing with unlawful activities. James Q. Wilson and Richard Herrnstein contended that the relatively minor gains from crime lose their power to reinforce deviant behavior as juveniles mature and develop increasing ties to conventional society.[138]
- *Developmental accounts for desistance.* One developmental explanation of desistance is that identity changes account for reduction or cessation of crime. Edward Mulvey and John LaRosa, focusing on the period from ages 17 to 20 years—the period they call the time of "natural" recovery—found that desistance was linked to a cognitive process taking place in the late teens when delinquents realized that they were "going nowhere" and that they had better make changes in their lives if they were going to be successful as adults.[139]
- *Rational choice accounts for desistance.* The main idea of the rational choice framework is that the decision to give up or continue with crime is based on a person's conscious reappraisal of the costs and benefits of criminal activity. Proponents of this

theory saw persisters and desisters as "reasoned decision makers."[140] David Farrington also noted that the severity of the adult penal system appeared to be a deterrent with the population he studied.[141]

- *Life-course perspective accounts for desistance.* The major objective of the life-course perspective, whose framework was discussed in Chapters 1 and 2, is to link social history and social structure. In 2003, Laub and Sampson published *Shared Beginnings, Divergent Lives,* which promises to be a classic study of life-course and developmental criminology. They argued that the data from the Gluecks' original study support the notion that explanations of desistance from crime and of persistence in crime are two sides of the same coin. From their analysis of offender narratives and life histories, Laub and Sampson perceived desistance as a process rather than an event—a process that operates simultaneously at different levels (individual, situational, and community) and across different contextual environments (especially family, work, and military service). They concluded that "offenders desist as a result of individual actions (choice) in conjunction with situational contexts and structural influences linked to key institutions that help sustain desistance."[142]

A central element in the desistance process, according to Laub and Sampson, is any change that "knifes off" individual offenders from their environment and at the same time offers them a new script for the future. The major turning points implicated in this study's desistance process included marriage/spouse, employment, reform school, the military, and neighborhood change. All of these turning points involve, to varying degrees, the following: "(1) New situations that knife off the past from the present. (2) New situations that provide both supervision and monitoring as well as new opportunities of social support and growth. (3) New situations that change and structure routine activities. (4) New situations that provide the opportunity for identity transformation."[143] In sum, offenders "choose to desist in response to structurally induced turning points that serve as the catalyst for sustaining long-term behavior change."[144]

Delinquency and Social Policy: Positive Youth Development

Positive Youth Development (PYD), previously discussed in Chapter 1, is a much different model for approaching adolescents and their issues. Supporters of this model claim that the traditional approaches to youth problems and societal interventions are based on a deficit-based perspective; instead, youth development activities and organizations should build on youths' resilience and competencies. They especially use the term *resilience* to describe the qualities that support healthy development in the face of adversity. Adolescents are seen not as objects that need to be acted upon but as self-directed, independent individuals who may deserve special care but who also merit the autonomy and dignity accorded other members of the community. The concepts of PYD propose that youths develop and flourish when they are connected to the right mix of relationships, opportunities, and social assets.[145]

This approach has long been present in the field of juvenile justice. The concepts of PYD can be seen in many prevention programs implemented through the years across the nation. Recently, the principles of PYD were championed throughout the federal government, including the White House, with the Helping America's Youth (HAY) initiative, launched by the Bush administration. The final report of the White House Task Force for Disadvantaged Youth highlighted research that shows that healthy adolescent development requires youth to have "caring adults in their lives, opportunities to learn marketable skills . . . and opportunities to contribute meaningfully in their communities and society."[146]

These are the basic principles of PYD practice:

- Youth development must strive to enhance individual and community capacities. One is not possible without the other.

- Youth development is predicated on youths exercising meaningful decision making over their programs.
- Youth development must break down racial/ethnic, gender, disability, sexual orientation, and class barriers and stereotypes.
- Youth development builds bridges between community-based organizations (formal and informal).
- Youth development activities must transform the environment in which youths live in the process of transforming the lives of participants.
- Youth development must provide participants with an opportunity to learn and at the same time to have fun.
- Youth development must provide youths with opportunities to serve their community.
- Youth development must provide youths with the necessary knowledge and skills that can be converted into meaningful lifelong employment.
- Youth development must actively integrate as many core elements as possible into all activities.[147]

PYD seems to be a particularly desirable approach for prevention programs as well as for those youths accused of less serious and nonviolent offenses, who make up three-quarters of the youths referred annually to juvenile justice authorities in the United States.[148]

Chapter Summary

This chapter examines individual-level explanations for delinquency, including personal decision making and the behavioral impact of rational choices made by young people. This chapter also points out the following:

- To justify punishing juveniles, theorists have turned to classical school principles or to the principles of rational choice theory, which build on classical thought. Both perspectives assert that individuals have free will and should be held responsible for their behavior.

- Policy makers in growing numbers are concluding that increasing the "cost" of crime to the perpetrator is the best way to reduce serious youth crime in the United States.

- Biological positivism and psychological positivism point to biological and psychological factors within the individual as the most significant determinants of delinquency.

- Biological and psychological factors may be very elusive, such as a difficult-to-condition autonomic nervous system or an inadequately developed superego, or they may be more easily discerned, such as inappropriate interpersonal relationships.

- Both early biological and psychological positivism theories have developed into more refined explanations of delinquent behavior. Early biological positivism has

largely been replaced by sociobiology, and psychoanalysis has been replaced by developmental models that give greater weight to the interactions between the individual and the environment.

- Children who have attention deficit hyperactivity disorder (ADHD) and learning disorders (LDs) tend to have problems in school; in turn, they tend to become involved with peers who demonstrate higher rates of delinquency.

- According to developmental perspectives, human behavior progresses along certain paths, with outcomes which are relatively predictable.

- Terrie Moffitt identified life-course-persistent (LCP) and adolescent-limited (AL) paths, in which young people either engage in persistent crime violation or temporarily experiment with delinquency.

- Richard Tremblay and colleagues' Montreal Longitudinal Experimental Study found that antisocial behavior was at its peak during the kindergarten years and that physical aggression during the kindergarten years is the best behavior predictor of later delinquency.

- In the Cambridge Study in Delinquent Development, David P. Farrington found that the types of acts that lead to convictions tend to be components of a larger pattern of antisocial behavior.

Key Terms

attention deficit hyperactivity
    disorder (ADHD), p. 67
autonomic nervous system, p. 66
biological positivism, p. 63
born criminal, p. 63
cognitive theory, p. 73
desistance, p. 79
determinism, p. 63

emotionality, p. 67
felicific calculus, p. 59
free will, p. 59
learning disability (LD), p. 67
orthomolecular imbalance, p. 68
positivism, p. 58
Progressive era, p. 62
psychoanalytic theory, p. 69

psychopath, p. 72
reinforcement theory, p. 71
routine activities approach, p. 60
social contract, p. 59
sociobiology, p. 63
trait-based personality model, p. 72
utilitarianism, p. 59

Review Questions

1. How do you explain the main contentions of the classical school?
2. How do you define positivism? Who were the early biological positivists?
3. How would you describe the psychopath? Why are psychopaths so difficult to treat?
4. What is sociobiology? What areas of sociobiology have findings related to delinquency?
5. What is psychological positivism? What has this position contributed to understanding delinquency?
6. What developmental studies were discussed in this chapter?

Discussion Questions

1. A rational choice theorist who studied the case of Billy would conclude that it was unfortunate that this young man had such a toxic and deprived family life but that this background did not take away his ability to make responsible decisions about his life. According to the concept of the rationality of crime, Billy freely chose to kill the old man; therefore he deserves to be punished for the murder. In your opinion, was Billy's decision rational? How much freedom did he have, and how much punishment did he deserve?
2. Does determinism negate the concepts of free will and choice? From your own experience, do you recall ever being so compelled to take some action that you could not avoid participation through the simple expedient of making a responsible choice? If so, what happened?
3. Does punishment deter delinquency or simply provoke escalation of delinquency as a retaliatory response?
4. Rational choice theory posits that crime and delinquency are the results of rational choices that people make. With this in mind, how might an increase in penalties associated with shoplifting impact the incidence of shoplifting in stores in your area? To what extent do you believe that increased punishments would reduce the number of offenses? What does that say about the rationality of crime?
5. Researchers seem to expend extraordinary effort seeking reliable means to predict delinquency and/or criminality. Do you think this indicates an unreasonable disregard for the roles of free will and personal choice in behavioral decisions? Explain your position.
6. A cynic might dismiss the causation research cited here as a waste of time, suggesting instead that human behavioral choices are simply elective decisions to behave one way or another. How would you respond?

Group Exercises

1. Have the class debate this question: Does the inability of the juvenile justice system to impose genuinely punitive responses to delinquency and criminality make a mockery of the concept of justice and, in fact, encourage continued delinquency/criminality?
2. Divide the class into two teams: the "Naturists" and the "Nurturists." Hold a debate on these two causational concepts.
3. Have students research the rates of learning disabilities (LDs) identified within the population of your state's prison system; then have them discuss their findings, specifically addressing whether they believe having an LD is a major causative contributor to criminality.

Introduction

F our Harlem teenagers were found guilty of second-degree murder of a New York University student for chasing him into a car's path during a robbery attempt on April 14, 2006.

Prosecutors said the boys held Broderick John Hehman in a bear hug, punched the side of his head, and tried to rob him. When Hehman broke free, they chased him into the street. Hehman was hit by a car, flew into the air, and smashed headfirst into the windshield. As he lay lifeless in the street, the boys stood on the corner laughing and didn't call for help afterwards. Hehman died three days later.

According to prosecutors, one of the boys had told the police that "he doesn't do robberies for money but for entertainment." A witness also reported that the attackers, who were black, said, "Get the white guy." Prosecutors, however, said the assault was not a hate crime because the assailants used race as a description, not a motive.

The two oldest assailants, ages 16 and 15, were sentenced to five and three years, respectively, in a state juvenile detention facility, with the possibility of extending their sentence year by year until they are 21 years old. The other assailants, both age 13, were sentenced to 18 months in juvenile detention, with extensions possible until they are 18 years old.

"This is just a 13-year-old kid who's just a baby," said the lawyer for one of the defendants. "He's really repentant." He added that his client attended school every day, is the child of a single mother, and had never been in trouble before.[1]

Chapters 4 through 6 examine sociological explanations for delinquency. This chapter looks closely at features of the social environment, termed **social structure**, that influence young people, causing some of them to commit delinquent acts.

The term *social structure* can have a variety of meanings. As used by sociologists, it can refer to entities or groups in relation to each other, to relatively enduring patterns of behavior and relationships within social systems, or to social institutions and norms embedded in social systems in such a way that they shape the behavior of actors within those systems. Social structure is related to delinquency by way of such factors as child poverty, racial disparity, disorganized communities, and unemployment.

Many of the social structural elements that we'll examine in this chapter could be found in the lives of the four youngsters in this chapter's opening story. They came from socially disorganized surroundings and, as lower-class youths, were part of a peer culture that had little stake in conventional values. Indeed, the pressure they felt to have more money, combined with their lack of ability to legitimately acquire it, was probably the determining factor in their attempt at robbery.

According to social structural theorists, explanations that focus on the individual fail to grasp the underlying social and cultural conditions that give rise to delinquent behavior. These theorists believe that the overall crime picture reflects conditions requiring collective social solutions. They urge that social reform, not individual counseling, be given the highest priority in efforts to reduce crime.

The causes of delinquency, as suggested by social structural theorists, include the social and cultural environment in which adolescents grow up and/or the subcultural groups in which they choose to become involved. Elijah Anderson's *Code of the Streets* is an influential book tracing the relationship between the structural breakdown of the community and the disorders of crime and drug use.[2]

social structure The relatively stable formal and informal arrangements that characterize a society, including its economic arrangements, social institutions, and values and norms.

EXHIBIT 4.1

Elijah Anderson and the Code of the Street

Elijah Anderson's *Code of the Streets*, which grew out of the ethnographic work Anderson did in two urban communities in Philadelphia, focused on the theme of interpersonal violence in the lives of inner-city youths. In questioning why so many inner-city adolescents are involved in violence and aggression, he concluded that in the economically deprived and drug-ridden communities in which they live, a "code of the streets" has replaced or at least weakened the rule of civil law.

A set of informal rules, or prescriptions for behavior, focuses on a search for respect. What is understood as respect is the "props" (or proper due). In this street culture, according to Anderson, respect is difficult to win and can be easily lost and requires constant vigilance. Respect is a form of social capital that is particularly valuable when other forms of capital are unavailable or have been lost.

The concept of "manhood" expresses respect and identity in the lives of these inner-city youths. This concept of manhood requires a certain ruthlessness and the ability to take care of oneself. It also requires having a sense of control, of being in charge, and of showing nerve. One's manhood must be communicated through words, gestures, and actions. Youths make it clear that everyone understands that if you mess with them, there will be "street justice or severe consequences because they are man enough to make you pay."

Source: Elijah Anderson, *Code of the Streets: Decency, Violence, and the Moral Life of the Inner City*; "The Code of the Street and African-American Adolescent Violence," *Research in Brief*, February 2009. www.ojp.usdoj.gov/nij; Karen F. Parker and Amy Reckdenwald, "Concentrated Disadvantage, Traditional Male Role Models, and African-American Juvenile Violence," *Criminology* 46 (2008), pp. 711–735; Nikki Jones, "Working 'the Code': On Girls, Gender, and Inner-City Violence," *Australian and New Zealand Journal of Criminology*, 41 (2008), pp. 63–83.

mycrimekit™

Video Introduction to Social Disorganization

social disorganization theory
An approach that posits that juvenile delinquency results when social control among the traditional primary groups, such as the family and the neighborhood, breaks down because of social disarray within the community.

Social structural theorists typically use official statistics as proof of their claim that forces such as social disorganization, cultural deviance, status frustration, and social mobility are so powerful that they induce lower-class youths to become involved in delinquent behavior. This chapter will examine several of these perspectives.

Social Disorganization Theory

Social disorganization can be defined as "the inability of a community structure to realize the common values of its residents and maintain effective social control."[3] **Social disorganization theory** suggests that macrosocial forces (e.g., migration, segregation, structural transformation of the economy, housing discrimination) interact with community-level factors (e.g., concentrated poverty, family disruption, residential turnover) to impede social organization. This sociological viewpoint focuses attention on the structural characteristics and mediating processes of community social organization that help explain crime while also recognizing the larger historical, political, and social forces that shape local communities.[4]

The intellectual antecedents of social disorganization theory can be traced to the work of Emile Durkheim; in Durkheim's view, anomie, or normlessness, resulted from society's failure to provide adequate regulation of its members' attitudes and behaviors. Loss of regulation was particularly likely when society and its members experienced rapid change and laws did not keep pace.[5]

Shaw and McKay

Social disorganization theory was developed by Clifford R. Shaw and Henry D. McKay during the first half of the twentieth century. Shaw and McKay, whose work helped found the Chicago School of Sociology, focused specifically on the social characteristics of the community as a cause of delinquency.[6] Their pioneering investigations established that delinquency varied in inverse proportion to the distance from the center of the city, that it varied inversely with socioeconomic status, and that delinquency rates in a residential area persisted regardless of changes in racial and ethnic composition of the area.[7]

Social Disorganization and the Community   Shaw and McKay viewed juvenile delinquency as resulting from the breakdown of social control among the traditional primary groups, such as the family and the neighborhood, because of the social

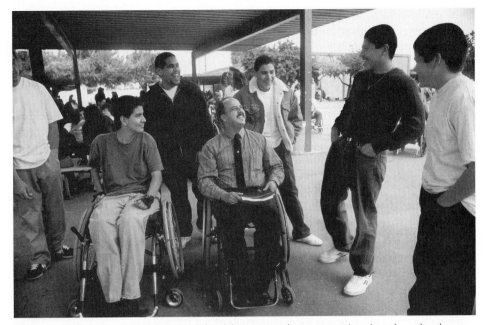

A former Hispanic gang member in a wheelchair counsels teens at a Los Angeles school.
▶ How might the social environment of a community contribute to delinquency?

disorganization of the community. Rapid industrialization, urbanization, and immigration processes contributed to the disorganization of the community. Delinquent behavior, then, became an alternative mode of socialization through which youths who were part of disorganized communities were attracted to deviant lifestyles.[8] The delinquent values and traditions, replacing traditional ones, were passed from one generation to the next.

Shaw and McKay turned to ecology to show this relationship between social disorganization and delinquency. Park and Burgess had earlier used the concept of ecology in explaining the growth of cities. Burgess, for example, suggested that cities do not merely grow at their edges but rather have a tendency to expand radially from their centers in patterns of concentric circles, each moving gradually outward.[9] Figure 4.1 is a diagram of the growth zones as Burgess envisioned them.

In 1929, Shaw reported that marked variations in rates of school truancy, juvenile delinquency, and adult criminality existed among different areas in Chicago. These rates varied inversely with the distance from the center of the city; that is, the nearer a given locality was to the center of the city; the higher its rates of delinquency and crime.[10] In 1942, Shaw and McKay published their classic work *Juvenile Delinquency and Urban Areas*, which developed these ecological insights in greater scope and depth.[11] They discovered that over a 33-year period, the vast majority of the delinquent boys came either from an area adjacent to the central business and industrial areas or from neighborhoods along two forks of the Chicago River.

Then, applying Burgess's concentric zone hypothesis of urban growth, they constructed a series of concentric circles, like the circles on a target, with the bull's-eye in the central city. Measuring delinquency rates by zones and by areas within the zones, they found that in all three periods the highest rates of delinquency were in Zone I (the central city), the next highest were in Zone II (next to the central city), and so forth, in progressive steps outward to the lowest rates in Zone V. Significantly, although the delinquency rates changed

FIGURE 4.1 Concentric Zones in Chicago

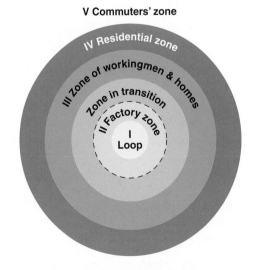

Source: Ernest W. Burgess, "The Growth of the City," in *The City*, edited by Robert E. Park, Ernest W. Burgess, and Roderick D. McKenzie (Chicago: University of Chicago Press, 1928), p. 51. Reprinted by permission.

Voices of Delinquency

Read "I Grew Up in New Orleans." How did the influence of his environment affect this youth? What aspects of Shaw and McKay's theory of social disorganization are found in the life of this youth?

from one period to the next, the relationships among the different zones remained constant, even though in some neighborhoods the ethnic compositions of the population had changed totally. During the first decade of the twentieth century, the largest portion of the population was German or Irish, but 30 years later it was Polish and Italian.[12]

Opportunity Structure and Delinquency   Shaw and McKay eventually refocused their analysis from the influence of social disorganization of the community to the importance of economics on high rates of delinquency. They found that the economic and occupational structures of the larger society were more influential in the rise of delinquent behavior than was the social life of the local community. They concluded that the reason members of lower-class groups remained in the inner-city community was less a reflection of their newness of arrival and their lack of acculturation to American institutions than a function of their class position in society.[13]

differential opportunity structure   The differences in economic and occupational opportunities open to members of different socioeconomic classes.

The consequences of this **differential opportunity structure** led to a conflict of values in local communities: Some residents embraced illegitimate standards of behavior, whereas others maintained allegiance to conventional values. Delinquent groups were characterized by their own distinctive standards, and Shaw and McKay became increasingly involved in examining the process through which delinquents came to learn and to pass on these standards.[14]

Cultural Transmission Theory   Shaw and McKay also elaborated on social disorganization theory by arguing that delinquent behavior became an alternative mode of socialization through which youths who were part of disorganized communities were attracted to deviant lifestyles.[15] This line of thought became known as the cultural deviance component of social disorganization theory.

Shaw and McKay further contended that the delinquent values and traditions that replaced traditional social standards were not the property of any one ethnic or racial group but were culturally transmitted from one generation to the next.[16] As evidence in support of this **cultural transmission theory**, these researchers found that certain inner-city areas continued to have the highest delinquency rates in Chicago despite shifts in population of nearly all of these areas.

cultural transmission theory   An approach that holds that areas of concentrated crime maintain their high rates over a long period, even when the composition of the population changes rapidly, because delinquent "values" become cultural norms and are passed from one generation to the next.

Shaw and McKay assumed that juvenile and adult gangs in these areas accounted for the transmission of this tradition of delinquency. Figure 4.2 diagrams the theoretical constructs of Shaw and McKay's social disorganization theory.

Evaluation of Shaw and McKay's Disorganization Theory   Few studies in the area of delinquency have been as influential in the development of research, theory, and social action as those of social disorganization theory. Let's survey the reasons why social disorganization theory has been so influential in the development of criminological theory:

- Shaw and McKay's studies addressed the problem of crime in terms of multiple levels of analysis. They shifted attention away from individual characteristics of delinquents and nondelinquents and toward group traditions in delinquency and the influence of the larger community. Thus, Shaw and McKay provided a theoretical framework bridging sociological and social psychological explanations.[17]
- Shaw and McKay's social disorganization theory also contributed to a rediscovery of the importance of macrolevels and the community in studies of delinquency. This rediscovery has led to the conclusion that an adequate understanding of the causes of illegal behavior requires an examination of the social structure, the individual, and other social contexts (such as primary groups) that mediate between the individual and that structure.[18]

FIGURE 4.2 Shaw and McKay's Social Disorganization Theory

Socially disorganized neighborhood → Failure of informal social controls → Increased gang activity → Cultural transmission of delinquent traditions → Increased delinquent activity

According to sociologist Albert Cohen, the destruction of property is a consequence of reaction formation, in which lower-class youths respond to the strain of being held to the standards of middle-class culture. ▶ What about middle-class youths who commit such acts? Does Cohen's theory hold true for them, or can their acts be attributed to other factors?

- Moreover, Shaw and McKay's theory has influenced research on how people and institutions adapt to their environment.[19] They saw the delinquent gang as a normal response to slum conditions and the social deprivations of local environments.

- Finally, recent examination of the social disorganization perspective has opened up exciting new avenues of research inquiry that to some extent have gone beyond Shaw and McKay's original work.[20] For example, Shaw and McKay's work has been updated by social ecology. The main contention of this position is that living in deteriorated environments, in which there is poverty, drugs, violence, and alienation, leads to high delinquency rates. According to social ecologists, such communities have high rates of disorder, gangs, fear, and change. A siege mentality can take place, with individuals feeling trapped and victimized. Later in this chapter, collective efficacy and the Project on Human Development in Chicago Neighborhoods are discussed, and both the possibility of collective efficacy and this project are promising approaches to deteriorating communities revitalizing themselves.[21] (See Web Extra 4.1 for more on the Project on Human Development in Chicago Neighborhoods.)

Social disorganization theory lost much of its vitality as a prominent criminological theory in the late 1960s and through the 1970s, because theory and research in that period focused primarily on individual rather than group and community characteristics.[22] Despite the criticisms it received, however, social disorganization theory experienced "a quiet, but significant revival" in the 1980s and later.[23] As the reemergence of interest in social disorganization theory shows, the work of Shaw and McKay and social ecology have had an enduring impact on the study of delinquency in the United States.

Cultural Deviance Theory and Delinquency

Social disorganization theory focused on the structural breakups of urban communities, but the next theory, **cultural deviance theory**, turns to the delinquent values that are found in some lower-class cultures. They are both cultural transmission theories;

mycrimekit

Web Extra 4.1

Project on Human Development in Chicago Neighborhoods (PHDCN)

cultural deviance theory A theory wherein delinquent behavior is viewed as an expression of conformity to cultural values and norms that are in opposition to those of the larger U.S. society.

in fact, the disorganization of the environment seen in social disorganization theory leads to cultural deviance theory, which is generally defined as viewing delinquent and criminal behavior as an expression of conformity to cultural values and norms that are in opposition to those of the larger society. According to Ruth Rosner Kornhauser, the necessary and sufficient cause of delinquency in cultural deviance models "is socialization to subcultural values condoning as right conduct what the controlling legal system defines as crime."[24]

Miller's Lower-Class Culture and Delinquent Values

Walter B. Miller's lower-class culture and delinquent values form a cultural deviance theory applied to the explanation of delinquent behavior. In his version of cultural deviance theory, anthropologist Miller argued that the motivation to become involved in delinquent behavior is endemic to lower-class culture:

> The cultural system which exerts the most direct influence on [delinquent] behavior is that of the lower-class community itself—a long-established, distinctively patterned tradition with an integrity of its own—rather than a so-called "delinquent subculture" which has arisen through conflict with middle-class culture and is oriented to the deliberate violation of middle-class norms.[25]

focal concerns of the lower class The values or focal concerns (trouble, toughness, smartness, excitement, fate, and autonomy) of lower-class youths that differ from those of middle-class youths.

Focal Concerns of Lower-Class Culture Miller argued that a set of **focal concerns of the lower class** characterizes this socioeconomic group. These concerns—trouble, toughness, smartness, excitement, fate, and autonomy—command widespread attention and a high degree of emotional involvement[26]:

- *Trouble.* Miller contended that staying out of trouble represents a major challenge for lower-class citizens and that personal status is therefore often determined in terms of this law-abiding/non-law-abiding dimension, but which of the two qualities an individual values depends largely on the individual and his or her circumstances. A person may make an overt commitment to abiding by the law while giving a covert commitment to breaking the law. Miller added that membership in adolescent gangs may be contingent on a commitment to the law-violating alternative.
- *Toughness.* Physical prowess, as demonstrated by strength and endurance, is valued in lower-class culture. In the eyes of lower-class boys, the tough guy who is hard, fearless, and undemonstrative as well as a good fighter is the ideal man. Miller contended that the intense concern over toughness is directly related to the fact that a significant proportion of lower-class males are reared in matriarchal households; he found a nearly obsessive concern with masculinity in these youths.
- *Smartness.* The capacity to outsmart, outfox, outwit, con, dupe, and "take" others is valued in lower-class culture; in addition, a man also must be able to avoid being outwitted, duped, or "taken" himself. Smartness also is necessary if people are to achieve material goods and personal status without physical effort.
- *Excitement.* The search for excitement or a thrill is another of the focal concerns of lower-class life. The widespread use of alcohol by both genders and gambling of all kinds spring from this quest for excitement. Going out on the town is the most vivid expression of searching for a thrill—but pursuits of this nature frequently lead to trouble. In between periods of excitement, lower-class life is characterized by long periods of inaction or passivity.
- *Fate.* Lower-class individuals, according to Miller, often feel that their lives are subject to a set of forces over which they have little control; they may accept the concept of destiny and may sense that their lives are guided by strong spiritual forces. They believe that good luck can rescue them from lower-class life; this belief in fate, in fact, encourages lower-class people to gamble.
- *Autonomy.* The desire for personal independence is an important concern, partly because the lower-class individual feels controlled so much of the time. A consequence of this desire for autonomy is an inability to deal with controlled environments such as those found in schools or correctional facilities.

Miller is contending that the lower class has a distinctive culture of its own and that its focal concerns, or values, make lower-class boys more likely to become involved in delinquent behavior. These boys want to demonstrate that they are tough and are able to outwit the cops. They also look at the pursuit of crime as a thrill. Yet they are likely to believe that if an individual is going to get caught, there is nothing he or she can do about it. Crime, then, permits lower-class youths to show personal independence from the controls placed on them and also provides an avenue through which youths hope to gain material goods and personal status with a minimum of physical effort.

See Figure 4.3 for the theoretical constructs of Miller's theory.

FIGURE 4.3 Miller's Theory of Lower-Class Culture

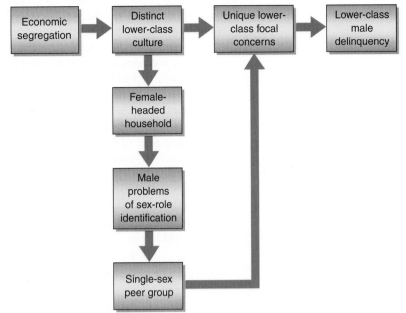

Evaluation of Miller's Theory Miller's theory appears most plausible when applied to the behavior of lower-class gang delinquents. These gang cultures appear to establish their own values and norms, distinct from the values and norms of the larger culture. Marvin E. Wolfgang and Franco Ferracuti also argued that a subculture of violence among young males in the lower social classes legitimates the use of violence in various social situations.[27]

Miller's contention that the lower classes have distinctive values has been widely criticized, however. Some critics argue that the evidence shows that lower-class youths hold the same values as those of the larger culture. For example, Richard A. Cloward and Lloyd E. Ohlin (discussed later in this chapter) as well as Albert K. Cohen have claimed that lower-class youths have internalized middle-class values and that their delinquent acts in fact reflect these middle-class values.[28]

Voices of Delinquency

Read "The Life and Times of Herron Lewiel, Jr." When Herron was growing up in Chicago, did he adhere to a set of lower-class values? What role did the gang play in accepting these values or norms?

Strain Theory and Delinquency

Strain theory proposes that delinquency results from the frustration individuals feel when they are unable to achieve the goals they desire.

Merton's Theory of Anomie

Robert K. Merton has made an important contribution to our understanding of how deviant behavior is produced by different social structures:

> Socially deviant behavior is just as much a product of social structure as conformist behavior. . . . Our primary aim is to discover how some social structures exert a definite pressure upon certain persons in the society to engage in nonconforming rather than conforming behavior.[29]

In *Social Theory and Social Structure*, Merton considered two elements of social and cultural systems: **culturally defined goals** and **institutional means**. The first is the set of "culturally defined goals, purposes, and interests held out as legitimate objectives for all or for diversely located members of the society."[30] These are the goals that people feel are worth striving for; they may be considered cultural goals. A second important aspect "defines, regulates, and controls the acceptable means of reaching out for these goals."[31] Although a specific goal may be attained by a variety of means, the culture does not sanction all of these means. The acceptable method is referred to as the institutionalized means. Merton contended that the two elements must be reasonably well integrated if a culture is to be stable and run smoothly. If

strain theory A theory that proposes that the pressure the social structure exerts on youths who cannot attain cultural success goals will push them to engage in nonconforming behavior.

culturally defined goals In Merton's strain theory, the set of purposes and interests a culture defines as legitimate objectives for individuals.

institutionalized means In Merton's theory, culturally sanctioned methods of attaining individual goals.

individuals believe that a particular goal is important, they should have a legitimate means to attain it, but when a culture lacks such integration, then a state of normlessness, or anomie, occurs. Merton further asserted that contemporary U.S. culture seemed to "approximate the polar type in which great emphasis upon certain success goals occurs without equivalent emphasis upon institutional means."[32] For example, the lower classes are asked to orient their behavior toward the prospect of accumulating wealth, but they are largely denied the means to do so legitimately. The opposition of the cultural emphasis and the social structure creates intense pressure for deviation.

Merton developed a typology of the modes of adaptation that individuals may use when confronted with anomie. Table 4.1 lists five types of individual adaptation: conformity, innovation, ritualism, retreatism, and rebellion. A plus sign (+) signifies acceptance, a minus sign (−) signifies rejection, and a plus/minus sign (±) signifies a rejection of the prevailing values and a substitution of new ones. Merton's theory uses these modes of adaptation to explain how deviant behavior in general is produced by the social structure, but they can also be applied specifically to juvenile law-breaking.[33]

Conformity   If a society is well integrated and therefore anomie is absent, conformity both to cultural goals and to institutionalized means will be the most common adaptation. Conforming juveniles accept the cultural goals of society as well as the institutional means of attaining them; they work hard in legitimate ways to become a success.

Innovation   When adolescents accept the cultural goal but reject the institutional means of attaining it, they may pursue other paths that frequently are not legitimate in terms of cultural values. Merton expressed the opinion that innovation resulting in deviant behavior is especially likely to occur in a society that offers success as a goal for all but at the same time withholds from a segment of the population the legitimate means of attaining that goal. For example, lower-class youths who have accepted the cultural goal of wealth are likely to steal if they are denied legitimate opportunities to achieve the goal they have internalized.[34] Unable to make it in socially acceptable ways, they tend to pursue the wealth goal in law-violating ways.

Ritualism   Although they may have abandoned the cultural goals, some juveniles will continue to abide by the acceptable means for attaining them. Ritualism consists of "individually seeking a private escape from the dangers and frustrations . . . inherent in the competition for major cultural goals by abandoning these goals and clinging all the more closely to the safe routines and institutional norms."[35] For example, some youngsters, while keeping their behavior within the confines of the

TABLE 4.1 Merton's Theory of Anomie		
Modes of Adaptation	**Cultural Goal**	**Institutional Means**
Conformity	+	+
Innovation	+	−
Ritualism	−	+
Retreatism	−	−
Rebellion	±	±

Source: This material appears in Robert K. Merton, "Social Structure and Anomie," *American Sociological Review* 3 (1938), p. 676.

law, stop trying to achieve in school, going through the motions of attending classes and studying but abandoning the goal of success.

Whereas innovation is a mode of adaptation typical of the lower class, ritualism is encountered more frequently in the lower middle class, because parents of lower-middle-class children exert continuous pressure on them to abide by the moral mandates of society.

Retreatism   When individuals have rejected both the goals of the culture and the institutionalized means of attaining them, they have, in effect, retreated from their society. Drug addicts have divorced themselves from the cultural goal of success and must break the law to obtain and use their drugs. Yet even though they have none of the rewards held out by society, these socially disinherited persons face few of the frustrations involved in continuing to seek those rewards.

Rebellion   Rebellion consists of rejecting the values and institutions of one's culture and substituting for them a new set of values and institutions. The rebellious juvenile, for example, may commit himself or herself to some ideology or movement promising a new social order with a "closer correspondence between merit, effort, and reward."[36]

Merton argued that his theory of anomie was "designed to account for some, not all, forms of deviant behavior customarily described as criminal or delinquent."[37] Thus, instead of attempting to explain all the behaviors prohibited by criminal law, Merton focused attention on the pressure or strain resulting from the discrepancy between culturally induced goals and the opportunities inherent in the social structure.[38] See Figure 4.4 for the theoretical constructs of Merton's theory.

Institutional Anomie Theory   Steven Messner and Richard Rosenfeld's book *Crime and the American Dream* refers to institutional anomie theory as a function of cultural and institutional influences in society. In agreeing with Merton that the success goal is widespread in society, they define this as the "American dream, which is both a goal and a process." As a goal, the American dream involves accumulating materialistic goods and wealth. As a process, Americans are socialized to dream that this goal is attainable and believe that this can take place. The desire to attain this goal generates pressures toward delinquency (see Library Extra 4.1).[39] According to Messner and Rosenfeld, what is unique about American society is that anomic conditions have been permitted to develop to such a high degree and that this, in turn, is what determines the high delinquency rates.[40] In a testing of cross-national data sets, Jukka Savolainen found support for the institutional anomie theory. This study indicated that the demonstrable effects of economic inequality on the level of lethal violence are limited to nations characterized by weak collective institutions of social protection.[41]

Evaluation of Merton's Theory   One of the main emphases of Merton's theory—an emphasis that has been largely ignored—is that it is "a theory of societal *anomie*, not of individually felt strain."[42] Merton's revision of anomie theory has been called "the most influential single formulation in the sociology of deviance in the last 25 years and . . . possibly the most frequently quoted single paper in modern sociology."[43] This theory's influence on the later theoretical contributions of Richard A. Cloward and Lloyd E. Ohlin as well as Albert K. Cohen demonstrates its importance to delinquency theory.[44]

Strain Theory and the Individual Level of Analysis

Strain theory, described below, dominated criminology in the 1960s before labeling theory gained acceptance in the late 1960s and early 1970s. A major reason for the wide acceptance of strain theory in that decade was that its central thesis of **blocked opportunity** resonated with Americans' growing concern over equal opportunity and with liberals' fear that injustice has serious costs. Strain theory also "did not require a broad rejection of the social order."[45]

FIGURE 4.4 Merton's Strain Theory

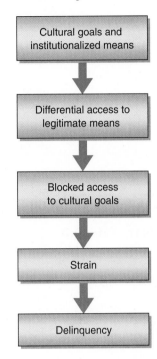

Library Extra 4.1
NIJ publication: *National Evaluation of the "I Have a Dream" Program*

blocked opportunity The limited or nonexistent chance of success; according to strain theory, a key factor in delinquency.

Strain theory met increased criticism in the 1970s. Many commentators at the time argued that strain theory had little empirical support and ought to be abandoned as a causal explanation of crime.[46] Strain theory survived those attacks, though it now plays a more limited role in explaining crime and delinquency.[47] In the 1980s, Thomas J. Bernard defended strain theory as not having been tested adequately.[48]

Robert Agnew's revised strain theory of delinquency points to another source of frustration and strain: the blockage of pain–avoidance behavior.[49] Agnew argued that when juveniles are compelled to remain in painful or aversive environments, such as family and school, the ensuing frustration is likely to lead to escape attempts or anger-based delinquent behavior. His examination of data from the Youth in Transition survey revealed that a juvenile's location in aversive environments in the school and family "has a direct effect on delinquency and an indirect effect through anger."[50]

General Strain Theory   Agnew also developed a general strain theory of crime and delinquency that distinguishes three different sources of strain: "failure to achieve positively valued goals, . . . the removal of positively valued stimuli from the individual, [and] the presentation of negative stimuli"[51] (see Library Extra 4.2). Anger and frustration are negative emotions resulting from such strain, and juveniles may cope with these strains through delinquent behaviors. Delinquency may be a way of escaping or reducing from strain (e.g., theft to achieve monetary goals). Certain strains are seen as more likely to lead to delinquency than others: (1) those high in magnitude, (2) those viewed as unjust, (3) those associated with lower self-control, and (4) those creating some pressure or incentive to engage in crime.[52] Agnew's general strain theory then presents guidelines, or a strategy, for measuring strain and explores under what conditions strain is likely to result in "nondelinquent and delinquent coping."[53]

In sum, after a period of neglect, individual-level strain theory has experienced a revival, primarily through the work of Robert Agnew, especially his general strain theory.[54] Subsequent studies examining the effects of strain have contributed to the revival of the individual-level strain theory.

Cohen's Theory of Delinquent Subcultures

Albert K. Cohen's thesis in his 1955 book *Delinquent Boys: The Culture of the Gang* stated that lower-class youths are actually internalizing the goals of middle-class culture but that they experience **status frustration**, or strain, because they are unable to attain them. This strain explains their membership in delinquent gangs and their nonutilitarian, malicious, and negativistic behavior.[55]

Delinquent Subculture   The social structure in American society, Cohen claimed, has an immense hold on citizens—even 12- or 13-year-old children know about the class system.[56] This class system defines the middle-class values and norms children are expected to aspire to and to achieve:

> These norms are, in effect, a tempered version of the Protestant ethic which has played such an important part in the shaping of American character and American society. In brief summary, this middle-class ethic prescribes an obligation to strive, by dint of rational, ascetic, self-disciplined, and independent activity, to achieve in worldly affairs. A not irrebuttable but common corollary is the presumption that "success" is itself a sign of the exercise of these moral qualities.[57]

Status at school especially is measured by these middle-class standards. First, the teacher is hired to foster the development of middle-class personalities. Second, the teacher is likely to be a middle-class person who values ambition and achievement and quickly recognizes and rewards these virtues in others. Third, Cohen pointed out, the educational system itself favors "quiet, cooperative, 'well-behaved' pupils" who make the teacher's job easier, and it greets with disapproval the "lusty, irrepressible, boisterous youngsters who are destructive of order, routine, and predictability in the classroom."[58]

Library Extra 4.2
"Robert Agnew's Strain Theory Approach"

Voices of Delinquency

Read "A Sad Story." What strain was present in this youth's life? How did he cope with his strain?

status frustration The stress that individuals experience when they cannot attain their goals because of their socioeconomic class.

A pivotal assumption in Cohen's theory is that lower-class males internalize middle-class norms and values but then are unable to attain middle-class goals. Status frustration occurs, and the mechanism of **reaction formation** is used to handle it. On the one hand, according to Cohen, the delinquent claims that the middle-class standards do not matter; but on the other hand, he or she directs irrational, malicious, unaccountable hostility toward the norms of the respectable middle-class society.[59]

Cohen defined nine norms that he claimed make up the middle-class measuring rod:

1. Ambition
2. Individual responsibility
3. Achievement
4. Temperance
5. Rationality
6. Courtesy and likeability
7. Less physical aggression
8. Educational recreation
9. Respect for property[60]

The delinquent subculture offers the lower-class male the status he does not receive from the larger culture, but the status offered by the delinquent subculture is status only in the eyes of his fellow delinquents. According to this theory, the same middle-class value system in America is instrumental in generating both respectability and delinquency.[61]

Cohen added that the delinquent subculture is nonutilitarian: Delinquents commit crimes "for the hell of it," without intending to gain or profit from their crimes. Cohen also claimed that malice is evident in the crimes of the delinquent subculture, that delinquents often display an enjoyment in the discomfort of others and a delight in the defiance of taboos. Further, the delinquent's conduct is right by the standards of the subculture precisely because it is wrong by the norms of the larger culture.[62] Moreover, the delinquent subculture demonstrates versatility in its delinquent behaviors; members of this subculture do not specialize, as do many adult criminal gangs and "solitary" delinquents. The delinquent subculture is characterized by "short-run hedonism." Its members have little interest in planning activities, setting long-term goals, budgeting time, or gaining knowledge and skills that require practice, deliberation, and study; instead, gang members hang around the corner waiting for something to turn up. A further characteristic of this subculture is its emphasis on group autonomy, which makes gang members intolerant of any restraint except the informal pressures of the gang itself.[63] See Figure 4.5 for the theoretical constructs of Cohen's theory.

Evaluation of Cohen's Theory   Cohen's *Delinquent Boys* made a seminal contribution to the delinquency literature. Cohen's theory is important because it views delinquency as a process of interaction between the delinquent youths and others rather than as the abrupt and sudden product of strain or anomie, as proposed by Merton's theory. Cohen contended that delinquency arises during a continuous interaction process whereby changes in the self result from the activities of others.[64] One of the most serious criticisms leveled at Cohen's theory is that of Travis Hirschi, who questioned the feasibility of using status frustration as the motivational energy to account for delinquency because most delinquent boys eventually become law abiding, even though their lower-class status does not change.[65] Also, Cohen does not

reaction formation The psychological strategy for dealing with frustration by becoming hostile toward an unattainable object.

Voices of Delinquency

Read "My Experiences as a Juvenile Delinquent." How did this middle-class youngster ever end up the way he did? How many of Cohen's norms did he rebel against? What turned him around?

FIGURE 4.5 Cohen's Theory of Delinquent Subcultures

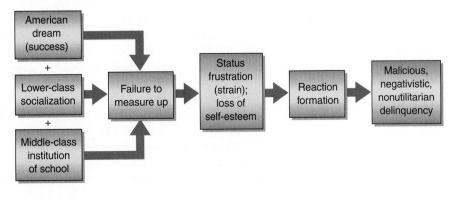

Three Hispanic members of the 18th Street Gang in Los Angeles, California. ▶ How might Cohen's notion of status frustration explain youth gang membership and delinquency?

Video Cloward and Ohlin

opportunity theory A perspective that holds that gang members turn to delinquency because of a sense of injustice about the lack of legitimate opportunities open to them.

offer any empirical evidence to support his theory, and the vagueness of such concepts as reaction formation and lower-class internalization of middle-class values makes it difficult to test his theory. Nevertheless, not only Cohen's theory but also the critiques and controversies surrounding this theory have done much to spark the development of delinquency theory, and much of the delinquency research since the publication of *Delinquent Boys* has built on Cohen's findings.

Cloward and Ohlin's Opportunity Theory

Richard A. Cloward and Lloyd E. Ohlin sought to integrate the theoretical contributions of Merton and Cohen with the ideas of Edwin H. Sutherland (see Chapter 5). Although Merton argued that lower-class youths strive for monetary success and Cohen contended that they strive for status, Cloward and Ohlin conceptualized success and status as separate strivings that can operate independently of each other. In their **opportunity theory**, Cloward and Ohlin portrayed delinquents who seek an increase in status as striving for membership in the middle class, whereas other delinquent youths try to improve their economic position without changing their class position.

Cloward and Ohlin contended that the most serious delinquents are those who experience the greatest conflict with middle-class values, since they "are looked down upon both for what they do want (i.e., the middle-class style of life) and for what they do not want (i.e., 'crass materialism')."[66] Cloward and Ohlin use Merton's theory to explain the particular form of delinquency that youths commit. They assume that these youths have no legitimate opportunities to improve their economic position and therefore that they will become involved in one of three specialized gang subcultures: "criminal," "conflict," and "retreatist."[67]

Criminal Subculture The criminal subculture is primarily based on criminal values. Within this subculture, illegal acts such as extortion, fraud, and theft are accepted as means to achieve economic success. This subculture provides the socialization by which new members learn to admire and respect older criminals and to adopt their lifestyles and behaviors. As new members master the techniques and orientations of the criminal world through criminal episodes, they become hostile toward and distrustful of representatives of the larger society, whom they regard as "suckers" to be exploited whenever possible.[68]

Conflict Subculture Violence is the key ingredient in the conflict subculture, whose members pursue status (or "rep") through force or threats of force. Warrior youth gangs exemplify this subculture. The "bopper," the basic role model, fights with weapons to win respect from other gangs and to demand deference from the adult world, and the bopper's role expectation is to show great courage in the face of personal danger and always to defend his or her personal integrity and the honor of the gang.[69]

A reputation for toughness—the primary goal of fighting gangs—ensures respect from peers and fear from adults and provides a means of gaining access to the scarce resources for pleasure and opportunity in underprivileged areas. Relationships with the adult world are typically weak, because gang members are unable to find appropriate adult role models who offer a structure of opportunity leading to adult success.[70]

Retreatist Subculture The consumption of drugs is the basic activity of the retreatist subculture. Feeling shut out from conventional roles in the family or occupational world, members of this subculture withdraw into an arena where the ultimate goal is the "kick," which may mean alcohol, marijuana, hard drugs, sexual experiences, hot music, or any combination of these. Whatever is chosen, retreatists are seeking an intense awareness of living and a sense of pleasure that is "out of this world."[71] The retreatist subculture generates a new order of goals and criteria of achievement, but instead of attempting to impose their system of values on the world of the "straights," retreatists are content merely to strive for status and deference within their own subculture.

Cloward and Ohlin noted that although these subcultures exhibit essentially different orientations, the lines between them may become blurred. For example, a subculture primarily involved with conflict may on occasion become involved in systematic theft, or members of a criminal subculture may sometimes become involved in conflict with a rival gang.[72] Figure 4.6 shows the main theoretical constructs of Cloward and Ohlin's theory.

Evaluation of Cloward and Ohlin's Theory Cloward and Ohlin's opportunity theory is important because of the impact it has had on the development of public policy and criminological theory.[73] However, the findings of several studies sharply

Voices of Delinquency

Read "I Want What Other Kids Want." How much did economic deprivation affect this youth? Is it hard to believe that this person later graduated from college and is now working with troubled youths?

FIGURE 4.6 Cloward and Ohlin's Opportunity Theory

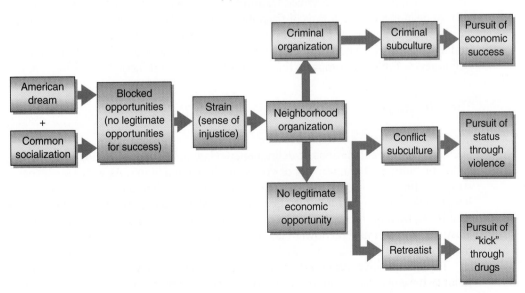

TABLE 4.2 Summary of Social Structural and Cultural Theories of Crime

Theory	Cause of Crime Identified in the Theory	Supporting Research
Cultural Deviance Theories		
Shaw and McKay	Delinquent behavior becomes an alternative mode of socialization through which youths who are part of disorganized communities are attracted to delinquent values and traditions.	Moderate
Miller	Lower-class culture has a distinctive culture of its own, and its focal concerns, or values, make lower-class boys more likely to become involved in delinquent behavior.	Weak
Wolfgang and Ferracuti	Subcultures of violence exist among lower-class males and legitimize the use of violence.	Weak
Strain Theories		
Merton	Social structure exerts pressure on individuals who cannot attain the cultural goal of success, leading them to engage in nonconforming behavior.	Moderate
Cohen	Lower-class boys are unable to attain the goals of middle-class culture, and therefore they become involved in nonutilitarian, malicious, and negative behavior.	Weak
Opportunity Theory		
Cloward and Ohlin	Lower-class boys seek out illegitimate means to attain middle-class success goals if they are unable to attain them through legitimate means, usually through one of three specialized gang contexts.	Moderate

disagree with the assumptions of Cloward and Ohlin's opportunity theory.[74] In 1978, Ruth Kornhauser, having reviewed the empirical research on the aspirations and expectations of delinquents, claimed that the research showed that delinquency was consistently associated with both low expectations and low aspirations—delinquents might not expect to get much, but they did not want much either. Thus, Kornhauser challenged the strain aspect of opportunity theory.[75]

In sum, strain theory explains that juveniles are "pushed" into delinquency as a result of a lack of access to opportunities for the realization of a set of success goals. In other words, those who are denied legitimate achievement of their success goals often turn to delinquency as a means of reaching desired goals or of striking back at an unfair system.[76] The role of blocked opportunity, whether found in Merton or Cloward and Ohlin, has received considerable attention in the sociological analysis of male delinquency. Table 4.2 compares the structural and cultural theories of delinquency.

Delinquency across the Life Course: Explanations of Delinquency

Social structure explanations of delinquency relate delinquent behavior to the structural and cultural characteristics of youths in the United States. As we've seen, social structure theorists suggest that a youth may become delinquent because he or she lives in a disorganized community, because he or she is unable to achieve middle-class standards, because he or she becomes part of a delinquent subculture due to status frustration, or because the lower class to which he or she belongs has values held by the subculture.

Three important structural explanations of delinquency across the life course point to the consequences of the reduced social capital that lower-class children have, the importance of disorganized communities in affecting the decisions of lower-class children, and the relationship between human agency and structure in the process of desistance from crime.

Reduced Social Capital

Lower-class youngsters often lack access to social capital—to the norms, networks, and supportive relationships they need if they are to realize their potential. They may be forced to struggle to meet their basic survival needs. Economic deprivation is first felt at home, and it is this deprivation that drives many youths to the streets.[77] Not surprisingly, the father frequently leaves, and the mother is gone much of the time simply trying to make ends meet. G. Roger Jarjoura, Ruth A. Triplett, and Gregory P. Brinker, using 14 years of longitudinal data for a national sample of younger adolescents, found that the exposure to poverty and the timing of such exposure are indeed related to an increased likelihood of delinquent involvement.[78]

Lower-class youngsters further encounter the difficulty of coping in constructive ways when they are not able to meet the success goals of society, an inability which usually becomes evident at school. Both lower- and middle-class youths may respond to lack of success with disruptive behavior, truancy, and crime. The inability to find a job or to compete in the marketplace further encourages these adolescents to pursue illegitimate means.[79] Robert Gillespie's survey of 57 studies shows considerable support for a relationship between unemployment and property crime; he found the relationship most evident in studies that use such variables as class, crime, and delinquency in a methodologically sophisticated manner.[80] Stephen W. Baron and Timothy F. Hartnagel's study of 200 homeless male street youths found that lengthy unemployment and lack of income, as well as anger, increase youths' criminal activities.[81] However, Steven F. Messner and his colleagues, using national data for 1967 through 1998, found that child poverty is positively related to arrest rates, but that changing unemployment yields a negative effect on youth offending.[82]

Disorganized Communities

In addition, lower-class children must deal with the impact of disorganized communities on their attitudes and worldview. In order to adapt to a disorganized community, adolescents may learn to accept cultural patterns that are conducive to delinquent behavior. For youths who experience economic deprivation at home, the streets offer the promise of attaining goods and services that their parents could never afford. In these disorganized communities, youth gangs typically are well established; in many communities youngsters may feel required to join a gang for safety. Disorganized communities also offer drugs of every type, frequent contact with adult criminals, and ongoing exposure to violence. Mary E. Pattillo's study of an African-American middle-class neighborhood in Chicago found that the neighborhood was closer to high-poverty and high-crime areas than were white middle-class neighborhoods and, as a result, had more problems with gang members and drug dealers.[83]

Thomas J. Bernard's article, "Angry Aggression among the 'Truly Disadvantaged,'" explained the high levels of anger and aggression among members of the underclass.[84] Bernard theorized that three social factors—urban environment, low social position, and racial and ethnic discrimination—increase the likelihood that the "truly disadvantaged" will react with frequent or intense physiological arousal. In Bernard's model, social isolation (a fourth social factor) concentrates the effects of the first three factors through multiple feedback loops, and the end result, according to Bernard's theory, is a "peak" of angry aggression that is comparable to learned helplessness.[85]

Thus, research evidence appears to support a relationship between social class, disorganization of the community, and delinquency.[86] The type of informal community controls found in the Chicago Area Projects during the 1930s and 1940s perhaps offers one of the most hopeful means to reduce the rates of delinquency in high-crime areas (see Chapter 12 for more description of the Chicago Area Projects). In their innovative work on neighborhoods and crime, Robert J. Sampson and colleagues developed the notion of "collective efficacy," which relates to informal social control and cohesion, or mutual trust, found among neighborhoods that effectively control youth crime.[87] This collective efficacy characterized the most effective of the Chicago Area Projects' communities and is found in present-day low-crime urban communities. The task of policy makers is to provide the structure or framework from which neighborhood solidarity and grassroots community organization can arise.

Human Agency and Social Structure

There has been an intense interest among sociological theorists in the relationship between human agency and structure. Margaret Archer contended that "the problem of structure and agency has rightly come to be seen as the basic issue in modern social theory."[88] In 1964, George Homans called for a move to "bring men in" and to return to an action theory grounded firmly in the instrumental, calculating, and purposive orientations of individuals.[89] In 1990, James Coleman's major work, *Foundations of Social Theory*, linked purposive action at the microlevel to interdependence at the macrolevel, showing that action is a complex social and interactive phenomenon.[90]

The theories presented in this chapter disclose how U.S. society imposes structural and cultural values on individuals without much concern for how individuals choose to respond to the influence of the sociocultural context and to the economic factors in their immediate environment. These theories leave two basic questions unanswered: What explains the fact that many youths in the same cultural setting do not become delinquent? Why is it that many culturally deprived youths who do become delinquent desist from delinquent behavior at the end of their teenage years, even when their social and economic situations remain the same?

John H. Laub and Robert J. Sampson, in their follow-up of the delinquent boys from the Gluecks' sample (see Chapter 3) to the age of 70 years, emphasized the importance of human agency in the desistance process. They viewed the men who desisted as "acting players" as those who accepted responsibility for what they had done and concluded that desistance takes place "as a result of individual actions (choice) in conjunction with situational contexts and structural influences linked to important institutions that help sustain desistance."[91]

In the Laub and Sampson study, work and employment, as well as the structured role stability that came from marriage and family, provided the desisters with the context in which they could choose to forge a new identity and from which they could receive support and encouragement. Those offenders who persisted were the individuals whose lives were characterized by a failure to maintain regular employment, by a tendency to abuse alcohol, and by an inability to receive the support of marriage and family. They seemed to be unable to rise above the lower-class background of their childhood and, in fact, continued much of the defiance that they had expressed in their younger years. Not surprisingly, their lives were characterized by ongoing contact with the criminal justice system and imprisonment.[92]

Delinquency and Social Policy: The Project on Human Development in Chicago Neighborhoods

The Project on Human Development in Chicago Neighborhoods (PHDCN) was launched with major support from the National Institute of Justice and the John D. and Catherine T. MacArthur Foundation. It was led by Felton Earls, M.D., at the Harvard University School of Public Health and Medical School. Project directors represent a variety of disciplines and major universities.[93]

The project is remarkable in both its scope and design. It combines (1) a longitudinal study of youths, with repeated interviews of more than 6,000 youths and their caregivers, with (2) a neighborhood study that included a survey of almost 9,000 neighborhood residents and systematic observation of levels of social and physical disorder in 80 neighborhoods. Analyzing these complex data has required using innovative statistical techniques.

The neighborhood study was conducted in 1995–96. Chicago was first divided into 343 neighborhoods of about 8,000 residents, composed of contiguous census tracts. Then 25 to 50 residents of each neighborhood were surveyed about neighborhood conditions and about their attitudes, yielding 8,782 surveys. Research teams also systematically observed and recorded conditions of physical and social disorder on each side of every street block in 80 neighborhoods, yielding approximately 27,000 observations.

The longitudinal study of youths was launched at the same time in 80 neighborhoods, which were chosen to vary in both racial and ethnic composition and socioeconomic conditions. With enough youths from enough neighborhoods, researchers can examine similar youths who live in very different neighborhoods, as well as youths who are not similar but live in similar neighborhoods.

The researchers enrolled 6,212 participants from 7 age cohorts (0, 3, 6, 9, 12, 15, and 18). Three waves of data collection were conducted. Each wave consisted of an interview with each youth who was at least 6 years old and an interview with a primary caregiver for youths younger than 18. Interviews were conducted about two and half years apart. This design, in which multiple-age cohorts are studied over overlapping ages, is referred to as an "accelerated longitudinal" design, because an age range (in this case, from 0 to about 25) can be studied in much less time than in a standard longitudinal study.

Data collection was conducted based on four separate components that focused on a variety of individual and community characteristics[94]:

1. *Community survey.* The dynamic structure of the local community, neighborhood organizational and political structures, cultural values, informal and formal social controls, and social cohesion were measured.
2. *Systematic social observation.* A standardized approach for directly observing the physical, social, and economic characteristics of neighborhoods, one block at a time, was applied to 80 of the 343 neighborhoods (i.e., over 23,000 blocks). These observations were coded to assess neighborhood characteristics such as land use, housing, litter, graffiti, and social interactions.
3. *Longitudinal cohort study.* An accelerated longitudinal design with seven cohorts was separated by three-year intervals. These randomly selected cohorts of children, adolescents, and young adults and their primary caregivers were followed over a period of seven years to study changes in their personal characteristics and circumstances.
4. *Infant assessment unit.* As part of the longitudinal cohort study, 412 infants from the birth cohort and their primary caregivers were studied during wave 1 (1994–1997) to examine the effects of prenatal and postnatal conditions on their growth and health, cognitive abilities, and motor skills.

Early Findings from the Neighborhood Study

Findings from the PHDCN's neighborhood study have received widespread attention in both the professional and general media. For example, in a widely cited article published in *Science* in 1997 and summarized in a National Institute of Justice *Research Review*, Robert Sampson, Stephen Raudenbush, and Felton Earls found that neighborhood social processes had a significant impact on homicide and violence in the community.

Homicide and violent victimization rates were found to be lower in neighborhoods where residents shared values, had common expectations that neighbors would intervene in problem behavior, and trusted each other. The researchers called this combination of shared values, trust, and expectations for social intervention "collective efficacy" to control crime and deviance. The level of collective efficacy, in turn, was strongly influenced by neighborhood conditions such as the extent of poverty and the lack of residential stability. Collective efficacy thus seems to be a mediating link between neighborhood conditions and crime and violence. Equally important, among neighborhoods with similar conditions, those with greater collective efficacy experienced less violence.

Robert J. Sampson and colleagues developed the concept of collective efficacy as characteristics of a community that they felt would work together to prevent and control crime. A community is high on collective efficacy to the extent that residents have mutual trust, share values, and have a disposition to intervene for the public good. Sampson and colleagues contended that the most important influence on a neighborhood's crime is neighbors' willingness to act, when necessary or needed, for one another's benefit, especially for the benefit of one another's children. Several studies have found that collective efficacy does function to mediate much of the effect of such community structural variables as high prevalence of poverty, unemployment, single-parent families, and racial/ethnic heterogeneity.[95]

The Project on Human Development in Chicago Neighborhoods (PHDCN), directed by Felton Earls and other researchers from the Harvard School of Public Health (including Sampson), has two main goals: to develop a coordinated approach to the study of human development and to enrich policy planning with new prevention, treatment, and rehabilitation strategies. The hoped for end result will be to enrich the understanding of collective efficacy in community life and to help more communities attain such collective efficacy.

This large-scale interdisciplinary study of the complex influences exerted on human development is one in which the National Institute of Justice has so far spent over $18 million; the MacArthur foundation has spent another $23.6 million on the project. Jerome Travis, director of the National Institute of Justice from 1994 to 2000, noted, "It is far and away the most important research insight in the last decade. I think it will shape policy for the next generation."[96]

The city of Chicago was selected as the research site because of its diversity in race, ethnicity, and social class. Data were collected in three waves: 1994–1997, 1997–1999, and 2000–2001. Researchers collapsed 847 census tracts into 347 neighborhood clusters (NC) based on seven groupings of racial/ethnic composition and three levels of socioeconomic status. The NCs were designed to be ecologically meaningful, composed of contiguous census tracts and based on both geographic boundaries and knowledge of Chicago neighborhoods. Each NC was composed of around 8,000 people.

As the immense data gathered by this project are analyzed in the years to come, it is hoped that they will provide resources and direction for policy makers not only in Chicago but also in other urban areas to develop more of what Sampson and colleagues call "collective efficacy."[97]

Chapter Summary

This chapter describes social structural theories of delinquency. The term *social structure* refers to the relatively stable formal and informal arrangements that characterize a society—including its economic arrangements and social institutions as well as its values and norms. Social structural theories propose that the structured arrangements within society can lead to delinquency, whereas structural and cultural disorder may result in high rates of crime and unsafe and disruptive living conditions. Among the best-known social structural approaches are the following:

- Clifford R. Shaw and Henry D. McKay, members of the Chicago School of Sociology, demonstrated the importance of social ecology, specifically the locations where young people live. The closer they live to the inner city, the researchers said, the more likely young people are to become involved in delinquency.

- Explanations for delinquency in inner-city areas go beyond social disorganization, however. It is well known, for example, that cultural traditions characteristic of the inner city pass criminogenic norms and values from one generation to the next.

- Walter B. Miller contends that lower-class youths do not aspire to middle-class values because they have their own lower-class values, or focal concerns, which encourage involvement in delinquent behavior.

- Robert K. Merton's anomie theory says that the social structure of a society influences the behavior that occurs in that society because of the way in which it structures opportunities. Merton notes that young people who are caught up in anomie, or normlessness, feel the strain that such conditions produce and are more likely to become deviant or delinquent than those who are not.

- Albert K. Cohen's theory of reaction formation contends that lower-class youths aspire to middle-class values but that their inability to attain those values causes them to invert the values and become involved in negativistic, malicious, and nonutilitarian behaviors.

- Richard A. Cloward and Lloyd E. Ohlin argue that youthful lower-class gang members aspire to middle-class values but become involved in illegitimate pursuits because they are unable to attain their goals legitimately.

All of the theories discussed in this chapter see delinquency as a response to inequalities built into the very structure of society.

Key Terms

blocked opportunity, p. 93
cultural deviance theory, p. 89
cultural transmission theory, p. 88
culturally defined goals, p. 91
differential opportunity structure, p. 88

focal concerns of the lower class, p. 90
institutionalized means, p. 91
opportunity theory, p. 96
reaction formation, p. 95

social disorganization theory, p. 86
social structure, p. 85
status frustration, p. 94
strain theory, p. 91

Review Questions

1. According to Shaw and McKay, what are the relationships among ecology, social disorganization, and transmission of deviant culture?
2. What are Miller's focal concerns, or values, of lower-class delinquency?
3. What is strain theory?
4. What has Merton contributed to strain theory?
5. What does Cohen contribute to strain theory?
6. What contribution do Cloward and Ohlin make to strain theory and delinquency?

Discussion Questions

1. Which of the theories in this chapter impressed you as being most logical? Why?
2. Are succeeding generations of researchers using Shaw and McKay's impressive body of work as starting points for inquiries that further advance our body of knowledge, or is present-day research simply slick repackaging of past successful efforts?
3. Do you believe that lower-class youngsters aspire to middle-class values, or do they have their own values?
4. What structural explanations of delinquency are most likely to explain middle-class delinquency?
5. Are Miller's focal concerns of the lower-class thesis valid? Should any of the concerns he includes be removed from the list? Are there other concerns you think should be added?
6. Do you think status frustration, which is described as being derived from an inability to attain desired goals, is unique to adolescents? Might it also explain adult criminal behavior?

Group Exercises

1. Have the class discuss/debate the merits and main criticisms of social disorganization theory.
2. Have the class debate/discuss the merits of Cohen's theory of delinquent subcultures.
3. Have the class debate/discuss the merits of Cloward and Ohlin's opportunity theory.
4. Have the students read Baron and Hartnagel's article, "Attributions, Affect, and Crime: Street Youths' Reactions to Unemployment," accessed at www.blackwell-synergy.com/doc/abs/10,111/j.1745-9125, 1997.tb01223.x; then have them discuss the material in class.

mycrimekit

Go to mycrimekit.com to explore the following study tools and resources specific to this chapter:

- **Practice Quiz:** Practice with multiple-choice, true/false, short-answer, and essay questions.

- **WebQuests:** Do web activities about the data-gathering methods used by the Project on Human Development in Chicago Neighborhoods' website.

- **Flashcards:** Use 13 flashcards to test your knowledge of the chapter's key terms.

Social Process Theories of Delinquency

*The theory I advocate
sees in the delinquent
a person relatively free
of the intimate
attachments, the
aspirations, and the
moral beliefs that bind
people to a life within
the law.*

—Travis Hirschi,
Causes of Delinquency

CHAPTER OBJECTIVES

After reading this chapter, you should be able to answer
the following questions:

- Do delinquents learn crime from others?
- Why is it that some young people routinely go from delinquent to nondelinquent acts and then back to delinquent behavior?
- What control mechanisms insulate teenagers from delinquent behavior?
- What role does a teen's self-concept play in delinquency?
- Does considering more than one theory increase our ability to explain delinquency?

Introduction

Dale Vincent Bogle, first imprisoned before age 20, went on to father nine children and quickly became a negative role model, steering most of them into lives of crime.

"Rooster," as he was called, grew up in Texas and as a young man moved to Oregon in 1961. Starting a family, he regularly beat his wife and taught his boys to shoplift at an early age. Bogle boys broke into liquor stores and stole tractor-trailer trucks, and Bogle girls turned to petty crimes to support drug habits.

The family patriarch died in 1998, and today 28 members of the Bogle clan, including Rooster's brothers and their families and Rooster's grandchildren, have served time. However, one of Rooster's daughters, who has never been arrested or abused drugs, has devoted her life to felons, helping to run halfway houses for newly released inmates.

Rooster may have been unusually prolific, but his legacy is not unusual. The U.S. Justice Department reports that 47% of inmates in state prisons have a parent or other close relative who has been incarcerated. Similarly, half of all juveniles in custody today have one parent or close relative with a criminal record.

Recognizing that parents "train" their children for a life of crime, Oregon correctional officials plan to identify families of offenders and set them on the right path with alcohol and drug counseling, anger management, and mental health guidance.

Experts do not entirely agree on why so many offspring of felons go into crime. While some cite poor role models and dysfunctional homes, others say it could also have to do with poverty, poor schooling, lack of opportunities, and even the parents' DNA.[1]

social process theory A theoretical approach to delinquency that examines the interactions between individuals and their environments, especially those that might influence them to become involved in delinquent behavior.

differential association theory The view that delinquency is learned from others and that delinquent behavior is to be expected of individuals who have internalized a preponderance of definitions that are favorable to law violations.

Video Differential Association

Library Extra 5.1
NIJ-sponsored research publication: *Trajectories of Violent Offending and Risk Status in Adolescence and Early Adulthood*

The various **social process theories** of delinquency, which provide the focus of this chapter, examine the interaction between individuals and their environments for clues to the root causes of delinquency. Most youngsters are influenced by the family, the school experience, and their peers, all of which are discussed in the next section on delinquency and environment. It is the process of socialization occurring within these social institutions that, along with social structure, provides the forces that insulate youths from or influence them to commit delinquent acts. Several theories focusing on social process have been widely used to explain juvenile delinquency. Differential association, drift, and social control theories, for example, became popular in the 1960s because they provided a theoretical mechanism for understanding aspects of the social environment as a determinant of individual behavior. Differential association theory examines how delinquents learn crime from others, drift theory proposes that any examination of the process of becoming deviant must take seriously both the internal components of the individual and the influence of the external environment, and social control theory provides an explanation for why some young people violate the law while others resist pressures to become delinquent. In addition to discussing these three social process perspectives, this chapter also describes and evaluates four integrated theories and considers process theories within a life-course perspective.

Differential Association Theory

Edwin H. Sutherland's formulation of **differential association theory** proposed that delinquents learn crime from others. His basic premise was that delinquency, like any other form of behavior, is a product of social interaction (see Library Extra 5.1). In developing the theory of differential association, Sutherland contended that individuals are constantly being changed as they take on the expectations and points of view

EXHIBIT 5.1

Edwin H. Sutherland's Background

Edwin H. Sutherland had much in common with Clifford R. Shaw and Henry D. McKay (see Chapter 4). All were born before the turn of the twentieth century and hailed from small midwestern towns. They all did their graduate work at the University of Chicago during the early decades of the twentieth century; they also knew one another personally and frequently responded to each other's work.

McKay and Sutherland, especially, were very good friends. They corresponded regularly and got together each year during the summer. Their friendship was not surprising because the two men were so alike in ancestry, geography, demeanor, and character. It was McKay who first identified the theory of differential association in the second edition of Sutherland's 1934 criminology textbook.

In a conversation with Sutherland in 1935, McKay referred to the "Sutherland theory." Sutherland sheepishly inquired what the "Sutherland theory" was, and McKay responded that he should read pages 51–52 of his own criminology text. Sutherland quickly located the pages and was surprised to find this statement: "The conflict of cultures is the fundamental principle in explanations of crime." In helping Sutherland discover his own theory in his own book, McKay actually stimulated the evolution of differential association theory.

Source: Derived from Jon Snodgrass, *The American Criminological Tradition: Portraits of the Men and Ideology in a Discipline*, Ph.D. dissertation, University of Pennsylvania, 1972.

---

of the people with whom they interact in intimate small groups.[2] Sutherland began with the notion that criminal behavior is to be expected of individuals who have internalized a preponderance of definitions that are favorable to law violations.[3] In 1939, he first developed the theory in his text *Principles of Criminology*, and he continued to revise it until its final form appeared in 1945. Exhibit 5.1 provides a look at the development of Sutherland's theory of differential association.

Propositions of Differential Association Theory

Sutherland's theory of differential association is outlined in these seven propositions:

1. Criminal behavior, like other behavior, is learned from others, that is, delinquent behavior is not an inherited trait but rather an acquired one.
2. Criminal behavior is learned through a youth's active involvement with others in a process of communication, a process which includes both verbal and nonverbal communication.
3. The principal learning of criminal behavior occurs within intimate personal groups. The meanings that are derived from these intimate relationships are far more influential for adolescents than is any other form of communication, such as movies and newspapers.
4. When criminal behavior is learned, the learning includes techniques of committing the crime, which are sometimes very simple, and the specific direction of motives, drives, rationalizations, and attitudes. For example, a youth may learn how to hot-wire a car from a delinquent companion with whom he is involved; he also acquires from the other boy the attitudes or mind-set that will enable him to set aside the moral bounds of the law.
5. The specific direction of motives and drives is learned from definitions of legal codes as favorable or unfavorable. Adolescents come in contact both with people who define the legal codes as rules to be observed and with those whose definitions of reality favor the violation of the legal codes. This creates culture conflict; the next proposition explains how this conflict is resolved (see Library Extra 5.2).
6. Differential associations may vary in frequency, duration, priority, and intensity. The impact that delinquent peers or groups have on a young person depends on the frequency of the social contacts, the time period over which the contacts take place, the age at which a person experiences these contacts, and the intensity of these social interactions.
7. Although criminal behavior is an expression of general needs and values, it is not explained by those general needs and values, because noncriminal behavior is an

Library Extra 5.2

Social Learning and Structural Factors in Adolescent Substance Use

FIGURE 5.1 Sutherland's Differential Association Theory

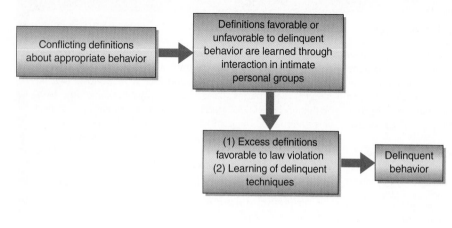

expression of the same needs and values. The motives for delinquent behavior are different from those for conventional behavior because they are based on an excess of delinquent definitions learned from others.[4]

These seven propositions of differential association theory consist of three interrelated concepts—normative (culture) conflict, differential association, and differential social organization. The interrelated concepts operate at two levels of the explanation: the society or group level and the individual level.[5]

Sutherland assumes that delinquents must be taught antisocial behavior. Those who do not engage in socially unacceptable behavior have been socialized or enculturated to conventional values, but those who become involved in delinquent behavior do so because they have been taught other values. Sutherland developed a quantitative metaphor, in which conventional and criminal value systems are composed of elementary units called "definitions." Each unit can be weighted by the modalities of frequency, priority, duration, and intensity of contact; delinquency or criminality is determined by the algebraic sum of these weighted units.[6] Figure 5.1 depicts Sutherland's explanation of differential association.

Evaluation of Differential Association Theory

Sutherland's differential association theory represented a watershed in criminology. Criminology was under heavy criticism before this theory was developed, because it lacked a general theoretical perspective to integrate findings and guide research.[7] In addition to providing this theoretical perspective, differential association theory offers the following strengths:

- It is difficult to reject the argument that juveniles learn crime from others. Needless to say, juveniles learn their basic values, norms, skills, and self-perceptions from others; accordingly, the idea that they also learn criminal behavior patterns from significant others seems irrefutable. The proposition that youngsters learn from people whose definitions are favorable to law violations appears to fit our understanding of juveniles and of their extreme vulnerability to the influence of the group.

- Differential association theory also has appeal in that it is seen as positive. It does not reduce delinquency to psychological and biological models, which postulate that personal inadequacies cannot be penetrated by outside influence. Instead, Sutherland sees individuals as changeable and as subject to the opinions and values of others. The chief task in delinquency prevention, then, is to strive for change in the small groups in which adolescents are involved rather than attempting to change an entire society.

- Differential association theory has had an enduring impact on the study of juvenile delinquency, as is apparent in the attempts to revise this theory. Daniel Glaser's modification of differential association theory, which is called **differential identification theory**, applied the interactionist concept of the self: "A person pursues criminal behavior to the extent that he identifies himself with real or imaginary persons from whose perspective his criminal behavior seems acceptable."[8] Robert J. Burgess Jr. and Ronald L. Akers's differential reinforcement theory proposed a step-by-step restatement of differential association according to such ideas as reinforcement and punishment (operant conditioning). This reformulation, now known as social learning theory, contended that criminal or

Voices of Delinquency

Read "The Athlete." How did peers influence her drug use? Did she, as Sutherland proposed, learn crime from others? What social process did this learning involve?

differential identification theory
A modification of differential association theory that applies the interactionist concept of the self, allows for choice, and stresses the importance of motives.

delinquent behavior is learned primarily "in those groups which comprise the individual's major source of reinforcements."[9] Marvin D. Krohn's network approach to delinquent behavior incorporates some of the elements of differential association theory. Krohn's term *network analysis* refers to sets of groups or organizations linked by the web of social relationships. Krohn suggested that the most important concept in accounting for delinquency is *multiplexity* (the tendency for social ties of different kinds to occur together)—if members of a social network participate jointly in a number of activities, they are likely to influence the behavior of actors within the network.[10]

Three of the most serious criticisms of differential association theory are as follows:

1. The terms of differential association theory are so vague that it is nearly impossible to test the theory empirically.[11] For example, how can an excess of definitions of criminality be measured statistically?[12] How can frequency, duration, priority, and intensity be studied? How can the learning process be more clearly specified?[13] What defines an intimate personal group? Exactly what techniques, motives, and rationalizations do youngsters learn from others?

2. Differential association theory has been accused of failing to deal with several critical questions relating to the process of learning crime from others. For example, why is it that one youth succumbs to delinquent definitions but another does not? Why do youths who are exposed to delinquent definitions still engage in conforming behavior most of the time? How did the first "teacher" learn delinquent techniques and definitions to pass on? Why do most youths desist from delinquent behavior at the age of 17 or 18 years? Why do youths frequently continue delinquent behavior even after the removal of the antisocial stimuli (delinquent peers)? Finally, what is the effect of punishment on delinquents?

3. Critics point out that differential association theory has no room for human purpose and meaning, because it ultimately reduces the individual to an object that merely reacts to the bombardment of external forces and cannot reject the material being presented.[14] According to the theory, then, the delinquent is a passive vessel into which various definitions are poured, and the resultant mixture is something over which the youth has no control.[15]

In the movie *Mean Girls*, this wannabe is hoping for acceptance from the Queen Bees. ▶ How **might the concept of differential association explain the interaction depicted here?**

On balance, although differential association theory has been subjected to sharp attacks over the years, it remains one of the best-known and most enduring theories of delinquent behavior. In 1988, Ross L. Matsueda offered a favorable analysis of differential association theory, proposing that research be done to specify "the concrete elements of the theory's abstract principles" and especially to identify "the content of definitions favorable to crime."[16]

Drift Theory and Delinquency

The process of becoming a delinquent, David Matza stated in *Delinquency and Drift* (1964), begins when a juvenile neutralizes himself or herself from the moral bounds of the law and "drifts" into delinquency. Drift means that "the delinquent transiently exists in limbo between convention and crime, responding in turn to the demands of each, flirting now with one, now the other, but postponing commitment, evading decision. Thus he drifts between criminal and conventional action."[17]

drift theory The theoretical perspective that juveniles neutralize the moral hold of society and drift into delinquent behavior.

Matza's concepts of drift and differential association have many assumptions in common, but Matza's **drift theory** does place far greater importance than differential association theory on the exercise of juveniles' choices and on the sense of injustice that juveniles feel about the discriminatory treatment they have received.

Having established that the delinquent is one who drifts back and forth between convention and deviancy, Matza then examines the process by which legal norms are neutralized. But fundamental to his analysis is the contention that delinquent youths remain integrated into the wider society and that a violation of legal norms does not mean surrendering allegiance to them.[18]

neutralization theory A theory examining how youngsters attempt to justify or rationalize their responsibility for delinquent acts.

Delinquency, then, becomes permissible when responsibility is neutralized. **Neutralization theory** provides a means of understanding how delinquents insulate themselves from responsibility for wrongdoing. There are five techniques of neutralization, or justifications, of delinquent behavior that precede delinquent behavior and that make such behavior possible by defining it as acceptable[19]:

1. Denial of responsibility ("I didn't mean it.")
2. Denial of injury ("I didn't hurt anyone.")
3. Denial of the victim ("They had it coming to them.")
4. Condemnation of the condemners ("Everyone is picking on me.")
5. Appeal to higher loyalties ("I didn't do it for myself.")[20]

A teenager argues with his mother. ▶ **What parental role might drift theory posit in the prevention of delinquency?**

The sense of responsibility, then, is the immediate condition of drift, but other conditions of drift include the sense of injustice, the primacy of custom, and the assertion of tort. Matza claimed that subcultural delinquents are filled with a sense of injustice because they depend on a memory file that collects examples of inconsistency. The primacy of custom relates to the male delinquent's observation of the virtues of his subculture; these virtues stress the "traditional precepts of manliness, celebrating as they do the heroic themes of honor, valor, and loyalty."[21] In the group setting, the delinquent must demonstrate valor and loyalty when faced with dare, challenge, and insult. The assertion of tort, which has to do with a private transaction between the accused and the victim, occurs when the subcultural delinquent considers a harmful wrong to be a tort instead of a crime. Subcultural delinquents frequently believe that the justice process cannot be invoked unless the victim is willing to file a complaint.[22]

The missing element that provides "the thrust or impetus by which the delinquent act is realized is *will*."[23] The will is activated both on mundane occasions and in extraordinary situations.[24] But the subcultural delinquent is not likely to have the will to repeat an old offense if he or she has failed in the past: "Few persons—clowns and fools are among them—like to engage in activities they do badly."[25] Desperation, reasoned Matza, also can activate one's will to commit infractions, and he saw desperation intertwined with the mood of fatalism—because the delinquent feels pushed around, he or she needs to make something happen to restore the mood of humanism. Crime then enables the subcultural delinquent to see himself or herself as cause rather than as effect.[26] Matza developed drift theory to account for the majority of adolescents who, from time to time, engage in delinquent behavior (see Figure 5.2).

Evaluation of Drift Theory

Drift theory has been largely ignored in recent analyses of delinquency, which is unfortunate because it does have several strengths:

- Drift theory builds on the assumption that delinquent behavior is a learning process that takes place in interactions with others. The theory examines how group influence can encourage youths to release themselves from the moral binds of the law.
- Drift theory can also help account for the fact that the majority of adolescents commit occasional delinquent acts but then go on to accept roles as law-abiding adults. Matza's explanation for the fact that delinquency declines as adolescents approach adulthood is that many teenage delinquents were not committed to delinquent norms in the first place.
- Additionally, drift theory helps us understand the situational aspects of delinquent behavior. Matza viewed the delinquent as a youth who is pressured to engage in delinquent behavior by a specific situational context and by the norms of that context. Matza rightly contended that youths are influenced by group processes to commit behaviors that they might not otherwise commit.
- In *Delinquency and Drift*, Matza challenged the notion that delinquents are "constrained" (compelled) to engage in delinquency, contending that hard determinism predicts far too much delinquency and that a **soft determinism** much more accurately explains delinquent behavior.[27] This argument for soft determinism, first found in drift theory, is similar to later versions of soft determinism or indeterminism found in control theory,[28] rational choice theory,[29] social learning theory,[30] and conflict theory.[31]
- Another important conjecture of drift theory is that the attitudes of delinquents and nondelinquents toward unlawful behaviors are basically the same. There are mixed findings in the literature concerning this conjecture.[32]
- John Hagan integrated drift theory with social control theory and a life-course conceptualization to study cultural stratification, finding that "adolescents adrift from parental and educational control are more likely than those with

FIGURE 5.2 Matza's Drift Theory

Feeling of injustice

Situational group justification

Neutralization of law

Delinquent activity

Voices of Delinquency

Read "She's Just a Party Animal." This is the story of a girl who did not see herself as a delinquent but who committed delinquent acts from time to time. Is her life, in any way, an expression of Matza's drift theory?

soft determinism The view that delinquents are neither wholly free nor wholly constrained in their choice of actions.

more controls to develop mild or more seriously deviant subcultural preferences [and that] among males with working-class origins, identification with the subculture of delinquency has a negative effect on trajectories of early adult status attainment."[33]

In sum, even though Matza's drift theory has received less attention than neutralization theory, it still is one of the most useful expressions of the dynamics of why individuals become involved in delinquent behavior. Sykes and Matza's neutralization theory has been more influential in the development of delinquency theory, but it appears to apply to some delinquent behaviors more than others.

Control Theory and Delinquent Behavior

Differential association and drift theories are both learning theories of crime, but **control theory** is focused more on an internal mechanism that helps youngsters avoid delinquent behavior. The core ideas of control theory have a long history, going back at least to the nineteenth century. Control theorists agree on one especially significant point: Human beings must be held in check, or somehow controlled, if delinquent tendencies are to be repressed. Control theorists also generally agree that delinquency is the result of a deficiency in something and that juveniles commit delinquency because some controlling force is absent or defective.[34]

Early versions of control theory include Albert J. Reiss Jr.'s theory of personal and social controls and F. Ivan Nye's family-focused theory of social control. Reiss described how the weak egos of delinquents lacked the personal controls to produce conforming behavior.[35] Nye added that the problem for the theorist was not to find an explanation for delinquent behavior; rather, it was to explain why delinquent behavior is not more common.[36] Walter C. Reckless's containment theory and Travis Hirschi's social control theory are the most developed examples of control theory, and we'll examine them next.

Containment Theory

Reckless developed **containment theory** in the 1950s and 1960s to explain crime and delinquency. Containment theory, which can explain both conforming behavior and deviancy, has two reinforcing elements: an inner control system and an outer control system. The assumption is that strong inner containment and reinforcing external containment provide insulation against deviant behavior.[37]

Elements of Containment Theory   Reckless defined the ingredients of inner containment as self-components, such as self-control, positive self-concept, well-developed superego, ego strength, high frustration tolerance, high resistance to diversions, high sense of responsibility, ability to find substitute satisfactions, goal orientations, and tension-reducing rationalizations.

Outer containment, or external regulators, represents the structural buffers in the person's immediate social world or environment that are able to hold him or her within bounds. External controls consist of such items as the presentation of a consistent moral front to the person; institutional reinforcement of his or her norms, goals, and expectations; effective supervision and discipline; provision for a reasonable scope of activity, including limits and responsibilities; and opportunity for acceptance, identity, and belongingness.

Internal pushes consist of the drives, motives, frustrations, restlessness, disappointments, rebellion, hostility, and feelings of inferiority that encourage a person to become involved in socially unacceptable behavior. Environmental pressures are those associated with poverty or deprivation, conflict and discord, external restraint, minority group status, and limited access to success in an opportunity structure. Finally, the pulls of the environment consist of distractions, attractions, temptations, patterns of deviancy, carriers of delinquent patterns, and criminogenic advertising and propaganda in society (see Library Extra 5.3).

Video Sykes and Matza

control theory Any of several theoretical approaches that maintain that human beings must be held in check, or somehow be controlled, if delinquent tendencies are to be repressed.

containment theory A theoretical perspective that strong inner containment and reinforcing external containment provide insulation against delinquent and criminal behavior.

Library Extra 5.3

OJJDP publication: *Causes and Correlates: Findings and Implications*

Relationship of Containment and Delinquency   If a youth has a weak outer containment, the external pressures and pulls need to be handled by the inner control system, but if the youth's outer buffer is relatively strong and effective, his or her inner defense does not have to play such a critical role. Similarly, if the youth's inner controls are not equal to the ordinary pushes, an effective outer defense may help to hold him or her within socially acceptable behavior, but if the inner defenses are in good working order, the outer structure does not have to come to the rescue. Juveniles who have both strong external and internal containment, then, are much less likely to become delinquent than those who have only either strong external containment or strong internal containment. Youths who have both weak external and internal controls are the most prone to delinquent behavior, although weak internal controls appear to result in delinquent behavior more often than do weak external controls (see Library Extra 5.4).

mycrimekit™

Library Extra 5.4
Testimony of John Wilson, Acting Administrator of the Office of Juvenile Justice and Delinquency Prevention, before the U.S. House of Representatives, Committee on the Judiciary, on October 2, 2000

Self-Concept as Insulation against Delinquency   Reckless and Dinitz concluded from their research that one of the preconditions of law-abiding conduct is a good self-concept. This insulation against delinquency may be viewed as an ongoing process reflecting internalization of nondelinquent values and conformity to the expectations of significant others—parents, teachers, and peers. Thus, a good self-concept, the product of favorable socialization, steers youths away from delinquency by acting as an inner buffer or containment against delinquency.

Several studies have found that a positive self-concept does help insulate adolescents from delinquent behavior.[38] Other studies have found little relationship between positive self-esteem and reduced rates of delinquency.[39] Still other researchers have argued that people behave in a fashion designed to maximize their self-esteem, so youngsters adopt deviant reference groups for the purpose of enhancing self-esteem.[40] Delinquent behavior then becomes a coping strategy to defend against negative self-evaluation.[41]

The major flaw of inner containment, or self-concept, theory is the difficulty of defining self-concept in such a way that researchers can be certain they are accurately measuring the key variables of this concept.[42] M. Schwartz and S. S. Tangri proposed that a poor self-concept might have other outcomes besides vulnerability to delinquency. They further disputed the adequacy of Reckless and Dinitz's measures of self-concept and questioned the effects of labeling on the subsequent behavior of both the "good" and "bad" boys.[43]

Social Control Theory

Travis Hirschi is the theorist most closely identified with **social control theory**, or bonding theory. In *Causes of Delinquency*, Hirschi linked delinquent behavior to the quality of the bond an individual maintains with society, stating that "delinquent acts result when an individual's bond to society is weak or broken."[44] In Hirschi's words, "We are all animals and thus all naturally capable of committing criminal acts."[45] Hence, he argued that humans' basic impulses motivate them to become involved in crime and delinquency unless there is reason for them to refrain from such behavior. Instead of the standard question "Why do they do it?" Hirschi asserted that the most important question becomes "Why don't they do it?"[46]

Hirschi theorized that individuals who are most tightly bonded to social groups such as the family, the school, and their peers are less likely to commit delinquent acts.[47] **Commitment to the social bond**, according to Hirschi, is made up of four main elements: attachment, commitment, involvement, and beliefs.

Attachment   An individual's attachment to conventional others is the first element of the social bond. Sensitivity toward others, argued Hirschi, relates to the ability to internalize norms and to develop a conscience.[48] Attachment to others also includes

social control theory A perspective that delinquent acts result when a juvenile's bond to society is weak or broken.

commitment to the social bond The attachment that a juvenile has to conventional institutions and activities.

A father helps his children with schoolwork. According to social control theorists, a child's attachment to and respect for his or her parents are the most important variables in preventing delinquency. ▶ What might rank third? Fourth?

the ties of affection and respect children have to parents, teachers, and friends. The stronger his or her attachment to others, the more likely it is that an individual will take this into consideration when or if he or she is tempted to commit a delinquent act.[49] Attachment to parents is the most important variable insulating a child against delinquent behavior, and even if a family is broken by divorce or desertion, the child needs to maintain attachment to one or both parents. "If the child is alienated from the parent," Hirschi asserted, "he will not develop an adequate conscience or superego."[50]

Commitment The second element of the social bond is commitment to conventional activities and values. An individual is committed to the degree that he or she is willing to invest time, energy, and self in attaining conventional goals such as education, property, or reputation. When a committed individual considers the cost of delinquent behavior, he or she uses common sense and thinks of the risk of losing the investment already made in conventional behavior.[51] Hirschi contended that if juveniles are committed to these conventional values and activities, they develop a stake in conformity and will refrain from delinquent behavior.

Involvement Involvement also protects an individual from delinquent behavior. Because any individual's time and energy are limited, involvement in conventional activities leaves no time for delinquent behavior: "The person involved in conventional activities is tied to appointments, deadlines, working hours, plans, and the like," reasoned Hirschi, "so the opportunity to commit deviant acts rarely arises. To the extent that he is engrossed in conventional activities, he cannot even think about deviant acts, let alone act out his inclinations."[52]

Beliefs The fourth element of the social bond is beliefs. Delinquency results from the absence of effective beliefs that forbid socially unacceptable behavior.[53] Such beliefs, for example, include respect for the law and for the social norms of society. This respect for the values of the law and legal system develops through intimate relations with other people, especially parents. Hirschi portrayed a causal chain "from attachment to parents, through concern for the approval of persons in positions of authority, to belief that the rules of society are binding on one's conduct."[54]

Empirical Validation of the Theory Travis Hirschi tested his theory by administering a self-report survey to 4,077 junior high and high school students in Contra Costa County, California, and he used school records and police records to analyze the data he received on the questionnaires. His analysis of the data yielded information on the basic elements of the social bond.

Hirschi analyzed attachment of respondents in the sample to parents, to the school, and to peers. The greater the attachment to parents, he found, the less likely the child was to become involved in delinquent behavior. But more than the fact of communication with the parents, the quality or the intimacy of the communication was the critical factor. The more love and respect found in the relationship with parents, the more likely it was that the child would recall the parents when and if a situation of potential delinquency arose.[55]

Hirschi also found that in terms of attachment to the school, students with little academic competence and those who performed poorly were more likely to become involved in delinquent behavior. Significantly, he found that students with weak affectional ties to parents tended to have little concern for the opinions of teachers and to dislike school.[56]

The attachment to peers, Hirschi added, did not imply lack of attachment to parents. The respondents who were most closely attached to and respectful of their friends were least likely to have committed delinquent acts. Somewhat surprisingly, delinquents were less dependent on peers than nondelinquents. Hirschi theorized from his data "that the boy's stake in conformity affects his choice of friends rather than the other way around."[57]

In terms of commitment, Hirschi found that if a boy claimed the *right* to smoke, drink, date, and drive a car, he was more likely to become involved in delinquency. The automobile, like the cigarette and bottle of beer, indicated that the boy had put away childish things. Also, the more a boy was committed to academic achievement, the less likely he was to become involved in delinquent acts. Hirschi further reported that the higher the occupational expectations of boys, the less likely it was that they would become involved in delinquent behavior.[58]

Hirschi found that the more a boy was involved in school and leisure activities, the less likely he was to become involved in delinquency. In other words, the more that boys in the sample felt that they had nothing to do, the more likely they were to become involved in delinquent acts. Hirschi theorized that the lack of involvement in and commitment to school releases a young person from a primary source of time structuring.[59]

Moreover, he found that the less boys believed they should obey the law, the less likely they were to obey it. He added that delinquents were relatively free of concern for the morality of their actions, so they were relatively amoral and differed significantly in values from nondelinquents. Additionally, the data in this study failed to show much difference between lower- and middle-class young people in terms of values. Figure 5.3 depicts the main constructs of Hirschi's theory.

FIGURE 5.3 Hirschi's Social Control Theory

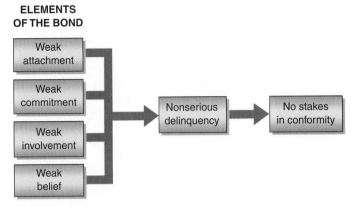

Voices of Delinquency

Read "My Father Was an Alcoholic." The writer of this story is on death row. Did this person's lack of social control, or bonding, contribute to his delinquencies as a juvenile and crimes as an adult? In your opinion, why did he turn out the way he did? If you, as one of the authors did, had a chance to work with him as a juvenile, what would your interventions have been?

Evaluation of Social Control Theory Social control theory has received wide support.[60] This theory of the causes of delinquent behavior has several strengths:

- Social control theory is amenable to empirical examination. Unlike other theorists discussed in this unit, Hirschi was able to test his theory with a population of adolescents. The basic theoretical constructs of control theory—concepts such as attachment to parents, involvement in school, and commitment to conventional activities—are clearly defined and measurable.
- Social control theory has provided valuable insights into delinquent behavior. For example, the importance of the intrafamily relationship has been substantiated.

TABLE 5.1 Summary of Social Process Theories of Delinquency

Theory	Proponents	Cause of Delinquency Identified in the Theory	Supporting Research
Differential association	Edwin Sutherland	Criminal behavior is to be expected in individuals who have internalized a preponderance of definitions favorable to law violations.	Moderate
Drift	David Matza	Juveniles neutralize themselves from the moral bounds of the law and drift into delinquent behavior.	Moderate
Containment	Walter Reckless	Strong inner containment and reinforcing external containment provide insulation against criminal behavior.	Moderate
Social control	Travis Hirschi	Criminal acts result when an individual's bond to society is weak or broken.	Strong

The relationship between the school and delinquency is another important area that social control theory addresses. Especially valid is the proposition that attachments and commitments to societal institutions (the social bond) are associated with low rates of delinquency.

■ Researchers are increasingly using this theory to develop integrated explanations of delinquent behavior.

In sum, although social control theory cannot explain all acts of delinquency, it still has more empirical support today than any other explanation of delinquency. However, even if Hirschi's theory adequately explains delinquency in juveniles who are involved only in relatively trivial offenses, whether its findings apply as well to serious delinquents can be earnestly questioned. Social control theory also fails to describe the chain of events that weakens the social bond, and it divides delinquents into either socialized or unsocialized youths.[61] As important as this theory is, greater attention must be given to the operational definitions of the elements of the social bond before the theoretical merits of social control theory can be fully ascertained.[62] Social process theories, including Hirschi's theory of social control, are summarized in Table 5.1.

Contextual Analysis: Integrated Theories of Delinquency

The theoretical development of integrated explanations for delinquency has been one of the most highly praised concepts in criminology.[63] Theory integration generally implies the combination of two or more contexts, including existing theories, levels of theory, social contexts, or individual contexts, on the basis of their perceived commonalities. Attempts to combine theoretical explanations of delinquency into a coherent sequence of connecting events and outcomes give rise to several issues and concerns:

■ Because the specific form of delinquent behavior to be explained may vary from one theory to another, variations will likely be present in the power and utility of the integrated theory.[64]

■ When theoretical expressions of delinquency are mixed, the question of which factors to use as a representation of theories used in the model becomes an issue. Differential association theory illustrates this second issue. It is divided into seven propositions and even further subcategories. The question becomes: Which proposition or propositions should be used as representative of differential association theory?[65]

■ In regard to synthesis efforts, an issue sometimes arises as to the generalizability of the theory to all segments of the population. For example, most theories of delinquency focus on lower-class adolescent males, but these theories may or may not apply to lower-class adolescent females or to middle- or upper-class adolescent males and females.[66]

■ Another concern is the fact that included theories may have different basic assumptions with respect to motivations, attitudes, and specific factors contributing to delinquency. Interdisciplinary theories, especially, offer opposing views on the feelings and attitudes of delinquents, and it is not uncommon for structural or process sociological theories to have widely divergent views both on delinquents' attitudes and motivations and on the effects of stimuli.[67]

Despite these daunting challenges, several integrated theories for delinquent behavior have been developed.[68] Four of the most important are Michael R. Gottfredson and Hirschi's general theory of crime, Delbert S. Elliott's integrated social process theory, Terence P. Thornberry's interactional theory, and J. David Hawkins and Joseph G. Weis's social development model.[69]

Gottfredson and Hirschi's General Theory of Crime

In their 1990 publication, *A General Theory of Crime*,[70] Gottfredson and Hirschi defined lack of self-control as the common factor underlying problem behaviors:

> People who lack self-control will tend to be impulsive, insensitive, physical (as opposed to mental), risk-taking, short-sighted, and nonverbal, and they will tend, therefore, to engage in criminal and analogous acts [which include smoking, drinking, using drugs, gambling, having children out of wedlock, and engaging in illicit sex]. Since these traits can be identified prior to the age of responsibility for crime, since there is [a] considerable tendency for these traits to come together in the same people, and since the traits tend to persist through life, it seems reasonable to consider them as comprising a stable construct useful in the explanation of crime.[71]

Thus, self-control is the degree to which an individual is "vulnerable to the temptations of the moment."[72] The other pivotal construct in this theory of crime is crime opportunity, which is a function of the structural or situational circumstances encountered by the individual. In combination, these two constructs are intended to capture the simultaneous influence of external and internal restraints on behavior[73] (see Figure 5.4).

More than two dozen studies have been conducted on the general theory of crime, and the vast majority have been largely favorable.[74] Self-control has been found to be related to self-reported crime among college students, juveniles, and adults; it tends to predict future criminal convictions and self-reported delinquency; and it is related to social consequences other than crime.

Gottfredson and Hirschi's theory of self-control is part of a trend that pushes the causes of crime and delinquency further back in the life course into the family. In some respects, it is a return to the emphasis found in the works of the Gluecks (see Chapter 3) and also resembles the important themes in Wilson and Herrnstein's reinforcement theory. This emphasis on early childhood socialization as the cause of crime, of course, departs from the emphasis on more proximate causes of crime found in rational choice theory and in most sociological theories.[75] Gottfredson and Hirschi's focus on a unidimensional trait also departs from the movement toward multidimensional and integrated theories of crime.[76]

Criticisms of the general theory of crime have focused largely on its lack of conceptual clarity.[77] It is argued that key elements of the theory remain to be tested,[78] that the theory does not have the power to explain all forms of delinquency and crime,[79] and that "questions remain regarding the ubiquity of self-concept."[80] Nevertheless, in spite of these criticisms, the general theory of crime will likely continue to spark continued interest and research.

mycrimekit

Video Self-Control Theory

FIGURE 5.4 Gottfredson and Hirschi's General Theory of Crime

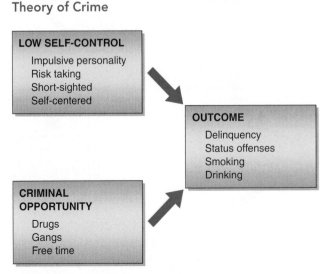

LOW SELF-CONTROL
Impulsive personality
Risk taking
Short-sighted
Self-centered

OUTCOME
Delinquency
Status offenses
Smoking
Drinking

CRIMINAL OPPORTUNITY
Drugs
Gangs
Free time

A group of Drug Free Youth gathers at Parrot Jungle in Miami, Florida. ▶ What does the general theory of crime say leads to low self-control among young people?

Elliott and Colleagues' Integrated Social Process Theory

Delbert Elliott and colleagues offer "an explanatory model that expands and synthesizes traditional strain, social control, and social learning perspectives into a single paradigm that accounts for delinquent behavior and drug use."[81] They argued that all three theories are flawed in explaining delinquent behavior: Strain theory is able to account for some initial delinquent acts but does not adequately explain why some juveniles enter into delinquent careers, whereas others avoid them; control theory is unable to explain prolonged involvement in delinquent behavior in light of there being no reward for this behavior; and social learning theories portray delinquents as passive and susceptible to influence when they are confronted with delinquency-producing reinforcements.

Integrating the strongest features of these theories into a single theoretical model, Elliott and colleagues contended that the experience of living in socially disorganized areas leads youths to develop weak bonds with conventional groups, activities, and norms. High levels of strain, as well as weak bonds with conventional groups, lead some youths to seek out delinquent peer groups, and these antisocial peer groups provide both positive reinforcement for delinquent behavior and role models for this behavior. Consequently, Elliott and colleagues theorized, there is a high probability of involvement in delinquent behavior when bonding to delinquent groups is combined with weak bonding to conventional groups[82] (see Figure 5.5).

This theory represents a pure type of integrated theory. It can be argued that both general theory and interactional theory are not fully integrated theories but are rather elaborations of established theories. In contrast, there is no question that integrated social process theory is an integrated theory.

FIGURE 5.5 Elliott and Colleagues' Integrated Social Process Theory

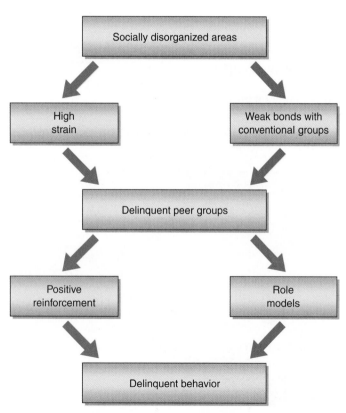

Examinations of this theory have generally been positive, yet some doubt has been raised about its application to various types of delinquent behaviors. Questions have even been raised about its power and utility with different types of drug activity. For example, integrated social process theory explained 59% of the variation in marijuana use but only 29%–34% of the distribution of hard drug use.[83]

Thornberry's Interactional Theory

In Thornberry's interactional theory of delinquency, the initial impetus toward delinquency comes from a weakening of the person's bond to conventional society, represented by attachment to parents, commitment to school, and belief in conventional values. Associations with delinquent peers and delinquent values make up the social setting in which delinquency, especially prolonged serious delinquency, is learned and reinforced. These two variables, along with delinquent behavior itself, form a mutually reinforcing causal loop that leads toward increasing delinquency involvement over time.[84]

Moreover, this interactive process develops over the person's life cycle. During early adolescence, the family is the most influential factor in bonding the youngster to conventional society and reducing delinquency. But as the youth matures and moves through middle adolescence, the world of friends, school, and youth culture becomes the dominant influence over his or her behavior. Finally, as the person enters adulthood, commitments to conventional activities and to family, especially, offer new avenues to reshape the person's bond to society and involvement with delinquent behavior.[85]

Finally, interactional theory holds that these process variables are systematically related to the youngster's position in the social structure. Class, minority group status, and social disorganization of the community all affect the initial values of the interactive variables as well as the behavioral trajectories. It is argued that youths from the most socially disadvantaged backgrounds begin the process least bonded to conventional society and most exposed to the world of delinquency. The nature of the process increases the chances that they will continue on to a career of serious criminal involvement; on the other hand, youths from middle-class families enter a trajectory that is oriented toward conformity and away from delinquency (see Figure 5.6).

Thornberry's theory essentially views delinquency as the result of events occurring in a developmental fashion. Delinquency is not viewed as the end product; instead, it leads to the formation of delinquent values, which then contribute to disconnections in social bonds, more attachments to antisocial peers, and additional involvement in delinquent behavior. As found in other developmental theories, some variables affect unlawful behavior at certain ages and other factors at other ages.[86]

Interactional theory has several positive features that should ensure its continued examination. It seems to make sense of much of the literature on explanations of delinquent behavior; in addition, studies that use an interactional framework not only are more

FIGURE 5.6 Thornberry's Interactional Theory

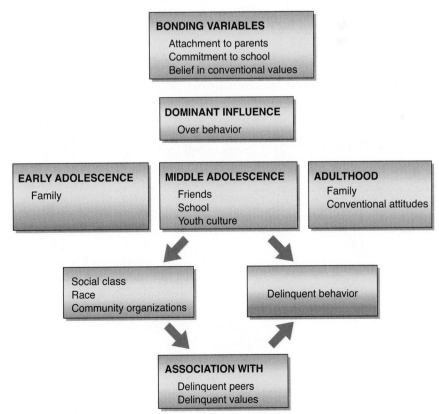

FIGURE 5.7 Hawkins and Weis's Social Development Model

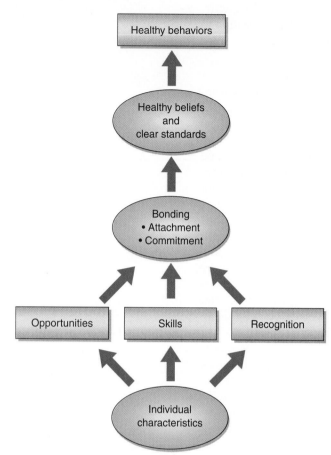

Source: James C. Howell, ed., *Guide for Implementing the Comprehensive Strategy for Serious, Violent, and Chronic Juvenile Offenders* (Washington, D.C.: Office of Juvenile Justice and Delinquency Prevention, 1995), p. 23.

social development model A perspective based on the integration of social control and cultural learning theories that proposes that the development of attachments to parents will lead to attachments to school and a commitment to education as well as a belief in and commitment to conventional behavior and the law.

commonly used among delinquency researchers but also are being increasingly used in interdisciplinary research. Furthermore, interactional approaches are consistent with the social settings in which individuals live and interact with others.[87]

Interactional theory also has several shortcomings. Most significantly, interactional theory fails to address the presence of middle-class delinquency and basically ignores racial and gender issues. Its viewpoint that delinquency will persist throughout adolescence and into adulthood (with which Gottfredson and Hirschi would agree) leaves little room for short-term discontinuation or permanent termination of illegal behavior patterns.[88]

Hawkins and Weis's Social Development Model

In terms of developing a new strategy, J. David Hawkins's and Joseph G. Weis **social development model** offers an integrated approach to delinquency prevention that could have long-range consequences for dealing with youth crime in American society.[89]

The social development model is based on the integration of social control theory and cultural learning theory. According to social control theory, the weakening, absence, or breakdown of social controls leads to delinquency[90]; cultural learning, or cultural deviance, theory emphasizes the role of peers and the community in the rise of delinquency, so in disorganized communities, youths are at greater risk of delinquency.[91]

Social control theory focuses on the individual characteristics that lead to delinquent behavior and the impact of the major socializing institutions on delinquency, whereas cultural learning theory examines the role of the community context in the process of learning criminal and delinquent attitudes and behaviors. Social control theory posits that youths become delinquent because of inadequate social controls; cultural learning theory adds that juveniles become socialized to delinquency in disorganized communities.

The social development model proposes that the development of attachments to parents will lead to attachments to school and a commitment to education, as well as a belief in and commitment to conventional behavior and the law. Learning theory describes the process by which these bonds develop: If juveniles are given adequate opportunities for involvement in legitimate activities and are able to acquire the necessary skills with a consistent reward structure, they will develop the bonds of attachment, commitment, and belief. Figure 5.7 presents a diagram of the social development model.

As a sound foundation for delinquency prevention, the social development model has linked families, schools, and peer groups as appropriate objects for intervention, depending on the child's developmental stage. Interventions that aim to increase the likelihood of social bonding to the family are appropriate from early childhood through early adolescence, and interventions that seek to increase the likelihood of social bonding to school are appropriate throughout the years of school attendance and are especially important as juveniles approach and enter adolescence.[92] Thus, the social development model offers communities an empirically grounded basis for designing, implementing, and assessing delinquency prevention programs.

Delinquency across the Life Course: Social Process

The theories in this chapter focus on social process. Delinquency, like other social processes, starts at a particular point and either continues or ceases. Crime continuation or desistance involves several ongoing processes: lack of competence in adolescence, cumulative disadvantage, and turning points and/or establishment of a new identity.

Lack of Competence in Adolescence

John Claussen's classic study of children of the Great Depression followed the study members of the Berkeley longitudinal studies for nearly 50 years, from childhood through the later years of the participants' lives. Claussen found that competence and social influence at the end of adolescence gave shape to the evolving life course.[93] Claussen defined what he called "planful competence" as comprising the dimensions of self-confidence, dependability, and intellectual investment. He found that a youth who demonstrated planful competence was "equipped with an ability to evaluate accurately personal efforts as well as the intentions and responses of others, with an informed knowledge of self, others, and options, and with the self-discipline to pursue chosen goals."[94]

Early competence in study participants, according to Claussen, meant fewer crises in every decade up to their fifties. Highly competent men were more likely to find the right job and to remain in this rewarding line of work, and highly competent women were more likely to find the right husband and to feel rewarded in family life. Choice and selection were both involved: A choice of attractive options and an ability to be selective permitted the most competent to take advantage of their opportunities. In contrast, Claussen concluded that adolescents who lacked planful competence had different trajectories or pathways and made choices that led to job difficulties, marital breakup, and personal difficulties with the law and with figures of authority.[95]

A young man accepts a job from an employer. ▶ **How does the social development model explain positive achievement? How does it explain delinquency?**

Cumulative Disadvantage

Most juvenile delinquents' lives are not characterized by the kind of planful competence that leads to one successful experience after another throughout the life course. Instead, delinquent youths deal with personal deficits that lead to a series of cumulative disadvantages. For example, Thornberry and Krohn's examination of the Rochester data revealed that individuals who begin antisocial behavior early have individual deficits (e.g., negative temperamental qualities) that both contribute to and are adversely affected by parental deficits (e.g., explosive physical disciplinary styles and low affective ties). Over time, these researchers contended, these parents and children develop a coercive interaction, the result being children who express persistent patterns of oppositional and aggressive behavior.[96]

The disorders in these adolescents' lives make delinquent behavior, drug use, and gang involvement more attractive. Involvement in various forms of delinquency then makes these young people more likely to drop out of school; to become pregnant or impregnate someone else; to be unemployed into their adult years; and to be arrested, convicted, and sentenced in the juvenile and later the adult system. Thus, distracted from conventional pathways, they become more involved in antisocial behaviors, which can continue from adolescence into adulthood.[97]

What this concept of cumulative disadvantage suggests is that each negative event in an offender's life tends to limit the positive options available to the individual and becomes a disadvantage in living a crime-free life (see Web Extra 5.1). Incarceration, especially, leads to cumulative disadvantage in other areas. Thus, arrest and incarceration may spark failure in school, unemployment, and weak community bonds, which in turn increase adult crime.[98]

Turning Points

As discussed in Chapter 2, Robert J. Sampson and John H. Laub explored the concept of a "turning point" in *Crime in the Making: Pathways and Turning Points through Life*[99] and further developed the idea in *Shared Beginnings, Divergent Lives*.[100] Sampson and Laub's social control explanation emphasizes the gradual buildup of investments that accrue in the presence of social bonds of attachment (see Web Extra 5.2). They found five turning points in the desistance process: marriage/spouses, employment, reform school, the military, and neighborhood change. These are "structurally induced turning points that serve as the catalyst for sustaining long-term behavioral change."[101]

Another view of the turning point emerges in the research that Shadd Maruna conducted on English ex-offenders. Maruna contended that ex-offenders desist from crime when they develop a coherent and prosocial identity for themselves. Accordingly, they need a coherent and credible self-story to explain to themselves and to others how their past could have led to their new identity. Maruna referred to this self-story as a "redemptive script" and described how interviewees used such scripts to link their past lives to positive outcomes.[102]

Peggy C. Giordano and colleagues developed a theory of cognitive transformation to explain desistance in their follow-up of a sample of serious adolescent female delinquents. These researchers found that four types of cognitive transformation take place as an integral part of the desistance process: (1) There is a shift in the actor's openness to change; (2) the individual is exposed to a hook or set of hooks for change; (3) the individual begins to envision and fashion an appealing and conventional "replacement self"; and (4) a transformation takes place in the way the actor views the former deviant behavior or lifestyle. These various cognitive transformations or shifts not only influence receptivity to one or more hooks of change but also inspire and direct behavior.[103]

In sum, desistance requires that a combination of positive attitudes, prosocial behaviors, and reinforcing transitions in marriage, family, and employment replace the negative patterns found in delinquency, criminality, and drug involvement. These processes not only require human agency but also are gradual, perhaps even unknown to the offender at the time.

Web Extra 5.1

Juvenile Justice Evaluation Center website, section titled "Serious, Violent, and/or Habitual Offenders"

Web Extra 5.2

National Youth Violence Prevention Resource Center website

Social Process Theories and Social Policy

Each of the social process theories discussed in this chapter can influence those who make social policy. Differential association theory suggests that delinquents learn from their association with small groups, so the more they are exposed to prosocial groups, the more likely it is that they will be deterred from delinquent behavior. Several treatment technologies, such as Positive Youth Development (PYD), suggest that some delinquent youths are influenced by positive group norms. The task, then, is to generate opportunities for delinquency-prone youths to be exposed to more positive definitions of the social order.

Social control theory suggests that the more attached youths are by social bonds, the more likely it is that they will refrain from delinquent behavior. Thus, attachment to the family, positive experiences in school, and exposure to prosocial groups in the community become important components in the design of delinquent prevention and control programs. Containment theory also proposes that positive experiences in the home, the school, and the community will lead to a good self-concept, thereby insulating youths from delinquent behavior.

Both drift theory and labeling theory suggest that a key element in the process of becoming delinquent is the reaction of society to unacceptable behavior. Delinquency in America is widespread throughout the social order, and the danger is that identifying and tagging individuals who have come to the attention of the justice system will increase their chances of continuing delinquent behavior or, even worse, that their official contacts with the system may encourage them to choose a delinquent career. Accordingly, policy makers would be wise to discourage the labeling of youths, both in the school system and in the justice system.

Chapter Summary

Each of the social process theories discussed in this chapter contributes to our understanding of how adolescents become delinquent. Among the perspectives discussed are the following:

- Differential association theory suggests that individuals learn from their association with small groups; if they are involved in antisocial groups, they are more likely to accept and internalize antisocial conduct norms and behavioral definitions.

- Social control approaches, including bonding theory, maintain that the more strongly adolescents are attached by positive social bonds, the more likely it is that they will refrain from delinquent behavior.

- Containment theory states that positive experiences in the home, the school, and the community will lead to the development of a positive self-concept, thereby insulating individuals from delinquency.

- Process theories, such as those discussed in this chapter, are also helpful in understanding the continuation of, or desistance from, delinquency across the life course. Bonding with significant others, drifting in and out of delinquent behavior, and developing a self-concept are key ideas in these theories.

- Theories of delinquency and drift, as well as other social control theories, emphasize the decision-making process at the individual level.

- Gottfredson and Hirschi's general theory of crime defines the lack of self-control as the common element underlying problem behaviors.

- Theory integration usually implies the combination of two or more existing theories on the basis of their perceived commonalities.

- Elliott and colleagues' integrated social process theory contends that the experience of living in socially disorganized areas leads young people to develop weak social bonds with conventional groups, activities, and norms. High levels of strain, as well as weak bonds, lead some youths to seek out delinquent peer groups.

- Thornberry's interactional theory suggests that delinquency leads to the formation of delinquent values, which then contribute to the disintegration of conventional bonds and greater attachment to antisocial peers.

- Criticisms of social process theories center on their level of analysis—which is the individual delinquent and the personal decision-making process. Critics point out that these theories fail to place sufficient emphasis on the impact of larger political and economic systems on adolescents and their development.

Key Terms

commitment to the social bond, p. 113

containment theory, p. 112

control theory, p. 112

differential association theory, p. 106

differential identification theory, p. 108

drift theory, p. 110

neutralization theory, p. 110

social control theory, p. 113

social development model, p. 120

social process theory, p. 106

soft determinism, p. 111

Review Questions

1. Why is differential association theory called a "learning" theory?
2. Self-concept, according to containment theory, is vitally important in affecting behavior. Do you agree?
3. Matza and Hirschi proposed different interpretations of the degree to which delinquents identify with the norms and values of society. What is the position of each theorist? Which position do you find more credible?
4. Which one of the four integrated theories makes the most sense to you? What are the advantages of integrated theory? What are its disadvantages?
5. Does Matza's drift theory seem to be present in the lives of delinquents? What forces seem to set in motion the drift toward delinquency?

Discussion Questions

1. Does differential association theory support the "nature" argument of crime causation? Explain your response.
2. Does cultural stratification naturally occur between generations? If so, how might it contribute to delinquency?
3. How does containment theory relate to the concept of peer pressure?
4. What do you think might account for youths reporting both the development of strong bonds to delinquent peers and the acceptance of the values of conventional society?

Group Exercises

1. Have students recount experiences when they were presented with opportunities to learn delinquent behavior (e.g., smoking and shoplifting), and ask them to explain what motivated them to take the course of action they ultimately took.
2. Have the class debate/discuss the merits and criticisms of each of the theories in this chapter. Have the students attempt to develop a workable definition of the term *self-concept*.
3. Have the class debate/discuss the merits and concerns of integrated theory.
4. Have the students read Mears and Field's article "A Closer Look at the Age, Peers, and Delinquency Relationship," accessible at http://wcr.sonoma.edu/v4nl/mears.html; have them discuss the authors' use of interactional theory in their research.
5. Take an anonymous poll of the class that asks these questions about their elementary and secondary school years: (1) Were you highly involved, moderately involved, or little involved in conventional activities? (2) Did you have a close, ambivalent, or distant relationship with your parents? (3) Did you become involved in delinquent behavior? Total the responses, and discuss the results with the class.

mycrimekit

Go to mycrimekit.com to explore the following study tools and resources specific to this chapter:

- **Practice Quiz:** Practice with multiple-choice, true/false, short-answer, and essay questions.

- **WebQuests:** Do web activities about Dr. Ross L. Matsueda's article explaining Sutherland's differential association theory.

- **Flashcards:** Use 11 flashcards to test your knowledge of the chapter's key terms.

Social Interactionist Theories of Delinquency

CHAPTER OBJECTIVES

After reading this chapter, you should be able to answer the following questions:

■ How important is the concept of labeling as a cause of future behavior?

■ What kinds of youngsters become more determined to succeed because they have been labeled?

■ Does peer evaluation affect some young people more than others?

■ How does social class affect the system's response to a troublesome youth?

We worry about what a child will become tomorrow, yet we forget that he is someone today.

—Stacia Tauscher, National Center for Juvenile Justice, Annual Report, 2003

Introduction

When 14-year-old Patrick V. was arrested for breaking into a boatyard in Kennebunkport, Maine, and starting a fire, he normally would have been charged with arson in state court. But due to the unusual circumstances of his case, he was convicted of a "terrorist act" and given a much longer sentence in a prison 600 miles away.

During the break-in, Patrick V. and a 19-year-old accomplice spotted what they thought were video surveillance cameras and started a fire to disable them. In addition to destroying the building and several boats, the fire ruined a boat engine owned by Kennebunkport's most prominent resident, former President George H. W. Bush.

Saying the incident raised national security concerns, Bush's Secret Service agents brought terrorism charges against the two boys in federal court under the then-newly passed PATRIOT Act. Federal officials reasoned that arson was "a crime of violence" and that it was a federal issue because the boatyard was engaged in interstate commerce.

Convicted in federal district court, the 19-year-old was sentenced to 57 months in a federal prison for adults and Patrick was sentenced to 30 months in federal prison. However, since the federal system does not run prisons for juveniles, Patrick was sent to a maximum-security juvenile facility run by the state of Pennsylvania, which houses juvenile offenders from the federal system.

In 2004, after Patrick's parents legally challenged having their son so far from home, a federal appeals court reopened the case and ordered Patrick into a Maine facility; the length of the sentence, however, went unchanged. Patrick's parents said their son had no previous criminal record and that the government overreacted because a former president was involved.[1]

This chapter discusses labeling theory, symbolic interactionist theory, and conflict theory. Labeling theory describes the creation and enforcement of society's rules and explains the important role those rules play in determining the nature and extent of delinquency. Symbolic interactionist theory considers the process by which deviant or delinquent behavior is influenced by reference groups and peers, and conflict theory sees delinquency as a by-product of the conflict that results when groups or classes with differing interests interact with one another.

These three perspectives are termed **social interactionist theories** of delinquency because they derive their explanatory power from the give-and-take that continuously occurs between social groups and between individuals and society.

social interactionist theory A theoretical perspective that derives its explanatory power from the give-and-take that continuously occurs between social groups and between individuals and society.

Labeling Theory

During the 1960s and 1970s, the labeling perspective was one of the most influential approaches to understanding crime and delinquency.[2] **Labeling theory** or the labeling perspective, sometimes called the interactional theory of deviance or the social reaction perspective, is based on the premise that society creates deviants by labeling those who are apprehended as different from other individuals when in reality they are different only because they have been tagged with a deviant label. Accordingly, labeling theorists focus on the processes by which individuals become involved in deviant behavior and stress the part played by social audiences and their responses to the norm violations of individuals.

The view that formal and informal social reactions to criminality can influence criminals' subsequent attitudes and behaviors has been recognized for some time. Frank Tannenbaum, Edwin M. Lemert, and Howard Becker, three of the chief proponents of the labeling perspective, focus on the process by which formal social control agents

labeling theory The view that society creates the delinquent by labeling those who are apprehended as different from other youths when in reality they are different primarily because they have been tagged with a deviant label.

A young woman mentors a girls' softball team. ▶ How can mentoring programs help young people avoid the potential negative consequences of labeling?

change the self-concept of individuals through these agents' reactions to their behavior. Recent work in labeling theory is also discussed in this section.

Frank Tannenbaum: Dramatization of Evil

Frederick M. Thrasher's 1927 study of juvenile gangs in Chicago was one of the first to suggest that the consequences of official labels of delinquency were potentially negative.[3] In 1938, Tannenbaum developed the earliest formulation of labeling theory in his book *Crime and the Community*. Tannenbaum examined the process whereby a juvenile came to the attention of the authorities and was labeled as different from other juveniles, and he theorized that this process produced a change in both how those individuals were then handled by the justice system and how they came to view themselves:

> The process of making the criminal, therefore, is a process of tagging, defining, identifying, segregating, describing, emphasizing, making conscious and self-conscious; it becomes a way of stimulating, suggesting, emphasizing, and evoking the very traits that are complained of.[4]

Tannenbaum called this process the "dramatization of evil," writing that the process of tagging a juvenile resulted in the youth becoming involved with other delinquents and that these associations represented an attempt to escape the society that was responsible for negative labeling. The delinquent then became involved in a deviant career, and regardless of the efforts of individuals in the community and the justice system to change his or her "evil" behavior, the negative behavior became increasingly hardened and resistant to positive values. Tannenbaum proposed that the less the evil is dramatized, the less likely youths are to become involved in deviant careers.[5]

Edwin Lemert: Primary and Secondary Deviation

The social reaction theory developed by Edwin M. Lemert provided a distinct alternative to the social disorganization theory of Shaw and McKay, the differential association notion of Edwin H. Sutherland, and the social structural approach of

Merton. Lemert focused attention on the interaction between social control agents and rule violators as well as on how certain behaviors came to be labeled criminal, delinquent, or deviant.[6]

Lemert's concept of primary and secondary deviation is regarded as one of the most important theoretical constructs of the labeling perspective. According to Lemert, **primary deviation** consists of the individual's behavior, and **secondary deviation** is society's response to that behavior. The social reaction to the deviant, Lemert charged, could be interpreted as forcing a change in status or role, that is, society's reaction to the deviant person resulted in a transformation in the individual's identity.[7] The social reaction to the deviant person, whether a disapproving glance or a full-blown stigmatization, is critical in understanding the progressive commitment of a person to a deviant mode of life.

Lemert observed this **process of becoming deviant** as having the following stages:

> The sequence of interaction leading to secondary deviation is roughly as follows: (1) primary deviation; (2) social penalties; (3) further primary deviation; (4) stronger penalties and rejection; (5) further deviation, perhaps with hostilities and resentment beginning to focus upon those doing the penalizing; (6) crisis reached in the tolerance quotient, expressed in formal action by the community stigmatizing of the deviant; (7) strengthening of the deviant conduct as a reaction to the stigmatizing and penalties; (8) ultimate acceptance of deviant social status and efforts at adjustment on the basis of the associated role.[8]

The social reaction to deviance is expressed in this process of interaction. *Social reaction* is a general term that summarizes both the moral indignation of others toward deviance and the action directed toward its control. This concept also encompasses a social organizational perspective; as an organizational response, the concept of social reaction refers to the capacity of control agents to impose such constraints on the behavior of the deviant person as are reflected in terms such as *treat, correct,* and *punish.*[9]

Howard Becker: Deviant Careers

Howard Becker, another major labeling theorist, conceptualized the relationship between the rules of society and the process of being labeled as an outsider:

> Social groups create deviance by making the rules whose infraction constitutes deviance, and by applying those rules to particular people and labeling them as outsiders. From this point of view, deviance is not a quality of the act the person commits, but rather a consequence of the application by others of rules and sanctions to an "offender." The deviant is one to whom that label has successfully been applied; deviant behavior is behavior that people so label.[10]

Becker argued that once a person is caught and labeled, that person becomes an outsider and gains a new social status, with consequences for both the person's self-image and his or her public identity. The individual is now regarded as a different kind of person.[11] Although the sequence of events that leads to the imposition of the label of "deviant" is presented from the perspective of social interaction, the analytical framework shifts to that of social structure once the label is imposed (see Web Extra 6.1). In other words, before a person is labeled, he or she participates in a process of social interaction, but once labeling has occurred, the individual is assigned a status within a social structure.[12] For the relationship among the theoretical constructs of labeling theory, see Figure 6.1.

Juvenile Justice Process and Labeling

There is a long history of arguments that the labeling found in the formal processing of youths through the juvenile justice system is what influences the secondary response of continued delinquent acts. Edwin Schur contended that most delinquent acts are insignificant and benign and that punishment is not needed. But when youths are arrested and brought before the juvenile court, they are stereotyped as different. Having acquired this label, they receive greater attention from authorities, and they

primary deviation According to labeling theory, the initial act of deviance that causes a person to be labeled a deviant.

secondary deviation According to labeling theory, deviance that is a consequence of societal reaction to an initial delinquent act.

process of becoming deviant In labeling theory, the concept that the process of acquiring a delinquent identity takes place in a number of steps.

Web Extra 6.1
Labeling theory from CrimeTheory.com

Voices of Delinquency

Read "I Have Come a Long Way." How big a factor is labeling in whether this youth becomes a delinquent or not? If he had been labeled, how would his life have turned out differently?

FIGURE 6.1 General Assumptions of Labeling Theory

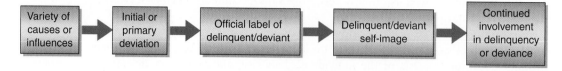

are likely to be processed more deeply in the justice system because of this increased attention. Delinquency laws are actually counterproductive, Schur stated, because they produce more delinquency than they deter. In 1973, Schur went so far as to argue for a policy of **radical nonintervention**, which simply means to "leave the kids alone whenever possible."[13]

> **radical nonintervention** A policy toward delinquents that advises that authorities should "leave the kids alone whenever possible."

More recently, several studies have suggested that under certain circumstances, "official punishment appears to increase the likelihood of subsequent deviance as suggested by labeling theory."[14] Francis T. Cullen and Joanne C. Gersten found that the formal reaction to delinquency affects the likelihood of subsequent delinquent behavior but that these effects are related to the types of reactions and the types of deviance.[15] Anthony Matarazzo, Peter J. Carrington, and Robert D. Hiscott investigated the relationship between prior and current youth court dispositions and found support for labeling theory; their findings indicated that prior juvenile court dispositions exerted a significant impact on current disposition, even with the control of relevant variables.[16]

New Developments in Labeling Theory

The early versions of labeling theory came under serious attack for theoretical flaws and lack of support.[17] Critics of this perspective charged that "labeling theorists had grossly exaggerated the role of labeling by suggesting that it is the only factor responsible for persistent deviance and by implying that it always increases the likelihood of subsequent rule breaking."[18] Assailed by these and other criticisms, the theory was under serious challenge by 1980 and, as Raymond Paternoster and Leeann Iovanni observed, was "pronounced dead by 1985."[19] However, the labeling perspective later enjoyed a resurgence because of its more sophisticated application.[20]

Recent Applications of Labeling Theory   Ruth Ann Triplett and G. Roger Jarjoura developed "new avenues for exploring the effects of labeling."[21] They separated labeling into formal and informal labeling: Formal labels, the emphasis of early labeling theorists, are the reactions by official agents of the justice system to illegal behaviors; in contrast, an informal label is "an attempt to characterize a person as a given 'type' . . . by persons who are not acting as official social control agents, and in social situations that are not formal social control 'ceremonies.'"[22] In other words, informal labels are those given by parents, neighbors, and friends. For example, John Braithwaite examined shaming in the family; his study showed that families use shaming, or reintegrative shaming, to bring an offender back into line with their beliefs.[23]

Triplett and Jarjoura also divided labels into subjective and objective labels. An audience's reaction to an actor is an objective label, whereas the actor's interpretation of that reaction is a subjective label. Although the importance of subjective labels has always been emphasized in symbolic interactionism, which is one of the important roots of labeling theory, it has remained largely unexplored in labeling theory and research.[24] Triplett, using the four waves of Elliott's National Youth Survey, concluded that the informal labels of significant others (parents) affect delinquent behavior both directly and indirectly for whites but that informal or subjective labels of significant others have no consistent direct or indirect effect on delinquent behavior for nonwhites.[25]

Students having lunch in the cafeteria of Oswego High School in New York. ▶ How do mode of dress, hairstyle, and so on signify a person's understanding of who he or she is? How do such understandings relate to social roles?

juvenile, perhaps contributing to the group's searching for another, more suitable alternative. (See Figure 6.2 for a model of reflected appraisals and behavior.) Matsueda suggested, "Whether or not a goal is achieved using unlawful means is determined by each individual's contribution to the direction of the transaction; those contributions, in turn, are determined by the individual's prior life experience or biography."[43]

This process by which role taking can lead to delinquent behavior, according to Matsueda, can be illustrated by several classic studies of delinquency. Scott Briar and Irving Piliavin's study found that gang youths who are committed to nonconventional lines of action are often incited into delinquent behavior by "situationally induced motives," which are verbal motives presented by other youths; free from considering how conventional others would react, they can take each other's role of presenting delinquent motives and adopting delinquent behavior.[44] James F. Short Jr. and Fred L. Strodtbeck noted that a youth's willingness to join a gang fight frequently revolved around the risk of losing status with the gang; in taking the role of the group and considering the group's negative reactions, these gang youths would join in for fear of losing status.[45] Donald Gibbons's study of delinquent boys further found that one result of group interaction was the emergence of novel shades of norms and values that influenced the direction of joint behavior.[46] (See Library Extra 6.1 for more information on juvenile offenders.)

Matsueda concluded that this discussion of role taking implies four features of a theory of the self and delinquent behavior. First, the self is formed by how an individual perceives that others view him or her and thus is rooted in symbolic interaction. Second, the self is an object that "arises partly endogenously within situations, and partly exogenously from prior situational self being carried over from previous experience." Third, the self as an object becomes a process that has been determined by the self at a previous point in time and by prior resolutions of problematic situations.

Library Extra 6.1
OJJDP publication: *Report of the Comprehensive Strategy Task Force on Serious, Violent and Chronic Juvenile Offenders—Part 1*

FIGURE 6.2 Alternative Models of Reflected Appraisals

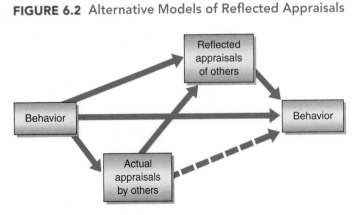

Source: Ross L. Matsueda, "Reflected Appraisals, Parental Labeling, and Delinquency: Specifying a Symbolic Interactionist Theory," *American Journal of Sociology* 97 (May 1992), p. 1585. Reprinted by permission of the University of Chicago Press.

Fourth, delinquent behavior takes place partly because habits are formed and partly because the stable perception of oneself is shaped by the standpoint of others.[47]

Using classic symbolic interactionist theory, Matsueda talked about the self as a consistent "me" that is relatively stable across situations. This self, which is called "a looking-glass self" by Charles H. Cooley[48] or the "self as an object" by Mead,[49] is a process that consists of three components: how others actually see us (others' actual appraisals), how we perceive the way others see us (reflected appraisals), and how we see ourselves (self-appraisals).[50] A person's self, then, is made up in part of a "reflected appraisal" of how significant others appraise or evaluate him or her.[51]

Matsueda used a sample from the National Youth Survey to test his theory. His findings supported a symbolic interactionist conceptualization of reflected appraisals and delinquency in a number of ways. Juveniles' reflected appraisals of themselves from the standpoint of parents, friends, and teachers "coalesced into a consensual self, rather than remaining compartmentalized as distinct selves."[52] This remained true whether the reflected appraisals were found in rule violators or socialized youths. In agreement with labeling theory, parental labels of youths as rule violators were more likely among nonwhites, urban dwellers, and delinquents. Delinquent youths' "appraisals of themselves are also strongly influenced by their parents' independent appraisals of them."[53] Moreover, prior delinquent behavior, both directly and indirectly, reflected appraisals of self. In addition, reflected appraisals as a rule violator exerted a large effect on delinquent behavior and mediated much of the effect of parental appraisals as a rule violator on delinquent behavior. Finally, age, race, and urban residence exerted significant effects on delinquency, most of which worked indirectly through prior delinquency and in part through the rule violator's reflected appraisal.[54]

Interactionist Perspectives on Gender, Race, and Delinquency   Heimer argued that "structural conflict gives rise to gender and race differences in motivations to break the law."[55] From the interactionist perspective, then, racial and gender inequalities are consequential for law violation because they restrict the positions of minorities and females and therefore constrain communication networks and the power needed to influence others.[56] She goes on to say:

> Hence, these forms of structural inequality influence definitions of situations because they partially determine the significant others and reference groups considered in the role-taking process. Through shaping definitions of situations, gender and racial inequality contribute to the patterning of crime and delinquency. Thus, consistent with the tradition of differential association in criminology, an interactionist theory of delinquency argues that there will be differences across groups in definitions of situations and the law to the extent that communication networks vary.[57]

Evaluation of Symbolic Interactionist Theory

The symbolic interactionist theory of delinquency has several strengths:

- It builds on symbolic interactionist theory, a great tradition in American sociology. This tradition has identified the locus of social control in the process of taking the role of the other and of linking with the broader social organization through role commitments, generalized others, and reference groups.[58]
- It builds on and adds to the insights of labeling theory. At a time in which labeling is being reformulated and is emerging in a more sophisticated form, the insights that Matsueda, Heimer, and their colleagues provide in relating symbolic interactionism and delinquency promise to further enrich labeling's contributions to our understanding of delinquency.
- The symbolic interactionist theory of delinquent behavior is insightful regarding how both law-abiding and delinquent youths form their conceptions of themselves and how these perceptions influence their decision making.
- This theory contributes helpful insights about the influence of delinquent peers and the group context on youths' self-appraisals.

An evaluation of symbolic interactionist theory, of course, is limited by the fact that it has been tested by Matsueda, Heimer, and colleagues in only a few settings.[59] At this point, it is uncertain how much delinquency it explains, even among group delinquents, and many of the criticisms aimed at labeling theory apply also to this theory. Nevertheless, symbolic interactionist theory is still a promising attempt to explain delinquent behavior. (See Library Extra 6.2 for additional information on juvenile offenders.)

Conflict Theory

Conflict theory sees social control as the end result of the differential distribution of economic and political power in any society, and conflict theorists view laws as tools created by the powerful for their own benefit.[60] The development of the conflict model is indebted to the concept of "dialectics." This concept, like that of order, can be traced back to the philosophers of ancient Greece. In antiquity the term *dialectics* referred to the art of conducting a dispute or bringing out the truth by disclosing and resolving contradictions in the arguments of opponents.[61]

Georg F. Hegel used this concept of dialectical thinking to explain human progress and social change. A prevailing idea, or "thesis," according to Hegel, would eventually be challenged by an opposing idea, or "antithesis." The resultant conflict usually would result in the merging of the two, or "synthesis." The synthesis gradually would be accepted as the thesis but then would be challenged by a new antithesis, and so it would go throughout history.[62] Karl Marx, rather than applying the method to ideas as Hegel did, applied the concept to the material world. Marx's theory became one of dialectical materialism, as he contended that the conflict was one of competing economic systems, in which the weak must ward off exploitation by the strong or powerful in society.[63]

Georg Simmel, a twentieth-century conflict theorist, argued that unity and discord are inextricably intertwined and together act as an integrative force in society. Simmel added that "there probably exists no social unity in which convergent and divergent currents among its members are not inseparably interwoven."[64] Simmel's notion of dialectics thus acknowledged the existence of tendencies for order and disorder.

More recently, Ralf Dahrendorf contended that functionalists misrepresented reality by being overconcerned with order and consensus, arguing that functionalists present a description of a utopian society—a society that never has existed and probably never will. Dahrendorf proposed that social researchers would be wise to opt for the conflict model because of its more realistic view that society is held together by constraint rather than consensus, not by universal agreement but by the coercion of some people by others.[65]

Richard Quinney has argued that criminal law is a social control instrument of the state "organized to serve the interests of the dominant economic class, the capitalist ruling class."[66] William Bonger earlier made this same point: "In every society which is divided into a ruling class and a class ruled, penal law has been principally constituted according to the will of the former."[67]

A more humane social order is the vision of some radical criminologists.[68] The goals of this ideal society are reduced inequality, reduced reliance on formal institutions of justice, and reduced materialism, and the social relations of this social order are committed to developing self-reliance, self-realization, and mutual aid.[69] This peaceful society can be attained by using compromise and negotiation on a community level to defuse violent social structures. Communities must organize themselves in such a way as to prevent crime and to help victims without punishing offenders when crime does occur.[70]

Dimensions of Conflict Criminology

A great deal of variation exists among the ideas of conflict criminologists. Some theories emphasize the importance of socioeconomic class, some focus primarily on power and authority relationships, and others emphasize group and cultural conflict.

Library Extra 6.2
OJJDP publication: *Report of the Comprehensive Strategy Task Force on Serious, Violent and Chronic Juvenile Offenders—Part 2*

conflict theory A perspective that holds that delinquency can be explained by socioeconomic class, by power and authority relationships, and by group and cultural differences.

Voices of Delinquency

Read "Wrong Place at the Wrong Time." Do you see elements of symbolic interactionist theory in the delinquent and adult crimes of the writer of this story? How did she take on roles during the years she talks about?

Video Basic Principles of Conflict Theory

radical criminology A perspective that holds that the causes of crime are rooted in social conditions that empower the wealthy and the politically well organized but disenfranchise the less fortunate.

Socioeconomic Class and Radical Criminology Even though Marx wrote very little on the subject of crime as the term is used today, he inspired a new school of criminology that emerged in the early 1970s. This school is variously described as Marxist, critical, socialist, left-wing, or new criminology as well as **radical criminology**. Marx was concerned both with deriving a theory of how societies change over time and with discovering how to go about changing society. This joining of theory and practice is called "praxis."[71]

Marx saw the history of all societies as the history of class struggles and viewed crime as a result of these class struggles.[72] He wrote in the *Communist Manifesto*:

> Freeman and slave, patrician and plebeian, lord and serf, guildmaster and journeyman, in a word, oppressor and oppressed, stood in constant opposition to one another, carried on an uninterrupted, now hidden, now open fight, a reconstruction of society at large, or in the common ruin of the contending classes.[73]

capitalism An economic system in which private individuals or corporations own and control capital (wealth and the means of production) and in which competitive free markets control prices, production, and distribution of goods.

Emerging with each historical period, according to Marx's theory, is a new class-based system of ranking. Marx contended that with **capitalism**, "society as a whole is more and more and more splitting up into two great classes directly facing each other—bourgeoisie [capitalist class] and proletariat [working class]."[74] The relations between the bourgeoisie and the proletariat become increasingly strained as the bourgeoisie comes to control more and more of the society's wealth and the proletariat is increasingly pauperized. In this relationship between the oppressive bourgeoisie and the pauperized proletariat lie the seeds of the demise of capitalism.[75]

Mark Colvin and John Pauly developed an integrated structural theory of delinquency, the purpose of which was to provide "a comprehensive theoretical approach to understanding the social production of serious patterned delinquent behavior," and using the empirical findings of others to support their model, they contended that the power relations to which most lower-class workers are subjected are coercive.[76]

Colvin and Pauly argued that the parents' experience of coerciveness in the workplace contributes to the development of coercive family control structures, which lead to alienated children. The coercive social milieu in which many people work reduces their capacity as parents to deal with their own children in anything other than a repressive fashion, frequently by using physical punishments—and this type of punishment hinders the development of positive bonds between children and their parents.[77]

The situation is exacerbated because juveniles with alienated parental bonds, according to Colvin and Pauly, are more likely to be placed in coercive school settings. Their alienation from both family and school encourages such juveniles to become involved with alienated peers, who form peer groups. These peer groups create two contrasting paths to delinquent involvement: In the first path, peer group coerciveness interacts with youngsters' earlier experiences of alienation to propel them into serious, patterned, violent delinquent behavior; in the second path, the experience of rewards from illegitimate sources builds a lasting attraction to serious and patterned delinquent behavior.[78]

Herman Schwendinger and Julia Siegel Schwendinger also stated that capitalism produces a marginal class of people who are superfluous from an economic standpoint.[79] They went so far as to say that "the historical facts are incontrovertible: capitalism ripped apart the ancient regime and introduced criminality among youth in all stations of life."[80]

The Schwendingers further argued that socialization agents within the social system, such as the school, tend to reinvent within each new generation the same class system: "The children of families that *have* more *get* more, because the public educational system converts human beings into potential commodities."[81] The schools tend to be geared toward rewarding and assisting those youths who exhibit early indications of achieving the greatest potential success in institutions of higher learning and later in the job market, but this selection is made at the expense of those who do not exhibit such potential in their early encounters with the educational system.[82]

In the Marxist perspective, the state and the law itself are ultimately tools of the ownership class and reflect mainly the economic interests of that class. Capitalism produces egocentric, greedy, and predatory human behavior. The ownership class is guilty of the worst crime: the brutal exploitation of the working class. Revolution is a means to counter this violence and is generally both necessary and morally justifiable. Conventional crime is caused by extreme poverty and economic disenfranchisement, products of the dehumanizing and demoralizing capitalist system.[83]

Power and Authority Relationships A second important dimension of conflict criminology is the focus on power and authority relationships. Max Weber, Ralf Dahrendorf, Austin T. Turk, and John Hagan have made contributions to this body of scholarship.

Weber's theory, like the Marxist perspective, contains a theory of social stratification that has been applied to the study of crime. Although Weber recognized the importance of the economic context in the analysis of social stratification, he did not believe that such a unidimensional approach could explain satisfactorily the phenomenon of social stratification. He added power and prestige to the Marxist emphasis on property and held these three variables responsible for the development of hierarchies in society. Weber also proposed that property differences led to the development of classes, power differences led to the creation of political parties and the development of classes, and prestige differences led to the development of status groups.[84] Further, Weber discussed the concept of "life chances" and argued that they were differentially related to social class; from this perspective, criminality exists in all societies and is the result of the political struggle among different groups attempting to promote or enhance their own life chances.[85]

Both Dahrendorf and Turk have extended the Weberian tradition in the field of criminology by emphasizing the relationships between authorities and their subjects. Dahrendorf contended that power is the critical variable explaining crime, arguing that although Marx built his theory on only one form of power, property ownership, a more useful perspective could be constructed by incorporating broader conceptions of power.[86]

Turk, constructing his analysis from the work of both Weber and Dahrendorf, argued that the social order of society is based on the relationships of conflict and domination between authorities and subjects.[87] Focusing on power and authority relationships, this perspective of conflict theory examines the relationships between the legal authorities who create, interpret, and enforce right–wrong standards for individuals in the political collectivity and those who accept or resist but do not make such legal decisions. Turk also made the point that conflicts between authorities and subjects take place over a wide range of social and cultural norms.[88]

John Hagan and his associates viewed the relationship between gender and nonserious delinquency as linked to power and control.[89] Using the data collected in Toronto, Ontario, they suggested that the presence of power among fathers and the greater control of girls explain why boys are delinquent more often than girls. Unlike Hirschi's control theory, Hagan and colleagues' **power-control thesis** based the measurement of class on the authority that parents have in their positions at work, and they assumed that the authority of parents at work translates into conditions of dominance in the household and in the degree of their parental control over their children.

Robert M. Regoli and John D. Hewitt's **theory of differential oppression** contends that in the United States, authority is unjustly used against children, who must "adapt to adults' conceptions of what 'good children' are." Children experience oppression, in this view, because they exist in a social world in which adults look on them as inferior and in which they lack social power relative to adults. Oppression takes place when adults use their power to prevent children from attaining access to valued resources or to prevent them from developing a sense of self as a subject rather than an object. Accordingly, children must submit to the power and authority of adults, and when children react negatively or fail to conform to these pressures, a process begins that results in delinquent acts.[90]

power-control thesis The view that the relationship between gender and delinquency is linked to issues of power and control.

theory of differential oppression The view that in the United States, authority is unjustly used against children, who must adapt to adults' ideas of what constitutes "good children."

These graffiti-covered row houses are in East Baltimore. According to the Marxist perspective, the very nature of capitalist society increases urban blight and contributes to the exploitation of lower-class youths, leading to an increased likelihood of crime. ▶ **Is this perspective valid? If so, how might capitalist societies lower their crime rates?**

The theory of differential oppression is organized around four principles:

1. Because children lack power on account of their age, size, and lack of resources, they are easy targets for adult oppression.
2. Adult oppression of children occurs in multiple social contexts and falls on a continuum ranging from benign neglect to malignant abuse.
3. Oppression leads to adaptive reactions by children. The oppression of children produces at least four adaptations: passive acceptance, exercise of illegitimate coercive power, manipulation of peers, and retaliation.
4. Children's adaptations to oppression create and reinforce adults' view of children as inferior subordinate beings and as troublemakers. This view enables adults to justify their role as oppressors and further reinforces children's powerlessness.[91]

Regoli and Hewitt recognized that the oppression of children falls along a continuum and that some children are oppressed to a greater degree than others. The very basis of their theory hinges on the belief that children who are reared in highly oppressive family conditions are more likely to become delinquent than those who are not raised in such aversive environments.[92]

Group and Cultural Conflicts   Another dimension of conflict criminology is **culture conflict theory,** which focuses on group conflict. Thorsten Sellin and George B. Vold advocated this approach to the study of crime. Sellin argued that to understand the cause of crime, it is necessary to understand the concept of **conduct norms,**[93] a concept referring to the rules of a group concerning the ways its members should act under particular conditions. The violation of these rules arouses a group reaction.[94] Each individual is a member of many groups (family group, work group, play group, political group, religious group, and so on), and each group has its own particular conduct norms.[95] According to Sellin:

> The more complex a culture becomes, the more likely it is that the number of normative groups which affect a person will be large, [and] the greater is the chance that the norms of these groups will fail to agree, no matter how much they may overlap as a result of a common acceptance of certain norms.[96]

culture conflict theory A perspective that delinquency or crime arises because individuals are members of a subculture that has conduct norms that are in conflict with those of the wider society.

conduct norms The rules of a group governing the ways its members should act under particular conditions, and the violation of these rules arouses a group reaction.

Sellin noted that an individual experiences a conflict of norms "when more or less divergent rules of conduct govern the specific life situation in which a person may find himself."[97] The act of violating conduct norms is "abnormal behavior," and crime represents a particular kind of abnormal behavior distinguished by the fact that crime is a violation of the conduct norms defined by criminal law.[98] Regarding criminal law, Sellin wrote:

> The criminal law may be regarded as in part a body of rules, which prohibit specific forms of conduct and indicate punishments for violations. The character of these rules . . . depends upon the character and interests of those groups in the population which influence legislation. In some states these groups may comprise the majority, in others a minority, but the social values which receive the protection of criminal law are ultimately those which are treasured by the dominant interest groups.[99]

Sellin also has developed a theory of "primary and secondary culture conflict." Primary culture conflict occurs when an individual or group comes into contact with an individual or group from another culture and the conduct norms of the two cultures are not compatible; secondary culture conflict refers to the conflict arising whenever society has diverging subcultures with conduct norms.[100]

Vold, like Sellin (and in the tradition of Simmel), analyzed the dimension of group conflict. He viewed society "as a congeries [an aggregation] of groups held together in a shifting, but dynamic equilibrium of opposing group interests and efforts."[101] Vold formulated a theory of group conflict and applied it to particular types of crimes, but he did not attempt to explain all types of criminal behavior. He stated that group members are constantly engaged in defending and promoting their group's status. As groups move into each other's territory or sphere of influence and begin to compete in those areas, intergroup conflict is inevitable. The outcome of a group conflict results in a winner and a loser, unless a compromise is reached—but compromises never take place when one group is decidedly weaker than the other. Like Simmel, Vold believed that group loyalty develops and intensifies during group conflict.[102] (See Library Extra 6.3 for information on a mentoring program.)

In sum, conflict criminologists can be divided into three basic groups: those emphasizing socioeconomic class, those emphasizing power and authority relationships, and those emphasizing group and cultural conflict. Those who emphasize socioeconomic class call themselves radical, Marxist, critical, humanist, or new criminologists and do not identify with the other two groups. Some significant differences do exist between radical criminologists and the other two groups: The non-Marxist conflict criminologists emphasize a plurality of interests and power and do not put a single emphasis on capitalism, as do the Marxist conflict criminologists, nor do the non-Marxist conflict criminologists reject the legal order as such or the use of legal definitions of crime.[103] Table 6.1 compares the three groups of conflict criminologists.

mycrimekit™

Library Extra 6.3
OJJDP's Juvenile Mentoring Program (JUMP)

TABLE 6.1 Comparisons of Conflict Perspectives

Perspective	Legal Definitions	Legal Order	Purpose of Conflict	Capitalism
Socioeconomic Class (Marxist)	Rejection	Rejection	Revolution	Rejection
Power and Authority Relationships	Acceptance	Acceptance	Reform	Acceptance
Group and Cultural Conflict	Acceptance	Acceptance	Reform	Acceptance

A teenager works a part-time job in a fast-food restaurant. Youths who don't have jobs are more likely to find other ways to provide for what they want. ▶ **What other ways might they choose?**

Evaluation of Conflict Theory

Conflict criminology's critiques of the social order do contribute two important pieces to the puzzle of why juveniles commit delinquent acts. First, the various conflict criminology perspectives call attention to the macrostructural flaws that contribute to high rates of juvenile delinquency. Second, radical humanism, also rooted in the structural inequalities of the social order, emphasizes the dignity of the person and is quick to identify instances where children experience oppression in the United States.[104]

Social Context of Delinquency: Restorative Justice and Peacemaking

For hundreds of years, community standards were passed to succeeding generations through interaction between adults and children in the community, and change in the standards came slowly. Conformity to those standards was enforced through both informal social mechanisms and the law. Because some of these standards enforced by the communities were sexist, racist, and classist and had nothing to do with the well-being of others or the community as a whole, the rebellion of the 1960s and 1970s attacked the potent existing informal social control mechanisms and began to rely more on the legal mechanisms for those standards essential for safe and fair communities.[105]

Advocates of restorative justice argue that after 25 years of relying on legal mechanisms, it is clear to many that legal standards are not sufficient to create healthy, ethical community behavior. The legal system is too distant from daily life to be effective and is too complicated and abstract for citizens to feel that they are a part of setting those standards or that they have responsibility for enforcing those standards in the community. In addition, because the legal system involves coercion and deprivation of liberty, it can set only minimum standards of behavior. Restorative-justice processes that encourage cooperation and voluntary engagement can establish standards for maximum behavior.[106]

One of the lessons of restorative justice taught to youths is empathy development. According to Kay Pranis and other proponents of restorative justice, we have allowed enormous distance to develop between ourselves and the children of others. We have not come to know them and have not invested emotionally, materially, and spiritually in their well-being. Moreover, we have not taught them by example to understand the interconnectedness of all things and the need to understand the impact of our actions on others.[107] The development of empathy requires (1) regular feedback about how our actions affect others, (2) relationships in which we feel valued and our worth is validated, and (3) experience of sympathy from others when we are in pain.[108]

Restorative justice also provides a framework for community members to reestablish a more appropriate relationship between community members and young people and to reduce the fear adults have of young people. The processes of restorative justice, especially face-to-face processes, involve the telling of personal stories in intimate settings. Stereotypes and broad generalizations about groups of people are difficult to sustain in the face of direct contact between youths and adults in a respectful setting. Restorative-justice processes assume value in every human being and therefore present individuals to one another in a respectful way, which draws out human dignity in everyone.[109]

Community Conferencing and Sentencing Circles

Community conferences make it possible for victims, youths, and community members to meet one another to resolve issues raised by an offender's trespass.[110] A particularly promising form of community conferences is termed **sentencing circles**. Historically, sentencing circles were found in U.S. native and Canadian aboriginal cultures. These circles were then adopted by the criminal justice system in the 1980s as First Nations Peoples of the Yukon and local criminal justice officials endeavored to build more constructive ties between the criminal justice system and the grassroots community. In 1991, Judge Barry Stuart of the Yukon Territorial Court introduced sentencing circles in order to empower the community to participate in the justice process.[111]

sentencing circles A form of restorative justice that incorporates principles of ancient, aboriginal tribal justice to address the harm suffered by crime victims and their families, the responsibilities of offenders, and the role of community.

One of the most intriguing developments in sentencing circles, as indicated by L. Parker, is the Hollow Water First Nations Community Holistic Healing Circle, which simultaneously addresses harm created by the offender, heals the victim, and restores community goodwill. Circles have been developed most extensively in the western provinces of Canada, and they have also experienced a resurgence in modern times among American Indian tribes (e.g., in the Navaho courts). Today circles may be found in most mainstream criminal justice settings. For example, in Minnesota, circles are used in a variety of ways for a variety of crimes and in varied settings[112]; a Hawaii minimum-security prison has a pilot reentry restorative circles program that began in 2005.[113]

How does a sentencing circle work? Participants in healing or sentencing circles typically speak out while passing around a "talking piece." Separate healing circles are initially held for the victim and the offender; after the healing circles meet, a sentencing circle (with feedback from the family, the community, and the justice system) determines a course of action, and other circles then follow up to monitor compliance, whether that involves, for example, restitution or community service.[114]

Evaluation of Restorative Justice

Restorative justice is rapidly gaining acceptance in juvenile and adult justice systems. Instead of relying on legal intervention to deal with youths' misbehavior and community conflicts, increasingly restorative-justice groups are intervening and seeking to find reconciliation between offenders, victims, and the community. Its basic approach of valuing youngsters, affirming their strengths, and seeking communication with them has much in common with the Positive Youth Development (PYD) approach that was previously discussed.

Nancy Rodriguez used official juvenile court data from an urban area and found that youths who participated in a restorative-justice program were less likely to recidivate than juveniles in a comparison group. Her study further revealed that male and female juveniles with a minimal offense history exhibited the most success from participating in these programs.[115] Another study of the long-term impact of restorative-justice referrals on prevalence of reoffense, number of later official contacts, and

TABLE 6.2 Restorative Justice and Treatment Interventions

Theory	Treatment Interventions
Provides a framework for community members to establish a communication network with young people to resolve minor disputes.	Community Conferencing and Peacemaking
Makes it possible for victims, youths, and community members to resolve issues of youthful members' trespasses; following a healing circle, a sentencing circle decides on the behavioral consequences.	Community Conferencing and Sentencing
Uses the family group decision-making model in order to try to stop family violence.	Family Group Conferences (FGCs)
Involves a reparations program track designed for offenders who commit nonviolent offenses and who are considered at low risk for reoffense.	Reparation and Restitution
Enables in-kind or actual return of what has been lost; it can be viewed within the larger context of "making amends."	Restitution Programs
Encourages one-on-one victim–offender reconciliation facilitated through a mediator.	Victim–Offender Conferencing

seriousness of later offending behavior over several follow-up periods also found a positive impact of restorative-justice programs in all of these categories.[116] Gwen Robinson and Joanna Shapland saw the possibility for restorative justice to be able to reduce recidivism.[117] Restorative justice appears to be one of the most hopeful approaches to juvenile crime, especially with minor forms of juvenile delinquency. See Table 6.2 for restorative-justice theory and the programs that have been developed from this approach to justice.

Delinquency across the Life Course: Labeling

One of the lessons to be learned from *Voices of Delinquency* is that those youngsters who were not apprehended and labeled by the juvenile justice system (first two sections) were able to move fairly easily from their adolescent behaviors into adult prosocial roles. Some had been deeply involved in drug use or drug trafficking, gang activities, and other forms of delinquency, but they did not have the disadvantage of the label "juvenile delinquent" or have the experiences of juvenile justice processing, including institutionalization. In contrast, those in the third and four sections of *Voices of Delinquency* were labeled. Some desisted in their late adolescence or early adulthood, but some went on to adult crime. Sadly, the final five stories were given by individuals who will spend the remainder of their lives in prison.

Certainly, more was involved than the label itself; there was the secondary response to the label. This secondary response sometimes included violent acts directed toward others. Interestingly, when the lives of those who have committed serious and violent acts are examined, they have many other factors in common: They tend to be the children of the poor, the have-nots, who have been abused in a variety of ways and who have become a marginal class. For example, street gang activity is more frequently found in those social settings where poverty, unemployment, drugs, violence, and police encounters are commonplace. They see violence, sometimes on a regular basis, and anticipate that they will end up either in prison or dead at a young age.[118]

One of the major challenges is finding ways to break this cycle of the wasted lives of alienated youths going from the juvenile to the adult correctional system and frequently spending a majority of their lives in prison. Restorative justice is one possibility, PYD is another, and effective prevention programs would be a third possibility. In addition, those who work with youths in various types of programming—ranging from probation to residential treatment to institutional care—can sometimes be instrumental in helping youths turn their lives around.

Voices of Delinquency

Read "I Grew Up in New Orleans" for insight into how a youngster in an urban setting can be exposed to violence, drugs, and gangs on a regular basis.

Delinquency and Social Policy: The Conflict Perspective

The conflict perspective has several contributions to make to handling youth crime in America. Its emphasis on improving human rights is a reminder to policy makers, as well as to all interest groups for children, that the ability of youths to achieve their maximum potential in American society is very much affected by the larger issue of human rights. Whether or not racial justice and the ability to earn an adequate standard of living are guaranteed affects whether minority children and those from impoverished families face discrimination and poverty as they grow up. Similarly, women's rights affect the thousands of children across the nation reared in one-parent homes. Finally, children's rights promise that youths will be granted or guaranteed more of the basic rights that adults enjoy.

Conflict criminology also has much to teach children's advocacy groups about how power and domination affect the creation of policy. For example, these theories contend that in our society control is gained by those groups that wield the most power and resources; that once a group achieves dominance over others, it seeks to use the available societal mechanisms to its advantage to maintain that dominance; that laws are formulated in the interests of the dominant groups, with the result that those behaviors common to the less powerful groups may be restricted; and that the law enforcement and control systems operate to process disproportionately the less powerful members of society.

Third, the conflict perspective points out that the opportunity structure and the economic exploitation of a society become key variables in understanding lower-class youth crime. Societies in which economic exploitation is extreme and in which opportunity is limited can be expected to have high rates of delinquency. Therefore, an adequate standard of living for all Americans and increased employment opportunities for teenagers become critical issues in deterring youth crime. Many of the stories in the *Voices of Delinquency*, especially those of youths who have gone on to the adult correctional system, reveal backgrounds of economic deprivation and abuse; they felt powerless and dominated, and they struck out in retaliation. In "Forgotten Children," an example of this would be the inmate who is serving life without parole: "I was taught by society that I was one of the unworthy children of its blessings because of my skin color. I had been raised by society to be a child of destruction, and so the respect that I should have had for another's rights, person, or property became unimportant to me. What had been instilled in an undeveloped mind, hurting soul, and unloved heart was that what I wanted or needed I could attain by force or brutality."[119]

Finally, conflict criminologists argue that **social injustice** prevails in American society. These criminologists believe that the formal juvenile justice system, as well as the informal justice system, administers different sorts of justice to the children of the haves than to the children of the have-nots, to boys who commit delinquent offenses than to girls who commit "moral" offenses, and to white youths than to nonwhite youths.[120]

social injustice According to many conflict-oriented criminologists, social injustice is found in apparent unfairness in the juvenile justice system arising from poor youths being disproportionately represented, female status offenders being subjected to sexist treatment, and racial minorities being dealt with more harshly than whites.

Chapter Summary

This chapter focuses on labeling theory, symbolic interactionist theory, conflict approaches to delinquency, and restorative justice and peacemaking. Some important points to remember are these:

- Reactions to deviance and crime play an important role in the creation of offender social identities.

- Reactions to deviance and crime occur within a social context, although the context may vary from the family to the group, to school settings, to official labeling

by the justice system, and even to society's political decision-making mechanisms.

- In individual experiences, social reaction occurs during the process of everyday interaction, and that process frequently involves the application of labels to what is perceived as unacceptable behavior.

- Societal responses to deviant behavior may result in the application of negative labels to individuals who engage in such behavior, and those labels may limit future possibilities for positive personal accomplishment.

■ Conflict criminologists relate delinquency to alienation and powerlessness among youths, especially lower-class youths; to the dominant class's creation of definitions of crime to control subordinate classes;

and to what they see as economic exploitation of the lower classes.

■ Restorative justice (and peacemaking) is an increasingly widely used method of communication between victims and youths and between youths and members of the community.

Key Terms

capitalism, p. 136
conduct norms, p. 138
conflict theory, p. 135
culture conflict theory, p. 138
labeling theory, p. 127
power-control thesis, p. 137

primary deviation, p. 129
process of becoming deviant, p. 129
radical criminology, p. 136
radical nonintervention, p. 130
secondary deviation, p. 129
sentencing circle, p. 141

social injustice, p. 143
social interactionist theory, p. 127
symbolic interactionist theory, p. 132
theory of differential oppression, p. 137

Review Questions

1. What is the labeling perspective's explanation for why adolescents become delinquent? Do you agree with this interpretation?
2. How is symbolic interactionist theory of delinquency an extension of, but different from, labeling theory?

3. What are the various dimensions of conflict theory? How do they differ?
4. What are the explanations of delinquency according to Marxist theory? Evaluate each of these explanations.

Discussion Questions

1. Were you ever labeled when you were a young child or juvenile? What influence did it have on your subsequent attitudes and behavior? Did the labels you received become a self-fulfilling prophecy?
2. Can you identify any groups beyond young children among which official labels may be more likely to influence subsequent attitudes and behavior?
3. How would you illustrate the application of symbolic interactionist theory to decision making in youth gangs or in adolescent peer groups? How did such reference group norms affect your decision making and behavior as an adolescent?

4. Reintegrative shaming is a form of shaming, imposed by a sanction by the criminal justice system, that is thought to strengthen the moral bond between the offender and the community. Can you think of any other methods of shaming? How effective do you believe they are?
5. Does role taking influence delinquent/criminal behavior in gang members, compelling them to perform wrongful acts because they perceive that is what is expected of them? If so, who imposes the expectations, their peers or conventional society? Explain your responses.

Group Exercises

1. Have the students read Regoli and Hewitt's article "Holding Serious Juvenile Offenders Responsible: Implications from Differential Oppression Theory," accessible at www.jcjc.state.pa.us/jcjc/lib/jcjc/publications/newsletter/2003/mar03pdf. Then discuss the article in class.
2. Have the class debate/discuss the merits and weaknesses of labeling theory.

3. Have the class debate/discuss the merits and weaknesses of conflict theory.
4. Have the students discuss the Schwendingers' claim that "the historical facts are inconvertible: capitalism ripped apart the ancient regime and introduced criminality among youth in all stations of life."

mycrimekit

Go to mycrimekit.com to explore the following study tools and resources specific to this chapter:

- **Practice Quiz:** Practice with multiple-choice, true/false, short-answer, and essay questions.

- **WebQuests:** Do web activities about the Office of Juvenile Justice and Delinquency Prevention's Statistical Briefing Book (SBB).

- **Flashcards:** Use 16 flashcards to test your knowledge of the chapter's key terms.

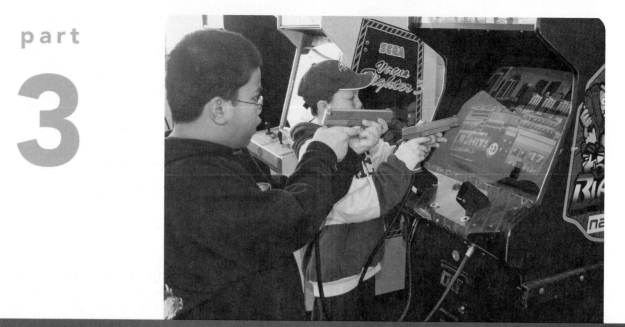

The Environmental Influences on and the Prevention of Delinquency

The chapters in this section provide an overview of the issues involved in preventing delinquency. Traditional approaches to delinquency have been preoccupied with explaining why males commit delinquent acts. In contrast to those perspectives, the first chapter in this section examines the world of the female delinquent. Various feminist perspectives are explored, and issues of gender, class, race, and ethnicity are examined to assess the influences they exert on the problem of female delinquency in American society today.

Chapters 8 and 9 deal with two of the most significant delinquency-related topics in the literature today. Chapter 8 asks how family relations affect the nature and extent of delinquent behavior, and it examines the all-too-frequent abusive treatment of young people within the family. Chapter 9 explores the school as an arena in which conventional success or failure and adaptation to peer pressures can affect the likelihood of delinquent behavior; violence, drug use, and other crimes that take place at school are also discussed.

Chapters 10 and 11 turn to two areas in which participation by adolescents tends to result in high rates of delinquency: gangs and drug use. Gangs, long a problem in our nation's cities, are quickly expanding into other parts of the country and can now be found in small cities and towns. Drug use includes the consumption and abuse of alcoholic beverages, the diversion of pharmacological substances for nonmedical purposes, and the illicit consumption of controlled substances. As these chapters will show, the good news is that both the number of gangs and gang membership have been decreasing since the late 1990s, and the rate of drug use among at least certain categories of juveniles is considerably lower than it was in the late 1970s. The bad news, however, is that both gang participation and drug use continue to result in dangerous and often deadly forms of behavior—affecting young people, their families, their schools, and the rest of society.

Chapter 12 covers the topic of the prevention of delinquency. It discusses goals of delinquency prevention as well as programs designed to help prevent delinquency, and it also deals with the victimization of children.

Gender and Delinquency

There has been growing concern that while most juvenile arrests have been decreasing, the number of female juvenile arrests in some offense categories (such as drug and alcohol violations) continues to rise.

—Girls Study Group (Research Triangle Institute)

CHAPTER OBJECTIVES

After reading this chapter, you should be able to answer the following questions:

■ How is gender important in an understanding of delinquency?

■ How are the categories of gender, class, and race helpful in understanding the issues faced by female delinquents and status offenders?

■ What strides toward gender equality have been made in the past few years? What led to these changes?

■ Are the categories of gender, class, and race interlocking forms of oppression? If so, is the whole greater than the sum of its parts?

Introduction

Police arrested Noemi's sister for trying to rob a woman on a Los Angeles sidewalk using a screwdriver and pepper spray in July 2001. They also arrested 16-year-old Noemi, who was waiting in the car. Noemi, whose last name has been withheld, was tried as an adult under the directives of Proposition 21, a newly passed voter initiative to curb serious juvenile crime, and she was convicted of armed robbery.

Prosecutors offered her a deal. She could spend three to five years in one of the state's youth prisons or just a year in the county jail and receive a "strike" under the state's three-strikes law that puts habitual offenders away for life. Noemi chose to serve a year in Los Angeles County's Twin Towers jail.

To protect young girls like Noemi, California law requires that they be segregated from boys and adult inmates. Since there were only two juvenile girls in the jail and no other place for them to go, Noemi was put into solitary confinement in the discipline ward.

Living with constant lighting, cold food, and only occasional contact with other inmates, who were some of the most disturbed in the facility, Noemi slipped into a depression. When she was eventually transferred to juvenile hall, she recalled that "I didn't even want to leave my room." After her release, she told a reporter, "I'd close myself in the bathroom and just sing the songs that I used to sing in there to try to relax."

"The effects of this type of confinement are profound and disabling," said Craig Haney, a psychology professor at the University of California at Santa Cruz who has studied solitary confinement. "For even the strongest of people, it's a test in maintaining sanity."[1]

Until recently, the study of delinquency had largely been the study of *male* delinquency. Meda Chesney-Lind, a professor at the University of Hawaii at Manoa and one of the country's most respected experts on female delinquency, said that the study of delinquency is gender biased and that delinquency theories are preoccupied with the delinquency of males. Consequently, she argued, the study of offending and of the juvenile justice process is shaped by male experiences and male understandings of the social world.[2]

Carol Smart and Dorie Klein were two of the first criminologists to suggest that a feminist criminology should be formulated because of the neglect of the feminist perspective in classical delinquency theories.[3] Klein's 1973 article ended in a call for "a new kind of research on women and crime—one that has feminist roots and a radical orientation."[4] In a 1995 update, Klein noted that the feminist critique of subjects such as women, crime, and justice "has exploded in volume and advanced light-years in depth, and interest."[5] Kathleen Daly and Chesney-Lind defined a feminist perspective as one "in which women's experiences and ways of knowing are brought to the fore, not suppressed."[6]

Feminist criminologists agree on gender-based differences in adolescents' experiences, developmental rates, and the scope and motivation of male and female patterns of offending.[7] There is also general agreement that female adolescents enjoy greater social support and are more controlled than are males. Further, a review of available data shows that females are less disposed to crime than males and have fewer opportunities for certain types of crimes,[8] and researchers commonly accept that high self-esteem has the effect of discouraging favorable risk-taking situations among female adolescents while encouraging risk-taking situations in males.[9]

There is disagreement, however, in how to address the male-oriented approach to delinquency, thought by many to be both persistent and dominant. One approach focuses on the question of generalizability. When samples include both males and females, researchers who emphasize cross-gender similarities routinely test whether given theoretical constructs account for the offending of both males and females; they also tend to pay little attention to how gender itself might intersect with other factors to create different meanings in the lives of boys and girls. Supporters of this gender-neutral position have examined such subjects as the family, social bonding, social learning, delinquent peer relationships, and, to a lesser degree, deterrence and strain.[10]

Some feminist theorists question the need for separate discussion of female delinquency, arguing that little evidence to date suggests that separate theories are needed to account for male and female delinquency. They also claim that latent structural analysis shows that female delinquency tends to operate through the same factors as male delinquency and add that empirical studies generally reveal that much more variation exists within each gender than between the sexes.[11] Thus, many feminist theorists would recommend that the subject of female delinquency be presented in textbooks as part of "a seamless whole rather than as a separate chapter."[12]

In contrast, other feminist theorists argue that new theoretical efforts are needed to understand female delinquency and women's involvement in adult crime. Sociologist Eileen Leonard, for example, questioned whether anomie, labeling, differential association, subculture, and Marxist theories can be used to explain the crime patterns of women and concluded that these traditional theories do not work and that they are basically flawed.[13] Chesney-Lind's application of male-oriented theories to female delinquency has posited that existing delinquency theories are inadequate to explain female delinquency, and she suggested that there is a need for a feminist model of delinquency because a patriarchal context has shaped the explanations and the handling of female delinquents and status offenders. She argued that the sexual and physical victimizations of adolescent females at home—and the relationship between these experiences and their crimes—have been systematically ignored.[14]

Leonard is one who has argued that new theoretical efforts to understand women's crime must include an analysis of the links among gender, race, class, and culture.[15] After accusing some feminists of ignoring racial, class, ethnic, religious, and cultural differences among women, Elizabeth V. Spelman concluded that it is only through an examination of such factors that oppression against women can be more clearly grasped and understood.[16] Chesney-Lind further extended this argument when she said that adolescent females and women are victims of "multiple marginality" because their gender, class, and race have placed them at the economic periphery of society. The labeling of a girl as delinquent takes place in a world, Chesney-Lind charged, "where gender still shapes the lives of young people in very powerful ways. Gender, then, matters in girls' lives and the way gender works varies by the community and the culture into which the girl is born."[17]

In the face of these two divergent positions—one seeking to explain away gender gaps and to be gender neutral, the other focusing on the importance of gender in understanding delinquency and crime—Darrell Steffensmeier and Emilie Allen have attempted to put the two approaches together. They contended that "[there] is no need for gender-specific theories," although they acknowledge that "qualitative studies reveal major gender differences in the context and nature of offending."[18] These researchers go on to develop a "middle road position,"[19] which has not received much acceptance or support in the literature.

Peggy C. Giordano and colleagues' sample from the Ohio Serious Offender Study led them to conclude that "the either/or dichotomy suggested by the contrast between traditional and feminist frameworks is neither necessary nor helpful to the theory-building process."[20] They suggested that the Ohio study "indicates that the basic tenets of these seemingly opposing viewpoints are not in themselves fundamentally incompatible, and the results require a more integrated approach," finding that this was particularly true when the focus is on the small subgroup of girls with serious delinquent histories.[21]

Giordano and colleagues' follow-up of their study of this subgroup of serious female offenders suggested that a comprehensive examination of their actions requires that we enlist the help of both classic explanations of delinquency and contemporary perspectives that emphasize uniquely gendered processes. Within the life histories of these girls, there is ample evidence of both types of social dynamics. Frequent themes within the narrative include disadvantaged neighborhood, economic marginality, and an "excess of definitions favorable to the violation of law." At the same time, parents' criminal involvement and/or severe alcohol and drug problems can be identified early on, and they continue throughout the women's childhood and adolescent years. The adult follow-up further supported the idea that some processes associated with continued crime or desistance seem to be "generic" (that is, they have a good fit with both women's and men's life experiences), whereas others appear to be more heavily gender specific.[22]

Gender Ratio in Offending

Important questions relate to the vastly different rates of criminal offending by gender: Why are females less likely than males to be involved in most crimes? Conversely, why are males more crime-prone than females? What explains these gender differences in rates of offending?[23] The issue of the gender ratio of crime leads to an inquiry into the factors that block or limit girls' or women's involvement in crime. It can be argued that this inquiry "reflects an androcentric [male-centered] perspective that makes men's behavior the norm from which women appear to deviate through their limited offending."[24]

Some feminist theorists propose treating gender as a key element of social organization rather than as an individual trait, an approach which permits a more complex examination of the gender gap. Data on crime trends, for example, reveal that a gender gap is more persistent for some offenses than others, fluctuates over time, and varies by class, race/ethnicity, and age.[25] Approaches that merely address the gender gap miss the opportunity to examine how causal factors differently shape men's and women's offending across important social dimensions. Miller and Mullins illustrated this point by noting evidence of a link between "underclass" conditions and African-American women's offending—a link that fails to have explanatory power for women's offending in other social contexts.[26]

Karen Heimer and colleagues examined the "economic marginalization thesis," which proposes "that the gender gap in crime decreases and females account for a greater proportion of crime when women's economic well-being declines."[27] "Not only are women more likely to live in poverty than men," they added, "but also the gender gap in poverty rates for women in the most crime-prone group continues to increase."[28] They concluded that continued economic oppression, instead of enhanced economic opportunities for women, may be the root cause of the narrowing of the gender gap in crime that has taken place over the past four decades.[29]

The most promising avenues for exploring the complexities of the gender ratio of offending are found in a conceptual scheme offered by Daly and consist of these three areas of inquiry:

1. *Gendered pathways.* What trajectories propel females and males into offending? What social contexts and factors facilitate entrance to and desistance from offending, and how are they gendered?
2. *Gendered crime.* What are the ways in which street life, sex and drug markets, criminal opportunities, informal economics, and crime groups are structured by gender and other social features? What observed variation occurs in the sequencing and contexts of women's and men's law-breaking?
3. *Gendered lives.* How does gender affect the daily lives of females and males? How does gender structure identities and courses of action? How do these experiences intersect with law-breaking?[30]

Social Context of Delinquency: Gender Roles and Delinquency

To a large degree, understandings of **gender** and gender-based roles are acquired through socialization. Children are socialized into preexisting gender arrangements and construct understandings of themselves and how they relate to others in terms of those frameworks. As Berkeley professor Barrie Thorne noted in her well-known book, *Gender Play*:

> Parents dress infant girls in pink and boys in blue, give them gender-differentiated names and toys, and expect them to act differently. Teachers frequently give boys more classroom attention than girls. Children pick up the gender stereotypes that pervade books, songs, advertisements, TV programs, and movies. And peer groups, steeped in cultural ideas about what it is to be a girl or a boy, also perpetuate gender-typed play and interaction. In short, if boys and girls are different, they are not born but *made* that way.[31]

An empirically based landmark study by the American Association of University Women (AAUW), which included girls of color and all social classes, examined the behavior and treatment of girls in the classroom. The most striking finding in this research was that white girls tend to lose their sense of self-esteem as they advance from elementary school to high school; African-American girls, in contrast, were found to maintain their self-esteem but too often would become dissociated from the school and schoolwork.[32]

Themes found to be unique to the high school–age girls in the AAUW study and in the girls described in the book *Schoolgirls*, by Orenstein were obsession with physical appearance and popularity based on external characteristics rather than achievement, lost of freedom in later adolescence associated with budding sexuality, close attention to relationships, and intense mother–daughter patterns of communication. Inner-city African-American and Latina girls were found to have somewhat unique issues related to life in tough neighborhoods, and the development of a tough exterior was seen as vital for their protection from gangs and violence; early pregnancy was a reality for many of them. In short, girls' victimization—from sexual harassment either at school or on the streets to full-blown sexual assaults—was a fact of girls' lives and had an important impact on their personalities and later development.[33]

In their gender-specific guidelines written for the state of Oregon, P. Patton and M. Morgan suggested that while these statements may not be true of every girl and boy, generally speaking the following can be assumed:

- Girls develop their identity in relation to other people while boys develop their identity in relation to the world.
- Girls resolve conflict based on relationships while boys resolve conflict based on rules.
- Girls focus on connectedness and interdependence while boys focus on independence and autonomy.
- Girls exhibit relational aggression while boys exhibit overaggression.[34]

Although there has been a recent resurgence in recognizing the importance of biology in determining sex-linked behavior, children in today's society continue to be effectively socialized into **gender roles**. Thorne reminds her readers that children have an active role in society and that the social construction of gender—an active and ongoing process in their lives—is most visible in play. When she observed children in middle school, she could identify the gender separation and integration that took place within the classroom, in the lunchroom, and on the playground. Children's active role in constructing gender could be seen as they formed lines, chose seats, gossiped, teased, and sought access to or avoided particular activities. Thorne particularly found extensive self-separation by gender on the playground, where adults have little control.[35]

In addition to the social construction of gender roles, there appears to be considerable evidence that girls develop differently than boys. Marty Beyer, a clinical

gender The personal traits, social positions, and values and beliefs that members of a society attach to being male or female.

gender role A societal definition of what constitutes either masculine or feminine behavior.

psychologist who has examined adolescent males and females across the nation since 1980, states that research "has identified different vulnerabilities and protective factors in girls"[36]; for example, girls have a greater tendency to internalize, and they experience higher rates of anxiety, depression, withdrawal, and eating disorders.[37]

Girls also are more focused on relationships than boys, Beyer noted. This focus on connection with others "makes it difficult for them to resolve the conflict between being selfish and selfless." Girls' failure to receive sufficient nurturing and success within the family may restrict their ability to feel lovable and capable, which in turn may hinder their identity development. Girls have more negative body images during adolescence than boys and tend to dislike themselves more than boys do. Early puberty and the simultaneous occurrence of physical development and transition to middle or high school are especially stressful for girls.[38]

The Female Delinquent

Many studies have pointed out the importance of gender in delinquent behaviors.[39] Gang studies confirm the pressures that young men and women experience in terms of appropriate displays of gender.[40] Gang experiences, for example, can be stigmatizing for girls, because gang participation violates traditional roles for females but not for males.[41] In a study of St. Louis gangs, Jody Miller and Scott H. Decker worked with young women and highlighted the significance of gender in shaping and limiting their involvement in violence and in shaping their victimization risks in gangs.[42] In addition, studies of adolescent gender reveal that boys report frequent sexual activity and early sexual intercourse more than girls and that patterns of male domination and female subordination are increasingly apparent during the adolescent years.[43]

A growing body of research has been devoted to the study of the characteristics of delinquent girls.[44] Researchers have identified basic demographic and offense patterns as well as background characteristics such as family dysfunction, trauma, physical abuse, mental health issues, substance abuse, risky sexual behavior, academic problems, and delinquent peers as common features among girls in custody.[45]

The profile of at-risk adolescent females that emerges identifies common characteristics, including stories of victimization, unstable family life, school failure, repeated status offenses, and mental health and substance abuse problems.[46] These risk factors are similar to those for boys but differ in terms of intensity for girls, except for school failure. Further female gender risk factors as singled out by the National Juvenile Justice Networking Forum, a project of the Girls Study Group, are early puberty and physical development, sexual assault, depression and anxiety, mother–daughter conflict, and cross-gender peer influence; for example, girls may be more influenced by romantic partners than boys, especially in the commission of minor delinquent acts.[47]

B. Bloom and S. Covington have outlined a profile of a female juvenile offender:

- She is 13 to 18 years old.
- She has experienced academic failure, truancy, and dropping out.
- She has a history of repeated victimization, especially physical, sexual, and emotional abuse.
- She is from an unstable family background that includes involvement in the criminal justice system, lack of connectedness, and social isolation.
- She has a history of unhealthy dependent relationships, especially with older males.
- She has mental health issues, including a history of substance abuse.
- She is apt to be a member of a community of color.[48]

Delinquent girls' problems in the school and in the family are correlated with depression, Beyer found. Delinquent girls have more frequently been sexually molested than boys and thus are more likely to develop post-traumatic stress disorder in response to the experience. Much of the behavior of delinquent girls, Beyer continued, occurs because of immature thinking; as is common with delinquent boys, delinquent girls react inappropriately to perceived threat, fail to anticipate or plan, make poor choices, and minimize danger.[49]

A young woman looks at herself in the mirror of a cosmetics case on the streets of New York City's East Village. ▶ **What gender differences does American delinquency display?**

Stephanie J. Funk's study on the need for separate risk assessment instruments for male and female delinquents found that varied assessments are helpful in identifying the risk for reoffending. Funk observed that the importance of social relationships for adolescent females increased their risk for delinquency in two ways: First, disruptions in family, community, and school relations affected females more negatively than males, so both potential and actual disruptions of relationships put females at risk for delinquency; second, the importance of connection introduced a greater risk for delinquency when the others in those relationships engaged in delinquent or criminal behaviors.[50]

According to Joanne Belknap and Kristi Holsinger, "The most significantly and potentially useful criminological research in recent years has been the recognition of girls' and women's pathways to offending."[51] To address these pathways, the National Council on Crime and Delinquency (NCCD) conducted a 1998 multidimensional study of girls in the California juvenile justice system.[52]

The first step along females' pathway into the juvenile justice system is victimization. The ages at which interviewed adolescent girls reportedly were most likely to be beaten, raped, stabbed, or shot were 13 and 14 years.[53] A large proportion of girls first entered the juvenile justice system as runaways, who frequently were attempting to escape abuse at home.[54]

Certain abuses follow these adolescent females into the juvenile justice system. Specific forms of abuse reportedly experienced by juvenile females include the consistent use of foul and demanding language by staff; inappropriate touching, pushing, and hitting by staff; placement in isolation for trivial reasons; and withholding of clean clothing. Some girls were strip-searched in the presence of male officers.[55]

A second step along females' pathway into the juvenile justice system involves substance abuse. Substance use in females is highly correlated with early childhood sexual victimization, especially among white females, with the literature consistently reporting a strong link between childhood abuse and the later development of alcoholism and other drug problems.[56] Significantly, at about the same age as the victimization occurred (usually when the girls were between 13 and 14 years old), the girls started using addictive substances.

A third step along females' pathway into the juvenile justice system involves girls acting out at home, in school, in sexual activity, in law-violating acts, and in gang involvement. The emotional problems troubled girls usually have tend to influence

FIGURE 7.1 Pathways to Delinquency

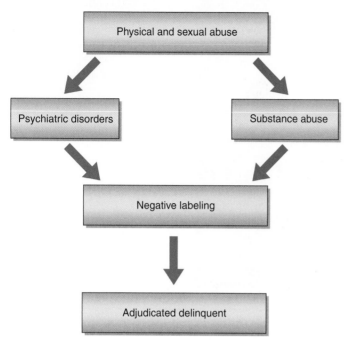

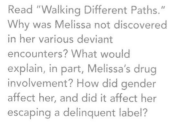

Web Extra 7.1

Center on Juvenile and Criminal Justice—girls in the criminal justice system

Voices of Delinquency

Read "Walking Different Paths." Why was Melissa not discovered in her various deviant encounters? What would explain, in part, Melissa's drug involvement? How did gender affect her, and did it affect her escaping a delinquent label?

their negative behaviors; as a result, they do poorly in school, are sometimes suspended or expelled, or drop out. They run away from home and come before the juvenile court, or they are referred to the court for their involvement in gangs or delinquent behaviors. The three pathways to delinquency in this discussion of the female delinquent are depicted in Figure 7.1.

Explanations of Female Delinquency

This section considers the important question of whether juvenile females commit delinquent acts for reasons different from those of males. Early explanations of female delinquency, which viewed adolescent females as having certain biological characteristics or psychological tendencies that made them more receptive to delinquency, focused on these biological and psychological factors. However, there is general agreement that the hopelessly flawed biological and psychological explanations of delinquency view troublesome adolescent females in our patriarchal society through the lens of sexism. More recent explanations of female delinquency have placed much greater emphasis on sociological factors.

Criminologists, as previously discussed, come to vastly different conclusions concerning the question of whether female juveniles commit delinquent acts for reasons different from those of young males. Some criminologists challenge whether gender-specific explanations are needed, because they claim that existing sociological theories can account for both males' and females' delinquency.[57] Still others argue for gender-specific explanations because, they say, traditional sociological theories of delinquent behavior fail to adequately explain the experience of being female. Gender-specific theories are found later in this chapter (see also Web Extra 7.1).

Biological and Constitutional Explanations

The early biological and constitutional explanations differ rather significantly from more recent ones. In *The Female Offender*, initially published in 1903, Cesare Lombroso dealt with crime as atavism, or the survival of "primitive" traits in female offenders[58]; he argued that women are more primitive, or lower on the evolutionary scale, because they are less intelligent and have fewer variations in their mental capacities than men.

Later in the twentieth century, with the biosocial revival in criminology, biological or physiological explanations for delinquency regained some popularity. T. C. N. Gibbens reported a high rate of sex chromosomal abnormalities in delinquent girls.[59] Furthermore, Cowie and colleagues noted the above-average weight of their institutional sample and suggested that physical overdevelopment tends to draw a girl's attention to sex earlier in life, resulting in sexual promiscuity.[60] In addition, they claimed that menstruation is a distressing reminder to females that they can never be males and that this distress makes them increasingly prone to delinquent acts.[61]

More recently, the focus has been on biopsychological vulnerability factors that are related to girls' delinquency. Five general categories have been considered: (1) stress and anxiety, (2) attention deficit hyperactivity disorder (ADHD) and conduct disorder (CD), (3) intellectual deficits, (4) early pubertal maturation, and (5) mental health issues. These factors apply also to boys' delinquency; in some cases, such as ADHD, boys have been labeled more often, but with others, girls appear to have greater vulnerability.[62] For example, recently discovered gender-related differences (especially in biological processes) may account for the sex differences in stress reactivity, and they contribute to a heightened vulnerability to behavioral problems with females in terms of their response to traumatic events[63] (see Library Extra 7.1).

Psychological Explanations

Psychological explanations of female delinquency also vary between the early and more recent explanations. W. I. Thomas, Sigmund Freud, Otto Pollak, Gisela Konopka, and others addressed this "innate" female nature and its relationship to deviant behavior.

Thomas's work marked a transition from physiological explanations to more sophisticated theories embracing physiological, psychological, and social structural factors. In *Sex and Society*, he suggested that there are basic biological differences between the sexes. Maleness, according to Thomas, is "katabolic," from the animal force that involves a destructive release of energy, and allows the possibility of creative work through this outward flow, but femaleness is "anabolic," meaning motionless, lethargic, and conservative.[64]

Freud also claimed that women are inferior because they are concerned with personal matters and have little social sense. Women, according to Freud, have weaker social interests and less capacity for the sublimation of their interests than men.[65] The Freudian orientation also suggests that at any stage of psychosexual development, faulty mechanisms, fixations, and other problems may occur, which would also lead to female delinquency.

Peter Bols was one of the researchers who focused on the sexual aspect of Freudian psychoanalytic theory. For example, Bols directly stated that "in the girl, it seems, delinquency is an overt sexual act, or to be more correct, a sexual acting out."[66] In a later work, Bols developed three constellations of female delinquency: Those in the first constellation view delinquency as a defense against regression, a denial of the need for a nurturing mother, and an attempt to avoid homosexual surrender; the delinquent female included in the second constellation sexually acts out as a revenge against the mother, who deserves this hostility because she has degraded the girl's oedipal father; and those in the third constellation are female delinquents who attempt through sexual misconduct to restore a sense of reality to their lives because they have become emotionally alienated from their families, which has detrimentally affected their egos. Bols saw female delinquency as much more destructive and irreversible in its consequences than male delinquency.[67]

Pollak's *The Criminality of Women* (1950) advanced the theory that women are more criminal than is usually believed but that their crimes largely go unreported or are hidden. Pollak credited the nature of women themselves for the traditionally low official rates of female crime, because women are inherently deceitful and, therefore, act as instigators rather than perpetrators of criminal activity. The roles played by women are a factor in hidden crimes as well, because their roles as domestics, nurses, teachers, and housewives enable them to commit undetectable crimes. The **chivalry factor**—the tendency of the police and the courts to forgive a girl for the same act for which they would convict a boy—is also advanced as a root cause of hidden crime.[68]

Konopka's study of delinquent females linked a poor home life with a deep sense of loneliness and low self-esteem. Her conception of delinquency relied heavily on the notion of individual pathology, and she concluded that only a female who is "sick" can become delinquent.[69] Konopka identified four key factors contributing to female delinquency: (1) a uniquely dramatic biological onset of puberty, (2) a complex identification process because of a girl's competitiveness with her mother, (3) the changing cultural position of females and the resultant uncertainty and loneliness, and (4) the hostile picture that the world presents to some young females.[70]

More recently, there has been a focus on psychiatric disorders and female delinquents. One study, consistent with other studies, found that along with their physical and sexual abuse, female delinquents tend to exhibit psychopathology, including

mycrimekit

Library Extra 7.1
OJJDP publication: *Juvenile Female Offenders: A Status of the States Report*

chivalry factor The idea that the justice system tends to treat adolescent females and women more leniently because of their gender.

post-traumatic stress disorder (PTSD), suicidal behavior, dissociative disorder, and borderline personality disorder.[71]

In sum, psychological studies of female delinquency shifted in the 1950s from the psychoanalytical to the familial–social and then to the psychiatric. As Chapter 3 noted, both advances in the neurological sciences and the work done in developmental psychology reflect a much greater understanding of why both male and female delinquents become involved in crime. (See Library Extra 7.2 for information on some promising programs for female juveniles.)

Sociological Explanations

Beginning in the late 1970s, numerous studies proceeded from the assumption that sociological processes traditionally related to males could also affect the delinquent involvement of females. General agreement exists among and between feminists and nonfeminists that literature approaching female delinquency from a sociological perspective appears to offer more promise than that which includes biological or psychological causes. Researchers have focused on sociological factors such as blocked opportunity, the women's liberation movement, social bonding, masculinity, power control, and peer group influence, among others. Research has discovered that the causal factors identified by these theories can explain much of the gender gap in delinquency.[72]

General Strain Theory   Males may be more likely to become involved in delinquency than females because males tend to experience strains conducive to delinquency and cope with strains through delinquency. Females, in turn, may experience certain strains that may exhibit other-directed delinquency. However, general strain theory explains female delinquency by contending that many females experience strains conducive to delinquency, such as harsh discipline, parental rejection, peer abuse, negative secondary school experiences, homelessness, and a strong need for money.[73]

Blocked Opportunity Theory   The role of blocked, or limited, opportunity has received considerable attention in the sociological analysis of male delinquency (see Chapter 4), but the usefulness of such variables in studying female delinquency has been largely ignored because males are seen as being concerned with achieving short- and long-term status and economic success, whereas juvenile females are viewed as possessing no such aspirations, instead being satisfied to occupy a role dependent on males.[74] Several studies found that the perception of limited opportunity was more strongly related to female delinquency than it was to male delinquency. Both African-American and white female delinquents regarded their opportunities less positively than did the male delinquents in their sample; status offenders also perceived their opportunities as being less favorable than did nondelinquents.[75]

Social Learning Theory   Social learning theory contends that males have higher rates of delinquency than females primarily because they tend to be associated with delinquent peers and belong to gangs more often than do females. It is also argued that female peer groups are less conducive to delinquency than mixed-gender or all-male peer groups; males, in turn, have beliefs more favorable to delinquency than do females. However, according to social learning theory, some females are more likely than others to become involved in delinquent behavior because they tend to associate with others who provide exposure to delinquent models, reinforce delinquent behaviors, and teach identities that are favorable to delinquency. In addition, research studies add that females may be inclined to engage in delinquency if they associate with older males or are part of mixed-gender or all-male peer groups.[76]

sex-role socialization The process by which boys and girls internalize their culture's norms, sanctions, and expectations for members of their gender.

Social Control Theory   Proponents of social control theory contend that females are less involved in delinquency than males because **sex-role socialization** results in more ties and stronger social bonds for females than for males.[77] In addition, adolescent females may have less opportunity to engage in delinquent behavior because in general they are more closely supervised by parents. Adolescent females are also more dependent on others, whereas adolescent males are encouraged to be more independent and achievement oriented. Consequently, differences in sex-role socialization supposedly promote a greater allegiance to the social bond among females, an allegiance which insulates them from delinquency more than it does males.[78]

Those females who are delinquent, according to social control theory, have less parental supervision, are less tied to their homes and families, are weakly bonded to parents and teachers, perform poorly in school, spend less time on homework, are involved in delinquent peer groups, and have less self-control.[79]

Differential Association Theory   Karen Heimer and Stacy De Coster, in a study on the relation between violent delinquency and gender, tested the explanatory power of differential association theory (see Chapter 6), which they reformulated to incorporate gender using feminist theory and gender studies. Heimer and De Coster's study emphasized process, particularly the ways in which gender is linked to delinquency through "interplay" among structural and cultural influences. The data revealed that emotional bonds to families were negatively related to the learning of violent definitions for girls but not for boys; coercive parental discipline and aggressive friends were positively related to the learning of violent definitions for boys but not for girls; and patriarchal beliefs about gender inhibited female violence without having any effect on male violence.[80]

Masculinity Hypothesis   Several studies of female delinquents have proposed a **masculinity hypothesis**. Adler contended that as females become more malelike and acquire more masculine traits, they become more delinquent.[81] Francis Cullen and coworkers found that the more male and female adolescents possessed "male" personality traits, the more likely they were to become involved in delinquency but that the relationship between masculinity and delinquency was stronger for males than for females.[82] William E. Thornton and Jennifer James found a moderate degree of association between masculine self-expectations and delinquency but concluded that males were still more likely to be delinquent than were females, regardless of their degree of masculinity.[83]

masculinity hypothesis The idea that as girls become more boylike and acquire more masculine traits, they become more delinquent.

Power-Control Theory   John Hagan and colleagues (discussed in Chapter 6) proposed a power-control theory to explain female delinquency.[84] Using a class-based framework and data collected in Toronto, Ontario, they contended that as mothers gain power relative to their husbands (usually by employment outside the home), daughters and sons alike are encouraged to be more open to risk taking. Parents in egalitarian families, then, redistribute their control efforts so that daughters are subjected to controls more like those imposed on sons; in contrast, daughters in patriarchal families are taught by their parents to avoid risks.[85] Hagan and colleagues concluded that "patriarchal families will be characterized by large gender differences in common delinquent behavior while egalitarian families will be characterized by smaller gender differences in delinquency."[86] Power-control theory thus concludes that when daughters are freed from patriarchal family relations, they more frequently become delinquent.[87]

Labeling Theory   Labeling theory focuses on the reaction to delinquency, both the formal reaction by the justice system and the informal reaction by parents, teachers, community residents, and friends. Labeling theorists claim that males are more likely to be labeled as delinquents than females both because the male cultural stereotype views males as troublemakers and because males engage in more delinquency. Labeling theory does argue that some females are more delinquent than others because they have been informally labeled as delinquents by parents, teachers, and others as well as formally labeled by the juvenile justice system.[88]

A teenage prostitute solicits a man near MacArthur Park in Los Angeles. Although the reasons offered for turning to prostitution may differ for white and African-American juveniles, some feminist theorists contend that the fundamental reason is the same: the social and economic inequities of a patriarchal capitalist system. ▶ Do you agree?

Interactionist Theory of Delinquency   Dawn Jeglum Bartusch and Ross L. Matsueda, in assessing whether an interactionist model can account for the gender gap in delinquency, used data from the National Youth Survey. Based on the symbolic interactionist model of delinquency (discussed in Chapter 6), they argued that "delinquency is determined in part by the self as conceived by symbolic interactionists, which in turn is determined by a process of labeling by significant others."[89] They did find some gender interactions: Parental labeling and reflecting appraisals had a larger effect on male delinquency, and parents were more likely to falsely accuse male delinquents.[90] Heimer reported that delinquency for both females and males occurred through a process of role taking, in which youths considered the perspectives of significant others, and among both boys and girls, attitudes favoring deviance encouraged delinquency. She also found that "girls' misbehavior can be controlled by inculcating values and attitudes, whereas more direct controls may be necessary to control boys' deviance."[91]

Deterrence, Rational Choice, and Routine Activities Theories   Three theories—deterrence theory, rational choice theory, and routine activities theory—would claim that males are more likely than females to be involved in delinquency because they see the costs of crime as low and the benefits as high. The explanation as to why females see the costs of crime as high and the benefits as low is related to their higher level of supervision, their moral beliefs, more self-control, less time spent in unstructured and unsupervised activities with peers, less association with delinquent peers, and less prior delinquency. Some females who see the costs of crime as low and the benefits as high differ from other females; for example, they may spend more unstructured and unsupervised time with peers. This is particularly true of those females who run away from home and spend a lot of time on the streets.[92]

Evaluation of Explanations of Female Delinquency

The discussion of female delinquency readily leads to the conclusion that biological explanations are the less predictive factors. Personal maladjustment hypotheses may have some predictive ability in determining the frequency of delinquency in girls, but sociological theories appear to be able to explain more of female delinquency and do it far more adequately. Some feminists are satisfied with the conclusion of sociological studies positing that males and females are differentially exposed or affected by the same criminogenic associations.[93] Strain theory, general theory, social learning theory, social control theory, differential association theory, power-control theory, labeling theory, and symbolic interactionist theory all have received some support.[94] Other feminists (as the next two sections of this chapter will show) contend that the unique experiences of females require gender-specific theories.

Types of Feminist Theories

Historically, feminist theory has at least seven expressions: liberal feminism, phenomenological feminism, socialist feminism, Marxist feminism, radical feminism, third-wave feminism, and postmodern feminism. Some of these approaches have focused squarely on juvenile delinquency, whereas others have been less concerned with law violations by adolescents. Chesney-Lind's radical feminist theory of delinquency, which is discussed in this chapter, is one of the most exciting efforts to explain delinquent behavior in adolescent females.[95] Following are brief explanations of the seven feminist theories:

1. *Liberal feminism.*   Liberal feminism, or egalitarianism, calls for equality of opportunity and enhanced freedom of choice for women. Liberal feminism

theorists do not believe that the system is inherently unequal or that discrimination is systematic. They hold that affirmative action, the Equal Rights Amendment, and other opportunity laws or policies provide evidence that men and women can work together to "androgynize" gender roles (blend male and female traits and characteristics) and eliminate discriminatory policies and practices.[96]

2. *Phenomenological feminism.* Phenomenological feminist theory pays more attention to the regulator than the regulated, that is, phenomenological feminists examine matters such as whether adolescent females receive the benefits of chivalrous treatment, why adolescent females have received discriminatory treatment by the juvenile justice system, and how juvenile laws penalize females. The assumption that adult female offenders are protected by the old norms of chivalry and receive more lenient treatment by the justice system is frequently accepted in adult corrections, but even if it is true for adult female offenders, strong evidence exists that it is not the case for adolescent females.

3. *Socialist feminism.* Socialist feminists, in contrast to other feminists, give neither class nor gender the higher priority. Instead, socialist feminists view both class and gender relations as equal as they interact with and co-reproduce each other in society. To understand class, socialist feminists argue, it is necessary to recognize how class is structured by gender; to understand gender requires that one see how it is structured by class. Crime results from the interaction of these relationships, because it is the powerful who have more legitimate and illegitimate opportunities to commit crime. Low female crime rates, then, are related to women's powerless position in society.[97]

4. *Marxist feminism.* Marxist feminists argue that as private property evolved, males dominated all social institutions, so gender and class inequalities result from property relations and the capitalist mode of production.[98] Sheila Balkan, Ronald Berger, and Janet Schmidt further contended that the foundation for a theory of women's criminality rests in a capitalist mode of production; sexism, they said, is the result of capitalist relations that structure women's and juveniles' power status and types of involvement in crime, and nonviolent female crimes such as shoplifting and prostitution reflect such conditions.[99]

5. *Radical feminism.* Radical feminists view masculine power and privilege as the root cause of all social inequality. The most important relations in any society, according to radical feminists, are found in patriarchy, which includes masculine control of labor power and the sexuality of women.[100] Alison M. Jaggar and Paula Rothenberg, two radical feminists, stated that women were the first oppressed group in history, that women's oppression is so widespread that it exists in virtually every known society, and that it is so deep that it is the hardest form of oppression to eradicate.[101] Radical feminists, especially, focus on sexual violence toward women.[102]

6. *Third-wave feminism.* Third-wave feminists, who are also called women-of-color feminists, womanists, and critical race feminists, object both to white feminists defining "women's issues" from their own standpoint without including women of color and third world concerns and to antiracist theory presuming that racial and ethnic minority women's experiences are the same as those of their male counterparts. These feminist theories focus on the significant roles that sexism, racism, class bias, sexual orientation, age, and other forms of socially structured inequality play in women's lives. They introduced the concept of intersectionalities to explain the interlocking areas of oppression and to examine how the categories of race, ethnicity, class, gender, sexuality, and age in intersecting systems of domination rely on each other to function. Third-wave feminism helps clarify not only those behaviors of women defined as criminal but also the many crimes against women. This approach makes clear the need to understand issues of social justice in evaluating the criminalization of women.[103] Furthermore, this form of feminist theory seeks ways for men and women to work together to eliminate racism, sexism, and class privilege.[104]

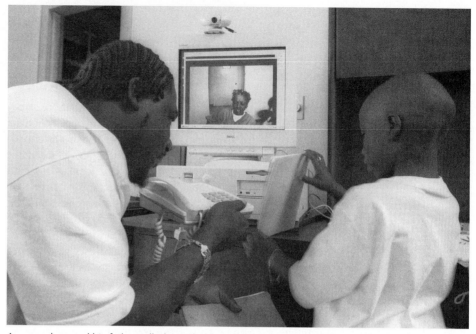

A young boy and his father talk through a camera-equipped speakerphone to the boy's mother, who is in prison hundreds of miles away. The boy is showing his recent drawings to his mother. The program is part of a virtual visitation pilot project run by the Florida Department of Corrections in an effort to strengthen mother–child bonds. ▶ **With increasing numbers of women being sent to prison, many children grow up without a mother at home. What can be done to address this issue?**

7. *Postmodern feminism.* Postmodern feminists criticize other feminists for assuming that women are a "clearly defined and uncontroversially given interest group."[105] Positivist feminists, as well as other modernists, claim that the truth can be determined, providing that all agree on responsible ways of going about it. Postmodern feminists question whether any knowledge is knowable and reject the idea that there is a universal definition of justice true for all people all of the time.[106]

Feminist Theory of Delinquency

feminist theory of delinquency A theory that adolescent females' victimization at home causes them to become delinquent and that this fact has been systematically ignored.

The **feminist theory of delinquency**, an expression of radical feminism, contends that girls' victimization and the relationship between that experience and girls' crime have been systematically ignored. Chesney-Lind, one of the main proponents of this position, stated that it has long been understood that a major reason for girls' presence in juvenile courts is their parents' insistence on their arrest. Researchers and those who work with female status offenders are discovering today that a substantial number are victims of both physical and sexual abuse.[107]

Chesney-Lind proposed that a feminist perspective on the causes of female delinquency include the following four propositions. First, girls are frequently the victims of violence and sexual abuse (estimates are that three-quarters of sexual abuse victims are girls), but unlike those of boys, girls' victimization and their response to that victimization are shaped by their status as young women. Second, their victimizers (usually males) have the ability to invoke official agencies of social control to keep daughters at home and vulnerable. Third, as girls run away from abusive homes characterized by sexual abuse and parental neglect, they are forced into the life of an escaped convict; unable to enroll in school or take a job to support themselves because they fear detection, female runaways are forced to engage in panhandling, petty theft, and sometimes prostitution to survive. Fourth, it is no accident that girls who are on the run from abusive homes or are on the streets because of impoverished homes become involved in criminal activities that exploit their sexuality. Because U.S. society has defined physically "perfect" young women as desirable, girls on the streets, who have little else of value to trade, are encouraged to utilize this resource. Not surprisingly, the criminal subculture also views them from this perspective.[108]

Considerable research supports the frequent victimization of adolescent females. Mimi Silbert and Ayala M. Pines found that 60% of the street prostitutes they interviewed had been sexually abused as juveniles.[109] R. J. Phelps and colleagues, in a survey of 192 female youths in the Wisconsin juvenile justice system, discovered that 79% of these youths (most of whom were in the system for petty larceny and status offenses) had been subjected to physical abuse that resulted in some form of injury.[110] Chesney-Lind's investigation of the backgrounds of adult women in prison underscored the links between their victimization as children and their later criminal careers, with interviews revealing that virtually all these women were victims of physical and/or sexual abuse as youngsters.

Gender Bias and the Processing of Female Delinquents

The underlying theme of this chapter is that adolescent females grow up in a culture that facilitates domination and control by males.[111] In this society, it is claimed that troublesome adolescent females are seen through lenses of discrimination, exploitation, and oppression.[112] Here are six corollaries:

1. *Adolescent females receive discriminatory treatment because of society's disapproval of sexual activity.*[113] Krohn, Curry, and Nelson-Kilger's analysis of 10,000 police contacts in a Midwestern city over a 30-year period found that adolescent females who were suspected of status offenses were more likely than their male counterparts to be referred to juvenile court for such offenses during all three decades.[114] Some studies have found that police officers adopt a more paternalistic and harsher attitude toward younger females to deter any further violation or inappropriate sex-role behavior.[115] Several studies have indicated that juvenile females are treated more harshly than boys because of their sexual history.[116]

2. *Offering another perspective, Rosemary C. Sarri concluded that juvenile law has long penalized females.* She claimed that although the law may not be discriminatory on its face, the attitudes and ideologies of juvenile justice practitioners administering it may result in violations of the Equal Protection Clause of the Fourteenth Amendment by leading them to commit females to longer sentences than males under the guise of "protecting" the female juveniles.[117] She added that "females have a greater probability of being detained and held for longer periods than males, even though the overwhelming majority of females are charged with status offenses."[118]

3. *Juvenile females, as a number of studies have documented, receive punitive processing through the juvenile justice system.* This results in their staying longer in detention and having longer stays in juvenile institutions than males for similar offenses.[119]

4. *According to another perspective, the oppressive treatment of adolescent females is hidden in the juvenile justice system.* Following the decriminalization of status offenses in 1979, Anne R. Mahoney and Carol Fenster reported that many girls appeared in court for criminal-type offenses that had previously been classified as status offenses, and they suggested that juvenile justice officials may have redefined these girls to be eligible for the kinds of protectionist sanctions that have been traditionally applied.[120]

5. *Another expression of the gender bias found in this "hidden justice" is that certain provisions of the Juvenile Justice and Delinquency Prevention Act provide that status offenders found in contempt of court for violating a valid court*

order may be placed in secure detention facilities, which permits juvenile judges to use their contempt power to confine repeat status offenders. If a runaway girl, for example, was ordered by the court to remain at home but she chose to run away again, she might be found in contempt of court—a criminal-type offense. There is reason to believe that juvenile judges apply their contempt power more often to female status offenders than to their male counterparts.[121]

6. *The early studies, especially, found that police officers, intake personnel, and judges supported a sexual double standard.* Female status offenders, as previously indicated, were more likely than their male counterparts to be petitioned to formal court proceedings, to be placed in preadjudicatory detention confinements, and to be confined in juvenile institutions. But at the same time, males who committed delinquent acts frequently received harsher treatment than their female counterparts. Consistent with what is known as the "chivalry" or "paternalism" thesis, police were less likely to arrest females suspected of property or person crimes; if arrested, female delinquents were less likely than male delinquents to be formally charged with criminal offenses, and if charged, they were less likely than males to be incarcerated for their offenses.[122]

Voices of Delinquency

Read "The Naïve Offender." Why did this youth, who had several offenses for which she could have come in contact with the justice system (engaging in sexual activity, transporting drug offenders, buying and using drugs), not come to the attention of the juvenile justice system? She is now working with troubled youths, but her life could have turned out much differently.

On balance, some evidence does exist that the discriminatory treatment of female status offenders may be declining since passage of the Juvenile Justice and Delinquency Prevention Act.[123] No longer do many states send status offenders to training schools with delinquents. But the long tradition of sexism in juvenile justice will be difficult to change. Due process safeguards for female delinquents, as well as for female status offenders, must be established to ensure greater social justice for them in the juvenile justice system. The intrusion of extralegal factors into the decision-making process in the juvenile court has led to discrimination against the adolescent female that must become a relic of the past.

Influence of Class

As part of the female delinquent's "multiple marginality," class oppression is another form of exploitation experienced by her.[124] In many ways, powerful and serious problems of childhood and adolescence related to poverty set the stage for a young person's entry into homelessness, unemployment, drug use, survival sex and prostitution, and ultimately even more serious delinquent and criminal acts. Even those adolescents coming from middle-class homes may be thrust into situations of economic survival if they choose to run away from abusive environments.

Traditional theories also fail to address the life situations of girls on the economic and political margins, because researchers typically fail to examine or talk with these girls. For example, almost all urban females identified by police as gang members have been drawn from low-income groups.[125] Lee Bowker and Malcolm Klein's examination of data on girls in gangs in Los Angeles stated the importance of classism as well as racism:

> We conclude that the overwhelming impact of racism, sexism, poverty and limited opportunity structures is likely to be so important in determining the gang membership and juvenile delinquency of women and girls in urban ghettos that personality variables, relations with parents and problems associated with heterosexual behavior play a relatively minor role in determining gang membership and juvenile delinquency.[126]

Class becomes important in shaping the lives of adolescent females in a number of other ways. Lower-class adolescent females tend to confront higher risk levels than middle- and upper-class adolescent females. They are more likely to have unsatisfactory experiences at school, to lack educational goals beyond high school, to experience higher rates of physical and sexual abuse, to deal with pregnancy and motherhood, to be involved in drug and alcohol dependency, to confront the risk of HIV/AIDS, and to lack supportive networks at home.[127] Although not all adolescent females at risk end up in the juvenile justice system, the likelihood of such a placement is greater for lower-class girls.[128]

Racial Discrimination

Young women of color, as well as other minority girls, often grow up in contexts very different from those of their white counterparts. Signithia Fordham's article "Those Loud Black Girls" showed that young African-American women resisted accepting the Anglo norm of femininity by being loud or asserting themselves through their voices. Yet this behavior led to negative school experiences, and it did not take long for these juvenile females to discover that it was the quiet ones who did well in school. Some of this population decided to "pass for white" or to adopt more acceptable norms of femininity in order to be successful in the school experience, but others refused to adopt this survival strategy, and their tool for liberation contributed to isolating or alienating them from school success.[129]

Because racism and poverty often go hand in hand, these girls are forced by their minority status and poverty to deal early and regularly with problems of abuse, drugs, and violence.[130] They also are likely to be attracted to gang membership.[131] H. C. Covey, Scott Menard, and R. Franzese summarized the effect of ethnicity on gang membership:

> Racial differences in the frequency of gang formation such as the relative scarcity of non-Hispanic, white, ethnic gangs may be explainable in terms of the smaller proportion of the non-Hispanic European American population that [lives] in neighborhoods characterized by high rates of poverty, welfare dependency, single-parent households, and other symptoms that characterize social disorganization.[132]

Minority girls' strategies for coping with the problems of abuse, drugs, violence, and gang membership, as Chesney-Lind has noted, "tend to place them outside the conventional expectations of white girls," and it also increases the likelihood that they will come to the attention of the juvenile justice system.[133]

There is also the belief that girls of color enjoy the benefits of chivalry much less than white girls do. Middle-class white girls—especially those who have committed minor offenses, not sexual ones—may be given greater latitude by the police, court intake officers, and juvenile court judges than their minority counterparts who have committed similar offenses. As with male minority offenders, female minority offenders are likely to be viewed as more dangerous to society and more likely to require long-term institutionalization.

The Whole Is Greater Than the Sum of Its Parts

An examination of the experience of African-American women reveals the geometric effects of multiple forms of oppression involving gender, class, and race.[134] Diane Lewis has noted that because feminist theories of women's inequality "focused exclusively upon the effects of sexism, they have been of limited applicability to minority women subjected to the constraints of both racism and sexism."[135] Lewis further noted that "black women . . . tended to see racism as a more powerful cause of their subordinate position than sexism and to view the women's liberation movement with considerable mistrust."[136]

The Combahee River Collective's 1977 statement about African-American feminism was an important historical contribution to the understanding of multiple simultaneous forms of discrimination. The group stated that it was committed to challenging all forms of "racial, sexual, heterosexual, and class oppression."[137]

Daly summarized this argument by saying that "unless you consider all the key relations of inequality—class, race, gender (and also age and sexuality)—you have considered none," adding that "unless you consider the inseparability of these relations in the life of one person, you do not understand what we are saying."[138] Spelman conceptualized the independence and multiple natures of gender, class, and race by saying that "how one form of oppression is experienced is influenced by and influences how another form is experienced."[139]

This suggests that gender, class, and race are interlocking forms of oppression and that the whole is greater than its parts. Thus, female delinquents, like adult women, suffer the consequences of multiple types of oppression as they face processing by the justice system.[140]

Delinquency across the Life Course: Gender and Delinquency

Jean Bottcher, in a study that targeted brothers and sisters of incarcerated teenagers, conceptualized gender as social practices and used these practices as the unit of analysis. Her study revealed social factors that intertwined with delinquent activities, limiting female delinquency while at the same time enabling and rewarding male delinquency: male dominance, differences in routine daily activities, variations in both sexual interests and transition to adulthood, and an ideology that defined both crime as male activity and child care as female activity.[141]

Longitudinal studies reveal that delinquent careers differ by gender. Male careers tend to begin earlier and to extend longer into the adult years. Studies of youth gangs show that female members are more likely than male members to leave the gang if they have a child. According to Bottcher, conventional life patterns—especially marriage, parenting, and work—draw both males and females away from gangs and delinquency but do so more quickly and completely for females.[142]

Amy C. D'Unger, Kenneth C. Land, and Patricia L. McCall, in a follow-up of the second Philadelphia cohort study, found both life-course-persistent and adolescence-limited delinquency (see Terrie Moffitt's classification scheme in Chapters 2 and 3) among the males, with a high and low category for each group. Among the females in this study, there were comparable adolescence-limited groups, although with lower overall offending levels. The high-rate adolescence-limited female offenders did share marked similarities with low-rate chronic male offenders; however, the chronic or persistent category of offender was less prominent among the females.[143]

Rebecca S. Katz, using waves 1 and 7 of the National Longitudinal Survey of Youth, found that much as in other studies, childhood victimization, sexual discrimination, adult racial discrimination, and domestic violence largely explained women's involvement in crime and deviance. Katz found some support for revised strain theory as an explanation for female involvement in criminal behavior, but she concluded that female crime also may require a unique theoretical model that more directly takes into account females' social and emotional development in a racist and patriarchal society.[144] See Exhibit 7.1 for a discussion of gender differences in the Dunedin Longitudinal Study.

Alex R. Piquero, Robert Brame, and Terrie E. Moffitt, using data from the Cambridge study of males and from the Dunedin, New Zealand, birth cohort, found that the vast majority of both males and females never experience a conviction, and for those who do, the number of convictions is quite small. They also stated that boys, more than girls, tend to become involved in crime when measured by conviction experience and that boys, once they are involved, exhibit more variations in conviction activity than do girls; the data further revealed that boys can be separated into low-, medium-, and high-frequency offender groups, whereas girls can be separated into low- and medium-frequency groups. Finally, their analysis found "that the process of continuity in criminal activity is formed by the end of adolescence similarly for both males and females" and that "there appear to be more similarities than differences across gender in how adolescent and adult patterns of offending are linked."[145]

There have been at least three studies that have examined the desistance process among women. I. Sommers, D. R. Baskin, and J. Fagan found that quality marriages led women to desist from crime, with some variation depending on the class and race of the women being studied.[146] A later study by Sommers and Baskin revealed that the desistance process was quite different for inner-city women of color, who were more likely to desist when they received alcohol and drug treatment or because they grew tired or fearful of repeated imprisonments.[147] Finally, as discussed in Chapter 5, Peggy C. Giordano and colleagues followed up on a sample of serious adolescent female delinquents and found neither marital attachment nor job stability to be strongly related to female desistance; instead, desisters underwent a cognitive shift, or

> > >   **EXHIBIT 7.1**   < < <

Gender Differences in the Dunedin Longitudinal Study

In *Sex Differences in Antisocial Behaviour*, Terrie E. Moffitt and colleagues reported on the findings of the Dunedin Longitudinal Study, which followed 1,000 males and females from age 3 to age 21 years. The basic findings indicate that young people develop antisocial behavior for two reasons. One form of antisocial behavior may be understood as a disorder with neurodevelopmental origins—a disorder that, like hyperactivity, autism, and dyslexia, shows a strong male preponderance, early childhood onset, subsequent persistence, and low prevalence in the population. Extreme gender differences are apparent in this form of antisocial behavior. The other form of behavior, representing the bulk of antisocial behavior (especially by females), is best understood as a social phenomenon originating in the context of social relationships, with onset in adolescence and high prevalence across the population. Gender differences in antisocial behaviors, according to this book, are negligible. Males' and females' antisocial behaviors are particularly alike when alcohol and drugs are involved, near the time when females reach puberty, and when females are yoked with males in intimate relationships. There were also other important insights:

- Increasing numbers of symptoms of CD predict increasingly poor young adult outcomes, regardless of gender.
- Antisocial behavior has disruptive effects on both females and males as they make the transition from adolescence to adulthood.

- The life-course-persistent antisocial female is extremely rare; approximately 1 in 100 females in a birth cohort seems to be on the life-course-persistent path.
- Females and males on the life-course-persistent path share similar risk factors of family adversity, poor discipline, cognitive deficits, hyperactivity, undercontrolled temperament, and rejection by peers.
- Almost all females who engage in antisocial behavior best fit the adolescence-limited type. Among adolescence-limited delinquency, the gender ratio is 1.5 males to 1 female.
- Males on the life-course-persistent path suffer from multiple poor outcomes as young adults, and youths on the adolescence-limited path also have some poor outcomes.

▶ **Why do you believe that this study found so few female life-course-persistent antisocial individuals? Why do females tend to be late-onset rather than early-onset offenders?**

Source: Terrie E. Moffitt, Avshalom Caspi, Michael Rutter, and Phil A. Silva, *Sex Differences in Antisocial Behaviour* (Cambridge, England: Cambridge University Press, 2001).

transformation, in which they experienced successful "hooks for change," which "facilitated the development of an alternative view of self that was seen as fundamentally incompatible with criminal behavior."[148]

Delinquency and Social Policy: Female Offenders

Another problem is that female offenders represented one of the least-serviced juvenile justice populations. There are only a few effective gender-specific programs nationally. The continuum of programs and services that are required to reduce females' entry into the juvenile justice system must be responsive both to gender and age and to developmental age.

A gender policy approach calls for a new vision for the juvenile justice system, one that recognizes the behavioral and social differences between female and male offenders that have specific implications for gender-responsive policy and practice.[149] Gender-responsive policy provides effective interventions that address the intersecting issues of substance abuse, trauma, mental health, and economic oppression, as Bloom and colleagues indicated; a focus on juvenile females' relationships with their family members is paramount as well.

Optimum environments for at-risk females of this age would be intensive family-based programs tailored to the needs of adolescent females.[150] Another possibility that has merit is a community-based all-girls school setting anchoring such services as family counseling, substance abuse prevention, specialized educational services (e.g., learning disabilities assessment), and mentoring services. A further gender-specific strategy is offering programs that provide the opportunity for the development of positive relationships between female offenders and their children.[151]

Chapter Summary

This chapter examines issues of gender as they relate to delinquency. Some of the most important points include:

- Female delinquency, like all other social behaviors, takes place in a world where gender shapes the lives of adolescents in powerful ways.

- Feminist theory, on which this chapter builds, starts with the assumption that adolescent females are socially positioned in society in ways that make them especially vulnerable to male victimization, including physical and sexual abuse and the negative effects of poverty.

- Feminist theory proposes that the meaning of gender and the nature of gender-related behavior depend heavily on the social context in which they are found.

- One area of agreement among feminists and non-feminists is that delinquency theories are primarily focused on why males commit delinquent acts and that not much attention has been given to the nature or causes of female delinquency.

- A major disagreement among theorists centers on whether separate perspectives are needed to explain female delinquency, with some writers charging that existing theories are inadequate to explain delinquency by females.

- Considerable evidence supports the position that female delinquency is produced by many of the same sociological factors as male delinquency and that more behavioral variation exists within genders than between them.

- An argument can be made that the relationship between the sexual and physical victimization of adolescent females at home and later law-violating behavior has been ignored and that new theoretical efforts are needed to deal with these experiences.

- Generally speaking, female delinquents are not treated more leniently by the juvenile justice system than are male delinquents when they commit status offenses, especially where disapproved sexual behavior is involved.

- Evidence shows that sexual offenses, incorrigibility, and running away from home do not make up the entire delinquent repertoire of girls; indeed, the offenses of male and female delinquents appear to be converging and are beginning to reflect similar patterns.

- Further examination of how gender, class, and race are interrelated will likely lead to additional insights into the problems facing female adolescents in the United States today.

Key Terms

chivalry factor, p. 155
feminist theory of delinquency,
   p. 160

gender, p. 151
gender roles, p. 151

masculinity hypothesis, p. 157
sex-role socialization, p. 156

Review Questions

1. What are different ways to handle the study of female delinquency?
2. How is an understanding of gender learned? What does this mean?
3. What are the main explanations of female delinquency?
4. What is the feminist theory of delinquency?
5. What are the various types of feminist theories?
6. How do gender, class, and race contribute to the victimization of the female delinquent or status offender?

Discussion Questions

1. Do you agree with Chesney-Lind's suggestion that a feminist model of delinquency is needed? Explain your response.
2. Which perspective should prevail in research, the one that pursues gender neutrality or the one that pursues gender specificity? If gender neutrality prevails, then would consistency demand race neutrality and ethnic neutrality as well? Explain your response.
3. Why is society seemingly so sensitive to the sexual behavior of adolescent girls?
4. Do you think these increased patterns of male domination and female subordination indicate emulation of behaviors observed in subcultural phenomena such as gangsta rap music videos? Explain your response.
5. Why is the relationship among gender, class, and race so important in understanding female delinquency?

Group Exercises

1. Appoint one male student to role-play Cesare Lombroso and four female students to role-play members of the National Organization for Women (NOW) meeting with the good doctor in a public forum (in front of the class) to discuss his theories regarding female offenders.

2. Try an anonymous poll of your students that asks the question: "During high school, were you greatly influenced, moderately influenced, or little influenced by peer pressure in making behavioral decisions?" Compile the results in male and female totals, and discuss the results in class.

mycrimekit™

Go to mycrimekit.com to explore the following study tools and resources specific to this chapter:

- **Practice Quiz:** Practice with multiple-choice, true/false, short-answer, and essay questions.

- **WebQuests:** Do web activities about female juvenile offending and effective strategies to prevent and reduce female involvement in delinquency and violence.

- **Flashcards:** Use 6 flashcards to test your knowledge of the chapter's key terms.

Families and Delinquency

CHAPTER OBJECTIVES

After reading this chapter, you should be able to answer the following questions:

- How do problems in the family affect adolescents?
- What factors in the family are most likely to affect the likelihood of delinquent behavior?
- What are the main forms of child abuse and neglect?
- What is the relationship of child abuse and neglect to delinquency and status offenses?
- How does the child welfare or juvenile justice system handle charges of child abuse?

The number of abused and neglected children has special significance for the juvenile justice system because many of these children end up in the system.

—Federal Advisory Committee on Juvenile Justice

Introduction

Law enforcement officials initially considered charges against an 11-year-old girl for selling heroin in South Miami, Florida, but it turned out that the girl, sometimes dressed in her school uniform or in a nightgown, was selling for her mother.

In a January 2004 stakeout of the girl's home, police saw her regularly selling $10 and $20 doses of heroin to drivers and pedestrians. On two occasions, they said, she sold heroin to undercover officers. Officials were surprised to learn her age because she looked to be age 15. The girl "did what her mother told her to do," said Charles Blazek, a spokesperson for the city of South Miami. "Whether she knows it's wrong or not, we don't know."

Within days of the girl's arrest, South Miami police decided not to prosecute her, and the state's attorney's office said it was inclined to agree. The girl's mother, Alison L. Davis, age 36, was charged with drug possession and trafficking; a child exploitation charge was also expected. The girl and her 7-year-old sister were placed in foster care.

Neighbors in the area, not known for drug dealing, said they had often seen the girl playing with other children. "We never thought she would do something like that," said Alda Larios, who had frequently invited the girl over to play with her daughters. "She was always sad, but she didn't cause problems."

Experts say using a child to deal drugs does occasionally happen. "We have kids being used as decoys or couriers or making actual sales, usually fronting for someone else on the street," said Joe Kilmer, a spokesman for the Drug Enforcement Administration.[1]

The family is the primary agent for the **socialization** of children. It is the first social group a child encounters and is the group with which most children have their most enduring relationships. The family gives a child his or her principal identity, even his or her name; teaches social roles, moral standards, and society's laws; and disciplines any child who fails to comply with those norms and values. The family either provides for or neglects children's emotional, intellectual, and social needs; as suggested above, the neglect of these basic needs can have a profound effect on the shaping of a child's attitudes and values.

This chapter discusses adolescents and family problems; the relationship between the family and delinquency; and the types and impact of child abuse and neglect, both at the time of their occurrence and across the life course.

socialization The process by which individuals come to internalize their culture; through this process, an individual learns the norms, sanctions, and expectations of being a member of a particular society.

Social Context of Delinquency: Impact of Families on Delinquency

The importance of the family in understanding delinquent behavior can be seen in the fact that most theories of delinquency rely heavily on the parent–child relationship and parenting practices to explain delinquency.[2] Social disorganization theories, subcultural theories, social control theories, and life-course theories all have this emphasis.[3] The theoretical emphasis on family processes, in turn, is supported by findings that family relationships and parenting skills are directly or indirectly related to delinquent behavior.[4]

A structure versus function controversy has been one of the important and continuing debates on the relationship between family and delinquency. The structural perspective focuses on factors such as parental absence, family size, and birth order, whereas the functional or quality-of-life view argues for the significance of parent–child interaction, the degree of marital happiness, and the amount and type of discipline.[5]

Judith Rick Harris challenged beliefs about the role of the family with her provocative 1995 claim that parental behavior has few, if any, enduring effects on the development of children, claiming that a youth's conduct, including delinquency, is predominantly influenced by peers or group socialization. She maintained that the relationship between parental socialization and child outcomes is largely due to the genes that are shared between parent and offspring. The media were struck by her central thesis that parenting does not affect children's behavior, and she was featured in a number of lead stories about her "truly revolutionary idea."[6] Her 1998 and 2006 books, *The Nurture Assumption: Why Children Turn Out the Way They Do* and *No Two Alike: Human Nature and Human Individuality*, continued to question whether families have any lasting effects on their children. Harris's research has led to other studies that have questioned the association between family life and child outcomes, and most of these studies are driven by findings from behavioral genetic research.[7] This line of research has argued that once the effects that the child has on the family are taken into consideration, the relationship between family factors and child outcomes vanishes.[8]

Family Factors

To return to the bulk of the research on family and delinquency, a number of family factors have been identified as having association with delinquency behavior, and these are covered in the following sections.

broken home A family in which parents are divorced or are no longer living together.

Broken Homes   The early research found a direct relationship between **broken homes** and delinquency[9]; later studies, however, questioned the relationship between broken homes and delinquency.[10] Researchers have shed further light on this debate. It has been reported that the factor of broken homes affects adolescent females more than males,[11] that broken homes have a larger impact on delinquency among African-Americans than on other racial groups,[12] and that the connection between broken homes and delinquency is more evident for status offenses than it is for more serious offenses.[13]

Below are six results of L. Edward Wells and Joseph Rankin's meta-analysis of 50 published studies dealing with broken homes and delinquency:

1. The prevalence of delinquency in broken homes is 10 to 15 percent higher than in intact homes.
2. The correlation between broken homes and juvenile delinquency is stronger for minor forms of juvenile misconduct (status offenses) and weakest for serious forms of criminal behavior (such as theft and interpersonal violence).
3. The type of family break seems to affect juvenile delinquency [because] the association with delinquency is slightly stronger for families broken by divorce or separation than by death of a parent.
4. There are no consistent or appreciable differences in the impact of broken homes between girls and boys or between black youths and white youths.
5. There are no consistent effects of the child's age at breakup on the negative effects of the separated family.
6. There is no consistent evidence of the often-cited negative impact of stepparents on juvenile delinquency.[14]

birth order The sequence of births in a family and a child's position in it, whether firstborn, middle, or youngest child.

Birth Order   Some evidence supports the significance of **birth order** in that delinquent behavior is more likely to be exhibited by middle children than by first or last children. The first child, according to this view, receives the undivided attention and affection of parents, and the last child benefits from the parents' experience in raising children as well as from the presence of other siblings, who serve as role models.[15] Other researchers found that children were initially stabilizing and later destabilizing in a marriage, because "firstborn children increase the stability of marriage through their preschool years, [but] older children and children born before marriage significantly increase chances of disruption."[16]

A sixteenth-century inscription on a plaque on the wall of Venice's Pieta church discouraging parents from abandoning their unwanted babies. ▶ What led some early writers to say that broken homes are possibly the single most important cause of delinquency? Do you agree?

Family Size   Research findings on **family size** generally reveal that large families have more delinquency than do small families. Hirschi explained the higher rate of delinquency with middle children as the result of family size rather than of birth position.[17] Rolf Loeber and Magda Stouthamer-Loeber suggested that a number of processes may explain why delinquency rates are greater in large families: First, parents in large families tend to have more difficulty disciplining and supervising their children than do parents with smaller families; second, some parents with large families delegate child rearing to older siblings, who may not be equipped to execute this task; and third, large families frequently are more exposed to illegitimacy, poverty, and overcrowding.[18]

family size The number of children in a family, a possible risk factor for delinquency.

Delinquent Siblings and Criminal Parents   Some evidence exists that siblings learn delinquency from others. The Gluecks reported that a much higher proportion of delinquents than nondelinquents had **delinquent siblings** and/or criminal mothers and fathers.[19] More recent research has substantiated the relationship between delinquent siblings or criminal parents and children's delinquent behavior.[20]

delinquent sibling A brother or sister who is engaged in delinquent behaviors; an apparent factor in youngsters' involvement in delinquency.

Quality of Home Life   Studies have generally reported that poor quality of home life, measured by marital adjustment and harmony within the home, affects the rate of delinquent behavior among children more than whether or not the family is intact (see Library Extra 8.1). Nye found the happiness of the marriage to be the key to whether or not children become involved in delinquent behavior.[21]

Library Extra 8.1
NIJ-sponsored publication: *Communitywide Strategies to Reduce Child Abuse and Neglect: Lessons from the Safe Kids/Safe Streets Program*

Family Rejection   Several studies have found a significant relationship between **rejection by parents** and delinquent behavior. Loeber and Stouthamer-Loeber's review of the literature found that 12 of 15 studies reported a significant relation between rejection and delinquency.[22] Although Nye found that the father's rejection is more often significantly related to delinquency than the mother's rejection,[23] a number of other studies concluded that rejection from mothers is more related to involvement with delinquency.[24] The study by McCord, McCord, and Zola, as well as a number of other studies, reported that only a small percentage of delinquents

rejection by parents The disapproval, repudiation, or other uncaring behavior directed by parents toward children.

A thoughtful-looking pregnant Hispanic teen girl leans against lockers at her school. ▶ Why do children born to young mothers face greater risks?

Web Extra 8.1
Center on Child Abuse and Neglect website

supervision and discipline The parental monitoring, guidance, and control of children's activities and behavior.

Voices of Delinquency

Read "It Has Been Quite a Ride." How did the chaos of this young woman's family life affect her? Why did she prevail in the midst of what seemed to be overwhelming problems?

had affectionate relationships with parents.[25] (See Web Extra 8.1 for a relevant website.)

Discipline in the Home Inadequate **supervision and discipline** in the home have been commonly cited to explain delinquent behavior. Hirschi found that the rate of delinquency increased with the incidence of mothers employed outside the home and attributed this finding to unemployed mothers spending more time supervising their children's activities and behavior.[26] Other studies have found mixed results in terms of discipline in the home.[27] Loeber and Stouthamer-Loeber concluded from their review of the literature that "the evidence suggests a stronger relation between lack of supervision and official delinquency than between lack of supervision and self-reported delinquency."[28]

John Paul Wright and Francis T. Cullen, in using data from the National Longitudinal Survey of Youth, advanced the concept of "parental efficacy" as an adaptation of Robert J. Sampson and colleagues' "collective efficacy" (see Chapter 4). Wright and Cullen employed parental efficacy because they wanted to evaluate the relationship between parental controls and supports in reducing delinquency with children. They found that support and control are intertwined and that parental efficacy exerts substantive effects on reducing children's inappropriate behaviors.[29]

Ronald L. Simons and colleagues, using data from a sample of several hundred African-American caregivers and their children, found that increases in collective efficacy within a community over time were associated with increases in authoritative parenting—which is defined as parents combining warmth and support with firm monitoring and control. Both authoritative parenting and collective efficacy, they added, served to deter affiliation with deviant peers as well as involvement in delinquent behavior, and this deterrent effect of authoritative parents was enhanced when it took place within a community with high collective efficacy.[30]

Conclusions

Conflicting findings make drawing conclusions about the relationship between delinquency and the family difficult, but the following seven observations have received wide support:

1. Family conflict and poor marital adjustment are more likely to lead to delinquency than is the structural breakup of the family.
2. Children who are intermediate in birth order and who are part of large families appear to be involved more frequently in delinquent behavior, but this is probably related more to parents' inability to provide for the emotional and financial needs of these children than to birth position or family size.
3. Children who have delinquent siblings or criminal parents may be more prone to delinquent behavior than those who do not.
4. Rejected children are more prone to delinquent behavior than those who have not been rejected, and children who have experienced severe rejection are probably more likely to become involved in delinquent behavior than those who have experienced a lesser degree of rejection.
5. Consistency of discipline within the family seems to be important in deterring delinquent behavior.
6. As the Gluecks predicted in 1950, lack of mother's supervision, father's and mother's erratic/harsh discipline, parental rejection, and parental attachment appear to be the most important predictors of serious and persistent delinquency.[31] Laub and Sampson's reanalysis of the Gluecks' data found that the mother's supervision, parental attachment, and parental style of discipline are the most

important predictors of serious and persistent delinquency.[32] Similarly, Loeber and Stouthamer-Loeber's meta-analysis identified parent–child involvement and supervision, child–parent rejection and discipline practices, parental criminality and deviant attitudes, and marital conflict and absence as the four dimensions of family functioning related to delinquency.[33]

7. The rate of delinquency appears to increase with the number of unfavorable factors in the home, that is, multiple risk factors within the family are associated with a higher probability of juvenile delinquency than are single factors.[34]

See Figure 8.1 for a representation of family factors and their relationship to delinquency.

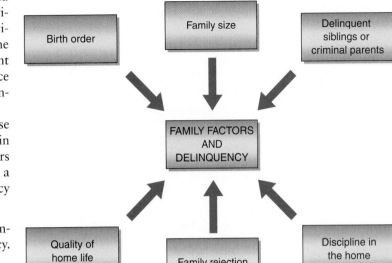

FIGURE 8.1 Family Factors and Relationships to Delinquency

Transitions and Delinquency

Divorced and single-parent families, blended families, out-of-wedlock births, homelessness, unemployment, alcohol and drug abuse, and violence are some of the family problems that affect adolescents today. Adolescents experiencing such problems are at a high risk of becoming involved in socially unacceptable behaviors.

The high divorce rate in the United States translates into an increasing number of single-parent families. In 2007, 67% of children below the age of 18 years lived with two married parents. The percentage, which decreased from 1980 to 1997, has remained the same at 67% to 69% from 1994 to 2007.[35] Divorce has affected African-American families more than white families: As many as 40% of white children and 75% of African-American children will experience divorce or separation before they reach 16 years of age. Many of these children will experience multiple family disruptions over the course of their childhood.[36]

What needs to be addressed is the relationship between the impact of family transitions and problem behaviors, such as delinquency and drug use. An examination of the Rochester, Denver, and Pittsburgh studies reveals a consistent relationship between a greater number of family transitions and a higher level of drug use and delinquent behavior, with the magnitude of the differences between juveniles with no family transitions and those with many family transitions being similar across the three cities.[37]

Poverty is a serious problem in the lives of children. In 2006, children living in female-headed families (with no husband present) continued to experience a higher poverty rate (42%) than their counterparts living in married-couple families (8%).[38] Economic hardship and lack of access to opportunity tend to undermine marital and parental functioning; furthermore, adolescents who experience family transitions may have difficulty managing anger and other negative emotions that may contribute to their involvement with delinquency or drugs. See Figure 8.2 for percentages of children under 18 years of age living in poverty, based on family type.

The majority of divorced parents remarry, and adolescents in these families must learn to adjust to a new parental figure. Blended families place stress on biological parents, stepparents, and children. In a typical blended family, the mother has custody of her children, and the stepfather lives with his wife's children; his biological children (if any) usually visit the home on an occasional or regular basis. Few adolescents escape the experience of a blended family without feeling resentment, rejection, and confusion. Some stepparents even subject their stepchildren to emotional, physical, or sexual abuse (see Library Extra 8.2).

Library Extra 8.2

NIJ-sponsored publication: *Co-Occurring Intimate Partner Violence and Child Maltreatment*

FIGURE 8.2 Percentage of Children under Age 18 in Poverty by Family Type, 1980–2005

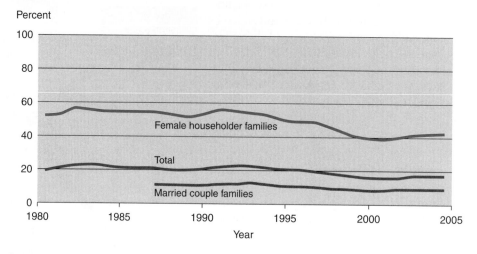

Source: Forum on Child and Family Service, *America's Children in Brief: Key National Indicators of Well-Being, 2007* (Washington, D.C.: Federal Interagency Forum on Child and Family Statistics, 2007), p. 14.

Childbearing is a life experience that many female adolescents have. In some instances, children are wanted and adolescent mothers are married; more often than not, however, pregnancy in adolescence leads to abortion or adoption. The birth rate of unmarried women has risen sharply since 2002, after having been relatively stable between the mid-1980s and 2002.[39] The birth rate for unmarried teenagers who are 15 years old to 17 years old in 2006 rose from 62% to 92% and went up from 40% to 81% for those ages 18 and 19 years old.[40]

Homelessness is a phenomenon that shapes the lives of an estimated 500,000 to 1.3 million young people each year. Many homeless youths leave their families after years of physical and sexual abuse, the addiction of a family member, strained interpersonal relations, and parental neglect. Homelessness, regardless of a child's age, is likely to expose him or her to settings permeated by substance abuse, promiscuity, pornography, prostitution, and crime.[41]

Unemployment also affects some family units in the United States. Between January 1994 and November 2004, the number of people 16 years old and older officially designated as unemployed declined from 6.6% to 5.4%.[42] The unemployment rate for African-American men ages 16 years and older declined from 12.1% in January 1994 to 10.5% in November 2004, and the rate for African-American women declined from 11.5% to 9%, but the bad news for African-American families is that nearly 10% of this population is still experiencing unemployment and all its consequences.[43]

Adolescents whose family members have substance abuse problems also have their sad stories to tell. Neglect, abuse, and economic hardship are common factors in family settings where alcohol misuse and substance abuse are ordinary behavior. Arrest data in *Crime in the United States 2007*, as previously discussed, reflect the nationwide scope of this problem in the general population. But while the prevalence of substance abuse is unarguable, its actual impact on adolescents is not easily measurable, since it is simply not possible to display the impact on a "one abuse instance = one adverse impact on one or more adolescent(s)"[44] basis. The impact is clearly visible, however, in the behaviors of the youths it affects.

Violence has long been a major characteristic of the problem family, and it is no stranger to family life today. Marital violence is a pervasive problem that affects nearly one-third of the married population. Numerous studies also show that some parents act out their aggression on their children,[45] and some families use physical violence for disciplinary purposes. Karen Heimer found that coercive discipline strategies teach youths to rely on force and coercion to resolve problems.[46] (See Web Extra 8.2 for information on the Child Welfare League of America.)

Web Extra 8.2

Child Welfare League of America website

Mass Media and Delinquent Behavior

Part of the challenge of being a parent today is dealing effectively with the influence that the mass media have on children. For our purposes, the term *mass media* refers to the Internet, radio, television, commercial motion pictures, videos, CDs, music, and the press (newspapers, journals, and magazines).

Violent TV Programs and Movies

Most people today watch a lot of television, and many seem to depend on media programming for their understandings of the surrounding world.[47] Consequently, criminologists have shown considerable interest in assessing the relationship between delinquent behavior and the exposure to violence viewed on television. Researchers in the area of delinquency generally conclude that TV violence is most likely to negatively impact the behavior of those children who are already predisposed toward violence and that it seems to have much less influence on young people who are not so predisposed.[48]

The influence of television and motion pictures also extends to the phenomenon of contagion. An example of the contagion effect of motion pictures can be seen in the movie *Colors*, whose showing in theaters across America led gang members nationwide to begin wearing their groups' colors; prior to seeing the movie, most gang members had not been wearing their gang colors.[49]

Walter B. Miller drew the following conclusion after examining the relationship between mass media content and the occurrence of gang violence:

> The influence of the media on the behavior of youth has long been a contentious issue. In recent years, increasing consensus has developed in support of the position that media images do have a significant influence, particularly on more susceptible youth.
>
> In the case of youth gangs, this contention would not be difficult to sustain. The lifestyle and subculture of gangs are sufficiently colorful and dramatic to provide a basis for well-developed media images. For example, the Bloods/Crips feud . . . caught the attention of media reporters in the early 1990s and was widely publicized. Gang images have served for many decades as a marketable media product—in movies, novels, news features, and TV dramas.[50]

Two teenagers playing video games. Some people think that violent video games can lead to violent behavior. ▶ **Do you agree?**

Violent Video Games

Video games involving violent scenarios, such as "Halo 2," "Grand Theft Auto," and "Asheron Call 2," are the focus of considerable controversy today. Some people accuse video game makers of promoting values that support violence. Not surprisingly, the software entertainment industry, with its annual $28 billion in sales paced by a nation's thirst for action, claims that their games are offered only for entertainment purposes.[51]

In August 2005, members of the American Psychological Association (APA) adopted a resolution calling for less violence in video and computer games marketed to children. One APA panelist, Kevin M. Kieffer, reported research that shows playing violent video games tends to make children more aggressive and less prone to helping behaviors.[52] Craig A. Anderson, one of the pioneers of research in this area, adds, "There really isn't any room for doubt that aggressive game playing leads to aggressive behavior."[53]

In the fall of 2005, the Federal Trade Commission (FTC) launched an investigation into the system used for rating video games, particularly what some saw as undeservedly low ratings that made the violent and sexually themed game "Grand Theft Auto" available to teens. Around the same time, a group of bipartisan senators proposed that the National Institutes of Health oversee a comprehensive $90 million study on the effects of violent media, including video games, on children's development.[54]

Internet-Initiated Crimes

Internet access is easily available to nearly everyone in the United States today, but the Web has become a new frontier for innovative forms of cybercrime. One source of Internet-initiated crime is the supremacist and hate groups that target young people through the Web. In like manner, youthful perpetrators of violent crimes are sometimes influenced by information collected or contacts made on the Internet, and child sexual abuse, where initial contacts are made through the Web, now accounts for up to 4% of all arrests for sexual assaults against juveniles.[55]

Gangsta Rap

Gangsta rap is a form of hip-hop music that some believe negatively influences young people by devaluing human life, the family, religious institutions, schools, and the justice system.[56] Gangsta rap, pioneered by Ice-T and other rappers influenced by Schoolly D's hard-core rap, portrays the lifestyles of inner-city gang members, and its lyrics relate stories of violence-filled lives. Guns play a prominent part in those lyrics and are frequently depicted as a means for attaining manhood and status.

Today's gangsta rap devotees seem to consist predominantly of white young people.[57] The subject matter of this music, which is available to children via television (especially MTV), the Internet, radio (including satellite radio), and retail CDs and DVDs, has created considerable controversy, with critics charging that the messages it espouses include misogyny, homophobia, racism, and materialism. Gangsta rappers usually defend themselves by pointing out that they are describing the reality of inner-city life and claim that when they are rapping, they are merely playing a character.[58]

In summary, today's parents must face the reality that their children's minds are being bombarded with extensive disturbing stimuli. Violence permeates movies and TV screens; video games are no less violent, and the most popular ones among teenagers are probably the most violent. Supremacist and hate groups are targeting young people through their websites; the Internet offers opportunities for the sexual abuse of vulnerable adolescent males and females. Finally, gangsta rap is filled with violence, appears to devalue human life, and contains lyrics promoting homophobia, misogyny, racism, and materialism.

Neglect and Child Abuse

Neglect and **child abuse**, like the other family problems addressed in this chapter, have a profound influence on shaping the behavior and attitudes of adolescents and adults.[59] Various categories of child abuse and neglect, also referred to as *child maltreatment*, are identified in Table 8.1. The specific issue of Internet-initiated sex crimes against minors is discussed in Exhibit 8.1. Kathleen M. Heide found it helpful to distinguish among three types of neglect (physical, medical, and emotional) and four types of abuse (physical, sexual, verbal, and psychological).[60] According to Heide, the types of abuse and neglect are frequently interrelated, with one type of child maltreatment often leading to another; for example, children who are sexually abused by parents become victims of neglect when their parents fail to seek medical attention for sexually transmitted diseases or resulting injuries.[61] Barbara Tatem Kelley, Terence P. Thornberry, and Carolyn A. Smith defined seven types of child maltreatment: physical abuse, sexual abuse, physical neglect, lack of supervision, emotional maltreatment, educational maltreatment, and moral–legal maltreatment[62] (for the definitions and levels of severity of each type, see Table 8.1).

Joan McCord's longitudinal study of 253 males revealed that abused, neglected, and rejected children had significantly higher rates of delinquency than did

neglect A disregard for the physical, emotional, or moral needs of children. Child neglect involves the failure of the parent or caregiver to provide nutritious food, adequate clothing and sleeping arrangements, essential medical care, sufficient supervision, access to education, and normal experiences that produce feelings of being loved, wanted, secure, and worthy.

child abuse The mistreatment of children by parents or caregivers. Physical abuse is intentional behavior directed toward a child by the parent or caregiver to cause pain, injury, or death. Emotional abuse involves a disregard of a child's psychological needs. Sexual abuse is any intentional and wrongful physical contact with a child that entails a sexual purpose or component, and such sexual abuse is termed *incest* when the perpetrator is a member of the child's family.

EXHIBIT 8.1

Internet-Initiated Sex Crimes against Minors

The goals of the National Juvenile Online Victimization (N-JOV) Study were to survey police agencies within the United States in order to document and enumerate arrests for Internet-related sex crimes committed against minors and to describe the offenders' characteristics. One area studied was the availability of child pornography (CP) on the Internet, and following are the key findings:

- Law enforcement agencies made an estimated 1,713 arrests for Internet-related crimes involving the possession of child pornography during the 12 months beginning July 1, 2000.
- Almost all of those arrested for CP possession were male; 91% were white, and 86% were older than age 25. Only 3% were younger than age 18.
- Most arrestees had images of prepubescent children (83%) and images graphically depicting sexual penetration (80%).
- Approximately 1 in 5 arrested CP possessors (21%) had images depicting sexual violence involving children, such as bondage, rape, and torture.
- About 39% of those arrested were in possession of at least one video containing moving images of child pornography.
- Roughly 53% of the cases involving pornography came to the attention of the justice system as CP possession cases, 31% could be classified as cases of child sexual victimization, and 16% were cases involving Internet sexual solicitations of undercover investigators posing as children.
- CP possession cases originated at all levels of law enforcement, with 25% beginning in federal agencies, 11% in Internet Crimes against Children (ICAC) Task Forces (which were not yet fully operational during the time frame covered by the study), 60% in other state and local agencies, and 3% in other agencies such as international law enforcement.
- Of the arrested CP possessors, 40% were "dual offenders" who sexually victimized children and also possessed child pornography, with both crimes uncovered during the same investigation; an additional 15% were dual offenders who attempted to sexually victimize children by soliciting undercover investigators who posed online as minors.

- One in six investigations beginning with allegations or investigations of CP possession discovered dual offenders.
- In the overall N-JOV study, 39% of arrested offenders who met victims online and 43% of offenders who solicited undercover investigators were dual offenders.
- Almost all arrested CP possessors (96%) were convicted or pleaded guilty, and 59% were incarcerated.
- Victims in these crimes were primarily 13- to 15-year-old adolescent girls who met adult offenders (76% of such offenders were older than age 25) in Internet chat rooms.
- The majority of offenders did not deceive victims about the fact that they were adults who were interested in sexual relationships.
- Most victims met and had sex with the adult offenders on more than one occasion, and half of the victims were described as feeling a close bond or being in love with the offenders.
- Almost all cases with male victims involved male offenders.
- Offenders used violence in 5% of the episodes recorded.[63]

▶ Why would an adolescent girl respond to an Internet solicitation and meet an adult who made it clear that he wanted to have a sexual relationship? Why would such a high percentage (half) develop a close relationship with the adult, with some of the victims describing themselves as "in love"? How are Internet-initiated sex crimes related to the failure of parents to assume responsibility for their children's well-being?

Sources: Janis Wolak, David Finkelhor, and Kimberly J. Mitchell, *Child-Pornography Possessors Arrested in Internet-Related Crimes: Findings from the National Juvenile Online Victimization Study* (Washington, D.C.: National Center for Missing and Exploited Children), pp. vii–viii; and Janis Wolak, David Finkelhor, and Kimberly J. Mitchell, "Internet-Initiated Sex Crimes against Minors: Implications for Prevention Based on Findings from a National Study," *Journal of Adolescent Health* 35 (2004), p. 424.

---

nonabused children (10%, 15%, and 29% versus 7%, respectively). Her study also found that, as adults, half of the abused or neglected adolescent males had been convicted of serious crimes or had become alcoholics or mentally ill.[64]

Cathy Spatz Widom's initial study of abuse and neglect found that 29% of those abused and neglected as children had a nontraffic criminal record as adults, compared with 21% of the control group.[65] Widom and Michael G. Maxfield's updated study, which followed 1,575 cases from childhood through adolescence and into young adulthood, was able to examine the long-term consequences of abuse and neglect[66]:

1. Being abused or neglected as a child increased the likelihood of arrest as a juvenile by 59%, as an adult by 29%, and for a violent crime by 30%.
2. Maltreated children were younger at the time of their first arrest, committed nearly twice as many offenses, and were arrested more frequently.
3. Physically abused and neglected (versus sexually abused) children were the most likely to be arrested later for a violent crime.

TABLE 8.1 Definitions of Child Maltreatment and Severity Ratings

Types of Maltreatment	Brief Definition	Examples of Least and Most Severe Cases
Physical Abuse	A caregiver inflicts a physical injury on a child by other than accidental means.	*Least*—Spanking results in minor bruises on a child's arm. *Most*—A child's injuries require hospitalization, cause permanent disfigurement, or lead to a fatality.
Sexual Abuse	Sexual contact or attempted sexual contact occurs between a caretaker (or responsible adult) and a child for the purposes of the caretaker's sexual gratification or financial benefit.	*Least*—A child is exposed to pornographic materials. *Most*—A caretaker uses force to make a child engage in sexual relations or prostitution.
Physical Neglect	A caretaker fails to exercise a minimum degree of care in meeting a child's physical needs.	*Least*—Food is not available for a child's regular meals, a child's clothing is too small, or a child is not kept clean. *Most*—A child suffers from severe malnutrition or severe dehydration due to gross inattention to his or her medical needs.
Lack of Supervision or Moral Neglect	A caretaker does not take adequate precautions (given a child's particular emotional and developmental needs) to ensure his or her safety in and out of the home.	*Least*—An eight-year-old is left alone for short periods of time (e.g., less than three hours) with no immediate source of danger in the environment. *Most*—A child is placed in a life-threatening situation without adequate supervision.
Emotional Maltreatment	Thwarting of a child's basic emotional needs (such as the need to feel safe and accepted) occurs persistently or at an extreme level.	*Least*—A caretaker often belittles or ridicules a child. *Most*—A caretaker uses extremely restrictive methods to bind a child or places a child in close confinement such as a closet or trunk for two or more hours.
Educational Maltreatment	A caretaker fails to ensure that a child receives an adequate education.	*Least*—A caretaker allows a child to miss school up to 15% of the time when the child is not ill and there is no family emergency. *Most*—A caretaker does not enroll a child in school or provide any educational instruction.
Moral–Legal Maltreatment	A caretaker exposes a child to or involves a child in illegal or other activities that may foster delinquency or antisocial behavior.	*Least*—A child is permitted to be present for adult activities, such as drunken parties. *Most*—A caretaker causes a child to participate in felonies such as armed robbery.

Source: Adapted from Barbara Tatem Kelley et al., "In the Wake of Childhood Maltreatment," *Juvenile Justice Bulletin* (Washington, D.C.: U.S. Department of Justice, Office of Juvenile Justice and Delinquency Prevention, 1997), p. 4.

4. Abused and neglected females also were at increased risk of arrest for violence as juveniles and adults.

5. White abused and neglected children were no more likely to be arrested for a violent crime than their nonabused and nonneglected white counterparts; in contrast, African-American abused and neglected children showed significantly increased rates of violent arrests compared with African-American children who were not maltreated.[67]

Thornberry and colleagues' ongoing study of delinquency examined direct child maltreatment as well as more general exposure to family violence. The 1994 study, which interviewed 1,000 seventh- and eighth-grade students and their caretakers every six months for four years, found that compared with youths who were not abused or neglected, these youths had higher rates of self-reported violence (705 versus 565).[68]

However, Matthew T. Zingraff and colleagues found from their study in Mecklenburg County, North Carolina, that although child maltreatment is an important correlate of delinquency, "the maltreatment–delinquency relationship has been exaggerated in previous research."[69] Furthermore, Zingraff and colleagues challenged the simple and direct relationship between maltreatment and delinquency, which was widely used in the studies of the 1970s and 1980s, when they concluded that delinquency is only one of many possible social, social–psychological, and behavioral consequences of maltreatment. Finally, Zingraff and colleagues added that status offenders appear to be affected by maltreatment more than property and violent offenders are.[70] (See Web Extra 8.3 and Web Extra 8.4 for additional sources of information on the welfare of children.)

Extent and Nature of the Problem

C. H. Kempe first exposed child abuse as a major social problem with his ground-breaking 1962 essay on the battered child syndrome.[71] Kempe's research led to an avalanche of writing on neglect, physical abuse, and sexual abuse. The passage of legislation in all 50 states in the late 1960s requiring mandatory reporting of child abuse and neglect cases also focused attention on these problems, as did the passage by Congress of the Child Abuse Prevention and Treatment Act and the establishment of the national Office on Child Abuse and Neglect in 1974. As an indication of the extent of maltreatment of children, an estimated 3.2 million referrals involving the maltreatment of approximately 5.8 million children were made to child protective services (CPS) during the fiscal year 2007, and of that number an estimated 794,000 children were found to be victims[72] (see Web Extra 8.5).

Victimization Statistics   Following are some figures from 2007:

■ Nearly 60% of child maltreatment victims experienced neglect.
■ More than 10% were physically abused.
■ Less than 10% were sexually abused.
■ Less than 5% were psychologically maltreated.[73]

See Figure 8.3 for victimization rates by maltreatment types.

Younger children make up the largest percentage of victims. Nearly 32% (31.9%) of all victims of maltreatment were younger than 4 years of age, an additional 23.8% were ages 4 to 7, and 19% were ages 8 to 11 (see Figure 8.4 for ages of victims). Victimization was split almost evenly between the sexes: 51.5% of the victims were girls and 48.2% were boys. Nearly one-half (46.1%) of all victims were white, one-fifth (21.7%) were African-American, and one-fifth (20.8%) were Hispanic. Figure 8.5 shows the race and ethnicity of victims for the year 2007.[74]

Web Extra 8.3

National Center for Missing and Exploited Children

Web Extra 8.4

Child Welfare Information Gateway

Voices of Delinquency

Read "A Small-Town Boy." How did his father's condition affect what happened to this young man? How did his mother affect what took place in his life? Are you surprised that he committed the crime he did?

Web Extra 8.5

Child Exploitation and Obscenity Section of the U.S. Department of Justice's Criminal Division

FIGURE 8.3 Victimization Rates by Maltreatment Type, 2000–2007

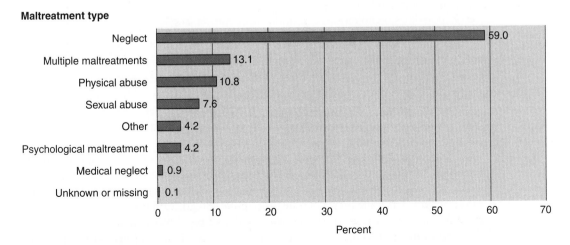

Source: Children's Bureau, *Child Maltreatment 2007* (Washington, D.C.: U.S. Department of Health and Human Services, 2007), p. 26.

FIGURE 8.4 Maltreated Children, by Age

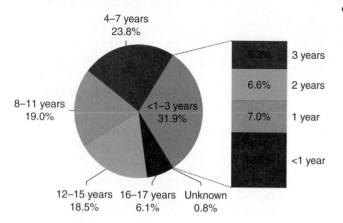

Source: Adapted from the Children's Bureau, *Child Maltreatment 2007* (Washington, D.C.: U.S. Department of Health and Human Services, 2007), p. 25.

Web Extra 8.6

Institute on Violence, Abuse, and Trauma website

Child fatalities represent the most tragic consequences of maltreatment. These statistics were reported for 2007:

- An estimated 1,760 children died due to child abuse or neglect.
- The overall rate of child fatalities was 2.35 deaths per 100,000 children.
- More than 30% (34.1%) of child fatalities were attributed to neglect only, but physical abuse was also a major contributor to child fatalities.
- More than three-quarters (75.7%) of the children who died because of child abuse and neglect were younger than 4 years old.
- Infant boys (younger than 1 year) had the highest rates of fatalities, 18.85 deaths per 100,000 boys of the same age in the national population.
- Infant girls less than 1 year of age had a rate of 15.39 deaths per 100,000 girls of the same age.[75]

Perpetrators of Maltreatment   In 2007 nearly 79.9% of child maltreatment victims were abused by their parents, with another 6.6% abused by other relatives (see Web Extra 8.6). Women comprised a larger percentage of perpetrators than men—56.5% compared to 42.4%. Nearly 75% of all perpetrators were younger than age 40.[76]

Neglect

The word *neglect* generally refers to disregard for the physical, emotional, or moral needs of children or adolescents. The Children's Division of the American Humane Association established a comprehensive definition of neglect, stating that physical, emotional, and intellectual growth and welfare are jeopardized when a child can be described in the following terms:

- Malnourished, ill-clad, dirty, without proper shelter or sleeping arrangement
- Unsupervised, unattended
- Ill, lacking essential medical care
- Denied normal experiences that produce feelings of being loved, wanted, secure, and worthy (emotional neglect)
- Failing to attend school regularly
- Exploited, overworked
- Emotionally disturbed due to constant friction in the home, marital discord, or mentally ill parents
- Exposed to unwholesome, demoralizing circumstances[77]

Defining neglect in legal or social terms, nevertheless, does not begin to capture an accurate picture of the neglected child. Such children must be seen if an observer is to realize the true hopelessness of their existence.[78] Newspapers frequently report the deaths of young children due to neglect or child abuse. As tragic as these cases are, however, Widom asked, "But what happens to the children who survive? The babies abandoned on streets or in hospitals, children left unattended for days without food in filthy roach-infested apartments, or children brutally abused?"[79]

Using data from two research projects, Polansky and colleagues developed the Childhood Level of Living (CLL) scale. Originally designed to assess families with children between the ages of four and seven, the CLL has since been used for a wider range of ages. The scale presents nine descriptive categories: Five assess physical care, and the other four assess cognitive, emotional, and psychological factors.[80] Realizing the limitations of the CLL scale, especially for issues of cultural diversity, a panel of child maltreatment experts in Ontario developed the Child Neglect Index (CNI), which assesses neglect in six areas: (1) supervision, (2) food and nutrition, (3) clothing and hygiene, (4) physical health care, (5) mental health care, and (6) developmental–educational care.[81]

Child Abuse

There are several types of child abuse, including physical, emotional, and sexual abuse. The term *physical abuse* refers to intentional behavior directed toward a child by the parent or caretaker to cause pain, injury, or death (see Web Extra 8.7). Richard Gelles and Claire Pedrick Cornell described a case in which a parent attempted to kill her child:

> Sue was a single parent who lived in a fourth-floor walk-up apartment. Her husband had left her three years earlier, and child support payments stopped within weeks of the final divorce decree. Poverty and illness were as much a part of Sue's home as the busy activity of her 4-year-old daughter Nancy. One cold gray March afternoon, Sue took Nancy out for a walk. Together they hiked up the steep pedestal of a suspension bridge that rose up behind their apartment. At the top of the bridge, Sue hugged Nancy and then threw her off the bridge. She jumped a moment later.[82]

What is unusual about this case is that both Nancy and Sue survived. Plucked from the icy water by a fishing boat, mother and child were taken to different hospitals. When Nancy was released from the hospital six months later, she was placed out of the home, and Sue's parental rights were terminated.[83]

Murray A. Straus has been one of the strongest proponents of defining corporal punishment as physical abuse. Straus examined the extent of physical abuse using data from a number of sources, notably the 3,300 children and 6,000 couples in the National Family Violence Survey, and he found that 90% of U.S. citizens used physical punishment to correct misbehavior. He claimed that although physical punishment may produce conformity in the immediate situation, its long-run effect is to increase the probability of delinquency in adolescence and violent crime inside and outside the family.[84]

Emotional abuse is more difficult to define than physical abuse because it involves a disregard for the psychological needs of a child or adolescent. Emotional abuse encompasses a lack of expressed love and affection as well as deliberate withholding of contact and approval and may include a steady diet of put-downs, humiliation, labeling, name-calling, scapegoating, lying, demands for excessive responsibility, seductive behavior, ignoring, fear-inducing techniques, unrealistic expectations, and extreme inconsistency.[85] Randy, a 16-year-old boy, tells about the emotional abuse he suffered:

> My father bought me a baby raccoon. I was really close to it, and it was really close to me. I could sleep with it, and it would snug up beside me. The raccoon wouldn't leave or nothing. A friend of mine got shots for it. My father got mad one night because I didn't vacuum the rug, and there were seven or eight dishes in the sink. He said, "Go get me your raccoon." I said, "Dad, if you hurt my raccoon I'll hate you forever." He made me go get my raccoon, and he took a hammer and killed it. He hit it twice on the head and crushed its brains. I took it out and buried it.[86]

Nature of Child Abuse Some theorists argue that child abuse has five basic explanations: (1) structural factors such as lower socioeconomic class, large family size, or single parenting; (2) the mental illness of a parent; (3) a parent's history of abuse as a child; (4) transitory situational factors, including such "triggers" as alcohol, drug use, or unemployment; and (5) a particularly difficult, demanding, or problematic child. Stephanie Amedeo and John Gartrell's study of 218 abused children found that the characteristics of parents, including being mentally ill and having been abused themselves, have the greatest explanatory power of predicting

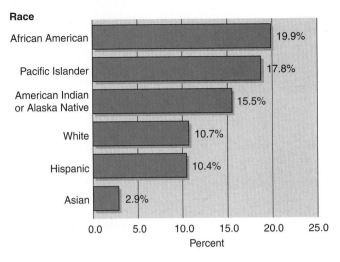

FIGURE 8.5 Race and Ethnicity of Child Maltreatment Victims, 2007

Race

- African American — 19.9%
- Pacific Islander — 17.8%
- American Indian or Alaska Native — 15.5%
- White — 10.7%
- Hispanic — 10.4%
- Asian — 2.9%

Percent (0.0, 5.0, 10.0, 15.0, 20.0, 25.0)

Source: Adapted from the Children's Bureau, *Child Maltreatment 2007* (Washington, D.C.: U.S. Department of Health and Human Services, 2007), p. 26.

Web Extra 8.7
National Center for Children Exposed to Violence

emotional abuse A disregard for the psychological needs of a child, including lack of expressed love, withholding of contact or approval, verbal abuse, unrealistic demands, threats, and psychological cruelty.

abuse; this study also revealed that triggers or stressors, such as alcohol and drug use, perform as factors that precipitate abuse.[87]

Blair Justice and Rita Justice contended that eight models explain the causes of abuse: (1) the psychodynamic model, (2) the character trait or personality model, (3) the social learning model, (4) the family structure model, (5) the environmental stress model, (6) the social–psychological model, (7) the mental illness model, and (8) the psychosocial systems model.[88]

Research findings disagree concerning the age at which a child is most vulnerable to parental abuse. The National Incidence and Prevalence of Child Abuse and Neglect study found that the incidence of physical abuse increased with age.[89] Gil found that half the confirmed cases of abuse involved children over six years of age and that nearly one-fifth were teenagers.[90] Yet while many adolescents may experience child abuse, the more serious cases still occur with infants and young children, who are more susceptible to injury; indeed, according to some researchers, three months to three years of age is the most dangerous period in a child's life.[91] Teenagers are more physically durable, are able to protect themselves better, and can leave the home if parents become too abusive.

Child abuse also seems to be more prevalent in urban areas than in suburban or rural settings. Urban areas having better resources to detect child abuse does not entirely explain why so many more cases are reported to urban police. Obviously, the congested populations and poverty of the city, which lead to other social problems, partly account for abuse being predominantly an urban problem.

The abusive situation is often characterized by one parent who is aggressive and one who is passive. The passive parent commonly defends the aggressive one, denies the realities of the family situation, and clings to the intact family and to the abusive partner. The passive parent behaves as though he or she is a prisoner in the relationship, condemned to a life sentence, and usually does not consider the option of separating from the aggressive partner because he or she is committed to the relationship, no matter how miserable the home situation may be.[92]

Children and adolescents may be victimized by either nonfamilial sexual abuse or incestuous sexual abuse. **Sexual abuse** of a child is intentional and wrongful physical contact with a child that entails a sexual purpose or component. Oral–genital relations, fondling of erogenous areas of the body, mutual masturbation, and intercourse are typical sexually abusive acts.[93]

Incest, according to the Office on Child Abuse and Neglect, is "intrafamily sexual abuse which is perpetrated on a child by a member of that child's family group and includes not only sexual intercourse, but also any act designed to stimulate a child sexually or to use a child for sexual stimulation, either of the perpetrator or of another person."[94] Incestuous sexual abusers may include a parent, grandparent, stepparent, sibling, aunt, uncle, or other member of the child's extended family. Nonfamilial sexual abusers may include any unrelated adult the child encounters outside the home (e.g., at school, church, recreational venues).

Linda Gordon's examination of incest from 1880 to 1930 found that incest appeared in 10% of case records of Boston child protection agencies and that 98% of these cases were father–daughter incest with a common pattern: The family relations made the girl victims into second wives. These victims took over many of the functions and roles of the mother, including housework, sexual relations, and child care, as they lived with their father. Despite their apparent acquiescence and obedience in these incestuous families, many of these girls actively sought escape from their victimization and loitered on the streets, where their low self-esteem made them easily exploitable.[95]

In more recent times, the number of sexual abuse cases substantiated by child protective service agencies in the United States underwent a dramatic 40% reduction between 1992 and 2000, with opinion being divided as to why the estimated annual incidence dropped from 150,000 to 89,500 cases (see Figure 8.6 for substantiated cases of child sexual abuse in the United States from 1990 to 2000). The trend has occurred in the majority of states; of 49 states, 39 experienced a total decline of 30% or more in substantiated cases of sexual abuse from their peak year to 2004.[96]

sexual abuse The intentional and wrongful physical contact with a person, with or without his or her consent, that entails a sexual purpose or component.

incest Any intrafamily sexual abuse that is perpetrated on a child by a member of that child's family group and that includes not only sexual intercourse but also any act designed to stimulate a child sexually or to use a child for sexual stimulation, either of the perpetrator or of another person.

Ronald Carroll McDonald (left), age 71 years old, of Lake Forest Park, Washington, pleads guilty in 1997 in a Seattle court to child rape and molestation charges. To many children, a photograph taken with McDonald was a Christmas tradition since he worked as Santa Claus in a local mall. ▶ Although cases involving sexual predators seem to appear in the news almost daily, national statistics show that the sexual abuse of children by their parents or guardians has declined significantly in the last decade or two. What might account for that decline?

The decline in child sexual abuse, according to National Child Abuse and Neglect Data System (NCANDS) data, appears to largely account for a concurrent 15% decline in child maltreatment. Although neglect cases fluctuated during the 1990s and had no overall decline, physical abuse has declined 30% since a peak in 1995. This decline in physical abuse is significant, but it is smaller and more recent than the decline in sexual abuse; in fact, the largest proportion of the decline in physical abuse

FIGURE 8.6 Estimated Number of Substantiated Cases of Child Sexual Abuse in the United States, 1990–2000

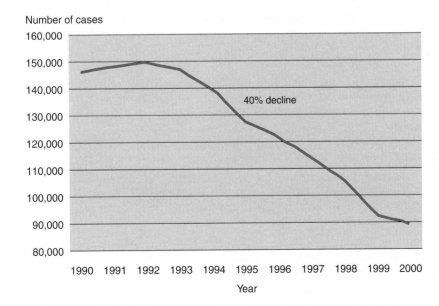

Source: David Finkelhor and Lisa M. Jones, *Explanations for the Decline in Child Sexual Abuse Cases* (Washington, D.C.: Office of Juvenile Justice and Delinquency Prevention, 2004), citing data from 1990–2000 National Child Abuse and Neglect Data System (NCANDS) reports (U.S. Department of Health and Human Services, 1992–2002).

(15%) occurred between 1998 and 1999, whereas the more gradual 40% decline in sexual abuse took place over an eight-year period.[97]

Incest reportedly occurs most frequently between a biological father or stepfather and a daughter but also may involve brother and sister, mother and son, and father and son.[98] Father–daughter incest usually is a devastating experience for the girl and sometimes has lifelong consequences. Stepfathers also sexually victimize stepdaughters, but biological fathers appear to be involved in more cases of sexual abuse than are stepfathers. Angela Browne and David Finkelhor's review of the literature on sexual abuse revealed that abuse by fathers or stepfathers has a more negative impact than abuse by others and that experiences involving genital contact and force seem to result in more trauma for the victim.[99] The average incestuous relationship lasts about three and one-half to four years.[100] The completed act of intercourse is more likely to take place with adolescents than with younger children.

Helen, a 16-year-old, was sexually victimized by her father for three years, and she had great difficulty getting anyone to believe that her father was committing incest. When the father was finally prosecuted, she made this statement:

> When I was thirteen, my father started coming into my room at night. He usually did it when he was drinking. He would force me to have sex with him. I told my mother. I told my teachers at school. But nobody would believe me.[101]

Some evidence exists that **brother–sister incest** takes place more frequently than **father–daughter incest,** but its long-term consequences are usually less damaging because it does not cross generational boundaries and often occurs as an extension of sex play.[102] But brother–sister incest can have damaging consequences for the sister if the act is discovered and she is blamed for being sexually involved with her brother. If the girl feels she has been seduced or exploited, then the damage may be even greater.

Mother–son incest is less common and only rarely reported, largely because of the strong stigmas and taboos attached to the idea of sex between boys and their mothers.[103] Mother–son incest usually begins with excessive physical contact, which eventually becomes sexually stimulating. "Don't leave me" or "Don't grow up" messages are communicated to the son as the mother seeks ways to prolong physical contact with him by sleeping with him, bathing him, or dressing him.[104]

Father–son incest also is rarely reported, largely because it violates both the moral code against incest and the taboo against homosexuality. The stress of an incestuous relationship, as well as the threat to masculinity, often results in serious consequences for the boy when father–son incest does occur. Sons who are involved in father–son incest usually experience acute anxiety because they feel damaged, dirty, and worthless, and they may cope by retreating into their own world and losing contact with reality.[105]

The National Center on Child Abuse and Neglect has identified five factors that are usually present when father–daughter incest takes place: (1) the daughter's voluntary or forced assumption of the mother's role, (2) the parents' sexual incompatibility, (3) the father's reluctance to seek a partner outside the family unit, (4) the family's fear of disintegration, and (5) the unconscious sanctioning by the mother.[106]

Justice and Justice developed a classification that is helpful in understanding the behavior of fathers who commit incest.[107] They divided incestuous fathers into four groups: symbiotic personalities, psychopathic personalities, pedophilic personalities, and a small group of "others."

Symbiotic personalities, who make up 70% to 80% of the incestuous fathers, have strong unmet needs for warmth and for someone to whom they can be close, and they hunger for a sense of belonging and intimacy. These fathers are out of touch with their needs and do not know how to meet them in healthy ways, so they look to the family to satisfy all their emotional needs more than the other types do. As relationships with their wives deteriorate, they turn to their daughters to satisfy their emotional and physical needs. They use a variety of rationalizations to justify their sexual abuse—for example, that physical intimacy is the highest form of love a father can show his daughter or that a father has exclusive property rights over the daughter and therefore can do whatever he wants. Alcohol is often used to loosen restraints on these fathers' behavior; after the sexual activity, they often blame the alcohol rather than themselves.

Psychopathic personalities seek stimulation and excitement through incestuous relationships. Sex is simply a vehicle to express the hostility they feel and to obtain the excitement they have felt deprived of in the past. The psychopath feels no guilt and has little capacity to love; he simply wants immediate gratification of his needs. Fortunately, this type of incestuous father is rare.

Pedophilic personalities are attracted to young children who show no signs of physical and sexual development. These extremely immature fathers have erotic cravings for children, and they want sexual activity with someone who will not reject or belittle them. Only a small amount of incest is committed by these immature and inadequate personalities.

The Justices' "others" include fathers who are psychotic and those who come from a subculture that permits incest. Psychotic fathers, who make up about 3% of incestuous fathers, experience hallucinations and delusions, and they are most often responsible for using force in incest. In some cultural groups, it is normal for the oldest daughter to assume her mother's role, both in the kitchen and in bed; the youngest daughter also is often introduced to sex by her father or brothers. This group of fathers accounts for only a small fraction of the cases of incest, because culturally sanctioned incest among certain immigrant groups has lost much of the acceptance it once had.

Neglect, Child Abuse, and Delinquency

Research findings have revealed that a neglected or abused child is more likely to become involved in delinquency or status offenses. Neglect or abuse may have a negative impact on the emotional development of the child; it may lead to truancy and disruptive behavior in school or running away from home or may generate so much pain that alcohol and drugs are sometimes viewed as a needed escape. Neglect or abuse may cause so much self-rejection, especially in victims of incest, that these youths may vent their self-destructiveness through prostitution or may even commit suicide. Neglect or abuse may also create so much anger that abused youngsters later commit aggressive acts against others.

Emotional Trauma of Neglect and Child Abuse   Victims of neglect and child abuse often have low self-esteem, considerable guilt, high anxiety, mild to serious depression, and high internal conflict.[108] Physically, they may experience disturbances in sleeping patterns, weight loss or gain, or continual illnesses, and they also tend to have poor social relationships.[109] A longitudinal sample of 500 juveniles confined to 48 correctional facilities in 20 states was assessed to examine the relationship between having been subjected to child maltreatment and experiencing anxiety and depression. The analysis revealed that confined youths who had experienced greater levels of child maltreatment had higher levels of both anxiety and depression and that higher levels of maltreatment were associated with increased depression over time.[110]

Runaways   Teenagers who have been abused frequently run away from home.[111] One sexually abused girl explained: "I never thought about where I was running to—only what I was running from."[112] **Running away** becomes a way of coping with the pain of neglect, physical abuse, and sexual abuse. The youth often sees running away as the only way to manage an unmanageable problem, or parents sometimes tell the child to get out because they want to rid themselves of the problems that the abusive situation has created. When abused adolescents are placed in foster homes, their running away may not stop because they often choose to reject their new family rather than risk the possibility of being rejected again. Unfortunately, sometimes children are removed from abusive homes only to experience abuse all over again in a foster home.

Voices of Delinquency

Read "A Sixteen-Year-Old Sexual Predator." Did this individual's sexual victimization contribute to his sexual deviancy? Do you believe that he belongs on a sex offender registry?

running away The act of leaving the custody and home of parents or guardians without permission and failing to return within a reasonable length of time; a status offense.

Disruptive and Truant Behavior in School Several studies have found that neglected and abused children have greater difficulty in school than children who are not maltreated.[113] According to R. S. Kempe and C. H. Kempe, "Many of these children become academic and social failures almost immediately upon entering school."[114] Neglected and abused school-age children tend to have deficiencies in language development,[115] are more frequently placed in special education classes,[116] are more likely to be assigned to classes for children with disabilities,[117] have more learning problems,[118] are more disobedient and have greater difficulty accepting authority,[119] and have more conflict with peers.[120]

Drug and Alcohol Abuse In an effort to blot out their pain and isolation, many abused children turn to drug and alcohol abuse.[121] Widom found that neglected and abused adolescent females were at increased risk for drug offenses,[122] and S. D. Peters found an association between sexual abuse and later alcohol abuse.[123] Richard Dembo and colleagues, in an examination of a sample of youths in a detention center, reported that sexual victimization had a direct effect on drug use, whereas physical abuse had an indirect and direct effect on drug use.[124] Abused children often feel they have nothing to lose by taking drugs; they are concerned only with forgetting their insecurity, anxiety, and lack of confidence. A type of loving and trusting relationship that they have never had with people before sometimes develops through drugs, so they can finally belong, experiencing closeness and security with peers who also take drugs.

Barbara L. Myers, former director of Christopher Street, Inc., and a victim of sexual abuse as an adolescent, tells why she turned to drugs:

> I was eleven years old when I first discovered that drugs could make the terrible world around me disappear. . . . When I was on drugs, I felt high, happy, and in control of my life. When I was high, I had peers; I finally belonged somewhere—in a group with other kids who took drugs. Whatever the others were taking, I took twice as much or more. I wasn't aware like the rest of them; I got high without worrying about how much I could handle or what it would do to me. It made me feel big and powerful because I didn't care what happened to me.
>
> People said that taking too many drugs would burn out your brains. I used to think that I could become a vegetable if only I could succeed in burning out my brains. I wanted to be a vegetable. I used to picture myself as a head of lettuce. I used to look at mentally

Dirty children stand behind run-down apartments in Los Angeles, California. Neglect is the most common form of child maltreatment today and can involve a lack of food, clothing, medical care, and parental supervision. When neglect occurs, siblings may be left to care for one another as best they can. ▶ What social and economic factors might lead to an increased incidence of child neglect?

EXHIBIT 8.2

Why Kids Kill Their Parents

Approximately 200 parents are killed each year by their children. Kathleen M. Heide has contended that killing a parent is frequently "an act of desperation—the only way out of a family situation of abuse [the killer-child] can no longer endure." She claimed that there are three types of youths who kill their parents: (1) the severely abused child who is pushed beyond his or her limits, (2) the severely mentally ill child, and (3) the dangerously antisocial child. According to Heide's research, the severely abused child is the most frequently encountered type of offender.

She found several characteristics of severely abused children who kill one or both parents:

- They are not violent.
- They are abused.
- Their parents are most likely substance abusers.
- They are isolated.

- They kill only when they feel there is no one to help them.
- They "block out" the murder, not revel in it.
- They see no other choice.
- They are sorry for what they did.

▶ If you were a social worker in a male institution and a severely abused juvenile on your caseload had killed his mother, how would you help him come to grips with what he had done? What would you do first, second, third, and so forth?

Source: Kathleen M. Heide, "Why Kids Kill," *Psychology Today* 25 (September–October 1992), pp. 62–77; Kathleen M. Heide, "Parents Who Get Killed and the Children Who Kill Them," *Journal of Interpersonal Violence* 8 (December 1993), pp. 531–544.

retarded people and think that they were so happy and didn't care about anything. I envied them because you could spit at them, and they would smile; they didn't seem to understand what hurt was.[125]

Sexual Behavior   A study of 535 young women who became pregnant as teenagers found that 66% had been sexually abused as children.[126] Considerable evidence shows that sexual abuse victims themselves often become involved in deviant sexual behavior; for example, promiscuity appears to be high among female sexual abuse victims.[127] Many female sexual abuse victims also become involved in prostitution,[128] and sexual abuse is frequently a part of the background of male prostitutes.[129] It is not surprising that female sexual abuse victims are attracted to prostitution, because they have come to see themselves as shamed, marked, and good only for delivering sex. The self-destructive aspect of prostitution serves as another way of expressing rage for never having been loved and for having been sexually and/or physically abused. In prostitution, sexual abuse victims take control by making strangers pay for sex. Detachment has already been learned in childhood; therefore, it is relatively easy for them to disassociate themselves from brief sexual encounters.[130] One recent study found that girls who experienced sexual abuse had more negative mental health, school difficulties, substance abuse, and risky sexual behavior as well as high rates of involvement with the juvenile justice system.[131]

Violence and Abuse   The idea that violence begets violence is firmly entrenched in the minds of both professionals and the general public. There is considerable support for the finding that abused and neglected male victims are more likely to express their anger in ways that hurt others, whereas female victims of mistreatment are more likely to become self-destructive.[132] There is also substantial support for the finding that those who have been abused or neglected in the past are more likely to abuse or neglect their children than those who have not experienced abuse or neglect. For example, in reviewing the research on family violence, Gelles noted: "One of the consistent conclusions of domestic violence research is that individuals who have experienced violent and abusive childhoods are more likely to grow up and become child and spouse abusers than individuals who have experienced little or no violence in their childhood."[133]

Several studies have found a positive relationship between neglect and abuse and later violent criminal acts. Thornberry, using data from the Rochester Youth Development Study, found that 69% of youths who were maltreated as children reported later involvement in violence, compared to 57% of those who were not maltreated.[134] Exhibit 8.2 presents a possible link between abuse and children who kill their parents. See Figure 8.7 for the risk factors of child maltreatment.

FIGURE 8.7 Possible Risk Factors of Child Maltreatment

There is some evidence that childhood maltreatment that does not persist into adolescence has minimal correlation with adolescent delinquency.[135] The negative influence of severe maltreatment, such as sexual abuse by parents or caretakers, is commonly seen as carrying into adulthood and perhaps even throughout the life course. However, Peggy Giordano, Stephen A. Cernkovich, and Jennifer L. Rudolph's study of women across the life course is a reminder that female offenders who suffered extremely abusive childhoods can still have cognitive transformations as adults and can desist from criminal behaviors.[136]

Child Abuse and the Juvenile Justice System

The term *child protective services* usually refers to services that are provided by an agency authorized to act on behalf of a child when parents are unwilling or unable to do so. In all states, these agencies are required by law to conduct assessments or investigations of reports of child abuse and neglect and to offer treatment services to families where maltreatment has taken place or is likely to occur.[137]

Although the primary responsibility for responding to reports of abuse and neglect rests with state and local child protective services agencies, the prevention and treatment of child maltreatment can involve professionals from many organizations and disciplines. Jurisdictions do differ in their procedures, but community responses to child maltreatment generally include the following sequence of events:

Identification

■ Individuals who are likely to identify abuse are often those in a position to observe families and children on a regular basis. These include educators, medical professionals, police officers, social services personnel, probation officers, day-care workers, and the clergy. Family members, friends, and neighbors also may be able to identify abuse.

Reporting

■ Some individuals—educators, child-care providers, medical and mental health professionals, social services providers, police officers, and clergy—often are required by law to report suspicions of abuse and neglect. Some states require such reporting by any person who has knowledge of abuse or neglect.

■ Child protective services or law enforcement agencies generally receive the initial report of alleged abuse or neglect. This initial report may include the identity of the child and information about the alleged maltreatment, the parent or other caretaker of the child, the setting in which maltreatment took place, and the person making the report.

Intake and Investigation

■ Protective services staff are required to determine whether the report constitutes an allegation of abuse or neglect and how urgently a response is needed. The initial investigation involves gathering and analyzing information about the child and family. Protective services agencies may work with law enforcement during this intake investigation.

■ In some jurisdictions, a police officer always accompanies the social worker on the child abuse or neglect investigation to protect the social worker, to help if the parents become assaultive, to use legal authority to take the child out of an

The U.S. Supreme Court building in Washington, D.C. In 2005, the Court considered the right of parents to be notified when their minor children seek abortions. The case, *Ayotte* v. *Planned Parenthood*, centered on New Hampshire's Parental Notification Prior to Abortion Act. The Court did not issue a definitive ruling and sent the case back to lower courts for further consideration. ▶ **Should parents be notified when their minor children seek abortions?**

abusive home if necessary, to gather evidence and take pictures if admissible evidence is present, and to permit the social worker to focus on the family rather than being preoccupied with the legal investigation.

- Caseworkers usually respond to reports of abuse and neglect within two to three days. An immediate response is required if it is determined that the child is at imminent risk of injury or impairment. If the intake worker makes the decision that the referral does not constitute an allegation of abuse or neglect, the case may be closed. If there is substantial risk of serious harm to the child or lack of supervision, state law allows the child to be removed from the home.

- If the decision is to take the child out of the home, the juvenile court judge must be called for approval as soon as the social worker and police officer leave the house. If the child has been taken out of the home, a temporary removal hearing normally is held in the juvenile court within three to five days. At this hearing, the juvenile judge can decide to leave the child in the temporary placement—a foster home, youth shelter, or group home—or return the child to the parents.

- Following the initial investigation, the protective services agency usually draws one of the following conclusions: (1) There is sufficient evidence to support or substantiate the allegation of maltreatment or risk of maltreatment; (2) there is insufficient evidence to support maltreatment; or (3) maltreatment or the risk of maltreatment appears to be present, although there is insufficient evidence to conclude or substantiate the allegation. When sufficient evidence does not exist, additional services may be provided if it is believed that there is risk of abuse or neglect in the future.

Assessment
- Protective services staff are responsible for identifying the factors that contributed to the maltreatment and for addressing the most critical treatment needs.

Case Planning
- Case plans are developed by protective services, other treatment providers, and the family to alter the conditions and/or behaviors that result in child abuse or neglect.

Treatment
- Protective services and other treatment providers have the responsibility to implement a treatment plan for the family.

Evaluation of Family Progress

■ After implementing the treatment plan, protective services and other treatment providers evaluate and measure changes in family behavior and conditions that led to child maltreatment. They also assess changes in the risk of maltreatment and determine when services are no longer required.

Case Closure

■ Some cases are closed because the family resists intervention efforts and the child is seen as being at low risk of harm. Other cases are closed when it has been determined that the risk of abuse or neglect has been eliminated or reduced to the point that the family can protect the child from maltreatment without additional intervention.

■ If the determination is made that the family will not protect the child, the child may be removed from the home and placed in foster care. If the decision is made that a child cannot be returned home within a reasonable time, parental rights may be terminated so that permanent alternatives can be found for the child.

Involvement of Juvenile or Family Court

■ An adjudication (fact-finding) hearing is held if a petition of abuse or neglect has been filed by the department of social services. Juvenile courts hear about 150,000 child abuse and neglect cases a year. Usually present at the adjudication hearing are the assistant district, state, or county attorney; the youth and his or her attorney; the parents and their attorney; the social worker assigned to the case; and the police officer who conducted the investigation. After the evidence has been presented, the juvenile court judge decides whether the petition charging neglect or abuse has been substantiated; if it has, a disposition hearing is set for about four weeks later.

■ States vary in the standard of proof needed to substantiate allegations of child abuse and neglect: 6 states rely on the caseworker's judgment; 18 states, on some credible evidence; 11 states, on credible evidence; 12 states, on the preponderance of evidence, and 3 states have no official reporting means. About 30% of all child abuse and neglect reports in the country are substantiated, which varies somewhat by type of maltreatment and by state.[138] For example, in Massachusetts, allegations were confirmed in 55% of investigations in 2002, whereas in New Hampshire, only 9% were substantiated.[139]

Termination of Parental Rights

■ In the most serious cases of child maltreatment, the state moves to terminate parental rights and to place a child for adoption. In 2000, parents of 64,000 children across the country had their parental rights terminated. However, not all terminations of parental rights resulted from child maltreatment; the overall rate of parental rights termination for substantiated child maltreatment cases is about 8%.[140]

Prosecution of Parents

■ The prosecution of parents in criminal court depends largely on the seriousness of the injury to the child and on the attitude of the district, county, or state attorney's office toward child abuse. The cases most likely to be prosecuted are those in which a child has been seriously injured or killed and those in which a father or stepfather has sexually abused a daughter or stepdaughter. The most common charges in prosecutions are simple assault, assault with intent to commit serious injury, and manslaughter or murder.

Reported cases of child abuse represent only the tip of the iceberg. Abuse and neglect cases among lower-class families are more likely to be reported than those among middle- or upper-class families. Procedures for dealing with abusive homes vary from one state to the next, as does their effectiveness. Moreover, much remains to be learned about dealing more effectively with abusive families, about determining the type of placements that will serve the best interests of the child, and about creating the kind of public policy that is necessary to reduce the amount of abuse and neglect in this nation.

Delinquency across the Life Course: Family-Related Risk Factors for Delinquency

With the emergence of the life-course perspective, there has been increased empirical and theoretical interest in the role played by family relations both in fostering and in protecting against delinquency and drug involvement. Studies have documented the family-related risk factors that increase delinquency propensity. Researchers have most frequently explored the impact on delinquency of the informal social control exercised by parents and within families.[141]

Gottfredson and Hirschi's self-control theory argues that the principal cause of individuals' low self-control is ineffective parenting. Ineffective parents are those who fail to monitor their children, to recognize deviant behavior when it takes place, and to punish such deviance. They are likely to have children who are low in self-control and therefore are more delinquent.[142] Carter Hay's findings from a sample of urban high school students generally supported Gottfredson and Hirschi's position, linking ineffective parenting, low self-control in children, and higher rates of delinquency.[143]

Some research has examined the links between corporal punishment and adolescent delinquent behavior or drug use. Ronald L. Simons and colleagues found that when parents engage in severe forms of corporal punishment coupled with the absence of parental involvement and warmth, children tend to feel angry and unjustly treated, resist parental authority, and are likely to become involved in delinquent behavior.[144] As mentioned earlier, Heimer also found that families who use coercive discipline merely teach their children that force and violence are appropriate tactics for solving problems; children thus learn definitions favorable to violence, which encourages them to be more prone to violent delinquent behavior.[145]

Shannon E. Cavanagh, using a sample drawn from the National Longitudinal Study of Adolescent Health, found that family structure at adolescence best predicted later emotional distress and that family structure at adolescence, along with cumulative family instability across childhood, best predicted current marijuana use.[146] Jennifer E. Lansford and colleagues, in a longitudinal study of 574 children followed from age 5 to age 21, found that individuals who had been physically abused in the first five years of life were at greater risk for being arrested as juveniles for violent, nonviolent, and status offenses. Moreover, physically abused youths were less likely to have graduated from high school and more likely to have been fired in the past year, to have been a teenage parent, and to have been pregnant or to have impregnated someone in the past year while not married.[147]

Robert J. Sampson, John H. Laub, and Christopher Wimer followed a sample of 500 high-risk boys from adolescence to age 32 and found that being married is associated with an average reduction of about 35% in the odds of crime compared to a nonmarried status. The data consisted of criminal histories and dated records for all 500 men along with personal interviews (using a life-history calendar), with a stratified subsample of 52 men who were followed to age 70. They concluded that "the results are robust, supporting the inference that the status of marriage causally [inhibits] crime over the life course."[148]

Delinquency and Social Policy: Child Maltreatment

Child maltreatment is a serious issue in the United States. This maltreatment can take place in a variety of contexts: from abusive or neglectful parents, from caretakers, from the Internet (in terms of child pornography), in the school, or even from religious leadership. We do know that some children are at greater risk of victimization than others:

- Children with allegations of multiple types of maltreatment were nearly three times more likely to be determined by authorities to be maltreated than were children with allegations of physical abuse.
- Children reported to be victims of sexual abuse were about 71% more likely to be considered victims than children with allegations of physical abuse only.
- Children who were reported to be disabled were 68% more likely to be a victim of maltreatment than children who were not disabled.
- Children who were reported by educational personnel were twice as likely to be considered maltreated as children reported by social and mental health personnel.
- Findings of victimization were inversely related to the age of a child. Children who were younger than four years old were most likely determined to be maltreated compared to all other age groups.[149]

We also know that child maltreatment can be an influential factor leading to such undesirable outcomes as emotional trauma, running away, disruptive and truant behavior in school, drug and alcohol abuse, sexual behavior, and violence and abuse. The more serious the maltreatment of a child, the more likely it is that he or she will become involved in these behaviors, which can have such negative consequences on his or her life course. The abused child, if seriously abused, can even become involved in taking a parent's life.

To reduce the extent of child abuse and neglect in the United States, a number of strategies or interventions are needed. Widom recommended the following six principles:

1. "The earlier the intervention, the better."
2. "Don't neglect neglected children."
3. "One size does not fit all," which means that "what works for one child in one context may not work for a different child in the same setting, the same child in another setting, or the same child in another period in his or her development."
4. "Surveillance is a double-edged sword," meaning intervention agents must be sensitive to the possibilities of differential treatment on the basis of race or ethnic background and take steps to avoid such practices.
5. "Interventions are not one-time efforts."
6. "Resources should be accessible."[150]

Chapter Summary

As this chapter notes, the family is the most important social institution in the lives of most young children. This chapter also makes some additional points:

- Studies of the relationship between the family and delinquency have generally concluded that the quality of life within the home is a more significant deterrent of delinquent behavior than the presence of both parents; that parental rejection is associated with delinquent behavior; and that inconsistent, lax, or severe discipline is associated with increased delinquency.

- Similar research concludes that delinquent behavior among children increases proportionately with the number of problems within the family. Divorced and single-parent families, blended families, births to unmarried women, alcohol and drug abuse, poverty, and violence are problems that some families encounter.

- Adolescents are exposed to a variety of seemingly negative media influences, including violent movies, TV shows, and video games; Internet pornography; and gangsta rap and other forms of music carrying violent themes.

■ Research findings show at least a partial link between child abuse and neglect and delinquent behavior and status offenses.

■ Children who have been neglected and abused may experience psychological problems, run away from home, become involved in truancy and disruptive behavior in school, and turn to drug and alcohol abuse.

■ Some neglected and abused youngsters become involved in deviant sexual behavior and assume an aggressive stance toward others.

■ In many cases of child maltreatment, authorities are reluctant to intervene unless severe physical injury, gross neglect, or sexual abuse can be demonstrated.

The failure of a family to provide for the needs of its children can have an effect on the attitudes and behaviors of those children that can last into their adult years—and even for the rest of their lives.

Key Terms

birth order, p. 170
broken home, p. 170
brother–sister incest, p. 184
child abuse, p. 176
delinquent sibling, p. 171
emotional abuse, p. 181

family size, p. 171
father–daughter incest, p. 184
father–son incest, p. 184
incest, p. 182
mother–son incest, p. 184
neglect, p. 176

rejection by parents, p. 171
running away, p. 185
sexual abuse, p. 182
socialization, p. 169
supervision and discipline,
   p. 172

Review Questions

1. How is the family the primary agent for the socialization of children?
2. What are the most serious problems facing the American family today? What are their effects on children?
3. What conditions within the family are more likely to result in delinquent behavior?
4. What is neglect? What are some examples of neglect within the home?
5. What are physical and emotional abuse? What are some examples of physical and emotional abuse within the home?
6. What is incest? What different kinds of incest exist? What type of father is most likely to become involved in incest?
7. How are child abuse and neglect related to status offenses and delinquent behavior?

Discussion Questions

1. Why do you think children born in the middle of the birth order are more likely to exhibit delinquent behavior?
2. Some advocate such dramatic measures as revocation of parental rights, removal of children from the home, and even forced sterilization of parents convicted of felony abuse or neglect. What is your position on the issue?
3. What factors do you think contribute to the fact that the rate of maltreatment by mothers alone is more than twice the rate of fathers acting alone?
4. Do you agree with Strauss's contention that corporal punishment legitimizes violence in children? Explain your response.
5. If you were a social worker, how would you handle the emotional abuse case described in the story of Randy and his raccoon?
6. Would you support or oppose legislation designating sexual abuse committed by a foster care provider a more egregious offense than other forms of sexual abuse and calling for more severe penalties? (Remember that legislation on hate crimes has established precedent for such unique categorization of especially reprehensible offenses.)

Group Exercises

1. Have students research data for their city and state on teen pregnancies, births, and abortions. Use the findings to guide a class discussion.

2. Take an anonymous poll of your students to determine how many came from broken homes. Ask volunteers to relate how being from a broken home has affected their participation in or rejection of delinquent behavior.

3. (a) Have one student research his or her state's law regarding the parental right to impose corporal punishment. (b) Then ask how many students believe corporal punishment is an appropriate way to discipline minor children and how many believe it is inappropriate. (c) Guide a discussion of the students' views on corporal punishment. During the discussion, have the lone researcher inform his or her classmates of what is permissible under state law.

4. Have the students read the case of the Menendez brothers, accessible at www.crimelibrary.com/notorious/murders/famous/menendez/index_1html; then have students discuss the case.

mycrimekit™

Go to mycrimekit.com to explore the following study tools and resources specific to this chapter:

■ **Practice Quiz:** Practice with multiple-choice, true/false, short-answer, and essay questions.

■ **WebQuests:** Do web activities about the Prevent Child Abuse America website.

■ **Flashcards:** Use 17 flashcards to test your knowledge of the chapter's key terms.

Schools and Delinquency

If a child cannot go to school without fear of being raped, robbed, or even murdered, then nothing else the government does really matters.

—National Policy Forum

CHAPTER OBJECTIVES

After reading this chapter, you should be able to answer the following questions:

- How has education evolved over time in the United States?
- What is the relationship between delinquency and school failure?
- What theoretical perspectives related to the school experience best explain delinquency?
- What rights do school students have?
- How has the partnership between the school and the justice system changed?
- Which intervention strategies seem to be most promising in the school setting?

195

Introduction

On March 21, 2005, 16-year-old Jeffrey Weise went to his grandfather's house on Minnesota's Red Lake Indian Reservation and used a .22-caliber rifle to shoot and kill his 58-year-old grandfather, a tribal policeman. Weise also killed his grandfather's 32-year-old girlfriend and stole his grandfather's police-issued handgun and a shotgun. He then drove to Red Lake Senior High School and shot dead an unarmed security guard at the school's main entrance before running inside and firing wildly at students and teachers. Weise chased down fleeing students, shooting some as they begged for their lives. School videotape shows him roaming through the school's hallways and classrooms, sometimes firing randomly. When 4 police officers responded to the incident, Weise fired several shots at them as they arrived at the school; when one of the officers returned fire, Weise went into a classroom and shot himself in the head. In addition to Weise, 5 students died, bringing the total number of people to die at his hand to 9.

The Red Lake school shooting was the deadliest school shooting in the United States since the 1999 Columbine High School shootings in Colorado, in which 2 students, Eric Harris and Dylan Klebold, shot and killed 12 students and a teacher before taking their own lives; 23 other people were wounded at Columbine.[1]

The public wants to know what is going on in the schools of this nation. Experts are ready to render explanations for the school killings, which range from "merely an aberration," to lack of impulse control in children today, to the breakdown of the family, to the abundance of guns in the hands of young people, to too much violence on television. What these killings certainly have done is focus attention on delinquency, especially violence, in school settings.[2]

Later in this chapter in "Scars on Their Souls," Chris Geschke, a sophomore at Santana High School in Santee, California, tells what impact school shootings have on students.[3] Geschke was walking to his classroom in the San Diego suburb about 9:15 A.M. on March 5, 2001. He passed by a bathroom, where inside a student senselessly began firing his weapon into a crowd of classmates. Before the student was subdued by an off-duty police officer, the young shooter had killed 2 students and wounded 13 others.

Geschke saw several classmates who had been shot stagger out of the bathroom and also saw a security guard race into the bathroom to try to subdue the crazed student. It later turned out that the security guard was wounded, but not fatally.

As Geschke was running to his classroom, which was about 10 feet from the bathroom, he spotted the shooter in hot pursuit of some students. The gunman shot 3 of Geschke's classmates who were running behind him and fired countless rounds toward him.

That Geschke was able to safely make it into the classroom and close the door was a miracle. Scores of bullets whizzed past his head (seven bullet holes were later found on the outside walls of that classroom).

On March 15, 2001, Geschke wrote a poignant recollection for his English class of the tragic events he was involved in at his school on March 5. Appropriately enough, his essay was titled "Scars on Their Souls." (See Table 9.1 for a timeline of recent worldwide school shootings.)

There is no question that an examination of delinquency in the United States must take a long look at the school experience. J. Feldhusen, J. Thurston, and J. Benning's longitudinal study found school relationships and experiences to be the third most predictive factor in delinquency, exceeded only by family and peer

TABLE 9.1 Recent School Shootings Worldwide

March 12, 2009, Germany	Tim Ktrydvhmrt Kretschmer killed 15 students and then himself at a German secondary school. An 18-year-old student was arrested for shooting another student at the school.
March 7, 2007, Greensville, Tex.	A 16-year-old male student fatally shot himself while in the band hallway area of the school.
January 3, 2007, Tacoma, Wash.	An 18-year-old male student was arrested for shooting a 17-year-old male student.
December 12, 2006, Springfield Township, Penn.	A 16-year-old male student shot and killed himself with an AK-47 assault rifle in the hallway of the high school.
October 17, 2006, Kaly, Tex.	A 16-year-old male high school sophomore committed suicide by shooting himself with a handgun in the school's cafeteria courtyard.
October 3, 2006, Nickel Mines, Penn.	Carl Charles Roberts IV, age 32, entered the one-room West Nickel Mines Amish School and shot 10 schoolgirls, ranging in age from 6 to 13 years old, and then killed himself; 3 of the girls died on-site, and 2 died later in an area hospital.
September 29, 2006, Cazenovia, Wis.	A 15-year-old student shot and killed Weston School's principal, John Klang.
September 27, 2006, Bailey, Colo.	An adult male held 6 students hostage at Platte Canyon High School; then he shot and killed Emily Keyes, age 16, and himself.
September 13, 2006, Montreal, Quebec, Canada	Kimveer Gill, age 25, opened fire with a semiautomatic weapon at Dawson College, killing Anastasia De Sousa, age 18, and wounding more than a dozen students and faculty before he killed himself.
August 24, 2006, Essex, Vt.	Christopher Williams, age 27, looking for his ex-girlfriend at Essex Elementary School, shot 2 teachers, killing 1 and wounding another. Before going to the school, he had killed the ex-girlfriend's mother.
November 8, 2005, Jacksboro, Tenn.	A 15-year-old shot and killed an assistant principal at Campbell County High School and seriously wounded 2 other administrators.
March 21, 2005, Red Lake, Minn.	Jeffrey Weise, age 16, killed his grandfather and his grandfather's girlfriend. He then drove to Red Lake High School where he killed a teacher, a security guard, 5 students, and finally himself, leaving a total of 10 dead.
September 28, 2004, Carmen de Patagones, Argentina	A 15-year-old Argentinean student killed 3 students and wounded 6 more in a town 620 miles south of Buenos Aires.
September 24, 2003, Cold Spring, Minn.	John Jason McLaughlin, age 15, killed 2 students at Rocori High School.
April 24, 2003, Red Lion, Penn.	James Sheets, age 14, killed Red Lion Area Junior High School principal Eugene Segro and then killed himself.
April 14, 2003, New Orleans, La.	One 15-year-old and 3 students were wounded at John McDonogh High School by gunfire from 4 teenagers, none of whom were students at the school. The motive was gang-related.
April 29, 2002, Vlasenica, Bosnia-Herzegovina	Dragoslav Petkovic, age 17, killed 1 teacher and wounded 1 teacher and then killed himself.
April 26, 2002, Erfurt, Germany	A total of 13 teachers, 2 students, and 1 policeman were killed and 10 were wounded by Robert Steinhaeuser, age 19, at the Johann Gutenberg Secondary School. Steinhaeuser then killed himself.
February 19, 2002, Freising, Germany	At a factory in Eching, 2 people were killed by a man who had been fired. He then traveled to Freising and killed the headmaster of the technical school from which he had been expelled; he also wounded another teacher before killing himself.
January 15, 2002, New York, N.Y.	A teenager wounded 2 students at Martin Luther King Jr. High School.
November 12, 2001, Caro, Mich.	Chris Buschbacher, age 17, took 2 hostages at the Caro Learning Center before killing himself.
March 30, 2001, Gary, Ind.	Donald R. Burt Jr., a 17-year-old student who had been expelled from Lew Wallace High School, killed 1 student.
March 22, 2001, Granite Hills, Calif.	Jason Hoffman, age 18, killed 1 teacher and wounded 3 students at Granite Hills High School before a policeman shot and wounded Hoffman.

(continued)

TABLE 9.1 Recent Worldwide School Shootings (*continued*)

March 7, 2001, Williamsport, Penn.	Elizabeth Catherine Bush, age 14, wounded student Kimberly Marchese in the cafeteria of Bishop Neumann High School. Bush, who was depressed, was frequently teased.
March 5, 2001, Santee, Calif.	Charles Andrew Williams, age 15, firing from a bathroom at Santana High School, killed 2 people and wounded 13.
January 18, 2001, Jan, Sweden	A student was killed by 2 boys, ages 17 and 19.
January 17, 2001, Baltimore, Md.	A student was shot and killed in front of Lake Clifton Eastern High School.
September 26, 2000, New Orleans, La.	During a fight at Woodson Middle School, 2 students were wounded with the same gun.
May 26, 2000, Lake Worth, Fla.	Teacher Barry Grunow was shot and killed at Lake Worth Middle School by Nate Brazill, age 13, with a .25-caliber semiautomatic pistol on the last day of classes.
March 10, 2000, Savannah, Ga.	Darrell Ingram, age 19, killed 2 students as they left a dance sponsored by Beach High School.
March 2000, Brannenburg, Germany	A teacher was killed by a 15-year-old student, who then shot himself; the shooter has been in a coma ever since.
February 29, 2000, Mount Morris, Mi.	A student, 6-year-old Kayla Rolland, was shot dead at Buell Elementary School near Flint, Michigan. The assailant was a 6-year-old boy with a stolen handgun.
December 7, 1999, Veghel, Netherlands	A 17-year-old student wounded 1 teacher and 3 students.
December 6, 1999, Fort Gibson, Okla.	A total of 4 students were wounded as Seth Trickey, age 13, opened fire with a 9mm semiautomatic handgun at Fort Gibson Middle School.
November 19, 1999, Deming, N.M.	Victor Cordova Jr., age 12, shot and killed Araceli Tena, age 13, in the lobby of Deming Middle School.
May 20, 1999, Conyers, Ga.	A total of 6 students were injured at Heritage High School by Thomas Solomon, age 15, who was reportedly depressed after breaking up with his girlfriend.
April 28, 1999, Tabler, Alberta, Canada	In the first fatal high school shooting in Canada in 20 years, 1 student was killed and 1 was wounded at W. R. Myers High School. The suspect, a 14-year-old boy, had dropped out of school after he was ostracized by his classmates.
April 20, 1999, Littleton, Colo.	A total of 12 students and 1 teacher were killed and 23 others were wounded at Columbine High School in the nation's deadliest school shooting. Eric Harris, age 18, and Dylan Klebold, age 17, had plotted for a year to kill at least 500 and blow up their school. At the end of their hour-long rampage, they also killed themselves.
June 15, 1998, Richmond, Va.	A 14-year-old boy killed 1 teacher and wounded 1 guidance counselor in the school hallway.
May 21, 1998, Springfield, Ore.	Kip Kinkel, age 15, killed 2 students and wounded 22 others in the cafeteria at Thurston High School; Kinkel had been arrested and released a day earlier for bringing a gun to school. His parents were later found dead at home.
May 19, 1998, Fayetteville, Tenn.	A student was killed in the parking lot at Lincoln County High School three days before he was to graduate. The victim was dating the ex-girlfriend of his killer, 18-year-old honor student Jacob Davis.
April 24, 1998, Edinboro, Penn.	Andrew Wurst, age 14, was charged with killing 1 teacher, John Gillette, and wounding 2 students at a dance at James W. Parker Middle School.
March 24, 1998, Jonesboro, Ark.	A total of 4 students and 1 teacher were killed and 10 others wounded outside as Westside Middle School emptied during a false fire alarm. Mitchell Johnson, age 13, and Andrew Golden, age 11, shot at their classmates and teachers from the woods.
December 15, 1997, Stamps, Ark.	Colt Todd, age 14, was hiding in the woods when he shot and wounded 2 students as they stood in the parking lot.
December 1, 1997, West Paducah, Ky.	Michael Carneal, age 14, killed 3 students and wounded 5 more as the students participated in a prayer circle at Heath High School.

TABLE 9.1 Recent Worldwide School Shootings (*continued*)

October 1, 1997, Pearl, Miss.	Luke Woodham, age 16, killed 2 students and wounded 7 more; he is also accused of killing his mother. He and his friends were said to be outcasts who worshiped Satan.
March 30, 1997, Sanaa, Yemen	A total of 8 people (6 students and 2 others) at two schools were killed by Mohammad Ahman al-Naziri.
February 19, 1997, Bethel, Alaska	Evan Ramsey, age 16, killed a principal as well as another student; 2 others were wounded.
March 13, 1996, Dunblane, Scotland	Thomas Hamilton killed 16 children and 1 teacher, and wounded 10 others, at Dunblane Primary School and then killed himself.
February 2, 1996, Moses Lake, Wash.	A 14-year-old student, Barry Loukaitis, opened fire on his algebra class, killing 2 students and 1 teacher and wounding 1 other.

Note: Incidents listed all involve students (or former students) as the perpetrators.

Source: Infoplease Information Please® Database, "Time Line of Worldwide School Shootings," © 2007 Pearson Education, Inc. All rights reserved. Reprinted by permission.

group relationships.[4] Delbert S. Elliott and Harwin L. Voss stated that "the school is the critical social context for the generation of delinquent behavior."[5] Arthur L. Stinchcombe believed that failure in school leads to rebelliousness, which leads to more failure and negative behaviors.[6] More recently, Eugene Maguin and Rolf Loeber's meta-analysis found that "children with lower academic performance offended more frequently, committed more serious and violent offenses, and persisted in their offending."[7]

In sum, there is considerable evidence that the school has become an arena for learning delinquent behavior. This chapter will look at the history of education in the United States, at the nature of crime in the schools, at different aspects of the relationship between the school setting and delinquent behavior, at the issue of students' rights, and at interventions used by some schools to prevent and control delinquency within school settings.

EXHIBIT 9.1

"Scars on Their Souls"

"In the aftermath of the shooting at Santana High, one thing certainly rings true: bullets can do more than just physical damage.

"This is not to diminish the tragic consequences for fifteen families. Two are dead, thirteen others injured. Their blood is red, their pain cruel. Their loss cannot be measured by words, nor can their grief be consoled. The bullets surely did physical damage that can be seen with the eye. We saw arm, facial, leg, chest, and back wounds. But the invisible damage—the pain—inflicted on the heart—will never go away. In time, that invisible damage will evolve into painful or distant memories, maybe even fade into the back of the mind. But there will always be scars on their souls.

"There is no rational reason for this irrational act. The media has tried to find a motive. Experts and Ph.D.s have pointed to a variety of reasons and social ills in attempts to justify their own theories.

"Talk show hosts have entertained thousands of callers, each with something to say and finding a new angle to say it. Was he bullied? Did bigger students abuse him? Did drugs cause this violent reaction? Was he a victim of a broken heart? Did the school not listen? Why didn't his friends do something? Where did the system fail?

"My question is, does it matter? Will an explanation bring back Brian Zuckor or Randy Gordon [two students who were killed]? Will a reason make things all better for 1,900 students, 300 faculty members and their families? Will a rational explanation help prevent my friends' mothers and fathers from worrying now every time they walk out the front door? Will an answer allow my mother to sleep peacefully again? Will a reason mean much to millions of other students at high schools just like Santana who watched us on TV and now worry the same thing could happen at their school?

"Their fear is real too. Again the invisible damage.

"I've learned a lot over the past couple of weeks. I've learned about my own mortality. I've learned about fate, and how easily one of those bullets could have hit me as I ran. I've retraced my steps in the past few days and felt the walls where the bullets hit. Bullets intended for me. I've learned that God was watching over me and has an important purpose for my own life. I've learned that people hurt, inside and outside.

"But more importantly, I've learned that bullets cause invisible damage. And they leave scars on the soul."

Reprinted with permission from Janet Christopulous.

Security personnel staff a booth at East Syracuse–Minoa Central High School in New York State. Since the Columbine High School shootings in Colorado in 1999 and numerous other attacks that have occurred since, school security has been given high priority. ▶ **What can be done to make schools safer still?**

Brief History of American Education

The U.S. Constitution says nothing about public schools, but by 1850 nearly all the northern states had enacted laws mandating free education. By 1918, education was both free and compulsory in nearly every state of the union. The commitment to public education arose largely from the growing need for a uniform approach to

An Amish buggy passes a stone farmhouse in Lancaster County, Pennsylvania, on the day after 32-year-old milk truck driver Charles Carl Roberts IV barricaded himself inside an Amish one-room schoolhouse in 2006, shot 10 young girls (5 of whom died), and then killed himself. ▶ **How can the recent spate of school shootings be explained?**

socialization of the diverse groups immigrating to this country. Joel H. Spring, a historian, writes of this movement:

> Education during the nineteenth century has been increasingly viewed as an instrument of social control to be used to solve the social problems of crime, poverty, and Americanization of the immigrant. The activities of public schools tended to replace the social training of other institutions, such as the family and church. One reason for the extension of school activities was the concern for the education of the great numbers of immigrants arriving from eastern and southern Europe. It was feared that without some form of Americanization immigrants would cause a rapid decay of American institutions.[8]

During most of the nineteenth century, U.S. schools were chaotic and violent places where teachers unsuccessfully attempted to maintain control over unmotivated, unruly, and unmanageable children through novel and sometimes brutal disciplinary methods.[9] For example, Horace Mann reported in the 1840s that in one school with 250 pupils, he saw 328 separate floggings in one week of five school days, an average of over 65 floggings a day.[10]

Widespread dissatisfaction with the schools at the turn of the twentieth century was one of the factors leading to the Progressive education movement (see Library Extra 9.1). Its founder, John Dewey, advocated reform in classroom methods and curricula so students would become more questioning, creative, and involved in the process of their own education. Dewey was much more concerned about individualism and personal growth than rigid socialization.[11]

The 1954 U.S. Supreme Court decision that ruled racial segregation in public schools unconstitutional was a pivotal event in the history of American education—it obligated the federal government to make certain that integration in schools was achieved "within a reasonable time limit."[12] The busing of children to distant schools, which arose out of the Supreme Court decision and which has resulted in the shift from neighborhood schools, remains a hotly debated issue.

During the 1960s, open classrooms, in which the teacher served as a "resource person" who offered students many activities from which to choose, were instituted as an alternative to the earlier teacher-oriented classrooms. As was the case with the Progressive education movement, the concept of the open classroom was accepted more widely in private schools than in public schools.

The baby boom of the 1950s resulted in increased enrollments and more formalized student–teacher contacts in public schools in the 1960s and early 1970s. Public education also became more expensive in the 1970s, because the increasing numbers of children in the classroom meant that more equipment (including expensive items such as computers, scientific equipment, and audiovisual aids) had to be purchased. At the same time, teachers' unions took a firmer stance during contract talks, and many larger cities experienced teachers' strikes during this decade.

Since at least the mid-1980s, instead of optimism, dire warnings have been issued by all sides concerning the state of education. An expert on schools put it this way in 1984:

> American schools are in trouble. In fact, the problems of schooling are of such crippling proportions that many schools may not survive. It is possible that our entire public education system is nearing collapse. We will continue to have schools, no doubt, but the basis of their support and their relationship to families, communities and states could be quite different from what we have known.[13]

School Crime

Crime in the schools, especially public schools, is a serious problem now facing junior and senior high schools across the nation. This high crime rate expresses itself through **vandalism**, **violence**, drug trafficking, and gangs. Vandalism and violence are examined in this section, and Chapters 10 and 11 will explore the difficulties that youth gangs and drugs bring to the school setting.

mycrimekit

Library Extra 9.1
OJJDP Fact Sheet: *Overcoming Barriers to School Reentry*

vandalism The act of destroying or damaging, or attempting to destroy or damage, the property of another without the owner's consent or destroying or damaging public property (except by burning).

violence A forceful physical assault with or without weapons. It includes many kinds of fighting, rape, other attacks, gang warfare, and so on.

Vandalism and Violence

There are two major reasons why so much youth crime is taking place in our schools. First, while urban schools are frequently criticized for failing to provide safe, orderly environments, the communities around these schools suffer from serious levels of crime and disorder. Unsafe schools, in other words, are lodged within unsafe neighborhoods. The level of school crime and violence is also dependent on the community context because most of the students are members of the community. For example, if a community has a large number of adolescent drug dealers, runners, and lookouts; youth gang leaders and followers; chronically disruptive youths; and juvenile property offenders, then local schools are likely to have high rates of youth crime. Similarly, schools with little vandalism or violence are usually lodged in supportive communities that have low rates of criminal or delinquent behavior.[14]

Second, schools' authoritarian atmosphere and the likelihood of failure by many students, especially those with limited learning abilities, create bored, frustrated,

---

EXHIBIT 9.2

Indicators of School Crime and Safety: 2005–2007

Violent Deaths at School

- From July 1, 2006, through June 30, 2007, there were 27 homicides and 8 suicides of school-age youths (ages 5–18) at school. Combined, this figure translates into about 1 homicide or suicide of a school-age youth at school per 1.6 million students enrolled during the 2006–2007 school year.

Nonfatal Student Victimization

- In 2006, students ages 12–18 were victims of about 1.7 million nonfatal crimes at school, including thefts and violet crimes.
- In 2006, more students ages 12–18 were victims of theft at school than away from school.
- In 2006, 10% of male students in grades 9–12 reported being threatened or injured with a weapon on school property in the past year, compared to 5% of female students.
- In 2006, a higher percentage of African-American students (10%) and Hispanic students (9%) reported being threatened or injured with a weapon on school property than white students (7%) and American Indian/Alaska Native students (6%).

Nonfatal Teacher Victimization

- In 2006, a greater percentage of secondary school teachers (8%) reported being threatened with injury by a student than elementary school teachers (6%). However, a greater percentage of elementary school teachers (4%) reported having been physically attacked than secondary school teachers (2%).
- In 2006, a greater percentage of public than private school teachers reported being threatened with injury (7% vs. 2%) or physically attacked (4% vs. 2%) by students in school. Among teachers in city schools, there were generally at least five times as many public school teachers as private school teachers who reported being threatened with injury (12% vs. 1%) and at least four times as many public school teachers as private school teachers who reported being physically attacked (5% vs. 1%).

School Environment

- In 2005–2006, 86% of public schools reported one or more serious violent incidents, thefts of items valued at $10 or greater, or other crimes, amounting to an estimated 2.2 million crimes. This figure translates into a rate of 46 crimes per 1,000 students enrolled in 2005–2006.
- In 2005–2006, 24% of public schools reported that student bullying was a daily or weekly problem. With regard to other discipline problems occurring at least once a week, 18% of public school principals reported student acts of disrespect for teachers, 9% reported student verbal abuse of teachers, 3% reported daily or weekly occurrences of racial/ethnic tensions among students, and 2% reported widespread disorder in classrooms. With regard to other discipline problems occurring at least once per school year, 17% of principals reported undesirable gang activities, and 4% reported undesirable cults or extremist activities during 2005–2006.
- In 2005–2006, a higher percentage of middle schools than primary schools reported various types of discipline problems, and a higher percentage of middle schools than high schools reported daily or weekly occurrences of student bullying and student sexual harassment of other students.
- In 2007, 23% of students ages 12–18 reported that street gangs were present at their school. Overall, a smaller percentage of white students (16%) and Asian students (17%) reported a gang presence at school than African-American students (38%) and Hispanic students (36%).
- In 2007, 22% of students in grades 9–12 reported that someone had offered, sold, or given them an illegal drug on school property in the past 12 months.
- In 2007, 10% of students ages 12–18 reported that someone at school had used hate-related words against them, and more than one-third (35%) reported seeing hate-related graffiti at school.

> ▶ If violence in public schools is declining, why do so many teachers feel unsafe in the school setting? What can be done to make public schools even safer?

Source: Rachel Dinkes, Jana Kemp, Katrina Baum, and Thomas D. Snyder, *Indicators of School Crime and Safety: 2008* (Washington, D.C.: U.S. Departments of Education and Justice, U.S. Government Printing Office, 2009), pp. v–vii.

dissatisfied, and alienated students. In one study, students consistently rated themselves as more bored in school than in any other setting.[15] The repressive methods of education, as Martin Gold noted, make school one of the most difficult experiences for adolescents in American society.[16] Urie Bronfenbrenner added that "the schools have become one of the most potent breeding grounds of alienation in American society."[17]

The need to establish a safe learning atmosphere is a serious issue in public education today, but the added security features of many public schools make them appear even more like prisons (see Library Extra 9.2). Uniformed police are stationed in many schools; other schools have their own security staff. Students must submit to a metal detector search to enter some schools, electronically locked doors are becoming more common, and locker searches for drugs and weapons are everyday occurrences in many schools. Identification tags or photo ID badges for students and silent panic buttons for teachers are other means schools are using to regain control of the environment. Until it was ruled unconstitutional by the courts, a school in Boston even gave a drug test (urinalysis) to every student during the physical examination performed by the school physician at the start of each academic year.[18]

In 2009, the National Center for Education Statistics published its eleventh annual report on school crime, *Indicators of School Crime and Safety: 2008*, which profiled school crime and safety and described the characteristics of the victims of these crimes (see Exhibit 9.2 for the report's basic findings). It can be argued that schools are safer for children than other areas because children experience higher rates of violence away from school than they experience when they are at school (as well as coming to or leaving school). In addition, there was some decline in violence from 1992 to 2008 (see Figure 9.1). Yet students still experience high rates of disorder in some schools, especially public urban schools[19]; they are more fearful of being attacked at school than away from school.[20] Some students avoid certain areas of their schools, and more students are faced with intimidation from bullies (see the discussion of ways to reduce bullying in the next section). Weapons, gangs, and drugs in schools are further indicators of school disorder.[21]

School Bullying

Bullying in school is a worldwide problem. Even though most of the research on bullying has taken place in Great Britain, Japan, and Scandinavian countries, it has been noted and discussed wherever formal schooling environments are found. Bullying consists of

Library Extra 9.2
Bureau of Justice Statistics (BJS) publication: *Indicators of School Crime and Safety*

bullying The hurtful, frightening, or menacing actions undertaken by one person to intimidate another (generally weaker) person, to gain that person's unwilling compliance, and/or to put him or her in fear.

A teenage girl bullying another girl. Students report being more afraid of attacks at school than when they are away from school. ▶ What can be done to reduce such fears?

FIGURE 9.1 Rate of Student-Reported Nonfatal Crimes against Students Ages 12–18 per 1,000 Students, by Type of Crime and Location, 1992–2003

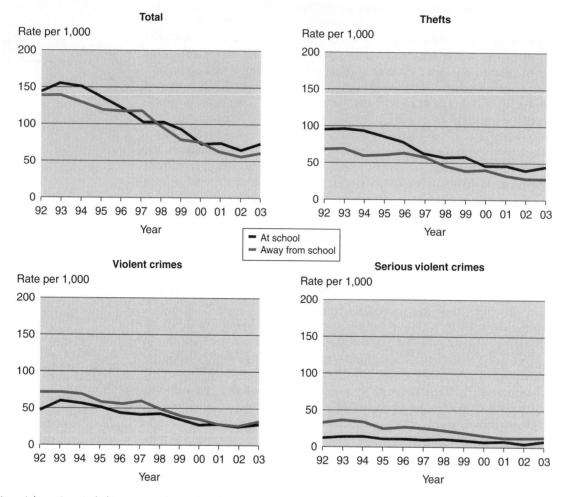

Note: Serious violent crimes include rape, sexual assault, robbery, and aggravated assault. Violent crimes include serious violent crimes and simple assault. Total crimes include violent crimes and theft. "At school" includes inside the school building, on school property, or on the way to or from school.

Source: U.S. Department of Justice, Bureau of Justice Statistics, *National Crime Victimization Survey* (NCVS), 1992–2003.

such direct behaviors as teasing, threatening, taunting, hitting, and stealing that have been initiated by one or more aggressive students against a weaker victim. In addition to such direct attacks, bullying may also be more indirect, causing a student to be socially isolated through intentional exclusion. Boys typically are involved in more direct bullying methods, whereas girls utilize more subtle strategies, such as spreading rumors and enforcing social isolation. Whether the bullying is direct or indirect, its key component is repeated physical or psychological intimidation that creates an ongoing pattern of harassment and abuse.[22] See Exhibit 9.3 for a description of the bullying problem and for information on intervention strategies that can reduce bullying in schools.

A number of studies have documented how bullying in the school context can create a climate of fear and discomfort in schools:

■ One study first summarized the literature, stating that bullying can be understood as both a dyadic and a peer group phenomenon, primarily situated in the heads (thinking) of those involved, in a lack of skill or experience, or in the delinquency of a bully who needs to be reformed. This study added that, unfortunately, typical antibullying strategies often simply train bullies to be better at bullying (meaning that they learn to bully more covertly and more expertly so as to inflict the same devastation without adult detection).[23]

> > > **EXHIBIT 9.3** < <

Facts about Bullying and Possible Intervention Strategies

Facts about Bullying

- Between 15% and 30% of students in U.S. schools are bullies or victims.
- In a recent report by the American Medical Association of over 15,000 sixth- through tenth-graders, it was estimated that approximately 3.7 million youths engage in, and more than 3.2 million are victims of, moderate or serious bullying each year.
- Bullying is often blamed as an important factor in school-related deaths.
- Membership in either bullying or victim groups is associated with dropping out of school, psychosocial adjustment problems, delinquent activity, and other long-term consequences.
- Physical bullying increases in elementary school, peaks in middle school, and declines in high school; verbal abuse, on the other hand, tends to remain constant.
- Over two-thirds of students believe that schools respond poorly to bullying.
- Only 25% of teachers see nothing wrong with bullying or put-downs and, as a result, intervene in only 4% of bullying incidents.

What Can Schools Do?

- *Early intervention.* Researchers advocate intervening in elementary or middle school or even as early as preschool. Social skills training is highly recommended, as are counseling and systematic aggression interventions for students demonstrating bullying and victim behaviors.
- *Parent training.* Parents must learn to reinforce their children's positive behavior patterns and must demonstrate appropriate interpersonal interactions.
- *Teacher training.* Training can help teachers identify and respond to potentially damaging victimization as well as implement positive feedback and modeling to address inappropriate social interactions. Support services personnel

who work with administrators can be helpful in designing effective teacher training modules.

- *Attitude change.* Researchers maintain that society must stop defending bullying behavior as part of growing up or by assuming the attitude that "kids will be kids." School personnel should never ignore bullying behaviors.
- *Positive school environment.* Schools with easily understood rules of conduct, smaller class sizes, and fair discipline practices report less violence and bullying behaviors.

What Can Parents Do?

- Parents should contact the school social worker, counselor, or school psychologist and ask for help concerning bullying or victimization concerns.
- Parents can provide positive feedback to their children for appropriate social behaviors that do not include aggression or bullying.
- Parents should use alternatives to physical punishment, such as the removal of privileges, as consequences for bullying behavior.
- Parents should stop bullying behavior when it takes place and help their children develop more appropriate social skills.

▶ As you think back to your own school years, did you have any experiences of being bullied? What did you feel at the time? If you were a bully instead of a victim, did you ever wonder why you were doing what you were doing? There tends to be a division between bullies and victims in the literature, but how about those who are bullies at some times and victims at other times? How frequently do you think this takes place?

Source: Adapted from Andrea Cohn and Andrea Canter, *Bullying: Facts for Schools and Parents.* (Bethesda, MD: National Association of School Psychologists, 2003). Available at: www.nasponline.org. Reprinted with permission of the publisher.

- Another study performed a meta-analysis and posited that an association existed between bullying and psychosomatic problems.[24]
- A further study found that students with mild disabilities were more likely to be perceived as bullies by both teachers and peers; in addition, teachers rated students with mild disabilities as being bullied by their peers significantly more often. Academically gifted students were seen by teachers as having the lowest rates of both bullying and being bullied.[25]
- The data from a survey of 24,345 youths on the evidence of racial/ethnic differences in children's self-report of being a victim of bullying revealed that African-American youths who were victimized tended to underreport being a victim of bullying.[26]

See Web Extra 9.1 and Web Extra 9.2 for more information on ways to deal with bullying.

Delinquency and School Failure

Lack of academic achievement, low social status at school, and dropping out are factors frequently cited as being related to involvement in delinquency. This section will look at the first two factors, and dropping out is considered later in the chapter.

Web Extra 9.1
Anti-Bullying Network

Web Extra 9.2
Bullying.org

Video   Travis Hirschi

FIGURE 9.2 Hirschi's Causal Chain

Source: Adapted from Travis Hirschi, *Causes of Delinquency* (Berkeley: University of California Press, 1969), pp. 131–132, 156.

Achievement

Considerable evidence indicates that, whether measured by self-report or by official police data, both male and female delinquency is associated with poor **academic performance** at school.[27] Travis Hirschi claimed that the causal chain shown in Figure 9.2 may eventually lead to delinquent behavior.[28] Numerous researchers have pointed out that delinquents' lack of achievement in school is related to other factors besides academic skills. For example, several studies have found that delinquents are more rejecting of the student role than are nondelinquents.[29] Delinquents' performance in school may be further affected by their relationships with classmates and teachers; several studies have concluded that the relationship between school performance and delinquency is mediated by peer influence.[30] Maguin and Loeber's meta-analysis of studies of academic performance and delinquency relationships found that children with lower academic performance committed more delinquent acts, committed more serious delinquent acts, and had a longer offending history than those with higher academic performance, an association which was stronger for males than for females and for whites than for African-Americans, and that academic performance also predicted delinquent involvement independent of socioeconomic status.[31]

Ann Arnett Ferguson spent three and a half years observing a middle school classroom in a western state and found that the classroom experience was anything but positive for many African-American children.[32] However, Richard B. Felson and Jeremy Staff, using the National Education Longitudinal Study, concluded that academic performance and delinquency have a spurious relationship.[33]

academic performance
Achievement in schoolwork as rated by grades and other assessment measures. Poor academic performance is a factor in delinquency.

Video Albert K. Cohen

In Canon City, Colorado, St. Scholastica Academy graduates hug each other before graduation at the Catholic boarding school for girls. ▶ **Studies have shown that delinquents tend to perform poorly at school. What factors contribute to poor school performance?**

Low Social Status

Albert K. Cohen's influential study of delinquent boys was one of the most comprehensive analyses ever undertaken of the role of the school in the development of delinquent subcultures. According to Cohen's theory, working-class boys (as discussed in Chapter 4) feel status deprivation when they become aware that they are unable to compete with middle-class youths in the school. Although avoiding contact with middle-class youths might solve the problem, working-class boys cannot do this because they are forced to attend middle-class schools established on middle-class values; consequently, they reject middle-class values and attitudes and form delinquent subcultures that provide them with the status denied in school and elsewhere in society.[34] Jackson Toby's study, based on a variation of Cohen's thesis, contended that a lower-class background makes school success difficult because lower-class youths lack verbal skills and encouragement from home.[35] John C. Phillips proposed steps by which low status in school can lead to deviant behavior (see Figure 9.3).[36] However, the proposed relationship between social class and delinquency in the school has been challenged. For example, one study found that any adolescent male who does poorly in school, regardless of class background, is more likely to become involved in delinquent behavior than one who performs well in school.[37]

FIGURE 9.3 Phillips's Steps Leading to Deviant Behavior

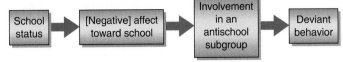

In short, most of the evidence points to three conclusions: Lack of achievement in school is directly related to delinquent behavior, most delinquents want to succeed in school, and the explanations for poor academic achievement are more complex than lack of general aptitude or intelligence. Although the existence of a relationship between social class and delinquency in the school has mixed support, a relationship between school achievement and delinquency is much clearer.

Theoretical Perspectives on School and Delinquency

Most major theories of delinquency see the school as a factor contributing to delinquent behavior. Blocked opportunity theory, strain theory, cultural deviance theory, social control theory, labeling theory, radical criminology, general theory of crime, and interactionist theories all make contributions to understanding delinquency in schools.

The majority of studies focusing on blocked opportunity have found that those most likely to commit delinquent acts are young people who do poorly in school or who believe that they have little chance of graduation. Observers say that when youthful offenders are unable to perform satisfactorily in school, they become disruptive, decide to drop out, or are suspended—all of which further reinforces involvement in deviant behavior.[38] Strain theorists contend that youngsters from certain social classes are denied legitimate access to culturally determined goals and opportunities and that the resulting frustration leads to either the use of illegitimate means to obtain society's goals or the rejection of those goals. Strain theory views the school as a middle-class institution in which lower-class children are frequently unable to perform successfully; these youths then turn to delinquency to compensate for feelings of status frustration, failure, and low self-esteem.[39]

Cultural deviance theorists argue that children learn delinquent behavior through being exposed to others and by mimicking or modeling others' actions—children may come to view delinquency as acceptable because of their exposure to others whose definitions of such behavior are positive. Because schools tend to reflect the characteristics of the community of which they are a part, attending school in high-crime areas increases the likelihood of association with delinquent peers.[40]

Social control theorists believe that delinquency varies according to the strength of a juvenile's bond to the social order. Social control theorists also posit that the school is one of the major socializing institutions, providing youths with structure, incentives, expectations, and opportunities for social bonding, and that delinquency is likely to result when a strong bond to school does not develop.[41]

Labeling theorists argue that once students are defined as deviant, they adopt a deviant role in response to their lowered status. Early on, schools attach labels on the basis of achievement and behavior, and these labels may influence the subsequent treatment of youths. For example, when students are labeled as aggressive, difficult to manage, or slow learners at an early stage, they may be put in a slow track for the remainder of their schooling. According to labeling theorists, this differential treatment contributes to delinquent identities and behaviors.[42]

Some radical criminologists view the school as a means by which the privileged classes maintain power over the lower classes. Subjected to the controlling forces of the state, lower-class children are exploited as they experience powerlessness and alienation, and they are more likely than middle- and upper-class children to be placed in the lowest tracks, to receive poor grades, to be suspended for disciplinary reasons, and to drop out of school. According to radical theorists, lower-class children are essentially being trained to accept menial roles in the social order.[43]

In the general theory of crime, once self-control has formed in childhood, it affects adolescents in the choices they make in peer relations, school conduct and achievement, drug and alcohol use, and delinquent activities. Thus, students with self-control will be able to abstain from activities in school that would affect teachers' negative evaluations; from unwholesome peer relations in and out of school that would affect their desire to succeed, including gang participation; and from behaviors that would garner the attention of the police and juvenile justice system officials.[44]

Interactional theory, as developed by Thornberry and colleagues, is an integrated theory that can be applied to the school. It originally stated that attachment to parents and commitment to school are important buffers against delinquency, so adolescents who are emotionally bonded to parents and who succeed at school are unlikely candidates for serious delinquency. Later versions of this theory have found that while weakened bonds to family and school do cause delinquency, delinquent behavior further reduces the strength of the bonds to family and school, thereby establishing a behavioral trajectory toward increasing delinquency.[45]

Another integrated theory related to the school is one developed by Wayne N. Welsh, Jack R. Greene, and Patricia H. Jenkins that draws on control theory, school climate theory, and social disorganization theory to examine the influence of individual, institutional, and community factors on misconduct in Philadelphia middle schools. One of the strong conclusions reached by these researchers is that the simplistic assumption that bad communities typically produce "bad children" or "bad schools" is unwarranted.[46]

Students' Rights

The school's authority over students comes from two principal sources: the concept of *in loco parentis* and state-enabling statutes.[47] E. Edmund Reutter Jr. summarized *in loco parentis* as follows:

in loco parentis The principle according to which a guardian or an agency is given the rights, duties, and responsibilities of a parent in relation to a particular child or children.

> The common law measure of the rights and duties of school authorities relative to pupils attending school is the *in loco parentis* concept. This doctrine holds that school authorities stand in the place of the parent while the child is at school. Thus, school personnel may establish rules for the educational welfare of the child and may inflict punishments for disobedience. The legal test is whether a reasonably knowledgeable and careful parent might so act. The doctrine is used not only to support rights of school authorities . . . but to establish their responsibilities concerning such matters as injuries that may befall students.[48]

State-enabling statutes authorize local school boards to establish reasonable rules and regulations for operating and keeping order in schools, which do not necessarily have to be in written form.[49] A classic statement on this type of authority was made in the 1966 case of *Burnside* v. *Byars*:

> The establishment of an educational program requires the formulation of rules and regulations necessary for the maintenance of an orderly program of classroom learning. In formulating regulations, including those pertaining to the discipline of schoolchildren, school officials have a wide latitude of discretion. But the school is always bound by the requirement that the rules and regulations must be reasonable. It is not for us to consider whether such rules are wise or expedient but merely whether they are a reasonable exercise of the power and discretion of the school authorities.[50]

The courts have become involved with schools in a number of important areas: procedural due process, freedom of expression, hair and dress codes, school searches, and safety.[51]

Procedural Due Process

Dixon v. *Alabama State Board of Education* (1961) was a major breakthrough for students' rights because the appeals court held for the first time that due process requires a student to receive notice and some opportunity for a hearing before being expelled for misconduct.[52] In 1969, the U.S. Supreme Court issued its far-reaching decision in *Tinker* v. *Des Moines Independent School District*, declaring that students do not shed their constitutional right of freedom of speech at the schoolhouse door. The issue that was involved in this case was whether students had the right to wear black armbands to protest the Vietnam War, and the Court ruled that school authorities did not have the right to deny free speech, even the expression of an unpopular view, unless they had reason to believe that it would interfere with the school operations.[53] In the 1986 *Bethel School District No. 403* v. *Fraser* case, the Court upheld a school system's right to suspend or discipline a student who uses profane or obscene language or gestures, reasoning that the use of lewd and offensive speech undermined the basic educational mission of the school.[54] In a 1988 decision, *Hazelwood School District* v. *Kuhlmeier*, the Court ruled that the principal could censor articles having to do with pregnancy and parental divorce in a student publication; the Court's majority justified this censorship because such publications were perceived to be part of the educational curriculum of the school.[55]

In January 1975, the U.S. Supreme Court took up the problem of **due process rights** in the schools, stating in *Goss* v. *Lopez* that schools may not summarily suspend students, for even one day, without following fundamentally fair fact-finding procedures.[56] In suspensions of 10 days or less, a student is entitled to oral or written notice of the charges, an explanation of the evidence, and an opportunity to be heard. The *Wood* v. *Strickland* ruling, issued a month after the *Goss* decision, found that school officials may be subject to suit and held financially liable for damages if they deliberately deprive a student of his or her clearly established constitutional rights.[57]

The issue of corporal punishment came before the U.S. Supreme Court in the 1975 *Baker* v. *Owen* and *Ingraham* v. *Wright* cases.[58] Although *Baker* v. *Owen* merely affirmed a lower-court ruling, *Ingraham* v. *Wright* held that reasonable corporal punishment is not cruel and unusual punishment under the Eighth Amendment to the U.S. Constitution.[59]

due process rights The constitutional rights that are guaranteed to citizens—whether adult or juvenile—during their contacts with the police, their proceedings in court, and their interactions with the public schools.

Freedom of Expression

Several court cases have defined students' rights to freedom of religion and expression in schools. In *West Virginia State Board of Education* v. *Barnette*, the Supreme Court held that students could not be compelled to salute the flag if that action violated their religious rights.[60] In *Tinker*, the wearing of black armbands was declared symbolic speech and therefore within the protection of the First Amendment.[61]

Hair and Dress Codes

Court cases testing the power of school administrators to suspend students for violations of hair and dress codes were widespread in the late 1960s and early 1970s. In *Yoo* v. *Moynihan*, a student's right to style his or her hair was held to be under the definition of the constitutional right to privacy[62]; then in *Richards* v. *Thurston*, the Court ruled that a student's right to wear long hair derived from his interest in personal liberty.[63] In *Crossen* v. *Fatsi*, a dress code prohibiting "extreme style and fashion" was ruled unconstitutionally vague and unenforceable as well as an invasion of the student's right to privacy.[64] Other decisions have held that schools cannot prohibit the wearing of slacks,[65] dungarees,[66] or hair "falling loosely about the shoulders."[67]

School Searches

The use of drugs and weapons is changing the nature of police–student relations in schools. In the 1990s, the police began to enforce the 1990 federal Gun-Free School Zones Act and increasingly, in communities across the nation, to enforce drug-free school zone laws. Drug-free zones usually include the school property along with the territory within a 1,000-foot radius of its perimeter. Alabama has the most aggressive law in this nation: Territory within three miles of a school is declared drug free.[68]

school search The process of searching students and their lockers to determine whether drugs, weapons, or other contraband is present.

The use of drug-sniffing dogs, Breathalyzers, hidden video cameras, and routine **school searches** of students' pockets, purses, school lockers, desks, and vehicles on school grounds appears to be increasing as school officials struggle to regain control over their schools. In some cases, school officials conduct their own searches; in other cases, the police are brought in to conduct the searches.

In the *New Jersey* v. *T.L.O.* decision (1985), the U.S. Supreme Court examined the issue of whether Fourth Amendment rights against unreasonable searches and seizures apply to the school setting.[69] On March 7, 1980, a teacher at Piscataway High School in Middlesex County, New Jersey, discovered two adolescent females smoking in a bathroom. He reported this violation of school rules to the principal's office, and the two females were summoned to meet with the assistant vice principal. When one of the females, T.L.O., claimed that she had done no wrong, the assistant principal demanded to see her purse; on examining it, he found a pack of cigarettes and cigarette rolling papers, some marijuana, a pipe, a large amount of money, a list of students who owed T.L.O. money, and letters that implicated her in marijuana dealing. T.L.O. confessed later at the police station to dealing drugs on school grounds.[70]

The juvenile court found T.L.O. delinquent and sentenced her to a year's probation, but she appealed her case to the New Jersey Supreme Court on the grounds that the search of her purse was not justified under the circumstances of the case. When the New Jersey Supreme Court upheld her appeal, the state appealed to the U.S. Supreme Court, which ruled that school personnel have the right to search lockers, desks, and students as long as they believe that either the law or school rules have been violated. The legality of a search, the Court stated, need not be based on obtaining a warrant or on having probable cause that a crime has taken place; rather, the legality of the search depends on its reasonableness, considering the scope of the search, the student's gender and age, and the student's behavior at the time.[71]

The significance of this decision is that the Supreme Court opened the door for greater security measures because it gave school officials and the police the right to search students who are suspected of violating school rules.[72] Of 18 cases in the years 1985–1991 that were decided by state appellate decisions applying the *T.L.O.* decision, school officials' intervention was upheld in 15 of them.[73]

In its 1995 *Vernonia School District 47J* v. *Acton* decision, the U.S. Supreme Court extended schools' authority to search by legalizing a random drug-testing policy for student athletes. This decision suggests that schools may employ safe-school programs, such as drug-testing procedures, as long as the policies satisfy the reasonableness test.[74]

In the 2002 *Board of Education of Independent School District No. 92 of Pottawatomie County* v. *Earls* decision, the U.S. Supreme Court reversed the judgment of the court of appeals and upheld the right of the school district to test students who participated in extracurricular activities; the Court found this to be a "reasonably effective means of addressing the School District's legitimate concerns in preventing, deterring, and detecting drug use by students."[75] The Court in *Pottawatomie* expanded the *Vernonia* decision by extending the drug testing of student athletes to the testing of students involved in extracurricular activities, which is an especially important issue, given the recent concern over steroid use on the part of professional, college, and high school athletes.

Safety

Court-imposed limitations on schools concerning the rules under which youths can be disciplined (*Tinker*) and the requirements for procedural due process relating to school administrators taking disciplinary action (*Goss, Ingraham,* and others) have made local school authorities increasingly wary of using tough methods to discipline students. Principals have become reluctant, for example, to suspend youths for acts such as acting insubordinate, wearing outlandish clothing, loitering in halls, and creating classroom disturbances; only a few decades earlier, such conduct would have drawn a quick notice of suspension. Increased judicial intervention in the academic area has contributed to (though not caused) an increase in unruly behavior, thereby reducing the safety of students in the public schools.[76]

In sum, judicial intervention in schools over the past three decades has had both positive and negative impacts. Students' rights are less likely to be abused than in the past because the courts have made it clear that students retain specific constitutional rights in school settings. However, school administrators who perceive themselves as handcuffed by court decisions have become reluctant to take firm and forceful action against disruptive students, and violence and delinquency in the schools have increased.

School and Justice System Partnerships

There is a growing trend toward increasing partnerships between schools and various agencies of the juvenile justice system.[77] Traditionally, school partnerships with juvenile justice agencies have centered on the use of police officers as informational sources, with their efforts aimed at prevention through education. Four well-known programs initiated through earlier police–school partnerships are Drug Abuse Resistance Education (D.A.R.E.), Police Athletic League (P.A.L.) programs, Gang Resistance Education and Training, and Law-Related Education (all are described in later chapters of this text). Police personnel who are involved with these programs use the school environment as a conduit for preventing youth crime through education and less intrusive intervention. Contemporary partnerships between schools and agents of the justice system are increasingly structured for student control and crime prevention rather than education, which signals important changes in the social control mechanisms used in schools and with children.[78]

The U.S. Department of Education's report titled *Violence and Discipline Problems in U.S. Public Schools 1996–1997* provided some preliminary indications on the extent of juvenile/criminal justice–public school collaboration. Taken from a national representative sample of elementary, middle, and secondary schools, this survey revealed that 97% of schools reported using some form of security measures; of the surveyed schools, 84% reported that they had low security measures (no police officers or guards, no metal detectors, but controlled access to campus), and 13% reported stringent to moderate security measures (full-time police officers or guards, metal detectors, and controlled access to campus), and of the schools with stronger security measures, 6% had police or other law enforcement personnel stationed for 30 hours or more at the school.[79] Despite the difficulty of gauging the extent of this collaboration, there did appear to be a growing number of schools using police officers, security personnel, or other security measures on a part-time basis (or more) to assist in maintaining school order, security, and control.[80]

The trends identified in the 1996–1997 report hold true today, and the changing nature of the partnership between criminal and juvenile justice agencies and the schools is as significant as the quantity of official presence. An indicator of this changing nature is the shift in language used by schools: Officers are brought into the school to "fight campus crime," maintain "discipline," "combat victimization," and support "zero tolerance"; justice personnel in the school, formerly called resource officers and liaisons, now increasingly are called "Independent School District (ISD) Police," "security officers," "guards," and "gang intelligence officers." Yet changes in the partnership go beyond semantics—criminal justice agencies in the school setting more frequently focus on identification and investigation, control of campus access, drug sweeps and drug testing, strip searches, surveillance, monitoring, and crowd control.[81]

Delinquency across the Life Course: Factors Involved in Dropping Out of School

One study that related the school to a life-course perspective was undertaken by Zeng-yin Chen and Howard B. Kaplan. Using a longitudinal panel data set collected at three developmental stages (early adolescence, young adulthood, and middle adulthood), Chen and Kaplan investigated how early school failure influenced status attainment at midlife, concluding that "early negative experiences set in motion a cascade of later disadvantages in the transition to adulthood, which, in turn, influences SES [socioeconomic status] attainment later in the life course."[82]

According to a 2001 report conducted by the Education Policy Center of the Urban Institute, the national graduation rate was 68%, with nearly one-third of all public high school students failing to graduate. Significant racial and economic gaps exist between those who graduate and those who do not:

■ Students from disadvantaged minority groups (American Indian, Hispanic American, African-American) have little more than a 50-50 chance of finishing high school with a diploma.
■ By comparison, national graduation rates for whites and Asians are 75% and 77%, respectively.
■ Males graduate from high school at a rate 8% lower than female students.
■ Graduation rates for students attending school in high-poverty, racially segregated urban school districts lag from 15% to 18% behind those of their peers.
■ A great deal of variation in graduation rates exists across regions of the nation as well as between the states.[83]

Wendy Schwartz analyzed information from the Educational Resource Information Center and determined the following:

■ Students in large cities are twice as likely to leave school before graduating as nonurban youths are.
■ More than one in four Hispanic youths drop out; of those, nearly half leave by the eighth grade.
■ Hispanics are twice as likely as African-Americans to drop out of school.
■ White and Asian youths are least likely to drop out.
■ More than 50% of all students who drop out of school leave by the tenth grade, 20% by the eighth grade, and 3% by the fourth grade.
■ In the last 20 years, the earnings level of **dropouts** doubled while it nearly tripled for college graduates.
■ Recent dropouts will learn $200,000 less than high school graduates and over $800,000 less than college graduates over the course of their lives.
■ Dropouts comprise nearly half of all heads of households on welfare.
■ Dropouts comprise nearly half of the nation's prison population.[84]

dropout A young person of school age who, of his or her own volition, no longer attends school.

John Sampson and John Laub have demonstrated that high school can be a turning point in an individual's life course (see Chapter 2).[85] Richard Arum and Irenee R. Beattie assessed the effects of high school educational experiences on the likelihood of adult incarceration.[86] Using event history analysis and the National Longitudinal Survey of Youth data, they found that high school educational experiences have a lasting effect on an individual's risk of incarceration. This study offered specifications of the high school context to identify how high school experiences can serve as a defining moment in an adolescent's life trajectory.[87]

Delinquency and Social Policy: Promising Interventions

Several intervention strategies promise to benefit schools in the United States: improved quality of the school experience; increased use of mentors for students who are encountering difficulties or experiencing problems; greater use of alternative schools for students who cannot adapt to the traditional education setting; development of a comprehensive approach to school success that includes home, school, church/synagogue, parents, and other institutions and persons who participate in school processes affecting students' lives; effective school-based violence-prevention programs; and more effective transitions from correctional contexts to the school setting. (See Figure 9.4 for a summary of this information.)

Improved School Experiences

Equality of the school experience begins with good teaching. Good teachers can make students feel wanted and accepted and can encourage students to have more positive and successful experiences in the classroom. Safety is another of the most important prerequisites of effective involvement in the educational process; unless students feel safe, they are unlikely to involve themselves very deeply in the school experience (see Library Extra 9.3). To ensure safety, a critical problem in large urban schools, administrators must take firm action to reduce violence and delinquency.

Mentoring Relationships

In 2005, 3 million adults had formal one-to-one mentoring relationships with young people, an increase of 19% since 2002.[88] Youth development experts generally agree that mentoring is a critical component in a child's social, emotional, and cognitive development and that it has the potential to build a sense of industry and competency, boost academic performance, and broaden horizons.[89] School-based mentoring is one of the most promising types of youth mentoring taking place today and is experiencing rapid growth. According to a Big Brothers Big Sisters of America survey, the number of school-based matches grew from 27,000 in 1999 to 90,000 in 2002, an increase of 233%.[90] Still, school-based mentoring is impacting only a small percentage of all youths who could be helped; for example, one of the findings of a 2002 survey is that of the 17.6 million young people who could benefit from having a mentor, only 2.5 million were in a formal one-to-one mentoring relationship.[91]

Library Extra 9.3
Office of Community Oriented Policing Services (COPS) publication: *Bullying in Schools*

FIGURE 9.4 Intervention Strategies to Improve Schools

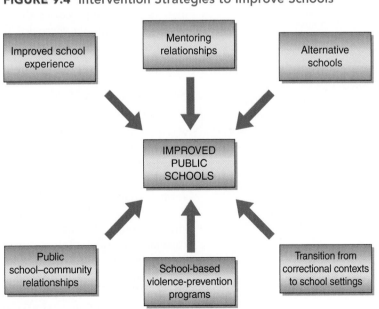

Alternative Schools

disruptive behavior
Unacceptable conduct at school. It may include defiance of authority, manipulation of teachers, inability or refusal to follow rules, fights with peers, destruction of property, use of drugs in school, and/or physical or verbal altercations with teachers.

Library Extra 9.4
OJJDP Fact Sheet: *Addressing the Problem of Juvenile Bullying*

Library Extra 9.5
OJJDP publication: *Juvenile Mentoring Program: A Progress Review*

Web Extra 9.3
National Education Association website, School Safety section
National Education Association, School Safety

Web Extra 9.4
National Youth Violence Prevention Resource Center website

alternative school A facility that provides an alternative educational experience, usually in a different location, for youths who are not doing satisfactory work in the public school setting.

Disruptive behavior is a very serious problem in many of this nation's classrooms (see Library Extra 9.4 and Library Extra 9.5 as well as Web Extra 9.3 and Web Extra 9.4). School administrators often suspend or expel students who cause trouble[92]; however, this policy of swift suspension stigmatizes troublemakers as failures and reinforces their negative behaviors. **Alternative schools** are deemed a much more satisfactory way of dealing with young people whom public schools cannot control or who are doing unsatisfactory work in a public school setting. The juvenile court sometimes requires disruptive students to attend an alternative school, but more frequently, students are referred by the public school system. In 2000–2001, 39% of public school districts had alternative schools and programs and served approximately 613,000 at-risk students in about 10,900 alternative schools and programs in the United States. Alternative schools and programs were found more frequently in large districts (those with 10,000 or more students) than in small districts (those with fewer than 10,000 students), in urban districts than in suburban or rural districts, and in southeastern districts than in districts in other regions of the nation.[93]

The ultimate goal of most alternative schools is to return students to the public school setting. They generally deal more effectively with disruptive students than does the public school system, and they tend to reduce absenteeism and dropout rates. In contrast, "the private schools' client/customer is the parents and everything is designed to satisfy them in order to attract students."[94]

Positive School–Community Relationships

"The legendary vision of the blackboard jungle," according to Stanley Cohen, has dominated social control policy in schools, adding that the desire for a safe and secure school has contributed to a "massive investment in hardware and preventive technology: video surveillance, ultrasonic detectors, hotline to the police, redesigning buildings into clusters of manageable space"; Cohen stated that administrators stress such problems as bomb threats, arson, violence, drug pushing, and mass disruption, concluding that the relevant literature often reads "like a blueprint for converting the school into a closed-security prison."[95] In contrast to efforts at reducing delinquency in the school by investing in hardware and preventive technology, an alternative intervention strategy is the development of a comprehensive, or multicomponent, approach that includes home, school, and other persons and institutions that participate in the social processes affecting the students' lives. Delinquency and the quality of the public school experience, then, must be analyzed within the larger context of school–community relationships.[96]

School-Based Violence-Prevention Programs

The real or perceived threat of school violence has influenced to a large degree the way principals manage, teachers teach, and students learn. In J. H. Price and S. A. Everett's national survey of secondary school principals, one-third indicated that they had already implemented some type of violence-prevention or safe-school program, and another third said that they were planning to implement such a program.[97] Delbert S. Elliott, Beatrix A. Hamburg, and Kirk R. Williams's 1998 book *Violence in American Schools: A New Perspective* argued that "the most effective interventions [for reducing school violence] use a comprehensive, multidisciplinary approach and take into account differences in stages of individual development and involvement in overlapping social contexts, families, peer groups, schools, and neighborhoods."[98] The final chapter of their book uses the ecological, life-course, and developmental approaches as a framework for organizing the previous chapters' research findings and prevention recommendations and integrates the book's various perspectives.

A police dog checks student lockers for contraband. In an attempt to provide a safe learning environment, some schools have adopted stringent security measures, leading some critics to compare today's public schools to prisons. ▶ **Are such strict measures necessary?**

From Correctional Contexts to School Settings

A new priority in juvenile justice is an emphasis on the role of schools in the transition of juvenile offenders from institutional confinement to life in the community. When an institutionalized delinquent returns to the public school setting, there are potential problems, and the needs of juvenile offenders, fellow students, teachers, and the community must all be considered.[99]

Chapter Summary

The costs of delinquency in schools can be measured in lost future earnings, reduction of a sense of safety in the school environment, and disruption of school activities. This chapter also points out the following:

- Delinquent behavior can be best understood as the product of complex socialization processes operating at many different levels within the school system.

- A student's lack of school achievement appears to be directly related to the likelihood of his or her delinquent behavior.

- Court decisions have mandated provision of specific constitutional rights to students, such as free speech and due process, in the school environment.

- Some school administrators perceive themselves as being handcuffed by court decisions and are reluctant to take firm and forceful action against disruptive students.

The school has long been acknowledged as important in the socialization of children, but public education is facing many sharp criticisms today:

- Public schools are failing to effectively educate and properly socialize American youths.

- Since the 1970s, vandalism, violence, and drug trafficking have become serious problems in many schools.

- High rates of school crime create unsafe conditions and an unwholesome environment for learning.

For schools to improve, a number of changes need to take place:

- Elevating the quality of the school

- Reducing the effects of bullying

- Increasing the use of mentoring

- Providing more effective alternative school experiences for disruptive students

- Finding ways to renew urban schools

- Developing more positive school–community relationships

- Making schools safe from violence

Key Terms

academic performance, p. 206
alternative school, p. 214
bullying, p. 203
disruptive behavior, p. 214

dropout, p. 212
due process rights, p. 209
in loco parentis, p. 208
school search, p. 210

vandalism, p. 201
violence, p. 201

Review Questions

1. How frequent are school shootings?
2. What crimes exist in public schools?
3. What factors are related to failure in school?
4. What theoretical explanations deal with delinquency and the school experience?

5. What rights do students have?
6. What interventions were mentioned that could be useful in reducing delinquency in the public schools?

Discussion Questions

1. Although schools may well be avenues for learning delinquent behavior, that behavior likely does not include shooting or bombing as an acceptable response to ordinary conflicts. Where are today's youths learning that resorting to such violence is an appropriate course of action?
2. Were you victimized by a bully, or did you observe violence during your elementary or secondary schooling? Relate the incidents.
3. What are the consequences of vandalism and violence in public schools?

4. Is increased criminality among dropouts a predictable result as they confront the economic realities of their limited earning capacities?
5. Do you think a program designed to reduce bullying in schools would have any effect on school violence and victimization?
6. Do you believe the various theoretical perspectives discussed here are useful for explaining the relationship between schools and delinquency?

Group Exercises

1. Show the film *Bowling for Columbine*, and then have a discussion of the incident.
2. Have the students research material related to the February 2000 shooting death of a six-year-old classmate in a Michigan elementary school; then discuss this incident.
3. Have the students research their county and state data on academic performance by adjudicated delinquents, comparing those data to the data on students not adjudicated as delinquent.

4. Have students research their county and state dropout rates.
5. Have the class review the University of Colorado at Boulder's "Evaluation of School-Based Violence Prevention Programs," accessible at www.colorado.edu/cspv/publications/factsheets/school/violence/FS-SV08.html; then discuss the material.

mycrimekit™

Go to mycrimekit.com to explore the following study tools and resources specific to this chapter:

- **Practice Quiz:** Practice with multiple-choice, true/false, short-answer, and essay questions.

- **WebQuests:** Do web activities about bullying and victims of bullying.
- **Flashcards:** Use 10 flashcards to test your knowledge of the chapter's key terms.

Gangs and Delinquency

Gang members' mutual support of criminal activities, and possession of a value system which condones such behavior, distinguishes gang members and gangs from all other offenders and groups.

—Michael K. Carlie,
Into the Abyss

CHAPTER OBJECTIVES

After reading this chapter, you should be able to answer the following questions:

- What is the relationship between peer groups and gang activity?
- How have gangs evolved in the United States?
- What is the relationship between urban-based gangs and emerging gangs in smaller cities and communities?
- How extensive is gang activity in this country?
- How does gang activity affect communities?
- Why do youths join gangs?

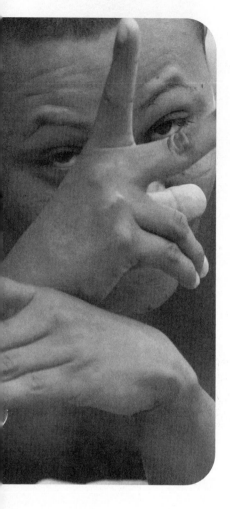

Introduction

Former San Francisco gang member Walter Simon has been confined to a wheelchair since 1993, when he was ambushed by a rival gang and shot eight times.

In a 2006 event convened by District Attorney Kamala Harris, following the murder of a witness in a gang-related homicide case, Simon strongly endorsed reporting criminals to authorities. He told assembled community leaders that there was a distinction between responsibly reporting criminals and just "snitching," such as when an arrestee names others to escape harsher punishment.

Simon, still on parole after serving half of a three-year state prison sentence for drug dealing, said he had joined a gang-intervention program and was attending college. But he wasn't able to keep out of trouble for long.

In July 2006, a month after the district attorney's event, police arrested Simon for possessing a gun, but Harris's office did not file charges. Then in April 2007, he was arrested in the killing of an innocent bystander caught in cross fire when Simon was shooting at an unidentified gunman. Police said Simon was sitting in front of a liquor store where he regularly dealt drugs. Kamala's office again declined to file charges and referred the matter to state officials to determine whether Simon had violated his parole. The state ultimately decided not to revoke Simon's parole for reasons that were unavailable to the media.

San Francisco authorities have been under fire for not adequately punishing repeat offenders, but in an e-mail to a San Francisco news site, Simon insisted he was innocent and demanded an apology from the police and media. "I guess since I'm just a crippled black ex-con, I don't fit the criteria for being considered worth an apology," he wrote.[1]

crack A less expensive but more potent form of cocaine.

Over the past 30 years, urban street gangs, armed with Israeli-made Uzis, Soviet AK-47s, diverted U.S. military M16s, and other automatic weapons, have evolved into small criminal empires fighting for control of thriving narcotics, auto theft, prostitution, gunrunning, and extortion operations. Illegal drugs form the backbone of most gang moneymaking criminal operations, with the manufacture and sale of **crack**, or rock cocaine, providing the bulk of the business. The crack trade, more than anything else, transformed street gangs into ghetto-based for-profit criminal organizations. Although most such gangs are led by adults, juveniles often play a central role in their day-to-day activities.[2]

As street gangs have become more business-like, they have formed associations with other organized crime groups, including Mexican drug cartels, Asian criminal groups, and Russian organized crime families. Gangs and their members are also becoming more sophisticated in their use of technology, including computers, cell phones, and the Internet. These new high-tech tools are frequently used to facilitate criminal activity and avoid detection by the police. Although some sources say that the number of gang members is in decline across the United States, some Hispanic gangs, such as *Mara Salvatrucha* (MS-13), are experiencing an influx of new members.[3]

This chapter focuses on youths who are involved in gangs. Youth gangs have become a problem in many nations and are widespread in the United States in urban, suburban, and rural areas.

Peer Groups and Gangs

The increased focus on the individual in delinquency theory in the 1970s and 1980s provided a necessary balance to the previous overemphasis on group processes. But by the late 1980s, there was some concern that most theories of delinquency had become social-psychological rather than sociological, with the result that the group aspects of delinquent behavior had ceased to be examined and at times were virtually ignored.[4] A number of 1990s studies on the relationship between peers and delinquency revealed a renewed interest in group processes.[5]

Peer Groups and Delinquent Behavior

Inquiry into group delinquency has resulted in conflicting findings. Some self-report studies have found that most delinquent behavior occurs in groups.[6] Maynard L. Erickson and Gary F. Jensen reported that regardless of their sex or whether they are in urban settings or small towns, juveniles tend to follow herd instincts when they violate the law. These authors did find that drug offenses have the highest group frequency and that status offenses—other than drinking and smoking—have the lowest.[7]

A *Mara Salvatrucha* (MS-13) gang member displays his tattoos. MS-13 is one of the nation's most violent gangs. ▶ What are the attractions of gangs like MS-13 for their members?

Other studies have also found that group delinquency may be overestimated.[8] Elizabeth S. Piper, using the 1958 Philadelphia cohort data, found an increasing tendency toward lone offending occurred later in the delinquent's career; another important finding of this study is a greater desistance rate among group offenders than among lone offenders, regardless of age at onset.[9]

There is considerable debate about the quality of delinquents' relationships with their friends or about the relationship between peers and delinquency. In terms of the quality of delinquents' relationships with their friends, Travis Hirschi believed that the causal significance of friendships has been overstated, and in referring to these relationships as **"cold and brittle,"** he argued that "since delinquents are less strongly attached to conventional adults than nondelinquents they are less likely to be attached to each other. . . . The idea that delinquents have comparatively warm, intimate social relations with each other (or with anyone) is a romantic myth."[10]

Peggy C. Giordano and S. A. Cernkovich, in examining the relationships involved in delinquent groups, found that delinquents and nondelinquents have similar **friendship patterns**, leading them to question Hirschi's "cold and brittle" assumption. Hirschi's position assumes social disability—"that is, that these kids are incapable of developing important and close friendships with each other and that they are just held together by the common quality of being losers"; in contrast, these researchers determined that delinquents are able to develop good and close primary relationships.[11] Mark Warr's analysis of the National Youth Gang Survey also found that delinquents are able to form close relationships with others. He stated that "delinquent friends tend to be 'sticky' friends (once acquired, they are not quickly lost) [but] . . . recent rather than early friends have the greatest effect on delinquency."[12]

The process of examining the relationship between delinquency and peers has generated considerable debate, which has largely focused on the question of causal order: Do delinquents merely seek friends like themselves, or do youths become delinquent because they associate with delinquent friends? One of the strongest findings of criminology, according to Ross L. Matsueda and Kathleen Anderson, is that "delinquent behavior is correlated with delinquency of one's peers."[13] Other studies support the idea that extensive association with peers who engage in serious delinquent behavior has a strong positive effect on delinquency but perhaps not as strong as formerly held.[14] For example, Dana L. Haynie and D. Wayne Osgood found that peer influence is not necessarily more powerful than that of gender, age, school, or family.[15]

Merry Morash, reporting that adolescent females belong to less delinquent groups (which is a significant factor in accounting for their lower levels of delinquency), contended that structural and situational constraints, as well as individual-level variables, explain why females end up in the least delinquent peer groups. Structural and situational factors, she suggested, may include the tendency of males to prefer

"cold and brittle" According to Travis Hirschi, the nature of interpersonal relationships among delinquents, specifically delinquents in gangs.

friendship pattern The type of peer relationships that exist within a teenage culture.

FIGURE 10.1 Age at First Arrest and Co-Offending

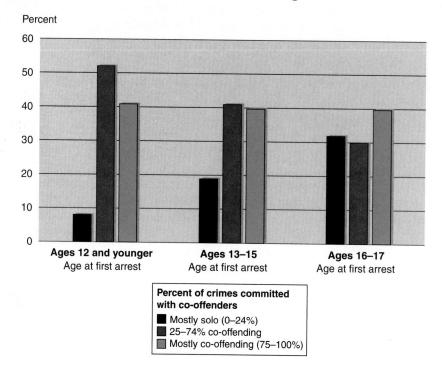

Source: Joan McCord and Kevin P. Conway, *Co-Offending and Patterns of Juvenile Crime* (Washington, D.C.: National Institute of Justice, Office of Justice Programs, 2005), p. 10.

Library Extra 10.1
OJJDP publication:
Co-Offending and Patterns of Juvenile Crime

to commit crime with other males, sex typing of females by males as inappropriate colleagues and leaders, and a crime environment emphasizing raw physical power (see Library Extra 10.1). Moreover, gender-related characteristics of females, such as an aversion to aggression and greater empathy, may restrain females from joining peers who are prone to violent acts.[16]

Joan McCord and Kevin P. Conway's 2005 publication, titled *Co-Offending and Patterns of Juvenile Crime*, reviewed the literature and reached the following conclusions:

- Offenders who are age 13 years and under are more likely to commit crimes in pairs and groups than are 16- and 17-year-old offenders (see Figure 10.1).
- About 40% of juvenile offenders commit most of their crimes with others.
- Co-offenders may learn through the influence of violent accomplices that violence can be an effective means of obtaining money or satisfying other desires.
- Youthful offenders are most at risk for subsequent crimes if they commit their crimes with accomplices.[17]

In sum, researchers generally agree that most delinquent behavior, especially more violent forms, is committed in groups, but they disagree on the quality of relationships within delinquent groups and on the influence of groups on delinquent behavior. There are a number of questions still to be answered: How do delinquent peers influence one another? What causes the initial attraction to delinquent groups? What do delinquents receive from these friendships that results in their continuing with them?[18]

Video Uniform Crime Report

Development of Gangs in the United States

Gangs have existed in this nation for centuries. In the War of 1812, for example, Jean Laffite led his band of pioneers and smugglers against the British in support of Andrew Jackson. The Younger and James gangs, two infamous gangs of the Wild West, have long been folk heroes.[19] Youth gangs, as we know them, also originated in the early decades of this nation's history. Some evidence indicates that youth gangs may have existed as early as the American Revolution[20]; other data suggest that they first emerged in the Southwest following the Mexican Revolution in 1813.[21] Youth gangs seemed to have spread into New England in the early 1800s, primarily because of the shift from agrarian to industrial society. Youth gangs, which began to flourish in Chicago and other large cities in the nineteenth century as immigration and population shifts reached peak levels, were primarily Irish, Jewish, and Italian.[22] During the twentieth century, the makeup of youth gangs changed rather significantly in nearly every decade.

Gangs and Play Activity: The 1920s through the 1940s

Frederick Thrasher's 1927 study, titled *The Gang: A Study of 1,313 Gangs in Chicago*, was a pioneering and as-yet unsurpassed work on gangs.[23] Thrasher viewed gangs as a normal part of growing up in ethnic neighborhoods. Adolescents who went to school together and played together in the neighborhood naturally developed a strong sense of identity, which led to their forming close-knit groups. Thrasher saw these gangs, evolving from neighborhood play groups, as bonded together without any particular purpose or goal and as largely transitory social groupings, typically with fewer than 30 members. They were generally organized in three concentric circles: a core composed of a leader and lieutenants, the rank-and-file membership, and a few occasional members. Finally, although each gang was different, the protection of turf was universally expected gang behavior.[24]

West Side Story Era: The 1950s

From the late 1940s through the 1950s, teenage gangs became more established in urban areas, such as Boston, New York, and Philadelphia. In addition to the time they spent hanging out, they partied together, and when necessary, they fought other gangs together. The musical *West Side Story*, later made into a movie, presented a picture of two 1950s New York youth gangs singing, dancing, and battling over turf; the Sharks, recent immigrants from Puerto Rico, defended their neighborhood while the Jets defended theirs, and territorial lines were confined to neighborhood ethnic boundaries.

The 1950s gangs did not have the lethal weapons that today's gangs have, but they were very capable of violent behavior. One of the authors was hired to work with a white gang in Newark, New Jersey, in 1960–1961. The job became available because his predecessor, who had been on the job for two weeks, had a knife held to his chest, cutting his shirt and drawing a little blood. The predecessor was warned that bad things would happen if he did not quit, so he chose to resign. The author received quite an education in how gangs operated that year, and unlike his predecessor, he did not have any threatening experience.

Millions of dollars in federal, state, and local money were spent on projects and programs designed to prevent and control the behavior of these fighting gangs. For example, the detached workers program, one of the most widely funded efforts, sent professional workers into the community to work with gang youths, but it proved to have little or no positive effect on reducing gangs' rates of delinquent behavior.[25]

Development of the Modern Gang: The 1960s

In the midst of a rapidly changing social and political climate in the 1960s, drugs influenced gang activity for the first time, "supergangs" emerged in several cities, and gangs became involved in social betterment programs and political activism.

Drugs led to reduced gang activity in some urban areas, and when gangs began to reduce their activities or even to disappear from some urban areas in the middle and late 1960s, some observers thought that the problem was coming to an end. New York City was one of the urban areas in which gang activity decreased significantly in the 1960s, with the major reason offered for this apparent reduction of activity being the use of hard drugs. Lesser reasons included the civil rights movement, urban riots, the growth of militant organizations, the war in Vietnam, and an exodus from the ghettos.[26]

A leader of a large Bronx gang in New York City reflected on the lack of gangs in the 1960s: "You can't keep a brother interested in clicking [gang activities] if he's high or nodding."[27] A college student who was a heroin addict for several years in Spanish Harlem in New York City during the 1960s also blamed drugs for the lack of gang activity:

> My brother was a big gang member. But we did not go for that kind of thing. Man, we were on drugs. That was cool. We were too busy trying to score to fool around with gang activity. It was everybody for himself.[28]

The 1960s was also the decade in which the major supergangs developed. Some neighborhood gangs became larger and more powerful than other gangs in surrounding neighborhoods, and they forced these groups to become part of their gang organization. Eventually a few gangs would control an entire city. For example, in the 1960s, the Crips, an African-American supergang, began as a small clique in a section of south Los Angeles[29]; in Chicago, the Vice Lords, Blackstone Rangers, and Gangster Disciples, all major supergangs today, also had their beginnings during that decade. (See the next section for an explanation of how the Gangster Disciples [GDs] developed at this time.)

During the late 1960s, the three Chicago supergangs became involved in social and political activism. The Vice Lords moved further than any of the other Chicago street gangs toward programs of community betterment.[30] Their involvement in social action began in the summer of 1967 when leaders of the Vice Lords attended meetings at Western Electric and Sears, Roebuck. Operation Bootstrap, which resulted from these meetings, formed committees for education and recreation as well as law, order, and justice. A grant from the Rockefeller Foundation in February 1967 enabled the Vice Lords to found a host of economic and social ventures, and they also worked with Jesse Jackson on Operation Breadbasket and, in the summer of 1969, joined with the Coalition for United Community Action to protest the lack of African-American employees on construction sites in African-American neighborhoods.

In 1968, all three street gangs worked against the reelection of Mayor Richard Daley's Democratic machine, and this political activism brought increased strain to their relationship with the Democratic Party's organization.[31] The interrelationships between the legal and political contexts became apparent on the streets of Chicago as street gangs experienced what they perceived as harassment from the police. As soon as he began a new term, Mayor Daley announced a crackdown on gang violence, and the state's attorney, Edward Hanrahan, followed by appraising the gang situation as the most serious crime problem in Chicago. The courts complied with this crackdown on gangs by increasing dramatically the number of gang members sent to prison in Illinois.[32]

Expansion, Violence, and Criminal Operations: The 1970s and Early 1980s

In the 1970s and 1980s, as their leadership was assumed by adults, street gangs became responsible for an even bigger portion of muggings, robberies, extortions, and drug-trafficking operations in the United States. One city after another reported serious problems with gangs in the early 1970s, and it became apparent that the gangs of the 1970s and early 1980s were both more violent than the gangs of the 1950s and more intent on making money from crime; furthermore, they were systematic in their efforts to extort local merchants, engage in robberies, shake down students for money, intimidate local residents, and sell stolen goods.

Some gangs became so sophisticated that the police regarded their activities as organized crime. Those gangs kept attorneys on retainer—some even printed business cards to further their careers in extortion, and they sold the cards to businesses to provide "protection" and to warn away rivals.[33]

The mid-1980s were a turning point for many ghetto-based street gangs, because crack cocaine had hit the streets and urban street gangs competed with one another

> > > **EXHIBIT 10.1** < < <

Origins of the Gangster Disciples

Larry Hoover, the chief of the Gangster Disciples, provides the following information on the beginnings of this gang.

I remember how close I came to death when I was 17. It was the night I was standing near the front of the Sarah Harrison Lounge drinking Wild Irish Rose, and David Barksdale, who was the sole leader of the Disciples, and his main people confronted me. I don't know how they got into my neighborhood that fast. They had me surrounded. There were only two of us, and there must have been 50 of them.

As David and I faced each other, I noticed he held a beer can in his hand. The next thing I knew, his fist was in my face. The 180 pounds of muscular raw power sternly admonished, "You are not going with Charlie Atkins. You guys are going to be Disciples." I firmly stated, "I am not going to be a Disciple." Guns were made visible. I thought, I will do anything to get out of this alive, but that is not what I said. For some reason, they didn't shoot us. That still surprises me.

My 20 soldiers and I became members of the Double 6 King Cobras, a faction of the Cobrastones led by Charles Atkins. Charlie was tough, dangerous, and very lethal. His slight build

didn't discourage him from quickly losing his temper. This [was?] a three-year period from 1966 to 1969, where we were alw[ays] fighting the Disciples. Out of the bloodbaths, two gangs emerged with tremendous power—the Blackstones and the Disciples.

Jeff Fort tried to make a deal with me to become a part of the Blackstone Nation. There were somewhere around 75 gang factions that made up the Nation. I did attend a few of their meetings, but he didn't offer to make me one of the Main 21. I remained bound to the Double 6 King Cobras until one night, [when] David and his main leaders got out of their cars holding their hands in the air. This indicated there would be no shooting. They offered to form a treaty with us. We agreed to stop fighting the Disciples.

It wasn't long after that he asked me if we could merge and each have the same amount of power. We would share the power, two kings, coexisting in one land. Neither of us would be higher or more important. He would lead the Devil Disciples. I would conduct the Gangster Disciples. The merger left us 6,000 strong. It was then that I realized my sovereign power. I was a king, and I was only 19 years old.

Courtesy of Linda Dippold Bartollas.

for the drug trade. For example, several Los Angeles gangs established direct connections to major Colombian smugglers, which ensured a continuous supply of top-quality cocaine; in some Chicago neighborhoods, heavily armed teams sold drugs openly on street corners, using gang "peewees" (youngsters) as police lookouts.

Development of Emerging Gangs: The Late 1980s and 1990s

In 1988–1989 and through the early 1990s, an upsurge of youth gangs suddenly occurred throughout the United States. Some of these youth gangs used names of the national urban gangs, such as the Bloods and Crips from Los Angeles or the Gangster Disciples, Vice Lords, or Latin Kings from Chicago. Other gangs made up their own names, based on neighborhoods or images they wanted to depict to peers and the community. By the mid-1990s, nearly every city, many suburban areas, and even some rural areas across the United States experienced the reality of youths who considered themselves gang members. The growth of these emerging gangs peaked by the early 1990s and began to decline by the end of the 1990s.

The Present

The number of gangs, as well as membership in these gangs, began to decline in the mid-1990s and has continued to decline overall throughout the United States, the exception to this decline being the recent growth of some ethnic gangs, such as MS-13. At the same time, federal law enforcement has had success in breaking up such urban gangs as the Gangster Disciples and the El Rukns. The street gang traditionally has been a cultural by-product in the United States, but ganglike structures are now being reported in numerous cities worldwide. Cities in Asian/Pacific nations reporting gangs are Beijing, Hong Kong, Melbourne, Papua New Guinea, and Tokyo, and European cities include Berlin, Frankfurt, London, Madrid, Manchester, and Zurich. There have also been indications that gang activity is taking place in Canada, Russia, and South America[34] (see Figure 10.2).

evelopment of Gangs in the Twentieth and Early Twenty-First Century

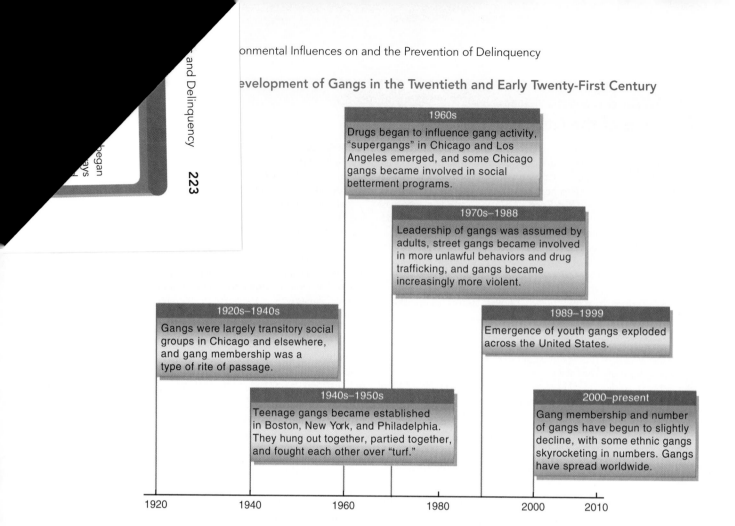

1960s
Drugs began to influence gang activity, "supergangs" in Chicago and Los Angeles emerged, and some Chicago gangs became involved in social betterment programs.

1970s–1988
Leadership of gangs was assumed by adults, street gangs became involved in more unlawful behaviors and drug trafficking, and gangs became increasingly more violent.

1920s–1940s
Gangs were largely transitory social groups in Chicago and elsewhere, and gang membership was a type of rite of passage.

1989–1999
Emergence of youth gangs exploded across the United States.

1940s–1950s
Teenage gangs became established in Boston, New York, and Philadelphia. They hung out together, partied together, and fought each other over "turf."

2000–present
Gang membership and number of gangs have begun to slightly decline, with some ethnic gangs skyrocketing in numbers. Gangs have spread worldwide.

1920   1940   1960   1980   2000   2010

Nature and Extent of Gang Activity

According to the 2006 National Youth Gang Survey, an estimated 785,000 gang members and 26,500 gangs were active in the United States. These estimates reflect a slight decline in gang problems since 1996, but in larger cities with a population of 50,000 or more, there is about the same number of gang problems. (See Figure 10.3,

Cambodian gang members are seen in California. Youth gangs appear to be spreading to our nation's smaller cities and towns. ▶ What accounts for this spread?

FIGURE 10.3 Law Enforcement Agency Reports of Gang Problems, 1996–2005

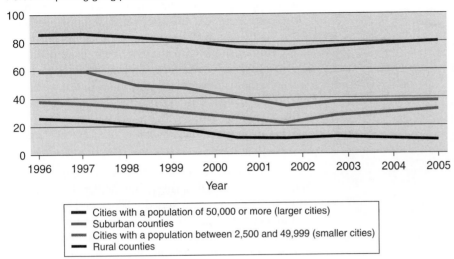

Percent reporting gang problems

Legend:
— Cities with a population of 50,000 or more (larger cities)
— Suburban counties
— Cities with a population between 2,500 and 49,999 (smaller cities)
— Rural counties

Note: For the random-sample groups, the observed variation in the percentage of agencies reporting gang problems from 2000 to 2005 is within the range attributable to sampling error; therefore, it does not represent a definitive change in the estimated number of jurisdictions with gang problems.

Source: Arlen Egley Jr. and Christina E. O'Donnell, *Highlights of the 2005 National Youth Gang Survey* (Washington, D.C.: Office of Juvenile Justice and Delinquency Prevention, 2006), p. 1.

which shows the percentage of law enforcement agencies reporting youth gang problems from 1996 to 2005.) In 2005, larger cities and suburban counties accounted for approximately 77% of the total number of gang members.[35]

Knowledge of the gang world requires an examination of the definition of gangs and the profile of gang members as well as an understanding of gangs' intimidation of the school environment, of the structure and leadership of urban street gangs, of emerging gangs in small communities across the nation, of racial and ethnic backgrounds of gangs, and of female delinquent gangs.

Definitions of Gangs

Considerable disagreement still exists about what parameters define a **gang**. Researchers differ on several questions:

■ How many youths make up a gang?
■ Must gang members commit crimes as a gang to be considered a gang?
■ Must gangs have some semblance of organizational structure?
■ Should motorcycle gangs, skinhead groups, and white supremacist groups be considered part of the youth gang problem?[36]

Thrasher's 1927 gang study was one of the first attempts to define a youth gang:

A gang is an interstitial group originally formed spontaneously and then integrated through conflict. It is characterized by the following types of behavior: meeting face to face, milling, movement through space as a unit, conflict, and planning. The result of this collective behavior is the development of tradition, unreflective internal structure, esprit de corps, solidarity, morale, group awareness, and attachment to local territory.[37]

W. B. Miller's studies in the 1970s defined a gang more through its organizational characteristics and dynamics, with a gang having "mutual interest," "identifiable leadership," and "well-developed lines of authority"; another organizational feature of the gang, according to Miller, is the desire to achieve a purpose, which usually includes "the conduct of illegal activity and control over a particular territory, facility, or type of enterprise."[38]

gang A group of youths who are bound together by mutual interests, have identifiable leadership, and act in concert to achieve a specific purpose that generally includes the conduct of illegal activity.

FIGURE 10.4 Age of Gang Members by Community Size, 2001

Percentage of gang members

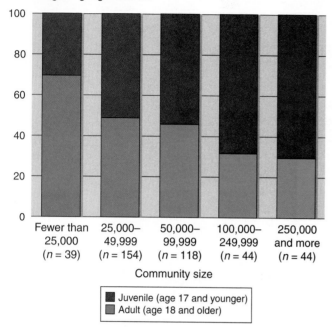

Community size

☐ Juvenile (age 17 and younger)
☐ Adult (age 18 and older)

Source: Adapted from Arlen Egley Jr., James C. Howell, and Aline K. Major, *National Youth Gang Survey 1999–2001* (Washington, D.C.: Office of Juvenile Justice and Delinquency Prevention, U.S. Government Printing Office, 2006), p. 18.

Web Extra 10.1

National Youth Gang Center website

In a 2000 publication, Finn-Aage Esbensen concluded that the following elements should be present for a group to be classified a youth gang:

■ The group needs to have more than two members.
■ Group members must fall within a limited age range, usually acknowledged as ages 12 to 24 years old.
■ Group members must take some steps to define their identity, such as naming the gang and/or using colors or symbols to claim gang affiliation.
■ Youth gangs must have some permanence, such as association with a geographic area.
■ Involvement in illegal activity is a central element of youth gangs.[39]

Thrasher does not specify that a gang's definition must include illegal activity, but Miller, Esbensen, and most other gang researchers do. Whereas Thrasher's definition focused on group interaction and Miller's observed organizational characteristics and dynamics, Esbensen was interested in clarifying group demographics (age range, sense of identity, and permanence within a specific area). Combining all three definitions could provide a useful and comprehensive definition of a youth gang.

Profiles of Gang Members

Gang profiles have at least four important dimensions: age of gang membership, size of the gang, commitment to the gang, and attraction of the gang.

Age of Gang Membership The smaller the community, the more likely it is that gang members will be juveniles. Sample surveys of urban street gang members indicate that 14% to 30% of adolescents join gangs at some point.[40] Nonetheless, the percentage of gang members who are juveniles has decreased over time: In 1996, 50% of all gang members were reported to be age 18 years or older, but by 2001, this number had grown to 67%. Juvenile gang members make up 70% of all gang members in small communities—a statistic that steadily declines as community size increases (see Figure 10.4).[41]

Juveniles become involved as young as 8 years of age, running errands and carrying weapons or messages. They are recruited as lookouts and street vendors and join an age-appropriate junior division of the gang. Gangs use younger and smaller members to deal cocaine out of cramped "rock houses," which are steel-reinforced fortresses. Gangs have long known that youngsters are invaluable because their age protects them against the harsher realities of the adult criminal justice system.[42]

Size of the Gang Gangs vary in size depending on whether they are traditional or specialty gangs in urban areas or emerging gangs in smaller cities or communities (see Web Extra 10.1). Large and enduring traditional (territorial) gangs in urban areas average about 180 members, whereas drug-trafficking gangs average only about 25 members. Some urban gangs (e.g., the supergangs of Chicago) have thousands of members, but gangs in emerging areas usually number less than 25 or so members.[43]

Commitment to the Gang Gang members have varying degrees of commitment to the gang. J. D. Vigil[44] and Vigil and J. M. Long[45] identified four basic types of gang involvement:

1. *Regulars.* The regulars are strongly attached to the gang and have few interests outside of the gang. The regulars are the hard-core, the inner clique who make key decisions, set standards, are the key recruiters, and enforce the sanctions against violators of group norms.

2. *Peripheral members.* The peripheral members are also strongly attached to the gang but participate less often than the regulars because they have other interests besides the gang.
3. *Temporary members.* The temporary members are marginally committed, joining the gang at a later age than the regulars and peripherals; they also tend to remain in the gang for only a short time.
4. *Situational members.* The situational members are very marginally attached, generally participate only in certain activities, and avoid violent activities whenever possible.[46]

A similar but somewhat different typology of gang commitment is contributed by Ira Reiner, who identified five different levels of commitment to the gang[47]:

1. *At-risk youths.* The at-risk youths are not really gang members but are pregang juveniles; they do not belong but have expressed some interest in gang participation.
2. *Wannabes.* The wannabes are recruits who are usually in their preteen years and have begun to emulate gang members' dress and values.
3. *Associates.* The associates make up the lowest level of gang membership. They are sometimes called Fringe, Li'l Homie, or soldiers, and it is not unusual for them to be assigned undesirable tasks or dangerous activities.
4. *Hard-core.* The hard-core, who are regarded as regular members and part of the inner clique, spend most of their time engaging in gang-related activities and are the most gang-bound in terms of lifestyle.
5. *Veteranos/original gangsters (O.G.s).* The *veteranos*/O.G.s are made up of men in their twenties or even thirties who continue to be active in gang activities. In Chicano gangs, *veteranos* are regarded as elder statesmen who may be retired but still command respect; in African-American gangs, O.G.s are men who have earned respect and who are often expected to teach younger members the ways of the gang.[48]

Attraction of the Gang   Why do young people join gangs? Willie Lloyd, legendary leader of a gang called the Almighty Unknown Vice Lords, explained why he became involved with gangs:

> I grew up on the streets of Chicago. When I was growing up, the Lords had a big impact on me. I never saw it as a gang but a cohesive and unified principle on which a person could organize his life. Even as a kid of nine, I was intrigued by the Lords when I first saw them outside of the Central Park Theater. It was the first time I had ever witnessed so many black people moving so harmoniously together. They were motored by the same sense of purpose and they all wore similar dress and insignia. There were over a hundred guys, all in black, with capes and umbrellas. To my young eyes, it was the most beautiful expression I had ever seen. They all seemed so fearless, so proud, so much in control of their lives. Though I didn't know one of them at the time, I fell in love with all of them. In retrospect, I made up my mind the very first time I saw the Vice Lords to be a Vice Lord.[49]

Mike Carlie, in his national overview of youth gangs, expanded on the question of why youths join gangs, asking why gangs form and what gangs offer to those who join them (see Table 10.1).

Voices of Delinquency

Read "From Gang Member to College Football Star." What was the attraction of gangs for this youth? How did he get out of the gang?

Types of Urban Gangs

Richard A. Cloward and Lloyd E. Ohlin's 1960 study identified criminal, conflict, and retreatist gangs (see Chapter 4),[50] and Lewis Yablonsky's research led him to conclude in 1962 that there were delinquent, violent, and social gangs.[51] More recently, Carl S. Taylor,[52] C. Ronald Huff,[53] Jeffrey Fagan,[54] and Malcolm W. Klein and Cheryl L. Maxson[55] found other types of gangs in the communities they studied.

Detroit urban gangs, according to Taylor, can be classified as scavenger, territorial, and corporate. Scavenger gangs have little sense of a common bond beyond

TABLE 10.1 Attraction of Gangs

Why Gangs Form	What Gangs Offer	Why Youths Join
Social discrimination or rejection	Acceptance	To avoid being discriminated against and to seek acceptance and a sense of belonging
Absence of a family and its unconditional love, positive adult role models, and proper discipline	Surrogate family	To be in a family and to have unconditional love, positive adult role models, and discipline
Feelings of powerlessness	Power	To overcome their powerlessness
Abuse, fear, and lack of security	Security	To reduce their feelings of fear and to feel secure
Economic deprivation	Means of earning money	To gain economically
School failure and delinquency	Alternative to school	To vent their frustration
Low self-esteem	Opportunities to build high self-esteem	To acquire high self-esteem
Lack of acceptable rites of passage into adulthood	Rite of passage to adulthood	To accomplish their passage from childhood to adulthood
Lack of legitimate free-time activities	Activity	To keep from being bored
Pathological needs	Setting in which to act out aggression	To vent their anger
Influence of migrating gang members	Any of the aforementioned	To get any of the aforementioned
Mass media portrayals of gangs and gang members	Any of the aforementioned	To get any of the aforementioned
Choice to follow in others' footsteps	Any of the aforementioned	To follow tradition and to gain acceptance
Ability to join	Any of the aforementioned	To get any of the aforementioned

Source: Adapted from Mike Carlie, *Into the Abyss: A Personal Journey into the World of Street Gangs* (www.faculty.missouristate.edu/m/mkc0961). Reprinted with permission from Michael K. Carlie.

their own impulsive behavior; without goals, purpose, and consistent leadership, these urban survivors prey on people who cannot defend themselves, and their crimes can be classified as petty, senseless, and spontaneous.[56] A territorial gang designates as a territory something that belongs exclusively to the gang, and one fundamental objective of a territorial gang is to defend its territory from outsiders. In doing so, this type of gang becomes the ruler of the streets. For example, a territorial gang defends its territory to protect its narcotic business.[57] The organized/corporate gang has a strong leader or manager, with the main focus of participating in illegal moneymaking ventures. Taylor concluded that "for the very first time in modern U.S. history, African Americans have moved into the mainstream of major crime. Corporate gangs in Detroit are part of organized crime in America."[58]

Huff's examination of gangs in Cleveland and Columbus identified three basic kinds:

1. *Informal hedonistic gang.* The basic concerns of informal hedonistic gangs were to get high (usually on alcohol and/or marijuana and other drugs) and to have a good time, and they were involved in minor property crimes more than in violent personal crimes.
2. *Instrumental gang.* The focal concerns of instrumental gangs were more economic, and they committed a high volume of property crimes for economic reasons; most of these gang members used drugs, and some used crack cocaine.
3. *Predatory gang.* The predatory gangs, which committed robberies, street muggings, and other crimes of opportunity, were more likely to use crack cocaine and to sell drugs to finance the purchase of more sophisticated weapons.[59]

Fagan's analysis of the crime–drug relationships in three cities identified four types of gangs. Type 1 was involved in a few delinquent activities and only in alcohol and marijuana use. Type 2 gangs were heavily involved in several types of drug sales, primarily to support their own drug use, and in one type of delinquency, vandalism. Type 3 gangs, representing the most frequent gang participation, included serious delinquents who had extensive involvement with both serious and nonserious offenses. Type 4 gangs had extensive involvement in both serious drug use and serious and nonserious offenses and had higher rates of drug sales. This cohesive and organized type, predicted Fagan, "is probably at the highest risk for becoming a more formal criminal organization."[60]

Klein and Maxson distinguished among five types of street gangs[61]:

1. *Traditional gang.* The traditional gangs, which have typically been in existence for 20 or more years, keep regenerating themselves. They tend to have a wide age range, sometimes including members from 9 or 10 years of age up to age 30 years or even older, and are usually large gangs, numbering a hundred or even several hundred members.

2. *Neotraditional gang.* The neotraditional gang resembles the traditional type but has not been in existence as long—probably no more than 10 years—and its members may number 50 to 100 (or even into the hundreds).

3. *Compressed gang.* The compressed gangs are small (usually 50 members or less) and have not formed subgroups. Their age range tends to be more narrow, with a difference of 10 years or less between the youngest and the oldest member.

4. *Collective gang.* The collective gang looks like the compressed type but is bigger and shows a wider age range—with perhaps 10 or more years between younger and older members.

5. *Specialty gang.* The specialty gangs narrowly focus their activities on a few offenses, and each gang comes to be characterized by its criminal specialty.[62]

A final typology is that of the supergangs, known as **People** and **Folks**, the two main groups of Chicago gangs. Beginning in the Illinois prison system at the end of the 1970s, Chicago gangs began to align themselves into the People (represented by a five-point star) and the Folks (represented by a six-point star). As of 1998, 31 Chicago gangs identified themselves as Folks and included the Gangster Disciples, Spanish Cobras, Imperial Gangsters, Latin Disciples, Latin Lovers, Braziers, Insane Popes, and Simon City Royals. The 27 gangs identifying themselves as People included the Vice Lords, El Rukns, Latin Kings, Future Stones, Gay Lords, Latin Lords, Bishops, and War Lords. There were also numerous factions within each major supergang.[63] For example, the Latin Kings had more than 13 and the Vice Lords had 11 different factions.[64]

People One of the two supergangs comprising the major Chicago street gangs.

Folks One of the two supergangs comprising the major Chicago street gangs.

Gangs in Schools

Schools have become fertile soil for violent youth gangs. G. David Curry and colleagues surveyed three St. Louis middle schools in 1996. Of the 533 respondents in the sample, 80 (15%) reported either currently or formerly being a gang member; of the 453 respondents who reported never having been a gang member, 260 (57.4%) reported at least one kind of gang involvement. With regard to gender, 55.6% of the girls and 59.1% of the boys who were never gang members reported some degree of gang involvement. With regard to race, 60.1% of the African-American youths and 37.5% of the white youths who were not gang members reported some degree of gang involvement. The authors' conclusion: The pervasive effect of gangs among middle school students in St. Louis was evident in the fact that the majority of non-gang members reported some level of gang involvement.[65]

In other research, R. C. Huff and K. S. Trump studied youth gangs in Cleveland, Ohio; Denver, Colorado; and southern Florida. They found that 50% of their

FIGURE 10.5 Percentage of Students Ages 12 through 18 Years of Age Reporting Street Gang Presence at School during the Previous 6 Months, by Urbanization and Race/Ethnicity, 2003

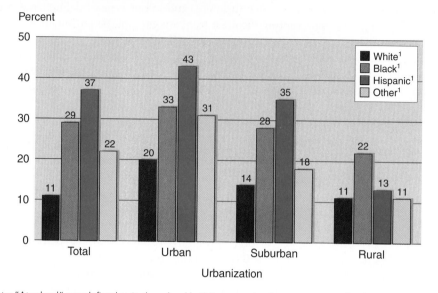

Note: "At school" was defined as in the school building, on school property, on a school bus, or in transit to and from school.

[1]"Other" includes Asians, Pacific Islanders, American Indians (including Alaska Natives), and students who indicated they were more than one race. For this report, non-Hispanic students who identified themselves as being of more than one race in 2003 (1% of all respondents) are included in the "Other" category. Respondents who identified themselves as being of Hispanic origin are classified as Hispanic regardless of their race.

Source: U.S. Department of Justice, Bureau of Justice Statistics, School Crime Supplement (SCS) to the *National Crime Victimization Survey, 2003.*

respondents reported that members of their gangs had assaulted teachers, 70% admitted that their gang had assaulted students, more than 80% said that gang members took guns and knives to school, and more than 60% claimed that gang members sold drugs at school.[66]

The violence perpetrated by gangs across the nation tends to vary from one school to the next, depending on the economic and social structures of the community, the gang tradition within that school, the gang's stage of development, and the extent of drug trafficking taking place. See Figure 10.5 for the percentages of students 12 through 18 years of age who reported that street gangs were present at school in 2003.

Gangs perpetrate school violence in a number of ways; for example, gang members are likely to bring concealed weapons into schools. George W. Knox, David Laske, and Edward Tromanhauser reported that high school students who are gang members are significantly more likely than nongang members to carry a firearm to school for purposes of protection.[67] Joseph F. Sheley and James D. Wright also found higher rates of ownership and carrying of firearms among gang members than among nongang members.[68] Furthermore, Charles M. Callahan and Ira Rivara determined that gang members are nearly three times as likely as nongang members to say firearm access is "easy."[69]

Gangs are also constantly recruiting new members, and nongang members are likely to be physically assaulted if they refuse to join. An African-American male who grew up in Chicago, went to college on a football scholarship, and graduated from law school told how he avoided gang membership: "They were always on me to join a gang. The only way I kept from getting beaten up all the time was to run home from football practice and to run to school every morning. I kept moving all the time, but I kept out of the gangs."[70]

Moreover, because more than one gang is typically present in a high school, conflict among gangs takes place on a regular basis. This conflict may be based on competition over the drug market, or it may relate to individual gangs within the school that are seeking to expand their turf. Fights may erupt in the school hallways, in the cafeteria, or during dances. Warring gang youths sometimes start a mass riot, with stabbings and shootings occurring during these altercations. The use of deadly weapons, of course, increases the likelihood of injuries or fatalities.

Finally, conflict among rival gangs in different schools also perpetrates violence. Fights commonly take place during athletic contests between competing schools. A drive-by shooting is the most serious violence that can erupt among rival gangs in the school setting. What usually occurs is that a gang youth is killed, and the victim's gang deems it necessary to retaliate, so before school, during lunch recess, or following school, a car speeds by, its occupants spraying bullets.[71]

A Portland, Oregon, high school head football coach told of an incident in which a group of Crips, dressed in blue, came speeding through the school's field house parking lot. His team was standing by him when he shouted, "Slow it down, fellas." They slowed down, pulled out a semiautomatic weapon, and pointed it at the coach and his team. The coach hit the deck and ordered his team to drop for cover. The coach said, "I thought I had bought the farm. Fortunately, they didn't pull the trigger. In my 20 years of teaching, I have never been afraid until this year."[72]

Gangs, Schools, and Drugs   Gangs in schools today have an economic base (drug dealing), which was not true in earlier years. By the 1980s, drug trafficking had become an attractive option, especially with the decline of economic opportunities for minority youths (see Web Extra 10.2). Jeffrey Fagan's study of gang drug use and drug dealing in three urban communities found the following:

> Drug use is widespread and normative among gangs, regardless of the city, the extent or nature of collective violence, or their organization or social processes. Serious and violent behaviors occur among the majority of the gangs.[73]

Elizabeth Huffmaster McConnell and Elizabeth Peltz's examination of gang activity in a Dallas urban high school found that drug distribution had become so extensive that the school required students to wear picture identification at all times in an attempt to control the number of "drug drops." Schools were an ideal setting for the distribution of drugs; mid-level distributors would come on campus, make their connections, and leave drugs with students who were street-level pushers, so a single stop for a mid-level distributor resulted in contacts with multiple street-level pushers.[74]

Gangs have a number of techniques for selling drugs in schools. In some schools, gang members prop doors open with cigarette packs and then signal from windows to nonstudents waiting to enter the building.[75] Some gang members sell drugs in the bathrooms, in the lunchrooms, or in parking lots. Daniel J. Monti's 1994 study of gangs and suburban schools told how one school's lunchroom had Bloods tables and Crips tables.[76] Gangs also use younger children in their drug trafficking: The children first serve as lookouts, but as they get older, they can become couriers (runners), who work as conduits between dealers and buyers.[77]

Web Extra 10.2
National Gang Crime Research Center (NGCRC) website

Urban Street Gangs

In urban settings, street gangs have become quasi-institutionalized and compete for status and authority within schools and other social institutions. Violence in schools and nearby neighborhoods has encouraged students to seek protection in gang membership. Youths hope that wearing the proper color and style of clothes and flashing the correct gang sign will keep them safe.

Urban gangs are sometimes able to effectively take control of schools, which permits them to collect fees from other students for the privilege of attending school, traversing the corridors, and avoiding gang beatings. Fear and intimidation keep both students and faculty from reporting gang activities to authorities. Many urban schools have had to adopt extreme security measures to protect themselves from gang violence and drug trafficking.

M. S. Jankowski contended that "one of the reasons that society does not understand gangs or the gang phenomenon very well is that there have not been enough systematic studies undertaken as to how the gang works as an organization," and he suggested that the most important organizational features of urban gangs are leadership, recruitment, initiation rites, role expectations and sanctions, migration patterns, and staying with the gang.[78]

Leadership   There are three types of gang leadership:

1. *Vertical/hierarchical type.* The vertical/hierarchical type divides leadership hierarchically into several levels, with authority and power being related to the position in the line of command.
2. *Horizontal/commission type.* Each horizontal/commission type is made up of several officeholders who share equal authority over the members and who share duties as well as power and authority.
3. *Influential type.* The influential types assign no written duties or titles to their leadership positions, but they usually have two to four members who are considered the leaders of the group and whose authority is based on their charisma.[79]

The most conspicuous example of the vertical/hierarchical type of leadership is found in the Chicago-based gangs. The best known of these gangs—the Gangster Disciples, the Vice Lords, the Black Disciples, and the El Rukns—have leaders who command great respect among gang members. Jeff Fort of the El Rukns (formerly Blackstone Rangers and Black P. Stone Nation), David Barksdale of the Disciples, and Larry Hoover of the Gangster Disciples are the three most legendary leaders of past decades. Exhibit 10.2 reveals some of the power that Jeff Fort had in the 1960s with the gang that was then called the Blackstone Rangers. The Bloods and the Crips, the two most notorious Los Angeles gangs, are representative of the horizontal/commission type. They are confederations among hundreds of subgroups or sets; the sets are formed along neighborhood lines, and most sets have 20 to 30 members.[80] Gangs in emerging gang communities, which are discussed later in the chapter, are examples of the third form of gang leadership, the influential type.

Recruitment   Gangs regularly go on recruiting parties, using three basic recruitment strategies:

1. In the "fraternity" type of recruitment, the gang presents itself as an organization that is the "in" thing to join.
2. The "obligation" type involves members who attempt to persuade potential members that it is their duty to join.
3. The "coercive" type uses physical and/or psychological pressure on potential members and threatens that either he or his family will be attacked if he fails to join.[81]

The recruitment of younger members is generally easy, because the life of a gang member looks very glamorous. Recruitment begins early in the grade school years; adolescent males are most vulnerable in the junior high years.[82] But even if a youth has enough support systems at home to resist joining a gang, it is very difficult to live in a neighborhood that is controlled by a street gang and not join. A gang leader explained: "You had two choices in the neighborhood I grew up in—you could either be a gang member or [be] a mama's boy. A mama's boy would come straight home from school, go up to his room and study, and that was it."[83]

Initiation Rites   Urban gangs have several methods of initiation:

■ A new member may be "blessed-in" to a gang. Those who are blessed-in to a gang usually have older brothers, fathers, mothers, or other relatives who are already in the gang.

> ### EXHIBIT 10.2

Jeff Fort and the Rise of the Blackstone Rangers

In 1959 a scrawny young boy by the name of Jeff Fort turned twelve years old in Woodlawn (Chicago) on the West Side. He and a few friends hung around the street corners, but nobody noticed. In the beginning they stole hubcaps and groceries, dividing the proceeds among themselves. The gang became the brightest light their young minds had ever dared to believe in, flickering through the darkness of the nights poisoned by danger, degradation, and despair. They were christened the Blackstone Rangers, and the light swelled brighter from its name alone.

Jeff Fort called twenty-one leaders to him, giving them responsibility and power, understanding intuitively that sharing his power would only make him stronger. They became known as the Main 21, but the gangs were well aware that they were the Enforcers. Bull, Mad Dog, Stone, Lefty, Thunder, Tom Tucker, Leto, Hutch, Bosco, Clark, Mickey Cogwell, Porgy, A.D., Old Man, Caboo, Moose, Dog, Crazy Paul, Bop Daddy, Cool Johnnie, and Sandman handled the problems that needed to be taken care of. The code dictated behavior. Punishment was meted out for not honoring the code. Everyone understood this. They could tell you to fight Louis, and out of sheer fear you would do it in a heartbeat.

Jeff and the Main 21 held meetings in the First Presbyterian Church at 6400 South Kimbark, where a large gymnasium held thousands of Blackstones. The Main 21 [members] were seated in a semicircle across the stage at the end of the gym. A microphone and podium were ready for the entrance of the awaited leader. He appeared out of nowhere, purposefully calm, controlled, loose, milking the crowd slowly, letting the heart rates increase steadily and build with the anticipation of what his next move would be.

He raised his fist, jerking it back hard, with power they all knew him to have. He yelled, "Blackstone," and together, as if one voice came from thousands of bodies, the thunderous roar resounded back: "Blackstone."

The spotlight circled the Main 21 [members]; then a second light appeared, dancing symmetrically with the first, increasing the rhythm, picking up a swaying motion that the bodies in the gym began to recognize and move to. A third spotlight flashed on, holding Jeff Fort in its sight, suggesting that the best was yet to come. It was.

Jeff, with his arms hanging loosely by his sides, began to feel the anticipation grow like a living thing. His breath quickening, nostrils [flaring], hair standing up on the back of his neck, his head slowly rotating back and forth [as he looked] across the crowd as if singling out each and every Stone in the audience, [his] piercing eyes [would hold them one at a time], looking directly at them.

In a deep, booming voice that sent static flying across the gym, he demanded, "Stones Run It!"

As if an electrical shock wave made its way through each nervous system, the brain registered a flight response translating to a simultaneous forward movement of thousands of bodies rising in a sea of exultation. There were thousands of voices singing praises to their master as they claimed, "Stones Run It!"

Jeff roared back, "Stones Run It!"

"Stones Run It!" they fired back.

Strangling the microphone, tap dancing to the energy bombarding off the four walls, Jeff screamed in a hoarse, rasping voice, "Blackstones!" moving the Main 21 [members] into action as they deliberately made their way down the stage onto the auditorium floor among the Stones, fists pounding in and out of the air above them, as if forcing it to perform with them, directing the Stones to thunder over and over and over again, "Blackstones, Blackstones, Blackstones!"

The Stones were literally everywhere in the late 1960s, incorporating other gangs into the nation like a confederacy under one flag. Known as America's most powerful gang, [its members] reveled in the notoriety acquired as a nation of Stones. Members were arrested for crimes ranging from reckless conduct and resisting arrest to armed robbery and murder.

> ▶ **Why do you think those who experienced this style of gang leadership responded with such enthusiasm? Why was Jeff Fort skillful in setting the stage for such a response?**

Source: Reprinted with permission from Linda Dippold Bartollas.

- A new male member more typically must be "*jumped-in,*" that is, he must fight other members. He may have to fight a specified number of gang members for a set period of time and demonstrate that he is able to take a beating and fight back, or he may have to either stand in the middle of a circle and fight his way out or run between lines of gang members as they administer a beating (under the latter circumstances, he is expected to stay on his feet from one end of the line to the other).
- A female is usually initiated into male-dominated gangs by providing sexual services for one or more gang members.
- A new member in some gangs is expected to play Russian roulette. Russian roulette involves loading a pistol's cylinder with one bullet, spinning the cylinder, closing it, pointing the gun to one's head, and pulling the trigger. If a player wins, he is in the gang. If he loses, well . . .
- A new member is often expected to participate in illegal acts, such as committing thefts or larcenies.

- A new member is frequently expected to assist in trafficking drugs.
- A new member in some gangs is expected to participate in "walk-up" or "drive-by" shootings.
- A new member is sometimes expected to commit a gang-assigned murder. Completing the procedure has sometimes been called a "blood-in" but is rarely part of initiation rites today.[84]

Role Expectations and Sanctions   A street gang's clothing, colors, and hand signs have traditionally been held sacred by gang members. In the world of gangs, warfare can be triggered by the way someone wears his hat, folds his arms, or moves his hands. Gang identity includes following codes for dress and behavior, making certain that the gang's name and symbol are scrawled in as many places as possible. Each gang has its own secret handshakes and hand signs, known as **representing**. Rival groups sometimes display the signs upside down as a gesture of contempt and challenge.[85] In recent years, however, urban gang members are much less open about their membership in an organization and are less likely to identify themselves by clothing, colors, and hand signs than in the past.

What has not changed is the expectation that members will be loyal to their gang (see Web Extra 10.3). Loyalty involves not giving up information about the gang to other gangs or law enforcement officials, doing what you are asked to do, and respecting other members (especially leaders) of the gang. If a gang member violates certain norms or expectations of the gang, he or she receives a violation. A violation usually means a physical beating; the second or third violation could result in the gang member being killed.

Migration Patterns   Another feature of urban gangs is gang migration, which can take place in at least three ways: (1) the establishment of satellite gangs in another location, (2) the relocation of gang members with their families, and (3) the expansion of drug markets.

Several studies have been unable to document the establishment of satellite gangs in other locations.[86] Maxson, Klein, and Cunningham, in surveying law enforcement agencies in over 1,100 cities nationwide, found that 713 reported some gang migration; the most typical pattern of this gang migration was the relocation of gang members with their families (39%), and the next most typical pattern was the expansion of drug markets (2%).[87]

Staying with the Gang   In recent decades, more juveniles have remained with urban gangs into their adult years. The major reasons for this continuation of gang activity into the adult years are the changing structure of the economy, resulting in the loss of unskilled and semiskilled jobs, and the opportunities to make money from the lucrative drug markets. Those juveniles who leave their urban gangs do it for many of the same reasons as other juveniles who mature out of committing delinquent behavior. Their leaving may involve the influence of a girlfriend, a move to another neighborhood or city, or the fear of arrest and incarceration in the adult system.[88] See Figure 10.6 for the major organizational characteristics of urban gangs.

Law-Violating Behaviors and Gang Activities

Despite the fluidity and diversity of gang roles and affiliations, it is commonly agreed that core members are involved in more serious delinquent acts than are situational or fringe members.[89] In the 2007 National Youth Gang Survey, most agencies with gang problems reported a decrease in gang-related crime (see Figure 10.7).

Gangs are increasingly using technology in the commission of crime. The most frequently reported use of technology involves cell phones with walkie-talkie or push-to-talk functions. Walkie-talkie cell phones enable gang members to alert one

representing The use by criminal street gangs of secret handshakes and special hand signs.

Web Extra 10.3

Mike Carlie's Into the Abyss: A Personal Journey into the World of Street Gangs

another to the presence of law enforcement officers or rival gang members. Gang members also use pay-as-you-go cell phones and call forwarding to insulate themselves from police; in addition, gang members make use of police scanners, surveillance equipment, and equipment for detecting microphones or bugs to insulate their criminal activity and to impede police investigations.[90]

Gangs are also making increased use of computers and the Internet. According to the *2005 National Gang Threat Assessment*, gangs use personal computers, laptops, and personal digital assistants to produce ledgers and maintain records of their criminal enterprises.[91] In addition, some evidence exists that gangs are using the Internet to track court proceedings and to identify witnesses; armed with publicly available records of legal proceedings, gangs can then identify and victimize witnesses. The Internet is sometimes used for soliciting sexual acts (a form of Internet-supported prostitution), and it provides a venue for the sale of gang-related clothing, music, and other paraphernalia; gangs are also using the Internet to become more involved in the pirating of movies and music.[92]

Studies of large urban samples found that gang members are responsible for a large proportion of violent offenses. In Rochester, New York, gang members made up 30% of the sample but self-reported committing 68% of all adolescent violent offenses, which is about seven times as many serious and violent acts as nongang youths.[93] A study in Columbus, Ohio, analyzed the arrest records of 83 gang leaders in the years 1980–1994; during these 15 years, the 83 gang leaders accumulated 834 arrests, 37% of which were for violent crimes (ranging from domestic violence to murder). The researchers theorized that violent crimes tended to increase as the gangs began engaging in drug activity and may have been connected to the establishment of a drug market.[94]

In the 2005 National Youth Gang Survey, a total of 173 cities with populations of 100,000 or more reported the number of homicides involving a gang member. In 2 cities, Los Angeles and Chicago, more than half of the combined nearly 1,000 homicides were considered to be gang related, and in the remaining 171 cities, approximately one-fourth of all the homicides were regarded as gang related. In 2004, the number of gang homicides recorded in these cities was 11% higher than the previous eight-year average. More than 80% of agencies with gang problems in both smaller cities and rural counties recorded no gang homicides.[95]

A final dimension of law-violating behaviors of urban street gangs is the extent to which they are becoming organized crime groups (see Library Extra 10.2). Scott Decker, Tim Bynum, and Deborah Weisel interviewed members of African-American and Hispanic gangs in San Diego and Chicago and found that only the GDs in Chicago are assuming the attributes of organized crime groups.[96] It can be argued that aspects of organized crime groups are

FIGURE 10.6 Major Organizational Characteristics of Urban Gangs

Library Extra 10.2

OJJDP Fact Sheet: *Highlights of the 2002–2003 National Youth Gang Surveys*

FIGURE 10.7 Changes in Reported Gang-Related Crime, 2006–2007

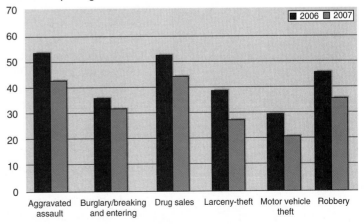

Source: National Gang Center, *National Youth Gang Survey Analysis: Gang Related Offenses* (Washington, D.C.: National Gang Center, 2008). Available at: http://www.nationalgangcenter.gov/Survey-Analysis/Gang-Related-Offenses.

found in such drug-trafficking gangs as the Bloods and Crips in Los Angeles, the Miami Boys of southern Florida, and the Jamaican Posses of New York and Florida. Beginning in the mid-1980s, these street gangs appeared to become criminal entrepreneurs, supplying illicit drugs, and in a brief period of several years, many of these street gangs developed intrastate and interstate networks for the purpose of expanding their illegal drug-market sales.

Gangs in Small Communities

emerging gang Any youth gang that formed in the late 1980s and early 1990s in communities across the nation and that is continuing to evolve.

Since the early 1990s, nearly every city, many suburban areas, and even some rural areas across the nation have experienced the reality of youths who consider themselves gang members. Thrasher's finding that no gangs he studied were alike appears to be true for these **emerging gangs** as well.[97] Curry and colleagues' 1992 national survey found that cities with emerging gangs reported that 90% of the gangs were made up of juveniles.[98]

This nationwide expansion began in the late 1980s and appeared to be fueled by four different situations. First, in some communities it took place when ghetto-based drug-trafficking gangs sent ranking gang members to a community to persuade local youths to sell crack cocaine; second, gang-related individuals operating on their own established drug-trafficking networks among community youths. Third, urban gang members whose families had moved to these communities were instrumental in developing local chapters of urban gangs, and fourth, youths in communities with little or no intervention from outsiders developed their own versions of gangs. The latter two types were less likely to become involved in drug trafficking than were the first two types.

Behind the first wave of nationwide gang expansion was urban gang leaders' knowledge that a lot of new markets were ripe for exploitation and that crack cocaine would command a high price in these new areas. To introduce the drug in these new markets, the representatives of most urban gangs promised the possibility of a gang satellite, that is, the emerging local gang would be connected by both name and organizational ties to the parent gang. However, urban gangs had neither the intent nor the resources to develop extensions of themselves in the emerging gang community, and the promise of being a gang satellite was only a carrot to persuade local youths to sell crack cocaine for the urban gang. The development of emerging gangs involved in drug trafficking throughout the nation has seven possible stages, and the degree and seriousness of gang activity in a community depend on the gang's stage of development[99]:

1. *Implementation.* The first stage begins when an adult gang member, usually a high-ranking officer, comes to a city that has no gangs. On arriving, this gang member goes to a low-income minority neighborhood where he recruits several juveniles to sell crack and be members of the new gang. The recruited juveniles are assured of a percentage of the money they make from the sale of crack; although the exact percentage seems to vary from gang to gang, it is typically about 10%.[100] The representative from the urban gang returns on a regular basis to supply drugs and pick up the money.

2. *Expansion and conflict.* In the second stage, the adult who came to the community tells the recruited juveniles enough about his gang that they are able to identify with it. They start to wear the proper clothing, learn gang signs, and experience a sense of camaraderie, yet their primary motivation is still to make money from selling drugs. One Midwestern youth claimed that he was making $40,000 a month selling crack for the Unknown Vice Lords when he was arrested and institutionalized.[101] Conflict inevitably arises as drug-trafficking gangs attempt to expand their markets, usually in the same neighborhoods. Fights may break out during school functions, at athletic events and shopping centers, and in parks and other common gathering places. Weapons may be used at this time, and the number of weapons increases dramatically in the community.

3. *Organization and consolidation.* In stage 3, youths identifying with a certain gang attempt to develop a group culture. The leadership is assumed by one or more members of the core group as well as by young adult males from the community. The increased visibility of the gang attracts a sizable number of "wannabes." The gang may be larger but is still relatively unorganized, consisting primarily of a group of males hanging around together. Recruitment is emphasized, and considerable pressure is put on young minority males to join the gang. One of these males noted, "If you are black, age 12 or so, they really put pressure on you to join. It's hard not to."[102]

4. *Gang intimidation and community reaction.* Several events typically take place during stage 4. Some whites join the minority gangs, and other whites form gangs of their own. One youth represented the spirit of this white reaction when he said, "The blacks ain't going to push us around."[103] Minority gangs are still more likely to wear their colors and to demonstrate gang affiliation. Drugs are also increasingly sold in the school environment, and gang control becomes a serious problem in the school. A high school teacher expressed her concern: "I've never had any trouble teaching in this school. Now, with these gang kids, I'm half afraid to come to school. It's becoming a very serious situation."[104] Gangs become more visible in shopping centers, and older people begin to experience some fear of shopping when gang youths are present. Equally disturbing—and much more serious in the long run—is that gangs become popular among children in middle school, with some allegiance being given to gangs among young children in first and second grades.

5. *Expansion of drug markets.* Drugs are openly sold in junior and senior high schools, on street corners, and in shopping centers during the fifth stage. Crack houses are present in some minority neighborhoods. Extortion of students and victimization of both teachers and students take place frequently in the public schools. The gangs are led by adults who remain in the community, the organizational structure is more highly developed, and the number of gang members shows a significant increase. Outsiders have been present all along, but during this stage they seem to be continually coming into and going out of the community. Men in their mid-twenties roll into the community driving high-status automobiles, wearing expensive clothes and jewelry, and flashing impressive rolls of money.

6. *Gang takeover.* Communities that permit the gangs to develop to stage 6 discover that gangs are clearly in control in minority neighborhoods, in the schools, at school events, and in shopping centers. The criminal operations of gangs also become more varied and now include robberies, burglaries, aggravated assaults, and rapes. Drive-by shootings begin to occur on a regular basis, and citizens' fear of gangs increases dramatically. The police, whose gang units usually number several officers, typically express an inability to control drug trafficking and violence.

7. *Community deterioration.* The final stage is characterized by the deterioration of social institutions and the community itself because of gang control. Citizens move out of the city, stay away from shopping centers, and find safer schools for their children. When an emerging gang community arrives at this stage of deterioration, it is fully experiencing the gang problems of urban communities.

In sum, while a community's reaction greatly affects the seriousness of the problem, nongang and sometimes low-crime communities across the nation in the late 1980s and early 1990s began to experience the development of gangs. These emerging gangs developed along different trajectories, but the most toxic to a community was the process that would take hold when ghetto-based drug-trafficking gang members were able to persuade minority youths to sell crack cocaine for them, and these youths, in turn, developed what they thought would be a satellite to the parent gang.

Racial and Ethnic Gangs

Hispanic/Latino, African-American, Asian, white, and Native American gangs constitute the basic types of racial and ethnic gangs in the United States. Hispanic/Latino and African-American gangs are generally more numerous and have more members

FIGURE 10.8 Race/Ethnicity of Gang Members, 1996, 1998, 1999, and 2001

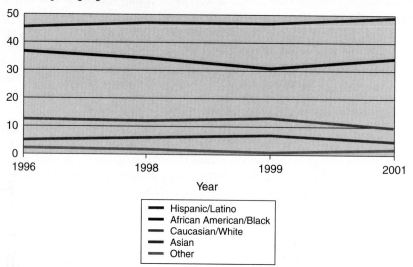

Source: Arlen Egley Jr., James C. Howell, and Aline K. Major, *National Youth Gang Survey 1999–2001* (Washington, D.C.: Office of Juvenile Justice and Delinquency Prevention, U.S. Government Printing Office, 2006), p. 21.

than other racial/ethnic gangs. In 2001, due to the steady increase in the percentage of Hispanic/Latino members, these gangs approached nearly one-half of all reported gang members (see Figure 10.8).

Hispanic/Latino Gangs   Hispanic/Latino gangs are divided into Mexican-American (or Chicano), Cuban, Puerto Rican, Dominican, Jamaican, and Central American members. According to the *2005 National Gang Threat Assessment*, law enforcement agencies across the nation reported that the most prominent Hispanic/Latino gangs in their jurisdictions were the Los Surenos (Sur 13), Latin Kings, MS-13, 18th Street, Nortenos, and La Raza, with more than 50% of reporting agencies indicating that Sur 13 was present in their jurisdiction and nearly 40% reporting moderate to high Sur 13 gang activity (Sur 13 was found to be present in 35 states).[105] Hispanic/Latino gang members frequently dress distinctively, display colors, communicate through graffiti, use monikers, and bear tattoos.[106]

African-American Gangs   African-American gangs have received more attention in this chapter than any other racial or ethnic group because most of the ghetto-based drug-trafficking gangs that have established networks across the nation are African-American. For example, the Bloods and Crips from Los Angeles, the People and Folks from Chicago, and the Detroit gangs are all mostly African-American. African-American gangs usually identify themselves by adopting certain colors in addition to other identifiers, such as the common hand signs shown in Figure 10.9.

Asian Gangs   There are varieties of Asian gangs in California, including Chinese, Vietnamese, Filipino, Japanese, and Korean groups. The Chinese gangs, especially, have spread to other major cities in this nation, and some of the other gangs also are active outside California. Asian gangs tend to be more organized and to have more of an identifiable leadership than is true of other street gangs. Ko-Lin Chin's examination of Chinese gangs found them to be involved in some of the nation's worst gang-related violence as well as heroin trafficking, but unlike other ethnic gangs, Chinese gangs are closely tied to the social and economic life of their rapidly developing and economically robust communities.[107] A study of Vietnamese youth gangs in southern California found that these youths experienced much marginality but attained the American dream by robbing Vietnamese families of large amounts of cash that such families keep at home.[108]

White Gangs Until the closing decades of the twentieth century, most gangs were made up of white youths. Today, according to Reiner, white youths make up about 10% of the gang population in the United States.[109] However, student surveys generally reveal a much larger representation of white adolescents among gang members.[110] For example, a survey of nearly 6,000 eighth-graders in 11 sites showed that 25% of the whites said they were gang members.[111] In the 1990s, the West Coast saw the solidification of lower- and middle-class white youths into groups who referred to themselves as *stoners*. These groups frequently abused drugs and alcohol and listened to heavy metal rock music, and some members practiced satanism, which included grave robbing, desecration of human remains, and sacrifice of animals.[112] Stoner groups can be identified by their mode of dress: colored T-shirts with decals of their rock music heroes or bands, Levis, and tennis shoes. They may also wear metal-spiked wrist cuffs, collars, and belts as well as satanic jewelry. The emerging white gangs across the nation have used many of the symbols of the stoner gangs, especially the heavy metal rock music and the satanic rituals, but they are not as likely to call attention to themselves with their dress, may refer to themselves as neo-Nazi skinheads, and are involved in a variety of hate crimes in addition to drug trafficking.[113]

Native American Gangs Attention also has been given to Navajo youth gangs.[114] In 1997, the Navajo Nation estimated that about 60 youth gangs existed in Navajo country. Gang values have encouraged such risky behaviors as heavy drinking and drug use, frequently leading to mortality from injuries and alcohol. A small percentage of Navajo male youths were involved in these groups, and at most 15% were peripherally affiliated with gangs. Many gang activities involved hanging around, drinking, and vandalizing, but gang members also robbed people, bootlegged alcohol, and sold marijuana.[115]

FIGURE 10.9 Common Gang Hand Signs

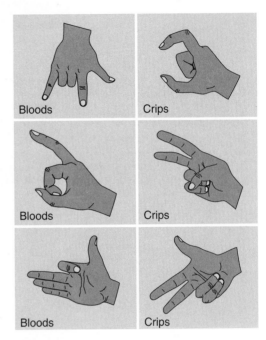

Source: Midwest Gang Investigators' Association, *Warning Signs for Parents* (n.d.).

Female Delinquent Gangs

Recent decades have brought increased awareness of adolescent girls who join gangs. Traditional sociologists once considered the female gang almost a contradiction in terms. A few studies have identified female gangs in Philadelphia and New York, with some of the gangs being extremely violent.[116]

A number of studies have found that adolescent females are connected to adolescent male gangs. The planning is done by the males, who usually exclude the females, but the female gang members would participate in violent crimes and drug-related gang activities.[117] Loyalty to the gang rivaled loyalty to the family, and most friends came from within the gang. The gang, according to J. C. Quicker, offered warmth, friends, loyalty, and socialization as it insulated its members from the harsh environment of the barrio.[118]

Finn-Aage Esbensen, Elizabeth Piper Deschenes, and L. Thomas Winfree Jr. found from their analysis of the Denver Youth Survey that girl gang participants committed a wide variety of offenses at only a slightly lower frequency than boys involved in gangs,[119] and Carl S. Taylor found that women were frequently represented in drug-trafficking gangs in Detroit.[120] Beth Bjerregaard and Carolyn Smith determined that involvement in gangs for both females and males was associated with increased levels of delinquency and substance abuse.[121] Joan Moore and John Hagedorn's 2001 summary of the research on female gangs reported that delinquency rates of female gang members are lower than those of male gang members but higher than those of nongang females and males; female gang members are also likely to be involved in property crimes and status offenses, they commit fewer violent crimes than their male counterparts, and they are heavily involved in drug dealing.[122] See Table 10.2 for gang-related charges for

TABLE 10.2 Gang-Related Charges for Female Arrestees in Chicago, 1993–1996

Offense[1]	Female Arrestees with Gang-Related Charge (%)			
	1993	**1994**	**1995**	**1996**
Violent (Total)	46.9	40.3	34.4	38.5
Homicide	0.2	0.1	0.0	0.1
Simple battery	17.6	16.1	14.1	14.9
Mob action	9.7	5.7	3.8	4.8
All other violent offenses	19.4	18.4	16.5	18.7
Drugs (Total)	36.4	37.9	44.4	37.7
Cocaine possession	14.3	9.8	8.8	2.6
Crack possession	7.0	11.6	13.9	15.6
All other drug offenses	15.1	16.5	21.7	19.5
Prostitution	0.8	1.5	4.1	9.8
Property	5.1	3.4	4.4	5.1
Weapons	3.7	4.3	2.5	2.8
Liquor	5.6	10.7	7.3	3.5
Other	2.2	1.7	2.7	2.3

Note: Percentages may not total 100 because of rounding. Total number (*n*) of cases per year: 1993, *n* = 2,023; 1994, *n* = 2,029; 1995, *n* = 2,021; 1996, *n* = 2,193.

[1]With the exception of vice offenses (drugs, prostitution, and gambling), authorities define gang-related offenses as such by referring to the motive of the offender. Vice offenses are considered gang-related if they involve a known gang member. Almost all liquor offenses involve underage drinking.

Source: Joan Moore and John Hagedorn, "Female Gangs: A Focus on Research," *Juvenile Justice Bulletin* (Washington, D.C.: Office of Juvenile Justice and Delinquency Prevention, 2001), p. 5. These data were drawn from special tabulations provided to the authors by the Illinois Criminal Justice Information Authority (1998).

female arrestees in Chicago from 1993 to 1996. Esbensen and colleagues' findings also failed to support the notion that girls involved in gangs were mere sex objects and ancillary members, and they also showed that girls aged out of gangs before boys and that girls received more emotional fulfillment from their involvement with gang activity.[123]

Jody Miller, in several articles as well as in her 2001 book, *One of the Guys*, has contributed to what is known about gender dynamics in gangs.[124] From research conducted in St. Louis, Missouri and Columbus, Ohio, Miller found that a female in a mixed-gender gang, an environment that supports gender hierarchies and the exploitation of young women, must learn to negotiate to survive in the gang milieu.[125] Gang involvement does expose young women to risks of victimization. Young women can choose to be "one of the guys" and expose themselves to higher risks of being arrested, injured, or even killed in conflicts with rival gangs, or they can use gender to decrease their risk of being harmed by not participating in "masculine" activities such as fighting and committing crime; however, females who opt out of violence and crime are then viewed as lesser members and may expose themselves to greater risks of victimization within their gangs.[126]

In sum, most studies found that female gangs still serve as adjuncts to male gangs, yet an increasing number of important studies show that female gangs provide girls with the necessary skills to survive in their harsh communities while allowing them a temporary escape from the dismal future awaiting them.[127] What these studies revealed is that females join gangs for the same basic reasons that males do—and share with males in their neighborhood the hopelessness and powerlessness of the urban underclass.[128]

Theories of Gang Formation

The classical theories about the origins of juvenile gangs and gang delinquency date from research done in the 1950s and were formulated by Herbert A. Bloch and Arthur Niederhoffer; Richard Cloward and Lloyd Ohlin; and Albert Cohen, Walter B. Miller, and Lewis Yablonsky.

Three Hispanic female 18th Street gang members strike a pose in South Central Los Angeles.
▶ What roles do females play in street gangs?

Bloch and Niederhoffer's theory was based on the idea that joining a gang is part of the experience male adolescents need to grow up to adulthood, so the basic function of the gang is to provide a substitute for the formalized puberty rites that are found in other societies.[129] Cloward and Ohlin's theory used the notion that lower-class boys interact with and gain support from other alienated individuals and that these youngsters pursue illegitimate means to achieve the success they cannot gain through legitimate means.[130] Cohen's theory stated that gang delinquency represents a subcultural and collective solution to the problem that faces lower-class boys of acquiring status when they find themselves evaluated according to middle-class values in the schools.[131] Miller held that there is a definite lower-class culture and that gang behavior is an expression of that culture; he saw gang leadership as based mainly on smartness and toughness and viewed the gang as very cohesive and highly conforming to delinquent norms.[132] Finally, Yablonsky suggested that violent delinquent gangs arise out of certain conditions, which are found in urban slums, that encourage the development of the sociopathic personality in adolescents, and such sociopathic individuals become the core leadership of these gangs.[133]

These classical theories of gangs focused on sociological variables such as strain (Cloward and Ohlin), subcultural affiliation (Miller and Cohen), and social disorganization (Yablonsky). Cohen, Cloward and Ohlin, and Miller also stressed the importance of the peer group for gang membership.[134] Each of the five theories of gang formation has received both support and criticism, but research into current expressions of gang activity is needed, because the existing theories were based primarily on 1950s gangs.[135]

Other theories of gangs are associated with social disorganization theory.[136] This theory is based on the assumptions that poor economic conditions cause social disorganization, that there is a deficiency of social control, and that this lack of social control leads to gang formation and involvement because youths in low-income neighborhoods seek the social order and security that gangs offer.[137]

More recently, underclass theory has been widely used to explain the origins of gangs.[138] In the midst of big-city ghettos and barrios filled with poverty and deprivation, it is argued, gangs are a normal response to an abnormal social setting.[139] Part of the underclass's plight, according to Fagan, is being permanently excluded from participating in mainstream labor market occupations, so members of the underclass are forced to rely on other economic alternatives, such as low-paying temporary jobs, part-time jobs, some form of welfare, or involvement in drug trafficking, prostitution, muggings, and extortion.[140] Hagedorn documented the loss of manufacturing jobs in Milwaukee during the 1980s, resulting in an increasingly segmented labor force in which minorities were consigned low-wage or even part-time work, welfare, and the illegal economy.[141] Vigil found that people who join gangs are pushed into these groups by their condition of poverty and their status as minorities—marginal to the wider society, their communities, and their families, they are subject to difficulties in all areas, and this multiple marginality makes them the most likely candidates for gang membership, because in a real sense, they have little else going for them—and he added that this "dialectic of multiple marginality [also] applies to why females now are more active in gangs."[142]

Jankowski contended that gang violence and the defiant attitude of young men are connected with the competitive struggle in poor communities and that being a product of their environment, they adopt a "Hobbesian view of life in which violence is an integral part of the state of nature."[143] The operations and survival rates of gangs vary greatly but, according to Jankowski's theory, can be accounted for by the interaction of four elements:

> [These four elements are] (1) inequality, and individual responses to reduce inequality; (2) the ability of the gang (both leadership and rank and file) to manage the desires and behavior of people with defiant individualist characters; (3) the degree to which a collective of individuals has been capable of developing a sophisticated organization to carry out its economic activities; and (4) the extent to which it has been able to establish ties to institutions belonging to the larger society.[144]

Moreover, Decker and Van Winkle stated that an explanation of why youths join gangs must be seen in the larger context of pulls and pushes.[145] Pulls relate to the attractiveness and benefits that the gang is perceived to offer a youth, and the benefits frequently cited are enhanced prestige or status among friends, excitement, and monetary profits from drugs. These personal advantages make gang involvement appear to be a rational choice. The pushes of gang membership come from the social, economic, and cultural forces of the larger society. Youths' experiences in response to these forces may include needing protection from other gangs, seeking an identity to overcome feelings of marginality, being recruited or coerced into gangs, or growing up in a neighborhood in which gang membership is a tradition.

Michael F. de Vries proposed that researchers need an integrated approach to understand why juveniles become involved with gangs, stating that for African-American youths, strain theory is "the heart of why African Americans find gang associations worthwhile." Gangs offer deprived African-American youths some opportunities to obtain status and financial gain that are denied to them in the larger culture. Asian immigrants, he argued, are also experiencing such strain: Although African-Americans are more "likely to engage in illicit drug distribution to counteract their inherited inferior position in society, Asians are more apt to engage in home invasions, theft, and intimidation as their way of coping with a similar strain." According to de Vries, subcultural theory appears to be helpful in explaining Hispanic gangs, which are largely separated from Anglo-American culture by their own traditions; he stated that "this subcultural group places a high degree of value on an individual's prowess (machismo), territorial identity, pride, and loyalty to their own group identity." Control theory, especially for middle-class whites, helps explain why these youths become involved in gang activity—social bonds are coming under attack as the family unit is becoming weaker.[146]

Delinquency across the Life Course: Gang Membership

The life-course perspective offers a number of insights regarding the study of gangs and their members. The most basic is that gang membership can be thought of as a trajectory, with some youngsters entering this trajectory and some not. Those who do enter it stay for varying lengths of time and become more or less involved in gang activities and behaviors. If gang membership is conceived as a trajectory with behavioral consequences, why some people enter it and some do not is an important consideration. The life-course perspective is a reminder that the origins of gang membership are found in several domains, are multidimensional, and include childhood risk factors, the social structural position of the family, family relationships, and unfolding influences of adolescence. Moreover, the life-course orientation suggests that for many people gang membership may act as a turning point with the potential to alter or redirect basic life-course pathways. Finally, the life-course perspective suggests that the duration of gang membership should intensify its consequences.[147]

Thornberry and colleagues contributed an important life-course orientation in their analysis of the gang behavior of Rochester youths as they aged into their young adult years. Following the sample in the Rochester Youth Development Study from age 13 to age 22, these researchers were able to separate selection effects (the extent to which delinquents seek out the gang) from facilitation effects (the extent to which the gang fosters delinquent behavior in its members). They have done this analysis for a variety of illegal behaviors related to gang activity, delinquency, drug use, drug selling, violence, and gun carrying and use and have found that gang membership seems to have a pronounced impact on facilitating all of these behaviors.[148]

Thornberry and colleagues also explored the longer-term consequences of joining a street gang. Does involvement in this strongly deviant form of adolescent social networks exact a toll in the later life of the person, or is gang membership merely a transitory adolescent phenomenon with few (if any) long-term consequences? The researchers concluded that "gang membership appears to have a pernicious impact on many aspects of life-course development. In addition, while the pattern of onset and duration of gang membership varies somewhat by gender, it has negative impacts on the life course of adolescent girls, as it does on adolescent boys."[149]

Delinquency and Social Policy: Prevention and Control of Youth Gangs

Surveys of youth gangs across the nation reveal that the numbers of gangs and gang members were decreasing but now are starting to rise again. There is no question that youth gangs are still a serious social problem. Gang involvement affects the quality of life for many youngsters and for most communities across the United States.

Even when gang youths are causing considerable problems at schools and in neighborhoods, communities across the nation have a tendency to deny that they have gangs.[150] Then if a dramatic incident occurs—such as the killing of an innocent victim or a shoot-out in which one or more gang youths are killed—what began as denial becomes repression, or the collective phenomenon of making the gangs "invisible." Meanwhile, despite such efforts as establishing gang units in police departments (or increasing the size of existing units) and harassing gang members at every opportunity, gangs begin an inexorable process of intimidation and terror that ultimately touches all aspects of community life.

Another reason for seeking successful interventions is that gangs are destructive to their members. Gangs that originate as play groups frequently become involved in dangerous, even deadly, games. Joining a gang may be a normal rite of passage for a youth, but gangs minister poorly to such basic adolescent needs as preparation for marriage, employment, and adaptation to the adult world. Adolescent males who join gangs for protection are often exposed to dangers that most nongang youths are able to avoid, and adolescent females who join because they are attracted to male members are often sexually exploited. Gang members are more likely both to commit delinquent acts and to become victims of crime than are youths who do not join gangs.[151] Finally, joining a gang may provide status and esteem in the present, but gang membership frequently leads to incarceration in juvenile and/or adult facilities.

Irving Spergel and colleagues' report on 45 cities with gang problems identified five strategies of intervention: (1) community organization, mobilization, and networking; (2) social intervention, focusing on individual behavioral and value change;

Voices of Delinquency

Read "From a Latino Gang Member to a Teacher in an Alternative School." Why was this youth able to make the transition from a gang to a nongang way of life? Why is he so motivated to work with gang youths as an adult?

Video Gangs: Community Prevention

Library Extra 10.3
Solutions to Address Gang Crime

(3) opportunities provision, emphasizing the improvement of basic education, training, and job openings for youths; (4) suppression, focusing on arrest, incarceration, monitoring, and supervision of gang members; and (5) organizational development and change, or the creation of special units and procedures.[152] (See Library Extra 10.3 for additional solutions to gang crime.)

In examining the implementation of these strategies, Spergel and colleagues found that suppression was most frequently used (44%), followed by social intervention (31.5%), organizational development (10.9%), community organization (8.9%), and opportunities provision (4.8%).[153] Community organization was more likely to be used by programs in emerging gang cities, whereas social intervention and opportunities provision tended to be favored strategic approaches in cities with chronic gang problems, but only 17 of the 45 cities saw any evidence of improvement in their gang situation.[154]

Spergel and colleagues, in developing a model for predicting general effectiveness in intervention strategies, stated:

> A final set of analyses across all cities [indicates] that the primary strategies of community organization and provision of opportunity along with maximum participation by key community actors [are] predictive of successful efforts at reducing the gang problem.[155]

Spergel and colleagues expanded their approach into the Comprehensive Community-Wide Approach to Gang Prevention, Intervention, and Suppression Program. This model contains several program components for the design and mobilization of community efforts by school officials, employers, street outreach workers, police, judges, prosecutors, probation and parole officers, and corrections officers.[156] The Gang Violence Reduction Program, an early pilot of this model, was implemented in Chicago, and after three years of program operations, the areas assessed in the preliminary evaluation of this project—lower levels of gang violence, few arrests for serious gang crimes, and hastened departures of youths from gang activities—were positive among the targeted group.[157]

The program was later implemented in five jurisdictions: Mesa, Arizona; Tucson, Arizona; Riverside, California; Bloomington, Illinois; and San Antonio, Texas.[158] These sites initially undertook the process of community mobilization as they identified or assessed the nature and extent of the gang problem; they then planned for

Members of the Miami Police Department's Gang Task Force monitor the crowd at Little Havana's annual Calle Ocho festival. ▶ **What can the police do to combat the growing influence of street gangs?**

program development and implementation in a problem-solving framework. It was not long thereafter that they began to implement appropriate interrelated strategies to target gang violence and its causes while they continued to reassess the changing nature and extent of the gang problem. Their strategies consisted of a combination of community mobilization, social intervention and outreach, provision of social and economic opportunities for youths, suppression or social control, and organizational change and development.[159]

What these efforts by Spergel and colleagues demonstrate is that only an integrated, multidimensional community-oriented effort is likely to have any long-term effect in preventing and controlling gangs in the United States. Such gang prevention, intervention, and control models must have several components: (1) The community must take responsibility for developing and implementing the model; (2) the model must take very seriously the structural hopelessness arising from the unmet needs of underclass children; (3) prevention programs, especially in the first six years of school, must be emphasized; (4) supporters must coordinate all the gang intervention efforts taking place in a community; and (5) sufficient financial resources must be available to implement the model.

Chapter Summary

The relationship between gang membership and delinquency is clearly documented in the literature, with both incidence and persistence of delinquency being directly tied to a youth's gang involvement. This chapter also explains the following:

- Young people derive meaning from and have their social needs met through contact with family members, peers, teachers, leaders, and participants in churches, community organizations, and school activities.

- Some youngsters find little reason to become involved in law-violating activities, whereas others become involved with various forms of delinquent behavior—often through the negative influence of peers.

- Some delinquents, with frustrated needs and nowhere else to find hope, become attracted to gangs.

- For these youths, gangs become quasi-families and offer acceptance and status, as well as a sense of purpose and self-esteem.

- Youth gangs are widespread throughout the United States; even small towns and rural areas are contending with the problem of gangs.

- Although youth gangs are not a recent phenomenon, many of today's gangs seem especially violent, and more than a few are characterized by the widespread use of automatic and semiautomatic weapons.

- Although gangs have historically trafficked in illicit drugs, drug trafficking provides a central focus for many of today's gangs.

- Drug gangs, or those whose primary purpose involves trafficking in illegal drugs, are much more prevalent today than in the past.

- Youth gangs of the past often transformed into street gangs, particularly in urban areas, with control of each gang in the hands of adults.

- In some urban areas, juveniles now constitute a minority of gang members.

- Many gang experts say that gangs thrive because of the poverty and lack of opportunity facing those who live in many of our nation's urban neighborhoods.

- The hopelessness of inner-city environments makes drug trafficking attractive and gang membership desirable for many young people, even in the face of a high possibility of being injured, imprisoned, or killed.

- Grassroots community groups have had some success in working with gang members, but gang reduction depends on providing children of the underclass with more positive options than they have today.

Key Terms

"cold and brittle," p. 219
crack, p. 218
emerging gang, p. 236

Folks, p. 229
friendship pattern, p. 219
gang, p. 225

People, p. 229
representing, p. 234

Review Questions

1. Why are gangs so popular among young people?
2. How have street gangs changed through the years?
3. What are the main organizational characteristics of gangs?
4. How do various racial/ethnic gangs differ?
5. What are some different ways that adolescent females can become involved in gangs?
6. What are the seven possible stages of development that an emergent gang may go through? How does the gang's stage of development relate to the degree and seriousness of gang activity in the community?

Discussion Questions

1. Discuss the development of gangs in recent years in your community. At what stage are they? What gang activities are evident? If gangs have not yet developed in your community, analyze why this is so.
2. In your community or nearby communities, what activities are females involved in with male youth gangs? Are there any separate female gangs?
3. Why have adults taken over so many youth gangs? With adults in leadership roles, what roles are reserved for youths?
4. Why is denial such a favorite strategy of police chiefs, school superintendents, and public officials for dealing with gangs? How much has this strategy been used in the community where you live or in a situation you know of?
5. What do you think is the most effective way to break up street gangs?
6. Are there any ways in which gangs could have a positive impact on adolescents?

Group Exercises

1. You have an opportunity to work with eight male gang members who are between 14 and 16 years of age. You have decided to design the 20 sessions around the theme of hopelessness. What would you do in these sessions to help instill more hope in the lives of these young men?
2. A particularly heinous crime has been committed by gang youths in your community. The community, which has been in a state of denial, is now alarmed. Community leaders invite you to speak to a group of concerned and leading citizens to develop a community-based plan to deal with gangs. You gather some friends together and develop a gang-prevention and gang-control plan for that community. What do you think will be the main steps in the plan that you and your group develop?

mycrimekit™

Go to mycrimekit.com to explore the following study tools and resources specific to this chapter:

- **Practice Quiz:** Practice with multiple-choice, true/false, short-answer, and essay questions.

- **WebQuests:** Do web activities about gang-related topics.
- **Flashcards:** Use 8 flashcards to test your knowledge of the chapter's key terms.

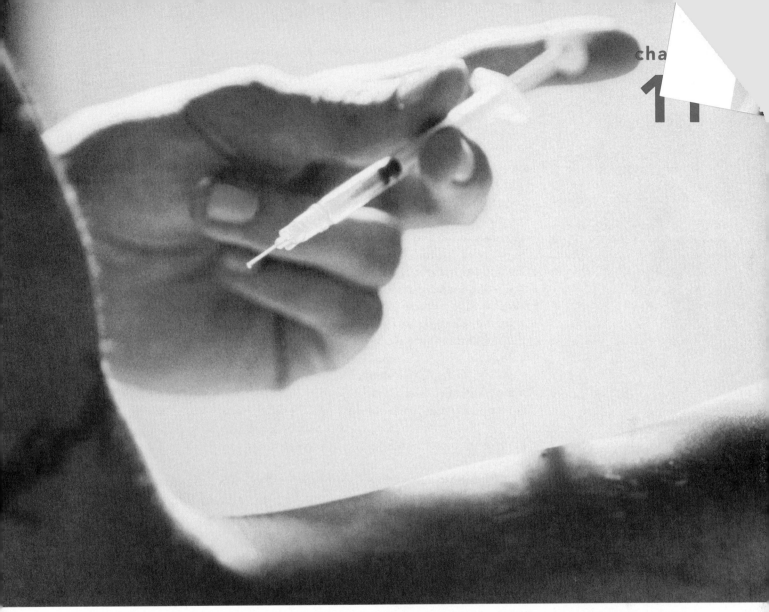

Drugs and Delinquency

For the foreseeable future, American youngsters will be aware of the psychoactive potential of many drugs and, in general, will have relatively easy access to them.

—*Monitoring the Future* Survey

CHAPTER OBJECTIVES

After reading this chapter, you should be able to answer the following questions:

- How are social attitudes related to drug use?
- How much drug use is there among adolescents in American society?
- What are the main types of drugs used by adolescents?
- What is the relationship between drug abuse and delinquency?
- What theoretical explanations best explain the onset of drug use?
- What can be done to prevent and control drug use among adolescents?

Introduction

Simon Curtis admits he led a reckless life in his early 20s in New York City, but he didn't think it would lead to two years in prison. Raised in a New Jersey suburb, he came to the city to study photography but said he ended up drinking too much, taking drugs, and making graffiti.

On July 14, 2001, at age 21, Curtis attended a photography show of Michelle Cortez, a friend he had a crush on. On a drunken whim, he pulled a $500 semi-nude self-portrait of Cortez off the wall and left, thinking it would be amusing to show it to her at a bar later that evening.

He was spotted, however, by the gallery's proprietor, Heather Stephens. She and her partner, Michael Delmonte, chased him out to a waiting SUV, driven by Curtis's friend, Sam Salganik. Delmonte jumped on the hood and Stephens somehow got inside. The vehicle drove away at 50 miles per hour, with Delmonte banging so hard that he cracked the windshield. Salganik stopped, got out, and repeatedly punched Delmonte, as Curtis looked on and Stephens ran away.

Curtis and Salganik were arrested and Salganik was sentenced to six months in prison and five years' probation, but Curtis skipped court. When police picked him up nearly two years later for making graffiti, he was finally called to account. Due to the violent nature of the theft, Curtis was found guilty of robbery, rather than larceny, and he began serving a one- to three-year sentence in an upstate prison.

"I've wasted a lot of time," Curtis said in May 2005, just before he was due for parole. As to his future, "I'm trying to get a plan together," he said.[1]

At 31 years of age, Simon Curtis's reckless life—involving years pursuing drugs, alcohol, and dubious fame as a storied graffiti artist—caught up with him. Released from state prison at age 35, life-course theory would suggest that he could make the best of his prison experience, see it as a turning point, and reorient his life. Should that not happen, he might continue abusing alcohol and drugs and become involved in additional destructive activities, which would likely mean that he'd suffer the consequences of those behavioral choices for the rest of his life.

Drug and alcohol use and juvenile delinquency have been identified as the most serious problem behaviors of adolescents.[2] The good news is that substance abuse among adolescents has dropped dramatically since the late 1970s; the bad news is that drug use has significantly increased among high-risk youths and is becoming commonly linked to juvenile law-breaking. More juveniles are also selling drugs than ever before in the history of the United States. Furthermore, the spread of AIDS within populations of intravenous drug users and their sex partners adds to the gravity of the substance abuse problem.[3]

Young people usually prefer substances that are not too costly. Beer and marijuana meet this criterion better than hard drugs do. Availability and potency are also important in drug use, for the substances are generally used as a means to other ends, such as achieving excitement. For example, marijuana and alcohol are used at rock concerts, parties, dances, football games, and outings to add to the excitement that is already present in such activities or to produce excitement when it seems to be lacking. In addition to enhancing excitement, substances can promote exploring new social spheres, sexual relationships, and unfamiliar places. Users also ingest narcotic substances to escape or retreat from the external world into a private inner self.

There is a difference between drug use and drug abuse. Drug use can be viewed as a continuum that begins with nonuse and includes experimental use, culturally endorsed use, recreational use, and compulsive use.[4] As an example of culturally endorsed use, peyote has been used sacramentally in the Native American church for centuries, and 23 states exempt this sacramental use of peyote from criminal penalties.[5]

Adolescent drug use becomes abuse only when the user becomes dysfunctional (e.g., is unable to attend or perform in school or to maintain social and family relationships; exhibits dangerous, reckless, or aggressive behavior; or endangers his or her health). The drug-dependent compulsive user's life usually revolves around obtaining, maintaining, and using a supply of drugs.[6] And as this chapter will show, drug use not only causes harm in itself but also is closely linked to delinquency.

Drug Use among Adolescents

Society focuses on youths' use of harder drugs, although alcohol remains the drug of choice for most adolescents (see Library Extra 11.1). Drug use among adolescents was extremely high during the late 1960s and into the 1970s, reaching epidemic proportions. Overall rates of illicit drug use appeared to peak sometime around 1979 and then leveled off, but even with the leveling off that took place, rates of illicit drug use among youths remained high for some time. Then, in 2001, there was a significant downturn in drug-use levels.[7] According to the 2007 *Monitoring the Future* study, overall illicit drug use by youths continued to decline further after 2001.[8]

According to the 2007 National Survey on Drug Use and Health, an estimated 19.9 million Americans age 12 or older were current (past-month) illicit drug users, which means they had used an illicit drug during the month prior to the survey interview, an estimate representing 8% of the population age 12 years or older. Illicit drugs include marijuana/hashish, cocaine (including crack), heroin, hallucinogens, inhalants, and prescription-type psychotherapeutic drugs used for nonmedical purposes.

This downward trend has also been evident for marijuana, although its use rose dramatically in the early 1990s. According to the Centers for Disease Control and Prevention, the use of marijuana among high school students has declined since 1999. In 2007, of high school students surveyed nationally, 40.2% had used marijuana during their lifetime, a decline from 42.4% in 2001 and 47.2% in 1999.[9] A similar downward

Library Extra 11.1
COPS publication: *Underage Drinking*

trend took place with cocaine, except that rates plateaued between 1979 and 1985 before starting to decline. Although cigarette use peaked in 1974, it did not begin declining significantly until about 1979. The highest rates of inhalant use were recorded in 1985, with slight reductions since that time. Table 11.1 reports the trends for several substances.

The results of this survey were quite similar to those of the 2008 *Monitoring the Future* survey, which found that 24.1% of twelfth-graders reported using drugs during 2003. Table 11.2 reports the 2008 percentages of students reporting drug use in the past month, in the past year, and over their lifetime.

Recent studies have shown a marked decrease in gender differences among drug users. Female high school students are slightly more likely than high school males to smoke cigarettes and to use some illicit drugs, including amphetamines; they use alcohol and marijuana at about the same rates as male high school seniors. Nevertheless, male adolescents are much more likely to be involved in heavy or binge drinking than female adolescents.[10]

The rates of illicit drug use in 2002 were about the same for white, African-American, and Hispanic/Latino youths. The highest use was found among those with two or more races—11.4%. American Indians/Alaska Natives had the second highest use (10.1%), followed by African-Americans (9.7%), whites (8.8%), Hispanics/Latinos (7.2%), and Asians (3.5%).[11]

In this 1871 engraving, a young boy is encouraged to smoke his first cigarette by two older girls while a shocked lady intrudes upon the scene. The use of drugs—both "soft" and "hard"—has a long history in our society, complicating efforts to identify the roots of modern-day drug abuse. ▶ **Why do people use drugs?**

TABLE 11.1 Percentages of Students Reporting Use of Specific Drugs, for Grades 8, 10, and 12 Combined, by Type, 1999–2008

	1999	2001	2008
Lifetime marijuana use	36.4%	35.3%	27.9%
30-day marijuana prevalence	16.9	16.6	12.5
Lifetime cocaine use	7.2	5.9	4.9
30-day cocaine prevalence	1.9	1.5	1.3
Lifetime inhalant use	17.5	15.3	13.1
30-day inhalant prevalence	3.3	2.8	2.6
Lifetime heroin use	2.2	1.7	1.3
Lifetime methamphetamine use	6.5	5.8	2.5
Lifetime MDMA (Ecstasy) use	5.3	8.0	4.1

Source: Adapted from Lloyd D. Johnston, Patrick M. O'Malley, Jerald G. Bachman, and John E. Schulenberg, *Monitoring the Future: National Results on Adolescent Drug Use* (Washington, D.C.: National Institutes of Health, 2009), Tables 1, 3, and 7.

Adolescents vary, of course, in terms of how frequently they use drugs and the type of drugs they use. The variables of age, gender, urban or rural setting, social class, and availability strongly affect the types of drugs used and have some effect on the frequency of drug use. Some users take drugs only at parties and on special occasions, some reserve them for weekends, and some use drugs every day.

Studies indicate that although fewer adolescents appear to be experimenting with drugs, those who use them tend to do so more frequently. Heavy users tend to be those who are male and white as well as youths who do not plan to attend college, and in schools, low achievers abuse drugs more than do high achievers.[12] Substance abuse is more common on the East and West Coasts than in the middle of the country.

In sum, although drug use among adolescents peaked during the late 1970s, rates of illicit drug use in this nation remain high, especially among high-risk youths.

Types of Drugs

The licit and illicit drugs used by adolescents, in decreasing order of frequency, are alcohol, tobacco, marijuana, cocaine, methamphetamine, inhalants, sedatives, stimulants (amphetamines and hallucinogens), steroids, prescription drugs, and heroin.

TABLE 11.2 Percentages of High School Students Reporting Drug Use, 2008

Student Drug Use	Eighth Grade	Tenth Grade	Twelfth Grade
Past-month use	9.7%	19.5%	24.1%
Past-year use	14.1	26.9	36.6
Lifetime use	19.6	34.1	47.4

Source: Adapted from Lloyd D. Johnston, Patrick M. O'Malley, Jerald G. Bachman, and John E. Schulenberg, *Monitoring the Future: National Results on Adolescent Drug Use* (Washington, D.C.: National Institutes of Health, 2009), Tables 1, 3, and 7.

EXHIBIT 11.1

Drugs: What's in a Name?

Drug names have been a source of confusion for many who have attempted to understand the drug problem. One drug may have a dozen or more names. Drugs may be identified by brand name, generic name, street name, or psychoactive category.

BRAND NAME

The name that a manufacturer gives a chemical substance is its brand name. Brand names are registered and are frequently associated with trademarks. This brand name identifies a drug in the pharmaceutical marketplace and may not be used by other manufacturers. Psychoactive substances without any known medical application or experimental use are not produced by legitimate companies and, as a result, have no brand name.

GENERIC NAME

The generic name is the chemical or other identifying name of a drug. Generic names are frequently used by physicians when they write prescriptions because generic drugs are usually less costly than brand-name drugs. Generic names are further used in most drug-abuse legislation at the federal and state levels to specify controlled substances. Generic names are sometimes applicable to the psychoactive chemical substances in drugs and not to the drugs themselves. For example, marijuana has the chemical tetrahydrocannabinol, or THC, as the active substance.

STREET NAME

Street names are slang terms. Many of them originated with the 1960s pop culture, and others continue to be produced in modern-day subculture. The street names for marijuana, cocaine, methamphetamine, and heroin are found in this chapter.

PSYCHOACTIVE CATEGORY

Psychoactive drugs are categorized according to their effects on the human mind. Stimulants, narcotics, depressants, and hallucinogens are typical psychoactive categories.

EXAMPLE

PCP and angel dust are street names for a veterinary anesthetic marketed under the brand name Sernylan. Sernylan contains the psychoactive chemical phencyclidine, which is classified as a depressant under the Controlled Substance Act.

Source: Frank Schmalleger, *Criminal Justice Today,* 9th ed., © 2007, p. 634. Reprinted by permission of Pearson Education, Inc., Upper Saddle River, N.J.

The licit drugs are those permitted for users who are of age (age 18 and older for tobacco and age 21 and older for alcohol); the illicit drugs are those forbidden by law (exceptions being drugs prescribed by a physician and marijuana in jurisdictions that permit the use of this drug). Exhibit 11.1 provides information on various drug names and categories. A number of illicit drugs take control of adolescents' lives when they become addicted. **Drug addiction,** according to noted drug-abuse researcher James A. Inciardi, is "a craving for a particular drug, accompanied by physical dependence, which motivates continuing usage, resulting in tolerance to the drug's effects and a complex of identifiable symptoms appearing when it is suddenly withdrawn."[13] See Figure 11.1 for figures on illicit drug use in 2007.

drug addiction The excessive use of a drug, which is frequently characterized by physical and/or psychological dependence.

alcohol A drug made through a fermentation process that relaxes inhibitions.

Alcohol and Tobacco

The reaction to Prohibition fostered the view of alcohol use as acceptable behavior that should be free from legal controls because the public did not perceive alcohol as a dangerous drug then (nor does it now). What makes **alcohol** so dangerous is that it relaxes inhibitions, and adolescents participate in risky behavior while under its influence. Adolescents' alcohol use can be linked to property destruction, fights, academic failure, occupation problems, and conflict with law enforcement officials.[14] Youths who are

FIGURE 11.1 Past-Month Illicit Drug Use among Persons Age 12 or Older: 2007

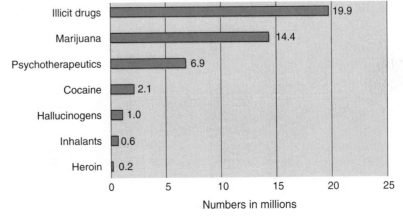

Source: Department of Health and Human Services, *Results from the 2007 National Survey on Drug Use and Health* (Washington, D.C.: Department of Health and Human Services, 2008), p. 16.

Voices of Delinquency

Read "Feeding the Monster." How did the addiction to alcohol and drugs control this person's life? The individual described in this story may be the best student that one of the authors ever had. How could such a capable person spend most of his life fighting addictions?

mycrimekit

marijuana The most frequently used illicit drug; usually smoked, it consists of dried hemp leaves and buds.

under the influence of alcohol may commit delinquent acts that they otherwise would not (see Web Extra 11.1).

The seriousness of alcohol use among adolescents can be seen in the data from the 2008 *Monitoring the Future*. According to this study, binge drinking (five or more drinks in a row during the prior two-week interval) peaked in 1979, held steady for a few years, and then declined substantially, from 41% in 1983 to a low of 28% in 1992, which represented a drop of almost one-third in binge drinking. In the 1990s, due to the rise of illicit drug use, binge drinking rose by only a small fraction, followed by some decline among eighth-, tenth-, and twelfth-graders. By 2008, the proportional declines following the most recent peak were 40%, 34%, and 22% for grades 8, 10, and 12, respectively.[15]

TV programs depicting the abuse of alcohol by adolescents, TV commercials aimed at adolescents saying "It is not cool" to drink, and talk shows dealing with underage drinking are all expressions of this growing public concern. The organization Mothers against Drunk Driving (MADD), which takes a strong stand against both teenage and adult drinking, started in 1980 when a 13-year-old California youth was killed by a hit-and-run driver. The child's mother, stunned that the operator of the automobile was not only drunk at the time but also out on bail for his third drunk-driving offense, launched MADD and initiated a nationwide campaign against driving under the influence (see Web Extra 11.2).

The use of cigarettes by adolescents is also a national public health concern. Due largely to efforts designed to steer young people away from the use of tobacco, cigarette smoking has declined sharply among American adolescents since the mid-1990s: Between the mid-1990s and 2005, daily cigarette usage declined from 10% to 4% among eighth-graders, from 18% to 8% among tenth-graders, and from 25% to 14% among twelfth-graders. Moreover, the proportion of students who start to smoke has been falling sharply since the 1990s.[16] In 2005, 4% of eighth-graders, 8% of tenth-graders, and 14% of twelfth-graders reported that they had smoked cigarettes daily in the past 30 days. Figure 11.2 shows the past-year cigarette initiates among persons age 12 or older.

Tobacco use is often neglected in a discussion of drugs because nicotine is not considered a mind-altering drug, yet there is considerable evidence that tobacco users suffer severe health consequences from prolonged use and that they subject others to the same consequences (see Web Extra 11.3). A 2000 analysis quantified the major factors contributing to death in the United States and found that tobacco contributed to 435,000 deaths annually, whereas alcohol contributed to 85,000 deaths and all illicit drugs combined contributed to 20,000 deaths.[17]

Marijuana

Marijuana, made from dried hemp leaves and buds, is the most frequently used illicit drug. An interesting indicator of the popularity of marijuana is the number of street terms that have been used to designate the substance: *A-bomb, Acapulco Gold, African black, ashes, aunt mary, baby, bammy, birdwood, California red, Colombian gold, dope, giggleweed, golden leaf, grass, hay, joints, Mexican brown, Mexican green, Panama gold, pot, reefer, reefer weed, seaweed, stinkweed, Texas tea,* and *weed.*[18]

Heated debates about the hazards of using marijuana have waged for some time. Research in the 1980s documented more ill effects of long-term marijuana use than had been suggested before. For example, several studies concluded that

FIGURE 11.2 Past-Year Cigarette Initiates among Persons Age 12 or Older, by Age at First Use: 2002–2007

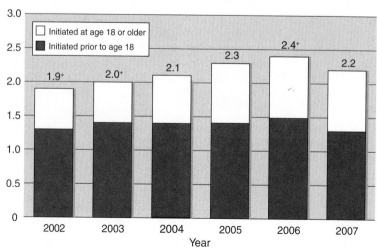

Numbers in millions

Source: Department of Health and Human Services, *Results from the 2007 National Survey on Drug Use and Health* (Washington, D.C.: Department of Health and Human Services, 2008).

EXHIBIT 11.2

A Risky Process

The following comes from an interview with a college student and former meth user, who recalls what it was like to use meth.

COOKING AND DEALING METH

Let me tell you about a drug I was addicted to for a long time. I even sold and manufactured this drug. Meth is made of common household products. Anyone can make it. It's really simple. You can buy the ingredients at Wal-Mart, hardware stores, and gas stations. When my boyfriend and I were cooking, we tried to play it smart, though. We'd buy ingredients from different people in different states in order to not get caught, because the authorities pay attention to people who make large purchases of the ingredients for the drug and would track them down. It is even worse now. If you go to Wal-Mart in my hometown, for example, and buy three things of drain cleaner or two packages of lithium batteries, your picture gets automatically taken at the register, and it is likely that the store will call the police on you.

The cooking process is complicated by the fact that you sometimes have to rely on a handful of people to assemble all the ingredients, and everyone wants a cut of the profit. One person might go to a farmer's field and steal anhydrous out of his tanks, another might buy ephedrine pills, and another might get the batteries or drain cleaner. If you do this all yourself, you increase the likelihood that you will get caught. Police are getting smarter all the time; they have even started setting up and monitoring anhydrous tanks on local farms.

Although it is made out of common household ingredients and is easy to cook, meth is very dangerous to make. I know people who have been burned and people who have had it blow up in their faces. It is really a risky process. You have to cover your face so that you don't breathe any of the materials; if you leave your face uncovered, you won't be happy (you will feel pain every time you breathe in). You also have to be careful what it touches. If any gets on your clothes, for example, it will burn holes right through your shirt, pants, shoes, or whatever fabric it comes in contact with.

Meth also stinks like mad when it is being made, which is why the Midwest and West are prime places for manufacturing the drug. With so many abandoned farmhouses, empty barns, and trailers and with so much land, it is much easier to find a safe place to cook. It would be virtually impossible to cook meth in New England because there is very little open space. If you were stupid and tried to cook it in a hotel or in your kitchen (as many have done), your neighbors would smell it, you would call attention to yourself, and it is likely that you would be busted.

As simple as it is, not just anyone can cook meth. You have to learn how. Most cookers learn by being "taken in" by another cooker/dealer. It usually works like this. You start using, you use more frequently, and you get to know the person you buy from. If the person you buy from is also a cooker and you can earn his or her trust or become a friend, he or she might show you how to cook. Once someone like that takes you under his or her wing, you are "in"—you are part of the inner circle. Being "taken in" is a very delicate process because meth makes people so paranoid. I remember thinking helicopters were following me, people were on my roof, and other crazy [stuff], and I always thought my friends were narcs. Everyone who used, cooked, or sold was constantly accusing each other of being narcs. This often led to violence in the ranks of the users—people getting jumped, beaten, stolen from, or threatened with guns or other violence.

Once you're in, though, once you're dealing, you don't want to be out. You have everyone's respect, everyone wants to talk to you, everyone wants what you have, everyone looks up to you, and you are making a lot of money. Add all of this to the physical addiction of the drug, and you might be able to begin to understand why people get "sucked in" once they are part of this lifestyle. This is what made it so hard for me to "leave the field." I was addicted to the drug and addicted to the money I was making. But when my best friend got busted cooking at age 20 (it was his first time getting in trouble *ever*) and got sent to prison for 91 years, I did not have to think twice—I have been sober and out of the "scene" for years.

METH AND THE "DRUG PROBLEM"

No one can deny that meth is a very serious problem in the Midwest. Kids here are into it. From what I've seen and according to national drug-use data, more people are using meth and the users are getting younger and younger. Anyone from upper-class kids to kids from the "other side of the tracks" is using it. Jocks, cheerleaders, debate team members, and drama club kids are just as likely to use it as a high school dropout. Meth is increasingly popular. It is not as popular as marijuana yet, but it is just as easy to get; it is everywhere. It is just as easy to get meth as it is to buy pot or to find someone to buy you alcohol if you are underage, if you know the right people.

Source: Personal interview with author.

---

marijuana smoking is a practice that combines the hazardous features of alcohol and tobacco as well as having a number of pitfalls of its own. Disturbing questions also remain about marijuana's effect on vital systems of the body, on immunity and resistance, on the brain and mind, and on sex organs and reproduction.[19]

Cocaine

Cocaine, the powder derivative of the South American coca plant, is replacing other illegal drugs in popularity. Street names for cocaine include *coke, lady snow, nose candy, Super Fly,* and *toot.* The major source of cocaine is Colombia, and its distribution is a major diplomatic issue in many Central and South American countries.

cocaine A coca extract that creates mood elevation, elation, grandiose feelings, and feelings of heightened physical prowess.

Voices of Delinquency

Read "Walking Away from Drugs Isn't Easy." Why does this person who graduated with a 3.9 grade point average from college say that it is hard to walk away from drugs? Why did she keep going back to drug use, regardless of the cost?

Cocaine is so expensive ($360 a gram on the streets according to the U.S. Office of National Drug Control Policy) that it is generally used in very sparing quantities. At one time, cocaine was believed to be less addicting than other illegal hard drugs, but users crave the extreme mood elevation, elation, grandiose feelings, and heightened physical prowess that cocaine induces, and when these begin to wane, a corresponding deep depression is experienced, so users are strongly motivated to use the drug again to restore their euphoria.

Snorting (inhaling) is the most common method of using cocaine, but freebasing (smoking) cocaine became popular in the 1980s. Freebase cocaine is derived from a chemical process in which the purified cocaine is crystallized; the crystals are crushed and smoked in a special heated glass pipe. Smoking freebase cocaine provides a quicker, more potent rush and a more powerful high than regular cocaine gives. Intravenous cocaine use also occurs, producing a powerful high, usually within 15 to 20 seconds. The method of speedballing (the intravenous use of cocaine in combination with another drug) intensifies the euphoric effect but can be quite dangerous.[20]

A less expensive but more potent version of cocaine—crack—achieved great popularity in the 1980s and 1990s. Crack apparently arrived in inner-city neighborhoods in Los Angeles, Miami, and New York between 1981 and 1983[21]; then it spread throughout the nation. Crack is known by users as *boulders, bricks, crumbs, doo-wap (two rocks), eight-ball (large rocks), flavor,* and *white (hard white).* Crack is most typically smoked in special glass pipes or makeshift smoking devices and is also smoked with marijuana in cigarettes, which are called *geek joints, lace joints,* or *pin joints.* A shotgun, which is secondary smoke exhaled from one crack user into the mouth of another, also provides the desired high.[22] Crack is frequently smoked in "crack houses," which may be abandoned buildings or the homes of crack dealers or users.

The addiction to crack by adolescent boys and young men can lead to abusive treatment of others; denial of responsibilities to family, school, and work; and increased rates of delinquent and criminal behavior. In addition to high rates of prostitution, other consequences of the addiction of adolescent girls and adult women to crack are widespread child abuse and child neglect and the toxic effects of crack during pregnancy.[23] The use of crack during pregnancy contributes to the premature separation of the placenta from the uterus, which results in stillbirths and premature infants, and infants who survive cocaine use in utero suffer withdrawal symptoms at birth and are at greater danger of stroke and respiratory ailments.[24] There is also a greater risk of sudden infant death syndrome (SIDS) among cocaine-exposed infants; such infants have a 17% incidence of SIDS, compared with 1.6% in the general population.[25] Furthermore, cocaine-exposed infants are more likely to experience emotional disorders, learning disabilities, and sensorimotor problems.[26]

Methamphetamine

Methamphetamine is a synthetic drug otherwise known by its street names: *chalk, crank, crystal meth, glass, ice,* and *meth* (to name just a few). It is a highly addictive stimulant, which can be injected, smoked, or snorted, whose effects last up to eight hours (with an initial rush at the beginning and a less intense high for the duration). This drug makes a user feel awake, aware, and happy but also agitated and paranoid. Methamphetamine is one of many of the so-called club drugs (see Exhibit 11.3).

According to the 2004 National Survey on Drug Use and Health, 11.7 million Americans over the age of 12 have used methamphetamine

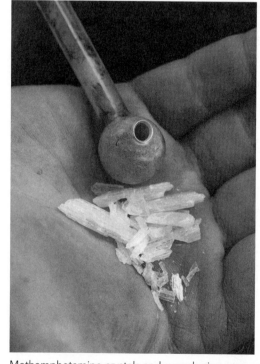

Methamphetamine crystals and a crack pipe are seen here. ▶ How much drug use is there among adolescents in American society today?

> > > **EXHIBIT 11.3** < <

Club Drugs

The term *club drugs* is a general one used for certain illicit substances (primarily synthetic) that are usually found at nightclubs, bars, and raves (all-night dance parties). Substances that are often used as club drugs include, but are not limited to, gamma hydroxybutyrate (GHB), ketamine, MDMA (Ecstasy), methamphetamine, and Rohypnol.

To some, club drugs seem harmless; in reality, however, these substances can cause serious psychological and physical problems, including death (see Web Extra 11.4). The raves where these drugs are used are sometimes promoted as alcohol-free events, which gives parents a false sense of security that their children will be safe attending such parties. But the effects of club drugs include the following:

- MDMA can cause a user's blood pressure and heart rate to increase to dangerous levels and can lead to kidney failure. It can also cause severe hyperthermia from the combination of the drug's stimulant effect and the often hot, crowded atmosphere of a rave.
- MDMA users may suffer long-term brain injury. Research has shown that MDMA can cause damage to the parts of the brain that are critical to thought and memory.

- GHB and Rohypnol are central nervous system depressants that cause muscle relaxation and loss of consciousness as well as an inability to remember what happened during the hours after the user ingests the drug. GHB and Rohypnol are often connected with drug-facilitated sexual assault, rape, and robbery.
- Ketamine is an animal anesthetic that, when used by humans, can cause impaired motor function, high blood pressure, amnesia, seizures, and respiratory depression.
- Methamphetamine (or meth) is a powerfully addictive stimulant that dramatically affects the central nervous system. Increased energy and alertness, decreased appetite, convulsions, high body temperature, shaking, stroke, and cardiac arrhythmia are all symptomatic of meth abuse.

▶ **Have you ever been to parties where club drugs were available? How do you explain their popularity?**

Source: In the Spotlight: Club Drugs: Summary (Washington, D.C.: National Criminal Justice Reference Service, 2004), pp. 1–2.

---

in their lifetime, which represents 4.9% of the U.S. population age 12 and older, and more than 583,000 (0.2%) reported using the drug in the past month.[27] (See Table 11.3 for the percentage of students reporting the use of methamphetamine in 2004 and 2008.)

The use of methamphetamine is growing. It originally was concentrated in California (especially in the San Diego area) but has widely spread to other states in the West and to states in the South and the Midwest.

Inhalants

Many types of **inhalants** are used by adolescents, but what these drugs have in common is that youths have to inhale the vapors to receive the high that they seek. One frequently used inhalant is butyl nitrite, commonly called *RUSH*, which is packaged in small bottles and can often be found in adult bookstores as well as on the street.

Web Extra 11.4

Clubdrugs.org

inhalant A volatile liquid that gives off a vapor, which is inhaled, producing short-term excitement and euphoria followed by a period of disorientation.

TABLE 11.3 Percent of Students Reporting Methamphetamine Use, 2004 and 2008

	Eighth Grade		Tenth Grade		Twelfth Grade	
	2004	2008	2004	2008	2004	2008
Past-month use	0.6%	0.7%	1.3%	0.7%	0.9%	0.6%
Past-year use	1.5	1.2	3.0	1.5	0.3	1.2
Lifetime use	2.5	2.3	5.3	2.4	3.4	2.8

Source: Adapted from Lloyd D. Johnston, Patrick M. O'Malley, Jerald G. Bachman, and John E. Schulenberg, Monitoring the Future: National Results on Adolescent Drug Use (Washington, D.C.: National Institutes of Health, 2009), Tables 1, 3, and 7.

Library Extra 11.2
OJJDP Fact Sheet: *Substance Abuse: The Nation's Number One Health Problem*

sedative A drug that is taken orally and affects the user by depressing the nervous system, causing drowsiness.

amphetamine A stimulant drug that occurs in a variety of forms.

Ecstasy A form of amphetamine (MDMA) that began to be used by adolescents in the United States in the 1980s and 1990s and is now rather widespread.

club drug A synthetic psychoactive substance often found at nightclubs, bars, raves, and dance parties. Club drugs include MDMA (Ecstasy), ketamine, methamphetamine (meth), gamma-butyrolactone (GBL), phencyclidine (PCP), and Rohypnol.

Other inhalants that are easier for young drug users to obtain are chlorohydrocarbons and hydrocarbons, which can be inhaled directly from gasoline, paint thinner, glue, or aerosol cans.

The use of these drugs brings about a feeling of excitement that is often followed by disorientation accompanied by slurred speech and a feeling of sleepiness. The use of inhalants can also be followed by mild to severe headaches and/or nosebleeds. Chronic use of some inhalants is associated with neurological damage and injury to the liver and kidneys.[28] See Library Extra 11.2 for more on the substance abuse problem among U.S. adolescents.

Sedatives

Like inhalants, many different **sedatives**, or barbiturates, are used by young people. The common factors among all sedatives is that they are taken orally and that they affect the user by depressing the nervous system and inducing a drowsy condition. On the street, they are known by the color of their capsule; for example, Seconal pills are known as *reds*, Amytals are called *blue devils*, and Tuinals are known as *rainbows*. Another popular sedative is methaqualone, which is known as *Quaaludes* or *Ludes* on the street.

Adolescents often abuse prescription drugs. Benzodiazepines (minor tranquilizers or sedatives) are among the most widely prescribed of all drugs. Valium, Librium, and Equanil are commonly prescribed for anxiety or sleep disorders, so to obtain them, some adolescents simply raid their parents' medicine cabinets. Adolescents can also get these prescription drugs from older teens or young adults or purchase them from Internet-based sources. The National Association of Boards of Pharmacy has identified about 200 websites that dispense prescription drugs but do not offer online prescribing services. According to a recent *Chicago Tribune* article that was cited by the American Medical Association, at least 400 websites both dispense and offer a prescribing service, and half of these sites are located in foreign countries.[29] Some adolescents have broken into pharmacies and stolen the drugs they want, whereas others obtain them through online trades in illicit clearinghouses called "pharms."

Amphetamines

Amphetamines were first made in Germany in the 1880s, but it was not until World War II that they were used by Americans. All the military branches issued Benzedrine, Dexedrine, and other types of amphetamines to relieve fatigue and anxiety, especially under battle conditions. Amphetamines became more readily available after the war and were widely used by students studying for examinations, by truck drivers trying to stay alert for extended periods of time, by people attempting to lose weight, and by people seeking relief from nasal congestion. Street names for the amphetamines that were used at the time included *bennies, black beauties, King Kong pills, pinks,* and *purple hearts.*[30]

In the late 1980s and early 1990s, methamphetamine (see earlier discussion) and MDMA arrived on the U.S. drug scene. MDMA, which was used by psychiatrists and other therapists because of its therapeutic benefits, had become a schedule I drug by 1986, which meant that its manufacture, distribution, and sale violated federal law, but it still maintained some popularity among undergraduate populations across the nation. In the 1990s, **Ecstasy**, the common name for MDMA, became popular on college campuses and with adolescents and was widely used at parties. Ecstasy is usually ingested orally in tablet or capsule form, is sometimes snorted, and is occasionally smoked; it is reported to produce profound pleasurable effects, such as acute euphoria and positive changes in attitude and self-confidence.[31] Ecstasy and various other substances are sometimes called **club drugs**.

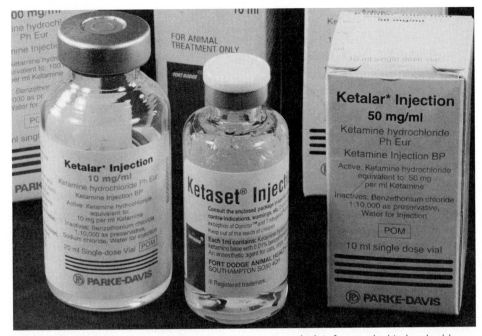

Pharmaceutical ketamine intended for injection. Ketamine, which is frequently dried and sold illegally as a powder for abuse, is a rapid-acting general anesthetic whose effects are similar to those of PCP. People who use it report feeling detached or disconnected from their surroundings.
▸ What other kinds of drugs are popular with young people today?

Hallucinogens

A parade of hallucinogens has been available over the years to adolescents interested in embracing mind-expanding experiences. Leading the parade in the 1960s was D-lysergic acid diethylamide, popularly known as LSD. Public antagonism arose in the late 1960s against LSD and other psychedelic substances, and its use dramatically declined in the 1970s.

Phencyclidine (PCP), a nervous system excitant which has analgesic, anesthetic, and hallucinogenic properties, was introduced in the late 1960s and became popular during the 1970s. First marketed as the PeaCe Pill, PCP was also known as *angel dust, animal tank, aurora borealis, buzz, devil dust, DOA, dummy dust, elephant, elephant juice, goon, rocket fuel,* and *THC.* Concern over PCP mounted during the 1970s, as its dangerousness became apparent.[32] In 1987, for example, hospital emergency rooms reported 8,000 incidents involving PCP, sometimes in combination with other drugs.[33] Use of PCP declined during the 1980s, with national samples of high school seniors who had used PCP at least once dropping from 13% in 1979 to less than 3% by 1990.[34]

Anabolic Steroids

Currently, 100 different types of anabolic steroids have been developed, and each requires a prescription to be used legally in the United States. Street terms include *Arnolds, Gym Candy, Juice, Pampers, Stackers,* and *Weight Trainers.* Anabolic steroids can be taken orally, injected intramuscularly, or rubbed on the skin in the form of creams or gels. Steroids are often used in patterns called *cycling,* which involves taking multiple doses of the drugs over a period of time, stopping for a period, and then starting again; users also often combine several different types of steroids in a process known as *stacking.* The reason for this, according to users, is that they believe the steroids will interact to produce a greater effect on muscle size than would happen using each drug individually.[35] A further method of steroid

TABLE 11.4 Reported Steroid Use by Grade Level

	Eighth Grade	Tenth Grade	Twelfth Grade
Past-month use	0.9%	0.9%	1.5%
Past-year use	1.4	1.4	2.2
Lifetime use	1.4	1.4	2.2

Source: Adapted from Lloyd D. Johnston, Patrick M. O'Malley, Jerald G. Bachman, and John E. Schulenberg, *Monitoring the Future: National Results on Adolescent Drug Use* (Washington, D.C.: National Institutes of Health, 2009), Tables 1, 3, and 7.

use is called *pyramiding*, a process in which users slowly escalate steroid use, reaching a peak amount at mid-cycle and gradually lowering the dose toward the end of the cycle.[36]

Results from the 2009 *Monitoring the Future* study, which surveyed students in eighth, tenth, and twelfth grades, showed that 1.7% of eighth-graders, 2.0% of tenth-graders, and 2.6% of twelfth-graders reported using steroids at least once in their lifetime (see Table 11.4). In terms of the difficulty of obtaining steroids, 18.1% of eighth-graders, 29.7% of tenth-graders, and 39.7% of twelfth-graders surveyed indicated that steroids were "fairly easy" or "very easy" to obtain.[37]

Anabolic steroid abuse has been associated with a wide range of adverse effects, ranging from those that are physically unattractive, such as breast development in men and acne, to others that are life-threatening. Although most of the effects are reversible if the abuser quits taking the drug, some can be permanent. In addition to their physical effects, anabolic steroids can cause increased irritability and aggression.[38] Furthermore, other health consequences occurring in both males and females using steroids include heart attacks, liver cancer, and elevated cholesterol levels, and those who inject steroids run the risk of contracting or transmitting bloodborne diseases, including HIV.[39]

Heroin

Opium, which is derived from certain poppy species, is the source of heroin, morphine, paregoric, and codeine, some of which are still used medically today. **Heroin**, a refined form of morphine, was introduced about the turn of the twentieth century, and its street names include *black tar, boy, brown, H, harry, henry, horse, shit,* and *smack*.[40]

Chronic heroin use, unlike the use of most other drugs, appears to produce relatively minor direct or permanent physiological damage. Nevertheless, street heroin users typically neglect themselves and, as a result, report such disorders as heart and lung abnormalities, scarred veins, weight loss, malnutrition, endocarditis (a disease of the heart valves), stroke, gynecological problems, hepatitis, local skin infections, and abscesses.[41] The danger of heroin overdose has for several decades marked heroin as a very dangerous drug; for example, the Drug Abuse Warning Network found that more than 20,000 heroin overdoses resulted in emergency room treatment each year and that 3,000 cases resulted in a stop at the morgue.[42]

Although individuals—especially people who have sensitivities and allergies to small amounts of substances—can differ in their reactions to drugs, it is obvious that the more drugs are used and the greater the frequency of their use is, the more serious the damage will be.[43] Table 11.5 provides a summary of the short- and long-term consequences of using alcohol and other drugs in adolescence.

heroin A refined form of morphine that was introduced around the beginning of the twentieth century.

TABLE 11.5 Consequences of Substance Abuse during Adolescence

Substance	Consequences	
	Short Term	**Long Term**
Cigarettes[1]		
Occasional Use	Vulnerability to other drugs	Excess morbidity, mortality
Frequent Use	Bad breath	Excess morbidity, mortality
	Respiratory problems	
Alcohol		
Occasional Use	None	None
Frequent Use	Drunk driving, leading to accidents, arrests, mortality	Alcoholism
	Impaired functioning in school	Cirrhosis of liver
	Family problems	Stomach cancer
	Depression	
	Accidental death (e.g., by drowning)	
Marijuana[2]		
Occasional Use	Vulnerability to other drugs	Inconclusive
Frequent Use	Impaired psychological functioning	Respiratory problems
	Impaired driving ability	Possible adverse reproductive effects
	Loss of short-term memory	Decrease in motivation
Cocaine[1,3]		
	Physical symptoms such as dry mouth, sweats, headache, nosebleeds, nasal passage irritation	Drug dependence
		Rhinitis, ulcerated nasal septum
	Loss of sleep	Hepatitis
	Chronic fatigue	Psychological effects such as depression, anxiety
	Feelings of depression	Convulsions
	Suicidal ideation	Social and financial problems
Multiple Substance Use[1]		
	Dysfunction	Drug dependence
	Dropping out of school	Chronic depression, fatigue
	Suspension from school	Truncated education
	Motor vehicle accidents	Reduced job stability
	Illegal activities	Marital instability
		Crime

[1]Adapted from M. Newcomb and P. Bentler, *Consequences of Adolescent Drug Use: Impact on the Lives of Young Adults* (Newbury Park, Calif.: Sage, 1988), pp. 219–222.

[2]R. Peterson, "Marijuana Overview," in *Correlation and Consequences of Marijuana Use* (National Institute on Drug Abuse, Washington, D.C.; *Research Issues* 34, 1984), pp. 1–19.

[3]Based on findings from a study reported by D. Chitwood, "Patterns and Consequences of Cocaine Use," in *Cocaine Use in America: Epidemiologic and Clinical Perspectives*, edited by N. Kozel and E. Adams (National Institute on Drug Abuse, Washington, D.C.; USDHHS, NIDA Research Monograph, 61, 1985), pp. 111–129.

Source: Adapted from Joy G. Dryfoos, *Adolescents at Risk: Prevalence and Prevention* (New York: Oxford University Press, 1990), p. 48. Reprinted by permission.

Web Extra 11.5
Office of National Drug Control
Policy website

Drug Use and Delinquency

An issue that has long been debated is whether drugs cause delinquency or delinquency leads to drug use or whether some other factors precede both delinquency and the onset of drug use[44] (see Web Extra 11.5). Considerable research has found that delinquency tends to precede the use of drugs.[45] Other research suggests that what might appear to be a causal association is in fact a product of shared antecedents.[46] It is possible that a common factor, or syndrome, exists that underlies both delinquent behavior and drug use; this common factor may explain the frequency and type of drug use.[47]

As previously discussed, a number of researchers have found that substance abuse is just one of an interrelated and overlapping group of adolescent problem behaviors, including delinquency, teen pregnancy, school failure, and dropping out of school.[48] Substance abuse, then, is one of the problem behaviors developed by adolescents during their early life course. John M. Wallace Jr. and Jerald G. Bachman summarized what is involved, using Richard and Shirley L. Jessor's "problem behavior" model:

> The basic theoretical structure of much present research can be subsumed under the "problem behavior" model posited by the Jessors. The Jessors' model is a comprehensive framework comprised of antecedent background variables and three systems of social-psychological and behavioral variables—the personality system, the perceived environment system, and the behavior system. The variables in the three primary systems interrelate to produce within the individual a greater or lesser proneness to become involved in problem behaviors. More specifically, the theory hypothesizes that young people who are less invested in traditional versus deviant behaviors, who are more strongly tied to peers than to parents, who are alienated from society, who have low self-esteem, and who hold unconventional beliefs, values, and attitudes are prone to become involved in problem behavior. The Jessors and their colleagues used their longitudinal dataset to test the theoretical model and found it to be quite successful in explaining adolescent problems—particularly drug use.[49]

In the early 1990s, longitudinal studies of high-risk youths in Denver, Pittsburgh, and Rochester also provided evidence of the overlap of substance abuse with other problem behaviors.[50] These three longitudinal studies found that substance abuse was significantly related to delinquency in youths regardless of race, that delinquent girls were at higher risk for drug use than were delinquent boys, and that delinquency was related to early sexual activity or pregnancy.[51] These studies concluded that "targeting delinquency and substance abuse simultaneously in intervention and prevention programs will more likely enhance the effectiveness of such programs in each problem area than will programs that focus uniquely on either substance abuse or delinquency."[52]

Other research has indicated large racial and ethnic differences in adolescent drug use, with the highest use among Native Americans, somewhat lower use among white and Hispanic youths, and lowest use among African-American and Asian youths.[53] In contrast, Delbert S. Elliott, David Huizinga, and Scott Menard's analysis of the National Youth Survey found no association between social class, race, and substance abuse: Although lower-class youths and African-Americans did have higher prevalence rates of serious delinquent behavior, whites had higher prevalence rates of minor delinquent acts and of alcohol, marijuana, and polydrug use; urban residents had higher rates of marijuana and polydrug use and were also more at risk of becoming sellers.[54] Wallace and Bachman found that controlling for background and lifestyle reduced or eliminated many of the racial and ethnic differences in drug use, and their data also revealed that several lifestyle factors, including time spent in peer-oriented activities, educational values and behaviors, and religious commitment, were strongly related to patterns of drug use and helped to explain the subgroup differences.[55]

Since the early 1990s, consensus has been increasing on the findings that explain the onset and continuing use of illicit drugs. First, there is widespread agreement that there is a sequential pattern of involvement in drug use during adolescence.[56] Denise B. Kandel and colleagues, using cross-sectional research and longitudinal data, proposed a developmental model for drug-use involvement: Alcohol use follows a pattern of minor delinquency and exposure to friends and parents who drink; the use of marijuana follows participation in minor delinquency and adoption of beliefs and values that are consistent with those held by peers but opposed by parents' standards; and adolescents' drug use proceeds to other illicit drugs if relationships with parents are poor and there is increased exposure to peers who use a variety of illegal drugs.[57]

Second, in examining drug use, it is important to identify in which of three major groups users belong. In the first group, youths or adults experiment once or twice and then discontinue drug use, whereas members of the second group continue drug use into young adulthood but do not allow drug use to interfere with their lives in any major ways; those in the third group become addicted or dependent on drugs, their entire lifestyle is likely to be designed around acquiring drugs daily, and they frequently commit crimes to maintain their drug supply.

Third, a number of risk factors appear to be related to delinquency and drug use. Early factors consist of perinatal difficulties, minor physical abnormalities, and brain damage, and later developmental risk factors are found in the family environment, including a family history of alcoholism, poor family management practices, and family conflict; other risk factors are early antisocial behavior and academic failure. Community risk factors include living in economically deprived areas and disorganized neighborhoods. According to J. David Hawkins, Richard F. Catalano, and Devon D. Brewer, the more of these risk factors a child has, the more likely it is that he or she will become involved in drug abuse.[58]

There is little debate that youths who use hard drugs are more likely to engage in chronic delinquent behavior.[59] Elliott and Huizinga found that nearly 50% of serious juvenile offenders were also multiple drug users, that 82% of these offenders reported use (beyond experimentation) of at least one illicit drug, that rates of alcohol use among serious offenders were 4 to 9 times those of nonoffenders, and that rates of marijuana use among serious offenders were 14 times those of nonoffenders.[60] Jeffrey Fagan and colleagues' survey of inner-city youths also determined that heavy substance use was more prevalent and frequent among serious delinquents but that the type of substance used was more strongly associated with delinquency than was the frequency of drug use.[61]

David M. Altschuler and Paul J. Brounstein's examination of drug use and drug trafficking among inner-city adolescent males in Washington, D.C., found that use and sale of drugs affected the frequency and seriousness of delinquent behavior: The heaviest users were significantly more likely than nonusers to commit property offenses, those who trafficked in drugs were significantly more likely to commit crimes against persons than youths who did not sell drugs, and adolescents who both used and sold drugs were the most likely to commit offenses against property and persons[62] (see Library Extra 11.3).

Library Extra 11.3
OJJDP Fact Sheet: *Assessing Alcohol, Drug, and Mental Disorders in Juvenile Detainees*

Drug-Trafficking Juveniles

Drug-trafficking juveniles can be divided into several groups. There are those who occasionally sell small amounts of drugs, usually to support their own drug appetites, but they commit few (if any) delinquent acts. They are most likely to sell marijuana to friends and classmates and usually avoid coming to the attention of the police or the juvenile justice system. Another group of drug-trafficking juveniles sells drugs frequently and may get their drugs from adult suppliers; they sell drugs in public places, such as on street corners, and are more likely to be arrested by the police and to be referred to the juvenile court. This group typically sells drugs independently of any gang affiliation, especially in suburban settings.[63] A third group sells drugs as part of their gang affiliation (especially in urban settings). Unlike the first two groups, drug trafficking within this group is controlled by adults, and participants in this group often end up in training schools or adult prisons. A student on academic scholarship in college told about his role in a gang's drug-trafficking operation:

> I must have been ten or eleven, and I was told to show up on this street corner. When I got there, they gave me a gun and told me to keep watch. If anyone came around, they told me to shoot them. They were taking care of business inside the crack house. Fortunately, nobody came around because I would have shot them. It surely would have changed my life.[64]

A street corner drug deal goes down. ▶ The text says that drug-trafficking juveniles can be divided into several groups. What are those groups?

Voices of Delinquency

Read "A Juvenile Drug Dealer." Why did this youth go from using to selling drugs? How could his life have turned out much differently?

Our understanding of juveniles and drug trafficking is heightened by Felix M. Padilla's 1992 book *The Gang as an American Enterprise*[65] and Daniel J. Monti's 1994 work *Wannabe Gangs in Suburbs and Schools*.[66] Padilla studied a Hispanic drug-dealing gang in Chicago and determined that this drug enterprise had an occupational hierarchy in which the cocaine and marijuana suppliers or distributors were on top, followed by "older guys," chiefs, and "mainheads." The street-level dealers, or mainheads, were juveniles who barely made a survival income and who usually had to supplement their drug income through stealing, yet they never quite got ahead because they would inevitably be arrested, the distributor would have his attorney bail them out, and it would then take them months to repay the distributor.[67]

Monti's examination of gangs in suburbs and schools focused on juveniles selling drugs. He found that gangs, especially the Gangster Disciples, had real control in the suburban schools he studied and that the Crips and Bloods were also represented in these schools. The drugs that were sold included marijuana, different types of pills, and some crack cocaine. The girls' involvement in drug trafficking typically consisted of holding drugs for boys, usually their boyfriends, when the boys thought they might be searched by the police or school officials. According to Monti, the youths who sold drugs kept the profits for themselves, not pooling their money with the gang; he also depicted drug dealing as a lucrative and exciting trade.[68] The chief effect of the so-called war on drugs has always been to make trafficking highly profitable. One interviewed youth commented:

> A third teenager from yet another gang was more deeply involved in drug dealing and gave no indication of leaving the trade. "It's an everyday thing now," he said. "[In one week] I made twenty-five hundred. At the first of the month you can make like ten thousand, because everybody gets their [welfare] checks then. They come to you and spend their whole check on it."[69]

Library Extra 11.4
National Drug Intelligence Center publication: *National Drug Threat Assessment*

Explanations for the Onset of Drug Abuse

As previously suggested, some adolescents never use drugs, others use drugs from time to time on an experimental or recreational basis, and still others go through a period of experimentation with substance use and become committed to continuous use (see Library Extra 11.4). This latter group is physically and/or emotionally addicted to the continued use of drugs.

There are at least two issues that can help us understand juveniles who use drugs. The first is determining whether it is the onset of drug use, the escalation of drug use, the addiction to drug use, or the cessation of drug use that is being addressed. We might ask: Why do some juveniles never try drugs? Why do some juveniles experiment with drugs from time to time but do not become addicted? Why do other adolescents go from the beginning stages of drug use to more serious stages? Why do still other juveniles become addicted to drugs? Why are some of those who become addicted able to quit, whereas other addicts seem unable or unwilling to terminate drug use?

The second issue is that there is no single comprehensive picture of what causes adolescents' use of drugs. Simons, Conger, and Whitbeck made this point when they said that "while research has established a number of correlates of drug use, no theoretical model has been developed which specifies the causal ordering of these associations and explicates their relationship to each other."[70] To express this another way, we might be aware of many of the reasons why juveniles become involved in drug use, but we do not know how all of the pieces of the puzzle fit together.[71]

The following sections specifically address adolescents' initial use of drugs by focusing on theories that attempt to explain substance use among adolescents.

Cognitive-Affective Theories

A number of theories have focused on how perceptions about the costs and benefits of drug use contribute to adolescents' decisions to experiment with these substances. Such models share two assumptions: (1) The decision to use substances rests in substance-specific expectations and perceptions held by adolescents, and (2) the effects of all other variables (e.g., adolescents' personality traits or their involvement with peers who use substances) are mediated through substance-specific cognitions, evaluations, and decisions.[72] The theory of reasoned action, which holds that the most important determinant of a person's behavior is behavioral intent, is the most encompassing of these cost-benefit/decision-making models.[73]

Addictive Personality Theory

Another explanation for the onset and continued use of drugs says that the typical addict has an addiction-prone personality and suffers from some deep-rooted personality disorder or emotional problem. Isidor Chein and colleagues' celebrated study, *The Road to H*, contended that youthful heroin addicts suffer from such personality disorders as "weak ego functioning," "defective superego," and "inadequate masculine identification"; for example, a young male with an addiction-prone personality, according to these authors, "[is unable] to enter into prolonged, close, friendly relations with either peers or adults, . . . [has] difficulties in assuming a masculine role, . . . is frequently overcome by a sense of futility, has an expectation of failure and general depression, . . . [is] easily frustrated and made anxious, . . . [and finds] frustrations and anxiety intolerable."[74]

Stress Relief Theory

The desire to get high, which is seen as a way to relieve stress, depression, or the boredom of everyday life, is common in adolescent peer culture. The desire to drink alcohol and get high is very much related to the desire to feel good, to be comfortable in social situations, and to gain acceptance in peer culture. This explanation for the appeal of substance abuse says that stress relief provides a sought-after high or peak experience.

Anthropologist Philippe Bourgois put it this way: "Substance abuse in general, and crack in particular, offers the equivalent of a born-again metamorphosis. Instantaneously the user is transformed from an unemployed, depressed high school dropout, despised by the world—and secretly convinced that his failure is due to his own inherent stupidity and disorganization." He becomes a person who has found life's purpose. "There is a rush of heart-palpitating pleasure," stated Bourgois, "followed by a jaw-gnashing crash and wide-eyed alertness that provides his life with concrete purpose: Get more crack—fast."[75]

Social Learning Theory

Drug use by peers is consistently found to be the strongest predictor of an individual's involvement in drug use. The argument can be made that drug use begins and continues primarily because juveniles or adults have contact with peers who use drugs and who provide both role models and social support for using drugs. Peer influence, not surprisingly, is especially important during adolescence. Peers appear to influence initial marijuana use but seem to be less important for those starting the use of alcohol or hard drugs; once peers persuade a person to begin using drugs, then a pattern of use is established that may eventually lead to addiction and continued use.[76]

Social learning theory posits that an adolescent's involvement in substance abuse has three sequential effects: It begins with the observation and imitation of substance-specific behaviors; it continues with social reinforcement, such as encouragement and support for drug use; and it culminates in a juvenile's expectation of positive social and physiological consequences from continued drug use. These anticipated consequences might be primarily social in nature, such as acceptance or rejection by peers, during experimental use and then become largely physiological in nature, such as positive or negative physiological reactions to the substances themselves, during subsequent stages. Social learning theory essentially says that an adolescent who anticipates that using substances will produce more personal benefits than costs will be at risk for continued use.[77]

Social Control Theories

Travis Hirschi's social control theory and Hawkins and Weis's social development model both assume that emotional attachments to peers who use substances is a primary cause of substance abuse. Unlike social learning theories, however, these two approaches pay specific attention to weak conventional bonds to society and to the institutions and individuals who might otherwise discourage deviant behavior.[78] Hirschi asserted that the deviant impulses that most adolescents share are held in check or controlled by strong bonds to conventional society, families, schools, and religions; however, adolescents who do not have such controlling influences will not feel compelled to adhere to convention or to engage in socially acceptable behaviors.[79]

The social development model proposes that adolescents become attached to substance-using peers if they feel uncommitted either to conventional society or to positive role models. Unlike Hirschi's social control theory that focuses largely on social systems, the social development model focuses more on individuals, their social development and their social interactions. This focus shifts developmentally, with parents dominating the preschool years, teachers dominating the preadolescent phase, and peers dominating the adolescent stage.[80]

Social Disorganization Theory

Social disorganization theory explains the onset and escalation of adolescents' drug use by claiming that a bleak economic environment for certain disenfranchised groups has created a generation of young adults in urban inner cities who regularly experience doubt, hopelessness, and uncertainty. According to this perspective, the hopelessness of the poor leads them to seek relief. Hence, drug use and alcohol abuse provide an immediate fix for hopelessness but, in the long run, create other problems.[81]

Integrated Theories

Delbert S. Elliott and colleagues offer a model that expands traditional strain, social control, and social learning theories into a single perspective that accounts for delinquent behavior and drug use.[82] They described the mechanisms by which neighborhood disorganization, attachment to families, and social values contribute to involvement with drugs.[83] This model was initially created to explain the causes of delinquency, but it was later more fully developed to explain adolescents' drug-using behavior[84] (see Web Extra 11.6).

Simons and colleagues expanded Ackers's social learning theory and attempted to "explain why adolescents join substance-using peer groups."[85] They did this

Web Extra 11.6
National Drug Intelligence
Center website

through their multistage social learning model that integrates social learning processes with several intrapersonal characteristics—including low self-esteem, emotional distress (e.g., anxiety, tension, depressed affect), inadequate coping skills (e.g., distraction or denial-avoidance), and social interaction skills (e.g., lack of compromise, overassertiveness, impoliteness, lack of empathy)—and a personal value system emphasizing a present orientation over long-term conventional goals concerning families, education, and religion.[86]

The attempt to explain a social phenomenon with a single theory has a long history in sociology, but substance abuse theory (like delinquency theory) owes its origins to several theoretical perspectives. For some individuals, drugs are an escape from the dreariness and toxicity of their home environments; for others, substance abuse is an attempt to escape from emotionally crippling problems; and for still others, substance abuse arises rather normally as part of peer influences. Integrated or interactionist models combining the effects of strain, control, and social learning theories probably make the most sense in explaining why adolescents start using alcohol and drugs.[87]

Delinquency across the Life Course: Drug Use

Two basic pathways are possible for substance-abusing youths. They may restrict themselves to substance abuse and not become involved in other delinquent activities; these offenders may desist from substance abuse after their adolescent years or continue to use drugs as adults. Alternatively, substance-abusing youths who also participate in other delinquent activities may desist from one or both types of activity during adolescence or continue to be involved in one or both as adults.

There is some evidence that about two-thirds of substance-abusing youths continue to use drugs after reaching adulthood but that about half desist from other forms of criminality. Researchers in the 1980s found that drug abusers who persisted in both crime and substance abuse as adults typically came from poor families, did poorly in school, used multiple types of drugs, were chronic offenders, and had an early onset of both drug use and delinquent behavior.[88]

Marvin D. Krohn, Alan J. Lizotte, and Cynthia M. Perez, in their 1997 analysis of the Rochester data, found that the use of alcohol and drugs in early adolescence increases a youngster's risk of becoming pregnant or impregnating someone, becoming a teenage parent, dropping out of school, and prematurely living independently from parents or guardians; in turn, the process of experiencing these early transitions increases the chances that individuals will use alcohol and drugs when they become young adults.[89] Krohn and colleagues suggested that the cumulative impact of experiencing various early transitions may be detrimental to the successful movement, or transition, to adult status and adult roles.[90] It is not surprising that an early or unsuccessful transition in one area will have implications for other trajectories.[91] Off-time and out-of-order transitions can be especially disruptive because the individual may not be prepared for the added responsibilities and obligations that frequently accompany these transitions, and precocious transitions can further lead to problematic consequences because of the increased economic burdens and reduced economic prospects facing those who experience them. For example, teenage parenthood can disrupt the order of transitions by leading youths to enter full-time employment before completing high school, which can derail career development. The person who leaves school before graduation may not have any choice but a low-paying unskilled job, which in turn produces job instability and ongoing economic disadvantages.[92]

Gary M. McClelland, Linda A. Teplin, and Karen M. Abram highlighted several generalizations about drug use and adolescent development that are widely recognized and accepted:

- Substance use commonly follows a sequence from tobacco and alcohol to marijuana and then to more dangerous substances.
- Substance use and abuse that begin in early adolescence are associated with more serious delinquency and longer deviant careers, antisocial personality disorders in later life, and more numerous risky behaviors.

Web Extra 11.7
Drug Enforcement
Administration (DEA) website

> > > **EXHIBIT 11.4** < < <

Overcoming Chemical Dependency

In a May 2004 interview, a former addict told his story.

My dad was an African-American. During his prime years, he was rated as one of the ten best baseball players in the country. He was always on the road; I didn't get to see him much. He finally stopped traveling when I was in the eighth grade, but all that did was put him in the nightclub business. He didn't take much interest in my life. I can count the number of extracurricular activities he went to; he would show up late or not at all. He would say that he would pick me up from school, but he wouldn't. The animosity I had for my dad continued up until the day he passed.

My mom is white. She was divorced and had two children from her first marriage. She married my father while he was in prison. He was in prison for writing bad checks. She stayed married to him for as long as she could, and then they divorced. I saw so little of my dad that I was raised in a white society. But when I stepped out of that door, I was a black man. I had quite a time adjusting to the two societies. There were a lot of days I had to fight to get home from school.

I can remember one time when I was eight or nine and I was laying on the bed and crying. I couldn't understand why people would treat me the way they did. My mom really couldn't explain it because she was a white female trying to educate a black young boy about racism within both the white community and the black community.

I felt a lot of pressure as a kid. Due to the fact that my dad owned clubs, I had access to alcohol. I didn't start drinking until I was 15 or 16 years old. But when I did start drinking, I really drank. I also began to smoke marijuana.

I went away to college on an academic scholarship. I didn't like school and only drank and smoked more pot. My alcohol intake was soaring, and my smoking was also increasing. I joined the military and for five years drank a lot of alcohol.

I got out of the military, got married, and had three children. My drug and alcohol use increased dramatically from 1985 to 1990. When crack came around, I got into that. I was what you call a weekend crack addict. That lasted until one day I went to a college football game with a cousin of mine. I cashed my check, and that weekend I smoked my whole paycheck up.

I didn't know what to tell my wife. I committed myself to an inpatient treatment program. I went in on a Monday, and as I was walking down the hall on a Thursday after Recreation, this warm feeling came over my body. I had to hold on to the wall because I almost lost my balance. It was like it was washed out of me. And since that day to the day right now, I haven't had a drink. I haven't smoked marijuana. I haven't done cocaine. I haven't smoked cigarettes.

Unfortunately, my wife had had it with me. She divorced me, but I have spent a lot of time with my children. I want to be a good father, something my father was not to me.

I do not define myself as an alcoholic. I do not consider myself to be a drug addict. I am a chemically dependent person. When I go to the doctor, I tell him not to prescribe anything that will ever be addictive to me.

Source: Personal interview with author.

- Substance abuse is associated with poor academic performance.
- More severe substance abuse and dependence are associated with serious criminal offenses in general.
- Substance use and abuse are associated with higher rates of psychiatric disorders and with disorders of greater severity.[93]

Drug addicts, like those with a history of delinquency and criminality, sometimes have a turning point, or change, when they walk away from drug use, but those who were deeply entrenched in the drug world as adolescents and continue this activity in their adult years find it particularly difficult to give up drugs. Those who are able to stay with the straight life typically have had a religious experience or have had an extremely positive experience in a therapeutic community for drug addicts.[94] (See Exhibit 11.4 for one person's account of how he walked away from his addiction to alcohol and drugs after several decades of dependency.)

Kandel and colleagues reported that significant status changes, including marriage and parenthood, were correlated with the cessation of marijuana smoking among users in their middle to late twenties.[95] L. A. Goodman and W. H. Kruskal found that reasons for cessation involved the imposition of both internal controls and external controls.[96] L. Thomas Winfree Jr., Christine S. Sellers, and Dennis L. Clason examined the reasons for adolescents' cessation of and abstention from substance use and determined that social learning variables clearly distinguished abstainers from current users, but they were less able to distinguish former users from current users or former users from abstainers.[97] Ryan D. Schroeder, Peggy C. Giordano, and Stephen A. Cernkovich investigated the effect of drug use on desistance processes using a sample of previously institutionalized youths and found that social network effects, particularly partner criminality, explain some of the negative impacts of drug use on life-course patterns of criminal offending.[98]

Delinquency and Social Policy: Solutions to the Drug Problem

Prevention programs, treatment interventions, strict enforcement, and harm reduction are all possible means of controlling drug use among adolescents. Prevention and treatment appear to be the most effective means of controlling drug abuse, but there is abundant evidence that deterrence tactics, such as the federal "war on drugs" (involving mostly strict enforcement), have been largely ineffective with both juveniles and adults.

Prevention Programs

The 1990s saw dramatic developments in drug-prevention programs. The Center for the Study and Prevention of Violence at the University of Colorado began an initiative called Blueprints for Violence Prevention, in which researchers evaluated 600 programs designed to prevent violence and drug abuse and to treat youths with problem behaviors.[99] The investigators were able to identify 11 model programs and 21 promising programs. Following are some of the more noteworthy: Life Skills Training (LST), which is designed to prevent or reduce the use of "gateway" drugs such as tobacco, alcohol, and marijuana[100]; (2) Midwestern Prevention Project (MPP), which is a comprehensive three- to five-year community-based prevention program targeting gateway use of alcohol, tobacco, and marijuana[101]; and (3) Project Toward No Drug Abuse (PROJECT TND), which targets high school youths who are at risk for drug abuse.[102] (See Chapter 12 for a wider description of these programs.) Significantly, Blueprints for Violence Prevention reported that both model programs and promising programs had positive outcome assessments when evaluated over a period of several years.[103] (See Library Extra 11.5 for information on another program.)

Police departments across the country conduct at least three substance abuse prevention programs in schools: Drug Abuse Resistance Education (D.A.R.E.), School Program to Educate and Control Drug Abuse (SPECDA), and Project Alert. The D.A.R.E. program is a widely replicated effort to prevent substance abuse. Although Chapter 14 notes that recent evaluations of D.A.R.E. are less than encouraging, yet it is the most popular school-based drug-education program in the United States and operates in about 70% of our nation's school districts, reaching 25 million students; it has also been adopted in 44 other countries.[104] New York City's SPECDA, a collaborative project of the city's police department and board of education, is another highly praised drug-prevention program.[105] Project Alert, a program originating in middle schools in California and Oregon, appears to have had some success in teaching students to avoid drugs and to resist peer pressure to use tobacco and alcohol.[106]

Effective programs need to incorporate early childhood and family interventions, school-based interventions, and comprehensive community-wide efforts. The important dimension of drug-prevention interventions, as is continually emphasized throughout this text, is a multidimensional approach centering on the family, school, and community (see Library Extra 11.6).

Treatment Interventions

Treatment for drug abusers takes place in psychiatric and hospital settings for youngsters whose parents can afford it or have third-party insurance benefits. Other youths, especially those substance abusers who have committed minor forms of delinquency, receive treatment in privately administered placements, which vary tremendously in the quality of program design and implementation. Substance abusers who are involved in serious forms of delinquency will likely be placed in county or state facilities whose basic organizational goals are custodial and security

Voices of Delinquency

Read "Selling Drugs Was My Downfall." Unlike the former story, this does not have a positive outcome. Can you identify why the life course of these two individuals ended up so differently?

Library Extra 11.5
General Counterdrug Intelligence Plan

Library Extra 11.6
University of Michigan's *Monitoring the Future* survey

Teen representatives of Drug Free Youth in Town are introduced at a Miami, Florida, workshop.
▶ **How can the success of drug-prevention programs be measured?**

oriented, and they generally receive some substance abuse counseling, especially in group contexts.

Substance-abusing youths with typical multiple problems may be more malleable than adult offenders, but there is little evidence that the majority of substance abuse programs are any more successful than those for adult substance abusers. Élan in Maine; Rocky Mountain in Colorado; Provo Canyon in Utah; and Cascade, Cedu, and Hilltop in California are privately administered therapeutic schools or emotional growth programs that may be better than the average substance abuse program for juveniles.[107]

Élan, a therapeutic community for juveniles in Poland Spring, Maine, is a treatment program for adolescents with emotional, behavioral, or adjustment problems. This coeducational and residential program serves juveniles in grades 8 through 12. Joe Ricci, a former drug addict and one of the success stories of Daytop (a therapeutic community for drug addicts) in New York City, and Dr. Gerald Davidson, a psychiatrist, started Élan in 1971.[108] The program involves intense peer pressure, guilt admittance, and often humiliating punishments and also stresses personal responsibility, honesty, self-control, and patience. The staff claim that the therapy is not as intense or encapsulated in negativity as it was in the past. Élan has grown into a finely tuned million-dollar operation. The 160 residents stay an average of 27 months, and the annual fees for a 12-month stay are $49,071. A high percentage of those who are admitted to this program graduate or receive "diplomas"; of this number, about 80% stay out of trouble, according to an in-house evaluation. Supporters think that Élan is an exemplary therapeutic experience for youths; foes, including some former residents, regard it as coercive and brutal.[109]

The philosophy of Élan, like that of similar therapeutic experiences for juveniles, is perhaps correct—that substance abusers need a confrontational environment with intense pressure from peers and staff to change. It may well be that the 60% to 70% of youths who stay at Élan to complete the two-year program are ready to change or to desist from drugs and negative behaviors and that this explains their high success rate. However, privately administered programs such as Élan do not have enough places available for all the juveniles who need such a therapeutic experience (see Library Extra 11.7).

Drug courts are another fairly recent treatment innovation for those who have a history of drug use (see Chapter 13). To address alcohol and drug problems, treatment services in drug courts have been based on formal theories of drug dependence

Library Extra 11.7
Office of National Drug Control Policy: *National Drug Control Strategy, 2009*

and abuse. They also attempt to employ the best therapeutic tools and to provide participants with the opportunities needed to build cognitive skills. Research findings generally show that drug courts can reduce recidivism and promote other positive outcomes, but research has been unable to uncover which court processes affect which outcomes and for what types of offenders.[110]

The balanced restorative-justice model (discussed further in Chapter 13) has been used as a form of treatment intervention with drug- and alcohol-abusing adolescents. It forms the guiding philosophy in 12 states and builds on restorative-justice conferencing that takes place in informal settings where voluntary negotiating encounters include victims, offenders, and their relevant communities.[111] Restorative-justice conferencing can also use more coerced restorative obligations, such as restitution or community service imposed by formal proceedings. What makes these processes and obligations "restorative," rather than rehabilitative or retributive, is the restorative intent underlying their imposition.[112]

Drug and alcohol abuse interventions have also been developed in a number of community-based and institutional settings. Some training schools, for example, conduct group sessions for those with histories of drug use. A social worker may conduct ongoing drug and alcohol abuse groups, and members from outside groups, such as Alcoholics Anonymous (AA) or Narcotics Anonymous (NA), may come into the institution and hold sessions.

Strict Enforcement

The "war on drugs" has not been won with juveniles any more than it has with adults. A disastrous consequence of this "war" is that increasing numbers of minority youths who were involved in using or selling crack cocaine have been brought into the justice system for extended periods of time. Some have even argued that the war on drugs has been a factor contributing to the spread of youth gangs.[113] Strict enforcement, however, has seemed to make a difference in several ways:

■ The destruction of overseas drug-producing crops has probably had some impact on the availability of drugs in the United States, raising prices and making some drugs harder to find.
■ Heavy penalties associated with the sale of illicit drugs appear to have been at least somewhat effective in deterring both juvenile and adult offenders.
■ Law enforcement's targeting of dealers has had some success in getting those offenders off the streets.
■ The policing of the sale of tobacco products, especially cigarettes, at convenience stores and other places has made it more difficult for minors to purchase or obtain tobacco products.
■ The strict enforcement of no-drug zones around schools has discouraged or at least reduced the number of persons trafficking drugs to school-age children.
■ Strict enforcement of adolescent drug trafficking at school and in neighborhoods may have reduced the availability of drugs to young people.

Harm Reduction

Harm reduction is an approach designed to reduce the harm done to youths by drug use and by the severe penalties resulting from drug use and sales. A number of harm-reduction strategies have been employed:

■ Programs in which health professionals administer drugs to addicts as part of a treatment and detoxification regimen
■ Drug-treatment facilities that are available for those drug addicts wishing to enter treatment
■ Needle exchange programs that are intended to slow the transmission of HIV and that provide educational resources about how HIV is contracted and spread

Juvenile drug users generally find a wide variety of treatment programs and facilities. Treatment programs are usually more readily available to middle- and upper-class youths than to lower-class youths, partially because wealthier parents can afford to pay for the care of their dependent children. The legalized administration of drugs to addicts and needle exchange programs are more typically found when working with adult drug users than with juveniles.

Chapter Summary

This chapter has discussed drug and alcohol use by adolescents. Some of the key points of the chapter are as follows:

- Drug use and alcohol abuse are forms of problem behavior, and their onset, duration, and termination are determined by the dynamics of the interplay between the environment and particular young people, which varies over developmental periods.

- The good news is that drug use appears to have declined significantly from the late 1970s, with perhaps slight increases since the early 1990s.

- It is also good news that the use of cigarettes has declined among American adolescents.

- The bad news is that alcohol abuse remains high among American adolescents and shows no signs of decreasing.

- The data seem to show that high-risk children are becoming increasingly involved in substance abuse.

- Although the use of crack cocaine may be declining across the nation, it remains the drug of choice for many disadvantaged youths.

- It is disconcerting that teenagers have increased their use of marijuana in the past decade.

- Recent increasing use of methamphetamine by adolescents may also be viewed as a matter of social concern.

- A number of theories examine why juveniles use drugs, but integrated theories appear to be the most adequate forms of explanation.

- Early prevention efforts in schools and in other social contexts appear to be making headway with low-risk children.

- The fact that substance abuse is usually one of several problems for high-risk youths makes it more difficult to achieve substantial success through therapeutic interventions.

Key Terms

alcohol, p. 251
amphetamine, p. 256
club drug, p. 256
cocaine, p. 253

drug addiction, p. 251
Ecstasy, p. 256
heroin, p. 258
inhalant, p. 255

marijuana, p. 252
sedative, p. 256

Review Questions

1. What drug remains the drug of choice for most adolescents? Why?
2. What drugs are used by adolescents? Why are some more widely used than others?
3. What is the debate about the relationship between drug use and delinquency?
4. What is known about drug-trafficking juveniles?

5. What are the various theories for the onset of drug use among adolescents and adults?
6. What is the relationship between drug use and the life course?
7. What approaches have been tried to solve the drug problem?

Discussion Questions

1. Why is drug use so popular in American society?
2. Why does the typical drug user use drugs up to a certain point and then go no further? At the same time, why do other youths who seem to be as committed to this stopping point continue using drugs?
3. Do you agree with exempting cultural drug use from criminal penalties? Explain your response.
4. Should nicotine be added to the list of controlled substances? Explain your response.

5. Why would a youth pursue only the drug pathway rather than the delinquency/drug pathway?
6. What factors do you think contribute to low drug-use rates among African-American and Asian adolescents?
7. Why do college students drink as much as they do? How is their drinking related to the subject matter of this chapter?

Group Exercises

1. Invite a medical expert to address the class regarding the short- and long-term health effects of the use of the various drugs discussed in this chapter.
2. Invite a leader of the local MADD chapter to address the class.
3. Invite a member of your local police department's drug-enforcement unit to address the class regarding drug-use patterns in your city and state.

4. Have the students clip newspaper or web articles related to Ecstasy use in your city and state, and have them share the articles with the class.
5. Invite a recovering addict from a local narcotics support group to address the class regarding his or her experiences in the postaddiction phase of his or her life.
6. Invite a drug counselor to address the class regarding his or her experiences trying to assist drug users.

mycrimekit™

Go to mycrimekit.com to explore the following study tools and resources specific to this chapter:

- **Practice Quiz:** Practice with multiple-choice, true/false, short-answer, and essay questions.

- **WebQuests:** Do web activities using the National Criminal Justice Reference Service (NCJRS) website.

- **Flashcards:** Use 10 flashcards to test your knowledge of the chapter's key terms.

Prevention of Delinquency

CHAPTER OBJECTIVES

After reading this chapter, you should be able to answer the following questions:

- What has been the history of juvenile prevention programs?
- What are promising prevention programs?
- What is the relationship between the victimization of children and the prevention of delinquency?
- What types of prevention programs are likely to work with high-risk youngsters?
- What are the ingredients of effective prevention programs?

When adults offer young people a chance, their love and support can show struggling youth the hope that lies beyond their future, and sometimes that hope makes all the difference.

—Former First Lady Laura Bush, leader of the Helping America's Youth Initiative

Introduction

Saul Alinsky, a community organizer, used to tell a story about social change. In this story, a man is walking by the riverside when he notices a body floating downstream. A fisherman also notices the body, leaps into the stream, pulls the body ashore, and gives mouth-to-mouth resuscitation, saving the person's life. The same thing happens a few minutes later, and then again and again. When yet another body floats by, the fisherman this time completely ignores the drowning man and starts running upstream along the bank. The observer asks the fisherman why he is not trying to rescue the drowning body. "This time," replies the fisherman, "I'm going upstream to find out who the hell is pushing those poor folks into the water."[1]

This story has an important message for students of delinquency: As long as we do nothing about original causes, we will just be pulling out bodies and mopping up the casualties. But Alinsky gave a twist to his story. While the fisherman was busy running up the bank to find the ultimate source of the problem, Alinsky asked, who was going to help those who continued to float down the river?

As this story indicates, the study of delinquency not only strives to find broad answers to the problem of youth crime but also seeks to help youths in trouble. Accordingly, as part of our examination of the broad questions about youth crime, this chapter discusses both the prevention and treatment of delinquency.

Prevention and treatment interventions largely take place in community programs, which depend on adequate funding to provide needed services. Effective programs typically have involved and committed staff who can establish rapport, provide mentoring, reinforce positive behaviors, and offer encouragement and guidance to struggling young people.

The Justice Policy Institute of the Center on Juvenile and Criminal Justice of the Northwestern University School of Law profiled 25 individuals who were petitioned into juvenile court as hard-core delinquents when they were young and who turned their lives around. The book, *Second Chances—100 Years of the Children's Court: Giving Kids a Chance to Make a Better Choice*, profiles these 25 young people. One of them was Derrick Thomas, whose story is in Exhibit 12.1.

Goal of Delinquency Prevention

The prevention of youth crime is certainly a desirable goal. An emphasis on prevention was written into federal law in the Juvenile Delinquency Prevention Act of 1972, the Juvenile Justice and Delinquency Prevention Act of 1974, and the Juvenile Justice Amendments of 1977 and 1980.[2] Despite this federal emphasis, prevention has been largely ignored in the study of delinquency, yet there is evidence that the declining but still disturbing levels of teenage violent behavior and use of firearms, the continuing problems with drugs and alcohol, and the emergence of nationwide gangs still call for the development and evaluation of delinquency prevention programs.

Three different levels of **delinquency prevention** have been identified: **Primary prevention** is focused on modifying conditions in the physical and social environments that lead to delinquency; **secondary prevention**, which is intervention in the lives of juveniles or groups identified as being in circumstances that dispose them toward delinquency, also takes place in diversionary programs, in which youngsters in trouble are diverted from formal juvenile justice programs; and **tertiary prevention** is directed at the prevention of recidivism, and it takes place in traditional rehabilitation programs.[3] Primary prevention receives the focus in this chapter, and Chapter 13 examines methods of secondary and tertiary prevention.

delinquency prevention An organized effort to forestall or prevent the development of delinquent behavior.

primary prevention The effort to reduce delinquency by modifying conditions in the physical and social environments that lead to juvenile crime.

secondary prevention The intervention in the lives of juveniles or groups identified as being in circumstances that dispose them toward delinquency.

tertiary prevention A program directed at the prevention of recidivism among youthful offenders.

> **EXHIBIT 12.1**

The Derrick Thomas Story

The following tells the story of a man named Derrick Thomas—his troubled early years and his later success in life. (Unfortunately, Thomas died on February 8, 2000, from complications following an automobile accident.)

Tears streamed down his face as his mother cradled fourteen-year-old Derrick Thomas, already over six feet tall, in her arms. After years of beating the system, of committing crimes and not getting caught, of conning adults with his engaging smile and winning personality, Thomas's number had finally come up. He was going to juvenile jail.

Placed on home confinement while awaiting trial on a burglary charge, his first juvenile court referral, Thomas repeatedly left the house. His pretrial services officer had reached her breaking point. She pulled Thomas out of class and summoned him and his mother to her office to break the bad news. For the next thirty days, Thomas would be locked up.

At the time, "getting locked up seemed like the worst thing that could happen to me," says Thomas, who went on to become a ten-time All-Pro linebacker for the Kansas City Chiefs and one of the National Football League's all-time sack leaders. But getting involved in the juvenile justice system actually turned out to be "one of the most important breaks I ever got." Through the court, Thomas would meet several people who helped him turn his life around. His juvenile court experiences led him to set up his own foundation for troubled inner-city youths and inspired him to use his life to make a difference on behalf of other troubled youths.

In public speaking engagements, Thomas told audiences the same thing he said in testimony before the United States Congress and the Missouri General Assembly, words that are a fitting epilogue to this profile: "I come to you today to say you can make a difference and to tell you that there are any number of success stories in the juvenile justice system, just like mine," he said.

Source: Office of Juvenile Justice and Delinquency Prevention, "Second Chances: Giving Kids a Chance to Make a Better Choice," in *Juvenile Justice Bulletin* (Washington, D.C.: U.S. Department of Justice, 2000), pp. 21–23.

History of Well-Meant Interventions and Present-Day Prevention Programs

History of Interventions

Delinquency prevention has a sad history, and the highway of delinquency prevention is paved with punctured panaceas.[4] A member of the Subcommittee on Human Resources of the Committee on Education and Labor put it this way: "The public is looking for an inexpensive panacea. . . . These periodic panaceas for delinquents

A police officer presents a delinquency prevention program to children in a Los Angeles classroom. ▶ **What would a successful delinquency prevention program consist of?**

EXHIBIT 12.2

Chicago Area Project

The Chicago Area Project (CAP) is a program that Clifford Shaw and his colleagues initiated in the 1930s. Shaw's group sought to discover by actual demonstration and measurement a procedure for the prevention of delinquency and the treatment of delinquents. In 1932, the first projects were set up in three ethnically homogeneous white neighborhoods: South Chicago, the Near West Side, and the Near North Side. The Near North Side and Near West Side area projects were located directly north and directly west of the Loop, Chicago's central business district, and both were areas with high delinquency rates. The third project was carried out in Russell Square on Chicago's southeast side, a heavily industrialized area consisting primarily of steel mills and railroad operations, but the area had a lower delinquency rate than the other two neighborhoods. Eventually 18 area projects were established in Chicago, including several in African-American Southside neighborhoods. (The concept of the area projects also spread to several other Illinois cities.)

Shaw and his colleagues had lost confidence in official agencies' ability to deal adequately with the needs of youths, so they recruited local leaders to intervene with neighborhood youths. CAP organizers believed that instead of throwing youths so quickly to the justice system, the community should intervene on their behalf. In the 60-year existence of CAP, community citizens have shown up in juvenile court to speak on behalf of youths in trouble, have organized social and recreational programs for youths, and also have given special attention to local youths who are having difficulties at home, in school, or with the law.

Some critics contend that CAP has been ineffective in coping with delinquency in its most serious forms in the areas of the city with the highest crime rates. CAP has also been criticized because it fails to attack the political and economic sources of power. Jon Snodgrass added that CAP's neglect of the realities of Chicago politics and economics essentially made this project a conservative response to the radical changes that are needed in disorganized communities.

Although this latter structural limitation of CAP is difficult to refute, it still has served as an exemplary model of what grassroots organizations in the community can achieve in preventing juvenile delinquency. Steven Schlossman and colleagues summarized the effectiveness of CAP by saying, "All of our data consistently suggest that the CAP has long been effective in organizing local communities and reducing juvenile delinquency."

▶ Why do you think this approach has generated so much enthusiasm through the years? How serious a flaw is it that CAP has ignored the political and economic sources of power?

Source: See Solomon Kobrin, "The Chicago Area Project: A 25-Year Assessment," *Annuals of the American Academy of Political and Social Sciences* 322 (March 1959), pp. 19–29; Steven Schlossman, Gail Aellman, and Richard Shavelson, *Delinquency Prevention in South Chicago: A Fifty-Year Assessment of the Chicago Area Project* (Santa Monica, Calif.: RAND, 1984); Steven L. Schlossman and Michael Smith, "The Chicago Area Project Revisited," *Crime and Delinquency* 26 (July 1983), pp. 398–462; and Jon Snodgrass, "Clifford Shaw and Henry D. McKay," in *Delinquency, Crime and Society*, edited by James Short Jr. (Chicago: University of Chicago Press, 1976), p. 16.

come along every 2 to 3 years in my experience. The harm they do is to divert the attention of the public from any long-term comprehensive program of helping youth, working to strengthen school systems, communities, job opportunities, housing and recreational programs."[5]

One reason that society seeks panaceas, or all-purpose remedies, is the human tendency to look for easy answers to complex problems[6]; another reason is the frustration and sense of futility in a continuous losing battle with juvenile crime that make policy makers eager to discover a solution. Furthermore, the receptivity toward panaceas stems from a cultural belief in prevention, as exemplified by the expression "An ounce of prevention is worth a pound of cure."

Prevention panaceas have ranged from biological and psychological interventions to group therapy, gang intervention, recreational activities, job training and employment, community organizations, and even structured reorganization of the entire society. The most widely known models of delinquency prevention are the Chicago Area Project (for a description, see Exhibit 12.2); the Cambridge-Somerville Youth Study in Massachusetts; the New York City Youth Board; the Mobilization for Youth Project in New York City; Boston's Midcity Project; and Walter C. Reckless and Simon Dinitz's self-concept studies in Columbus, Ohio:

■ *Cambridge-Somerville Youth Study.* One of the best known of the prevention programs identified those youths who were headed for trouble with the law. It took place in Cambridge and Somerville, Massachusetts, from November 1937 to December 31, 1945. This individual approach to delinquency prevention presumed that psychological disturbances lead to delinquent behavior, so it focused on efforts made through a counseling relationship to alter the psychological states of respondents as well as their ability to function in school and at home. In a 30-year follow-up, Joan McCord found that "none of the measures confirmed hopes that treatment had improved the lives of those in the treatment group."[7]

■ *New York City Youth Board.* Another study also presumed that psychological disturbances led to delinquent behavior and provided psychiatric and social work services to identified predelinquents through the New York City Youth Board. The study was conducted from 1952 to 1953, when researchers used the Glueck social prediction table to examine 223 boys in two public schools located in high-delinquency areas in the New York City school system. This prediction table was made up of five family-related factors: discipline of boy by father, supervision of boy by mother, affection of father for boy, affection of mother for boy, and family cohesiveness. The evaluation at the conclusion of the study (like that of the Cambridge-Somerville Youth Study) revealed disappointing results. The Glueck social prediction table did not accurately predict delinquency, nor did the psychiatric and social work services appear to have any positive effect on those youths identified as predelinquent.[8]

■ *Mobilization for Youth Project.* In 1961, one of the most ambitious attempts to prevent and control juvenile delinquency took place in a 67-block area of Manhattan's Lower East Side in New York City. This endeavor—New York's Mobilization for Youth (MFY) Project—built on Richard A. Cloward and Lloyd E. Ohlin's delinquency and opportunity theory and sought to reduce the gap between the social and economic aspirations of youths and their opportunities to achieve these goals through legitimate means. This approach to delinquency prevention became the major strategy for the new federal delinquency initiatives endorsed by the President's Committee on Juvenile Delinquency and Youth Crime as well as the prototype project for many of the federally funded "war on poverty" programs during the 1960s. Five major delinquency prevention projects later replicated the MFY model. The MFY Project was multidimensional in its scope and extremely ambitious in its goals, but it was nearly impossible to evaluate. Supporters claimed that the MYF Project was on the right track but was not taken far enough; detractors countered that the danger in trying to do too much was to end up doing too little.[9]

■ *Boston's Midcity Project.* The Midcity Project began in inner-city Boston in 1954 largely as a result of widely publicized gang violence. Detached gang workers served as intermediaries between gang members and employers, school officials, and the police. Walter B. Miller's evaluation of this program found that there was no significant measurable inhibition of law-abiding behavior.[10] This project did lead to the detached gang worker projects, based on the strategies which assume that delinquency stems from the influence of peers and from weak attachments between youths and conforming members of society; they were widely used in Boston, Chicago, Los Angeles, and New York during the 1950s and 1960s but were found to be unsuccessful. Interestingly, the intervention of the detached gang workers usually resulted in the group becoming involved in higher rates of delinquency than before the arrival of the workers.

■ *Self-Concept and the Prevention of Delinquency.* Walter C. Reckless and Simon Dinitz used role development and educational strategies in order to improve the self-concept of students who were veering toward delinquency (see Chapter 5). In the late 1950s and early 1960s, the Columbus, Ohio, school system permitted Reckless and Dinitz to set up pilot projects in elementary schools in high-delinquency areas, with the basic purpose of improving the self-concept of male students who had been identified as prone to delinquency. In all, 1,762 boys were examined at four consecutive yearly periods—at the end of the seventh, eighth, ninth, and tenth grades—but the researchers found that in none of the outcome variables were the experimental subjects significantly different from the controls.[11]

A number of studies in the 1970s examined the effectiveness of delinquency prevention programs (see Library Extra 12.1). Michael C. Dixon and William W. Wright concluded from their examination of these programs that "few studies show significant results."[12] Richard J. Lundman, Paul T. McFarlane, and Frank Scarpitti drew the same pessimistic conclusion in 1976: "It appears unlikely that any of these [delinquency prevention] projects prevented delinquent behavior."[13] Lundman and Scarpitti collaborated on a later study of delinquency prevention; after adding 15 projects to the 25 previously studied, they concluded in 1978 that "a review of forty past or continuing attempts at the prevention of juvenile delinquency leads to the nearly inescapable conclusion that none of these projects has successfully prevented delinquency."[14] These researchers even went on to say that given the poor history of past attempts at delinquency prevention, there was little reason to expect any greater success with any efforts.[15]

Prevention programs have received a number of other criticisms besides those dealing with their ineffectiveness. Critics accuse the programs of widening the nets of social control over children because they have resulted in sweeping more children into some program, agency, or system; critics also charge that prevention programs are far too expensive (as part of its national evaluation of delinquency prevention, the U.S. Justice Department spent more than $20 million to provide intervention and services to 20,000 juveniles in 68 cities) and that prevention programs offer only piecemeal solutions to the profound problems that lead to juvenile crime. Finally, the rights of children, critics say, are sometimes compromised in prevention interventions.[16]

In the 1990s, the Office of Juvenile Justice and Delinquency Prevention (OJJDP) began targeting the prevention of serious and violent juvenile offending, recognizing that these serious and violent juvenile offenders are responsible for a disproportionate number of crimes and that reducing chronic juvenile delinquency is a critical challenge facing society.[17] A multifaceted and coordinated approach toward these youths was identified, with prevention as a critical first step,[18] and pilot programs were established in a number of sites across the United States in the final few years of the twentieth century.

Promising Prevention Programs

The juvenile justice system has traditionally focused on youths after they have had initial contact with law enforcement authorities. The last 20 years, however, have witnessed the emergence of a proactive approach to preventing juvenile crime, an approach sometimes termed the "public health model of crime prevention."[19]

This public health model, which grew out of the disease prevention efforts of a century ago, focuses on reducing risk and increasing opportunities for success. With its proactive emphasis on the prevention of social problems, the public health approach offers an appealing alternative to a reactive focus on rehabilitation or punishment. The public health approach employs the following four-step procedure to identify issues that need attention and to develop solutions: (1) Define the nature of the problem using scientific methods or data; (2) identify potential causes using analyses of risk and protective factors associated with the problem; (3) design, develop, and evaluate interventions; and (4) disseminate successful models as part of education and outreach.[20]

Some researchers have recently begun advocating a shift in the prevention field intended to concentrate exclusively on building resiliency rather than trying to reduce risks.[21] They contend that an emphasis on risks focuses primarily on deficits, whereas a prevention strategy can produce more significant outcomes by concentrating instead on building strengths. Research has shown, however, that delinquency prevention programs focusing too heavily on improving resiliency without addressing the source of the risks are largely unsuccessful.[22] The *Model Programs Guide* of the OJJDP argues that the design of effective prevention programs and strategies

mycrimekit™

Library Extra 12.1
OJJDP publication: *Blueprints for Violence Prevention*

EXHIBIT 12.3

OJJDP *Model Programs Guide*

The Office of Juvenile Justice and Delinquency Prevention's *Model Programs Guide* (MPG) is designed to assist practitioners and communities in implementing evidence-based prevention and intervention programs that can make a difference in the lives of children and communities. The MPG database of evidence covers the entire continuum of youth services from prevention through sanctions to reentry. The MPG can be used to assist juvenile justice practitioners, administrators, and researchers to enhance accountability, ensure public safety, and reduce recidivism. The MPG is an easy-to-use tool that offers the first and only database of scientifically proven programs across the spectrum of youth services.

The following prevention programs are presented:

Academic Skills Enhancement
Afterschool/Recreation
Alternative School
Classroom Curricula
Cognitive Behavioral Treatment
Community and Policy-Oriented Policing
Community Awareness/Mobilization
Drug, Alcohol Therapy/Education
Family Therapy
Gang Prevention

Leadership and Youth Development
Mentoring
Parent Training
School/Classroom Enhancement
Truancy Prevention
Vocational/Job Training
Wraparound/Case Management

CONCLUSION

The MPG contains summary information (program description, evaluation design, research findings, references, and contact information) on evidence-based delinquency prevention and intervention programs. Programs are categorized into exemplary, effective, and promising, based on a set of methodological criteria and the strength of the findings.

▶ **Why is a program guide that includes treatment and prevention programs by state a potentially helpful resource for both policy makers and practitioners?**

Source: Adapted from *OJJDP Model Programs Guide* (www .dsgonline.com/mpg2.5/mpg_index.htm).

---

needs to consider the interrelationships between reducing risk factors and building resiliency (see Exhibit 12.3 for an introduction to the OJJDP guide).

The Blueprints for Violence Prevention report, developed by the Center for the Study and Prevention of Violence at the University of Colorado–Boulder and supported by the OJJDP, identified 11 model programs and 21 promising violence-prevention and drug abuse–prevention programs that have received rigorous evaluation.[23] Table 12.1 presents a complete list of the promising model programs the researchers identified, and the following discussion will briefly describe the 11 model programs.

Big Brothers Big Sisters of America (BBBSA)   With a network of more than 500 local agencies throughout the United States that maintain more than 145,000 one-to-one relationships between youths and volunteer adults, Big Brothers Big Sisters of America (BBBSA) operates as the best-known and largest mentoring program in the nation. The program serves youths ages 6 to 18 years old, a significant number of whom are from single-parent and disadvantaged households. Mentors meet with their matches for three to five hours at least three times a month and participate in a variety of activities, and the supervision of the match relationship is one of the program's hallmarks.[24] An 18-month evaluation found that compared with a control group waiting for a match, youths in this mentoring program were 46% less likely to start using drugs, 27% less likely to start drinking, and 32% less likely to hit or assault someone; they also were less likely to skip school and more likely to have improved family relationships.[25]

Bullying Prevention Program   This model program, called the Bullying Prevention Program, aims to restructure the social environment of primary and secondary schools in order to provide fewer opportunities for bullying and to reduce the peer approval and support that reward bullying behavior. Adults in the school setting are seen as the driving force of this program; the program seeks to ensure that adults in

TABLE 12.1 Promising Model Programs and Age Groups of Targeted Juveniles

Blueprints Program	Pregnancy/Infancy	Early Childhood	Elementary School	Junior High School	High School
Model Programs					
Big Brothers Big Sisters of America (BBBSA)			X	X	X
Bullying Prevention Program			X	X	
Functional Family Therapy (FFT)				X	X
Incredible Years		X	X		
Life Skills Training (LST)				X	
Midwestern Prevention Project (MPP)				X	
Multidimensional Treatment Foster Care (MTFC)				X	X
Multisystemic Therapy (MST)				X	X
Nurse–Family Partnership	X				
Project Toward No Drug Abuse (Project TND)					X
Promoting Alternative Thinking Strategies (PATHS)			X		
Promising Programs					
Athletes Training and Learning to Avoid Steroids					X
Brief Strategic Family Therapy			X	X	X
CASASTART			X	X	
Fast Track			X		
Good Behavior Game			X		
Guiding Good Choices			X	X	
High/Scope Perry Preschool		X			
Houston Child Development Center	X	X			
I Can Problem Solve		X	X		
Intensive Protective Supervision				X	X
Linking the Interests of Families and Teachers			X		
Preventive Intervention				X	
Preventive Treatment Program			X		
Project Northland				X	
Promoting Action through Holistic Education				X	X
School Transitional Environmental Program				X	X
Seattle Social Development Project			X	X	
Strengthening Families Program: Parents and Children 10–14			X	X	
Student Training through Urban Strategies				X	X
Syracuse Family Development Program	X	X			
Yale Child Welfare Project	X	X			

Source: Table 1.1 in Sharon Mihalic et al., *Blueprints for Violence Prevention* (Washington, D.C.: Office of Juvenile Justice and Delinquency Prevention, 2004).

the school are aware of bullying problems and are actively involved in their prevention. Classroom-level intervention involves the creation of class rules regarding bullying behavior and regular meetings in class to discuss issues as well as rule infractions.[26] This program has proved effective in large samples evaluated in South Carolina and Norway. In rural South Carolina, for example, children in 39 schools in grades four through six reported that they experienced a 25% decrease in the frequency at which they felt bullied by other children.[27]

Functional Family Therapy (FFT) Functional Family Therapy (FFT) is a short-term family-based prevention and intervention program that has been successfully applied in a variety of contexts to treat high-risk youths and their families from various backgrounds. Specifically designed to help underserved and at-risk youths ages 11 to 18 years old, this multisystemic clinical program provides 12 one-hour sessions of **family therapy** spread over three months, and more difficult cases may receive up to 30 hours of therapy[28]; the success of this program has been demonstrated and replicated for more than 25 years. Evaluations using controlled follow-up periods of one, three, and five years have demonstrated significant and long-term reductions, ranging from 25% to 60%, in the reoffending of youths.[29]

family therapy A counseling technique that involves treating all members of a family; a widely used method of dealing with a delinquent's socially unacceptable behavior.

Incredible Years: Parent, Teacher, and Child Training Series The Incredible Years model program has a comprehensive set of curricula designed to promote social competence and to prevent, reduce, and treat conduct problems in young children. The target population of this program is children ages two to eight who exhibit or are at risk for conduct problems. In the parent, teacher, and child training programs, trained facilitators use videotaped scenes to encourage problem solving and sharing of ideas. The parent program teaches parents interactive play and reinforcement skills, logical and natural consequences, and problem-solving strategies; the teacher training component is designed to strengthen teachers' skills in classroom management; and the child training component emphasizes building empathy with others, developing emotional competency, managing anger, solving interpersonal difficulties, and succeeding at school.[30] All three series of this program have received positive evaluations as meeting their original goals.[31] (See Library Extra 12.2 for information on a youth-focused publication.)

Library Extra 12.2
OJJDP publication: *YouthBuild U.S.A.*

Life Skills Training (LST) Consisting of a three-year intervention curriculum designed to prevent or reduce the use of gateway drugs such as tobacco, alcohol, and marijuana, the lessons in Life Skills Training (LST) emphasize social resistance skills training to help students identify pressures to use drugs. This intervention is meant to be implemented in school classrooms by teachers but also has been taught successfully by health professionals and peer leaders. LST targets all middle/junior high school students, using an initial 15-lesson intervention in grade six or seven and booster sessions over the following two years (10 sessions in year two and 5 sessions in year three), with lessons averaging 45 minutes in length and using a variety of techniques. Components of the program are designed to teach youths personal self-management skills, social skills, and negative attitudes toward the use of drugs.[32] Using outcomes from more than a dozen studies, evaluators have found LST to reduce tobacco, alcohol, and marijuana use by 50% to 75% in intervention students compared to control students.[33]

Midwestern Prevention Project (MPP) The intervention called Midwestern Prevention Project (MPP) includes school normative environment change as one of the components of a comprehensive three- to five-year community-based prevention program that targets gateway use of alcohol, tobacco, and marijuana. A central component of the program is the school-based intervention, which is designed as a primary prevention program. The program begins in either sixth or seventh grade and includes 10 to 13 classroom sessions taught by teachers trained in the curriculum; 5 booster sessions are offered in the second year of the program. A parent component follows the school sessions and is designed to develop family norms (shared standards of behavior) that discourage drug use, and the community component takes place during the last stages of the prevention effort and involves the support of community leaders.[34] Researchers followed students from eight schools who were randomly assigned to treatment or to control groups for three years and found that the program brought net reductions of up to 40% in adolescent smoking and marijuana use, with results maintained through high school graduation.[35] (Web Extra 12.1 provides a website listing funding sources for after-school programs.)

Web Extra 12.1
AfterSchool.gov

Multidimensional Treatment Foster Care (MTFC) For adolescents who have had problems with chronic antisocial behavior, delinquency, and emotional disturbance, Multidimensional Treatment Foster Care (MTFC) has been a cost-effective alternative to group or residential treatment, confinement, or hospitalization. This intervention provides short-term (generally about seven months) highly structured therapeutic care in foster families. Its goal is to decrease negative behaviors, including delinquency, and to increase youths' participation in appropriate prosocial activities, including school, hobbies, and sports. The program recruits, trains, and supervises foster families and provides youngsters with weekly skilled and focused therapy, and youths also participate in a structured daily behavioral management program implemented in the foster home. Counseling is further provided for the youngsters' biological (or foster) families in either an individual or a group format.[36] Evaluations of MTFC demonstrated that youths who participated in the program had significantly fewer arrests (an average of 2.6 offenses versus 5.4 offenses) and spent fewer days in lockup than youths placed in other community-based programs.[37]

Multisystemic Therapy (MST)   Multisystemic Therapy (MST) provides cost-effective community-based clinical treatment to chronic and violent juvenile offenders who are at high risk of out-of-home placement, specifically targeting the multiple factors contributing to antisocial behavior. The overarching goal of the intervention is to help parents understand and help their children overcome their behavior problems. MST uses strengths in each youth's social network to promote positive change in his or her behavior. Typically working in the home, at school, and in other community locations, therapists (who have low caseloads of four to six families) are available 24 hours a day, 7 days a week. Treatment usually lasts about 4 months, which includes about 60 hours of therapist–family contact.[38] Program evaluations have revealed 25% to 70% reductions in long-term rates of rearrest and 47% to 64% reductions in out-of-home placements. These and other positive results were maintained for nearly 4 years after treatment ended.[39]

Nurse–Family Partnership   Formerly called Prenatal and Infancy Home Visitation by Nurses, this model program, Nurse–Family Partnership, sends nurses to the homes of lower-income unmarried mothers, beginning during pregnancy and continuing for two years following the birth of the child. Tested with both white and African-American families in rural and urban settings, this program is designed to help women improve their prenatal health and the outcomes of their pregnancy by encouraging good health habits, giving them the skills they need to care for their infants and toddlers, and improving their own personal development.[40] Follow-up showed that this program's positive outcomes had long-term effects for both mothers and children: During the first 15 years after delivery of their first child, unmarried women who received nurse visits had 31% fewer subsequent births, longer intervals between births, fewer months on welfare, 44% fewer behavioral problems due to alcohol and drug abuse, 69% fewer arrests, and 81% fewer criminal convictions than those in the control group; adolescents whose mothers had received nurse home visits more than a decade earlier were 60% less likely to have run away, 56% less likely to have been arrested, and 80% less likely to have been convicted of a criminal violation than adolescents whose mothers had not received visits.[41]

Project toward No Drug Abuse (Project TND)   Project toward No Drug Abuse (Project TND) targets high school youths (ages 14 to 19 years old) who are at risk for drug abuse. Over a four- or five-week period, 12 classroom-based lessons offer students cognitive motivation enhancement activities, information about the social and health consequences of drug use, correction of cognitive misperceptions, help with stress management, instruction in active listening, and training in self-control to counteract risk factors for drug abuse.[42] At a one-year follow-up, participants in 42 schools revealed reduced usage of cigarettes, alcohol, marijuana, and hard drugs.[43]

Promoting Alternative Thinking Strategies (PATHS)   A comprehensive program for promoting social and emotional competencies, Promoting Alternative Thinking Strategies (PATHS) focuses on the understanding, expression, and regulation of emotions. The yearlong curriculum is designed to be used by teachers and counselors with entire classrooms of children in kindergarten through fifth grade, and lessons include such topics as identifying and labeling feelings, assessing the intensity of feelings, expressing feelings, managing feelings, and delaying gratification. The basic outcome goals are to provide youths with tools to achieve academically and to enhance both the classroom atmosphere and the learning process[44]; evaluations of

EXHIBIT 12.4

Victimization and Its Results

"I am the by-product of a mixed marriage. I say by-product of a marriage, because I never actually felt wanted, or even loved, for that matter. Both of my parents were alcoholics and very abusive, my father more so than my mother. My mother was the recipient of so many beatings from my father that I am unable to remember how many times it happened.

"One morning I got up to go to school, and as always, I checked on Dennis, who like me had asthma. I was responsible for taking care of Dennis. That morning he was not breathing. I had to wake my parents from an alcoholic stupor, the result of the night before. They checked on Dennis, found he was not moving or breathing, and called an ambulance. The ambulance and police finally arrived, but nothing could be done, and they just took him away. Both of my parents accused me of killing Dennis.

"My life took a 360-degree turn after the death of my brother. With the guilt of his death came feelings of isolation, aloneness, hate, despair, and an attitude that I did not care what happened anymore. I used those feelings and attitude to create an impenetrable wall that still exists to this day.

"The next four years became a nightmare, like we were living in the twilight zone. I thought the first six years of my life were bad, but I was sadly mistaken. We moved from the slums of the projects to a dilapidated house with a backyard full of junk and an infected creek. My father's beatings increased in severity, my mother and I getting the worst of it.

"My father's favorite idea of a joke was to unscrew a light bulb from a light socket, stick his finger in it, and hold the hand of one of my sisters. We created a chain where all three of my sisters would be holding hands, and one would be holding mine. My other hand held onto the water tap in the sink. He would laugh, and my sisters would scream and cry. I would simply grit my teeth while I filled up with hatred.

"One day I watched my father slap my mother around, and something clicked in my head; pure hatred took over my entire being. I patiently waited until my father went to sleep. I then snuck into the kitchen and got a butcher knife and boldly walked into their bedroom. My mother was sitting up in bed reading a magazine and saw me walk into their bedroom with a knife in hand. She screamed just as I put the point of the knife to my father's throat. He awoke with a start, and the top of the knife nicked his neck, drawing blood. He looked at me and then at the big old butcher knife I had at his throat and said nothing. In a very calm and childlike voice, I said to him, 'If you ever touch my mother or my sisters ever again, I will kill you in your sleep.' I walked out of their bedroom and back to mine, still holding the knife. The next morning I ran away from home."

This youth lasted on the streets for a month before he was arrested and then began his journey from one juvenile placement to another throughout the remainder of his adolescence. His adjustments to these placements were extremely problematic: He was sexually victimized in several and pushed a victimizing counselor down two flights of stairs in one institution (he broke both legs and an arm and received a concussion); in this same institution, he set a housemaster's office on fire.

Upon becoming 18 years old, he graduated from juvenile crime to adult crime, as he became involved with an older individual whom he accompanied on armed robberies. He was arrested when he committed murder, was convicted, and sent to prison. He was paroled 20 years later and remained in the community for several years; he eventually began to commit armed robberies again. He escaped from jail, carjacked a vehicle, and executed the owner of the vehicle, an 18-year-old. He is now on death row in Ohio, his appeals have run out, and he will face execution in the near future.

▶ Are you surprised that this person, based on his childhood, has been convicted of murder twice? How did abusive treatment influence him to become involved in delinquency and later in adult crime?

Source: One of the authors was involved in a death penalty court case with this individual, and his story is used with his permission.

---

this program have found positive behavioral changes related to peer aggression, hyperactivity, and conduct problems.[45]

These prevention programs, which are promising in their diversity and range of offerings, work to prevent delinquency through family-, school-, peer-, and community-based interventions.

Victimization of Children

Victimization cannot be separated from the prevention of delinquency or from other forms of problem behaviors. The child who is victimized, whether at home, in the school, or in the community, has been maltreated. This victim has not had some (and perhaps many) of his or her needs met and is likely at that time or later to respond with some form of socially unacceptable behavior, including delinquency. Victimization, then, can be seen as a pathway to delinquency, and the more serious the victimization, the more likely it is that the youth—and later the adult—will become involved in serious forms of delinquency and crime. See Exhibit 12.4 for one story of how victimization led to crime.

A number of studies have identified a strong association between juvenile victimization and juvenile delinquency. It can be argued that juvenile delinquency and victimization co-occur extensively in the youth population, particularly because delinquents become involved in risky activities.[46] Carlos A. Cuevas and colleagues, using the Developmental Victimization Survey (a national sample of 1,000 youths ages 10 to 17 years old), found support for three distinct types for the group of delinquent-victims—bully-victims, property delinquent-victims, and delinquent/maltreatment-victims; for a large group of youths who are primarily delinquent but not seriously victimized; and for the group of juveniles who are primarily victimized but not delinquent.[47] Following are the characteristics of each group:

Voices of Delinquency

Read "A Sixteen-Year-Old Sexual Predator." What was the possible relationship between the abuse he received and his becoming involved in sexually inappropriate behaviors?

- *Delinquent-victims.* Three groups are identified who fall into the delinquent-victim category. Bully-victims are defined as youths who in the past year engaged in violent interpersonal acts or weapon carrying and who also experienced a high level of violent victimization. The property delinquent-victims were involved in delinquency that was solely in the property crime domain. A third group, the delinquent/maltreatment-victims, experienced sexual victimization or a form of child maltreatment and engaged in an above-average amount of delinquency.
- *Primarily delinquents.* Another category is made up of youths who are primarily delinquent; they have committed acts of property delinquency or violent acts and have a low rate of victimization. They are subdivided into property delinquents, who engaged in at least one act of property delinquency but no violent delinquency and experienced little or no victimization, and assaulters, who engaged in at least one violent act of delinquency (but experienced little or no victimization).
- *Primarily victims.* Those youths who are primarily victims and have low rates of delinquency are broken into two groups. One group, reflecting a mild level of delinquency, had above-average levels of victimization but committed no acts of property delinquency or violence. A second group contains those who experienced sexual victimization or a form of child maltreatment but only had a low level of delinquency.

Table 12.2 summarizes the above typology.

TABLE 12.2 Typology Groups: Delinquency and Victimization Criteria

	Name	Delinquency Criteria	Victimization Criteria
Delinquent-victims	Bully-victim	Any interpersonal violence or weapon carrying	≥ 3 violent victimizations
	Property delinquent-victim	Property delinquency, no interpersonal violence	≥ 3 victimizations
	Delinquent/maltreatment-victim	≥ 2 acts of delinquency	Any sexual victimization or child maltreatment
Primarily delinquents	Assaulter	Any interpersonal violence or weapon carrying	< 3 violent victimizations
	Property delinquent	Property delinquency, no interpersonal violence	< 3 victimizations
Primarily victims	Nondelinquent/ maltreatment-victim	< 2 acts of delinquency	Any sexual victimization or child maltreatment
	Mild delinquency-victim	No violence and no acts of property delinquency	≥ 3 victimizations
None	Mild delinquency-nonvictim	No violence and no acts of property delinquency	< 3 victimizations

Source: Adapted Carlos A. Cuevas, David Finkelhor, Heather A. Turner, and Richard K. Ormrod, "Juvenile Delinquency and Victimization," *Journal of Interpersonal Violence* 22 (December 2007), p. 1587. Reprinted by permission of Sage Publications.

As has been done by those who examined the typology of victimization in other social contexts, the authors found that there were cases of youths who met criteria for more than one group. The strong relationship between victimization and delinquency can be seen in the correlation in this study between total number of different types of victimization and total number of endorsed delinquent acts.[48]

In sum, the prevention of delinquency and other problem behaviors in children begins in a social context where their needs are met. The more their needs are met and the less they experience victimization or maltreatment, the more likely it is that these children will refrain from serious delinquent acts; if they do become involved in an occasional delinquent activity, it will be something that they move through as they are in the process of accepting adult responsibilities. These insights are reflected in several of the stories in the first sections of *Voices of Delinquency*.

Successful Programs

Joy Dryfoos's 1990s analysis of the 100 most successful delinquency prevention programs tried through the 1980s identified their common features:

- High-risk children are attached to a responsible adult who is responsive to their needs. Techniques typically include individual counseling and small-group meetings, individual tutoring and mentoring, and case management (see Web Extra 12.2).
- A number of different kinds of programs and services are in place in a collaborative community-wide multiagency approach. Partners in the community-wide network include schools, businesses, community health and social services agencies, church groups, police, courts, and universities.
- In successful programs, an emphasis is placed on early identification and intervention, in which children and families are reached in the first stages of problem behaviors. As demonstrated in data on pregnancy, school achievement, substance abuse, and delinquency prevention, early identification and intervention have both short- and long-term benefits.
- The more successful programs located outside the school generally provide needed though controversial services, such as family planning and overnight

Serena Williams visits with children at a Boys and Girls Club in Los Angeles. ▶ **How do young people benefit from having role models like Williams?**

shelter for homeless and runaway youths. These programs appeal to youngsters turned off by the school system and also have the advantage of being able to offer weekend and summer programs.

- Many successful programs feature professional or nonprofessional staff who require training to implement the program. For example, LST, school-based management, cooperative learning, and team teaching require extensive in-service training and ongoing supervision.

- Personal coaching and social skills training are also found in many of these programs; these involve teaching youths about their own risky behavior, providing them with coping skills, and helping them make healthy decisions about their future.

- Several of the successful approaches use older peers to influence or help younger children, either in social skills training or as tutors. The training and supervision by the peer mentors appear to be important aspects of this component.[49]

In sum, the two program components that appear to have the greatest significance are (1) providing individual attention to high-risk youngsters and (2) developing broad community-wide interventions. Dryfoos's analysis appears to be equally cogent today (see Web Extra 12.3).

Web Extra 12.3
National Youth Violence Prevention Resource Center website

Comprehensive Delinquency Prevention Strategy

Another prevention strategy emerged in the 1990s. Based on research spearheaded and funded by the OJJDP, a consensus developed that the most effective strategy for juvenile corrections is to focus comprehensive prevention and diversion efforts on high-risk juveniles who are involved in violence; these juveniles—the ones whom officials are quick to dump into the adult system—commit the most frequent and more serious delinquent acts. At the same time that the seriousness of their behaviors was affecting changes in juvenile codes across the nation, research was beginning to find that these high-risk youths can be impacted by well-equipped and well-implemented prevention and treatment programs.[50]

Such programs are based on the assumption that the juvenile justice system does not see most serious offenders until it is too late to intervene effectively.[51] This strategy also presumes that if the goal is to reduce the overall violence in American society, it is necessary to successfully intervene in the lives of high-risk youthful offenders, who commit about 75% of all violent juvenile offenses.[52]

Several general characteristics are found in these comprehensive programs: They address key areas of risk in youths' lives, they seek to strengthen the personal and institutional factors contributing to healthy adolescent development, they provide adequate support and supervision, and they offer youths a long-term stake in the community.[53] These prevention programs for high-risk youths must be integrated with local police, child welfare, social services, school, and family preservation programs because comprehensive approaches to delinquency prevention and intervention require strong collaborative efforts between the juvenile justice system and other service provision systems, including health, mental health, child welfare, and education. An important component of a community's comprehensive plan is to develop mechanisms that effectively link these service providers at the program level.[54]

The comprehensive or multisystemic aspects of these programs are designed to deal simultaneously with many aspects of youths' lives. They are intensive, often involving weekly or even daily contacts with at-risk youths, and build on youths' strengths rather than focusing on their deficiencies. These programs operate mostly (though not exclusively) outside the formal justice system under a variety of public, nonprofit, or university auspices. Finally, they combine accountability and sanctions with increasingly intensive rehabilitation and treatment services, which is achieved through a system of graduated sanctions in which an integrated approach is used to stop the penetration of youthful offenders into the system.[55] See Figure 12.1 for an overview of this comprehensive prevention strategy.

FIGURE 12.1 Overview of a Comprehensive Delinquency Prevention Strategy

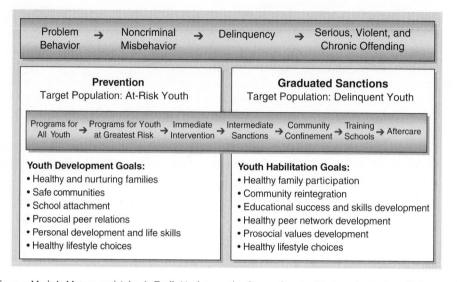

Source: Mark A. Matese and John A. Tuell, *Update on the Comprehensive Strategy for Serious, Violent, and Chronic Juvenile Offenders* (Washington, D.C.: Office of Justice Programs, Office of Juvenile Justice and Delinquency Prevention, 1998), p. 1.

In 1996, three communities—Lee and Duval Counties in Florida and San Diego County in California—collaborated with the OJJDP to apply the processes and principles set forth in OJJDP's comprehensive strategy statement; initial evaluations of the three pilot projects reported that each of the three sites had benefited significantly from the comprehensive planning process.[56] The following were among the accomplishments identified in a 2000 report:

■ Enhanced community-wide understanding of prevention services and sanction options for juveniles

■ Expanded networking capacity and better coordination among agencies and service providers

■ Institution of performance measurement systems

■ Hiring of staff to spearhead ongoing comprehensive strategy planning and implementation efforts

■ Development of comprehensive five-year strategic action plans[57]

Delinquency and Social Policy: The Importance of Early Intervention

Research seems to show that the younger a child is when first involved with the juvenile justice system, the more likely it is that the child will persist in delinquency; that the more contact a juvenile has with the juvenile justice system, the more likely it is that he or she will persist in delinquent behavior; and that the further a youngster is processed into the juvenile justice system, the less chance there is that he or she will be diverted successfully from the system.[58] These findings readily lead to the conclusion that primary (or early) prevention is much more desirable than later means of delinquency control.

There is also common agreement among experts on a number of concepts. First, no one solution exists to the delinquency prevention problem; that is, no one program component is available that by itself can alter the outcomes for all high-risk children. Second, high-risk behaviors are interrelated, so prevention programs should have broad and comprehensive goals. Third, each community requires a package of services that need community-wide planning. Fourth, the focus of prevention should

EXHIBIT 12.5

Delinquency Prevention

The desirable goal is for a child not to become involved in delinquent behavior, but if that goal cannot be achieved in a child's life, then the next desirable goal is for his or her delinquent behavior to be minor and limited to a few acts. If that goal cannot be achieved, then the next goal is for the delinquency to be confined to a youth's adolescent years. The purpose of prevention ultimately is for a child to live a productive and fulfilling life. In *Voices of Delinquency*, each individual describes the pain of a wasted life, a life in which each has also taken other lives, with the result that most will spend the remainder (or most) of their life in prison and one will be executed by the state. Reading these final stories in *Voices of Delinquency* is a vivid reminder of the importance of delinquency prevention to this society.

STORIES FROM *VOICES OF DELINQUENCY*

"The Thinker"

"I still long for freedom but have accepted my fate. If I could change it, I would, but I don't dwell on freedom like some guys do. . . . I'll never give up hope or the dream of freedom, but I'm not going to obsess over it. I have my life, and I'll get as much out of it as I can."

"Forgotten Children"

"With thirty-two days before being released, I was charged with two counts of murder, tried, convicted, and sentenced to two life sentences. Since that time, some twenty-six years have passed. Here I sit in prison seeking to overcome the need for attention and seeking to overcome the deprivations of my childhood."

"A Small-Town Boy"

"One evening I made a terrible decision while under the influence of this drug combination [alcohol and tranquilizers]. It resulted in the death of a girlfriend and cost me the rest of my life in prison. I truly regret my actions."

"My Father Was an Alcoholic"

"I have come to the realization that the beatings were only a small part of my childhood. My abusive background certainly influenced my life of crime, but there is more to it than that. My mental disability has no doubt influenced my life of crime. There were also all those drugs I took. I guess I will never know what really went wrong inside of me. What I do know is that I am now the living dead."

"Selling Drugs Was My Downfall"

"So I went to the store to get a pack of cigarettes, and I saw him pumping gas at the same point. I pointed and aimed, and I shot and killed this young man. To this day I wish I could definitely turn the clock back. I have a few friends who have been gunned down, and it makes me depressed that I have put myself in that pair of shoes. It does not make me feel very good about myself at all."

Individuals have human agency (i.e., they exercise free choice), and in spite of the social environment in which they live, they still make choices about what they are going to do with their lives—including whether they will become involved in delinquent acts or not. Human agency (choice) is still available, regardless of what pathway they take through their adolescent and adult years. For prevention efforts to work in their lives, they need support from a variety of sources, and viable prevention programs can also be helpful to them as they receive reinforcement for the positive decisions they make.

---

be on changing institutions rather than on changing individuals. Fifth, the timing of interventions is critical in achieving a successful outcome; preschool and middle school periods are when problems develop and ought to receive more focus in prevention interventions. Finally, a continuity of efforts must be maintained because one-shot efforts have little or no effect.[59]

The social development model implies the following six principles for the prevention of delinquency in those neighborhoods characterized by high rates of serious and violent delinquency:

1. A key to delinquency prevention is community organization against delinquency.
2. Community control of prevention efforts and other services for youth should be encouraged.
3. The participation of youths, as well as adults, should be encouraged.
4. Delinquent groups and gangs should be co-opted into constructive activities or disbanded.
5. Access to legitimate opportunities should be restricted, and legitimate educational, employment, and social activities should be accessible to all youths.
6. Efforts to improve the control mechanisms of the family should be directed at enhancing its direct control function and its ability to develop self-control among children.[60]

Voices of Delinquency

Excerpts in Exhibit 12.5 taken from the five final stories.

Chapter Summary

This chapter points out that the prevention of youth crime, which is the top priority of juvenile justice agencies, has several aspects:

- Three different levels of delinquency prevention programs have been identified in this chapter: primary, secondary, and tertiary.

- Primary prevention is focused on modifying general conditions in the physical and social environments that lead to delinquency.

- Secondary prevention programs target particular juveniles who have been identified as living in circumstances that dispose them toward delinquency.

- Tertiary prevention efforts are directed at the root causes of recidivism and usually work through traditional rehabilitation programs.

- A number of promising delinquency prevention programs were developed in the late nineteenth and early twentieth centuries.

- For prevention programs to have a continuing impact on youth crime in the United States, it will be necessary to modify the underlying social, economic, and political conditions in American society that lead to crime.

- Until those modifications are made, primary and secondary delinquency prevention programs will merely chip away at the tip of the iceberg rather than deal with the root of the delinquency problem.

Key Terms

delinquency prevention, p. 273
family therapy, p. 279

primary prevention, p. 273
secondary prevention, p. 273

tertiary prevention, p. 273

Review Questions

1. What is primary prevention? What is secondary prevention? What is tertiary prevention? How are they different?
2. What were the well-known prevention intervention programs of the past? What was the outcome of these programs?
3. What was different about the Chicago Area Project?
4. What are some of the more promising programs? Why are they defined as more promising?
5. What is the relationship between prevention, victimization, and delinquency?

Discussion Questions

1. Why have delinquency prevention programs been so popular in the United States?
2. Do you believe that prevention programs will have any effect on high-risk offenders? If they were to prove effective, how would that change youth crime in this nation?
3. Review the Institute on Family and Neighborhood Life's Olweus Bullying Prevention Program, available at www.clemson.edu/olweus/index.html. Can you think of any changes you might make to this program?
4. Considering the threat that violent youths present to society at large, should high-risk juvenile offenders identified as violent be removed from the juvenile justice program and dealt with more severely? Explain your response.
5. Some blame what they call the "Syndrome Society" for socializing youths to believe that they are not responsible for their own behavior because it was caused by some individual or social condition over which they have no control. How would you respond to this thesis?

Group Exercises

1. Have the students research the legislation cited in this chapter, beginning with the Juvenile Delinquency Prevention Act of 1972, and extract the sections of the laws that address prevention. Discuss the material in class.

2. Divide the class into six groups, one for each of the models listed here (excluding the Chicago Area Project). Have the six groups prepare and present a briefing to the class about their assigned project.

3. Have the students access the National Criminal Justice Reference Service (NCJRS) Delinquency Prevention webpage, available at www.ncjrs.gov/APP/Topics/Topic.axpx?topicicd=1333, and review the resources and programs it presents. Discuss the material in class.

mycrimekit™

Go to mycrimekit.com to explore the following study tools and resources specific to this chapter:

- **Practice Quiz:** Practice with multiple-choice, true/false, short-answer, and essay questions.

- **WebQuests:** Do web activities about the programs and services Homeboy Industries offers.

- **Flashcards:** Use 5 flashcards to test your knowledge of the chapter's key terms.

part 4

The Juvenile Justice System

Part Four of the text provides an overview of the issues involved in the juvenile justice system. Chapter 13 looks at the juvenile justice process and describes the many agencies and types of officials who play important roles in the handling of juvenile offenders. The chapter begins with a description of the historical development of the juvenile justice system and then outlines the structure and functions of today's system. It also explores perspectives on correcting youthful offenders, including the increasingly popular restorative-justice model. Racial inequalities within the system, the impact on the system of the Juvenile Justice and Delinquency Prevention Act of 1974, and the influence of graduated sanctions are all explored.

Chapter 14 looks at the pivotal role that the police play in responding to juvenile crime and in marshaling efforts to prevent it. Police discretion in the handling of juvenile offenders is an especially significant element that may determine the kinds of dispositions that juveniles receive. The chapter also discusses the rights that juvenile offenders have when they are taken into custody.

Chapter 15 focuses on the role of the juvenile court, including how expectations facing the court have changed. The various stages of juvenile court proceedings and the changing sentencing structure of juvenile courts are also explored. The chapter concludes with a discussion of an especially important recent U.S. Supreme Court decision preventing the execution of offenders who commit any crime, no matter how serious, if they are under the age of 18 years old.

Chapter 16, this section's (and text's) final chapter, explores juvenile corrections, including probation, community-based treatment programs, short- and long-term juvenile confinement, and aftercare. Underlying this chapter is the important question: What do we do about those youths who have committed a serious or violent crime or who continue to violate the law?

Juvenile Justice Process

CHAPTER OBJECTIVES

After reading this chapter, you should be able to answer the following questions:

- How has the juvenile justice system developed?
- What is diversion, and how is it important?
- What is the juvenile justice process?
- What are the stages in the juvenile justice process?
- In what ways are the juvenile and adult justice systems the same? In what ways are they different?
- What are the basic models used in juvenile corrections to deal with law-violating behaviors?
- Why is minority overrepresentation such a serious issue for the juvenile justice system?
- What will the juvenile justice system look like in the future?

The current [juvenile justice] system, a relic from a more innocent time, teaches youthful offenders that crime pays and that they are totally immune and insulated from responsibility.

—National Policy Forum

Introduction

Lionel Tate, still a young man, has led a violent and confused life. He was the youngest child in modern times to be sentenced to life in prison, but that sentence was overturned. Seven years later, however, he was back in prison, convicted of a robbery that netted just over $30.

In 1998, when Tate was age 12, he battered to death 6-year-old Tiffany Eunick in Broward County, Florida. Tate claimed that he had been practicing wrestling moves on her, but Eunick had a lacerated liver, skull fracture, and broken ribs. The sentencing judge said the injuries "were not the playful acts of a child [but] were cold, callous, and indescribably cruel."

Tate was convicted in 2001 of first-degree murder. But after a public outcry against this unusually tough sentence, a state appeals court overturned the conviction, saying he had been incapable of understanding the criminal proceedings against him. He was released on 1 year's house arrest and 10 years' probation. In September 2004, however, he was found carrying a four-inch knife outside his home, and his probation was extended to 15 years.

Eight months later, in May 2005, Tate robbed a pizza deliveryman with a gun for four pizzas and $33.60 in cash. Tate accepted a plea bargain for the robbery and was to be sentenced to 10 to 30 years in prison, but he was allowed to withdraw his guilty plea for the robbery and was sentenced to 30 years in prison for gun possession.

In February 2008, however, Tate pleaded no contest to the pizza robbery and was sentenced to 10 years in prison, running concurrently with his 30-year sentence. Tate's mother left court saying, "I'm tired of the whole system, the whole case, I'm just tired."[1]

Society has long considered how best to process and treat juvenile offenders and how to determine at what age a person is able to form the mental intent necessary for the commission of a crime. Some observers suggest children are too immature to form the "evilness" required to plan and commit certain acts of violence and therefore deserve compassion.[2] However, in support of the "get tough with juveniles" position, the argument is frequently made that society has some 15-, 16-, and 17-year-old youthful offenders who function on adult levels; traditional treatment, this position contends, does not hold much promise in dealing with these kids.

The juvenile justice system is responsible for controlling and correcting the behavior of law-violating juveniles. The system's inability to accomplish its basic mission has resulted in massive criticism from all sides. Indeed, both conservatives and liberals want to reduce the scope of the juvenile court's responsibilities: Conservatives want to refer serious youthful offenders to the adult court, whereas some liberals recommend divesting the juvenile court of its jurisdiction over status offenders.

Development of the Juvenile Justice System

This chapter examines juvenile justice through the lenses of the past, the present, and the future. Beginning with the development of juvenile justice in the United States, its structures, functions, and issues are discussed, and future possibilities are suggested.

Origins of the Juvenile Court

The first juvenile court was founded in Cook County (Chicago), Illinois, in 1899 when the Illinois legislature passed the Juvenile Court Act. The *parens patriae* doctrine provided a legal catalyst for the creation of the juvenile court, furnishing a rationale for the use of informal procedures for dealing with juveniles and for expanding state power over children. *Parens patriae* was also used to justify the juvenile court's authority to determine the causes of delinquent behavior and to make decisions on the disposition of cases. The kindly parent, the state, could thus justify relying on psychological and medical examinations rather than on trial by evidence. Once the *parens patriae* rationale was applied to juvenile proceedings, the institution of the juvenile court followed.

In his book *The Child Savers*, Anthony Platt discussed the political context of the origin of the juvenile court, claiming that the juvenile court was established in Chicago and later elsewhere because it satisfied several middle-class interest groups. He saw the juvenile court as an expression of middle-class values and of the philosophy of conservative political groups. In denying that the juvenile court was revolutionary, Platt charged:

> The child-saving movement was not so much a break with the past as an affirmation of faith in traditional institutions. Parental authority, education at home, and the virtues of rural life were emphasized because they were in decline at this time. The child-saving movement was, in part, a crusade which, through emphasizing the dependence of the social order on the proper socialization of children, implicitly elevated the nuclear family and, more especially, the role of women as stalwarts of the family. The child savers were prohibitionists, in a general sense, who believed that social progress depended on efficient law enforcement, strict supervision of children's leisure and recreation, and the regulation of illicit pleasures. What seemingly began as a movement to humanize the lives of adolescents soon developed into a program of moral absolutism through which youths were to be saved from movies, pornography, cigarettes, alcohol, and anything else which might possibly rob them of their innocence.[3]

Lionel Tate, dressed in prison stripes, entered a guilty plea Wednesday, March 1, 2006, during a Fort Lauderdale, Fla., court hearing where Tate plead guilty to armed robbery and probation violation. Tate, who received a 30-year prison sentence on those charges, was the youngest child in modern times to be sentenced to life in prison for a death that he caused when he was 12 years old. ▶ Do you think he should get another chance?

Platt contended that the behaviors the **child savers** deemed worthy of penalty—such as engaging in sex, roaming the streets, drinking, fighting, frequenting dance halls, and staying out late at night—were found primarily among lower-class children. Therefore, juvenile justice from its inception, he argued, reflected class favoritism that resulted in the frequent processing of poor children through the system while middle- and upper-class children were more likely to be excused.[4]

The children of the poor were a particular problem to the child savers because the juvenile court emerged in the wake of unprecedented industrial and urban development in the United States. This process was closely connected with large-scale immigration to urban centers of people who had different backgrounds from the indigenous population. These immigrants brought new social problems to Chicago and other urban centers, and the child savers were determined to "rescue" the immigrant children and to protect them from their families.[5]

child savers A name given to an organized group of progressive social reformers of the late nineteenth and early twentieth centuries who promoted numerous laws aimed at protecting children and institutionalizing an idealized image of childhood innocence.

Emergence of Community-Based Corrections

The first application of community-based corrections for juveniles grew out of juvenile aftercare, or parole, used to supervise juveniles after their institutionalization. Such programs are nearly as old as juvenile correctional institutions. By the 1820s, superintendents of houses of refuge had the authority to release juveniles when they saw fit; some juveniles were returned directly to their families, and others were placed in the community as indentured servants and apprentices who could reenter the community as free citizens once they finished their terms of service. This system became formalized only in the 1840s, when states set up inspection procedures to monitor the supervision of those with whom youths were placed.

Juvenile **aftercare** was influenced by the development of adult parole in the late 1870s. Zebulon Brockway, the first superintendent of Elmira Reformatory in New York State, permitted parole for carefully selected prisoners. When they left the institution, parolees were instructed to report to a guardian on arrival, to write immediately to the superintendent, and to report to the guardian on the first of each month.

Juvenile aftercare programs spread throughout the United States in the early decades of the twentieth century and took on many of the features of adult parole.

aftercare The supervision of juveniles who are released from correctional institutions so that they can make an optimal adjustment to community living; also, the status of a juvenile conditionally released from a treatment or confinement facility and placed under supervision in the community.

probation A court-ordered non-punitive juvenile disposition that emphasizes community-based services and treatment and close supervision by an officer of the court. Probation is essentially a sentence of confinement that is suspended so long as the probationer meets the conditions imposed by the court.

Juveniles were supervised in the community by aftercare officers, whose jobs were similar to those of parole officers in the adult system. The parole board did not become a part of juvenile corrections, for in more than two-thirds of the states, institutional staff continued to decide when youths would return to the community.

Probation as an alternative to institutional placement for juveniles arose from the effort of John Augustus, a Boston cobbler, in the 1840s and 1850s. Augustus, who is called "the father of probation," spent considerable time in the courtroom and in 1841 persuaded a judge to permit him to supervise an offender in the community rather than sentencing the offender to an institution. Over the next two decades, Augustus worked with nearly 2,000 individuals, including both adult and juvenile offenders. As the first probation officer, Augustus initiated several services still used in probation today: investigation and screening, supervision, educational and employment services, and provision of aid and assistance.[6]

Expansion and Retrenchment in the Twentieth Century   In the twentieth century, probation services spread to every state and were administered by both state and local authorities. The use of volunteer probation workers had disappeared by the turn of the twentieth century, only to return in the 1950s. Probation became more treatment oriented: Early in the twentieth century, the medical treatment model was used; later, in the 1960s and 1970s, probation officers became brokers who delivered services to clients. The upgrading of standards and training also was emphasized in the 1960s and 1970s.

Residential programs, the third type of community-based juvenile corrections to appear, had their origins in the Highfields Project, a short-term guided-interaction group program. Known officially as the New Jersey Experimental Project for the Treatment of Youthful Offenders, this project was established in 1950 on the former estate of Colonel and Mrs. Charles Lindbergh. The Highfields Project housed adjudicated youths who worked during the day at the nearby New Jersey Neuro-Psychiatric Institute and met in two guided-interaction groups five evenings a week at the Highfields facility. Similar programs were initiated in the 1960s at South Fields in Louisville, Kentucky; Essexfields in Newark, New Jersey; Pinehills in Provo, Utah; the New Jersey centers at Oxford and Farmingdale for boys and at Turrell for girls; and the START centers established by the New York City Division for Youth.

In the late 1980s and 1990s, a decline in federal funding, along with the "get tough" mood of society, meant the closing of some residential and day-treatment programs. Although probation remained the most widely used judicial disposition, both probation and aftercare services were charged to enforce a more hard-line policy with juvenile offenders. See Table 13.1 for a timeline of the most important events in the evolution of community-based corrections for juveniles.

residential program A program conducted for the rehabilitation of youthful offenders within community-based and institutional settings.

TABLE 13.1 Timeline of Community-Based Corrections for Juveniles in the United States

Date	Event
1820s	Superintendents of houses of refuge had the power to release juveniles from the institution.
1840s	States set up inspection procedures to monitor the supervision of those with whom juveniles were placed.
1841	John Augustus began to supervise juvenile and adult offenders in Boston.
1869	The Commonwealth of Massachusetts established a visiting probation agent system that supervised youthful offenders.
1890	Probation was established statewide in Massachusetts.
1950	The Highfields Project was established.
1980s–present	Retrenchment took place in community-based corrections.

Development of Juvenile Institutions

Before the end of the eighteenth century, the family was commonly believed to be the source or cause of deviancy, so the idea emerged that perhaps the well-adjusted family could provide the model for a correctional institution for children. The house of refuge, the first juvenile institution, reflected the family model wholeheartedly; it was designed to bring order, discipline, and care of the family into institutional life. The institution was to become the home; the peers, the siblings; and the staff, the parents.[7]

The New York House of Refuge, which opened on January 1, 1825, with six girls and three boys, is usually acknowledged as the first house of refuge. Several similar institutions already existed in England and Europe.[8] Over the next decade or so, Boston, Philadelphia, Bangor (Maine), Richmond, Mobile, Cincinnati, and Chicago followed suit in establishing houses of refuge for males; 23 schools were chartered in the 1830s and another 30 in the 1840s. Some houses of refuge were established by private philanthropists, some by the state government or legislature, and some jointly by public authorities and private organizations. The vast majority of the houses of refuge were for males. The average capacity was 210, but the capacity ranged from 90 at Lancaster, Massachusetts, to 1,000 at the New York House of Refuge for Boys.[9]

The development of the **cottage system** and the construction of these juvenile institutions outside cities were two reforms of the mid-nineteenth century. The cottage system, which was introduced in 1854 and quickly spread throughout the nation, housed smaller groups of youths in separate buildings, usually no more than 20 to 40 youths per cottage. Early cottages were log cabins; later cottages were built from brick or stone. Now called **training schools** or industrial schools, these juvenile facilities were usually constructed outside cities so that youths would be reformed through exposure to the simpler rural way of life. It was presumed that residents would learn responsibility and new skills as they worked the fields and took care of the livestock, and their work would enable the institution, in turn, to provide its own food and perhaps even realize a profit.

cottage system A widely used treatment practice that places small groups of training school residents into cottages.

training school A correctional facility for long-term placement of juvenile delinquents; may be public (run by a state department of corrections or youth commission) or private.

Twentieth-Century Changes

Several significant changes occurred in juvenile institutionalization during the first several decades of the twentieth century. One change was that reformers advocated treatment on several fronts. Case studies were used to prescribe treatment plans for residents; reception units were developed to diagnose and classify new admissions; individual therapies, such as psychotherapy and behavior modification, were used; and group therapies, such as guided-interaction groups, became popular means of transforming the inmate subculture. Institutional programs also became more diverse. Confined juveniles could graduate from state-accredited high school programs; home furloughs and work-release programs were permitted in many training schools and included printing, barbering, welding, and repairing automobiles. Furthermore, the types of juvenile correctional facilities increased to include ranches and forestry camps as well as the traditional prison-like training schools. Finally, several experimental forms of training schools developed that offered the promise of changing juvenile corrections.

In spite of the improvements in many reform schools, as well as the truly experimental efforts in a few, the story of the twentieth-century training school is one of scaled-down prisons for juveniles.[10] In the 1960s and 1970s, reformers began to accuse training schools of being violent, inhumane, and criminogenic.[11] Widespread criticism of training schools, various court decisions, and pressure groups in state legislatures led to a number of reforms in the mid- and late 1970s. These innovations included the decision to no longer confine status offenders with delinquents in training schools, an increase in staff training programs, the growing acceptance of grievance procedures for residents, and the establishment of coeducational facilities.

In the late 1980s and 1990s, a number of disturbing changes took place in juvenile institutionalization. Training schools became overcrowded and more violent.

TABLE 13.2 Timeline of Juvenile Institutionalization	
Date	**Event**
1825	New York House of Refuge was opened.
1854	The cottage system was introduced.
1850s–1860s	Juvenile facilities were called training schools or industrial schools.
1880–1899	The public became disillusioned, realizing that training schools were primarily custodial institutions.
1900–1950s	Training schools underwent a period of reform, especially with the introduction of varied forms of treatment.
1960s–1970s	Training schools came under great criticism.
Late 1970s	Training schools underwent another period of reform.
Late 1980s–present	Training schools became overcrowded, grew more violent, and confined increased numbers of minority youths.

Members of minorities made up a greater proportion of the population of juvenile correctional institutions, especially for drug offenses. Status offenders and juveniles who had committed nonserious delinquent acts continued to be committed to private training schools, but private placements also began to admit youngsters who had committed serious delinquent offenses. More youths were transferred to adult court for violent crimes and received long-term prison sentences. (See Table 13.2 for a timeline of juvenile institutionalization.)

Diversion from the Juvenile Justice System

diversion programs Dispositional alternatives for youthful offenders that exist outside of the formal juvenile justice system.

In the late 1960s and early 1970s, **diversion programs** sprouted up across the nation. *Diversion*, a term which refers to keeping juveniles outside the formal justice system, can be attempted either through the police and the courts or through agencies outside the juvenile justice system. The main characteristic of diversion initiated by the courts or police is that the justice subsystems retain control over youthful offenders, and youths who fail to respond to such a program usually will be returned to the juvenile court for continued processing within the system.

In the 1970s, youth service bureaus (YSBs) and runaway centers were the most widely used diversion programs outside the juvenile justice system. More recently, family counseling, substance abuse, and juvenile mediation programs have been used by juvenile courts and probation departments to divert juveniles from the formal justice system; gang intervention programs have been implemented in some communities across the nation to divert gang youths from formal processing.

In the 1990s, new forms of diversion developed in the United States and included community courts, alternative dispute resolution, gun courts, youth courts, and drug courts. Youth courts and drug courts are described in more detail.

Youth Courts

Youth courts, also known as *teen courts, peer courts,* or *student courts,* are juvenile justice programs in which youths are sentenced by their peers (see Figure 13.1 for a history of youth courts). Established and administered in a variety of ways, most youth courts are used as a sentencing option for first-time offenders ages 11 to 17 years old who are charged with nonviolent misdemeanor offenses. The offender has typically acknowledged his or her guilt and participates in a youth court voluntarily rather than going through the more formal juvenile justice procedures.[12] In 2005, more than

FIGURE 13.1 History of Youth Courts

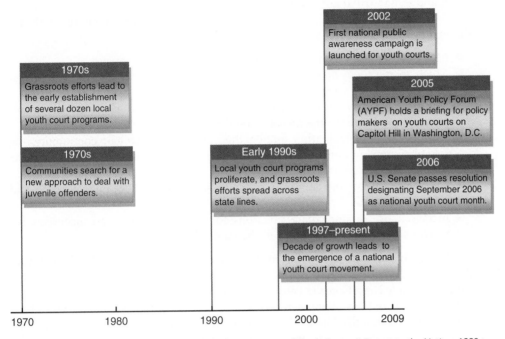

Source: Adapted from Scott B. Peterson and Jill Beres, "History of Youth Courts," *Report to the Nation, 1993 to 2008: The Global Youth Justice Movement—15 Year Update on Youth Courts and Teen Courts.* Courtesy of Scott B. Peterson.

110,000 youths volunteered to hear more than 115,000 juvenile cases, and more than 20,000 adults volunteered to be facilitators for peer justice in youth court programs; 1,158 youth court programs in 49 states and the District of Columbia provided restorative justice for youthful offenders.[13]

Four possible case-processing models are used by these courts:

1. *Adult judge.* An adult serves as judge and rules on legal terminology and court-room procedures. Youths serve as attorneys, jurors, clerks, bailiffs, and so forth.
2. *Youth judge.* This is similar to the adult judge model except that a youth serves as the judge.
3. *Tribunal.* Youth attorneys present the case to a panel of three youth judges, who decide the appropriate disposition for the defendant. A jury is not used.
4. *Peer jury.* This model does not use youth attorneys. The case is presented to a youth jury by a youth or adult, and the youth jury then questions the defendant directly.[14]

Youth courts usually handle first-time offenders who are charged with offenses such as theft, misdemeanor assault, disorderly conduct, and possession of alcohol. The majority of these teen courts (87%) reported that they rarely or never accepted any juveniles with prior arrest records. The most common disposition used by these courts is community service, followed (in level of use) by victim apology letters (86%), apology essays (79%), teen court jury duty (75%), drug/alcohol classes (59%), and monetary restitution (34%).[15]

Juvenile Drug-Court Movement

By 2003, approximately 300 juvenile drug courts had opened, with another 100 being planned. The juvenile drug-court movement, which is dedicated to juveniles, is part of an expanding adult drug-court movement that has been stimulated by Title V of the Violent Crime Control and Law Enforcement Act of 1994, an act that authorizes the attorney general to make grants to various agencies to establish drug courts. These agencies include states, state and local courts, units of local government, and Indian tribal governments.[16]

A number of strategies are common to juvenile drug courts compared with traditional juvenile courts:

- Much earlier and much more comprehensive intake assessments
- Much greater focus on the functioning of the juvenile and the family throughout the juvenile court system
- Much closer integration of the information obtained during the assessment process as it relates to the juvenile and the family
- Much greater coordination among the court, the treatment community, the school system, and other community agencies in responding to the needs of the juvenile and the court
- Much more active and continuous judicial supervision of the juvenile's case and treatment process
- Increased use of immediate sanctions for noncompliance and incentives for progress for both the juvenile and the family[17]

Currently six states operate juvenile drug courts, with the greatest activity in California (two programs) and Florida (four programs). For example, the Escambia County Juvenile Drug Court in Pensacola, Florida, began operating in April 1996. It is a 12-month three-phase approach to treating substance use and abuse, with Phase I lasting about 2 months, Phase II lasting 4 months, and Phase III lasting 6 months. The drug-court judge supervises treatment of up to 40 offenders by reviewing reports from treatment personnel to determine the need for either positive or negative incentives to encourage participation and involvement.[18]

The most positive characteristic of diversion programs is that they minimize the penetration of youthful offenders into the justice system, but empirical studies of diversion generally have not demonstrated that doing something (treatment or services) is necessarily better than doing nothing. Researchers warn that the overlooked negative consequences of diversion challenge the viability of this concept.[19] Some of these negative effects include widening the net of juvenile justice by increasing the number of youths under the control of the system, increasing the size of the system (budget and staff), ignoring clients' due process rights or constitutional safeguards, and labeling minor offenders.[20]

Juvenile Justice System Today

Like most systems (private or public), the juvenile justice system is most concerned with maintaining its equilibrium and surviving. The system is able to survive by maintaining internal harmony while simultaneously managing environmental inputs. The police and the juvenile court, juvenile probation, residential and day-treatment programs, detention facilities, long-term juvenile institutions, and aftercare are all closely interrelated, so changes in one organization have definite consequences elsewhere within the system.

Structure and Functions

The juvenile justice system is made up of three basic subsystems—police, juvenile court, and corrections—that consist of between 10,000 and 20,000 public and private agencies, with annual budgets totaling hundreds of millions of dollars. Many of the 40,000 police departments across the nation have juvenile divisions, and over 3,000 juvenile courts and about 1,000 juvenile correctional facilities exist in the United States.[21] Of the 50,000 employees in the juvenile justice system, more than 30,000 are employed in juvenile correctional facilities, 6,500 are juvenile probation officers, and the remaining

mycrimekit™

Review History of the Juvenile Justice Court

Dr. Jerome G. Miller is seen in this 1972 photo. In the early 1970s, Miller undertook a radical social experiment, closing down virtually all Massachusetts training schools and dispersing delinquent children to community-based programs. ▶ **What would be the consequences of such an action today?**

> > > **EXHIBIT 13.1** < < <

Lee Boyd Malvo

Following is the story of Lee Boyd Malvo—his background, his school years, and his choices that eventually brought him in contact with the U.S. justice system.

Lee Boyd Malvo (alias John Lee Malvo or Malik Malvo) was born in Kingston, Jamaica, on February 18, 1985, to Leslie Malvo, a bricklayer, and Una James, a seamstress.

Malvo's parents never married and separated when he was a toddler. The father rarely saw his son after that. Ms. James often traveled to find work, and Lee was left for long periods of time in the care of relatives and friends.

Malvo and his mother left Jamaica when he was about fourteen years of age and moved to the island of Antigua. In 2000, while they were in Antigua, they met John Allen Muhammad (born John Allen Williams). The mother claimed that she was not intimate with Muhammad, but that she and her son formed a strong bond with him. She reported that her son had spent most of his life seeking a father figure.

Ms. James eventually left Antigua for Fort Myers, Florida, traveling on false documents and living there illegally. She left Lee with Muhammad, and her son was supposed to join her a few months later.

In 2001, Malvo joined his mother for a brief period in Florida, before moving to Bellingham, Washington, where he and Muhammad lived in a homeless shelter. The two would spend their evenings in a local coffee shop playing chess. Malvo enrolled

in high school, falsely listing Muhammad as his father. Classmates said that he was good in school, polite, well-dressed, and willing to state his opinions, but he did not make any friends.

While in the Tacoma, Washington, area, Malvo shoplifted a Bushmaster XM-15 rifle from Bull's Eye Shooter Supply, a retail gun dealer. About this time, Lee converted to Islam.

The pair left Bellingham in the summer of 2002 and turned up in Baton Rouge, Louisiana, where one of Muhammad's ex-wives lived. Months later, Malvo was arrested along with Muhammad and charged with participating in the infamous D.C.-area sniper shootings that took place during three weeks in October 2002 and claimed the lives of ten people.

Malvo was charged with murder, but his defense team claimed that he was a defenseless young person who had been brainwashed by Muhammad. Although Malvo pleaded not guilty by reason of insanity, a Virginia court convicted him of two capital crimes and the unlawful use of a firearm. Five days later, on December 23, 2003, the jury recommended a sentence of life in prison without the possibility of parole. On March 10, 2004, a judge formally imposed that sentence.

Source: This article is licensed under the GNU Free Documentation License. It uses material from the Wikipedia article, "Lee Boyd Malvo." Adapted from http://en.wikipedia.org/wiki/Lee_Boyd_Malvo.

---

personnel are aftercare (parole) officers and staff who work in residential programs. In addition, several thousand more employees work in diversion programs and private juvenile correctional systems.[22]

The functions of the three subsystems differ somewhat. The basic work of the police is maintaining order and enforcing the law. The function of maintaining order, which occupies most of police officers' time, involves such responsibilities as settling family disputes, providing emergency ambulance service, directing traffic, furnishing information to citizens, preventing suicides, giving shelter to drunks, and checking the homes of families on vacation. The law enforcement function requires that the police deter crime, make arrests, obtain confessions, collect evidence for strong cases that can result in convictions, and increase crime clearance rates. The police must also deal with juvenile law-breaking and provide services juveniles need.

The juvenile courts are responsible for disposing of cases referred to them by intake divisions of probation departments (see Chapter 15), supervising juvenile probationers, making detention decisions, dealing with cases of child neglect and dependency cases, and monitoring the performance of youths who have been adjudicated delinquent or status offenders. The *parens patriae* philosophy of the juvenile court charges the court with treating rather than punishing youngsters appearing before juvenile judges, but the treatment arm of the juvenile court goes only so far, and youths who commit serious crimes or persist in juvenile law-breaking may be sent to training schools or transferred to adult court (see Library Extra 13.1).

The corrections system is charged with the care of youthful offenders sentenced by the courts. Juvenile probation, the most widely used judicial disposition, supervises offenders released to probation by the courts, ensuring that they comply with the conditions of probation imposed by the courts and desist from delinquent behavior in the community (see Library Extra 13.2). Day-treatment and residential programs (see Chapter 16) are charged with preparing youths for their return to the

Library Extra 13.1
OJJDP publication: *Juvenile Offenders and Victims: 2006 National Report* (Chapter 4)

Library Extra 13.2
OJJDP publication: *How the Justice System Responds to Juvenile Victims: A Comprehensive Model*

community, with preventing unlawful behavior in the program or in the community, and with providing humane care for youths directed to the programs. Long-term juvenile correctional institutions have similar responsibilities, but the officials of these programs also are charged with deciding when each youth is ready to be released to the community. Officials of long-term institutions must also ensure that residents receive their constitutional and due process rights. Aftercare officers, the final group in the juvenile justice system, have the responsibility of supervising youths released from long-term juvenile correctional institutions; like probation officers, aftercare officers are expected to make certain that youthful offenders fulfill the terms of their aftercare agreements and avoid delinquent behavior.

Stages in the Juvenile Justice Process

The means by which juvenile offenders are processed by juvenile justice agencies are examined throughout this text. The variations in the juvenile justice systems across the nation make it difficult to describe this process, but Figure 13.2 is a flowchart of the juvenile justice system and the criminal justice system that shows what these systems have in common. The process begins when the youth is referred to the juvenile court. Some jurisdictions permit a variety of agents to refer the juvenile, whereas in others the police alone are charged with this responsibility. The more common procedure is that the youth whose alleged offense has already been investigated is taken into custody by the police who have made the decision to refer the juvenile to the juvenile court (see Web Extra 13.1).

The intake officer, usually a probation officer (see Chapter 16), must decide whether the juvenile should remain in the community or be placed in a shelter or

Review   Adjudication Process

Web Extra 13.1

OJJDP PowerPoint presentation: "Juvenile Justice System Structure and Process"

FIGURE 13.2 Stages of Delinquency Case Processing in the Juvenile Justice System

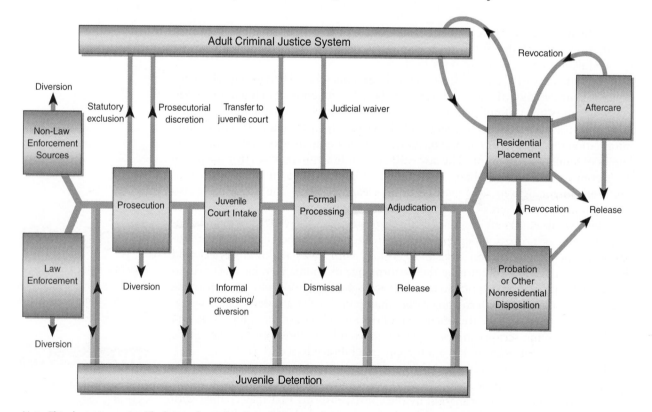

Note: This chart gives a simplified view of case flow through the juvenile justice system. Procedures vary among jurisdictions.

Source: Adapted from Howard N. Snyder and Melissa Sickmund, *Juvenile Offenders and Victims: 2006 National Report* (Washington, D.C.: Office of Juvenile Justice and Delinquency Prevention, 2006), p. 205.

detention facility. As indicated in Figure 13.2, the intake officer has a variety of options in determining what to do with a youth, but in more serious cases, the juvenile generally receives a petition to appear before the juvenile court.

The juvenile court judge (or the referee in many jurisdictions) hears the cases of juveniles referred to the court. If the juvenile is to be transferred to adult court, this must be done before any juvenile proceedings take place; otherwise, an adjudicatory hearing, the primary purpose of which is to determine whether the juvenile is guilty of the delinquent acts alleged in the petition, takes place. The court hears evidence on these allegations. *In re Gault* (see Chapter 15) usually is interpreted to guarantee to juveniles the right to representation by counsel, freedom from self-incrimination, and the right to confront and cross-examine witnesses, and some states also give juveniles the right to a jury trial.

A disposition hearing takes place when a juvenile has been found delinquent in the adjudicatory stage. Most juvenile court codes now require that the adjudicatory and disposition hearings be held at different times. The number of dispositions juvenile judges have available to them varies from one jurisdiction to the next. In addition to the standard disposition of warning and release, placement on juvenile probation, or adjudication to the department of youth services or corrections, some judges can place juveniles in a publicly or privately administered day-treatment or residential program, and some jurisdictions even grant juvenile judges the authority to send a juvenile to a particular correctional facility.

The juvenile adjudicated to a training school is generally treated somewhat differently in small states than in large states. In small states with one training school for males and (usually) one for females, a youth adjudicated to a training school usually is sent directly to the appropriate school, but large states that have several facilities for males and perhaps more than one for females may send the youth to a classification (or diagnostic) center to determine the proper institutional placement. Training school residents currently are not confined as long as they were in the past and frequently are released within a year. Institutional release takes place in a variety of ways, but the juvenile released from the training school is generally placed on aftercare status. To be released from this supervision, the juvenile must fulfill the rules of aftercare and must avoid unlawful behavior.

Juvenile court judge Jeanne Meurer of Austin, Texas, gazes intently at a young defendant represented by a public defender during a detention hearing. ▶ **How does the juvenile justice system differ from the adult criminal justice system?**

> > > **EXHIBIT 13.2** < <

Similarities and Differences between the Juvenile and Adult Justice Systems

SIMILARITIES

- Police officers use discretion with both juvenile and adult offenders.
- Juvenile and adult offenders receive *Miranda* warnings and other constitutional rights at time of arrest.
- Juveniles and adults can be placed in pretrial facilities.
- The juvenile court and the adult court use proof beyond a reasonable doubt as the standard for evidence.
- Plea bargaining may be used with both juvenile and adult offenders.
- Convicted juvenile and adult offenders may be sentenced to probation services, residential programs, or institutional facilities.
- Boot camps are used with juvenile and adult offenders.
- Released institutional juvenile and adult offenders may be assigned to supervision in the community.

DIFFERENCES

- Juveniles can be arrested for acts that would not be criminal if they were adults (status offenses).

- Age determines the jurisdiction of the juvenile court; age does not affect the jurisdiction of the adult court.
- Parents are deeply involved in the juvenile process but not in the adult process.
- Juvenile court proceedings are more informal, whereas adult court proceedings are formal and open to the public.
- Juvenile court proceedings, unlike adult proceedings, are not considered criminal. Juvenile records are generally sealed when the age of majority (usually age 16 or 17) is reached. Adult records are permanent.
- Juvenile courts cannot sentence juveniles to jail or prison; only adult courts may issue such sentences.

▶ How much harm would it do to juveniles if juvenile proceedings were abolished and juveniles were handled in adult court? What would be the advantages if juvenile offenders were handled with adult proceedings and procedures?

---

recidivism The repetition of delinquent behavior by a youth who has been released from probation status or from training school.

A cohort study conducted in the late 1990s in Maricopa County Juvenile Court (Phoenix, Arizona) found a somewhat favorable picture of youths' contact with the juvenile justice system. Using records that captured the complete juvenile court careers of more than 150,000 youths who were born between 1962 and 1977, researchers found that 54% of males and 73% of females who entered the juvenile justice system never returned on a new referral. **Recidivism** was much higher for males than females, with 19% of males but only 5% of females accruing four or more arrests. Because there was a standing policy in this county that all youths arrested be referred to the juvenile court for screening, this study provides a complete history of local youths' official contact with the juvenile justice system.[23]

In *Shared Beginnings, Divergent Lives*, John H. Laub and Robert J. Sampson reported on interview respondents who identified the time they spent at the Lyman School for Boys, a training school in Massachusetts, as a turning point in their lives. For some men, the school provided a setting in which they could acquire the discipline and structure that had been absent from their lives, some saw their Lyman School experience as a deterrent that would keep them away from crime in the future, others felt that the school provided an environment for learning important lessons about life, and some credited Lyman School (and their military service) with offering needed boundaries and strictness. However, some men defined the Lyman School as a horrible experience for them.[24]

In recent decades, training schools have had far more critics than supporters. Although the old argument that juvenile institutions are "schools of crime" is much too simplistic, there is convincing evidence that the recidivism rates are very high among those who have been confined in training schools. A 1989 review demonstrated that the rearrest rates of juveniles in several jurisdictions that rely heavily on institutions ranged from a low of 51% to a high of 70%.[25] An analysis of youths released from state correctional and private facilities in Minnesota in 1985 and 1991 found that 53% to 77% continued their criminal careers into adulthood.[26] Peter Greenwood and Franklin Zimring stated that most state training schools "fail to reform . . . [and] make no appreciable reductions in the very high recidivism rates, on the order of 70 to 80 percent, that are expected for chronic offenders."[27]

William P. Evans, Randall Brown, and Eric Killian analyzed two 2001 surveys administered to 197 youths in two Nevada juvenile detention facilities and found that the youths who possessed high levels of decision-making competence scored higher on a postdetention success scale.[28] This study is a reminder that human agency is involved in juveniles' outcomes—affecting whether juveniles use an experience as a positive or a negative transition in their lives. It is also reasonable to conclude that youths with higher decision-making abilities would find more reason to desist from crime.

Comparison of the Juvenile and Adult Justice Systems

There is much similarity between the juvenile and adult justice systems. Both systems are made up of three basic subsystems (police, court, and corrections) and numerous interrelated agencies. The flow of justice in both is supposed to progress from law violation to police apprehension, judicial process, judicial disposition, and rehabilitation in correctional agencies. The basic vocabulary is usually the same in the juvenile and adult systems, but even when the vocabulary differs, the intent remains the same (see Table 13.3).

Both juvenile and adult systems are under fire to "get tough on crime," especially on offenders who commit violent crimes. Both must deal with case overloads and institutional overcrowding; both must operate on fiscal shoestrings; and both face the ongoing problems of staff recruitment, training, and burnout. Exhibit 13.3 further describes the common ground and differences between the juvenile and adult justice systems.

Basic Correctional Models

To correct the behavior of the juvenile delinquent, there have traditionally been four basic correctional models applicable to the juvenile justice system: (1) the rehabilitation model, (2) the justice model, (3) the balanced and restorative model, and (4) the crime-control model. An emerging model in juvenile justice, which is based more on a balanced approach between treatment and punishment, is much more focused on punishment and accountability than has been the case in juvenile justice in the past.

TABLE 13.3 Juvenile and Adult Justice System Terms

Juvenile Terminology	Adult Terminology
Adjudicatory hearing	Trial
Aftercare	Parole
Commitment	Sentence to confinement
Detention	Holding in jail
Dispositional hearing	Sentencing hearing
Juvenile court officer	Probation officer
Offender	Defendant
Petition	Indictment
Petitioner	Prosecutor
Respondent	Defense attorney
Taking into custody	Arrest

adjudicatory hearing The stage of juvenile court proceedings that usually includes the youth's plea, the presentation of evidence by the prosecution and by the defense, the cross-examination of witnesses, and a finding by the judge as to whether the allegations in the petition can be sustained.

commitment A determination made by a juvenile judge at the disposition stage of a juvenile court proceeding that a juvenile is to be sent to a juvenile correctional institution.

detention The temporary restraint of a juvenile in a secure facility, usually because he or she is acknowledged to be dangerous either to self or to others.

dispositional hearing The stage of the juvenile court proceedings in which the juvenile judge decides the most appropriate placement for a juvenile who has been adjudicated a delinquent, a status offender, or a dependent child.

juvenile court officer A probation officer who serves juveniles (the term is used in some but not all probation departments).

petition A document filed in juvenile court alleging that a juvenile is a delinquent and asking that the court assume jurisdiction over the juvenile or asking that an alleged delinquent be waived to criminal court for prosecution as an adult.

petitioner In the juvenile justice system, an intake officer (prosecutor) who seeks court jurisdiction over a youthful offender.

respondent The defense attorney in the juvenile court system.

taking into custody The process of arresting a juvenile for socially unacceptable or unlawful behavior.

> > > **EXHIBIT 13.3** < < <

Restorative Philosophy

A restorative philosophy has been a major development in criminological thinking, being grounded in traditions of justice from the ancient Arab, Greek, and Roman civilizations. The purpose of restorative justice is to restore or "make whole" victims, offenders, and communities through the participation of a plurality of stakeholders. Restorative justice is seen as an alternative to either rehabilitation or retribution in juvenile justice. Its appeal to liberals is a less punitive juvenile justice system; its appeal to conservatives is an emphasis on empowerment both for victims and for families and on fiscal savings due to the parsimonious use of punishment.

In adult justice, restorative justice is found in victim–offender mediation, victim notification, victim input in sentencing and in plea bargaining, family group conferences, healing circles, restorative probation, reparation boards (based on the Vermont model), and Chinese Bang Jiao programs.

Restorative justice is increasingly found in juvenile justice approaches such as restorative probation, antibullying programs in school, conflict resolution in school, youth courts, drug courts, healing circles, victim mediation, victim notification, and victim input in juvenile court dispositional matters.

▶ In what types of cases is restorative justice more likely to be used? In what cases would it be rarely used?

Source: Adapted from John Braithwaite, "Restorative Justice: Assessing Optimistic and Pessimistic Accounts," in *Crime and Justice: A Review of Research*, Vol. 25, edited by Michael Tonry (Chicago and London: University of Chicago Press, 1999), pp. 1, 4.

---

mycrimekit™

Review   Difference between the Adult and Juvenile Justice Systems

rehabilitation model   A correctional model whose goal is to change an offender's character, attitudes, or behavior so as to diminish his or her delinquent propensities. The medical, adjustment, and reintegration models are variants of this model because they are all committed to changing the offender.

medical model   A correctional model whose proponents believe that delinquency is caused by factors that can be identified, isolated, treated, and cured—much like a disease.

adjustment model   A rehabilitative correctional approach that emphasizes helping delinquents demonstrate responsible behavior.

reintegration model   A perspective that holds that offenders' problems must be solved in the community in which they occur and that community-based organizations can help offenders readjust to community life.

justice model   A contemporary model of imprisonment based on the principle of just deserts.

Rehabilitation Model   The goal of the **rehabilitation model** is to change an offender's character, attitudes, or behavior patterns to diminish his or her propensities for youth crime.[29] The three variations of the rehabilitation model—the medical model, the adjustment model, and the reintegration model—all are expressions of rehabilitative philosophy.

The **medical model**, the first treatment model to be developed from the rehabilitative philosophy, contends that delinquency is caused by factors that can be identified, isolated, treated, and cured. Its proponents believe that delinquents should be treated as though they had a disease and that punishment should be avoided, because it does nothing to solve delinquents' problems and only reinforces the negative self-image these troubled youths have.

The **adjustment model** was developed in the late 1960s and 1970s when some proponents of rehabilitation became dissatisfied with the medical model. According to the adjustment model, delinquents need treatment to help them deal with the problems that led them to crime, with an emphasis on delinquents' responsibility at the present time. Youthful offenders cannot change the facts of their emotional and social deprivations of the past, but they can demonstrate responsible behavior in the present and avoid using past problems as an excuse for delinquent behavior. The various therapies used are not based on punishment, because punishment is seen as only increasing delinquents' alienation and behavior problems.

A basic assumption of the third rehabilitative approach, the **reintegration model,** is that delinquents' problems must be solved in the community where they began and that society has a responsibility for helping law violators reintegrate themselves back into community life. The reintegration model recommends community-based corrections for all but hard-core offenders, offers those hard-core offenders who must be institutionalized a wide variety of reentry programs, and provides the necessary services so that delinquents can restore family ties and obtain employment and education.[30] Supporters of the reintegration model established a wide variety of community-based programs in the 1970s, including diversion programs, residential and day-treatment programs, and programs to treat drug abusers.

Justice Model   The **justice model** holds to the belief that punishment should be the basic purpose of the juvenile justice system. Among the variants of the justice model for youth crime are those proposed by David Fogel, by the Report of the Committee for the Study of Incarceration, and by the Report of the Twentieth Century Fund.[31]

The concept of **just deserts** is the pivotal philosophical basis of the justice model. According to Fogel's model of **justice as fairness**, offenders are volitional and responsible human beings, so they deserve to be punished if they violate the law because punishment shows that the delinquent is blameworthy for his or her conduct. The decisions concerning delinquents should be based not on their needs but on the penalties that they deserve for their acts.[32] Punishment is not intended to achieve social benefits or advantages, such as deterrence or rehabilitation; the only reason to punish an offender is because he or she deserves it, but the punishment given an offender must be proportionate to the seriousness of the crime.

Balanced and Restorative Model Building on research and practical experience dating back to the early 1980s, the **balanced and restorative model** is an integrated effort to reconcile the interests of victims, offenders, and communities through programs and supervision practices. (For more on the background and philosophy of this model, see the section titled "Delinquency and Social Policy" later in this chapter.) The word *balanced* refers to system-level decision making by administrators to ensure accountability to crime victims, to increase competency in offenders, and to enhance community safety[33] (see Figure 13.3).

These three goals are summarized in accountability, competency, and community protection. In this model, "accountability" refers to a sanctioning process in which offenders must accept responsibility for their offenses and the harm caused to victims and make restitution to victims, assuming that community members are satisfied with the outcome. "Competency" refers to the rehabilitation of offenders, that is, when offenders improve their educational, vocational, emotional, social, and other skills, they can become responsible adults and live successfully in the community. In this model, "community safety" refers to the ability of citizens to prevent crime, resolve conflict, and feel safe because offenders have matured into responsible citizens. Subsequently, the overall mission of the balanced and restorative model is to develop a community-oriented approach to the control of offenders rather than relying solely on punishment.[34]

The juvenile justice system, in implementing the balanced and restorative model, uses many of the same principles as the justice model to develop effective systems for the supervision of juvenile offenders in the community[35] (see Library Extra 13.3).

Crime-Control Model The public has become increasingly intolerant of serious youth crime and is more and more receptive to the **crime-control model**, which emphasizes punishment as the remedy for juvenile misbehavior. The crime-control model is grounded on its adherents' conviction that the first priority of justice should be the protection of the life and property of the innocent, and supporters of the crime-control model, which is based on the classical school of criminology (examined in Chapter 3), charge that punishment is the preferred correctional model because it both protects society and deters crime. Youthful offenders are taught not to commit further crimes while noncriminal youths receive a demonstration of what happens to a person who breaks the law.[36]

Comparison of the Four Models The rehabilitation model is more concerned that juvenile delinquents receive therapy than that they be institutionalized; the crime-control model, on the other hand, is a punishment model that contends juveniles must pay for their crimes. Those who back the crime-control model also claim that punishment has social value for both offenders (deterrence) and society (protection). The justice model strongly advocates that procedural safeguards and fairness be granted to juveniles who have broken the law, yet proponents of this model also firmly hold that juveniles should be punished according to the severity of their crimes. The balanced and restorative model is an accountability model that is focused

FIGURE 13.3 Balanced and Restorative-Justice Model

Source: Gordon Bazemore and Mark S. Umbreit, *Balanced and Restorative Justice* (Washington, D.C.: Office of Juvenile Justice and Delinquency Prevention, 1994), p. 1.

just deserts A pivotal philosophical underpinning of the justice model that holds that juvenile offenders deserve to be punished and that the punishment must be proportionate to the seriousness of the offense or the social harm caused.

justice as fairness A justice model that advocates that it is necessary to be fair, reasonable, humane, and constitutional in the implementation of justice.

balanced and restorative model An integrative correctional model that seeks to reconcile the interests of victims, offenders, and communities through programs and supervision practices.

Library Extra 13.3
OJJDP Juvenile Justice Bulletin: "Restorative Justice Conferences as an Early Response to Young Offenders"

crime-control model A correctional model supporting discipline and punishment as the most effective means of deterring youth crime.

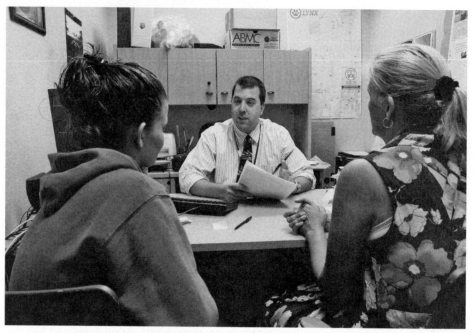

A neighborhood restorative-justice coordinator conducts an intake interview with a new program client. The juvenile offender was referred to the program by a judge. ▶ **What are the goals of the balanced and restorative model of corrections?**

on recognizing the needs of victims, giving proper attention to the protection of society, and providing competency development for juveniles entering the system. Table 13.4 compares the four models.

Emergent Approaches to Handling Youthful Offenders

There is wide support for using the crime-control model with serious and violent juvenile offenders. For example, from 1992 through 1997, legislatures in 47 states and the District of Columbia enacted laws that made their juvenile justice systems more punitive[37] (see Table 13.5). Many states added to the purpose clauses of their juvenile codes such phrases as "provide effective deterrents"; "hold youths accountable for criminal behavior"; "balance attention to youthful offenders, victims, and the

TABLE 13.4 Comparison of Key Elements of the Rehabilitation, Justice, Balanced and Restorative, and Crime-Control Models

Elements	Models			
	Rehabilitation	Justice	Balanced and Restorative	Crime Control
Theory of why delinquents offend	Behavior is caused or determined; based on positivism	Free will; based on the classical school	Free will; based on the classical school	Free will; based on the classical school
Purpose of sentencing	Change in behavior or attitude	Justice	Community protection	Restoration of law and order
Type of sentencing advocated	Indeterminate	Determinate	Determinate	Determinate
View of treatment	Goal of correctional process	Voluntary but necessary in a humane system	Voluntary but necessary in a humane system	Ineffective and actually coddles offenders
Crime-control strategy	Use therapeutic intervention to eliminate factors causing crime	Provide fairness for victims, for offenders, and for practitioners in the system	Make juvenile offenders accountable for their behavior	Declare war on youth crime by instituting "get tough" policies

TABLE 13.5 Changes in State Juvenile Justice Systems (1990s)

From 1992 through 1997, legislatures in 47 states and the District of Columbia enacted laws that made their juvenile justice systems more punitive.

State	Changes in Law or Court Rule[1]			State	Changes in Law or Court Rule[1]		
Alabama	T		C	Montana	T	S	C
Alaska	T		C	Nebraska			
Arizona	T	S	C	Nevada	T		C
Arkansas	T	S	C	New Hampshire	T	S	C
California	T		C	New Jersey		S	C
Colorado	T	S	C	New Mexico	T	S	C
Connecticut	T	S	C	New York			
Delaware	T	S	C	North Carolina	T		C
District of Columbia	T	S		North Dakota	T		C
Florida	T	S	C	Ohio	T	S	C
Georgia	T	S	C	Oklahoma	T	S	C
Hawaii	T		C	Oregon	T	S	C
Idaho	T	S	C	Pennsylvania	T		C
Illinois	T	S	C	Rhode Island	T	S	C
Indiana	T	S	C	South Carolina	T		C
Iowa	T	S	C	South Dakota	T		
Kansas	T	S	C	Tennessee	T	S	C
Kentucky	T	S	C	Texas	T	S	C
Louisiana	T	S	C	Utah	T		C
Maine			C	Vermont			
Maryland	T		C	Virginia	T	S	C
Massachusetts	T	S	C	Washington	T		C
Michigan		S	C	West Virginia	T		C
Minnesota	T	S	C	Wisconsin	T	S	C
Mississippi	T		C	Wyoming	T		C
Missouri	T	S	C				

[1]T = Transfer provisions, S = Sentencing authority, C = Confidentiality.

Source: Howard N. Snyder and Melissa Sickmund, *Juvenile Offenders and Victims: 1999 National Report* (Washington, D.C.: Office of Juvenile Justice and Delinquency Prevention, 1999), p. 89.

community"; and "impose punishments consistent with the seriousness of the crime."[38] (For information on the Juvenile Justice Committee of the American Bar Association, see Web Extra 13.2.)

In Table 13.6, it can also be seen that in 1997 about as many states were emphasizing prevention/diversion/treatment philosophical goals as were advocating punishment philosophical goals. At the same time, nearly twice as many states placed importance on both sets of goals in their juvenile codes. The trend toward a balanced and restorative approach also was seen in the late 1990s, and by the end of the 1997 legislative session, 17 states had adopted the language of the balanced and restorative-justice philosophy, emphasizing offender accountability, public safety, and competency development.[39]

Race and Juvenile Justice

One of the most disturbing issues facing the juvenile justice system today is the long-standing and pronounced disparities in the processing of white and minority youths. Northeastern University's Donna Bishop concluded: "Despite decades of research, there is no clear consensus on why minority youths enter and penetrate the juvenile justice system at such disproportionate rates."[40] According to Bishop, two explanations have been given: "The first is that minority overrepresentation reflects race and

mycrimekit

Web Extra 13.2
American Bar Association's Juvenile Justice Committee

TABLE 13.6 Philosophical Goals in Juvenile Code Purpose Clause

Prevention/Diversion/Treatment	Punishment	Both Prevention/Diversion/Treatment and Punishment	
Arizona[1]	Arkansas	Alabama	New Hampshire
District of Columbia	Georgia	Alaska	New Jersey
Kentucky	Hawaii	California	New Mexico
Massachusetts	Illinois	Colorado	New York
North Carolina	Iowa	Connecticut	North Dakota
Ohio	Louisiana	Delaware	Oklahoma
South Carolina	Michigan	Florida	Oregon
Vermont	Missouri	Idaho	Pennsylvania
West Virginia	Rhode Island	Indiana	Tennessee
		Kansas	Texas
		Maryland	Utah
		Maine	Virginia
		Minnesota	Washington
		Mississippi	Wisconsin
		Montana	Wyoming
		Nebraska	
		Nevada	

- Most states seek to protect the interests of the child, the family, the community, or some combination of the three.
- In 17 states, the purpose clause incorporates the language of the balanced and restorative-justice philosophy, emphasizing offender accountability, public safety, and competency development.
- Purpose clauses also address court issues such as fairness, speedy trials, and even coordination of services. In nearly all states, the code also includes protections of the child's constitutional and statutory rights.

[1]Arizona's statutes and court rules did not contain a purpose clause; however, the issue is addressed in case law.

Source: Adapted from Patricia Torbet and Linda Szymanski's *State Legislative Responses to Violent Juvenile Crime: 1996–97 Update.* Office of Juvenile Justice and Delinquency Prevention, "1999 National Report Series," *Juvenile Justice Bulletin* (Washington, D.C.: U.S. Department of Justice, 1999), p. 3.

ethnic differences in the incidence, seriousness, and persistence of delinquent involvement (the 'differential offending' hypothesis)" and "the second is that overrepresentation is attributable to inequities—intended or unintended—in juvenile justice practice (the 'differential treatment' hypothesis)."[41]

University of Missouri–St. Louis Professor Janet L. Lauritsen, in examining what is known about racial and ethnic differences in juvenile offending, offered the following conclusions that have wide support in the literature:

- Rates of juvenile homicide are higher for minorities than rates for white youthful offenders. Similarly, variations exist in rates of lethal violence between minority groups.
- Official data suggest disproportionate involvement in nonlethal violence on the part of African-American youths. When arrest data are restricted to specific forms of nonlethal violence, African-American youths appear to be disproportionately involved in robbery, aggravated assault, and rape.
- Juvenile property crime data show that African-American youths are slightly more involved in such offenses than white youths, although the level of involvement varies by type of property crime.
- Arrest data show that white youths are disproportionately involved in alcohol offenses and that American Indian youths are slightly more likely than African-American or Asian-American youths to be arrested for these crimes.
- African-American youths are disproportionately arrested for drug abuse violations and illicit drug use, but self-report data from juveniles on their own drug

involvement do not confirm the differences between African-American and white youths suggested by arrest data. In fact, white youths are somewhat more likely to report using marijuana, selling any drug, and selling marijuana.

- Weapons violations arrest data indicate that African-American youths are disproportionately likely to be arrested for weapons possession or use.[42]
- Although the most commonly occurring crimes exhibit few group differences, the less frequent and serious crimes of violence show generally higher levels of African-American and Latino-American involvement.[43]

See Table 13.7 for a summary of racial and ethnic differences in juvenile offenses. Lauritsen concluded that this kind of empirical evidence suggests that the relationship between race and ethnicity and juvenile involvement in delinquency is complex and contingent on the type of offense. In contrast, Bishop suggested that minority overrepresentation in the juvenile justice system is attributable to inequities in system practices rather than differences in the incidence, seriousness, or persistence of offending.

Minorities are overrepresented among youths held in secure detention, petitioned to juvenile court, and adjudicated delinquent. Among those who are adjudicated delinquent, minorities are more often committed to the "deep end" of the juvenile system: When confined, they are more likely to be housed in large public institutions rather than in privately run specialized treatment facilities or group homes, and prosecutors and judges seem quicker to relinquish jurisdiction over minorities, transferring them to criminal court for prosecution and punishment[44] (see Web Extra 13.3).

mycrimekit™

Web Extra 13.3
Coalition for Juvenile Justice website

Disproportionate Minority Confinement

Carl E. Pope and William H. Feyerherm's highly regarded assessment of the issue of discrimination against minorities revealed that two-thirds of the studies they examined found "both direct and indirect race effects or a mixed pattern (being present at

---

TABLE 13.7 Summary of Racial and Ethnic Differences in Juvenile Offending by Crime Type

Pattern Found in Arrest Data	Source of Confirmation
Lethal Violence • Black youth most disproportionately involved • Latino youth disproportionately involved in some cities • American Indian youth disproportionately involved	Witness reports, case evidence
Nonlethal Violence • Black youth disproportionately involved	Victim reports, self-reports, parent and teacher reports
Property Crime • White youth more involved for some offenses • Black youth more involved for some offenses • Overall, minimal differences across groups	Self-reports
Alcohol Violations • White youth disproportionately involved • American Indian youth disproportionately involved	Self-reports (for white youth); no sufficient data for American Indian youth involved
Drug Abuse Violations • Black youth disproportionately involved	Self-report data contrary to arrest data; white youth report higher levels in self-report data
Weapons Violations • Black youth disproportionately involved	Self-reports (also show higher prevalence for Hispanic youth)

Source: Janet L. Lauritsen, "Racial and Ethnic Differences in Judicial Offending," in *Our Children, Their Children: Confronting Racial and Ethnic Differences in American Juvenile Justice,*" edited by Darnell F. Hawkins and Kimberly Kempf-Leonard (Chicago: University of Chicago Press, 2005), p. 96. Reprinted by permission of University of Chicago Press.

some stages and not at others)."[45] They added that selection bias can take place at any stage and that small racial differences may accumulate and become more pronounced as minority youths are processed into the juvenile justice system.[46]

The Coalition for Juvenile Justice (then the National Coalition of State Juvenile Justice Advisory Groups) brought national attention to the problem of **disproportionate minority confinement** in its 1988 annual report to Congress. In that same year, Congress responded to evidence of disproportionate confinement of minority juveniles in secure facilities by amending the Juvenile Justice and Delinquency Prevention Act (JJDPA) of 1974 to provide that states must determine whether the proportion of minorities in confinement exceeded their proportion in the population of the state; if there was overrepresentation, states must demonstrate efforts to reduce it.[47]

During the 1992 reauthorization of the JJDPA, Congress substantially strengthened the effort to address disproportionate confinement of minority youths in secure facilities. Elimination of disproportionate minority confinement was elevated to the status of a "core requirement" alongside deinstitutionalization of status offenders, removal of juveniles from adult jails and lockups, and separation of youthful offenders from adults in secure institutions. The 2002 reauthorization of the JJDPA also changed the disproportionate minority confinement (DMC) mandate to reduce minority contact with the system. See Exhibit 13.4 for a summary of state compliance with DMC core requirements as of December 2002.

Michael J. Leiber's 2003 book, *The Contexts of Juvenile Justice Decision Making*, examined four jurisdictions in Iowa and revealed the presence of race effects that were not accounted for by legal and relevant extralegal factors. Race effects began at the intake stage in all four jurisdictions; interviews with juvenile court personnel, as well as an analysis of community and historical factors, provided insights into the contexts of court decision making and the roles played by race in this decision making. The race effects vary in other stages of juvenile justice processing, sometimes involving both more severe and more lenient outcomes in the same jurisdiction. Leiber's study found that although decision making is more complex than is often suggested by previous research, the cumulative effect is still the disproportionate confinement of minorities, especially African-Americans, in the juvenile justice system[48] (see Web Extra 13.4, Library Extra 13.4, and Library Extra 13.5).

disproportionate minority confinement The court-ordered confinement, in juvenile institutions, of members of minority groups in numbers disproportionate to their representation in the general population.

Web Extra 13.4
OJJDP: DMC Chronology

Library Extra 13.4
OJJDP publication:
Disproportionate Minority Contact

Library Extra 13.5
NIJ article: *Brick by Brick: Dismantling the Border between Juvenile and Adult Justice*

Delinquency across the Life Course: Effects of the Juvenile Justice System on Juvenile Offenders

Early cohort studies certainly did not present a favorable picture of the effect of the juvenile justice process on juvenile delinquents. The Philadelphia studies found that the probability of becoming an adult offender increased dramatically for individuals with a record of juvenile delinquency. The Philadelphia, Racine, and Columbus cohort studies found that stricter punishments by the juvenile justice system were likely to encourage rather than to eliminate recidivism (further delinquent behavior).[49] The Racine cohort studies found that an increase in frequency and seriousness of misbehavior typically occurred in the periods following the administration of sanctions by the justice system and that those who had police contacts as juveniles were more likely to have police contacts as adults.[50] The Columbus cohort study further found that the impact of institutional treatment was basically negative; in fact, after institutionalization, the length of time between arrests decreased dramatically.[51] These studies found that the probabilities of continuing with juvenile crime and going on to adult crime increased for individuals who were brought to the attention of the juvenile justice system.

More recent longitudinal studies have not been more positive about the impact of the juvenile justice system. As Chapters 2 and 3 revealed, the earlier youths come to the attention of the juvenile justice system, the more likely they are to continue with juvenile crime; the more time they spent in the juvenile justice system, the more

> > > **EXHIBIT 13.4** < <

Summary of State Compliance with the DMC Core Requirement

The following summary of state compliance with the DMC core requirement, pursuant to Section 31.303(j) of the JJDP Formula Grants Regulation (28 C.F.R. Part 31), is based on FY 2002 Formula Grant applications as of December 2002.

- In addition to completing the identification and assessment phases in earlier years, three states continue to monitor their DMC trends each year, update their assessment studies, implement intervention strategies to address identified factors that contribute to DMC, and conduct evaluations of their DMC efforts:

  Colorado   Pennsylvania   Washington

- The District of Columbia and twenty states have completed the identification and assessment phases, are implementing the intervention phase, and also have submitted updated DMC data, demonstrating ongoing monitoring efforts:

Alaska[1]	Idaho	New York
Arkansas	Minnesota	North Dakota
California[1]	Mississippi	Oklahoma
Connecticut	Missouri	Oregon
Delaware[2]	Montana	South Carolina[3]
District of Columbia	Nevada	Tennessee[1]
Georgia	New Jersey	Virginia

- Four states have completed the identification and assessment phases, are implementing the intervention phase, and plan to update DMC identification data and/or assessment studies:

  Indiana   Kansas   Michigan   New Mexico[3]

- One state has completed the identification phase, is implementing the intervention phase, and [is] conducting a formal assessment study:

  Alabama

- Four states have completed the identification phase, are implementing the intervention phase, and plan to conduct formal assessments:

  Louisiana   North Carolina   Ohio   West Virginia

- Eleven states have completed the identification and assessment phases and are implementing the intervention phase:

Arizona	Iowa	Texas
Florida	Maryland	Utah
Hawaii	Massachusetts[3]	Wisconsin
Illinois	Nebraska	

- One state became a participating state in the Formula Grants Program in 1999. It has completed the identification phase and is conducting an assessment study:

  Kentucky[3]

- Two states in which the minority juvenile population recently exceeded 12 percent of the total juvenile population, which requires them now to comply with the DMC requirement, have partially completed the identification phase:

  Maine   Vermont

- Four territories have completed the identification phase, which revealed that minority juveniles were not being disproportionately detained:

American Samoa	Guam
Northern Marianas	Virgin Islands

- One territory has been exempted by the U.S. Census Bureau from reporting racial statistics and, therefore, is exempt from complying with the DMC requirement:

  Puerto Rico

- Two states are under a draw down restriction of 25 percent of the FY 2002 Formula Grant allocation pending submission of required information:

  New Hampshire   Rhode Island

- Two states did not participate in the FY 2002 Formula Grants Program:

  South Dakota   Wyoming

---

[1]Began to receive intensive DMC technical assistance in January 2002 to further enhance DMC efforts.

[2]Received intensive DMC technical assistance from November 2000 to July 2001 to further enhance DMC efforts.

[3]Received intensive DMC technical assistance since November 2000 to further enhance DMC efforts.

Source: Heidi M. Hsia, *Disproportionate Minority Confinement: 2002 Update* (Washington, D.C.: Office of Juvenile Justice and Delinquency Prevention, 2004), pp. 10–11.

---

likely they are to go on to adult crime; and the deeper they go into the system, the higher the rates of recidivism when they leave and the more serious crimes they tend to commit as adults.

Delinquency and Social Policy: Dissatisfaction with Juvenile Institutionalization

There is widespread dissatisfaction in many jurisdictions with how the juvenile justice system, especially long-term juvenile institutionalization, is functioning today. In the mid-2000s, two evaluations of juvenile institutions in California and Texas were

Voices of Delinquency

Read "I Want to Stay Out of Places Like This." Why is the justice experience such a negative experience for youths?

completed. California's evaluation said that "it is not reform that is needed. Everything needs to be fixed."[52] In 2007, in response to the reports of sexual abuse of youths at the Texas Youth Commission institutions, Governor Rick Perry placed the Texas Youth Commission under conservatorship to guide reform of the agency.[53] If California and Texas were the only states dissatisfied with the performance of juvenile facilities, then the issue of juvenile institutionalization would not be considered such a serious matter; however, the mounting evidence from other states indicates that dissatisfaction with juvenile institutionalization is a mounting national concern.

It is likely that this dissatisfaction, as well as the extreme cost of juvenile institutionalization, will lead to reform of long-term institutional care. Improving the quality of institutional care—and it is possible to do this, as some facilities are demonstrating—is an important step in improving the quality of juvenile justice for those youths who must be committed to these placements, and with the improved quality of institutional life, perhaps the recidivism rates of youthful offenders will be reduced.

Trends for the Future

There are several changes that are taking place in juvenile justice today and will likely continue in the future:

- *Expansion of restorative justice.* As mentioned in several chapters of this text, restorative justice is one of the most exciting movements in corrections today, and it has recently been coupled with intermediate sanctions. From the grassroots level to local and state headquarters, restorative justice is rapidly gaining momentum within the United States. Victim–offender conferencing (sometimes called mediation) is the oldest and most widely used expression of restorative justice, with more than 1,300 programs in 18 countries.[54] While stressing accountability for offenses committed, restorative strategies operate with the goal of repairing injuries to victims and to communities in which crimes have taken place. Whether these conferences occur before, during, or after adjudication, they promote education and transformation within a context of respect and healing. These models neither are mutually exclusive nor compete in and of themselves and can be combined or adapted depending on the special situation at hand.[55]
- *Increased use of technology.* Rather than rely on traditional methods of security and control, the correctional system is now entering a new phase of technocorrections, which involves using technology rather than personnel to monitor probation, aftercare, and institutional populations. Today, technology-driven security is designed to maintain security, both in the community and in institutions. Community corrections has relied for quite some time on technology to monitor offenders; for example, electronic monitoring (EM) has been increasingly used in probation services. Now, new methods of technology are being explored to provide probation and parole officers with tools to better manage their caseloads and do their jobs more effectively and efficiently.
- *Greater use of evidence-based practice principles and approaches.* Evidence-based practice principles are increasingly used in juvenile justice today. It is contended that programs that go by the following principles have a better chance of succeeding than those that do not: (1) Target criminogenic needs, (2) target programs to high-risk offenders, (3) base design and implementation on a proven theoretical model, (4) use a cognitive-behavioral approach, (5) disrupt the delinquency network, (6) provide intensive services, (7) match offender's personality and learning style with appropriate program settings and approaches, (8) include a prevention component in release decisions, (9) integrate juvenile justice with community-based services, and (10) reinforce integrity of services. Effective programs continually monitor program development, organizational structure, staff development and training, and other core organizational processes, and an

important part of this effective offender intervention treatment approach is program evaluation.[56]

Clearly, some of these changes are more likely to occur than others, and resources may constrain certain agencies from fully implementing all of them.[57]

Chapter Summary

The juvenile justice system is responsible for controlling and correcting the behavior of law-violating juveniles. Of special note are the following points:

- It can be argued that the juvenile justice system has improved since the mid-1970s, but the improvements hardly seem to have scratched the surface in terms of designing a justice system that will effectively deal with juvenile delinquency in the United States.

- The problem of continued serious juvenile delinquency in the United States challenges the juvenile justice system to mobilize a coordinated and effective approach to dealing with youth crime.

- Racial and ethnic inequities represent one of the most serious issues facing the juvenile justice system today.

- Conflicting philosophies and strategies for dealing with youth crime and a fragmented juvenile justice system that varies from one jurisdiction to another make it nearly impossible for the juvenile justice process to handle delinquency cases effectively.

- The balanced and restorative model is rapidly gaining acceptance in more and more jurisdictions as a promising modality that should be employed in the fight against juvenile crime.

- Efforts to coordinate a continuum of increasing sanctions for violent and chronic youthful offenders offer hope and represent positive directions for the juvenile justice system.

Key Terms

adjudicatory hearing, p. 303
adjustment model, p. 304
aftercare, p. 293
balanced and restorative
   model, p. 305
child savers, p. 293
commitment, p. 303
cottage system, p. 295
crime-control model, p. 305
detention, p. 303

dispositional hearing, p. 303
disproportionate minority
   confinement, p. 310
diversion programs, p. 296
just deserts, p. 305
justice as fairness, p. 305
justice model, p. 304
juvenile court officer, p. 303
medical model, p. 304
petition, p. 303

petitioner, p. 303
probation, p. 294
recidivism, p. 302
rehabilitation model, p. 304
reintegration model, p. 304
residential program, p. 294
respondent, p. 303
taking into custody, p. 303
training school, p. 295

Review Questions

1. What is the purpose of the juvenile justice system?
2. What were the origins of the juvenile court?
3. How did community-based corrections for juveniles develop?
4. How did probation develop?
5. How did juvenile institutions develop?
6. What is diversion, and why is it important?

7. How is a juvenile processed through the juvenile justice system?
8. What comparisons are there between the juvenile and adult justice systems?
9. What are the basic correctional models?
10. What are some future trends for juvenile justice?

Discussion Questions

1. The juvenile justice system has devised four ways to deal with delinquency: the rehabilitation model, the justice model, the balanced and restorative model, and the crime-control model. Which do you think works best? Why? Why is the balanced and restorative model gaining such popularity nationwide?

2. After reading this chapter, do you feel encouraged or discouraged about the ability of society to deal effectively with delinquency? Why?

3. Does society really need a juvenile justice system that is separate from the adult system used with criminals? Be able to defend your explanation.

4. Some suggest today's youths are far more sophisticated than were the youths of earlier generations, so they should be held responsible for their behavior at an earlier age. Do you agree? Explain your response.

5. Should terminologies be standardized for the adult and juvenile justice systems? Explain your response.

Group Exercises

1. Have students research their county and state data to determine how many juveniles are currently incarcerated and how many are currently on probation. Discuss their findings.

2. Have students research their county and state data to determine the applicable juvenile recidivism rate. Discuss their findings.

3. Appoint teams to research juvenile justice processing in the 10 most populated countries (excluding the United States and Germany); then have each team prepare and present a briefing to the class.

4. Have students research their county and state data to determine the rate of minority juvenile confinement. Discuss their findings.

mycrimekit™

Go to mycrimekit.com to explore the following study tools and resources specific to this chapter:

- **Practice Quiz:** Practice with multiple-choice, true/false, short-answer, and essay questions.

- **WebQuests:** Do web activities using the Federal Advisory Committee on Juvenile Justice's report regarding major issues that face the nation's juvenile justice system.

- **Flashcards:** Use 28 flashcards to test your knowledge of the chapter's key terms.

chapter 14

Police and the Juvenile

The vast majority of youth are good citizens who have never been arrested for any type of crime.

—Shay Bilchik, President, Child Welfare League of America

CHAPTER OBJECTIVES

After reading this chapter, you should be able to answer the following questions:

- What has been the history of police–juvenile relations?
- How have the attitudes of juveniles toward the police changed?
- How are juvenile offenders processed?
- What are the legal rights of juveniles in encounters with police?
- What kinds of efforts do the police make to deter delinquency?
- How does community policing impact juveniles?

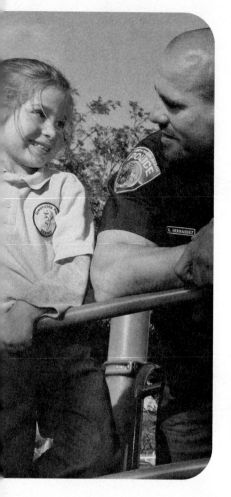

Introduction

A juvenile justice official once described an exemplary juvenile officer as follows.

> Darrell Dirks, a juvenile officer, is beautiful. He talks like a kid. He walks down the halls of school. Kids will punch him in the shoulder. He'll smile and punch them back. He prevents crimes simply because he talks with the kids and hangs out with them. They'll tell him who is doing what. The kids have more respect for him than I've ever seen with a juvenile police officer.[1]

Juvenile crime represents one of the most demanding and frustrating areas of police work. A common complaint of police officers is that arrested juvenile offenders are back on the streets before the officers have had a chance to complete the necessary paperwork. Also, with the rise of youth gangs and with increased numbers of juveniles carrying weapons, policing juveniles is much more dangerous than it used to be. Finally, police departments give little status to those dealing with youth crime because they regard arresting a juvenile as a poor "bust."

Policing juveniles is similar in some ways to policing adults, yet in other ways it is quite different. It is similar in that both juveniles and adults have constitutional protections; that juveniles can be as hostile to the police as adults can be; that armed juveniles, of course, are as dangerous as armed adults; that both juveniles and adults are involved in gangs, some of which are involved in drug trafficking; and that alcohol and drugs affect the functioning of both juveniles and adults. A major difference is the belief that juveniles are more salvageable than adults—few would argue against the widely held tenet that juveniles are more likely than adults to experience a turning point where they can walk away from crime.

Accordingly, the importance of police–juvenile relations cannot be minimized. The police are usually the first contact a youth has with the juvenile justice system. As the doorway into the system, the police officer can use his or her broad discretion to either detour youths or involve them in the system. In a real sense, the police officer becomes an on-the-spot prosecutor, judge, and correctional system when dealing with a juvenile offender.

Juveniles' Attitudes toward the Police

The subject of juveniles' attitudes toward the police received considerable attention in the 1970s, less attention in the 1980s, and more attention in the 1990s. Robert Portune's 1971 study of almost 1,000 junior high students in Cincinnati found that whites had more favorable attitudes toward the police than African-Americans, that girls had more favorable attitudes than boys, and that students from middle- and upper-class families had more positive attitudes than those from lower-class families; he also found that hostility toward the law and police increased progressively during grades seven through nine.[2]

Several studies have reported that juveniles who have had contact with the police have more negative attitudes toward police than those who have not had contact. L. Thomas Winfree Jr. and Curt T. Griffiths's 1977 study of students in 17 high schools found that, to a considerable degree, juveniles' attitudes toward the police are shaped by contacts with police officers; that negative contacts influence juvenile attitudes more than do the factors of gender, race, residence, or socioeconomic status; and that negative contacts appear to be twice as important as positive contacts in determining juvenile attitudes toward police officers.[3]

William T. Rusinko and his colleagues, in examining about 1,200 ninth-grade students in three junior high schools in Lansing, Michigan, in 1978, explored the importance of police contact in shaping juveniles' attitudes toward the police. They found that positive police contacts with the white youths in their study clearly neutralized their encounters with police that had negative connotations, but these researchers found that positive police contact did not reduce the tendency for African-American youths to be less positive in their opinions of police. Their findings agree with several other studies that show the development of a culturally accepted view of police among African-Americans independent of their arrest experience.[4]

Scott H. Decker's 1981 review of the literature on attitudes toward the police concluded that youths had more negative attitudes toward the police than did older citizens and that race, the quality of police services, and previous experiences with the police also affected citizens' attitudes.[5]

Komanduri S. Murty, Julian B. Roebuck, and Joann D. Smith found in a 1990 Atlanta study that "older, married, white-collar, educated, and employed respondents reported a more positive image of the police than their counterparts—younger, single, blue-collar, low-educated, unemployed/underemployed respondents."[6] Murty and colleagues offered support for previous findings that younger African-American males are particularly hostile toward the police; these researchers demonstrated that the chances that respondents will have negative attitudes toward the police also vary, in descending order, with residence in high-crime tracts, single marital status, negative contacts with the police, and blue-collar occupations.

Michael J. Leiber, Mahesh K. Nalla, and Margaret Farnworth's 1998 study challenged the traditional argument that juveniles' interactions with the police are the primary or sole determinant of youths' attitudes toward the police. Instead, according to these authors, "[juveniles'] attitudes toward authority and agents of social control develop in a larger sociocultural context, and global attitudes toward police affect youths' assessment of specific police contacts."[7]

Data from the *Monitoring the Future* survey of high school seniors from the mid-1980s through the mid-1990s indicated that high school seniors' attitudes toward the police became more negative during those decades across all subsets of the sample. For example, in response to a question about their attitudes toward the police and law enforcement agencies, the percentages of youths responding "good" and "very good" tended to decline throughout the 1980s and into the early 1990s across the categories of gender, race, and geographic region; however, these general downward trends showed some improvement in later years. The *Monitoring the Future* data for 2007 revealed that 35.8% of high school seniors (up from 26.6% in 1996) responded either "good" or "very good." If the 30.2% of "fair" responses were added to the "good" and "very good" categories, roughly 61% of high school seniors could be considered to have a positive attitude toward the police.[8]

Youthful offenders, as anyone who has worked with this population can testify, are the most negative toward the police. Many juveniles claim that they have experienced police harassment on a regular basis and police brutality at least occasionally. They often charge that police "run them off" the streets without justification, that police stop and arrest them without probable cause, and that police are quick to put their hands on them.

Summing up, as Leiber and colleagues pointed out, juveniles' attitudes toward the police are formed in a larger sociocultural context. Most youths appear to have positive attitudes toward the police: Younger juveniles have more positive attitudes than older ones; whites are usually more positive than African-Americans; girls are more positive than boys; and middle- and upper-class youngsters tend to be more positive than lower-class ones. The more deeply committed a juvenile is to crime, the more hostile he or she is toward the police. But the findings about the influence of contacts with the police are mixed. Some researchers have found that the more contacts a juvenile has with the

An officer reads the *Miranda* rights to a handcuffed juvenile following an arrest for drug possession. Respect for and deference to police officers may result in leniency, but youths who are disrespectful, hostile, or abusive toward police officers are more likely to end up in juvenile court.
▶ Should police officers be allowed to exercise such discretion?

police, the more negative he or she feels about the police; others have concluded that for white youths, positive contacts tend to neutralize the effect of negative contacts. Finally, a survey of high school seniors revealed that the attitudes of juveniles toward the police today seem to be more positive than they were during the 1980s and 1990s.

Processing of Juvenile Offenders

When responding to juvenile lawbreakers, police are influenced by a variety of individual, sociocultural, and organizational factors. They can choose a more or less restrictive response to an individual offender.

Factors Influencing Police Discretion

police discretion A police officer's ability to choose from among a number of alternative dispositions when handling a situation.

Police discretion can be defined as the choice a police officer makes between two or more possible means of handling a situation. Discretion needs to be both professional and personal. Discretion is important, for the police actually act as a court of first instance in initially categorizing a juvenile. The police officer thus becomes a legal and social traffic director who can use his or her wide discretion to detour juveniles from the justice system or involve them in it (see Web Extra 14.1).

Police discretion has come under attack because many believe the police abuse their broad discretion, but most police contacts with juveniles are impersonal and nonofficial and consist simply of orders to "Get off the corner," "Break it up," or "Go home." Studies generally estimate that only 10% to 20% of police–juvenile encounters become official contacts.[9] In 2004, Stephanie M. Myers, reporting on data collected for the Project on Policing Neighborhoods (POPN), a study of police in Indianapolis, Indiana, and St. Petersburg, Florida, found that 84 (13%) of the 654 juvenile suspects were arrested.[10]

The point can also be made that the juvenile justice system could not function without police discretion. Urban courts, especially, are overloaded; probation officers' caseloads are entirely too high; and many juvenile correctional institutions are jammed to capacity. If police were to increase by two to three times the number of youths they referred to the system, the resulting backlog of cases would be unmanageable.

The police officer's disposition of the juvenile offender is mainly determined by 11 factors: (1) offense, (2) citizen complaints, (3) gender, (4) race, (5) socioeconomic status, (6) individual characteristics of the juvenile, (7) police–juvenile interactions, (8) demeanor, (9) police officer's personality, (10) departmental policy, and (11) external pressures (see Table 14.1).

Offense The most important factor determining the disposition of the misbehaving juvenile is the seriousness of the offense. Donald J. Black and Albert J. Reiss Jr. pointed out that the great bulk of police encounters with juveniles pertain to matters of minor legal significance, but the probability of arrest increases with the legal seriousness of the alleged offense.[11]

Citizen Complaints A number of studies have found that the presence of a citizen or the complaint of a citizen is an important determining factor in the disposition of an incident involving a juvenile.[12] If a citizen initiates a complaint, remains present, and wishes the arrest of a juvenile, chances are that the juvenile will be arrested and processed.[13] If the potential arrest situation results from police patrol, the chances are much greater that the youth will be warned and released.

Gender Traditionally, girls have been less likely than boys to be arrested and referred to the juvenile court for criminal offenses, but there is some evidence of the erosion of police "chivalry" in the face of youthful female criminality.[14] Yet, as Chapter 7 noted, girls are far more likely to be referred to the court if they violate traditional role expectations for girls through behaviors such as running away from home, failing to obey parents, or being sexually promiscuous.[15]

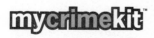

TABLE 14.1 Factors Influencing Disposition
Individual Factors
Personality characteristics of the juvenile
Personality characteristics of the police officer
Interaction between the police officer and the juvenile
Sociocultural Factors
Citizen complaints
Gender of the juvenile
Race/ethnicity of the juvenile
Socioeconomic status of the juvenile
Influence of cultural norms in the community and values of the wider society on both juveniles and police officers
External pressures in the community to arrest certain types of juvenile offenders
Organizational Factors
Nature of the offense
Departmental policy

Race   Studies differ on the importance of race in determining juvenile disposition. On the one hand, several studies (after results were corrected to account for offense seriousness and prior record) have found that the police are more inclined to arrest minority juveniles[16]; the strongest evidence showing race as a determining factor is found in the Philadelphia cohort study.[17] However, several other studies failed to find much evidence of racial bias. It is difficult to appraise the importance of race in the disposition of cases involving juveniles, because African-Americans and members of other minority groups appear to be involved in serious crimes more often than whites. Nonetheless, it does seem that racial bias makes minority juveniles special targets of the police.[18] See Exhibit 14.1 for a discussion of racial profiling and the police.

Socioeconomic Status   Substantiating the effect of class on the disposition of cases involving juveniles is difficult because most studies examine race and socioeconomic status together, but lower-class youngsters, according to many critics of the juvenile justice system, receive different "justice" than middle- or upper-class youths. What the critics mean by this is that lower-class youths are dragged into the net of the system for the same offenses for which white middle- and upper-class juveniles often are sent home. Patrol and juvenile police officers generally agree that there is more concern about "saving" middle- and upper-class juveniles than lower-class ones, but they justify this use of discretion by saying that the problematic behaviors of middle- and upper-class children are more likely to be corrected, because their parents can afford psychotherapy and other such resources.

Individual Characteristics of the Juvenile   Such individual factors as prior arrest record, previous offenses, age, peer relationships, family situation, and conduct of parents also have a bearing on how the police officer handles each juvenile.[19] A juvenile who is older and has committed several previous offenses is likely to be referred to the

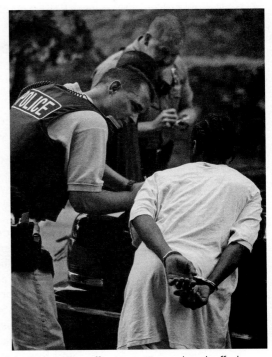

A white police officer questions a handcuffed African-American juvenile. ▶ What constitutes racial profiling? Is racial profiling ever justified?

> > > **EXHIBIT 14.1** < <

Racial Profiling and the Police

Minority motorists, especially African-Americans, have long complained that the police, especially in suburban areas, stop them for no legitimate reason but solely because they are African-Americans—a practice known as racial profiling. Furthermore, during such stops, African-Americans may be subjected to detailed questioning and searches and given little or no explanation of why they were stopped. This phenomenon has achieved such notoriety among African-Americans that it is called "driving while black."

The use of race as a key factor in police decisions to stop and interrogate citizens has received attention from the mass media, civil rights groups, and political leaders. In 1999, President Clinton condemned racial profiling and directed federal agencies to collect information on the race of individuals they stop and interrogate. More recently, President George W. Bush labeled profiling as "wrong" and argued that it must end. Congressional hearings on racial profiling have been held, and several states are considering or have passed legislation that would require law enforcement agencies to collect demographic data on persons they stop. More than 80% of U.S. citizens said in a 1999 Gallup poll that they "disapproved" of racial profiling. Profiling has been blamed for ills ranging from increased friction between the police and minority communities to overall reduced confidence in and cooperation with the police.

A Bureau of Justice Statistics survey of police–public contact found that in 1999 African-Americans were somewhat more likely than Hispanics and whites to report being stopped by the police. African-Americans who had been stopped were more likely than whites to report that they had been ticketed, handcuffed, arrested, or searched by police officers; they also were more likely to say that officers had threatened or used force against them. In this survey, African-Americans also were much less likely than whites or Hispanics to feel that the physical search or the vehicle search was legitimate.

Ronald Weitzer and Steven A. Tuch analyzed national survey data on citizens' views of racial profiling and found that both race and personal experience are strong predictors of attitudes toward profiling. They also found that African-Americans' social class affects their view of the prevalence and acceptability of this practice. Yet there is evidence that even middle-class African-Americans feel they have experienced racial profiling when they drive through predominantly white areas.

The importance of this finding is that regardless of the reality, the perception of racial profiling reinforces the feeling in the African-American "collective consciousness" that the police serve an oppressive function. Police can do much to dispel beliefs that stops are racially motivated by offering more information to justify stops, and officers who are polite, listen to individuals they stop, and explain their actions also are likely to receive cooperation from citizens.

▶ Is it racial profiling when a police officer tells a group of African-American juveniles hanging around a corner to scatter and go home? Does your answer change if the police officer believes that these particular juveniles are members of a criminal gang? Is it unacceptable for a police officer to stop a new BMW full of African-American juveniles who, in the judgment of the officer, are involved in drug trafficking?

Source: Adapted from Tom R. Tyler and Cheryl J. Wakslak, "Profiling and Police Legitimacy: Procedural Justice, Attributions of Motive, and Acceptance of Police Authority," *Criminology* 42 (May 2004), pp. 253–281; Ronald Weitzer and Steven A. Tuch, "Perceptions of Racial Profiling: Race, Class, and Personal Experience," *Criminology* 40 (May 2002), pp. 435–456; and Albert J. Meehan and Michael C. Ponder, "Race and Place: The Ecology of Racial Profiling African American Motorists," *Justice Quarterly* 19 (September 2002), pp. 399–430.

juvenile court.[20] The family of the juvenile is also an important variable. An assistant police chief who had spent several years working as a juvenile officer put it this way:

> Most juvenile problems derive from the parents. You've got to get the parents involved to be successful. You've some parents who are concerned, and you can tell they'll take things by the handle when they're dealing with the problem. Other parents simply don't care. If you want to make any headway in this work, it is necessary to stay on top of the family.[21]

Police–Juvenile Interactions   Three studies found that a juvenile's deference to a police officer is influential in determining disposition. In 1964, Irving Piliavin and Scott Briar discovered that if a youth is polite and respectful, the chances for informal disposition are greatly increased, but if the juvenile is hostile, police will probably judge him or her to be in need of juvenile court intervention.[22] Carl Werthman and Irving Piliavin found in 1967 that the hostility and scorn that African-American gang members displayed toward the police resulted in a high rate of court referral.[23] Richard J. Lundman, Richard E. Sykes, and John P. Clark's 1980 replication of Black and Reiss's study concluded that in encounters in which no evidence links a juvenile to an offense, the demeanor of the juvenile is the most important determinant of whether or not formal action is taken.[24]

Demeanor In the 1990s, the relationship between demeanor and arrest of adult offenders stirred up considerable controversy among criminologists. David A. Klinger's 1994 and 1996 studies of police behavior in Dade County, Florida, spearheaded this debate in challenging the long-standing belief that police officers are more likely to arrest citizens who do not show them an acceptable level of deference, his basic argument being that demeanor had been measured improperly and had not been controlled adequately for other important variables.[25] Robert E. Worden and Robin L. Shepard's 1996 reanalysis of data collected for the Police Services Study, however, supported the original finding of the importance of disrespectful or hostile demeanor toward the police in influencing the likelihood of arrest.[26]

Police Officer's Personality The factor of police officer personality has received some support for shaping the nature of police–juvenile interactions. An officer who has little tolerance for adolescents may more frequently become involved in a confrontation requiring an official contact.

Departmental Policy Police departments vary in their policies on handling misbehaving juveniles.[27] James Q. Wilson found that the more professional police departments had higher numbers of juveniles referred to the juvenile court, because they used discretion less often than departments that were not as professional.[28]

External Pressures The attitudes of the press and the public, the status of the complainant or victim, and the philosophy and available resources of referral agencies usually influence the disposition of juvenile lawbreakers.

In sum, sufficient studies have been done to provide an outline of an empirical portrait of the policing of juveniles. Of the 11 factors influencing police officers' dispositions of juveniles, the seriousness of the offense and complaints by citizens appear to be more important than the other 9 factors. However, individual factors, departmental policy, and external pressures also are highly influential in determining how police–juvenile encounters are handled.

Informal and Formal Dispositions

A patrol officer or **juvenile officer** has at least five options (see Figure 14.1) when investigating a complaint against a juvenile or arriving at the scene of law-violating behavior:

1. *Warning and release.* The least severe sanction is applied when the patrol officer decides merely to question and release the youth. Commonly, this occurs when a juvenile is caught committing a minor offense. The patrol officer usually gives an informal reprimand to the youth on the street or takes the juvenile in for a longer interview at the police station. In 1997, about 25% of juveniles were handled informally within the department and released.[29]
2. *Station adjustment.* The juvenile can be taken to the station, where the juvenile will have his or her contact recorded, will be given an official reprimand, and then will be released to the parents. In a **station adjustment**, the first thing the department does when the juvenile is brought to the station is to contact the parents. In some police departments, juveniles can be placed under police supervision and remain under supervision until released from probation.[30]
3. *Referral to a diversion agency.* The juvenile can be released and referred to a diversion agency. In some jurisdictions, the police operate their own diversion program; more typically, juveniles are referred to agencies such as Big Brothers Big Sisters, a runaway center, or a mental health agency. In 1997, about 1% were referred to diversion programs.[31]
4. *Citation and referral to juvenile court.* The police officer can issue a **citation** and refer the youth to the juvenile court. The intake counselor of the juvenile court,

FIGURE 14.1 Juvenile Dispositional Alternatives Available to the Police

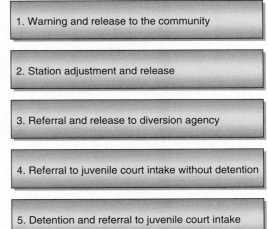

Possible Outcomes of Police–Juvenile Encounters

1. Warning and release to the community

2. Station adjustment and release

3. Referral and release to diversion agency

4. Referral to juvenile court intake without detention

5. Detention and referral to juvenile court intake

juvenile officer In some police departments, a police officer who has received specialized training to work effectively with juveniles, and who is tasked primarily with such work.

station adjustment One of several disposition options available to a police officer whereby a juvenile is taken to the police station following a complaint, the contact is recorded, and the juvenile is given an official reprimand and then released to his or her parents or guardians.

citation A summons to appear in juvenile court.

TABLE 14.2 Percentages of Delinquency Cases Referred by Law Enforcement, 2006

Most Serious Offense	Percent
Delinquency	82%
Person	87
Property	91
Drugs	90
Public order	61

Source: Howard N. Snyder and Melissa Sickmund, *Juvenile Offenders and Victims: 2006 National Report* (Washington, D.C.: National Center for Juvenile Justice, Office of Juvenile Justice and Delinquency Prevention, 2006), p. 157.

who is usually a probation officer, then decides whether or not a formal petition should be filed and whether the youth should appear before the juvenile judge; the juvenile is then returned to the family with this disposition. Today, more than four-fifths of the delinquency cases handled in juvenile court are referred by law enforcement agencies. Property delinquency cases are referred by law enforcement most often, followed by drug cases, and then offenses involving violence against persons. A smaller proportion of public-order cases are referred to juvenile court by law enforcement, primarily because this offense category contains cases involving contempt of court and probation violations that are most frequently referred by probation or court personnel.[32] Table 14.2 gives the percent of delinquency cases referred to juvenile court by police agencies in 2006.

5. *Detention.* The police officer can issue a citation, refer the youth to the juvenile court, and take him or her to a detention center. An intake worker at the detention center then decides whether the juvenile should be returned to the parents or left at the detention center. A juvenile is left in detention when he or she is thought to be dangerous to self or others in the community or has no care in the home. Taking youths out of their own homes and placing them in detention facilities clearly must be a last resort.

Legal Rights of Juveniles

The rights of juveniles in custody have changed dramatically since the days when the "third degree" was given at the station. Although some departments have lagged behind others in granting due process rights to juveniles under **arrest**, the majority of them now comply with court decisions concerning the rights of juveniles. Yet because few juvenile cases are appealed, police practices by which juveniles are denied their due process rights are usually known only at the local level.[33]

Search and Seizure

The Fourth Amendment to the Constitution of the United States protects citizens from unauthorized **search and seizure**. In 1961, the Supreme Court decision in *Mapp v. Ohio* affirmed Fourth Amendment rights for adults, stating that evidence gathered in an unreasonable search and seizure—that is, evidence seized without probable cause and without a proper search warrant—was inadmissible in court.[34] In *State v. Lowry* (1967), the Supreme Court applied the Fourth Amendment ban against unreasonable searches and seizures to juveniles:

> Is it not more outrageous for the police to treat children more harshly than adult offenders, especially when such is violative of due process and fair treatment? Can a court countenance a system, where, as here, an adult may suppress evidence with the usual effect of having the charges dropped for lack of proof, and, on the other hand, a juvenile can be institutionalized—lose the most sacred possession a human being has, his freedom—for "rehabilitative" purposes because the Fourth Amendment right is unavailable to him?[35]

arrest The process of taking a person into custody for an alleged violation of the law. Juveniles who are under arrest have nearly all the due process safeguards accorded to adults.

search and seizure The police procedure used in the investigation of crimes for the purpose of gathering evidence.

Police officers take information from handcuffed gang members in Phoenix, Arizona.
▶ **What rights do juvenile offenders have when facing processing by the juvenile justice system?**

Juveniles thus must be presented with a valid search warrant unless they have waived that right, have consented to have their person or property searched, or have been apprehended in the act. When these conditions have not been met, courts have overturned rulings against juveniles. For example, a 1966 District of Columbia ruling suppressed evidence seized when the police entered a juvenile's apartment without a warrant at 5 A.M. to arrest him; the court held that "the Fourth Amendment to the United States Constitution is a protection designed to secure the homes and persons of young and old alike against unauthorized police searches and seizures."[36]

In another case, a Houston police officer stopped a car being driven without lights and issued the driver, a youth, a traffic ticket for that offense as well as for driving without a driver's license. The youth was taken to a police station because the officer had some questions about the automobile's ownership. Five hours after the initial contact, another police officer searched the youth without his consent and without a search warrant and discovered 50 milligrams of marijuana; for this possession of marijuana, the youth was committed to the Texas Youth Council. An appellate court released the youth from training school, finding that a search some five hours after the original arrest for driving without lights "can hardly be justified as incidental to the arrest for a traffic offense."[37]

Interrogation Practices

The Fourteenth Amendment of the Constitution affirms that police must adhere to standards of fairness and due process in obtaining confessions. Current standards also require that the courts must take into consideration the totality of circumstances under which a confession was made in determining the appropriateness of the confession.

The Supreme Court decision *Haley* v. *Ohio* is an early example of excesses in **police interrogation**. In the *Haley* case, a 15-year-old youth was arrested at his home five days after a store robbery in which the owner was shot. Five or six police officers questioned the boy for about five hours; he then confessed after being shown what were alleged to be the confessions of two other youths. No parent or attorney

police interrogation The process of interviewing a person who has been arrested with the express purpose of obtaining a confession.

was present during the questioning. The Supreme Court invalidated the confession, stating:

> The age of the petitioner, the hours when he was grilled, the duration of his quizzing, the fact that he had no friend or counsel to advise him, the callous attitude of the police toward his rights combine to convince us that this confession was wrung from a child by means which the law should not sanction. Neither man nor child can be allowed to stand condemned by methods which flout constitutional requirements of due process of law.[38]

The Supreme Court also ruled in *Brown* v. *Mississippi* that police may not use force to obtain confessions[39]; in this case, police had used physical force to extract a confession. Other confessions have been ruled invalid because the accused was too tired; was questioned too long; and/or was not permitted to talk with spouse, friends, or lawyer either while he or she was being interrogated or until he or she confessed.[40]

Miranda v. Arizona The landmark 1966 U.S. Supreme Court ruling that suspects taken into police custody must, before any questioning can take place, be informed that they have the right to remain silent, that anything they say may be used against them, and that they have the right to legal counsel.

Juveniles taken into custody are entitled to the rights stated in the 1966 decision of **Miranda v. Arizona**. This Supreme Court decision prohibits the use of a confession in court unless the individual was advised of his or her rights before interrogation, especially the right to remain silent, the right to have an attorney present during questioning, and the right to be assigned an attorney by the state if the individual could not afford one.[41] *In re Gault* (see Chapter 15) made the right against self-incrimination and the right to counsel applicable to juveniles.[42] However, the *Gault* decision failed to clarify whether or not a juvenile could waive the protection of the *Miranda* rules and also failed to specify what is necessary for a juvenile to waive his or her *Miranda* rights intelligently and knowingly. For example, is a juvenile's ability to waive *Miranda* rights impaired if the youth is under the influence of drugs or alcohol or in a state of shock?

The 1979 *Fare* v. *Michael C.* decision applied the "totality of the circumstances" approach to the interrogation of juveniles. The circumstances behind this case were that Michael C. was implicated in a murder that took place during a robbery, so the police arrested the 16-year-old youth and brought him to the station. After he was advised of his *Miranda* rights, he requested to see his probation officer; when this request was denied, he proceeded to talk to the police officer, implicating himself in the murder. The Supreme Court ruled in this case that Michael C. appeared to understand his rights and that when his request to talk with his probation officer was denied, he expressed his willingness to waive his rights and continue the interrogation.[43]

Thomas Grisso, who studied juveniles interrogated by the St. Louis police in 1981, found that virtually all of them had waived their *Miranda* rights, so he questioned whether juveniles were even "capable of providing a meaningful waiver of the rights to avoid self-incrimination and to obtain legal counsel."[44] After surveying a sample of juveniles, Grisso found that almost everyone younger than 14 years of age and half the juveniles in the 15- to 16-year-old age bracket had less than adequate understanding of what their *Miranda* rights entailed.

Several court cases have held that the minority status of a juvenile is not an absolute bar to a valid confession. A California case upheld the confession of two juveniles from Spanish-speaking families; although both had been arrested before, one had an IQ of 65–71, with a mental age of 10 years and 2 months.[45] Similarly, a North Carolina court of appeals approved the confession of a 12-year-old youth who was charged with shooting out a window in a camper truck.[46] A Maryland appellate court approved the confession of a 16-year-old youth, a school dropout with an eighth-grade education, who was charged with firebombing and burning both a store and a school during a racial confrontation.[47]

To protect juveniles against police interrogation excesses, many jurisdictions have a statutory requirement that a parent, someone acting *in loco parentis* for the child, or counsel for the child must be present at police interrogation in order for a confession to be admissible. In *Commonwealth* v. *Guyton* (1989), the Massachusetts court held that no other minor, not even a relative, can act as an interested adult.[48] Other courts have ruled that the interested adult may be a child's relative.[49] Some states attempt to protect the juvenile by requiring that the youth be taken to the juvenile detention center or to juvenile court if he or she is not returned immediately to the parents' custody, obviously preferring that police interrogation take place within juvenile facilities rather than at a police station.[50]

Fingerprinting

Fingerprinting, along with other pretrial identification practices, has traditionally been highly controversial in juvenile corrections. Some juvenile court statutes require that a judge approve the taking of fingerprints of juveniles, control access to fingerprint records, and provide for fingerprint destruction under certain circumstances.[51] In many other jurisdictions, the police department determines policy, with some police departments routinely fingerprinting all juveniles taken into custody and suspected of serious wrongdoing. The Juvenile Justice and Delinquency Prevention Act of 1974 recommended that fingerprints be taken only with the consent of the judge, that juvenile fingerprints not be recorded in the criminal section of the fingerprint registry, and that the records be destroyed after their purpose has been served.

A 1969 Supreme Court decision that reversed a Mississippi ruling is the most important case dealing with juvenile fingerprints. In this case, the U.S. Supreme Court ruled, among other things, that fingerprints taken by the police could not be used as evidence. The youth in question was detained by the police without authorization by a judicial officer, was interrogated at the time he was first fingerprinted, and was fingerprinted again at a later date; the Court ruled that the police should not have detained the youth without authorization by a judicial officer, that the youth was unnecessarily fingerprinted a second time, and that the youth should not have been interrogated at the first detention when he was fingerprinted.[52]

fingerprinting A pretrial identification procedure used with both juveniles and adults following arrest.

Pretrial Identification Practices

Among other **pretrial identification practices**, both photographing and placing juveniles in lineups are highly controversial. Another recent practice is to notify the school district regarding juveniles who have been convicted of serious or violent crimes.

A lineup consists of the police placing a number of suspects in front of witnesses or victims, who try to identify the person who committed the crime against them. If no one can be identified, the suspects are released to the community, but if one of the persons is identified as the perpetrator, the police then proceed with their prosecution. The courts have been careful to set standards for the police to follow because innocent youths could end up labeled as delinquents and confined in an institution; one important standard is that the offender must have an attorney at the initial identification lineup in order to ensure that the identification of the offender is not tainted.

In one important case, *United States* v. *Wade* (1967), the Supreme Court ruled that the accused has a right to have counsel present at postindictment lineup procedures.[53] In *Kirby* v. *Illinois* (1972), the Court went on to add that the defendant's right of counsel during postindictment lineup procedures goes into effect as soon as the complaint or the indictment has been issued.[54] In the *In re Holley* decision (1970), a juvenile accused of rape had his conviction reversed by the appellate court because of the lack of counsel during the lineup identification procedure.[55]

At the end of 1997, 45 states and the District of Columbia had statutes permitting photographing of juveniles under certain circumstances for criminal history record purposes, and juvenile codes in 42 states allowed names—and sometimes even pictures and court records—of juveniles who were involved in delinquency proceedings to be released to the media.[56] Since 1997, still more states have permitted similar pretrial identification practices.

Photographs also can play an important part in the identification of offenders. For example, in one case, a rape victim was shown a photograph of one suspect only, and she could not identify the offender from that photograph but then later identified her attacker in a probation office. A California appellate court noted that

pretrial identification practices The procedures such as fingerprinting, photographing, and placing juveniles in lineups for the purpose of identification prior to formal court appearance.

Review   Legal Rights of Juveniles

permitting the identification of offenders on the basis of only one photograph was inappropriate because it could prejudice the victim.[57]

Another problem with photographs is their permanency and potential stigmatizing effects on youths in the community. Because photographs are filed and frequently reviewed by police officers, the police examine these photographs whenever something happens in the community, so innocent youths may never be able to escape the stigma of such labeling. For these reasons, some states require that judges give the police written consent to take photographs, that the photographs not be published in the media, and that the photographs be destroyed when the youths become adults.

Social Context of Delinquency: The Police and the Prevention of Juvenile Offenses

Now we move to the final section of this chapter, which examines what police can do about preventing and deterring juvenile crime. Juvenile delinquency poses a difficult problem for police officers who must deal with a wide range of behaviors, from drug-trafficking street gangs to status and runaway offenders. That more juveniles own handguns and that they are exhibiting violent behavior are two of the major challenges facing the police today.

Police–juvenile relations today take place in the larger context of community-oriented policing (COP), which has focused on developing a cooperative relationship between police officers and communities. Law enforcement officers are quite cognizant that fear of crime makes people reluctant to participate in their neighborhoods; the result is that citizens cede control to criminals. COP attempts to empower citizens by helping them regain ownership and pride in their neighborhoods, thereby fostering a greater feeling of well-being, an increased interest in community affairs and events, and a greater willingness to participate in efforts to reduce crime. By encouraging community building, COP endeavors to enhance the preventive capacity of neighborhood institutions, and it also attempts to empower police officers by expanding officers' discretion and encouraging them to solve problems creatively, in ways that do not necessarily involve arrest (Library Extra 14.1).[58]

Library Extra 14.1

Police Encounters with Juvenile Suspects

COP appears to be especially useful in juvenile justice for a number of reasons. It moves police officers from anonymity in the patrol car to direct engagement with a community, thus giving them more immediate information about neighborhood problems and insights into their solutions, and frees officers from an emergency response system and permits them to engage more directly in proactive crime prevention. In addition, COP makes police operations more visible to the public, which increases police accountability to the public; decentralizes operations, which allows officers greater familiarity with the workings and needs of various neighborhoods; encourages officers to view citizens as partners, which improves relations between the public and the police; and moves decision making and discretion to those who best know the community's problems and expectations.[59]

Three ways police departments are attempting to implement community-based policing in the prevention and deterrence of youth crime are community-based, school-based, and gang-based interventions.

Community-Based Interventions

Community relations are a major focus of police officers who work with juveniles. They must cultivate good relations with school administrators and teachers, with the staff of community agencies, with the staff of local youth organizations and youth shelters, with the juvenile court, and with merchants and employees at popular juvenile hangouts. Of course, juvenile police officers also must develop good relations with parents of youthful offenders as well as with the offenders themselves. The officer who has earned the respect of the youths of the community will be aware of what is happening in the community and will be called on for assistance by youths in trouble. Special Agent Ann Miller gives an example of good community relations:

> The most challenging task of working with juveniles is to get them to realize the importance of the decisions they make. Lots of juveniles have an attitude in which they think they are untouchable and nothing will happen to them.
>
> I don't think juveniles respond to me differently than they would to a male police officer. The bottom line is the type of rapport you build with juveniles. If you are a jerk, juveniles will respond in negative ways. But if you treat juveniles with decency and respect, the chances are that they will respond to you in the same way.
>
> What I find exciting about working with juveniles is that you can have a positive effect on kids. Kids want to learn. The challenge is to be there and to encourage kids to make something positive happen even though they have had trouble in the past. There are some kids I've arrested three or four times before they are able to get some positive things going in their lives.[60]

One of the important challenges the police face today is finding missing children. The AMBER Alert system began in 1996 when Dallas–Fort Worth broadcasters teamed with local police departments to develop an early-warning system to assist in finding abducted children, which they called the Dallas AMBER Plan. AMBER, which stands for America's Missing: Broadcast Emergency Response, was named in memory of nine-year-old Amber Hagerman, who was kidnapped while riding her bicycle and brutally murdered in Arlington, Texas, in 1996. Other states and communities soon set up their own alert plans, and the AMBER Alert network was adopted nationwide.[61] Exhibit 14.2 describes AMBER Alerts.

The police are called on to intercede in a variety of juvenile problems. These include enforcing the curfew ordinances that more and more communities across the nation are passing,[62] enforcing drug laws,[63] preventing hate crimes committed by teenagers against minority groups (Jews, other ethnic groups, and homosexuals),[64] focusing attention on serious habitual offenders, enhancing the quality and relevance of information that is exchanged through active interagency collaboration, and controlling gun-related violence in the youth population.

A police officer talks to a preschool class about home safety in Port Angeles, Washington. Establishing good community relations is crucial for police officers who work with juveniles.
▶ **What are these children likely to remember from this experience?**

EXHIBIT 14.2

AMBER Alert

The following material, which describes the AMBER Alert system in a question-answer format, comes from the federal Office of Justice Programs.

HOW DOES PROJECT AMBER WORK?

Once law enforcement has determined that a child has been abducted and the abduction meets the AMBER Alert criteria, law enforcement notifies broadcasters and state transportation officials. AMBER Alerts interrupt regular programming and are broadcast on radio and television and appear on highway signs. AMBER Alerts can also be issued on lottery tickets, to wireless devices such as mobile phones, and over the Internet. Through the coordination of local, state, and regional plans, the Department of Justice (DOJ) is working toward the creation of a seamless national network.

HOW EFFECTIVE HAS IT BEEN?

AMBER Alert has been very effective. The programs have helped save the lives of 200 children nationwide.

Over 84% of those recoveries have occurred since October 2002, when President George W. Bush called for the appointment of an AMBER Alert Coordinator at the first-ever White House Conference on Missing, Exploited, and Runaway Children.

AMBER Alerts serve as deterrents to those who would prey on children. Program data have shown that some perpetrators release the abducted child after hearing the AMBER Alert on the radio or seeing it on television.

NOW THAT ALL 50 STATES HAVE AMBER ALERT PLANS, HOW DOES THIS HELP CHILDREN AND FAMILIES?

The establishment of AMBER Alert plans in all 50 states marks an important milestone in the efforts to prevent child abductions. No matter where a child is abducted, communities and law enforcement work together to recover missing children quickly and safely. The numbers of recovered children speak for themselves. In 2001, only 2 children were recovered via AMBER Alert; in 2004, that number rose to 71. Interstate expansion has had a marked impact in saving children's lives.

WHAT ARE THE CRITERIA FOR ISSUING AMBER ALERTS?

Each state AMBER Alert plan has its own criteria for issuing alert notices. The PROTECT Act, passed in 2003, which established

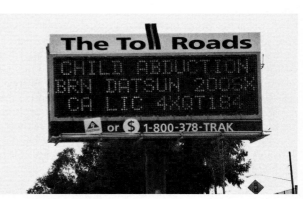

An AMBER Alert sign informs motorists of a child abduction incident in Orange County, California.
▶ How does the AMBER Alert system work?

the role of AMBER Alert Coordinator within the DOJ, calls for the DOJ to issue minimum standards or guidelines for AMBER Alerts that states can adopt voluntarily. The DOJ's Guidance on Criteria for Issuing AMBER Alerts follows:

- Law enforcement must confirm that an abduction has taken place.
- The child is at risk of serious injury or death.
- There is sufficient descriptive information of the child and the captor or captor's vehicle to issue an alert.
- The child must be 17 years old or younger.
- It is recommended that AMBER Alert data be immediately entered into the FBI National Crime Information Center. Text information describing the circumstances surrounding the abduction of the child should be entered, with the case flagged as "child abduction."

Most states' guidelines adhere closely to DOJ's recommended guidelines.

▶ What is the significance of the AMBER Alert program for local communities and for the nation? How do local media and national law enforcement networks serve as a deterrent to those who might consider abducting children?

Source: Adapted from www.amberalert.gov/faqs.html.

In many larger cities, police departments form juvenile units to handle youth crime. A 2000 survey of law enforcement agencies (those with 100 or more sworn officers) reported that a large proportion of these agencies had special units targeting juvenile justice concerns (see Table 14.3).[65]

School-Based Interventions

Developing effective delinquency prevention programs in schools is one of the most important challenges facing the police at the present time (see Library Extra 14.2). Community predelinquent programs have included courses in high school, junior

Library Extra 14.2
OJJDP Juvenile Justice Bulletin: "Effective Intervention for Serious Juvenile Offenders"

TABLE 14.3 Special Units Targeting Juvenile Justice Concerns

Type of Special Unit	Type of Agency	
	Local Police	State
Drug education in schools	70%	30%
Juvenile crime	62	10
Gangs	45	18
Child abuse	46	8
Domestic violence	45	10
Missing children	48	31
Youth outreach	33	6

Source: Howard N. Snyder and Melissa Sickmund, Office of Juvenile Justice and Delinquency Prevention, *Juvenile Offenders and Victims: 2006 National Report* (Washington, D.C.: U.S. Government Printing Office, 2006), p. 153.

high school, and elementary school settings addressing school safety, community relations, drug and alcohol abuse, city government, court procedures, bicycle safety, and juvenile delinquency. The Officer Friendly Program and McGruff "Take a Bite Out of Crime" were established throughout the nation to develop better relations with younger children.

More recently, popular prevention programs have included Gang Resistance Education and Training (G.R.E.A.T.) and Law-Related Education (LRE). As of June 1997 more than 2,400 officers from 47 states and the District of Columbia had completed G.R.E.A.T. training, and the program is now found in school curricula in all 50 states and the District of Columbia.[66] A 1995 evaluation, based on a cross-sectional survey of 5,935 eighth-graders from 42 schools where G.R.E.A.T. was taught, found that students who completed these lessons reported more prosocial behaviors and attitudes than their peers who did not finish the program or who failed to participate in the first place.[67] In a 1999 evaluation, Finn-Aage Esbensen and D. Wayne Osgood found that students who had completed the G.R.E.A.T. curriculum four years before did not show levels of gang or delinquency involvement significantly different from those of a control group, but this evaluation also revealed that students who had finished the curriculum continued to have more prosocial attitudes than those who had not.[68]

LRE is designed to teach students the fundamental principles and skills needed to become responsible citizens in a constitutional democracy.[69] A 1985 national curriculum survey reported that LRE had been added to the curriculum in more than half of the 46 states involved in the study.[70] One of the few studies evaluating LRE programs found that these programs, when properly conducted, can reduce tendencies toward delinquent behavior and improve a range of attitudes related to responsible citizenship and that successful students were also less likely to associate with delinquent peers and to use violence as a means of resolving conflict.[71]

Today, the need for substance abuse prevention programs demands creativity and involvement on the part of the police. The Drug Abuse Resistance Education (D.A.R.E.) program (discussed in the section on social policy below) is a widely replicated effort by the police to prevent substance abuse. New York City's School Program to Educate and Control Drug Abuse (Project SPECDA), which is a collaborative effort of the city's police department and board of education, is another highly praised drug-prevention program; in this project, a 16-session curriculum, with the units split evenly between fifth and six grades, imparts basic information about the risks and effects of drug use, makes students aware of the social pressures that cause drug use, and teaches acceptable methods of resisting peer pressure to experiment with drugs.[72]

In addition to drug-prevention programs, the police respond to incidents ranging from student fights and assaults to drug and weapon possession. Officers also regularly drive by schools during night and weekend patrol to prevent vandalism and burglary to school property, and the police are responsible for providing security and safety to the school. In some schools, this requires conducting searches of students as they come into the school, monitoring the halls, doing conflict mediation when necessary, and protecting students as they come to and go home from school. The police are frequently called on to assist the school in searching for weapons and drugs on school property and are charged to enforce drug-free school zone laws and the federal Gun-Free School Zones Act. The police are also expected to enforce school attendance programs in a few school districts across the nation.

The federal Office of Community Oriented Policing Services (COPS) has awarded almost $715 million to more than 2,900 law enforcement agencies to fund more than 6,300 school resource officers (SROs) through the COPS in Schools (CIS) program. In addition, COPS has appropriated nearly $21 million to train COPS-funded SROs and school administrators in partnering schools or school districts to work more collaboratively through the CIS program. SROs in schools can serve in a variety of ways: They may function not only as law enforcement officers but as problem solvers, LRE educators, and community liaisons; they may teach classes in crime prevention, substance abuse awareness, and gang resistance; they may monitor and assist troubled students through mentoring programs; and they may promote social and personal responsibility by encouraging student participation in community service activities. Moreover, these officers help schools develop policies to address delinquent activity and school safety.[73]

Gang-Based Interventions

As discussed in Chapter 10, the number of street gangs rose dramatically across the nation beginning in the late 1980s. The characteristics of these gangs vary widely from one city to another. Some of the gangs are simply groups of adolescents who hang around together and who seldom get into any serious trouble, other gangs engage in extensive drug activity, and some have become involved in violent drive-by shootings in which innocent citizens have been killed.

Drugs and violence have made gangs a problem for the police (see Library Extra 14.3). For example, police officers caught a group of Los Angeles Crips conducting a drug sales seminar in St. Louis, Missouri.[74] Once a community becomes aware of the seriousness of the gang problem—usually after a violent gang incident has taken place—then pressure is typically put on the police to solve the problem. Police departments have frequently responded to this pressure by setting up one of three types of intervention units to work with gangs.[75]

The Youth Service Program, which is one such unit, is formed to deal with a specific gang problem and is not a permanent unit within the police department; officers continue to perform their regular duties and are not exclusively concerned with gang problems. The gang detail is a second type of unit, and the officers in these units generally are pulled from detective units or juvenile units. The gang detail differs from the Youth Service Program in that its officers are assigned solely to gang problems and do not routinely work on other assignments. The **gang unit** is the third type of unit, and the members of these permanent units see themselves as specialists who are working on gang problems; for example, many gang units will develop extensive intelligence networks with gang members in the community.[76]

Delinquency across the Life Course: Effects of Police Discretion

The police are the first line of contact with law-violating juveniles. They frequently have the discretion to divert a youth or refer him or her to the attention of the juvenile justice system, especially when the juvenile is involved in a minor offense. As repeatedly

---

Voices of Delinquency

Read "What Would I Say to Urban Gang Kids?" In this story, a former gang member, who is now a university graduate and a police officer working with youths (including gang youths), relates a speech that he makes to these youths. Is this likely to be an effective presentation?

mycrimekit

Library Extra 14.3

NIJ-sponsored publication: *Children in an Adult World: Prosecuting Adolescents in Criminal and Juvenile Jurisdictions*

mycrimekit

Review Gangs: Community Prevention

gang unit A specialized unit established by some police departments to address the problem of gangs.

stated in this text, there is no question that the juvenile who has an early onset of crime and comes to the attention of the justice system is more likely to be involved with the justice system longer and go on to the adult system more than the youth who is diverted from the system or begins his or her onset of crime at a later date in adolescence. The police, who must try everything possible to avoid contributing to the ongoing delinquency and later criminality of individuals, can do the following:

- Develop relationships with juveniles so that they can feel connected with police officers and feel that they are being treated fairly.
- Avoid any form of abusive treatment of juveniles.
- Do not target certain juveniles and thereby make them heroes to their peers.
- Expand the ways in which they work with the community to deal with problem-oriented juveniles.
- Develop and evaluate prevention programs, especially for predelinquent youths.

Voices of Delinquency

Read "Feeding the Monster." In this story, the writer tells how the police enhanced their department's reputation in the community. He says, "Hell, the cops were doing more for our egos than we were." How likely is this to occur elsewhere?

Delinquency and Social Policy: Project D.A.R.E.

The most popular school-based drug-education program in the nation is Drug Abuse Resistance Education (D.A.R.E), a program that receives over $200 million annually in public funding despite strong evidence of its ineffectiveness. This program is designed to equip elementary school children with skills for resisting peer pressure to experiment with tobacco, drugs, and alcohol. Using a core curriculum consisting of 17 hour-long weekly lessons, D.A.R.E. gives special attention to fifth- and sixth-graders to prepare them for entry into junior high and high school, where they are most likely to encounter pressure to use drugs. Since it was founded, D.A.R.E. has expanded to encompass programs for middle and high school students, gang prevention, conflict resolution, parent education, and after-school recreation and learning. As the most popular school-based drug-education program in the United States, it is administered in about 75% of this nation's school districts, reaching 26 million, and has been adopted in more than 50 countries.[77]

It has been widely evaluated, and there are several disappointing findings:

- The D.A.R.E. program has some immediate beneficial effects on student knowledge of drugs, social skills, attitudes about drug use, and attitudes toward the police.
- These effects dissipate quickly and are typically gone within one to two years.
- The effects of D.A.R.E. on drug-use behavior (measured in numerous ways) are extremely rare.
- The identified effects tend to be small in size and also dissipate quickly.[78]

Dennis Rosenbaum summarized this collective evidence:

In sum, the results were very disappointing despite high expectations for the program. Across more than 30 studies, the collective evidence from evaluations with reasonably good scientific validity suggests that the core D.A.R.E. program does not prevent drug use in the short term, nor does it prevent drug use when students are ready to enter high school or college. Students who receive D.A.R.E. are indistinguishable from students who do not participate in the program.[79]

Rosenbaum raised a question that has been widely raised elsewhere—"How can we reconcile this state of knowledge with the reality of worldwide support for D.A.R.E.?"—and goes on to say, "The irony for the drug prevention field (and other fields as well) is that a program known to be ineffective receives millions of dollars in support, whereas programs known to be effective or promising are sidelined and remain unfunded."[80]

Dozens of communities in the 1990s and early 2000s have dropped the D.A.R.E. program, but the debate whether to continue funding has been waged both nationally and internationally. Proponents of D.A.R.E. are a strong interest group and presently are able to maintain federal funding for this drug-prevention program.

Chapter Summary

This chapter has focused on the relationship between the police and juveniles in U.S. society. Policing juveniles is similar in some ways to policing adults, yet in other ways it is quite different:

- Because the police usually represent the first contact a juvenile has with the justice system, effective police–juvenile relations are vitally important.

- In the late nineteenth and early twentieth centuries, the policing of juveniles came to be viewed differently than the policing of adults.

- This change, which coincided with reforms in community-based and institutional care of delinquents, emphasized the importance of delinquency prevention.

- Specialized police units were soon created in many of our country's large cities and were charged with delinquency prevention and the apprehension of juveniles who broke the law.

- In the late 1970s and early 1980s, budgetary constraints led to reduced police involvement in delinquency prevention and in diversionary programs for juveniles.

- By the late 1980s and early 1990s, however, a rise in juvenile violence, growing juvenile drug abuse, and proliferation of youth gangs again led to an expanded police emphasis on delinquency prevention and to an examination of the problems faced by juveniles.

- Juveniles today generally demonstrate a better attitude toward the police than in the past, and police officers today are typically more positive about the handling of juveniles, showing that efforts to enhance police–juvenile relations have been at least partly successful.

- The most important elements in understanding police–juvenile relations today may be the public's expectation that the police should address the problems of juvenile crime and prevent youth crime in rich and poor communities alike.

- Today's police have wide discretion in dealing with juvenile lawbreakers, and several studies have found that 80% to 90% of police–juvenile encounters result in diversion from official processing by the juvenile justice system.

- Although a number of factors influence how police officers respond to juvenile offenders, the most important element influencing police discretion and disposition of the juvenile offender is the nature of the offense committed.

- Over time, juveniles have been granted a number of significant due process rights by the courts, and those rights have placed increased requirements on the police for the proper handling of juveniles.

- Of special concern today is the need for the police to deal with the problem of violent youth crime—a challenge made all the more difficult by the fact that many juveniles possess handguns, gangs are widespread, juvenile drug abuse remains at significant levels, and some juveniles have become involved in hate crimes.

Key Terms

arrest, p. 322
citation, p. 321
fingerprinting, p. 325
gang unit, p. 330

juvenile officer, p. 321
Miranda v. *Arizona*, p. 324
police discretion, p. 318
police interrogation, p. 323

pretrial identification
   practices, p. 325
search and seizure, p. 322
station adjustment, p. 321

Review Questions

1. Overall, how do juveniles feel about the police?
2. What are the most important factors affecting the processing of juveniles?
3. What are the juvenile dispositional alternatives available to the police?

4. What are the most important legal rights of juveniles?
5. How do the police attempt to prevent and deter delinquency?

Discussion Questions

1. Why do the attitudes of minority and white youths toward the police tend to differ? Why would youthful offenders feel differently toward the police than nonoffenders? Have your experiences with the police made a difference in how you feel about the police?
2. What are the rights of a juvenile taken into custody?
3. What is your evaluation of D.A.R.E.? Did you participate in a D.A.R.E. program in high school? If so, did it make a difference in your using or not using drugs?
4. Why is the police role in working with juveniles more difficult today than it was in the past?
5. Do you think police discretion leads to discriminatory decision making?
6. Is "by-the-book" policing the wisest course of action to prevent charges of discrimination? Explain your response.

Group Exercises

1. Have students research data from their county and state to determine how many police departments have dedicated juvenile crime units or officers.
2. Invite a two- or three-member panel from your local police department, including at least one supervisor (sergeant or lieutenant), to discuss police discretion with the class.
3. Invite a member of your local police department's juvenile crime unit to address the class regarding juvenile justice issues in your community.
4. Invite a member of your local police department's gang unit to address gang issues in your community.

mycrimekit™

Go to mycrimekit.com to explore the following study tools and resources specific to this chapter:

- **Practice Quiz:** Practice with multiple-choice, true/false, short-answer, and essay questions.

- **WebQuests:** Do web activities about Terrence T. Allen's article *Taking a Juvenile Into Custody: Situational*

Factors That Influence Police Officers' Decisions and Project Safe Neighborhoods fact sheet *Do After School Programs Reduce Delinquency?*

- **Flashcards:** Use 11 flashcards to test your knowledge of the chapter's key terms.

Juvenile Court

CHAPTER OBJECTIVES

After reading this chapter, you should be able to answer the following questions:

- How did the juvenile court begin?
- What pretrial procedures are involved in juvenile court proceedings?
- How is a trial conducted in juvenile court?
- What are the various forms of sentencing available to a juvenile court judge?
- What can be done to improve the juvenile court?

Under our Constitution the condition of being a boy does not justify a kangaroo court.

—*In re Gault*, 387 U.S. 1 (1967)

Introduction

The U.S. Supreme Court's 2005 decision barring the execution of minors used a Missouri murder as a test case on whether executing offenders under age 18 is ever allowable, even in the case of remorseless killers.

Christopher Simmons, age 17, told friends he wanted to break into 46-year-old Shirley Crook's home, hog-tie her, and throw her into the Meramec River near St. Louis. He said they could "get away with it" because they were minors. One friend dropped out of the scheme, but Simmons and a 15-year-old accomplice followed through.

The younger accomplice was given life in prison, and Simmons was sentenced to death. Missouri was one of 20 states at the time that allowed the execution of youths ages 16 and 17, but the Missouri Supreme Court threw out Simmons's death sentence and banned all executions for minors, which brought the case to the U.S. Supreme Court.

The high court had previously ruled on juvenile executions in 1988, striking down death sentences for 15-year-olds based on the "cruel and unusual punishment" clause of the Eighth Amendment to the U.S. Constitution.

A year later, however, the Supreme Court upheld the death penalty for 16- or 17-year-olds—a decision that met with worldwide opposition. The International Covenant on Civil and Political Rights bars juvenile executions, and only three other countries—Somalia, Iran, and Congo—allowed them, according to the Death Penalty Information Center.

In its 2005 decision *Roper* v. *Simmons*, the Court ruled 5 to 4 that executing minors violates "the evolving standards of decency that mark the progress of a maturing society" and that American society has come to regard juveniles as less culpable than adult criminals.[1]

Although the *Simmons* case set a precedent in making juveniles immune from execution for the crimes they commit, no matter how serious, it is significant for yet another reason: In the face of calls by many for reform of the juvenile court and for the imposition of adult punishments on juvenile offenders, the case reinforces the line separating juveniles from adults. In so doing, it seemed to echo the sentiments of Judge Gustav L. Schramm, who, as first juvenile court judge of Allegheny County (Pittsburgh), Pennsylvania, made clear the duties of juvenile court when he said:

> Neither umpire nor arbiter, [the juvenile judge] is the one person who represents his community as *parens patriae*, who may act with the parents, or when necessary even in place of them, to bring about behavior more desirable. As a judge in a juvenile court, he does not administer criminal law. The child before him is not a defendant. There is no conviction, no sentence. There is no lifelong stigma of a criminal record. In a juvenile court the judge administers equity; and the child, still immature and unable to take his place as an adult before the law, is the recipient of consideration, of guidance and of correction. The stake is no less than the saving of [a] human being at a time more favorable than any in an uncertain future.[2]

Judge Schramm claimed, as do other advocates of the **juvenile court,** that the informal setting of juvenile court and the parental demeanor of the judge enable wayward youths to be saved or rescued from possible lives of crime. Indeed, during the first half of the twentieth century, the juvenile court, a unique contribution to the world of jurisprudence, was widely praised for its attempt to redeem wayward youths.[3]

Critics eventually challenged these idealistic views of the juvenile court, claiming that the juvenile court had not succeeded in rehabilitating youthful offenders, in bringing justice and compassion to them, or even in providing them with their due

juvenile court Any court that has jurisdiction over matters involving juveniles.

process rights.[4] Some investigators even accused the juvenile court of doing great harm to the juveniles who appeared before it.[5]

Today three different positions have emerged concerning the role of the juvenile court. One position continues to support the *parens patriae* philosophy, or the state as parent, and holds to "the best interest of the child" standard for decision making. According to Judge Leonard P. Edwards, implicit in this standard is the position that "children are different from adults, that they have developmental needs which they cannot satisfy without assistance and that care and supervision are critical to their upbringing."[6] Edwards made this telling statement: "If children were no different from adults, the juvenile court would be unnecessary."[7] This position contends that the juvenile court is superior to the criminal court because the juvenile court offers the rehabilitation of offenders, the protection of youths, and the flexibility to provide the needed individualized justice for youths in their formative years.[8] The concept of individualized justice is actually the hallmark of the juvenile court:

> Individualized justice for children is the legitimate goal of the juvenile justice system. The court must, within the bounds of state and constitutional law, tailor its response to the peculiar needs of the child and family, with goals of (1) rehabilitating the child; (2) reuniting the family; and (3) protecting the public safety.[9]

A second position proposes that the justice model (see Chapter 13) replace the *parens patriae* philosophy as the basis of juvenile court procedures. In the 1980s, proposed procedural changes such as decriminalization of status offenses, determinate sentencing, mandatory sentencing, and opening up of juvenile proceedings and records struck at the very heart and core of traditional juvenile court proceedings.[10] The wide acceptance of these recommendations, as Barry C. Feld noted in 1991, was seen in the fact that "about one-third of the states now use the present offense and prior record [in the juvenile court] to regulate at least some sentencing decisions through determinate or mandatory minimum sentencing statutes or correctional administrative guidelines."[11] The proposed Model Juvenile Justice Code, which attracted considerable attention, also was based on the principles of the justice model.[12] The 1994 revisions in Minnesota's juvenile code showed how one state was influenced by the justice model in the remodeling of its juvenile code.[13]

A third position advocates that the juvenile court be abolished.[14] For example, Proposition 102 amended the Arizona Constitution in 1996 so that juvenile courts no longer have "exclusive" or "original" jurisdiction for offenders under 18 years of age.[15] Feld is one of the most articulate spokespeople for this position, arguing that an integrated criminal court with a youth discount (juveniles would receive lesser sentences than adults for similar violations of the law) would provide youthful offenders with greater protections and justice than they currently receive in the juvenile justice system and with more proportional and humane consequences than judges currently inflict on them as adults in the criminal justice system.[16] He contended that "a statutory sentencing policy that integrates youthfulness and limited opportunities to learn self-control with principles of proportionality and reduced culpability" would give youthful offenders with categorical fractional reductions of sentences given to adults.[17] This categorical approach is what Feld meant by an explicit "youth discount" at sentencing. For example, a 14-year-old delinquent might receive 25% to 33% of the adult penalty; a 16-year-old, 50% to 66%; and an 18-year-old adult, the full penalty.[18] In his 1997 article "Abolish the Juvenile Court," Feld made his point even stronger (see Juvenile Law 15.1).[19] Although the juvenile court would likely survive the implementation of the justice model, perhaps in a much altered form, the success of this movement would sound the death knell of the juvenile court.[20]

In sum, significant changes are clearly sweeping through the almost 110-year-old corridors of the juvenile court. As we approach the completion of the first decade of the twenty-first century, what is actually taking place is that all three positions are represented: For minor offenses, as well as for status offenses in most

Juvenile Law 15.1

Abolish the Juvenile Court?

Barry Feld writes:

[Since the mid-1970s] judicial decisions, legislative amendments, and administrative changes have transformed the **juvenile court** from a nominally rehabilitative social welfare agency into a scaled-down, second-class criminal court for young people. The reforms have converted the historical ideal of the juvenile court as a social welfare institution into a penal system that provides young offenders with neither therapy nor justice. The substantive and procedural convergence between juvenile and criminal courts eliminates virtually all the conceptual and operational differences in strategies of criminal social control for youths and adults. No compelling reasons exist to maintain, separate from an adult criminal court, a punitive juvenile court whose only remaining distinctions are its persisting procedural deficiencies. Rather, states should abolish juvenile courts' delinquency jurisdictions and formally recognize youthfulness as a mitigating factor in the sentencing of younger criminal offenders. Such a policy would provide younger offenders with substantive protections comparable to those afforded by juvenile courts, [en]sure greater procedural regularity in the determination of guilt, and avoid the disjunctions in social control caused by maintaining two duplicative and inconsistent criminal justice systems.

▶ **How do you feel about abolishing the juvenile court? What would be the disadvantages of such a move across the United States?**

Source: Barry C. Feld, "Abolish the Juvenile Court: Youthfulness, Criminal Responsibility, and Sentencing Policy," *Journal of Criminal Law and Criminology* 88 (Fall 1997), p. 68. Reprinted by special permission of Northwestern University School of Law, *The Journal of Criminal Law and Criminology.*

states, the "best interest of the child" position is the guiding standard of juvenile court decision making; for offenders who commit more serious delinquent acts, the principles of the justice model are increasingly used in adjudicatory and disposition hearings; and repetitive or violent youthful offenders are commonly transferred quickly to the adult court and handled as adults. Perhaps the question is not whether the traditional juvenile court will change but whether the court will survive (see Exhibit 15.1).

Changes in Juvenile Court

The concept of the juvenile court was rapidly accepted across the nation—31 states had instituted juvenile courts by 1905, and by 1928, only 2 states did not have a juvenile court statute. In Cook County, the amendments that followed the original act brought the neglected, the dependent, and the delinquent together under one roof. The "delinquent" category comprised both status offenders and actual violators of criminal law.

Juvenile courts throughout the nation were patterned on the Chicago court. Juveniles in trouble were offered informal and noncriminal hearings, their records generally were kept confidential, the hearings were not open to the public, and juveniles were detained separately from adults. Reformers then proposed that the noncriminal aspects of the proceedings be echoed in the physical surroundings of the court:

The courtroom should be not a courtroom at all; just a room, with a table and two chairs, where the judge and the child, the probation officer and the parents, as occasion arises, come into close contact, and where in a more or less informal way the whole matter may be talked over.[21]

Reformers further advocated that the juvenile judge sit at a desk rather than on a bench and that he occasionally "put his arm around [the delinquent's] shoulder and draw the lad to him."[22] But the sympathetic judge was instructed not to lose any of his judicial dignity. The goals of the court were defined as investigation, diagnosis, and prescription of treatment. Lawyers were deemed unnecessary because these civil proceedings were not adversary trials but informal hearings in which the best interests of the youths were the chief concern.

EXHIBIT 15.1

In Family Court, Child Defendant's Welfare Takes Priority

There is no jury, no media gallery, no victim impact statement, no public eye at all in the Family Court trial of a child accused of killing someone, as a 9-year-old Brooklyn girl was yesterday in a juvenile petition.

The process is not called a trial at all, but a fact-finding. And juvenile court judges issue dispositions, never sentences.

On paper at least, the language of juvenile justice in New York reflects a gentler application of criminal law than the one used in the adult model. It is a system informed in part by the principles of child welfare and in part by the 19th-century prison-reform ethic of rehabilitation over punishment.

"The overarching goal of the process is to protect the child's welfare," said Laurence Busching, chief of the Family Court division of the City Law Department. In the adult world, Mr. Busching's agency would fill the role as prosecutor of the 9-year-old defendant (known in the juvenile system as the respondent), who is accused of fatally stabbing her 11-year-old friend on Monday afternoon during a quarrel over a ball.

"The standard the court uses is to meet the needs and best interests of the child while considering the needs and protection of the community," Mr. Busching said. Depending on the finding of facts in her case, the 9-year-old will probably face no more than 18 months in a detention center, though a judge could seek to hold her for longer, even until her 18th birthday, he said. New York excludes children under 13 from being prosecuted as adults, no matter the crime.

But in 23 other states, including Florida and Pennsylvania, there is no such age barrier in homicide cases. "A child of 6 can be charged with murder as an adult" in those states, though no such case has gone to trial, said Marsha Levick, legal director of the Juvenile Law Center, a Philadelphia-based organization that advocates for children in the court system.

Ms. Levick helped direct the legal appeal for Lionel Tate, a 12-year-old Florida boy initially sentenced as an adult to life in prison for the 1999 killing of a 6-year-old playmate, Tiffany Eunick. She recently filed a friend-of-the-court brief in a United States Supreme Court case, *Roper* v. *Simmons*, weighing the issue of the death penalty for juveniles, which the court ultimately ruled unconstitutional.

In her brief to the Supreme Court, Ms. Levick presented evidence compiled by Laurence Steinberg, a psychologist and psychology professor at Temple University, indicating that the human brain may not reach full maturity until well past puberty. "New research on brain maturation shows there is continued development—in regions of the brain important for impulse control and foreseeing the consequences of one's actions—into the early and mid-20's," Professor Steinberg said in a telephone interview.

In response to a significant rise in juvenile crime from 1987 to 1994, much of it attributed to the crack epidemic, most states

This family court building is located in the Bronx, New York.
▶ **What does this text mean when it says that "the language of juvenile justice reflects a gentler application of criminal law than the one used in the adult model"?**

in the country, including New York, New Jersey and Connecticut, amended juvenile court laws to make it easier to prosecute children as adults, especially in cases of violent crime. But while many of those laws took effect in 1996 or later, juvenile crime rates began declining in 1994 and have continued to fall, Ms. Levick said.

Studies show that sparing the rod often spares the child. "There is growing evidence that kids who are sentenced as adults come out worse than they would have if they are sentenced as juveniles," Professor Steinberg said. All states require schooling for juveniles serving time in detention centers, and most also provide psychiatric counseling and treatment, he said. In adult prisons, services are far more stinted, and the environment often brutalizing.

Leslie Acoca, a therapist based in Oakland, Calif., and the director of a health study focusing on girls in the juvenile court system, said a vast majority had experienced domestic violence, sexual abuse, substance abuse or combinations of those.

In a study of 1,000 California girls in juvenile detention, 88 percent suffered one or more serious physical or mental disorders, Ms. Acoca said.

In short, the juvenile court was founded on several basic ideals: that the court should function as a social clinic designed to serve the best interests of youths in trouble; that youths who were brought before the court should be given the same care, supervision, and discipline as would be provided by a good parent; that the aim of the court is to help, to restore, to guide, and to forgive; that youths should not be treated as criminals; and that the rights to shelter, protection, and proper guardianship are the only rights of youths.[23]

Changes in Legal Norms

In the twentieth century, the group known as the **constitutionalists**, one of the most formidable foes of the juvenile court, contended that the juvenile court was unconstitutional because under its system the principles of a fair trial and individual rights were denied. The constitutionalists were particularly concerned that the youths appearing before the court have procedural rights as well as the rights to shelter, protection, and guardianship. They also believed that dependent and neglected youths are different than youths who break the law and therefore must be dealt with through separate judicial proceedings; that diagnostic and treatment technologies are not sufficiently developed to ensure that the delinquent can be treated and cured of his or her misbehavior; and that the state must justify interference with a youth's life when his or her freedom is at stake.[24] Their recommendations included modifications of juvenile court procedures by the adoption of separate methods for dealing with dependent and neglected youths and those accused of criminal behavior, by the use of informal adjustments to avoid official court actions as frequently as possible, and by the provision of rigorous procedural safeguards and rights for youths appearing before the court at the adjudicatory stage.[25]

A series of decisions by the U.S. Supreme Court in the 1960s and 1970s demonstrated the influence of the constitutionalists on juvenile justice. As Figure 15.1 shows, the five most important cases were ***Kent v. United States*** (1966), ***In re Gault*** (1967), ***In re Winship*** (1970), ***McKeiver v. Pennsylvania*** (1971), and ***Breed v. Jones*** (1975).

Kent v. United States (1966)   *Kent* is the first decision in which the U.S. Supreme Court dealt with a juvenile court case dealing with the matter of **transfer** (see Juvenile Law 15.2). The juvenile judge did not rule on the motions of Kent's counsel and held no hearings, nor did he confer with Kent, Kent's mother, or Kent's counsel. The judge instead entered an order saying that after full investigation he was transferring jurisdiction to the adult criminal court; he made no findings and entered no reasons for the waiver.

constitutionalists The name given to a group of twentieth-century reformers who advocated that juveniles deserve due process protections when they appear before the juvenile court.

Kent v. United States A 1966 U.S. Supreme Court decision on the matter of transfer; the first decision in which the Supreme Court dealt with a juvenile court case.

In re Gault A 1967 U.S. Supreme Court case that brought due process and constitutional procedures into juvenile courts.

In re Winship A 1970 case in which the U.S. Supreme Court decided that juveniles are entitled to proof beyond a reasonable doubt during adjudication proceedings.

McKeiver v. Pennsylvania A 1971 U.S. Supreme Court case that denied juveniles the right to trial by jury.

FIGURE 15.1 Timeline of U.S. Supreme Court Decisions of Special Relevance to Juvenile Justice

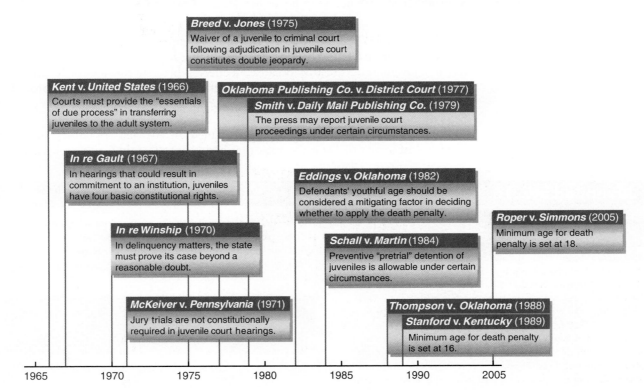

Source: Adapted from Office of Juvenile Justice and Delinquency Prevention, *Juvenile Offenders and Victims: 2006 National Report* (Washington, D.C.: OJJDP, 2006), p. 101.

Juvenile Law 15.2

Kent v. United States

Morris A. Kent Jr., a 16-year-old youth living in Washington, D.C., was on juvenile probation and was charged with three counts each of housebreaking and robbery and two counts of rape. His mother retained an attorney who had Kent examined by two psychiatrists and a psychologist. The attorney then filed a motion for a hearing on the question of waiver, together with a psychiatrist's affidavit that certified that Kent was "a victim of severe psychopathology," and recommended hospitalization for psychiatric observation. Counsel contended that psychiatric treatment would make

Kent a suitable subject for juvenile court rehabilitation. His counsel also moved for access to juvenile court probation records.

▶ What did Supreme Court Justice Fortas mean when he said that "there may be grounds for concern that the child receives the worst of both worlds"? Do you agree with his criticism of the juvenile court?

Source: Kent v. United States, 383 U.S. 541, 86 S.Ct. 1045, 16 L.Ed.2d 84 (1966).

Breed v. Jones A 1975 double jeopardy case in which the U.S. Supreme Court ruled that a juvenile court cannot adjudicate a case and then transfer the case to the criminal court for adult processing of the same offense.

transfer The process of certifying a youth over to adult criminal court. It takes place by judicial waiver and legislative waiver.

On appeal, the U.S. Supreme Court, holding that the juvenile court proceedings were defective, found that during a transfer hearing, Kent should have been afforded an evidential hearing; that he should have been present when the court decided to waive jurisdiction; that his attorney should have been permitted to examine the social worker's investigation of the youth, which the court used in deciding to waive jurisdiction; and that the judge should have recorded a statement of reasons for the transfer. Justice Abe Fortas, in the decision, stated:

> There is evidence, in fact, that there may be grounds for concern that the child receives the worst of both worlds; that he gets neither the protection accorded to adults nor the solicitous care and regenerative treatment postulated for children.[26]

The Court decided that withholding Kent's record essentially meant a denial of counsel. The Court also held that a juvenile has a right to be represented by counsel, that a youth charged with a felony has a right to a hearing, and that this hearing must "measure up to the essentials of due process and fair treatment"; finally, a juvenile's attorney must have access to his or her social or probation records.[27]

In re Gault (1967)   In May 1967, the U.S. Supreme Court reversed the conviction of a minor in *In re Gault*. This influential and far-reaching decision represented a new dawn in juvenile court history because, in effect, it brought the light of constitutional procedure into juvenile courts—no longer could due process and procedural safeguards be kept out of the adjudication proceedings. Juvenile Law 15.3 gives the facts of this case.

In *Gault*, the U.S. Supreme Court overruled the Arizona Supreme Court for its dismissal of a writ of *habeas corpus* that had sought Gerald Gault's release from a

Juvenile Law 15.3

In re Gault

Gerald Gault, a 15-year-old Arizona boy, and a friend, Ronald Lewis, were taken into custody on June 8, 1964, on a verbal complaint made by a neighbor. The neighbor had accused the boys of making lewd and indecent remarks to her over the phone. Gault's parents were not notified that he had been taken into custody, he was not advised of his right to counsel, he was not advised that he could remain silent, and no notice of charges was made either to Gerald or to his parents; additionally, the complainant was not present at either of the hearings. In spite of considerable confusion about whether or not Gerald had made the alleged phone

call, what he had said over the phone, and what he had said to the judge during the course of the two hearings, Judge McGhee committed him to the State Industrial School "for the period of his minority (that is, until age 21) unless sooner discharged by due process of law."

▶ What due process rights did this case grant juveniles? What due process rights did juveniles still lack after this decision?

Source: In re Gault, 387 U.S. 1, 18 L.Ed.2d 527, 87 S.Ct. 1428 (1967).

training school.[28] Justice Fortas, for the Court majority, ruled on four of the six issues raised in the appeal:

1. Notice, to comply with due process requirements, must be given sufficiently in advance of scheduled court proceedings so that reasonable opportunity to prepare will be afforded, and it must "set forth the alleged misconduct with particularity."

2. The due process clause of the Fourteenth Amendment requires that in respect of proceedings to determine delinquency which may result in commitment to an institution in which the juvenile's freedom is curtailed, the youth and his parent must be notified of the youth's right to be represented by counsel retained by them; if they are unable to afford counsel, counsel will be appointed to represent the youth.

3. The constitutional privilege against self-incrimination is as applicable in the case of juveniles as it is with respect to adults.

4. No reason is suggested or appears for a different role in respect of sworn testimony in juvenile courts than in adult tribunals. Absent a valid confession adequate to support the determination of the juvenile court, confrontation and sworn testimony by witnesses available for cross-examination are essential for a finding of "delinquency" and an order committing Gerald to a state institution for a maximum of six years.[29]

Justice Fortas, in delivering the Court's opinion, recalled other cases that had provided juveniles with due process of law. In both *Haley* v. *Ohio* (1948) and *Gallegos* v. *Colorado* (1962), the Supreme Court had prohibited the use of confessions coerced from juveniles; in *Kent,* the Court had given the juvenile the right to be represented by counsel.[30] Justice Fortas concluded his review of legal precedent with the sweeping statement that juveniles have those fundamental rights that are incorporated in the due process clause of the Fourteenth Amendment to the U.S. Constitution. For more information on juvenile offenders, see Library Extra 15.1 and Web Extra 15.1.

The *In re Gault* decision affirmed that a juvenile has the right to due process safeguards in proceedings in which a finding of delinquency can lead to institutional confinement. The decision also established that a juvenile has the right to notice of the charges, right to counsel, right to confrontation and cross-examination, and privilege against self-incrimination. However, the Court did not rule that juveniles have the right to a transcript of the proceedings or the right to appellate review.

In choosing not to rule on these two latter rights, the Court clearly did not want to turn the informal juvenile hearing into an adversary trial. The cautiousness of this decision was underlined by a footnote stating that the decision did not apply to preadjudication or postadjudication treatment of juveniles.

In re Winship (1970) In *Winship*, the Supreme Court decided that juveniles are entitled to proof **beyond a reasonable doubt** during the adjudication proceedings[31] (Juvenile Law 15.4 presents the facts of this case). In ruling that "preponderance of evidence" is not a sufficient basis for a decision when youths are charged with acts that would be criminal if committed by adults, the *Winship* decision not only expanded *Gault* but also reflected other concerns of the justices. The Court desired

Library Extra 15.1

OJJDP publication: *Juvenile Offenders and Victims: 2006 National Report* (Chapter 6)

Web Extra 15.1

OJJDP PowerPoint presentation: "Juvenile Offenders in Court"

beyond a reasonable doubt A legal standard establishing the degree of proof needed for a juvenile to be adjudicated a delinquent by the juvenile court during the adjudicatory stage of the court's proceedings.

Juvenile Law 15.4

In re Winship

The *Winship* case involved a New York boy who was sent to a state training school at the age of 12 for taking $112 from a woman's purse. The commitment was based on a New York statute that permitted juvenile court decisions on the basis of a "preponderance of evidence," a standard that is much less strict than "beyond a reasonable doubt."

▶ What is the actual difference between "preponderance of evidence" and "proof beyond a reasonable doubt"? What was the importance of this difference in this case?

Source: In re Winship, 397 U.S. 358, 90 S.Ct. 1968, 25 L.Ed.2d 368 (1970).

Juvenile Law 15.5

McKeiver v. Pennsylvania

Joseph McKeiver, age 16, was charged with robbery, larceny, and receiving stolen goods, all of which were felonies under Pennsylvania law. This youth was found delinquent at an adjudication hearing and was placed on probation after his request for a jury trial was denied.

In re Terry

Edward Terry, age 15, was charged with assault and battery on a police officer, misdemeanors under Pennsylvania law. His counsel's request for a jury trial was denied, and he was adjudicated a delinquent on the charges.

In re Barbara Burrus

Barbara Burrus and approximately 45 other youths, ranging in age from 11 to 15 years old, were the subjects of juvenile court summonses in Hyde County, North Carolina. The charges arose out of a series of demonstrations in the county in late 1968 by African-American adults and youths protesting school assignments and a school consolidation plan. These youths were charged with willfully impeding traffic. The several cases were consolidated into groups for hearing before the district judge, sitting as a juvenile court. A request for a jury trial in each case was denied, and each juvenile was found delinquent and placed on probation.

▶ Some states now permit jury trial for juveniles. How can they grant a jury trial with this Supreme Court decision?

Source: McKeiver v. Pennsylvania, 403 U.S. 528, 535 (1971); In re Terry, 215 Pa. Super 762 (1970); and In re Barbara Burrus, 275 N.C. 517, 169 S.E.2d 879 (1969).

both to protect juveniles at adjudicatory hearings and to maintain the confidentiality, informality, flexibility, and speed of the juvenile process in the prejudicial and postadjudicative states. The Court obviously did not want to bring too much rigidity and impersonality to the juvenile hearing.

McKeiver v. Pennsylvania (1971)   During the 1969 through 1971 sessions, the Supreme Court heard three cases together (*McKeiver v. Pennsylvania, In re Terry*, and *In re Barbara Burrus*) concerning whether the due process clause of the Fourteenth Amendment guaranteeing the right to a jury trial applies to the adjudication of a juvenile court delinquency case.[32] The decision, which was issued in *McKeiver v. Pennsylvania*, denied the right of juveniles to have jury trials. Juvenile Law 15.5 summarizes the facts of these three cases.

The Supreme Court gave the following five reasons for its ruling:

1. Not all rights that are constitutionally assured for the adult are to be given to the juvenile.
2. The jury trial, if required for juveniles, may make the juvenile proceedings into a fully adversary process and will put an end to what has been the idealistic prospect of an intimate, informal protecting proceeding.
3. A jury trial is not a necessary part even of every criminal process that is fair and equitable.
4. The jury trial, if injected into the juvenile court system, could bring with it the traditional delay, the formality, and the clamor of the adversary system.
5. There is nothing to prevent an individual juvenile judge from using an advisory jury when he or she feels the need. For that matter, there is nothing to prevent individual states from adopting jury trials.[33]

A number of states do permit jury trials for juveniles, but most adhere to the constitutional standard set by the Supreme Court. Surveys of states report that juveniles choose jury trials in only about 1% to 3% of cases.[34] The significance of the *McKeiver* decision is that the Court indicated an unwillingness to apply further procedural safeguards to juvenile proceedings, especially during the preadjudicatory and postadjudicatory treatment of juveniles.

Breed v. Jones (1975)   The question of transfer to an adult court, first considered in the *Kent* case, was taken up again in the *Breed v. Jones* decision.[35] This case raised

Teenage sniper Lee Boyd Malvo is flanked by police officers as he is brought into a Maryland courtroom. ▶ **Did Malvo deserve to be treated as an adult for purposes of the law?**

the issue of **double jeopardy**, questioning whether a juvenile could be prosecuted as an adult after an adjudicatory hearing in the juvenile court. The increased use of transfers, or the binding over of juveniles to the adult court, makes this decision particularly significant today (see Juvenile Law 15.6).

The U.S. Supreme Court ruled that Breed's case did constitute double jeopardy—a juvenile court cannot adjudicate a case and then transfer the case over to the criminal court for adult processing on the same offense. The significance of *Breed* is that **prosecutors** must determine which youthful offenders they want to transfer to the adult court before juvenile court adjudication; otherwise, the opportunity to transfer, or certify, those youths is lost.[36]

Today nearly every state has defined the specific requirements for transfer proceedings in its juvenile code (discussed in more detail later in this chapter). At present, when a transfer hearing is conducted in juvenile court, due process law usually requires (1) a legitimate transfer hearing, (2) a sufficient notice to the juvenile's family and defense attorney, (3) the right to counsel, and (4) a statement of the court order regarding transfer.

Some evidence exists that youths who have counsel may get more severe dispositions than those without counsel.[37] For example, studies reported in 1980 and 1981

double jeopardy A common law and constitutional prohibition against a second trial for the same offense.

prosecutor The representative of the state in court proceedings. Also called *county's attorney, district attorney,* or *state attorney.*

Juvenile Law 15.6

Breed v. *Jones*

In 1971 the juvenile court in California filed a petition against Jones, who was then 17 years old, alleging that he had committed an offense that, if committed by an adult, would have constituted robbery. Jones was detained pending a hearing. At the hearing, the juvenile judge took testimony, found that the allegations were true, and sustained the petition. At the dispositional hearing, Jones was found unfit for treatment in the juvenile court, and it was ordered that he be prosecuted as an adult offender. At a subsequent preliminary hearing,

Jones was held for criminal trial. An information hearing was held against him for robbery, and he was tried and found guilty. Counsel objected that Jones was being subjected to double jeopardy, but the defendant was committed to the California Division of Juvenile Justice.

▶ **What is double jeopardy? Why is it important for juveniles and adults in the legal process?**

Source: Breed v. Jones, 421 U.S. 519, 95 S.Ct. 1779 (1975).

Juvenile Law 15.7

Detention Facilities

Detention centers are administered by state agencies, city or county government, welfare departments, juvenile courts, or private vendors, but the majority of detention facilities are administered by the county. In 1997, of 44 states responding to a survey conducted by the National Council on Crime and Delinquency, 73% operated detention facilities at the county level and 36% at the state level; 30% were under multiple jurisdictions; 16% had court-administered or -operated detention facilities; and 11% contracted with private vendors to provide detention services.

The traditional model of detention for youths was woefully inadequate. A grim-looking detention facility usually was attached to the building that housed the administrative offices and hearing rooms of the juvenile court, and locked outer doors and high fences or walls prevented escapes. The lack of programming made it clear that these facilities were intended merely to be holding centers. A former resident, interviewed in May 1981, described her experience in a traditional detention home:

> It [the facility] sucks. It was the worst place I've ever been in. They're [the staff] cruel. They used to give work details for punishment. For an entire hour, I scrubbed the kitchen floor with a toothbrush. They can get away with this, and it is not against the law. The place is falling apart. They are just not very caring people. They didn't do much for me except scare me.

Fortunately, the nationwide movement to develop standards for detention as well as more innovative detention programs resulted in marked improvement in the overall quality of detention facilities and programs [in the 1980s and 1990s]. The bureau of detention standards, in those states that have such oversight units, usually inspects detention centers once a year; this inspection ensures better-quality detention practices.

Attention homes, which were initiated in Boulder, Colorado, by the juvenile court to improve the detention process for juveniles, have spread to other jurisdictions. The stated purpose of the attention homes program is to give youths attention rather than detention. Problem resolution is the focus of the program, and professional services are provided to residents on a contractual basis. These nonsecured facilities have no fences, locked doors, or other physical restraints and are characterized by more extensive programming and by more intensive involvement between residents and staff than are typical in other facilities.

In-home detention, a nonresidential approach to detention, was first used in St. Louis (Missouri), Newport News and Norfolk (Virginia), and Washington, D.C., and now is used throughout the United States. The in-home detention program is commonly within the organizational structure of the juvenile court and is administered by the community services unit of the probation department. An in-home detention coordinator typically meets with the intake officer, a field probation officer, and sometimes a juvenile officer before the detention hearing to decide whether a youth is an appropriate candidate for in-home detention. Some jurisdictions use a release risk evaluation to decide whether in-home detention for a particular youth should be recommended to the juvenile judge. A youth who is placed on in-home detention is required to remain at home 24 hours a day; the in-home detention worker visits the youth and family 7 days a week and also makes random phone calls throughout the day to make certain that the juvenile is at home. As will be discussed in Chapter 16, electronic monitoring is starting to be used as part of in-home detention programs.

▶ What are the detention facilities like in your jurisdiction? Are you familiar with attention homes or in-home detention programs?

Source: Adapted from Kelly Dedel, "National Profile of the Organization of State Juvenile Correctional Systems," *Crime and Delinquency* 44 (October 1998), p. 514. Copyright © 1998 by Sage Publications. Reprinted by permission of Sage Publications, Inc.

Library Extra 15.2

OJJDP publication: *Juvenile Court Statistics 2000*

that juveniles with counsel were more likely to receive an institutional disposition than those without counsel.[38] When it exists, there are two possible explanations for this positive relationship between counsel and punitive dispositions: First, the juvenile judge is punishing youths who choose to be represented by counsel; second, the youths who have committed more serious crimes are the ones requesting counsel and are the ones most likely to be adjudicated to training school or transferred to adult court. Although the former may have been true in the past, the latter is typically true today (see Library Extra 15.2). Juvenile Law 15.7 covers the different types of detention facilities used for juvenile offenders.

Pretrial Procedures

The types of cases that are under the jurisdiction of the juvenile court vary widely among and even within states, but they generally include those involving delinquency, neglect, and dependency. In 2005, juvenile courts handled an estimated 1,697,000 delinquency cases. Figure 15.2 shows that between 1960 and 2005, juvenile court delinquency caseloads increased more than 300%.[39] Juvenile courts also may deal with

FIGURE 15.2 Delinquency Cases, 1960–2005

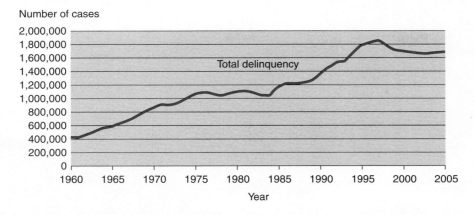

Source: Adapted from Charles Puzzanchera and Melissa Sickmund, *Juvenile Court Statistics 2005* (Pittsburgh, Penn.: National Center for Juvenile Justice, 2008), p. 36. Reprinted by permission.

cases involving adoption, termination of parental rights, appointment of guardians for minors, custody, contributing to delinquency or neglect, and nonsupport.

Pretrial procedures in the juvenile justice system include the detention hearing, the intake procedure, and the transfer procedure, all of which take place before the adjudication stage of juvenile court proceedings.

Detention Hearing

Legislative acts that govern the juvenile court normally require that the police either take a youth to an intake officer of the court or a detention facility or release the youth to his or her parents. At a **detention hearing,** the criteria for detention are based on the need to protect the youth and to ensure public safety. The decision to detain must be made within a short period of time, usually 48 to 72 hours, excluding weekends and holidays. Urban courts, which have intake units on duty 24 hours a day for detention hearings, frequently act within a few hours.[40]

In some states, intake officers of the juvenile court, rather than juvenile judges, conduct detention hearings. Such a procedure represents a progressive move because having the same judge preside over both the detention hearing and the adjudication hearing is a poor practice. Some states still require that the juvenile judge be responsible for the policies and operations of the detention facility; juvenile judges also are usually required to decide whether a youth who was admitted to detention a few days earlier must remain locked up to preclude inappropriate or overly long detention.

In 2005, the offense profile of detained delinquency cases was as follows: drug-law violations, 12%; person cases, 25%; public-order cases, 28%; and property cases, 35%.[41] Juveniles who are held in detention may be assigned to one of several different types of placements. The **detention center** (detention hall or detention home) physically restricts youths for a short period, whereas **shelter care** is physically nonrestrictive and is available for those who have no homes or who require juvenile court intervention. A third type of placement is **jail** or police lockup. A fourth is **home detention**; in-home detention restricts a juvenile to his or her home and is supervised, normally by a paraprofessional staff member. Finally, **attention homes** offer services and staff support in a nonrestrictive setting.

Five states have legislated a hearing on probable cause for detained youths, and appellate cases in other states have moved in the direction of mandating a probable cause hearing to justify further detention. Courts in Alaska and Georgia have ruled that a youth is entitled to counsel at a detention hearing and to free counsel if the youth is indigent. The supreme courts of Alaska and California and an appellate court in Pennsylvania all have overturned cases in which no reason or inadequate reason was stated for continuing detention. Finally, courts in Baltimore, the District

detention hearing A hearing, usually conducted by an intake officer of the juvenile court, during which the decision is made as to whether a juvenile will be released to his or her parents or guardians or be detained in a detention facility.

detention center A facility that provides custodial care for juveniles during juvenile court proceedings. Also called juvenile halls and detention homes, detention centers were established at the end of the nineteenth century as an alternative to jails for juveniles.

shelter care A facility that is used primarily to provide short-term care for status offenders and for dependent or neglected youths.

jail A police lockup or county holding facility for adult offenders. Jails have few services to offer juveniles.

home detention House arrest. This form of detention is used in some jurisdictions, and an adjudicated juvenile remains at home under the supervision of juvenile probation officers.

attention home An innovative form of detention facility, found in several locations across the nation, that is characterized by an open setting.

A teenage defendant (right) and his court-appointed defender stand before a juvenile court judge in Orange, California. ▶ **What is the role of juvenile defense counsel?**

bail The money or property pledged to the court or actually deposited with the court to effect the release of a person from legal custody. Juveniles do not have a constitutional right to bail as do adults.

of Columbia, and Nevada have ruled that a juvenile who is in detention is entitled to humane care. The appeals court in the District of Columbia stated that there is a statutory obligation to provide a juvenile with care "as nearly as possible equivalent to that which should have been given him by his parents."[42]

Court decisions have differed concerning **bail** for a juvenile. Decisions have found that juveniles have a constitutional right to bail; that juvenile act procedures, when applied in a manner consistent with due process, provide an adequate substitute for bail; or that juveniles do not have a constitutional right to bail. Nine states (Arkansas, Colorado, Connecticut, Georgia, Massachusetts, Nebraska, Oklahoma, South Dakota, and West Virginia) have enacted laws granting juveniles the right to bail; on the other hand, Hawaii, Kentucky, Oregon, and Utah deny juveniles the right to bail.

The U.S. Supreme Court decision in the *Schall* v. *Martin* (1984) case represents an example of a fundamental change that seems to be occurring in detention practices.[43] The plaintiffs originally filed a lawsuit in federal district court claiming that the New York Family Court Act was unconstitutional because it allowed for the preventive detention of juveniles:

> The District Court struck down the statute as permitting detention without due process and ordered the release of all class members. The Court of Appeals affirmed, holding . . . the statute is administered not for preventive purposes, but to impose punishment for un-adjudicated criminal acts, and that therefore the statute is unconstitutional.[44]

The Supreme Court, however, reversed the decision of the appeals court. Justice William H. Rehnquist, in writing the opinion for the majority, declared that the "preventive detention under the statute serves the legitimate state objective held in common with every State, of protecting both the juvenile and the society from the hazards of pretrial crime."[45] Some experts believe that the Court's ruling may encourage a significant expansion of preventive, or secure, detention for juveniles.

The constitutionality of preventive detention may have been confirmed by the Supreme Court in *Schall*, but this policy still raises several controversial issues. First, there is the technical difficulty of accurately predicting which offenders should be detained to prevent their commission of further offenses before trial; second, the detainee considers preventive detention as punitive confinement, regardless of the stated purpose of the practice; and third, there are issues of the propriety of incarceration

TABLE 15.1 Offense Profile of Delinquency Cases, 2005		
Most Serious Offense	**Nonpetitioned**	**Petitioned**
Person	24%	26%
Property	37	34
Drugs	11	12
Public Order	27	28

Note: Detail may not total 100% because of rounding.

Source: Charles Puzzanchera and Melissa Sickmund, *Juvenile Court Statistics 2005* (Pittsburgh, Penn., National Center for Juvenile Justice, 2008), p. 36. Reprinted by permission.

before the determination of guilt and of the procedural safeguards that must accompany such a practice. Indeed, evaluations of the detention process indicate that the majority of juveniles who are preventively detained are not charged with serious offenses.[46]

Intake Process

Intake essentially is a preliminary screening process to determine whether a court should take action—and if so, what action—or whether the matter should be referred elsewhere. Larger courts usually handle this function through a specialized intake unit, and probation officers or other officers of the court screen incoming cases in smaller courts.[47]

Between 1985 and 2005, the likelihood that a delinquency case would be handled informally decreased. The largest increases of petitioned cases between 1985 and 2005 were seen in drug cases (232%) followed by public-order cases (205%) and person offenses cases (151%). Table 15.1 shows the offense profile of delinquency cases for 2005.

Intake procedures follow **complaints** to authorities against youths. Juvenile law varies from state to state regarding who is permitted to sign such a complaint. Typically, most complaints are filed by the police, although they may be initiated and signed by a victim or by the youth's parents. In some states, parents, victims, probation staff, social services staff, neighbors, or anyone else may go directly to the court to file a complaint. Complaints also may be brought by school officials and truant officers.

After the intake officer receives the complaint, he or she must first decide whether the court has statutory jurisdiction. If the statutory guides are unclear, the intake officer should seek the advice of the prosecuting attorney. Once legal jurisdiction is established, the second step is to conduct a preliminary interview and investigation to determine whether the case should be adjudicated nonjudicially or petitioned to the court. This evaluation procedure varies from jurisdiction to jurisdiction, principally because so many juvenile courts have failed to provide written guidelines, so the intake officer usually has broad and largely unregulated discretion in making the intake decision.

Options for the Disposal of Cases The intake unit, especially in larger urban courts, may have up to five options for the disposal of cases: (1) outright dismissal of the complaint, (2) informal adjustment (chiefly diversion to a nonjudicial agency), (3) informal probation, (4) consent decree, and (5) filing of a petition.

Outright dismissal of the complaint takes place when legal jurisdiction does not exist or when the case is so weak that the intake officer questions the feasibility of petitioning the youth to the juvenile court. **Informal adjustment** means that the intake officer requires restitution from the youth (see Chapter 16), warns him or her, and then dismisses the case or diverts the youth to a social services agency. The diversion agency supervises such referrals and generally reports to the intake unit on the youth's progress; status offenders and juveniles charged with minor offenses typically are dealt with under this option.

intake The first stage of juvenile court proceedings, in which the decision is made whether to divert the juvenile being referred or to file a formal petition in juvenile court.

complaint A charge made to an intake officer of the juvenile court that an offense has been committed.

informal adjustment An attempt to handle a youthful offender outside of the formal structures of the juvenile justice system.

Juvenile Law 15.8

Informal Sanctions

Informal processing is considered when decision makers (police, intake workers, probation officers, prosecutors, or other screening officers) believe that accountability and rehabilitation can be achieved without the use of formal court intervention.

Informal sanctions are voluntary, and consequently, the court cannot force a juvenile to comply with an informal disposition. If the court decides to handle the matter informally (in lieu of formal prosecution), a youthful offender agrees to comply with one or more sanctions such as voluntary probation supervision, community service, and/or victim restitution. In some jurisdictions, before juveniles are offered informal sanctions, they must agree that they committed the alleged act.

When informally handled, the case is usually held open pending the successful completion of the informal disposition.

Upon successful completion of these arrangements, the charges against the offender are dismissed. But if the offender does not fulfill the court's conditions for informal handling, the case is likely to be reopened and formally prosecuted.

Informal handling is less common than in the past but is still used in a large number of cases. According to *Juvenile Court Statistics 2001–2002*, 42 percent of delinquency cases disposed in 2002 were handled informally, compared with more than half in 1987.

▶ **What is your opinion of informal sanctions? What do you see as their strengths and weaknesses?**

Source: Howard N. Snyder and Melissa Sickmund, *Juvenile Offenders and Victims: 2006 National Report* (Washington, D.C.: U.S. Department of Justice, Office of Justice Programs, Office of Juvenile Justice and Delinquency Prevention., 2006).

---

informal probation An arrangement in which, instead of being adjudicated as a delinquent and placed on probation, a youth is informally assigned to the supervision of a probation officer.

consent decree A formal agreement between a juvenile and the court in which the juvenile is placed under the court's supervision without a formal finding of delinquency.

adult court Criminal courts that hear the cases of adults charged with crimes and to which juveniles who are accused of having committed serious offenses can be waived (transferred). In some states, adult criminal courts have jurisdiction over juveniles who are accused of committing certain specified offenses.

Informal probation, which has been under increased criticism since the 1970s, involves the casual supervision of a youth by a volunteer or probation officer who reserves judgment on the need for filing a petition until the intake officer (or other designated person) sees how the youth fares during the informal probation period. See Juvenile Law 15.8 for more information on informal sanctions.

A **consent decree** is a formal agreement between the youth and the court in which he or she is placed under the court's supervision without a formal finding of delinquency. Consent decrees provide an intermediate step between informal handling and probation; the consent decree is used less often than the other options that are currently open to the intake officer. The consent decree, it should be noted, comes after the petition but before the adjudication hearing.

If none of these options is satisfactory, the intake officer can choose to file a petition. Unfortunately, the broad discretionary power given intake workers has often been abused. For example, Duran Bell Jr. and Kevin Lang's study of intake in Los Angeles County revealed the importance of extralegal factors, especially cooperative behavior, in reducing the length of detention and the effect of age in increasing the length of detention.[48]

Research is needed to determine which approach to intake will result in the greatest services to youths and the least misuse of discretion, but until a systematic examination of the intake process is done, the principles of being fair and of doing the least harm possible to youths should guide the intake screening process.

Transfer Procedure

All state legislatures have passed laws permitting juveniles to be transferred to **adult court.** The peak year for the number of delinquency cases waived to criminal court was 1994, but this increase was followed by a 51% decline between 1994 and 2001; then between 2001 and 2005, the number of judicially waived delinquency cases increased 7%.[49] Some states have implemented transfer procedures by lowering the age of judicial waiver, some by excluding certain offenses from juvenile court jurisdiction, and others by passing legislation aimed at transfer of serious juvenile offenders. Indeed, between 1992 and 1995, 41 states passed laws that facilitated trying juveniles in adult court.[50]

Every state currently has some provision for transferring juvenile offenders to adult criminal courts. Vermont (at age 10), Montana (at age 12), and Georgia, Illinois, and Mississippi (at age 13) transfer youths at very young ages; more states transfer youths at 14 years old than at any other age, and 7 states transfer youths at either 15 or 16 years of age.

Several states grant prosecutors, rather than juvenile court judges, the nonreviewable discretionary power to determine the court before which juveniles will be required to appear. For example, in the early 1980s the state of Florida expanded the discretionary power of prosecutors in dealing with juveniles who are 16 years old or older.[51] Table 15.2 indicates which states allow prosecutors to try juveniles in either juvenile or criminal court.

In 15 states, murder is excluded from juvenile court jurisdiction; 10 states exclude rape, 8 exclude armed robbery or robbery, 6 exclude kidnapping, and 3 exclude burglary. A total of 11 states use a combination of offense categories.[52]

Judicial waiver and legislative waiver (also called *remand, certification,* and *waiver of jurisdiction*) are the two basic mechanisms for transferring juvenile offenders to the adult criminal justice system. Judicial waiver, the more common, takes place after a judicial hearing on a juvenile's amenability to treatment or his or her threat to public safety.[53]

Judicial waiver, as previously discussed in regard to the *Kent* v. *United States* and *Breed* v. *Jones* decisions, contains certain procedural safeguards for youthful offenders. The criteria that are used to determine the **binding over** (transfer) decision typically include the age and maturity of the youth; the seriousness of the referral incident; the youth's past record; the youth's relationship with parents, school, and

judicial waiver The procedure of relinquishing the processing of a particular juvenile case to adult criminal court; also known as certifying or binding over to the adult court.

binding over The process of transferring (also called certifying) juveniles to adult criminal court. Binding over takes place after a judicial hearing on a juvenile's amenability to treatment or his or her threat to public safety.

TABLE 15.2 States Permitting Prosecutorial Discretion

State	Minimum Age for Concurrent Jurisdiction	Concurrent Jurisdiction Offense and Minimum Age Criteria, 2004							
		Any Criminal Offense	Certain Felonies	Capital Crimes	Murder	Certain Person Offenses	Certain Property Offenses	Certain Drug Offenses	Certain Weapon Offenses
Arizona	14		14						
Arkansas	14		16	14	14	14			
California	14		14	14	14	14	14	14	
Colorado	14		14		14	14	14		
Dist. of Columbia	16				16	16	16		
Florida	NS	16	16	NS	14	14	14		14
Georgia	NS			NS					
Louisiana	15				15	15	15	15	
Michigan	14		14		14	14	14	14	
Montana	12				12	12	16	16	16
Nebraska	NS	16	NS						
Oklahoma	15		16		15	15	15	16	15
Vermont	16	16							
Virginia	14				14	14			
Wyoming	13		14		14	14	14		

Notes: Ages in the minimum age column may not apply to all offense restrictions but represent the youngest possible age at which a juvenile's case may be directly filed in criminal court. "NS" indicates that in at least one of the offense restrictions indicated, no minimum age is specified.

In states with concurrent jurisdiction, the prosecutor has discretion to file certain cases in either criminal court or juvenile court.

Source: Howard N. Snyder and Melissa Sickmund, *Juvenile Offenders and Victims: 2006 National Report* (Washington, D.C.: U.S. Department of Justice, Office of Juvenile Justice and Delinquency Prevention, 2006), p. 113.

community; and the dangerousness of the youth. Court officials also decide if they believe the youth may be helped by juvenile court services. Most juvenile court judges appear to be influenced primarily by the youth's prior record and the seriousness of the present offense.

legislative waiver A legislative action that narrows juvenile court jurisdiction, excluding from juvenile courts those youths charged with certain offenses.

Legislative waiver is accomplished in five ways. The first occurs when legislatures simply exclude certain offenses from juvenile court jurisdiction, meaning that any juvenile who commits a specified offense automatically goes before the adult court. The second lowers the age over which the juvenile court has jurisdiction; for example, if a state's age of juvenile court jurisdiction is 18 years old, the legislature may lower the age to 16 years old. The third form of legislative waiver specifies that juveniles of specific ages who commit specific crimes are to be tried by adult court, a method of legislative waiver which focuses as much on the offense as it does on the age of the offender. The fourth method of legislative waiver involves statutes that simply state that anyone who commits a specific crime may be tried in adult court, an approach which is attractive to those who believe that any youth who violates the law should receive an appropriate punishment. The fifth method is for state legislatures to give both the juvenile and the adult courts concurrent jurisdiction over all juveniles who are under the jurisdictional age of the juvenile court.

reverse waiver A provision that permits a juvenile who is being prosecuted as an adult in criminal court to petition to have the case transferred to juvenile court for adjudication or disposition.

Statutes mandating that the decision to prosecute a juvenile as an adult be made on the basis of the seriousness of the offense charged are inconsistent with the rehabilitative philosophy of the juvenile court. Legislative waiver also is problematic because it usually has a rationale of incapacitation of chronic offenders through longer sentences than those provided by the juvenile process.[54]

blended sentencing The imposition of juvenile and/or adult correctional sanctions on serious and violent juvenile offenders who have been adjudicated in juvenile court or convicted in criminal court.

Reverse waiver and **blended sentencing** must also be considered in discussing waiver. In reverse waiver, some state laws permit youths who are over the maximum age of jurisdiction to be sent back to the juvenile court if the adult court believes the case is more appropriate for juvenile court jurisdiction; for a reverse waiver, defense counsel and prosecutors attempt to make their case for their desired action, with some evidence and testimony being allowed and arguments being presented. When each side has had a chance to present its case and to rebut the opponents' arguments, the judge makes the decision.[55]

In blended sentencing, some states permit juvenile court judges at the disposition hearing to impose both an adult and a juvenile sentence concurrently. In these cases, the juvenile is given both sentences but is ordered first to fulfill the requirements of the juvenile disposition. If the juvenile meets the requirements of this disposition satisfactorily, then the adult disposition is suspended, but if the juvenile does not fulfill the conditions of the juvenile disposition, then he or she is required to serve the adult sentence. In some states, the juvenile may be ordered to abide by the requirements of the juvenile disposition until reaching the age of majority; at this point, the juvenile begins serving the adult sentence minus the time already spent under juvenile court supervision.[56]

Scott Dyleski, age 16, appears behind a protective glass barrier in Judge David Flinn's courtroom in Martinez, California, on October 27, 2005. Dyleski was charged as an adult with first-degree murder in the death of Pamela Vitale, the wife of well-known attorney Daniel Horowitz. Convicted in 2006, he was sentenced to life in prison without possibility of parole. ▶ **Are such lengthy sentences appropriate for juvenile offenders who commit crimes like Dyleski's?**

In sum, although waivers are still relatively infrequent, they remain an important issue in juvenile justice. Significantly, juveniles waived to adult court are not always the most serious or violent offenders. Donna Bishop and colleagues' examination of 583 prosecutorial waivers of 16- and 17-year-old youths in Florida from 1981 to 1984 revealed that most transferred juveniles were property offenders and low-risk offenders.[57] Examinations of waivers have found that little consensus exists as to which criteria should be used in making waiver decisions.[58] Furthermore, although remanded youths are receiving severe penalties, waiver generally does not result in more severe penalties for juvenile offenders than they would have received in juvenile court. Several states have attempted to develop a process that might identify juveniles unfit for retention in juvenile court; using such criteria as age, offense, and prior record, for example, Minnesota has codified transfer procedures to be followed by judges and prosecutors. An evaluation undertaken by

Lee Ann Osburn and Peter A. Rose, however, concluded that Minnesota's procedures were inadequate for making effective transfer decisions.[59] With adult courts' massive caseload and their limited judicial experience in sentencing juveniles, little evidence exists that adult judges know what to do with juveniles who appear before them.[60]

Juvenile Trial Proceedings

The trial stage of juvenile court proceedings is divided into the adjudicatory hearing, the disposition hearing, and judicial alternatives. There is usually also a (statutory) right to appeal.

Adjudicatory Hearing

Adjudication is the fact-finding stage of the court's proceedings. The adjudicatory hearing usually includes the following steps: the youth's plea, the presentation of evidence by the prosecution and by the defense, the cross-examination of witnesses, and the judge's finding. The number of cases in which the juvenile was adjudicated delinquent rose steadily from 1985 to 2002, except for property cases[61] (see Figure 15.3).

adjudication The court process wherein a judge determines if the juvenile appearing before the court committed the act with which he or she is charged. The term *adjudicated* is analogous to convicted in the adult criminal justice system and indicates that the court concluded that the juvenile committed the act.

FIGURE 15.3 Adjudicated Cases in Juvenile Court

Between 1985 and 2005, the number of cases in which the youth was adjudicated delinquent increased 85% (from 337,100 to 623,900).

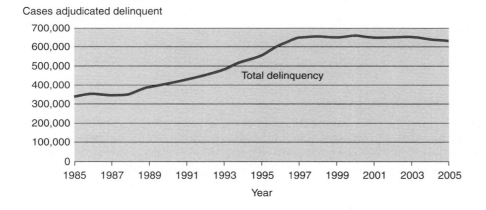

Between 2000 and 2005, the number of cases adjudicated delinquent increased for cases involving person and public-order offenses but decreased for cases involving property and drug offenses.

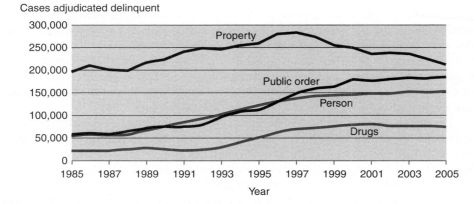

Source: Adapted from Charles Puzzanchera and Melissa Sickmund, *Juvenile Court Statistics 2005* (Pittsburgh, Penn.: National Center for Juvenile Justice, 2008), p. 46. Reprinted by permission.

The steps followed in the adjudicatory hearing serve as protections to ensure that youths are provided with proof beyond a reasonable doubt when they are charged with an act that would constitute a crime if it had been committed by an adult and that the judge follows the rules of evidence and dismisses hearsay from the proceedings. Hearsay is dismissed because it can be unreliable or unfair, inasmuch as it cannot be held up for cross-examination. The evidence must be relevant and must contribute to the belief or disbelief of the act in question.

Prosecutors in most juvenile courts begin the adjudication proceedings by presenting the state's case. The arresting officer and witnesses at the scene of the crime testify, and any other evidence that has been legally obtained is introduced. The defense attorney then cross-examines the witnesses. Defense counsel also has the opportunity at this time to introduce evidence that is favorable to his or her client, and the youth may testify in his or her own behalf; the prosecutor then cross-examines the defense witnesses. The prosecution and the defense present summaries of the case to the judge, who reaches a finding or a verdict.

jury trial The court proceeding in which a panel of the defendant's peers evaluate evidence and render a verdict. The U.S. Supreme Court has held that juveniles do not have a constitutional right to a jury trial, but several jurisdictions permit juveniles to choose a jury trial.

There are 10 states that provide for a **jury trial** for juveniles, but jury trials are seldom demanded. Statutory provisions often close juvenile hearings to the general public, although this decision varies from one jurisdiction to the next. The right to a speedy trial has been provided by state court decisions and by statutes that limit the amount of time that can elapse between the filing of a complaint and the actual hearing.[62]

In sum, the typical adjudication hearing has come a long way since the *In re Gault* decision. Although some judges and defense attorneys are exemplary in the support they give to the due process protection of juveniles during this stage of the court's proceedings, other judges and defense attorneys fall short in living up to either the spirit or the letter of post-*Gault* juvenile law. This is particularly true of defense attorneys who lack knowledge of juvenile court procedures or the juvenile law itself. Significantly, largely because of the changing standards for transfer to the adult court, the prosecutor has become a prominent figure at these proceedings.

Disposition Hearing

Once a youth has been found delinquent at the adjudicatory stage, some juvenile court codes still permit judges to proceed immediately to the disposition (sentencing) hearing. However, the present trend is to hold a **bifurcated hearing**, or a split adjudicatory and dispositional hearing, because a split hearing gives the probation officer appointed to the case an opportunity to prepare a social study investigation of the youth.

bifurcated hearing A split adjudication and disposition hearing, which is the present trend of the juvenile court.

The disposition stage of the court's proceedings normally is quite different from the fact-finding stage, especially when it is held at a different time. The traditional purpose has been to administer individualized justice and to set in motion the rehabilitation of the delinquent; therefore, the judge is not limited by constitutional safeguards as much as he or she was at the adjudication hearing. Rules of evidence are relaxed, parties and witnesses are not always sworn in, and hearsay testimony may be considered.[63] The starting point of the disposition hearing is usually the written social study of the juvenile prepared by the probation officer, a report which examines such factors as school attendance and grades, family structure and support, degree of maturity and sense of responsibility, relationships with peers, participation in community activities, and attitudes toward authority figures. In this final stage of the proceedings, juveniles are permitted to have legal counsel, and the *Kent* decision ensures the right of counsel to challenge the facts of the social study.

The factors that influence judicial decision making at the dispositional stage can be separated into formal and informal factors. The three most important formal factors are (1) the recommendation of the probation officer and the information contained in the social study investigation, (2) the seriousness of the delinquent behavior and previous contacts with the court, and (3) the available options. The recommendation of the probation officer in the social study report is usually followed by the juvenile judge. The seriousness of the delinquent behavior and previous contacts with the court probably have the greatest impact on judicial decision making at this stage. Terence Thornberry confirmed that seriousness of the current offense and the number of previous offenses have the greatest impact.[64] M. A. Bortner's examination of disposition decision making in a large Midwestern county revealed that the youth's age, his or her prior referrals, and the detention decision surfaced as the most important influences.[65] Studies of the juvenile courts in Colorado, Pennsylvania, and Tennessee also indicated that prior decisions by juvenile court personnel were related more strongly to disposition than any other factor.[66] Finally, the juvenile judge is influenced by the options that are available—the most desirable placement may not be available in that jurisdiction, or the desired placement may have no space for the youth.

The informal factors that sometimes influence judicial decision making at the disposition stage are the values and philosophy of the judge; the social and racial background of the youth, as well as his or her demeanor; the presence or absence of a defense counsel; and the potential political repercussions of the delinquent acts. In terms of the values and philosophy of the judge, some judges work from a legal model, some from an educational model, and some from a medical model, and the model that a particular judge emphasizes will, of course, affect his or her handling of juvenile delinquents.[67] Ruth D. Peterson found that racial, ethnic, gender, and age factors affected the disposition of older adolescents in New York's state courts. Race and ethnicity did not significantly influence disposition decisions in New York City, but outside the city, minority youths tended to become targets of stereotypes and to receive harsh treatment.[68]

Judicial Alternatives

The alternatives that are available to different juvenile courts vary significantly (see Library Extra 15.3 and Web Extra 15.2; see also Chapter 16). Large urban courts have all or most of the following 11 alternatives at their disposal, but rural courts may have only a few:

1. *Dismissal.* Dismissal is certainly the most desired disposition for juveniles. The fact-finding stage may have shown the youth to be guilty, but the judge can decide, for a variety of reasons, to dismiss the case.
2. *Restitution.* Also usually very desirable is restitution, where youths may be required to work off their debt with a few hours each week, but their lives are not seriously interrupted.
3. *Outpatient psychiatric therapy.* Whether in the court clinic, in the community mental health clinic, or with a private therapist, outpatient therapy is a treatment-oriented decision and is often reserved for middle-class youths to keep them from being sent to "unfitting" placements (see Web Extra 15.3).
4. *Probation.* As the most widely used disposition, probation seems to be a popular decision with delinquents and a good treatment alternative for the court. Probation is sometimes set for a specific length of time, usually a maximum of two years. The judge can direct the probation officer to involve the youth in special programs, such as alternative schools, speech therapy, or learning disability programs.
5. *Foster home placement.* Foster home placements are more restrictive, inasmuch as youths are removed from their natural homes. These placements are used most frequently for status offenders and dependent and neglected youths.
6. *Day-treatment program.* Day-treatment programs are a popular alternative with juveniles because the youths who are assigned to these programs return home in the evening, but these programs are few in number and are available in only a few states.
7. *Community-based residential program.* There are different types of community-based residential programs, such as group homes and halfway houses, that are available to many judges. These residential facilities may be located in the community or in a nearby community, but they are not as desirable as community-based day-treatment programs because youths are taken from their homes to live in these facilities (see Library Extra 15.4).
8. *Institutionalization in a mental hospital.* Institutionalization may be seen as appropriate for a youth's needs but requires a psychiatric evaluation; after the evaluation, the doctor may recommend that the court initiate proceedings for commitment to a mental hospital.

Library Extra 15.3
OJJDP publication: *Juvenile Drug Court Programs*

Web Extra 15.2
Juvenile Detention Alternatives Initiative from the Annie E. Casey Foundation

Web Extra 15.3
National Institute of Mental Health's Child and Adolescent Mental Health Center website

Library Extra 15.4
OJJDP Juvenile Justice Bulletin: "Alternatives to the Secure Detention and Confinement of Juvenile Offenders"

appeal The review of juvenile court proceedings by a higher court. Although no constitutional right of appeal exists for juveniles, the right of adjudicated juveniles to appeal has been established by statute in some states.

appellate review The review of the decision of a juvenile court proceeding by a higher court. Decisions by appellate courts, including the U.S. Supreme Court, have greatly affected the development of juvenile court law and precedent.

determinate sentencing A model of sentencing that provides fixed terms of sentences for criminal offenses. Terms are generally set by the legislature rather than determined by judicial discretion.

indeterminate sentencing In juvenile justice, a sentencing model that encourages rehabilitation through the use of general and relatively unspecific sentences. Under the model, a juvenile judge has wide discretion and can commit a juvenile to the department of corrections or youth authority until correctional staff make the decision to release the juvenile. This type of sentencing is used with juveniles in most jurisdictions other than those that have mandatory or determinate sentencing.

Juvenile Justice Standards Project A project jointly sponsored by the Institute of Judicial Administration and the American Bar Association that proposes that juveniles' sentences be based on the seriousness of the offense committed rather than on the needs of the youth.

9. *County or city institution.* Some county or city institutions are available to a few judges across the nation. Placement in these facilities may be deemed appropriate for a youth who needs more security than probation offers but who does not require long-term placement in the state training school.

10. *State or private training school.* The state or private training schools are usually reserved for youths who have committed serious crimes or for whom everything else has failed. In some states, state training schools include minimum-security (forestry camps, farms, and ranches), medium-security, and maximum-security institutions.

11. *Adult facility or youthful offender facility.* In a few states, if the youth has committed a serious offense and is seen as too hard-core for a juvenile correctional institution, he or she is placed in an adult facility or a youthful offender facility.

Right to Appeal

Although juveniles do not yet have a constitutional right to make an **appeal** of their cases to a higher judiciary, practically all states grant them the right to appeal by statute. The states are following the lead of the U.S. Supreme Court, which pointed out in *Gault* that juveniles should have the same absolute right to appeal as do adults under the Equal Protection Clause of the Constitution. Since that ruling, most state legislatures have passed laws granting juveniles the right to appeal; state courts have also ruled that state statutes granting the right to appeal for juveniles must be applied uniformly to all juveniles, a decision which effectively undermines the past practice in which some courts gave judges the discretion to determine which juvenile cases could be appealed. The common practice today is to give juveniles the same rights to appeal that adults have.[69]

The right to appeal is limited for the most part to juveniles and their parents. States may appeal in some circumstances, but this right is seldom exercised, and few cases have come before the courts. Another issue of appeal concerns the type of orders that may be appealed—although states generally permit the appeal of final orders, what is "final" varies from state to state. Most state statutes call for the case to be appealed to an appellate court, but a few states call for a completely new trial. Other common statutory rights of juveniles at appeal are the right to a transcript of the case and the right to counsel.[70]

Organizational factors limit the use of the **appellate review** of juvenile court decisions. Many juveniles lack counsel at trial who can make a record and obtain a transcript, and even more juveniles lack access to appellate counsel. In addition, juvenile public defenders' caseloads frequently preclude the luxury of filing appeals; many public defenders neither authorize their clients to file appeals nor advise their clients of the possibility of an appeal. The only study that compared rates of appeals by criminal defendants and juvenile delinquents found that convicted adults appealed more than 10 times as often as did juveniles.[71]

Juvenile Sentencing Structures

Determinate sentencing (fixed sentences for specified offenses) is a new form of sentencing in juvenile justice, and in some jurisdictions it is replacing the traditional form, **indeterminate sentencing** (sentencing at the judge's discretion). In addition, increasing numbers of juvenile courts are using a blended form of sentencing.

Criticism of the decision-making outcomes of juvenile courts has increased since the 1970s. Early on, the criticism focused on the arbitrary nature of the decision making that violated the due process rights of juveniles; more recently, this criticism has been based on the belief that the juvenile court is too "soft" on crime. This latter criticism, especially, has led to a number of attempts to change sentencing and other juvenile procedures.

One of the first efforts at reform was the **Juvenile Justice Standards Project**, jointly sponsored by the Institute of Judicial Administration and the American Bar

Association. Officially launched in 1971 by a national planning committee under the chairmanship of Judge Irvin R. Kaufman, the project proposed comprehensive guidelines for juvenile offenders that would base sentences on the seriousness of the crime rather than on the needs of the youth. The guidelines represented radical philosophical changes and still are used by proponents to attempt to standardize the handling of juvenile lawbreakers.

The belief that disparity in juvenile sentencing must end was one of the fundamental thrusts of the recommended standards. To accomplish this goal, the commission attempted to limit the discretion of juvenile judges and to make them accountable for their decisions, which would then be subject to judicial review. Also important in the standards was the provision that certain court procedures would be open to the public, although the names of juveniles still would remain confidential.

At the beginning of the twenty-first century, juvenile court judges remain quite concerned about these proposed standards. Their basic concerns are that these standards attack the underlying philosophy and structure of the juvenile court and that these standards would limit their authority. They see the influence of the hard-liners behind this movement toward standardization and feel that the needs of youths will be neglected in the long run; they also challenge the idea that it is possible, much less feasible, to treat all youths alike.

Nevertheless, the adoption of the standards has been taking place across the nation. New York State was the first to act on them through the Juvenile Justice Reform Act of 1976, which went into effect on February 1, 1977. The act orders a determinate sentence of five years for class A **felonies**, which include first-degree kidnapping, first-degree arson, and murder, and the initial term can be extended by at least one year. The juvenile, according to the act, should be placed in a residential facility after the first year; then, if approved by the director of the division, the confined youth can be placed in a nonresidential program for the remainder of the five-year term, but the youth must remain under intensive supervision for the entire five-year term.

In 1977, the state of Washington also created a determinate sentencing system for juveniles in line with the recommendations of the Juvenile Justice Standards Project. In the 1980s, a number of states stiffened juvenile court penalties for serious juvenile offenders, either by mandating minimum terms of incarceration (Colorado, Kentucky, and Idaho) or by enacting a comprehensive system of sentencing guidelines (Arizona, Georgia, and Minnesota).[72]

felony A criminal offense punishable by death or by incarceration in a state or federal correctional institution, usually for one year or more.

A recent report by Congress found that the nation's juvenile detention centers have become warehouses for mentally ill youths. ▶ **Why are those children locked up?**

In 1995, the Texas legislature introduced such "get tough" changes in the juvenile justice system as lowering the age at which waiver could occur to 14 years old for capital, first-degree, and aggravated controlled substance felony offenses and greatly expanding the determinate sentence statute that was first enacted in 1987. Under determinate sentences, any juvenile—regardless of age—can be sentenced for up to 40 years in the Texas Youth Commission, with possible transfer to the Texas Department of Corrections. Finally, prosecutors can choose to pursue determinate sentence proceedings rather than delinquency proceedings, but they first must obtain grand jury approval.[73] Daniel P. Mears and Samuel F. Field's examination of the determinate sentencing statute for Texas found the increased proceduralization and criminalization of juvenile courts did not eliminate consideration of age, gender, or race/ethnicity in sentencing decisions.[74]

In the 1990s, nearly every state enacted **mandatory sentencing** for violent and repetitive juvenile offenders. The development of graduated, or accountability-based, sanctions was another means that states used in the 1990s to ensure that juveniles who are adjudicated delinquent receive an appropriate disposition by the juvenile court. Several states have created a blended sentencing structure, which is a mechanism for holding juveniles accountable for their offenses, for cases involving repeat and serious juvenile offenders. This expanded sentencing authority allows criminal and juvenile courts to impose either juvenile or adult sentences—or at times both—in cases involving juveniles.[75] See Figure 15.4 for blended sentencing options.

mandatory sentencing The requirement that individuals who commit certain offenses be sentenced to a specified length of confinement if found guilty or adjudicated delinquent.

Graduated Sanctions

In adult corrections, increased attention has been given to intermediate sanctions, and in recent decades these intermediate sanctions have included a system of graduated sanctions, ranging from fines, day-reporting centers, drug courts, and intensive probation to residential placements.

This same movement has gained some momentum in juvenile justice, but in juvenile justice the system of graduated sanctions is focused on serious, violent, and chronic juvenile offenders. These offenders are moved along a continuum through a well-structured system that addresses both their needs and the community's safety. At each level, juvenile offenders are subject to more severe sanctions if they continue in their delinquency offenses.[76]

Social Context: Core Principles of Graduated Sanctions

According to John J. Wilson and James C. Howell, a model graduated system combines the treatment and rehabilitation of youths with fair, humane, reasonable, and appropriate sanctions,[77] offering a continuum of care that consists of diverse programs. Included in this continuum are immediate sanctions within the community both for first-time nonviolent offenders and for more serious offenders, secure care programs for the most violent offenders, and aftercare programs providing high levels of both social control and treatment services.[78]

Each of the graduated sanctions is intended to consist of gradations, or sublevels, that together with appropriate services constitute an integrated approach. This approach is designed to stop the youthful offender's further penetration into the juvenile system by inducing law-abiding behavior as early as possible through the combination of treatment sanctions and appropriate interventions. The family must be involved at each level in the continuum, and aftercare must be actively involved in supporting the family and in reintegrating the youth into the community. Programs will need to use risk and needs assessments to determine the placement that is appropriate for the offender. The effectiveness of interventions depends on their being swift, certain, and consistent and incorporating increased sanctions that include the possible loss of freedom. As the severity of sanctions is increased, so

FIGURE 15.4 Blended Sentencing Options in Juvenile Cases

Blended sentencing options create a middle ground between traditional juvenile and adult sanctions.

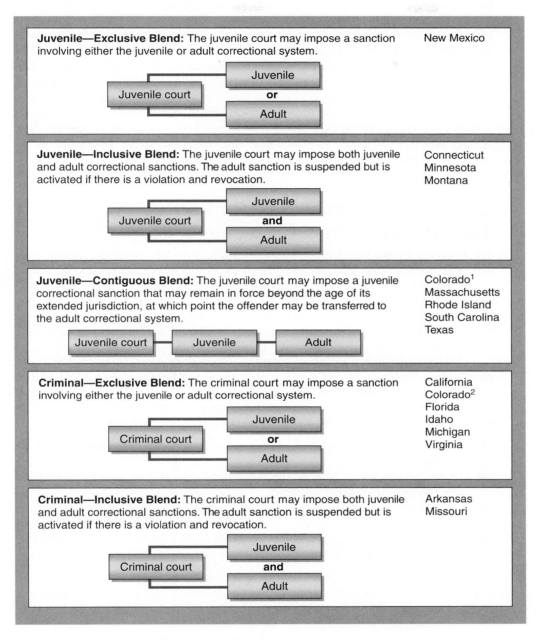

Juvenile—Exclusive Blend: The juvenile court may impose a sanction involving either the juvenile or adult correctional system.

New Mexico

Juvenile—Inclusive Blend: The juvenile court may impose both juvenile and adult correctional sanctions. The adult sanction is suspended but is activated if there is a violation and revocation.

Connecticut
Minnesota
Montana

Juvenile—Contiguous Blend: The juvenile court may impose a juvenile correctional sanction that may remain in force beyond the age of its extended jurisdiction, at which point the offender may be transferred to the adult correctional system.

Colorado[1]
Massachusetts
Rhode Island
South Carolina
Texas

Criminal—Exclusive Blend: The criminal court may impose a sanction involving either the juvenile or adult correctional system.

California
Colorado[2]
Florida
Idaho
Michigan
Virginia

Criminal—Inclusive Blend: The criminal court may impose both juvenile and adult correctional sanctions. The adult sanction is suspended but is activated if there is a violation and revocation.

Arkansas
Missouri

Note: Blends apply to a subset of juveniles specified by state statute.

[1]Applies to those designated as "aggravated juvenile offenders."
[2]Applies to those designated as "youthful offenders."

Source: Adapted from Office of Juvenile Justice and Delinquency Prevention, *1999 National Report Series* (Washington, D.C.: U.S. Department of Justice, 1999), p. 19.

must the intensity of treatment be increased. These sanctions could ultimately mean confinement in a secure setting, ranging from a secure community-based facility to a public or private training school, camp, or ranch. The programs that are most effective for hard-to-handle youths address key areas of risk in their lives, provide adequate support and supervision, and offer youths a long-term stake in the community.[79]

In 2005, an Office of Juvenile Justice and Delinquency Prevention (OJJDP) author cited research indicating that "many incarcerated youth can be managed effectively in well-structured community-based programs."[80] Consequently OJJDP has sponsored the implementation of small community-based or regional facilities to provide secure economical confinement for a population of serious, violent, and/or chronic juvenile offenders. Federal funding now provides states that are considering new facilities with an opportunity to replace large traditional training schools with smaller regional or community-based facilities that are part of a continuum of sanctions and services supported by local justice systems and communities. According to Shelley Zavick, president of the International Partnership for Youth/Justice Solutions Group, "Such facilities are more likely to be rooted in local values, engender community support and involvement, and reflect the needs of local jurisdictions. Equally important, these smaller facilities can target programming and operations to be responsive to the specific treatment and supervision needs of the youth in their care."[81]

Delinquency across the Life Course: The Impact of Transfer on Juveniles

The process of transferring juveniles to the adult court has generated considerable debate in juvenile justice circles and has raised a number of questions: Who should be transferred? What are the consequences in terms of criminal sanctions, as compared to juvenile court sanctions? What effect does the prison system have on juveniles? What are the consequences of transfer to the individuals involved? The answers to these questions help determine how transfer affects delinquents across the life course.

One finding is that transferred offenders, especially violent offenders, are significantly more likely to reoffend than those who have not been transferred.[82] L. Lanza-Kadace and colleagues conducted a Florida study that included 950 young adult offenders (half were transferred to the adult system in 1995 or 1996, and the other half remained in the juvenile justice system).[83] They found the following:

- Overall, 49% of the transferred offenders reoffended, compared with 35% of the retained offenders.
- For violent offenders, 24% of the transferred offenders reoffended, compared with 16% of the retained offenders.
- For drug offenses, 11% of the transferred offenders reoffended, compared with 9% of the retained offenders.
- For property offenses, 14% of the transferred offenders reoffended, compared with 10% of the retained offenders.[84]

Richard E. Redding proposed that juveniles tried as adults have higher recidivism rates because of the stigmatization and other negative effects, the sense of resentment and injustice juveniles feel about being tried and convicted as adults, the learning of criminal mores and behaviors in prison, and the decreased focus on rehabilitation and family support in the adult system.[85]

What Redding does not mention is that juveniles are more likely to be victimized, including sexually assaulted, in the adult system than they are in the juvenile system (something that is discussed in Chapter 16). One of the authors worked for over four years with juveniles who had been sexually victimized in a juvenile facility, and our follow-ups revealed that these sexual victims did not generally do well in the community and that it was not unusual for them to commit violent offenses.[86]

It can be argued that at least juveniles who commit a violent crime before they are 18 years old can no longer be executed—but as this book goes to press, they still can be placed in prison for life. The sentence of life without parole is an option that has been used in most states to deal with convicted adult as well as juvenile offenders. Sometimes, juveniles as young as 13 or 14 years old receive what amounts to being sentenced to die in prison. An organization known as the Equal Justice Initiative has documented

74 cases where children 14 years of age or younger have been given this sentence.[87] In November 2009, the U.S. Supreme Court agreed to hear two cases that challenge the constitutionality of life sentences for juveniles. One of the cases involves 34-year-old Joe Sullivan, a Florida prisoner who was sent away for life for raping an elderly woman when he was 13. The other case involves Terrance Graham, now 22, who was convicted of armed robberies that were committed when he was 16 and 17 years old. Bryan Stevenson, one of the defense attorneys appearing before the Court, told reporters that his basic argument is "to say to any child of 13 that you are only fit to die in prison is cruel," and cruel and unusual punishments are prohibited by the U.S. Constitution.[88]

Delinquency and Social Policy: Excellence in Juvenile Courts

What excellence in the juvenile court means is one of the topics that merits discussion among policy makers. The National Council of Juvenile and Family Court Judges provides its answer to this question, taking a somewhat broader approach and identifying the functions of the court and its judges. The council believes that the juvenile court should have exclusive jurisdiction in all matters affecting juveniles and families in delinquency cases, should have the same status as general trial courts, and should have the power and authority to "order, enforce, and review delivery of court ordered services and treatment for children and families."[89] Following are their 16 key principles for developing a juvenile court of excellence:

1. Juvenile delinquency court judges should engage in judicial leadership and encourage system collaboration.
2. Juvenile delinquency systems must have adequate staff, facilities, and program resources.
3. Juvenile delinquency courts and juvenile abuse and neglect courts should have integrated one family–one judge case assignments.
4. Juvenile delinquency judges should have the same status as the highest level of trial court in the state and should have multiple-year or permanent assignments.
5. All members of the juvenile delinquency court should treat youths, families, crime victims, witnesses, and others with respect, dignity, courtesy, and cultural understanding.
6. Juvenile delinquency court judges should ensure that their systems divert cases to alternative systems whenever possible and appropriate.
7. Youths charged in the formal juvenile delinquency court must have qualified and adequately compensated legal representation.
8. Juvenile delinquency court judges should ensure that crime victims have access to all phases of the juvenile delinquency court process and should receive all services to which they are entitled by law.
9. Juvenile delinquency courts should render timely and just decisions, and trials should conclude without continuances.
10. Juvenile delinquency system staff should engage parents and families at all stages of the juvenile delinquency court process to encourage family members to participate fully in the development and implementation of the youth's intervention plan.
11. The juvenile delinquency court should engage the school and other community support systems as stakeholders in each individual youth's case.
12. Juvenile delinquency court judges should ensure that court dispositions are individualized and that they include graduated responses, both sanctions and incentives.
13. Juvenile delinquency court judges should ensure that effective postdisposition review is provided to each delinquent youth as long as the youth is involved in any component of the juvenile justice system.
14. Juvenile delinquency court judges should hold their systems and the systems of other juvenile delinquency court stakeholders accountable.

15. Juvenile delinquency court judges should ensure that the court has an information system that can generate the data necessary to evaluate performance.
16. The juvenile delinquency court judge is responsible to ensure that the judiciary, court staff, and all system participants are both individually trained and trained across systems and roles.[90]

Chapter Summary

This chapter has examined the juvenile court. Key points are as follows:

- The juvenile court concept, as originally formulated, was built on the idea of *parens patriae*, that is, the state acting as substitute parent in keeping with the best interests of the child.

- Another ideal underlying the juvenile court concept is that youths are malleable and that their personalities are not yet fully formed, offering the opportunity for reformation and rehabilitation.

- The classic purposes of the juvenile court have come under scrutiny as policy makers, facing public outcry over what some see as an increasingly violent and dangerous juvenile population, have been forced to rethink the proper role of the court.

- The resolution of the current debate, whatever its outcome, will have long-term repercussions for American juvenile justice.

- Beginning in the 1960s, important U.S. Supreme Court decisions accorded juveniles a significant number of due process rights. As a consequence, the typical juvenile court hearing today has many of the trappings of an adult criminal trial.

- Noteworthy decisions of the 1970s show that the Supreme Court has been unwilling to transform the activities of the juvenile court completely into an adversarial battleground like proceedings in adult criminal court.

- The pretrial procedures of the juvenile court consist of the detention hearing, the intake process, and the transfer procedure.

- The adjudicatory hearing is the fact-finding stage in juvenile court. The judge, the defense attorney, and the prosecutor are typically present at the adjudicatory hearing, especially in larger jurisdictions; witnesses are cross-examined, and proof beyond a reasonable doubt must be established.

- Once a youth is found delinquent, the judge then determines the most fitting disposition. Available judicial alternatives may range from dismissal to placement in a state or private training school.

- Juvenile court sentencing structures have expanded in many jurisdictions; having gone beyond the indeterminate sentence model, today they include various forms of determinate sentencing.

- The 2005 U.S. Supreme Court case of *Roper* v. *Simmons* precludes execution of anyone who commits a crime while under the age of 18 years old.

Key Terms

adjudication, p. 351

adult court, p. 348

appeal, p. 354

appellate review, p. 354

attention home, p. 345

bail, p. 346

beyond a reasonable doubt, p. 341

bifurcated hearing, p. 352

binding over, p. 349

blended sentencing, p. 350

Breed v. *Jones*, p. 339

complaint, p. 347

consent decree, p. 348

constitutionalists, p. 339

detention center, p. 345

detention hearing, p. 345

determinate sentencing, p. 354

double jeopardy, p. 343

felony, p. 355

home detention, p. 345

indeterminate sentencing, p. 354

informal adjustment, p. 347

informal probation, p. 348

In re Gault, p. 339

In re Winship, p. 339

intake, p. 347

jail, p. 345

judicial waiver, p. 349

jury trial, p. 352

juvenile court, p. 335

Juvenile Justice Standards Project, p. 354

Kent v. *United States*, p. 339

legislative waiver, p. 350

mandatory sentencing, p. 356

McKeiver v. *Pennsylvania*, p. 339

prosecutor, p. 343

reverse waiver, p. 350

shelter care, p. 345

transfer, p. 339

Review Questions

1. What are the three positions concerning the role of the juvenile court described in this chapter?
2. What were the most important U.S. Supreme Court cases concerning the rights of juveniles during the court process? What did each contribute?
3. What are the three important hearings that take place during pretrial procedures, and why are they important?

4. How is the transfer procedure different from one state to another?
5. What takes place during the trial stage of juvenile court proceedings?
6. How have juvenile sentencing structures changed in many jurisdictions?

Discussion Questions

1. What is your opinion of the interesting present-day view of the constitutional perspective in Sheldon Richman's article "Phoney-Baloney Constitutionalist"? (It is available at www.ff.org/comment/'com0305n.asp.)
2. Should transfer to adult court be limited to violent juvenile offenders? Explain your response.
3. Only 10 states currently allow jury trials for juvenile offenders. Do you think jury trials should be allowed

for all juveniles? What do you see as the benefits and liabilities of doing so? Explain your response.
4. Do you think the structure of the juvenile court should be changed? Why or why not?
5. How should the juvenile justice system deal with status offenders?
6. How should juveniles who commit serious crimes be handled?

Group Exercises

1. Poll the students to determine who supports the *parens patriae* philosophy, who advocates the justice model, and who favors the abolition of juvenile courts. Moderate a discussion between the groups.
2. Divide the class into two groups: those who agree with the U.S. Supreme Court's ruling in *Kent* v. *United States* (1966) and those who disagree. Moderate a discussion between the groups.
3. Divide the class into two groups: those who agree with the U.S. Supreme Court's ruling in *In re Gault* (1967) and those who disagree. Moderate a discussion between the groups.
4. Divide the class into two groups: those who agree with the U.S. Supreme Court's ruling in *In re Winship*

(1970) and those who disagree. Moderate a discussion between the groups.
5. Divide the class into two groups: those who agree with the U.S. Supreme Court's ruling in *McKeiver* v. *Pennsylvania* (1971) and those who disagree. Moderate a discussion between the groups.
6. Divide the class into two groups: those who agree with the U.S. Supreme Court's ruling in *Breed* v. *Jones* (1975) and those who disagree. Moderate a discussion between the groups.
7. Invite a local juvenile court judge to address the class regarding his or her role in the juvenile court process.

mycrimekit™

Go to mycrimekit.com to explore the following study tools and resources specific to this chapter:

- **Practice Quiz:** Practice with multiple-choice, true/false, short-answer, and essay questions.

- **WebQuests:** Do web activities about the National Council of Juvenile and Family Court Judges (NCJFCJ).
- **Flashcards:** Use 40 flashcards to test your knowledge of the chapter's key terms.

Juvenile Corrections

CHAPTER OBJECTIVES

After reading this chapter, you should be able to answer the following questions:

- What types of experiences do juveniles have in various institutional placements?
- Why do some juveniles benefit more from institutionalization than others? How effective are institutions at correcting juvenile crime?
- What rights do juveniles have while confined?
- What can be done to improve juvenile correctional institutions in the United States?

Our society is fearful of our kids. I think we don't know how to set limits on them. They begin to behave in severely outrageous ways, and nobody stops them.

—David York, Cofounder of Tough Love International

Introduction

Child advocates have harshly condemned the conditions under which youth offenders are housed in institutional care. California juvenile facilities, according to a recent report, are failing their children. They have little chance of leaving improved, and some are worse off than when they arrived.[1] In March 2007, responding to the reports of sexual abuse of youths at the Texas Youth Commission institutions, Texas Governor Rick Perry placed the Texas Youth Commission under conservatorship to guide reform of the agency. A report documents the violence, sexual abuse, and lack of accountability in the juvenile facilities of this state.[2] The Connecticut Juvenile Training School has been a headache for state authorities since its opening in 2001. Its high-security perimeter fence, thick steel doors, and small cells with slits for windows make it feel more like a prison than a rehabilitation facility for juveniles. The problems are increasing in 2010, as Connecticut is raising the maximum age for juvenile offenders from 15 to 17 years old, moving many of the 250 to 300 16- and 17-year-olds who now go to adult prisons each year into juvenile facilities.[3] The U.S. Department of Justice (DOJ) has filed lawsuits against facilities in 11 states for supervision that is either abusive or harmfully negligent. While the DOJ does not have the power to shut down juvenile correctional facilities, through litigation it can force a state to improve its facilities and protect the civil rights of jailed youths.[4] In a nationally conducted survey, the Associated Press contacted each state agency that oversees juvenile correctional centers and asked for information on the numbers of deaths as well as the numbers of allegations and confirmed cases of physical, sexual, and emotional abuse by state members since January 1, 2004. According to this survey, more than 13,000 claims of abuse were identified in juvenile correctional facilities around the nation from 2004 through 2007—a disturbing number given that the total population of detained youths was about 46,000 at the time the states were surveyed.[5]

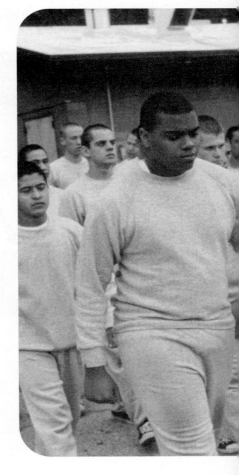

This chapter examines juvenile corrections, including corrections both in the community and in long-term institutions. The basic forms of **community-based corrections** are probation, residential and day-treatment programs, and aftercare. These services are alternatives to institutional placements and keep juvenile delinquents out of training schools, jails, and adult prisons. This chapter also focuses on long-term juvenile institutional placements, which include reception and diagnostic centers, ranches and forestry camps, boot camps, and public and private training schools. Juveniles may also be sent to adult prisons; Figure 16.1 gives thumbnail descriptions of these various types of long-term institutional placement alternatives for juveniles. Finally, this chapter considers aftercare and transition services back to the community for juveniles as they are released from institutional care. (See Web Extra 16.1 for information on juveniles in correctional facilities.)

Probation

Probation permits juvenile offenders to remain in the community under the supervision of a probation officer, subject to certain conditions imposed by the court. Probation, which many consider to be the brightest hope of corrections, has several different connotations in the juvenile justice system: It is a legal system in which an adjudicated delinquent can be placed, an alternative to institutionalization, and a subsystem of the juvenile justice system.

community-based corrections A corrections program that includes probation, residential and day-treatment programs, and parole (aftercare). The nature of the linkages between community programs and their social environments is the most distinguishing feature of community-based corrections. As frequency, duration, and quality of community relationships increase, the programs become more community based.

Web Extra 16.1
OJJDP PowerPoint presentation: "Juvenile Offenders in Correctional Facilities"

probation A court sentence under which the juvenile's freedom in the community is continued or only briefly interrupted, but the person is subject to supervision by a probation officer and the conditions imposed by the court.

FIGURE 16.1 Long-Term Institutional Placement Alternatives for Juveniles

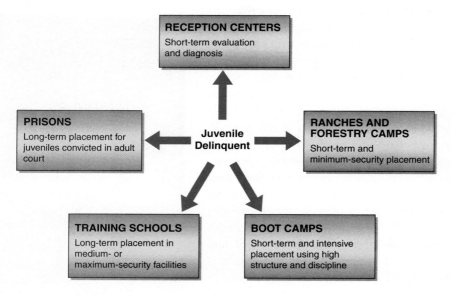

The *Desktop Guide to Good Juvenile Probation Practice*, a publication of the National Center for Juvenile Justice, states that "good juvenile probation practice is mission-driven, performance-based, and outcome-focused.[6]" "Mission-driven" means that "the work of juvenile probation must be directed at clearly articulated and widely shared goals" that must guide everyday procedures, budget allocations, and staff assignments[7]; "performance-based" means that it should move from general goals to specific objectives and should designate "concrete activities that are calculated to achieve its goals and hold itself responsible for performing them."[8] "Outcome-focused" means that it "systematically measures the tangible results of its interventions, compares those results to its goals, and makes itself publicly accountable for any differences."[9]

Operation of Probation Services

The basic functions of probation services—intake, investigation, and supervision—operate using an increasingly "get tough" approach to juvenile crime. In intake, the initial decision is made about what to do with the law-violating juveniles. Preparation of the social history report, which assists the juvenile judge at the disposition stage of the court proceedings, is the most important process during investigation. The supervisory function is divided into managing a caseload, providing treatment services, and maintaining surveillance (see Exhibit 16.1).

probation officer An officer of the court who is expected to provide social history investigations, to supervise individuals who have been placed on probation, to maintain case files, to advise probationers on the conditions of their sentences, to perform any other probationary services that a judge may request, and to inform the court when persons on probation have violated the terms of that probation.

Intake The intake officer is usually a **probation officer**, although larger probation departments may have separate intake units in which intake officers are not probation officers. Regardless of the organizational structure, the intake officer is the chief decision maker for juveniles prior to the juvenile court proceeding and has two important decisions to make: what to do with the case and whether to detain the youth until a detention hearing can be scheduled.

The intake officer is commonly faced with one of the following situations: Parents bring a child in on their own, parents bring a child in because of a letter requesting their presence, or a police officer brings in a child who has been apprehended on suspicion of committing an unlawful act. Parents who walk in with their child typically complain, "My kid won't obey," "My kid won't do the chores," "My kid won't come home at night," or "My kid is running around with the wrong crowd." They want someone in authority to say, "You're going to get punished unless you clean up your act." After interviewing both the youth and parents—sometimes separately—the intake officer might make a contract with the child and parents in which each agrees to an acceptable compromise solution, or the intake officer might decide to refer the youth to a diversion agency.[10]

Parents whose child has been apprehended by the police for a criminal act are commonly instructed by letter to bring their child to the intake unit at a particular time. The intake officer must conduct a preliminary investigation at this time and, on the basis of the findings, decide what to do about the petition. Ordinarily, the youth is not retained in a detention facility but is released to the parents.

Police officers also frequently bring juveniles who have been apprehended committing an unlawful act to the intake unit. As part of the preliminary investigation, the intake officer must get in touch with the parents and make an immediate decision about the need for detention. The youth is detained if he or she is judged dangerous to self or others or lacks supervision in the home.

EXHIBIT 16.1

Is the System Broken?

Changes are coming in juvenile justice, and some states, like California, are bound to lead the charge toward reforming the system. This box contains some of the summary statements contained in a 2006 report commissioned by California's Division of Juvenile Justice when it sought guidance on how to go about reforming the state's juvenile correctional institutions.

The Division of Juvenile Justice has many good people working for it—hardworking, dedicated, and well meaning. The current leadership is professional, knowledgeable, and committed to reform. But if reform is to happen, they will need help, for this is not a system that needs tinkering around the edges—this is a system that is broken almost everywhere you look:

- High levels of violence and fear in its institutions
- Unsafe conditions for both residents and staff
- Antiquated facilities unsuited for any mission
- An adult corrections mentality with an adult/juvenile mix
- Management by crisis with little time to make changes
- Frequent lockdowns to manage violence, with subsequent program reductions
- Time added for infractions that extends average lengths of stay more than eight months
- Lengths of stay that are almost triple the average for the nation
- Hours on end when many youths have nothing to do
- Vocational classrooms that are idle or running at half speed

- Capitulation to gang culture with youths housed by gang affiliation
- Low levels of staffing amidst huge living units
- Abysmal achievement despite enormous outlays for education
- Information systems incapable of adequately supporting management
- Little partnership with counties and a fragmented system
- Poor reentry planning and too few services in parole
- Enormous costs with little to show for it

It is not just reform that is needed. Everything needs to be fixed.

▶ Juvenile institutions in California have long been acknowledged as models for the rest of the nation. Why is it, then, that juvenile institutionalization in California appears to have ended up in such dismal shape? Does this report blame staff commitment, performance, or loyalty? If not, what do you think are the underlying problems plaguing this state's juvenile correctional system?

Source: Christopher Murray, Chris Baird, Ned Loughran, Fred Mills, and John Platt, *Safety and Welfare Plan: Implementing Reform in California* (Sacramento: California Department of Corrections and Rehabilitation, Division of Juvenile Justice, 2006), p. 1.

Investigation   Investigation requires that probation officers prepare a **social history report** on a youth ruled delinquent to aid the judge in making the correct disposition. If a juvenile court uses a bifurcated hearing (separate adjudicatory and disposition stages), the judge orders a social history when a juvenile is found delinquent at the

social history report A written report of a juvenile's social background that probation officers prepare for a juvenile judge to assist the court in making a disposition of a youth who has been ruled delinquent.

Police and probation officers talk with young members of the Crips street gang outside a Los Angeles high school. A recent publication discussed in this text says that "good juvenile probation practice is mission-driven, performance-based, and outcome-focused." ▶ What does that mean?

Juvenile Law 16.1

Probation Rules

These rules are to be followed by probationers:

1. Obey all federal, state, and local laws.
2. Contact Juvenile Court Officer by the next working day if taken into custody for questioning on a new law violation(s).
3. May not possess or use alcohol or drugs, unless prescribed by a doctor.
4. Obey parental rules, including assigned household chores.
5. Attend all scheduled appointments with Juvenile Court Officer, assigned Tracker, and/or Volunteer Juvenile Court Officer.
6. Continue to be involved in a school program (this includes supervision and monitoring by Juvenile Court School Liaison).
7. Obey curfew regulations.
8. Participate in family therapy until successfully discharged (if deemed appropriate).
9. Participate in individual counseling until successfully discharged (if deemed appropriate).
10. Make reasonable restitution as agreed upon in the Restitution Contract.
11. Complete _____ hours of Community Service Work Project.
12. Participate in tutoring (if deemed appropriate).
13. Write a letter of apology to the victim(s) for your actions.
14. Do not use verbal/physical violence or intimidation.
15. Participate in outpatient substance evaluation, cooperate with recommended counseling, and pay service fee to ensure completion of evaluation.
16. Attend Alcoholics Anonymous (AA)/Narcotics Anonymous (NA) meetings weekly (if deemed appropriate).
17. Do not frequent establishments or residences where controlled substances and alcohol are served or associate with the individuals involved.
18. Do not leave the county without permission from Juvenile Court Officer.
19. Do not use or possess weapons of any kind.
20. Actively seek and maintain employment.

Failure to comply with the above rules will result in one (or a combination) of the following consequences/recommendations to the court:

1. Grounding
2. Tightening of curfew hours
3. Assignment of Community Service Work Project hours
4. Tracking and monitoring
5. Supervision by Juvenile Court School Liaison/ participation/completion in School Violence Program
6. Day-Treatment Program
7. Additional appointments with Juvenile Court Officer
8. Assignment of two hours of Community Service Work Project for each hour (or part of an hour) of unauthorized school absence
9. Detention for 48 hours
10. Return to court for modification of last court order

▶ **As a juvenile, would you have found the above rules restrictive? Are they too restrictive? What would you add or omit?**

Source: Adapted from "Probation Rules" courtesy of Juvenile Court Services of Black Hawk County.

adjudicatory or fact-finding stage, but if the court combines the adjudicatory and disposition stages, the social history must be completed before a juvenile appears in front of the judge, who waits until the youth has been found delinquent to read the report.

The probation officer usually has 30 to 60 days to write this report. He or she will review the youth's arrest record, reports of the current offense, any available psychiatric or psychological evaluations, and any information from social agencies; interview the youth and the parents, usually at least once in the home; and may also interview the arresting officer, school administrators or teachers, neighborhood religious leaders, and peers who know of or were involved in the alleged offense. Peers often volunteer information, saying to the probation officer, "I hear you're Fred's PO. I want you to know that he's a real crazy and did the crime," or "John is a real loser. Let me tell you some of the other [stuff] he's done."

Supervision When a juvenile judge sentences a youth to probation, the probation officer generally takes the youth aside and explains the meaning of probation. The probationer is informed of how frequently he or she will report to the probation officer and of the importance of complying with the conditions of probation. See Juvenile Law 16.1 for some of the probation rules for one juvenile probation office.

The length of time a youth must spend on probation varies from state to state. In some states, the maximum length is until the juvenile reaches the age of majority (normally 16 or 18 years old but sometimes 21 years old). Other states limit the length of time a juvenile or adult can spend on probation—for example, in Illinois it is limited

EXHIBIT 16.2

Decisions Facing Probation Officers

To make the decision of whether to revoke probation, modify the conditions of probation, or place a juvenile outside the home, probation officers consider some questions:

1. Is the juvenile a danger to self or others?
2. Is the juvenile exceeding the limits in the home, community, and school?
3. Is the family amenable to services?
4. How can the scarce resources be used wisely with this juvenile?
5. What other consequences (e.g., community service) can be imposed without court intervention?

To make the decision on what to do with a juvenile on an informal adjustment agreement who is not following home rules and who is violating curfew, getting dirty urine analyses (U.A.s), or failing to attend the Second Chance Program, probation officers consider several questions:

1. Does the juvenile show any remorse for his or her actions?
2. Does the juvenile want to change or make an adjustment to the contract?
3. Have all other options been utilized?

4. Is the charge worth sending to the court to get compliance? (For example, is a simple misdemeanor worthy of the expense of court action?)

To answer the question of what to do with a juvenile who is already adjudicated delinquent with the charge of possession with intent to deliver a controlled substance and who continues to get dirty U.A.s, probation officers consider these questions:

1. Does use of evaluation/treatment help?
2. Does a 48-hour lockup work?
3. Have we tried all other services and consequences?
4. Would it be fair to modify the court order with a mittimus withheld to placement or commitment to the training school in Eldora?

▶ **Which questions do you think would have the most influence on probation officers in these three scenarios? Why?**

Source: "Decisions Facing Probation Officers" courtesy of Juvenile Court Services of Black Hawk County.

to five years; in New York, to two years; in Washington, D.C., to one year; and in California, to six months.

The supervisory function is divided into casework management, treatment, and surveillance. Effective casework management requires that a probation officer keep an up-to-date casework file, carry out periodic reviews, decide how each client is to be handled, and divide probationers into several categories, depending on their needs and the risk they present to the community. Those with more serious needs and who present a greater risk to the community are required to report to their probation officer more frequently.

Surveillance requires that the probation officer make certain that probationers comply with the conditions of probation and that they do not break the law. The probation officer has a number of opportunities to observe the behavior of a probationer in the office, at home, and perhaps at school and also visits the probationer's parents. If a probationer's behavior is unacceptable, the probation officer is likely to receive reports from school or from law enforcement agencies.

The importance of surveillance was underscored in the mid-1970s when, with the emphasis on law and order, probation services were accused of failing to protect society. If a youth does not comply with the conditions of probation or commits another delinquent act, the probation officer must inform the judge by filing a notice of violation, and if the violation is serious enough, the probation officer must recommend that probation be revoked. Thus the probation officer has a law enforcement role as well as a treatment role. In Exhibit 16.2, probation officers reveal the questions that they consider in making decisions; the answers to these questions clearly place the probation officer in an enforcement role.

Risk Control and Crime Reduction

The current emphasis in juvenile probation, as in adult probation, is on programs fostering risk control and crime reduction, including restitution and community service, intensive supervision, house arrest, and electronic monitoring (EM).

The main goals of **restitution** and community service programs are to hold youthful offenders responsible for their crimes. Over the past 30 years, restitution

surveillance The observation of probationers by probation officers, intended to ensure that probationers comply with the conditions of probation and that they do not break the law.

restitution The court-ordered repayment to the victim; often used together with community service as a condition of juvenile probation.

programs and community service orders have had significant growth, much of it resulting from the Office of Juvenile Justice and Delinquency Prevention (OJJDP). In 1977, the OJJDP launched a major restitution initiative by spending $30 million to fund the use of restitution in 85 juvenile courts throughout the United States, and the OJJDP followed this initiative with the National Restitution Training Program in 1983 and the Restitution Education, Specialized Training, and Technical Assistance (RESTTA) Project in 1985. These initiatives are directly responsible for most of the growth of restitution programs.[11]

Three broad types of restitution can be ordered by the juvenile court: straight financial restitution, community service, and direct service to victims. Community service is the most common, probably because it is the easiest to administer. Direct service takes place less frequently, largely because of victim reluctance to have contact with offenders. However, the three program types frequently blend together. For example, a local jurisdiction may organize work crews and even enter into recycling, janitorial, and other service contracts with public or private agencies in order to provide youthful offenders with jobs so that they can pay restitution. The most common goals of restitution programs are holding juveniles accountable, providing reparation to victims, treating and rehabilitating juveniles, and punishing juvenile offenders[12] (see Library Extra 16.1 and Web Extra 16.2).

When it comes to making restitution and overseeing community service work, probation officers are key players, and in many jurisdictions it is up to these officers to do some or all of the following[13]:

- Determine participation eligibility.
- Calculate appropriate amounts of restitution to be made.
- Assess offenders' ability to pay.
- Determine payments/work schedules.
- Monitor performance.
- Close cases.

With community work restitution, juveniles are generally ordered to perform a certain number of work hours at a private, nonprofit, or government agency. Some large probation departments have established up to 100 sites where this service may be performed, and these sites typically include public libraries, parks, nursing homes,

Library Extra 16.1

OJJDP publication: *Juvenile Offenders and Victims: 2006 National Report* (Chapter 7)

Web Extra 16.2

Juvenile Justice Trainers Association

Young offenders paint fences as part of their sentence to community service. ▶ What are the responsibilities of juvenile probation officers who work with offenders sentenced to community service?

animal shelters, community centers, day-care centers, youth agencies, YMCAs and YWCAs, and local streets. Some restitution programs involve supervised work crews; in these situations, juveniles go to a site and work under the supervision of an adult.

Youthful offenders in Hennepin County (Minneapolis), Minnesota, find themselves very quickly dispatched by the juvenile judge to the Saturday work squads for **community service projects**. A first-time property offender will usually be given a sentence of 40 hours. Each Saturday morning, youths who are assigned to the work squad are required to be at the downtown meeting place at 8 A.M.; the coordinator of the program, who is on the staff of the probation department, then assigns each to a specific work detail, which includes recycling bottles and cans, visiting with patients at a nursing home, doing janitorial work, cleaning bus stops, planting trees or removing barbed-wire fences at a city park, and working at a park reserve. This program sends out five trucks each Saturday with 10 youths and 2 staff members in each truck.[14]

community service project
A court-required restitution in which a juvenile spends a certain number of hours working in a community project.

Intensive Supervision In the 1980s and 1990s, as probation continued to be criticized as a lenient measure that allowed offenders to escape punishment, intensive supervision programs (ISPs) became more widely used in juvenile probation. Georgia, New Jersey, Oregon, and Pennsylvania are experimenting with statewide programs for juveniles.[15] But more and more juvenile judges, especially in metropolitan juvenile courts, are placing high-risk juveniles on small caseloads and assigning them more frequent contact with a probation officer than would be true of traditional probation.

The Juvenile Court Judges' Commission in the Commonwealth of Pennsylvania developed an intensive probation project because of its concern with increased commitments to training schools. In addition to investing $1,868,014 to support intensive probation and aftercare programs, the commission also provides program guidelines and monitoring to each county that is willing to set up an intensive probation program. By the end of 1989, 32 counties had established intensive probation programs that featured such standards as providing a caseload size of no more than 15 high-risk delinquents for each intensive probation officer, requiring a minimum of three face-to-face contacts per week with each of these youths and a minimum of one contact per week with the family and/or guardian, and establishing intensive probation services for a minimum of 6 months and a maximum of 12 months.[16]

ISPs are widely used in adult corrections and have received considerable praise for their effectiveness in keeping high-risk offenders out of long-term confinement. However, two national reviews of ISPs in juvenile probation discovered that "neither the possible effectiveness nor the possible ineffectiveness of these programs had been carefully examined. As a result, their status in this regard, including their impact on recidivism, was essentially unknown."[17]

Some criminologists have sought to develop an integrated social control (ISC) model of intensive supervision addressing the major causal factors identified in delinquency theory and research. This proposed model, which integrates the central components of strain, control, and social learning theories, contends that the combined forces of inadequate socialization, strains between educational and occupational aspirations and expectations, and social disorganization in the neighborhood lead to weak bonding to conventional values and activities in the family, community, and school; weak bonding, in turn, can lead youths to delinquent behavior through negative peer influence. Figure 16.2 shows a diagram of this model.[18]

House Arrest and Remote Location Monitoring House arrest is a sentence imposed by the court whereby youths are ordered to remain confined in their own homes for the length of their sentence, although they may be allowed to leave their homes for medical reasons, school, employment, and approved religious services. They may also be required to perform community service. EM equipment may or may not be used to monitor juveniles' presence in a residence where they are required to remain.

FIGURE 16.2 Integrated Strain–Control Paradigm

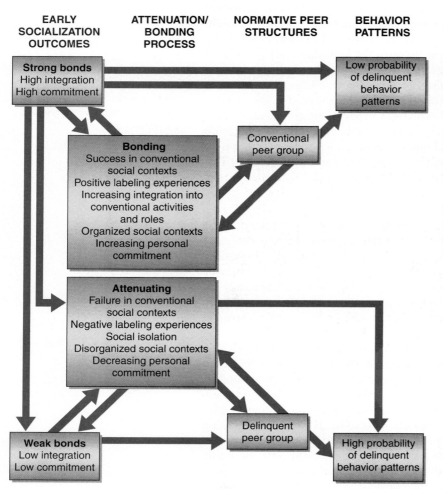

Source: Barry Krisberg et al., *Juvenile Intensive Planning Guide* (Washington, D.C.: Office of Juvenile Justice and Delinquency Prevention, 1994), p. 7.

remote location monitoring The use of electronic equipment to verify that an offender is at home or in a community correctional center during specified hours or to track his or her whereabouts; also called *electronic monitoring.*

Remote location monitoring was inspired by a New Mexico district court judge's reading of a comic strip in which the character Spiderman was tracked by a transmitter affixed to his wrist. The judge approached an engineer, who designed an electronic bracelet to emit a signal picked up by a receiver placed in a home telephone. The bracelet was designed so that if the offender moved more than 150 feet from the home telephone, the transmission signal would be broken, alerting the authorities that the offender had fled his or her home.[19]

Today's EM equipment receives information about monitored offenders and transmits the information to a computer at the monitoring agency. There are several EM methods:

- Continuous signaling devices use a transmitter attached to the probationer that emits a continuous radio signal.
- Programmed contact devices call the juvenile probationer at scheduled or random times and use various technologies to determine the identity of the person who answers (voice verification, a device worn by the probationer that is inserted into a verifier box attached to the phone, or a digital camera for visual verification).
- Global positioning systems, worn by juvenile probationers, have a transmitter that communicates signals to a satellite and back to a computer monitor, pinpointing offenders' whereabouts at all times.

- Remote alcohol testing devices may be used alone or with other devices listed above. The probationer is required to blow into a device (Alco-Sensor) which transmits results to a computer that records the amount of alcohol in the offender's blood. Such devices may also be attached to automobile ignition systems in order to prevent an offender who has been drinking from driving.[20]

In 1997, an estimated 89,095 adults—3.5% of all probationers—were on EM surveillance. Nearly every state has adults on EM surveillance, although the courts in some states limited the use of EM by banning certain types of monitoring equipment and allowing monitoring only by consent.[21] The use of EM in juvenile justice has been gradually gaining acceptance. For example, according to a November 1988 survey, only 11 juvenile programs used EM[22]; today EM programs are widely used in juvenile justice programs throughout the United States. EM programs are used for a variety of reasons:

- They increase the number of juveniles safely released into existing home confinement programs.
- They reduce the number of juveniles returned to juvenile detention for violating home confinement restrictions.
- They reduce the number of field contacts required of home confinement officers.
- They provide a reasonably safe alternative to confinement for low-risk offenders.

Seen here is a youthful offender's remote location monitoring ankle bracelet. ▶ **What are the different kinds of electronic monitoring that can be employed in the supervision of juvenile offenders?**

- They provide for early reunification of youths with their families.
- They allow juveniles to return to school.[23]

EM tends to be more effective when used as a tool in conjunction with other programs rather than when operating alone as a supervision program, yet there seems to be no consistent findings that successful completion of EM programs leads to a decrease in recidivism.[24]

Volunteer Programs

As stated earlier, probation was initially staffed with volunteers, and professional staff did not begin appearing until the turn of the twentieth century. But in the 1950s, Judge Keith J. Leenhouts initiated a court-sponsored volunteer program in Royal Oak, Michigan, that sparked the rebirth of the volunteer movement. Today over 2,000 court-sponsored **volunteer programs** are in operation, using volunteers to assist probation officers in a variety of ways, and the use of volunteers has become one of the most valuable ways to help offenders adjust to community life.

The National Information Center on Volunteers in Court has identified several areas in which **community volunteers** can work effectively with juvenile offenders. They can provide a one-to-one support relationship for the youth with a trustworthy adult; can function as a child advocate with teachers, employers, and police; can be good role models; can set limits and teach prosocial values; can teach skills or academic subjects; and can help youths develop a realistic response to their environment.

In addition to these areas of direct contact, volunteers can assist in administrative work; help to recruit, train, and supervise other volunteers; serve as consultants to the regular staff; become advisers to the court, especially in the policy-making area; develop good public relations with the community; and contribute money, materials, or facilities. Volunteers can also improve the morale of the regular probation staff because volunteers are usually positive and enthusiastic about the services they are providing; since many volunteers are professionals (physicians, psychiatrists, psychologists, dentists, etc.), they can provide services that the probation department may not have the financial resources to obtain. Finally, their contributions can reduce the caseload of the regular staff.

volunteer program The use of unpaid adult community members to assist probation officers in a variety of ways.

community volunteer An individual who donates his or her time to work with delinquents in the community.

Several criticisms have been leveled at volunteer programs. Critics say that volunteers sometimes create more work than they return in service and that volunteers cannot handle serious problems and sometimes can harm their clients. Parents may view a volunteer as an untrained worker and resist his or her help. But proper screening, training, and supervision can do much to ensure a high quality of probation services from volunteers (see Library Extra 16.2 and Web Extra 16.3).

Residential and Day Treatment

Residential and day-treatment programs are usually reserved for juvenile probationers who are having difficulty dealing with the looseness of probation supervision. In residential programs, which are usually group homes or foster care placements, delinquents are taken away from the supervision of parents and are assigned 24 hours a day to their new placement. Some group homes are like the halfway houses used in adult corrections and serve as a placement for juveniles on aftercare status who have nowhere else to go. In day-treatment programs, juveniles attend morning and afternoon program sessions and return home in the evening.

Types of Programs

Group homes, day-treatment programs, and wilderness programs are the main types of community-based programs. Group homes are a residential placement to which juveniles are adjudicated, either while on probation or when released from a training school. Day-treatment programs are nonresidential programs that juveniles attend during the day, returning home in the evening. Wilderness programs, sometimes called "survival programs," take place in such settings as the mountains, the woods, the sea, and the desert, and the intent of these survival programs is to improve youths' self-confidence and sense of self-reliance.

group home A placement for youths who have been adjudicated by the court that serves a group of about 13 to 25 youths as an alternative to institutionalization; also called *group residence, halfway house,* or *attention home.*

Group Homes   Such terms as *group residence, halfway house, group home,* and *attention home* are used in various parts of the United States to identify a small facility serving about 13 to 25 youths. These types of **group homes** fulfill several purposes: They provide an alternative to institutionalization; they serve as a short-term community placement, wherein probation and aftercare officers can deal with youths' community problems; and they serve as a "halfway-in" setting for youths having difficulty adjusting to probation and as a "halfway-out" placement for delinquents who are returning to the community but lack an adequate home placement.

Intake criteria, treatment goals, length of stay, target population services, available services, physical facilities, location in reference to the rest of the city, and house rules of group homes throughout the United States are extremely diverse. Some homes are treatment oriented, using a modality such as guided group interaction (GGI) to generate a supportive environment among residents and staff. In GGI, residents are expected to support, confront, and be honest with one another so that they can help each other deal with their problems.[25]

group home model A form of community-based residential program that has had some success with youthful offenders.

One well-developed **group home model** is the **teaching family group model**, which was developed in 1967 with the establishment of the Achievement Place group home in Lawrence, Kansas. The teaching family group model has been used in more than 40 homes in 12 states.[26] The Criswell House in Tallahassee, Florida, established in 1958, housed 25 youths on probation and parole and used GGI, and in the 1970s, Florida developed a network of 9 group homes modeled on the Criswell House.[27] The DARE Program in Massachusetts is another widely used model; established in 1964, this program had 10 specialized programs and 13 community residences, including 9 group homes, 4 programs of **foster care**, 2 residential schools, shelter care programs, and a high-security intensive care facility.[28]

teaching family group model A community-based residential program that has had some success with delinquent youths.

foster care A home setting for juveniles who are lawfully removed from their birth parents' homes.

Unfortunately, such exciting programs as the Achievement Place are not typical of group homes across the nation. In too many group homes, beds (vacancies) are hard to find, and group homes may even have long waiting lists. Residents also

A staff member talks with a future program participant at the Center for Young Women's Development in San Francisco. The center reaches over 3,500 young women each year through street-based outreach efforts. Its staff are comprised entirely of women under 25 years old.
▶ **What kinds of services are likely to be of greatest interest to marginalized young women?**

typically have longer stays than they would have in training schools, which raises real questions about whether group homes are a less punitive placement than juvenile institutions.

Day-Treatment Programs Nonresidential **day-treatment programs** multiplied nationwide during the early 1970s. Their popularity can be traced to the advantages they offer community-based corrections: They are more economical because they do not provide living and sleeping quarters, they make parental participation easier, they require fewer staff members, and they are less coercive and punishment oriented than residential placements.

day-treatment program A court-mandated, community-based corrections program that juveniles attend in the morning and afternoon. They return home in the evening.

Nonresidential programs usually serve male juveniles, although California operates two such programs for girls as well as several coeducational programs. These nonresidential programs have been used widely by the California Community Treatment Project. The New York Division for Youth has also established several nonresidential programs, called STAY, which also expose youths to a GGI experience.

Another nonresidential program, conducted by the Associated Marine Institutes (AMI), offers 25 of its 40 schools and institutes as nonresidential facilities. Funded by state and private donations, this privately operated program tailors its institutes to the geographic strengths of each community, using the ocean, wilderness, rivers, and lakes to stimulate productive behavior in juvenile delinquents. In the nonresidential programs that include both males and females, the 14- to 18-year-old trainees live at home or in foster homes. Youths are referred to this program either by the courts or by the Division of Youth Services[29] (see Exhibit 16.3).

For the Marine Institutes, which constitute most of AMI's schools, the contract that the youth signs on entering the program sets individual goals for the training period in a dozen categories, including diving, ship-handling skills, ocean science, life-saving, and first aid, as well as such electives as photography and marine maintenance. The major incentive for youths is the opportunity to earn official certification as scuba divers. Other incentives that are designed to maintain enthusiasm include sew-on patches; certificates awarded for short-term achievement in first aid, ship-handling skills, and diving; trophies for trainee of the month; and field trips, such as a cruise to the Bahamas or the Florida Keys.[30]

> > > **EXHIBIT 16.3** < <

Programs of the Associated Marine Institutes

Since 1969, programs of the Associated Marine Institutes (AMI) have been developed to work with juvenile delinquents. Over the years, new institutes were started throughout the United States and in the Cayman Islands.

AMI's main objective is to develop attitudes in the youths it serves that will help them meet their responsibilities, develop employable skills, increase self-confidence, and encourage further education. After attending the program, each youth is placed in a school, a job, or the armed forces. Aftercare coordinators monitor youths for three years after they graduate to offer assistance.

In September 1993, Attorney General Janet Reno and President Bill Clinton visited the Pinellas Marine Institute in St. Petersburg, Florida, one of AMI's 40 schools. In a nationally televised program where he announced his crime bill, the president said, "These programs are giving young people a chance to take their future back, a chance to understand that there is good inside them."

One of the ingredients of AMI's programs is a strong commitment to meaningful work. AMI looks upon work as one of the most beneficial forms of therapy and teaches that nothing worthwhile is achieved without hard work.

Academic success is also emphasized. The intent of the AMI programs is to motivate students and to give them the right tools and opportunities so that they can succeed in school. Indeed, the goal of the AMI teaching staff is to prepare youths to take their General Educational Development (GED) exam and then attend a vocational school, a community college, or a four-year college.

A further important ingredient of this program is modeling. AMI staff support the belief that what they do is more important than what they say. Their philosophy on modeling is: Tell me, I'll forget. Show me, I may remember. Involve me, I'll be committed.

▶ What are the advantages that AMI has over other community-based programs for juveniles? Is the emphasis given to aftercare in this program one that should be pursued more by other programs?

Source: Associated Marine Institutes.

Library Extra 16.3

OJJDP National Report Series publication: *Juvenile Residential Facility Census*

Outward Bound A wilderness-type survival program that is popular in many states as an alternative to the institutionalization of juveniles.

The better-known programs, such as AMI, continue to thrive, but with the decline of federal funding sources in the late 1970s and early 1980s, many day-treatment programs had to close their doors. There is no question that these programs play a much smaller role in community-based corrections than they did in the 1970s (see Library Extra 16.3).

Wilderness Programs **Outward Bound** is the most widely used wilderness program. Its main goal is to use the overcoming of a seemingly impossible task to gain self-reliance, to prove one's worth, and to define one's personhood.[31] The first Outward Bound program in the United States was established in Colorado in 1962, and today Outward Bound offers 750 wilderness courses, including rock climbing, kayaking, dog sledding, sailing, rappelling, backpacking, and more, to adults, teens, and youths. Over 10,000 students participate in wilderness courses. Outward Bound offers multiyear partnerships with 125 schools across the United States, and it encourages over 30,000 students and 4,000 teachers to reach high levels of achievement and to discover their potential. Outward Bound also has urban programs in Atlanta, Baltimore, Boston, New York, and Philadelphia.[32]

Types of Institutional Placement

Library Extra 16.4

OJJDP *Juvenile Justice Bulletin:* "Psychiatric Disorders of Youth in Detention"

Youthful offenders who do not adequately adjust to community-based programs or who commit another offense while under community supervision may be adjudicated to a public or private institutional placement (see Library Extra 16.4). Public institutional facilities are sometimes administered by the county, but the vast majority of them are under state control. Reception and diagnostic centers, ranches, forestry camps, boot camps, and training schools are the main forms that juvenile correctional institutions take. (Recently, however, it should be noted that juveniles have increasingly been sent to adult prisons.) Private facilities play a somewhat significant role in the long-term custody of juveniles; although there are more than twice as many privately operated juvenile facilities as publicly operated ones, private facilities hold less than half as many youths as do public facilities.[33]

In 2003, 307 juvenile offenders were in custody for every 100,000 juveniles in the United States. Nationwide, the total number of youthful offenders in residential placement facilities rose 41% from 1991 to 1999 but then declined 10% from 1999 to 2003, the result being an overall increase of 27% between 1991 and 2003. The number of status offenders in juvenile facilities peaked in 1995 but then declined 36% between 1995 and 2003.[34]

In terms of the most serious offense leading to confinement in 2003, 38% of confined juveniles were being held for person offenses, 31% for property offenses, and 12% for technical offenses. Public-order offenses ranked fourth, at 10%, and drug offenses (perhaps a little surprisingly) ranked last among all the types of offenses on which statistics were kept, making up only 9% of all committed juvenile offenders.[35]

There were 14,590 female juvenile offenders held in custody throughout the country in 2003, accounting for 15% of all offenders in custody (the proportion of females had increased from 13% in 1991 to 15% in 2003). The female proportion was greater among status offenders (40%) than among delinquents (14%) and for detained (18%) than for committed (12%) delinquents.[36] In 2003, more than 59,000 minority offenders were in residential placement in juvenile facilities in the United States, which was 61% of the custody population nationwide; of the 96,655 in placement in 2003, 37,347 were white, 36,740 were African-American, 18,422 were Hispanic/Latino, 1,771 were American Indian, 1,462 were Asian, and 913 were of other or mixed races.[37]

The 2006 report *Implementing Reform in California* reveals the skyrocketing cost of juvenile institutional care. It costs California $115,129 per year to institutionalize each juvenile resident (Figure 16.3). California's 2004's average length of stay was 25.9 months—nearly three times as long as the average of 19 states that participated in a nationwide survey (Figure 16.4). It should be noted, however, that juvenile offenders in California may be kept in institutional care until they are 24 years old, something which has contributed significantly to the average length of stay for those sentenced to juvenile facilities in California.[38]

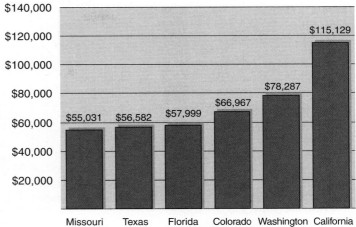

FIGURE 16.3 Cost per Youth per Year of Confinement in Selected States, 2005

Source: Christopher Murray, Chris Baird, Ned Loughran, Fred Mills, and John Platt, *Safety and Welfare Plan: Implementing Reform in California* (Sacramento: California Department of Corrections and Rehabilitation, Division of Juvenile Justice, 2006), p. 5.

Reception and Diagnostic Centers

The purpose of **reception and diagnostic centers,** which are managed and operated by either public or private agencies, is to determine which treatment plan suits each adjudicated youth and which training school is the best placement. The evaluation of each resident used to take 4 to 6 weeks, but the process has been condensed today to an average length of 34 days. Evaluations are normally done by a psychiatrist, a clinical psychologist, a social worker, academic staff, and a chaplain. Each youth undergoes a psychiatric evaluation and a battery of psychological tests to measure intelligence, attitude, maturity, and emotional problems, and a social case study is completed. During this orientation period, the academic staff determine the proper school placement and attempt to identify any debilitating learning problems; physical and dental examinations also typically are given to the youth at this time, and child-care workers in living units evaluate institutional adjustment and peer relationships. When all the reports have been prepared, a case conference is held on each resident to summarize that youth's needs and attitudes and recommend the best institutional placement.

In large youth commissions or departments of youth services, the recommendation must be approved by an institutional coordinator. Upon approval, the youth is transferred to the selected institution, accompanied by the diagnostic report. Because many training schools have their own orientation programs, however, it is not unusual

reception and diagnostic center A facility where juveniles who have been committed to correctional institutions frequently are first sent. This type of center diagnoses youths' problems and develops individualized treatment plans.

FIGURE 16.4 Average Length of Stay in Juvenile Residential Placement in Months for Selected States, 2005 (Males)

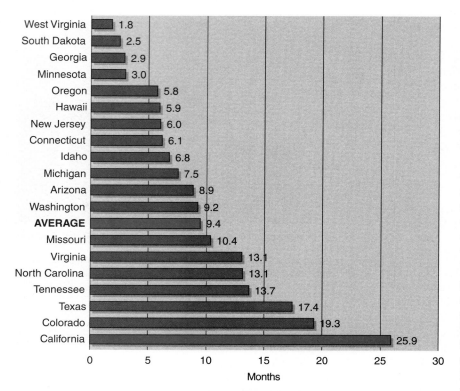

State	Months
West Virginia	1.8
South Dakota	2.5
Georgia	2.9
Minnesota	3.0
Oregon	5.8
Hawaii	5.9
New Jersey	6.0
Connecticut	6.1
Idaho	6.8
Michigan	7.5
Arizona	8.9
Washington	9.2
AVERAGE	9.4
Missouri	10.4
Virginia	13.1
North Carolina	13.1
Tennessee	13.7
Texas	17.4
Colorado	19.3
California	25.9

Source: Christopher Murray, Chris Baird, Ned Loughran, Fred Mills, and John Platt, *Safety and Welfare Plan: Implementing Reform in California* (Sacramento: California Department of Corrections and Rehabilitation, Division of Juvenile Justice, 2006), p. 2.

forestry camp A correctional facility where residents usually do conservation work in state parks, including cleaning up, cutting grass and weeds, and doing general maintenance.

ranch A public or private juvenile correctional institution that, like a forestry camp, is usually less secure than a training school and that has a more normal atmosphere.

for the report to receive little attention and for the youth to undergo nearly the same process again in the training school cottage.

Forestry Camps and Ranches

Minimum-security institutions, such as **forestry camps** and **ranches**, are typically reserved for youths who have committed minor crimes and for those who have been committed to the youth authority or private corrections for the first time. In forestry camps, which are popular in a number of states, residents usually do conservation work in a state park, including cleaning up, cutting grass and weeds, and doing general maintenance. Treatment programs usually consist of group therapy, individual contacts with social workers and the child-care staff, and one or two home visits a month. Residents also may be taken to a nearby town on a regular basis to make purchases and to attend community events. Escapes are a constant problem because of the nonsecure nature of these facilities.

Horseback riding is a popular recreational activity on ranches, but work details usually consist of taking care of the livestock, working in the garden, and performing general maintenance duties. GGI is the most widely used treatment, and as part of a continuum of care, one or two home visits a month help residents reintegrate themselves into community living.

A resident in the Hennepin Cou̅ Home School spends time with horses. Riding horses and canoeing are two of the activitie̅ ̅ ̅ ̅ ̅ ̅ ̅ ̅ ake this placement very different from most institutional settings. ▶ How do such activities further the treatment goals of institutions that employ them?

EXHIBIT 16.4

Hennepin County Home School

The Hennepin County Home School (HCHS) is a state-licensed residential institution for juvenile males and females between the ages of 13 and 18 years old who have been committed by the Hennepin County Juvenile Court. This innovative facility, which combines features of camps and ranches, is located on a beautiful 167-acre wooded lake site in Minnetonka, Minnesota, approximately 17 miles from downtown Minneapolis. The campus includes seven 24-bed residential cottages, a school facility with a full gymnasium, an administration and services building with a 16-bed secure internal support unit, a new 16-bed transitional living unit (TLU), a horse barn and arena, and playing fields. Hennepin County Home School is licensed for 168 open and 16 secure beds.

The Adolescent Male Treatment Program (Cottages 5, 6, and 7) is a corrective treatment program with development specialization for residents who have committed major property offenses and crimes against persons. The length of commitment is determined by the juvenile court and ranges from 10 to 13 months, including a 45-day transition and a 2-month furlough component, during which time the juvenile returns to the community at the conclusion of his institutional stay. The Female Offender Program (Cottage 2) is a corrective treatment program for property and person offenders. The length of the commitment is determined by the juvenile court and ranges from 10 to 13 months, with a specialized 45-day transition and a minimum 2-month furlough. The Juvenile Sex Offender Program (Cottage 3) is a corrective treatment program for boys who have committed sexual offenses. The length of the commitment is indeterminate, with a furlough option after 12 months. The Beta Program (Cottage 1) is for less serious offenders; the length of stay is 3 to 6 weeks, and the focus of the program's activities is on work for repayment of court-ordered restitution and public-service projects.

One of the exciting new programs is the Intensive Aftercare Program (IAP). Residents are offered a continuum of services, including successful community reintegration and aftercare, to meet their full range of needs. This continuum-of-care model reflects the Intensive Community-Based Aftercare Model developed by the Office of Juvenile Justice and Delinquency Prevention (OJJDP). The County School's IAP model includes six intertwined phases: assessment, case planning, institutional treatment, prerelease, transition, and community reintegration.

Superintendent Theresa E. Wise had this to say about HCHS:

The value of Hennepin County Home School is that we provide a safe and secure environment where the youth has an opportunity to look at himself or herself. Some youth are afraid at home and school, and we want them to be and feel safe here. This institution believes that a safe and secure environment helps youth internalize change. We are also concerned about the whole youth, and, therefore, we attempt to partner with the external community and work with families.

▶ **What does the photograph of the resident and the horses suggest about this school? How does this facility seem to be different from the average public or private training school? Why is the continuum-of-care model such an important program?**

Source: Based on information from brochures and other materials developed by the Hennepin County Home School, its website, and interviews conducted in 2006.

Residents are generally much more positive about a placement at a forestry camp or ranch than about placement at a training school. They like both the more relaxed approach to security and the more frequent community contact. Residents also respond to the generally shorter stays at these minimum-security institutions, and given the looser atmosphere of these settings, it is not surprising that they have better relations with staff members here than in training schools. Yet some youths who are homesick or are victimized by peers cannot handle these settings and repeatedly run away until they are transferred to more secure institutions. For a description of the Hennepin County Home School, see Exhibit 16.4; for information on community-based facilities for violent juvenile offenders, see Library Extra 16.5.

Boot Camps

Boot camps for youthful offenders, like those for adult offenders, developed in the mid-1980s and 1990s. Emphasizing military discipline, physical training, and regimented activity for periods typically ranging from 30 to 120 days, these programs endeavor to shock juvenile delinquents out of committing further crimes.

The rationale for juvenile boot camps is consistent with the juvenile justice system's historical emphasis on rehabilitation, usually incorporating explicit assumptions about the needs of delinquent youths and providing remedial, counseling, and aftercare programs to address these needs.[39] All the programs employ military customs and courtesies, including uniformed drill instructors, a platoon structure, and the summary punishment of participants (including group punishment under some circumstances).

mycrimekit™

Library Extra 16.5

OJJDP Juvenile Justice Bulletin: "Planning Community-Based Facilities for Violent Juvenile Offenders as Part of a System of Graduated Sanctions"

boot camp A military-style facility used as an alternative to prison in order to deal with prison crowding and public demands for severe punishment.

mycrimekit

Library Extra 16.6

NIJ publication: *National Study Comparing the Environments of Boot Camps with Traditional Facilities for Juvenile Offenders*

Although there are differences in emphases, with Denver creating the most militaristic environment, juvenile boot camp programs have generally discovered that they must tailor their environment to participants' maturity levels.[40]

Boot camps for juveniles are generally reserved for mid-range offenders, those who have failed with lesser sanctions such as probation but who are not yet hardened delinquents (see Library Extra 16.6). The shock aspect of the boot camp experience includes incarceration as the environment within which the program takes place.[41] These programs typically focus on youths in their middle to late teens and exclude sex offenders, armed robbers, and violent offenders. Yet only a few programs limit themselves to nonviolent youths who have committed their first serious offense or are being confined for the first time; for example, the Orleans Parish program accepts anyone who is sentenced by the juvenile judge.[42]

A fair assessment may be that the quality of boot camps depends largely on how much they tailor their programs to participants' maturity levels and how effective they are in implementing and sustaining effective aftercare services. In 2000, Doris MacKenzie and colleagues completed a study of 26 juvenile boot camps, comparing them with traditional facilities (the experiences of 2,668 juveniles in 26 boot camps were compared to those of 1,848 juveniles in 22 traditional facilities).[43] They found that, overall, juveniles in boot camps perceived their environments as more positive or therapeutic, less hostile or dangerous, and more structured than juveniles in traditional facilities perceived their environments; moreover, this study revealed that, over time, youths in boot camps became less antisocial and less depressed than youths in traditional facilities.[44]

Other follow-ups on juvenile boot camps have almost all found recidivism rates of boot camps to be slightly higher than or about the same as those of traditional juvenile facilities.[45] Charges of abuse in boot camps have been made in Arizona, Georgia, Maryland, and South Dakota. For example, in the summer of 1999, a 14-year-old girl in South Dakota died from dehydration during a long-distance run.[46] On July 1, 2001, Anthony Haynes, a 14-year-old boy from Arizona, died at a boot camp where troubled juveniles were allegedly kicked and forced to eat mud; in this camp, the regimen includes forced marches, in-your-face discipline, and a daily diet of an apple, a carrot, and a bowl of beans.[47]

Corrections officers demand the attention of a new recruit on the first day of orientation at the Greene County Impact Incarceration Program in Illinois. The program, a military-style boot camp for first-time juvenile offenders who have been convicted of felonies, is supposed to shock residents into conforming their behavior to the requirements of the law. ▶ **How successful have such programs been?**

The combined disappointing recidivism results, as well as the charges of abuse, have prompted Arizona, Georgia, Maryland, and South Dakota to shut down or reevaluate the "get tough with juveniles" approach popularized in the early 1990s. Arizona removed 50 juveniles from the boot camp in which Haynes died; Maryland shut down one boot camp and suspended the military regimens at its other two facilities after reports of systematic assaults, and the charges of abuse led to the ouster of the state's top five juvenile justice officials.[48]

Panaceas die hard in juvenile corrections, and this highly acclaimed approach of the 1980s and 1990s will continue to be used across the nation. However, criticisms of boot camps and disappointing recidivism data probably will result in fewer new programs being established and in greater scrutiny of existing programs.

Public and Private Training Schools

Some training schools look like prisons, others resemble college campuses, and still others have a homelike atmosphere, yet regardless of what they look like, training schools are used more today than they were in the 1970s and 1980s. Youth gangs are becoming a serious problem in some training schools. In California Division of Juvenile Justice (the former California Youth Authority) institutions, for example, gangs dominate daily life in bulging dormitories, in crowded cafeterias, and on the recreational fields.[49] The gang organization that is present in the California Division of Juvenile Facilities is relatively absent in training schools elsewhere, but gang members are increasingly being sentenced to public training schools in other states.

The larger states, such as California, Illinois, Michigan, and New York, have several training schools each.[50] Smaller states commonly have one training school for boys and another for girls, but Massachusetts and Vermont have no training schools. Coeducational institutions gained some acceptance in the 1970s, when several states opened one or more coeducational campuses, but that trend seems to have passed.

The physical structure of training schools ranges from the homelike atmosphere of small cottages to open dormitories with little privacy to fortress-like facilities with individual cells and fences. The level of security is usually higher for public than for private facilities because a larger proportion of the public facilities are detention centers designed to control residents' movement through staff monitoring and physical restrictions such as fences.[51]

Programs and Services   The programs that public and private training schools offer are superior to those of other juvenile institutions. The medical and dental services that residents receive tend to be very good, and most larger training schools have a full-time nurse on duty during the day and a physician who visits one or more days a week. Although institutionalized delinquents frequently complain about the medical and dental care they receive, most youths still receive far better care than they did before they were confined.

According to research that one of the authors has conducted in six states, the educational program is usually accredited by the state and is able to grant high school diplomas. The majority of training schools also offer classes to prepare residents for the General Educational Development (GED) high school equivalency certificate examinations. College preparation classes are sometimes provided in some training schools, but this seems to have been more true in the past than at present. Additionally, basic skills education classes are usually available in reading, writing, and mathematics, and special education and literacy or remedial reading are also provided in most training schools. Classes tend to be small, and students are permitted to progress at a rate that fits their needs.[52]

The vocational training provided by training schools usually depends on the size of the school. Larger training schools for boys may offer courses such as computer repair; auto shop/engine repair; small appliance repair; carpentry/building trades; printing, electrical, and welding trades; and forestry/agriculture. Schools for girls may offer courses in cosmetology, computer training, secretarial trades, and food

Library Extra 16.7

NIJ Research in Brief: *Resources for Juvenile Detention Reform*

services. Generally speaking, vocational training is often not helpful in finding employment; some released residents have difficulty being admitted to labor unions, and some may not come away with a sufficient skill set. Nonetheless, a few residents do leave the institution and find excellent jobs with the skills they have acquired.[53]

The rehabilitation of juvenile delinquents remains the avowed purpose of most training schools (see Library Extra 16.7). In the twentieth century, seemingly every conceivable method was used in the effort to rehabilitate residents so they would refrain from unlawful behavior. The treatment technologies still in use include classification systems, treatment modalities, skill development, and prerelease programs, and the most widely used treatment modalities are transactional analysis, reality therapy, psychotherapy, behavior modification, GGI, positive peer culture, and drug and alcohol treatment. Rational therapy, sometimes called the "errors-in-thinking modality" or Cognitive Skills Training Program (CSTP), is a relatively recent treatment modality in juvenile corrections that has been implemented in a number of public and private training schools across the nation.

In their 2000 meta-analysis of 83 studies on interventions with institutionalized offenders, Mark W. Lipsey, David B. Wilson, and Lynn Cothern found that 74 involved youthful offenders who were in the custody of juvenile justice institutions and 9 involved residential institutions that were administered by mental health or private agencies; all the juveniles in these placements had committed serious offenses that warranted confinement or close supervision in an institutional setting.[54] Table 16.1 compares treatment types in order of effectiveness with both noninstitutionalized and institutionalized offenders.

TABLE 16.1 Comparison of Treatment Types in Order of Effectiveness

Noninstitutionalized Offender Treatments	Institutionalized Offender Treatments
Positive Effects, Consistent Evidence	
Individual counseling Interpersonal skills Behavioral programs	Interpersonal skills Teaching family homes
Positive Effects, Less Consistent Evidence	
Multiple services Restitution, probation/parole	Behavioral programs Community residential Multiple services
Mixed But Generally Positive Effects, Inconsistent Evidence	
Employment-related training Academic programs Advocacy/casework Family counseling Group counseling	Individual counseling Guided group counseling Group counseling
Weak or No Effects, Inconsistent Evidence	
Reduced caseload, probation/parole	Employment-related training Drug abstinence Wilderness/challenge
Weak or No Effects, Consistent Evidence	
Wilderness/challenge Early release, probation/parole Deterrence programs Vocational programs	Milieu therapy

Source: Mark W. Lipsey et al., *Effective Intervention for Serious Juvenile Offenders* (Washington, D.C.: Office of Juvenile Justice and Delinquency Prevention, 2000), p. 5.

One of the serious shortcomings of programming in many training schools is the lack of attention given to the needs of adjudicated female offenders. The 1992 Amendment to the 1974 Juvenile Justice and Delinquency Prevention Act addressed the issue of gender bias, requiring states to analyze the need, types, and delivery of gender-specific services. As an example of gender-biased treatment, a comparative study of 348 violent juvenile females and a similar number of males reported in 1992 that half the males were admitted to rehabilitative or alternative programs, but only 29.5% of females received treatment in any form.[55]

Recreation has always been emphasized in training schools. Male residents are usually offered such competitive sports as softball, volleyball, flag football, basketball, and sometimes even boxing or wrestling. Cottages may compete against each other, and the institution may have a team that competes against other institutional teams. Other popular recreational activities include attending weekly movies; building model cars; participating in talent shows, dramatics, and choir; decorating the cottage during holidays; and playing Ping-Pong, pool, and chess. Some training schools offer sailing or canoeing for residents, some have swimming pools, and some sponsor dances with residents of nearby training schools.

Religious instruction and services are always provided in state training schools. A full-time Protestant chaplain and a part-time Roman Catholic chaplain are available in most schools; unlike in adult prisons, Muslim, Buddhist, Native American, and Jewish religious leaders generally are not available. Religious services that are offered include Sunday Mass and morning worship, confession, baptism, instruction for church membership, choir, and religious counseling. Usually few residents respond to these religious services unless attendance is compulsory, and then residents respond with considerable resistance.

The punishment of misbehaving residents varies from school to school. Fortunately, blatant staff brutality has disappeared from most schools—adult correctional systems have had enough problems with the federal courts that state governments do not want confinement conditions in their juvenile institutions to be declared unconstitutional. The amount of time residents spend in solitary confinement, or maximum isolation, is also generally less than it was in the 1980s. The use of force and mechanical restraints in training schools increased in the 1990s when training schools began to use handcuffs, anklets, security belts, four-point ties, and straitjackets.[56] Increasing numbers of staff seemed to believe that restraints were needed to control residents.[57] The danger is that improperly applied mechanical restraints that are applied for excessively long periods of time can result in serious physical injury or emotional trauma to a juvenile.

Evaluation of Public versus Private Training Schools   One of the debates that has raged for years concerns the comparison of public and private training schools. Privately administered training schools are usually better known to the public than are state institutions because private institutions' soliciting of funds has kept them in the public eye. Proponents of private institutions claim that they are more effective than public training schools; they have a limited intake policy, which allows them to choose whom they want to admit, and they can be more flexible and innovative.

A real problem of evaluating **private juvenile placements** is that few studies have examined the accuracy of these claims or the effects of institutional life on residents. Peter W. Greenwood, Susan Turner, and Kathy Rosenblatt's 1989 evaluation of the Paint Creek Youth Center (PCYC) in southern Ohio is probably the most positive evaluation of a private institutional placement for juveniles.[58] Their evaluation claimed that this program is different from the traditional training school because it is small (33 beds); because it features a comprehensive and integrated therapeutic approach that emphasizes accountability, social learning, and positive peer culture; and because it has been able to implement family therapy and intensive aftercare services.[59]

Examining a group of youths who supposedly were randomly assigned to PCYC or to the Training Institution Central Ohio (TICO) or to other Department of Youth Services (DYS) institutions, Greenwood and colleagues found that the experimental subjects (those who had been assigned to PCYC) were less likely to

private juvenile placement A training school that operates under private auspices. The county or state generally pays the school a per diem rate for the care of youths committed to these facilities.

have been recommitted to a correctional institution on new charges than were the controls (those who had been assigned to TICO and other DYS facilities).[60]

David Shichor and Clemens Bartollas's 1990 examination of the patterns of public and private juvenile placements in one of the larger probation departments in southern California revealed that relatively few differences were apparent between juveniles who were sent to public and private placements. Although youths in public institutions appeared to be somewhat more delinquent and youths who were placed in private facilities had more personal problems, the two populations did not vary markedly. Several other claims made by advocates of private placements also were not documented by this study, especially the claims that private placements provide more professional and treatment services to juveniles than do public placements and that private placements have lower staff–client ratios than do public placements; furthermore, this study found that hard-core delinquents in private placements were not separated from those who had committed more minor offenses.[61]

A fair assessment of private placements is that, with some glaring exceptions, private training schools are usually more flexible and innovative than state facilities. The smaller size of private training schools is somewhat balanced by the fact that one-half of them still house 100 or more residents, numbers that are too large for effective work with institutionalized juveniles. Perhaps the old adage is right after all: The best institutions are private ones, and the worst juvenile institutional placements are also private ones.

Social Context: Training School Life

The nature of the **residential social system** (the social hierarchy established by inmates) is an important factor in the quality of life in a training school. The many empirical studies on the residential social system have consistently challenged the efficacy of juvenile institutionalization. Too many of these studies present a frightening picture of what a juvenile experiences during confinement, and these studies also have found that there are more similarities than differences in residential life in single-sex and coeducational institutions.

mycrimekit

Review Juvenile Institutionalization

residential social system The social hierarchy that is established by residents in an institution.

The Glen Mills School, which has been at its present location in Concordville, Pennsylvania, for over 100 years, is the oldest existing residential school for court-adjudicated male delinquents in the country. ▶ How large a role does residential placement play in the juvenile justice system?

Training Schools for Boys

Many studies of training schools for boys reflect an inmate society in which the strong take advantage of the weak. In their study of the State Industrial School for Boys in Golden, Colorado, Gordon E. Barker and W. Thomas Adams found two types of residential leaders: One held power through brute force, and the other ruled through charisma. According to these researchers, residents were involved in an unending battle for dominance and control.[62]

Howard W. Polsky studied a cottage in a residential treatment center in New York and found that the staff in Cottage 6 were unable to keep residential leaders from exploiting peers. The social hierarchy the researchers identified in this cottage had a pecking order, with those at the bottom of the status hierarchy finding life so debilitating that most of them ended up in mental hospitals.[63]

Sethard Fisher studied a small training school in California and identified victimization and patronage as two of the major behaviors taking place; he defined *victimization* as "a predatory practice whereby inmates of superior strength and knowledge of inmate lore prey on weaker and less knowledgeable inmates."[64] The word *patronage* referred to youths building "protective and ingratiating relationships with others more advantageously situated on the prestige ladder"; Fisher also saw victimization as being made up of physical attack, agitation, and exploitation.[65]

Clemens Bartollas, Stuart J. Miller, and Simon Dinitz's *Juvenile Victimization: The Institutional Paradox* examined the culture that end-of-the-line delinquents established in a maximum-security institution in Columbus, Ohio (TICO). In this training school, dominant youths exploited submissive ones in every way possible: 90% of the 150 residents were involved in this exploitation matrix, with 19% of exploiters never being exploited, 34% being exploiters and victims at different times, 21% being occasionally victims and never exploiters, 17% being chronic victims, and 10% being neither victims nor exploiters.[66]

In a 15-year follow-up evaluation of this training school, in 1989, Miller, Bartollas, and Dinitz found that the negative youth culture described in the 1976 study still thrived and that the strong still victimized the weak. Staff members were more disillusioned than they were at the time of the first study and also were more fearful of victimization from residents.[67]

M. Forst, J. Fagan, and T. S. Vivona, relying on data collected in both juvenile facilities and adult correctional facilities, found that 1.7% of youths in training schools reported having been sexually attacked while in the facility and that 8.6% (five times as many) of juveniles in adult correctional facilities reported such victimization while incarcerated during the previous 12 months.[68]

Following the passage and signing of the Prison Rape Elimination Act (PREA) of 2003, three major government-sponsored research effectors have provided additional insights about the conditions and scope of sexual victimization of confined juveniles. The first drew on a nationally representative sample of 7,073 youths held in 203 facilities and found that 3.6% of juveniles (1 in every 28) in residential facilities reported having been sexually victimized at least one time, that two-thirds (65%) of victimized youths reported that another youth victimized them, and that almost one-half (48%) reported that a staff member victimized them (totals are more than 100% due to some youths being victimized by multiple others and/or on multiple occasions).[69]

A second study involved the administrative records data collected by the Bureau of Justice Statistics because of the PREA-mandated study of the incidence and prevalence of sexual violence in U.S. correctional institutions. Data specific to juvenile institutions were available for 2004, and the rates of sexual victimization reported by authorities in juvenile institutions were more than 5% of confined juveniles.[70]

The third study conducted testing during 2007 in 12 facilities, which were located in six states and included 9 male facilities, 1 female facility, and 2 coeducational facilities. Across the sample, 19.7% of responding youths reported at least one incident of sexual victimization during the previous 12 months of confinement, and of these surveyed youths, 8.8% reported victimization as a result of force or threat of force, 8.7% reported it as a result of force or threat of force, and 8.7% reported it as a result of an exchange of sex for money, favors, or protection; in addition, 1 in every 13 youths (7.9%) reported having engaged in some form of nonconsensual sexual activity with a facility staff member.[71]

In sum, while there are many exceptions to the lawless environment described in these studies, an environment in which the strong take advantage of the weak, the fact is that the quality of life for residents in too many training schools is extremely problematic. Even more troubling are the high rates of staff involvement in the sexual victimization of residents.

Training Schools for Girls and Coeducational Institutions

training school for girls A correctional facility for long-term placement of adjudicated female juvenile delinquents.

Until 1960, studies on confined juvenile girls were as numerous as those on incarcerated adult females. The early studies found that girls in training schools became involved in varying degrees of lesbian alliances and pseudo-family relationships. Since 1970, only three major studies have been done on females' adjustment to training schools[72]:

1. Rose Giallombardo's *The Social World of Imprisoned Girls* examined three **training schools for girls** in various parts of the United States and found that a kinship system existed (with some variation) in each of the training schools. A pseudo-family membership organization was pervasive in all three institutions, whether it was called the "racket," the "sillies," or "chick business," and encompassed 84% of the girls at the eastern institution, 83% at the central, and 94% at the western.[73] Some of the social roles identified were "true butches," "true fems," "trust-to-be butches," "trust-to-be fems," "jive time butches," "jive time fems," "straights," "squealers," "pimps," "foxes," "cops," and "popcorns."[74]

2. Alice Propper's *Prison Homosexuality* examined three coeducational and four female training schools scattered through the East, Midwest, and South, of which five were public and two were private Catholic training schools, with residents reporting homosexual behavior involving from 6% to 29% of the inmates in the various institutions. Propper found that the best indicator of homosexual participation during a juvenile's present term of institutionalization was previous homosexuality. In contrast to previously held assumptions, Propper found very little overlap between pseudo-family roles and homosexual behavior: Participation in homosexuality and make-believe families was just as prevalent in coeducational as in single-sex institutions, and homosexuality was as prevalent in treatment-oriented as in custody-oriented facilities. She also reported that residents sometimes continued homosexual experiences when they were released, even when their first experience was as the unhappy victim of a homosexual rape.[75]

3. Christopher M. Sieverdes and Clemens Bartollas's study of six coeducational institutions in a southeastern state drew the following conclusions: Females adhered more strongly to inmate groups and peer relationships than did males; they felt more victimized by peers than did males; they did not harass or manipulate staff as much as males did; and they were more satisfied with institutional life than were males.[76] Unlike Propper's study, these researchers found that pseudo-families existed among girls but were based much less on homosexual alliances than were those in all-girls training schools.[77] Status offenders, who made up 70% of the girls and 30% of the boys, were the worst victims in these training schools and had the most difficulty adjusting to institutional life.[78] White males and females experienced high rates of personal intimidation and victimization by African-American and American Indian youths.[79]

Rights of Confined Juveniles

The rights of institutionalized juveniles have been examined by the federal courts and addressed in the Civil Rights of Institutionalized Persons Act (CRIPA). CRIPA gives the Civil Rights Division of the U.S. Department of Justice (DOJ) the power to bring actions against state or local governments for violating the civil rights of institutionalized persons.

U.S. Courts

The U.S. courts long paid less attention to juvenile institutions than to adult prisons because juvenile facilities were assumed to be more humane and to infringe less on the constitutional rights of offenders. However, deteriorating conditions in juvenile correctional facilities, including the overcrowded living conditions, the frequent assaults among residents and against staff, and the growing presence of gang youths, led to a wave of litigation in the latter decades of the twentieth century. The courts have mandated three major rights: the right to treatment, the right to be free from cruel and unusual punishment, and the right to access to the courts.

Right to Treatment   Several court decisions have held that a juvenile has a **right to treatment** when he or she is committed to a juvenile institution.[80] In the *Morales* v. *Turman* decision (1973), the U.S. District Court for the Eastern District of Texas issued the most extensive order ever justified by a child's right to treatment[81]: The court held that the state of Texas had to follow a number of criteria to ensure that proper treatment would be provided to confined juveniles.[82] Among these criteria were minimum standards for assessing and testing a youth committed to the state; minimum standards for assessing educational skills and handicaps and for providing programs aimed at advancing a youth's education; minimum standards for delivering vocational education and medical and psychiatric care; and minimum standards for providing a humane institutional environment. But the order was vacated by the Fifth Circuit Court of Appeals on the grounds that a three-judge court should have been convened to hear the case. The U.S. Supreme Court, however, reversed the Fifth Circuit Court of Appeals and remanded the case, and the order of the U.S. District Court for the Eastern District of Texas has withstood the assault against it and ultimately prevailed.[83]

right to treatment The entitlement of a juvenile who has been committed to a training school to receive any needed services (e.g., therapy, education).

Right to Be Free from Cruel and Unusual Punishment   Considerable case law has also been established ensuring confined juveniles the right to be free from **cruel and unusual punishment**.[84] Federal courts have held that extended periods of solitary confinement and the use of Thorazine and other medications for the purpose of control represent cruel and unusual punishment.[85] In a 1995 case, *Alexander* v. *Boyd and South Carolina Department of Juvenile Justice*, the district court ruled that the use of gas in three training schools to punish juveniles for disciplinary infractions violated the juveniles' due process rights; in its decision, the court noted that the use of gas irritates the mucous membranes of those who are exposed to it and causes instant pain and spasms in the eyelids, breathing problems, and coughing fits.[86]

cruel and unusual punishment A guarantee provided by the Eighth Amendment to the U.S. Constitution against inhumane punishments. Accordingly, juveniles in correctional custody must not be treated with unnecessary harshness.

Right to Access to the Courts   Juveniles committed to training schools have a constitutional right of access to the courts.[87] In *Germany* v. *Vance* (1989), the first Circuit Court of Appeals held that the stigma of violating the law, being arrested, and being incarcerated is similar for juveniles and adults, so juveniles have a constitutional right to court access like that enjoyed by adults.[88] Finally, in *John L.* v. *Adams* (1992), the Sixth Circuit Court of Appeals held that juveniles have a constitutional right of access to the courts, finding that, for purposes of access, no substantial legal differences could be found between an incarcerated juvenile and an incarcerated adult.[89]

CRIPA and Juvenile Correctional Facilities

Through November 1997, the Civil Rights Division had investigated 300 institutions under CRIPA; 73 of these institutions, or about 25%, were juvenile detention and correctional facilities. The Civil Rights Division was monitoring conditions in 34 juvenile correctional facilities through consent decrees in Kentucky, New Jersey, and Puerto Rico. The consent decree filed in Kentucky included all 13 juvenile facilities in the state, the decree in New Jersey was with 1 facility, and the decree in Puerto Rico was with 20 facilities.[90]

Review Rights of Institutionalized Juveniles

Juvenile Aftercare

Release is the prime goal of a confined youth. The days, weeks, months, and sometimes years spent in confinement are occupied by thoughts and fantasies of release or even escape. The entire juvenile justice system is focused on release. Staff are responsible for guiding residents throughout their confinement, with punishment, education and vocational training, and rehabilitative techniques being used in an effort to guarantee that a resident's return to the community will be permanent and positive.

juvenile aftercare The supervision of juveniles who are released from correctional institutions so that they can make an optimal adjustment to community living.

Parole, or **juvenile aftercare**, as it is usually called, is concerned with the release of a youth from an institution when he or she can best benefit from release and can make an optimal adjustment to community living. A major concern in juvenile justice in the past 40 years has been the development of a workable philosophy and concept of aftercare. A number of objectives for juvenile aftercare or parole have been developed through the years:

1. Release residents from confinement at the most favorable time for community adjustment.
2. Prepare youths for their successful community completion of aftercare.
3. Reduce the crimes committed by released juveniles.
4. Reduce the violent acts committed by released offenders.
5. Increase the confidence of the community in the system of parole.
6. Alleviate overcrowding of training schools.
7. Monitor youthful offenders as they refrain from trafficking in or abusing drugs.
8. Discourage the return of youths to street gangs.

The achievement of these objectives requires extensive planning and research. For example, determining the most favorable time for release requires far more knowledge than is presently available. Many new and innovative techniques for prediction can be devised, and research must enable releasing authorities to compare the costs of leaving juveniles in institutions with the possible harm to society if they are released.

There is some question whether any method is effective in knowing when to release an institutionalized youth. For example, a study of 16,779 juveniles in Florida released from community programs to the community found that there was no consistent relationship between length of confinement and recidivism. The length of confinement, this 2008 study found, was only significant for male offenders released from high-risk facilities.[91]

Once a youth is adjudicated to a state training school, the state normally retains jurisdiction until his or her release. The authority to make the decision about when to release a youth from training school is usually given to institutional staff, although a number of states give other agencies and boards the authority to parole juveniles. Often the cottage staff will review the progress of each youth at designated intervals, and when the staff recommend release, the recommendation is reviewed by a board made up of staff from throughout the institution. If this board concurs, the recommendation must be approved by an institutional coordinator at the youth authority or youth commission.

Administration and Operation of Aftercare Services

Aftercare is the responsibility of the state and is administered by the executive branch in 44 states. In 4 states, aftercare is under the organization of the probation department and is administered by probation officers, and in 4 states, other means of organizing and administering aftercare are used.[92]

halfway house A residential setting for adjudicated delinquents, usually those who need a period of readjustment to the community following institutional confinement.

The aftercare or probation officer (probation officers in many jurisdictions have aftercare youths as part of their caseloads) who is responsible for the case sometimes corresponds with or may even visit the institutionalized youth in training school. In many states, a youth cannot be released until the aftercare officer approves the home placement plan submitted by the institutional home worker, which usually involves a visit to the home by the officer to make certain that the home is a good placement. At other times, the aftercare officer must locate an alternate placement, such as a foster home, group home, or **halfway house**.

An **interstate compact** is sometimes initiated when a youth has no acceptable home placement within his or her own state. The institutional social worker usually contacts the appropriate agency in another state where the youth has a possible placement and submits an interstate compact for the transfer of the youth to that state after release from training school. The state of original jurisdiction retains authority over the youth and is kept advised of the juvenile's status.

Part of the problem in juvenile aftercare is that youthful offenders usually are sent back to the same communities (and same families) and exposed again to the same problems they could not handle earlier. Most of their friends are still around, and it is not long before a friend suggests that they commit another crime together. If the returnee is determined, he or she may be able to say, "Hey, get out of my face. I don't want to hear that business." But if the young person cannot find a job—and jobs are scarce for delinquent youths, who frequently are school dropouts—or is under financial pressure, it becomes harder and harder not to return to crime.

Most youths on aftercare status are placed on supervision in the community for a year or more after their release. The aftercare officer, who is expected to monitor the behavior of youths under supervision, provides each youth with a list of rules; these rules usually resemble those given to adult parolees and pertain to such matters as obeying parents, maintaining a satisfactory adjustment at school or at work, being home at a certain time every night, avoiding contact with other delinquents, avoiding use or possession of any narcotic, and reporting to the aftercare officer as requested.

interstate compact The procedure for transferring a youth on probation or aftercare/parole from one state to another.

Risk Control and Crime Reduction

The current emphasis in aftercare is on short-term behavior control. The OJJDP has developed an intensive aftercare program that incorporates the principles of preparing youths for release to the community, facilitating youth–community interaction and involvement, and monitoring youths' reintegration into the community.[93]

Similar to juvenile probation, ISPs are being increasingly used—as of 1992, there were over 80 aftercare ISPs in the United States.[94] The most noteworthy of these intensive programs are the ones in the 30 counties of Pennsylvania; "Lifeskills 95", the Violent Juvenile Offender Research and Development Program in Boston, Memphis,

A 15-year-old juvenile lives in separate housing for juveniles in an Orange County, Florida, jail. The color of the teenager's ID bracelet identifies him as a high-risk maximum-security inmate.
▶ **Why should juveniles be separated from adults when confined?**

FIGURE 16.5 Intervention Model for Juvenile Intensive Aftercare

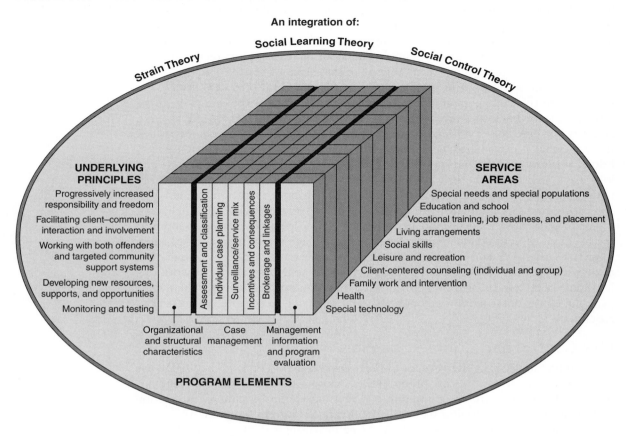

Source: David Altschuler et al., *Reintegration, Supervised Release, and Intensive Aftercare* (Washington, D.C.: Office of Juvenile Justice and Delinquency Prevention, 1999).

Library Extra 16.8

OJJDP Juvenile Justice Bulletin: "Aftercare Services"

Newark, and Detroit; the Skillman Intensive Aftercare Project; the Michigan Nokomis Challenge Program; the PARJO program in New York; and OJJDP's Intensive Aftercare Program (IAP).

There has also been a focus on developing an integrated theoretical framework for guiding intensive supervision of chronic juvenile offenders (see Library Extra 16.8). Based largely on combinations of social control, strain, and social learning theories, the IAP model focuses on the reintegrative process[95] (Figure 16.5 shows the program elements of this model). Underlying assumptions of this model are that chronic and serious delinquency is related to weak controls produced by social disorganization, inadequate socialization, and strain; that strain is produced by social disorganization independent of weak controls; and that peer group influences intervene as a social force between youths with weak bonds and/or strain on the one hand and delinquent behaviors on the other.[96]

This IAP model was initially implemented in Clark County (Las Vegas), Nevada; Arapaho, Douglas, and Jefferson Counties and metropolitan Denver, Colorado; Essex, Newark, and Camden Counties, New Jersey; and the city of Norfolk, Virginia. The participation of the New Jersey counties ended in 1997, but the other three programs have carried through on preparing high-risk offenders for progressively increased responsibility and freedom in the community. These programs' well-developed transition components, which begin shortly after a youth is adjudicated to an institution and continue through the early months of community adjustment, are particularly striking (see Table 16.2 for these transition components). The results of the first five years of implementation (1995–2000) revealed a dramatically improved level of communication and coordination between institutional and aftercare staff as well as the ability to involve parolees in community services almost immediately after institutional release.[97]

TABLE 16.2 Transition Components of Intensive Aftercare Programs			
	Intensive Aftercare Programming Site		
Transition Component	**Colorado**	**Nevada**	**Virginia**
Early Parole Planning	Initial plan complete at 30 days after institutional placement; final plan complete at 60 days prior to release.	Initial plan complete at 30 days after institutional placement; final plan complete 30 days prior to furlough.	Initial plan complete 30 days after institutional placement; final plan complete 30 days prior to release.
Multiple Perspectives Incorporated in Plan	Case manager, institutional staff, youth, parents, and community providers all routinely involved.	Parole officer, institutional community liaison, institutional staff, and youth; parent participation limited.	Parole officer, institutional case manager, youth, interagency "Community Assessment Team," and parent.
Parole Officer Visits to Institution	One to two times per week; routine.	Once per month; routine since spring 1997.	One to two times per month; routine.
Treatment Begun in Institution and Continued in Community	Via community providers. Includes multifamily counseling, life skills training, individual counseling, and vocational skills training; done routinely.	Via an institution–community liaison and parole officers. Includes life skills and drug/alcohol curriculums; done routinely until liaison vacancy.	Via one provider at Hanover only. Drug/alcohol treatment; sporadic use; state policy discourages contract services by community providers for institutionalized youth.
Youth Prerelease Visits to Community	Supervised day trips to community programs, beginning 60 days prior to release.	Not allowed.	Not allowed.
Preparole Furlough	Overnight/weekend home passes, beginning 30 days prior to release.	Thirty-day conditional release to community, prior to official parole.	Not allowed.
Transitional Residence	Not part of the design, but occurs for some youth.	Not part of the design.	Two group homes in Norfolk; 30- to 60-day length of stay; used for most youth.
Transitional Day Programming	Two day-treatment programs in Denver; used for almost all youth during the first few months after release.	One day-treatment supervision/treatment program; used for most youth.	Day treatment used for youth who do not go to group homes.
Phased Supervision Levels on Parole	Informal system: contact once per week during the first few months, down to once per month later.	Four-phase system: contact four times per week during furlough; three times per week next 90 days; two times per week next 60–90 days; once per week next 30–60 days.	Four-phase system: group home; contact five to seven times per week next 60 days; three to five times per week next 60 days; three times per week last 30 days.

Source: Richard G. Wiebush, Betsie McNulty, and Thao Le, *Implementation of the Intensive Community-Based Aftercare Program* (Washington, D.C.: Office of Juvenile Justice and Delinquency Prevention, 2000), p. 2.

In-house detention and EM programs still have not received the attention that they deserve in juvenile aftercare.[98] Juvenile aftercare also emphasizes drug and alcohol urinalyses (sometimes called "drug drops") and continues to use boot camp programs as a means of releasing juveniles early from training schools.

In both traditional and intensive aftercare, if a rule is violated or a law is broken, a youth may be returned to a training school. Although guidelines for the **revocation of aftercare** for juveniles have not been formulated by court decisions, revocation of a youth's aftercare status is no longer based solely on the testimony of the aftercare officer, who could be influenced by personality clashes or prejudice toward the client. Today most jurisdictions have formal procedures for the revocation of aftercare. The aftercare officer may initially investigate the charge; if the finding is that the youth did commit the offense, the officer will report the parole violation to the supervisor. The supervisor may review the case and make the decision, or a revocation committee may

revocation of aftercare The cancellation of parole and return of the offender to an institution. It takes effect if a juvenile on aftercare commits another offense or violates the conditions of parole.

examine the violation. The aftercare officer may be required to submit a written recommendation for revocation but is not allowed to testify, and the youth is permitted to speak in his or her own defense.

Juveniles in Adult Prison

Juveniles who end up in prison have usually been transferred to the adult court and been given a prison sentence. They soon discover that adult correctional institutions are a world apart from nearly all training schools: Prisons are much larger, some containing several thousand inmates, and can cover acres of ground; life on the inside is typically austere, crowded, and dangerous; and the violent and exploitative relationships that are found in adult correctional institutions make this disposition a hard one for juveniles, who are particularly vulnerable to sexual victimization and physical assault.[99]

Some variations on the practice of confining juveniles in adult institutions exist among the states. In some jurisdictions, judges have no alternative but to place juveniles in adult institutions if the law requires it, but judges in a few states (under special circumstances) can place youths in either juvenile or adult institutions, whereas judges in some other states can refer juveniles back to juvenile court, but they are then transferred to adult institutions when they come of age.[100]

In October 2000, Indiana stopped sending juveniles convicted of adult crimes into the general prison population. Those with lesser offenses are now held at the medium-security Plainfield Correctional Facility or at the minimum-security Medaryville Correctional Facility, but Indiana juveniles who commit violent or serious offenses are sent to Wabash Valley, a maximum-security facility.[101]

In 2002, an estimated 4,100 new court commitments involving juveniles younger than 18 years old were sent to adult state prison. Between 1985 and 2002, the annual number of new court commitments to state prisons involving juveniles younger than age 18 increased 22%, with new commitments overall increasing 114%.[102]

In one study, Kelly Dedel Johnson, director of One in 37 Research, Inc., in Portland, Oregon, found that 13 states permit the transfer of juveniles to adult facilities: California, Colorado, Hawaii, Indiana, Kentucky, Massachusetts, New Jersey, New York, Rhode Island, South Carolina, Texas, Washington, and Wisconsin. The court has authority to make such transfers in one-third of these states, the commitment agency has authority in one-third, and the transfer decision is a joint agreement between two authorities (e.g., agency and court or juvenile and adult agency) in one-third. The reasons for such transfers include age of the offender, seriousness of the offense, failure to benefit from the program, and poor institutional adjustment. A violent attack on a staff member by an older resident with an initial serious offense, for example, would be the type of case most likely leading to a transfer from a juvenile facility to an adult prison.[103]

Delinquency across the Life Course: The Impact of Institutionalization on Juveniles

We do know that the recidivism rates in juvenile corrections have consistently been extremely high[104]; we also know that youths who are released from institutions of the juvenile justice system have a high percentage of going on to adult crime.[105] As one study put it, "Institutionalized juveniles, particularly violent offenders, constitute the population most at risk of becoming the next generation of adult prisoners."[106] We further know that violent juveniles pose particular challenges to institutional staff and have high rates of subsequent recidivism.[107]

There have been two schools of thought concerning institutional impact. One school questions the efficacy of what takes place in long-term institutional stays, arguing that juvenile institutionalization provides a "school of crime" that has existed for generations; in addition, as previously discussed, most juveniles experience some form of victimization, and some even experience sexual assaults. More recently, a number of studies have also questioned the efficacy of juvenile institutionalization: One study found that little evidence exists that increased lengths of stay in juvenile institutions have reduced recidivism[108]; a second study found that the longer the length of the initial confinement was, the greater the number of subsequent convictions[109]; and another study asserted that incarcerating juveniles beyond the point of rehabilitation may make them more dangerous than they were when initially incarcerated and may impede successful community reintegration following release.[110]

The other school of thought has reached opposite conclusions about the value of juvenile institutionalization: One study found recidivism to be much higher among noninstitutionalized youths than among those who had been institutionalized[111]; a second study evaluating youths in Maryland concluded that institutionalization seemed to be more effective in reducing crime than noninstitutionalization.[112]

More research is clearly needed to further examine the positive and negative effects of confinement on juvenile reoffending. Future research must include an analysis of program quality and treatment and needs to consider institutional impact on various types of youths.[113] The fact remains that those released from juvenile institutions currently have high rates of recidivism, that they too frequently go on to commit adult crimes, and that sometimes they end up spending much— if not most—of their lives in prison or even on death row.

Voices of Delinquency

Read "My Father Was an Alcoholic." Did training school have any effect on the person featured in this article? What could have been done for this youth so that he had a positive outcome? Would it bother you if someone you worked with (as one of the authors worked with this youth) ended up on death row?

Delinquency and Social Policy: Juveniles' Safety during Institutionalization

For policy makers, one of the most serious issues related to juvenile institutionalization is providing for the safety of residents. PREA (2003) is a reminder of the importance of residents' safety. Various studies have identified a number of factors related to higher levels of sexual violence:

- Being in a long-term secure facility
- Having been physically assaulted
- Having been robbed in the facility
- Being under 14 years of age
- Being female
- Having a longer term of commitment (but victimization is most likely early in the resident's stay)
- Having a gang presence in the facility
- Being a member of a gang
- Having serious charges (those with the most serious charges in their units have the highest risk of victimization)
- Being of mixed or "other" race
- Having high amounts of contraband in the facility[114]

The National Prison Rape Elimination Commission has proposed a set of standards designed to create zero-tolerance policies for juvenile correctional institutions. These 2008 standards emphasized the need for heightened protection of those youths identified as vulnerable to sexual assault without restricting their access to the programs and other rights and privileges of the other confined youths, and they specifically rejected the policies of some facilities of placing lesbian, gay, bisexual, and transgender youths in segregation housing or in isolation. The standards go on to say that whenever possible, facilities should transfer victims of sexual abuse to outside health care providers for forensic medical exams to avoid a conflict of interest or a potential conflict and that all juvenile residents should have access to outside victim advocates and mental health professionals for emotional support that is needed to deal with sexual abuse. Moreover, upon receiving an allegation of sexual abuse, the head of the juvenile facility must report the allegation to the head of the juvenile agency, the juvenile court that adjudicated the victim's case, and the parents or guardians of the victims (in most cases).[115]

Chapter Summary

This chapter examines juvenile corrections, including probation, community-based treatment, institutionalization, and aftercare. Among the most important issues discussed in this chapter are the following:

- Today more delinquents are treated in the community than are adjudicated to training schools, because juvenile judges remain supportive of the least restrictive or soft-line approach for minor offenders.

- Community-based corrections include probation, residential and day-treatment programs, and aftercare.

- Clients placed on probation or in aftercare are more likely to participate in intensive supervision programs than in the past.

- Youths who have failed on probation or who have committed serious crimes are likely to be assigned to a public or private juvenile correctional placement.

- Long-term juvenile institutions consist of forestry camps and ranches, boot camps, and training schools.

- Although the proportion of juveniles who are sent to long-term facilities is small, these institutions of last resort are an integral part of society's efforts to exercise control over juveniles who break the law.

- Training schools tend to be quite expensive, but the length of time residents spend there, the programs that are offered, and the nature of the peer subcultures that exist within them tend to vary from state to state and even from training school to training school.

- Aftercare (or parole, as it is called in some states) has much in common with probation. Indeed, in some jurisdictions, the same officer is responsible for both a probation and aftercare caseload.

- Juveniles who are transferred to adult court may be sentenced to spend time in an adult prison.

Key Terms

boot camp, p. 377
community-based
   corrections, p. 363
community service project, p. 369
community volunteer, p. 371
cruel and unusual
   punishment, p. 385
day-treatment program, p. 373
forestry camp, p. 376
foster care, p. 372
group home, p. 372

group home model, p. 372
halfway house, p. 386
interstate compact, p. 387
juvenile aftercare, p. 386
Outward Bound, p. 374
private juvenile placement, p. 381
probation, p. 363
probation officer, p. 364
ranch, p. 376
reception and diagnostic
   center, p. 375

remote location monitoring, p. 370
residential social system, p. 382
restitution, p. 367
revocation of aftercare, p. 389
right to treatment, p. 385
social history report, p. 365
surveillance, p. 367
teaching family group
   model, p. 372
training school for girls, p. 384
volunteer program, p. 371

Review Questions

1. What is the purpose of probation?
2. What are the three basic functions of probation services?
3. What are the various forms of risk control being used today? How does each work?
4. What are the three types of residential and day-treatment programs? How does each function?

5. What are the main types of juvenile institutions? How do these types differ?
6. What are the main types of programs that take place during an institutional stay?
7. What is aftercare? Why is this transition to the community so important?

Discussion Questions

1. What are the job responsibilities of a probation officer?
2. Given their notoriously heavy caseloads, is it responsible to blame probation officers when a juvenile probationer reoffends? Are probation officers made scapegoats by the media? Explain your responses.
3. What are the differences between probation and aftercare services?
4. Of the programs discussed in this chapter, which do you believe is the most effective for helping offenders reintegrate into the community?
5. How effective are community-based corrections programs? What can be done to improve the effectiveness of community-based corrections?
6. How effective are training schools? What can be done to make training schools more effective?

Group Exercises

1. Invite a local probation officer to address the class regarding his or her role in the juvenile justice process.
2. Have the students clip newspaper articles related to residential and day-treatment programs for juvenile offenders in your state. Discuss them in class.
3. Have the students compare recidivism rates for juveniles who have completed the Outward Bound and Associated Marine Institutes programs and compare them to the recidivism rates for juvenile offenders on conventional probation. Discuss their findings in class.
4. Have the students research how many juvenile offenders are currently electronically monitored and the annual cost of such monitoring compared to the cost of conventional supervision.

mycrimekit™

Go to mycrimekit.com to explore the following study tools and resources specific to this chapter:

- **Practice Quiz:** Practice with multiple-choice, true/false, short-answer, and essay questions.

- **WebQuests:** Do web activities about juvenile corrections officer work.
- **Flashcards:** Use 29 flashcards to test your knowledge of the chapter's key terms.

Glossary

This glossary includes all of the key terms listed in each of the chapters and incorporates selected terms adapted from the FBI's *Uniform Crime Reporting Handbook,* the *Juvenile Court Statistics* report series, and the Census of Juveniles in Residential Placement. The National Center for Juvenile Justice's *State Juvenile Justice Profiles* was also influential in determining the content of selected definitions.

academic performance The achievement in schoolwork as rated by grades and other assessment measures. Poor academic performance is a factor in delinquency.

adjudication The court process wherein a judge determines if the juvenile appearing before the court committed the act with which he or she is charged. The term *adjudicated* is analogous to convicted in the adult criminal justice system and indicates that the court concluded that the juvenile committed the act.

adjudicatory hearing The stage of juvenile court proceedings that usually includes the youth's plea, the presentation of evidence by the prosecution and by the defense, the cross-examination of witnesses, and a finding by the judge as to whether the allegations in the petition can be sustained.

adjustment model A rehabilitative correctional approach that emphasizes helping delinquents demonstrate responsible behavior.

adolescence The life interval between childhood and adulthood; usually the period between the ages of 12 and 18 years.

adult court Criminal courts that hear the cases of adults charged with crimes and to which juveniles who are accused of having committed serious offenses can be waived (transferred). In some states, adult criminal courts have jurisdiction over juveniles who are accused of committing certain specified offenses.

aftercare The supervision of juveniles who are released from correctional institutions so that they can make an optimal adjustment to community living; also, the status of a juvenile conditionally released from a treatment or confinement facility and placed under supervision in the community.

age of onset The age at which a child begins to commit delinquent acts; an important dimension of delinquency.

alcohol A drug made through a fermentation process that relaxes inhibitions.

alternative school A facility that provides an alternative educational experience, usually in a different location, for youths who are not doing satisfactory work in the public school setting.

amphetamine A stimulant drug that occurs in a variety of forms.

appeal The review of juvenile court proceedings by a higher court. Although no constitutional right of appeal exists for juveniles, the right of adjudicated juveniles to appeal has been established by statute in some states.

appellate review The review of the decision of a juvenile court proceeding by a higher court. Decisions by appellate courts, including the U.S. Supreme Court, have greatly affected the development of juvenile court law and precedent.

arrest The process of taking a person into custody for an alleged violation of the law. Juveniles who are under arrest have nearly all the due process safeguards accorded to adults.

attention deficit hyperactivity disorder (ADHD) A cognitive disorder of childhood that can include inattention, distractibility, excessive activity, restlessness, noisiness, impulsiveness, and so on.

attention home An innovative form of detention facility, found in several locations across the nation, that is characterized by an open setting.

autonomic nervous system The system of nerves that govern reflexes, glands, the iris of the eye, and activities of interior organs that are not subject to voluntary control.

bail The money or property pledged to the court or actually deposited with the court to effect the release of a person from legal custody. Juveniles do not have a constitutional right to bail as do adults.

balanced and restorative model An integrative correctional model that seeks to reconcile the interests of victims, offenders, and communities through programs and supervision practices.

behavior modification A psychological treatment method that rewards appropriate behavior positively, immediately, and systematically and assumes that rewards increase the occurrence of desired behavior.

beyond a reasonable doubt A legal standard establishing the degree of proof needed for a juvenile to be adjudicated a delinquent by the juvenile court during the adjudicatory stage of the court's proceedings.

bifurcated hearing A split adjudication and disposition hearing, which is the present trend of the juvenile court.

binding over The process of transferring (also called certifying) juveniles to adult criminal court. Binding over takes place after a judicial hearing on a juvenile's amenability to treatment or his or her threat to public safety.

biological positivism The belief that juveniles' biological characteristics and limitations drive them to delinquent behavior.

birth order The sequence of births in a family and a child's position in it, whether firstborn, middle, or youngest child.

blended sentencing The imposition of juvenile and/or adult correctional sanctions on serious and violent juvenile offenders who have been adjudicated in juvenile court or convicted in criminal court.

blocked opportunity The limited or nonexistent chance of success; according to strain theory, a key factor in delinquency.

body-type theory The theory developed by William Sheldon, Sheldon Glueck, Eleanor Glueck, and others, who proposed that youths with the mesomorphic (bony, muscular, and athletic) body type are more likely to be delinquent than are those with the endomorphic (soft, round, and fat) and ectomorphic (tall, thin, and fragile) body types.

boot camp A military-style facility used as an alternative to prison in order to deal with prison crowding and public demands for severe punishment.

born criminal An individual who is atavistic, who reverts to an earlier evolutionary level and is unable to conform his or her behavior to the requirements of modern society; thus, an individual who is innately criminal.

Breed* v. *Jones   A 1975 double jeopardy case in which the U.S. Supreme Court ruled that a juvenile court cannot adjudicate a case and then transfer the case to the criminal court for adult processing of the same offense.

broken home   A family in which parents are divorced or are no longer living together.

brother–sister incest   Sexual activity that occurs between brother and sister.

bullying   The hurtful, frightening, or menacing actions undertaken by one person to intimidate another (generally weaker) person, to gain that person's unwilling compliance, and/or to put him or her in fear.

capitalism   An economic system in which private individuals or corporations own and control capital (wealth and the means of production) and in which competitive free markets control prices, production, and distribution of goods.

child abuse   The mistreatment of children by parents or caregivers. Physical abuse is intentional behavior directed toward a child by the parent or caregiver to cause pain, injury, or death. Emotional abuse involves a disregard of a child's psychological needs. Sexual abuse is any intentional and wrongful physical contact with a child that entails a sexual purpose or component, and such sexual abuse is termed *incest* when the perpetrator is a member of the child's family. Also see *child sexual abuse.*

child savers   A name given to an organized group of progressive social reformers of the late nineteenth and early twentieth centuries who promoted numerous laws aimed at protecting children and institutionalizing an idealized image of childhood innocence.

child sexual abuse   Any intentional and wrongful physical contact with a child that entails a sexual purpose or component. Such sexual abuse is termed *incest* when the perpetrator is a member of the child's family.

chivalry factor   The idea that the justice system tends to treat adolescent females and women more leniently because of their gender.

chronic youthful offender   A juvenile who engages repeatedly in delinquent behavior. The Philadelphia cohort studies defined chronic offenders as youths who had committed five or more delinquent offenses. Other studies use this term to refer to a youth involved in serious and repetitive offenses.

citation   A summons to appear in juvenile court.

clearance by arrest   The solution of a crime by arrest of a perpetrator who has confessed or who has been implicated by witnesses or evidence. Clearances can also occur by exceptional means, as when a suspected perpetrator dies prior to arrest.

club drug   A synthetic psychoactive substance often found at nightclubs, bars, raves, and dance parties. Club drugs include MDMA (Ecstasy), ketamine, methamphetamine (meth), gamma-butyrolactone (GBL), phencyclidine (PCP), and Rohypnol.

cocaine   A coca extract that creates mood elevation, elation, grandiose feelings, and feelings of heightened physical prowess.

cognitive theory   A perspective on human development that says children develop cognitive abilities through interaction with the physical and social worlds.

cohort   A generational group as defined in demographics, in statistics, or for the purpose of social research.

cohort study   Research that usually includes all individuals who were born in a specific year in a particular city or country and follows them through part or all of their lives.

"cold and brittle"   According to Travis Hirschi, the nature of interpersonal relationships among delinquents, specifically delinquents in gangs.

commitment   A determination made by a juvenile judge at the disposition stage of a juvenile court proceeding that a juvenile is to be sent to a juvenile correctional institution.

commitment to delinquency   David Matza's term for the attachment that a delinquent juvenile has to a deviant identity and values.

commitment to the social bond   The attachment that a juvenile has to conventional institutions and activities.

committed juvenile   A youth whose case has been adjudicated and disposed of in juvenile court or who has been convicted and sentenced in criminal court.

community-based corrections   A corrections program that includes probation, residential and day-treatment programs, and parole (aftercare). The nature of the linkages between community programs and their social environments is the most distinguishing feature of community-based corrections. As frequency, duration, and quality of community relationships increase, the programs become more community based.

community service project   A court-required restitution in which a juvenile spends a certain number of hours working in a community project.

community volunteer   An individual who donates his or her time to work with delinquents in the community.

complaint   A charge made to an intake officer of the juvenile court that an offense has been committed.

conduct norms   The rules of a group governing the ways its members should act under particular conditions, and the violation of these rules arouses a group reaction.

conflict theory   A perspective that holds that delinquency can be explained by socioeconomic class, by power and authority relationships, and by group and cultural differences.

consensual model   A model of society that views the social order as a persistently stable structure that is well integrated and that is based on a consensus of values.

consent decree   A formal agreement between a juvenile and the court in which the juvenile is placed under the court's supervision without a formal finding of delinquency.

constitutionalists   The name given to a group of twentieth-century reformers who advocated that juveniles deserve due process protections when they appear before the juvenile court.

containment theory   A theoretical perspective that strong inner containment and reinforcing external containment provide insulation against delinquent and criminal behavior.

control theory   Any of several theoretical approaches that maintain that human beings must be held in check, or somehow be controlled, if delinquent tendencies are to be repressed.

cottage system   A widely used treatment practice that places small groups of training school residents into cottages.

crack   A less expensive but more potent form of cocaine.

crime-control model   A correctional model supporting discipline and punishment as the most effective means of deterring youth crime.

criminal opportunity theory   A theory claiming that criminals tend to be attracted to targets that offer a high payoff with little risk of legal consequences.

criminal street gang   A formal or informal group or association of three or more individuals who commit two or more gang crimes in two or more separate criminal episodes.

critical criminologist   A social scientific thinker who combines Marxist theory with the insights of later theorists, such as Sigmund Freud.

cruel and unusual punishment   A guarantee provided by the Eighth Amendment to the U.S. Constitution against inhumane punishments. Accordingly, juveniles in correctional custody must not be treated with unnecessary harshness.

cultural deviance theory   A theory wherein delinquent behavior is viewed as an expression of conformity to cultural values and norms that are in opposition to those of the larger U.S. society.

culturally defined goals   In Merton's strain theory, the set of purposes and interests a culture defines as legitimate objectives for individuals.

cultural transmission theory   An approach that holds that areas of concentrated crime maintain their high rates over a long period, even when the composition of the population changes rapidly, because delinquent "values" become cultural norms and are passed from one generation to the next.

culture conflict theory   A perspective that delinquency or crime arises because individuals are members of a subculture that has conduct norms that are in conflict with those of the wider society.

curfew violation   The violation of an ordinance forbidding persons below a certain age from being in public places during set hours; a status offense.

day-treatment program   A court-mandated, community-based corrections program that juveniles attend in the morning and afternoon. They return home in the evening.

deinstitutionalization   The process of closing long-term institutions and moving residents to community-based corrections facilities. *Deincarceration* is another term used to describe this process.

Deinstitutionalization of Status Offenders (DSO) Project   A project that evaluated the effects of deinstitutionalization of status offenders in eight states and prompted a national evaluation.

delinquency prevention   An organized effort to forestall or prevent the development of delinquent behavior. See also *primary prevention, secondary prevention,* and *tertiary prevention.*

delinquent act   An act committed by a juvenile for which an adult could be prosecuted in a criminal court but when committed by a juvenile is within the jurisdiction of the juvenile court. Delinquent acts include crimes against persons, crimes against property, drug offenses, and crimes against public order when juveniles commit such acts.

delinquent sibling   A brother or sister who is engaged in delinquent behaviors; an apparent factor in youngsters' involvement in delinquency.

desistance   The termination of a delinquent career or behavior.

detention   The temporary restraint of a juvenile in a secure facility, usually because he or she is acknowledged to be dangerous either to self or to others.

detention center   A facility that provides custodial care for juveniles during juvenile court proceedings. Also called *juvenile halls* and *detention homes,* detention centers were established at the end of the nineteenth century as an alternative to jails for juveniles.

detention hearing   A hearing, usually conducted by an intake officer of the juvenile court, during which the decision is made as to whether a juvenile will be released to his or her parents or guardians or be detained in a detention facility.

determinate sentencing   A model of sentencing that provides fixed terms of sentences for criminal offenses. Terms are generally set by the legislature rather than determined by judicial discretion.

determinism   A philosophical position that suggests that individuals are driven into delinquent or criminal behavior by biological or psychological traits that are beyond their control.

developmental life-course (DLC) theory   A framework suggesting that four key factors determine the shape of the life course: location in time and place, linked lives, human agency, and timing of lives.

differential association theory   The view that delinquency is learned from others and that delinquent behavior is to be expected of individuals who have internalized a preponderance of definitions that are favorable to law violations.

differential identification theory   A modification of differential association theory that applies the interactionist concept of the self, allows for choice, and stresses the importance of motives.

differential opportunity structure   The differences in economic and occupational opportunities open to members of different socioeconomic classes.

disorderly conduct   The unlawful interruption of the peace, quiet, or order of a community. It includes offenses such as disturbing the peace, vagrancy, loitering, unlawful assembly, and rioting.

dispositional hearing   The stage of the juvenile court proceedings in which the juvenile judge decides the most appropriate placement for a juvenile who has been adjudicated a delinquent, a status offender, or a dependent child.

disproportionate minority confinement   The court-ordered confinement, in juvenile institutions, of members of minority groups in numbers disproportionate to their representation in the general population.

disruptive behavior   Unacceptable conduct at school. It may include defiance of authority, manipulation of teachers, inability or refusal to follow rules, fights with peers, destruction of property, use of drugs in school, and/or physical or verbal altercations with teachers.

diversion   The act of officially stopping or suspending a case prior to court adjudication and referring the juvenile to a community education, treatment, or work program in lieu of adjudication or incarceration. Successful completion of a diversion program results in the dismissal or withdrawal of formal charges.

diversion programs   Dispositional alternatives for youthful offenders that exist outside of the formal juvenile justice system.

double jeopardy   A common law and constitutional prohibition against a second trial for the same offense.

drift theory   The theoretical perspective that juveniles neutralize the moral hold of society and drift into delinquent behavior.

dropout A young person of school age who, of his or her own volition, no longer attends school.

drug addiction The excessive use of a drug, which is frequently characterized by physical and/or psychological dependence.

drug and alcohol abuse intervention A treatment modality in which drug-abusing juveniles are usually treated in a group context.

due process rights The constitutional rights that are guaranteed to citizens—whether adult or juvenile—during their contacts with the police, their proceedings in court, and their interactions with the public schools.

Ecstasy A form of amphetamine (MDMA) that began to be used by adolescents in the United States in the 1980s and 1990s and is now rather widespread.

electronic monitoring See *remote location monitoring.*

emerging gang Any youth gang that formed in the late 1980s and early 1990s in communities across the nation and that is continuing to evolve.

emotional abuse A disregard for the psychological needs of a child, including lack of expressed love, withholding of contact or approval, verbal abuse, unrealistic demands, threats, and psychological cruelty.

emotionality An aspect of temperament. It can range from a near absence of emotional response to intense, out-of-control emotional reactions.

escalation of offenses An increase in the frequency and severity of an individual's offenses; an important dimension of delinquency.

family size The number of children in a family; a possible risk factor for delinquency.

family therapy A counseling technique that involves treating all members of a family; a widely used method of dealing with a delinquent's socially unacceptable behavior.

father–daughter incest Sexual activity between a father and his daughter. Also refers to incest by stepfathers or the boyfriend(s) of the mother.

father–son incest Sexual activity between father and son. Also refers to incest by stepfathers or the boyfriend(s) of the mother.

felicific calculus A method for determining the sum total of pleasure and pain produced by an act; also the assumption that human beings strive to obtain a favorable balance of pleasure and pain.

felony A criminal offense punishable by death or by incarceration in a state or federal correctional institution, usually for one year or more.

feminist theory of delinquency A theory that adolescent females' victimization at home causes them to become delinquent and that this fact has been systematically ignored.

financial restitution See *restitution.*

fingerprinting A pretrial identification procedure used with both juveniles and adults following arrest.

focal concerns of the lower class The values or focal concerns (trouble, toughness, smartness, excitement, fate, and autonomy) of lower-class youths that differ from those of middle-class youths.

Folks One of the two supergangs comprising the major Chicago street gangs.

forestry camp A correctional facility where residents usually do conservation work in state parks, including cleaning up, cutting grass and weeds, and doing general maintenance.

foster care A home setting for juveniles who are lawfully removed from their birth parents' homes.

free will The ability to make rational choices among possible actions and to select one over the others.

friendship pattern The type of peer relationships that exist within a teenage culture.

gang A group of youths who are bound together by mutual interests, have identifiable leadership, and act in concert to achieve a specific purpose that generally includes the conduct of illegal activity.

gang unit A specialized unit established by some police departments to address the problem of gangs.

gender The personal traits, social positions, and values and beliefs that members of a society attach to being male or female.

gender role A societal definition of what constitutes either masculine or feminine behavior.

group home A placement for youths who have been adjudicated by the court that serves a group of about 13 to 25 youths as an alternative to institutionalization; also called *group residence, halfway house,* or *attention home.*

group home model A form of community-based residential program that has had some success with youthful offenders.

guided group interaction (GGI) An interaction occurring in the community or in an institution that places youthful offenders in an intensive group environment under the direction of an adult leader. The guided group interaction process substitutes a whole new structure of beliefs, values, and behaviors for the values of delinquent peer subcultures.

halfway house A residential setting for adjudicated delinquents, usually those who need a period of readjustment to the community following institutional confinement.

heroin A refined form of morphine that was introduced around the beginning of the twentieth century.

hidden delinquency Any unobserved or unreported delinquency.

home detention House arrest. This form of detention is used in some jurisdictions, and an adjudicated juvenile remains at home under the supervision of juvenile probation officers.

house of refuge An institution that was designed by eighteenth- and nineteenth-century reformers to provide an orderly, disciplined environment similar to that of the "ideal" Puritan family.

human agency The active role juveniles take in their lives; the fact that juveniles are not merely subject to social and structural constraints but make choices and decisions based on the alternatives that they see before them.

incest Any intrafamily sexual abuse that is perpetrated on a child by a member of that child's family group and that includes not only sexual intercourse but also any act designed to stimulate a child sexually or to use a child for sexual stimulation, either of the perpetrator or of another person.

incidence of delinquency The frequency with which delinquent behavior takes place.

incorrigible The characteristic of a juvenile who is beyond the control of parents, guardians, or custodians; also called *ungovernable.*

indeterminate sentencing In juvenile justice, a sentencing model that encourages rehabilitation through the use of general and relatively unspecific sentences. Under the model, a juvenile judge has wide discretion and can commit a juvenile to the department of corrections or youth authority until correctional staff make the decision to release the juvenile. This type of sentencing is used with juveniles in most jurisdictions other than those that have mandatory or determinate sentencing.

index offense The most serious type of offense reported in the FBI's Uniform Crime Reporting Program, including murder and nonnegligent manslaughter, forcible rape, robbery, aggravated assault, burglary, larceny-theft, motor vehicle theft, and arson.

informal adjustment An attempt to handle a youthful offender outside of the formal structures of the juvenile justice system.

informal probation An arrangement in which, instead of being adjudicated as a delinquent and placed on probation, a youth is informally assigned to the supervision of a probation officer.

inhalant A volatile liquid that gives off a vapor, which is inhaled, producing short-term excitement and euphoria followed by a period of disorientation.

in loco parentis The principle according to which a guardian or an agency is given the rights, duties, and responsibilities of a parent in relation to a particular child or children.

In re Gault A 1967 U.S. Supreme Court case that brought due process and constitutional procedures into juvenile courts.

In re Winship A 1970 case in which the U.S. Supreme Court decided that juveniles are entitled to proof beyond a reasonable doubt during adjudication proceedings.

institutionalized means In Merton's theory, culturally sanctioned methods of attaining individual goals.

instrumental Marxists The name of a group whose members view the entire apparatus of crime control as a tool or instrument of the ruling class.

instrumental theory A perspective developed by Herman Schwendinger and Julia Siegel Schwendinger that holds that the most important variable predicting delinquency in teenagers is their status relative to that of their peers.

intake The first stage of juvenile court proceedings, in which the decision is made whether to divert the juvenile being referred or to file a formal petition in juvenile court.

intake decision The decision made by a juvenile court intake officer that results in a case either being handled informally at the intake level or being petitioned and scheduled for an adjudicatory or waiver hearing.

interstate compact The procedure for transferring a youth on probation or aftercare/parole from one state to another.

jail A police lockup or county holding facility for adult offenders. Jails have few services to offer juveniles.

judicial decision The decision made in response to a petition that asks the court to adjudicate or waive the youth. This decision is generally made by a juvenile court judge.

judicial disposition The definite action taken or treatment plan decided on or initiated regarding a particular case after the judicial decision is made. For the *Juvenile Court Statistics* report series, case dispositions are coded into the following categories: (1) waived to criminal court (cases that were transferred to criminal court as the result of a waiver hearing in juvenile court); (2) placement (cases in which youths were placed in a residential facility for delinquents or were otherwise removed from their homes and placed elsewhere); (3) probation (cases in which youths were placed on informal/voluntary or formal/court-ordered probation or supervision); (4) dismissed (cases that were dismissed—including those warned, counseled, and released—with no further action anticipated) and (5) miscellaneous (a variety of actions that were not included above, including fines, restitution and community service, referrals outside the court for services with minimal or no further court involvement anticipated, and dispositions coded as "other" by the reporting courts).

judicial waiver The procedure of relinquishing the processing of a particular juvenile case to adult criminal court; also known as *certifying* or *binding over* to the adult court.

jury trial The court proceeding in which a panel of the defendant's peers evaluate evidence and render a verdict. The U.S. Supreme Court has held that juveniles do not have a constitutional right to a jury trial, but several jurisdictions permit juveniles to choose a jury trial.

just deserts A pivotal philosophical underpinning of the justice model that holds that juvenile offenders deserve to be punished and that the punishment must be proportionate to the seriousness of the offense or the social harm caused.

justice as fairness A justice model that advocates that it is necessary to be fair, reasonable, humane, and constitutional in the implementation of justice.

justice model A contemporary model of imprisonment based on the principle of just deserts.

juvenile A youth at or below the upper age of juvenile court jurisdiction in a particular state.

juvenile aftercare The supervision of juveniles who are released from correctional institutions so that they can make an optimal adjustment to community living; see also *aftercare*.

juvenile court Any court that has jurisdiction over matters involving juveniles.

juvenile court officer A probation officer who serves juveniles (the term is used in some but not all probation departments).

juvenile court statistics The data about youths who appear before the juvenile court, compiled annually by the National Center for Juvenile Justice.

juvenile delinquency An act committed by a minor that violates the penal code of the government with authority over the area in which the act occurs.

juvenile drug court A special court designed for nonviolent youthful offenders with substance abuse problems who require integrated sanctions and services such as mandatory drug testing, substance abuse treatment, supervised release, and aftercare.

Juvenile Justice and Delinquency Prevention (JJDP) Act of 1974 A federal law that established a juvenile justice office within the then-existing Law Enforcement Assistance Administration to provide funds for the prevention and control of youth crime.

Juvenile Justice Standards Project A project jointly sponsored by the Institute of Judicial Administration and the American Bar Association that proposes that juveniles' sentences be based on the seriousness of the offense committed rather than on the needs of the youth.

juvenile officer In some police departments, a police officer who has received specialized training to work effectively with juveniles, and who is tasked primarily with such work.

juvenile petition See *petition*.

kadi justice   A judicial approach similar to that of a Muslim judge who sits in the marketplace and makes decisions without any apparent reference to established or traditional rules and norms.

Kent v. United States   A 1966 U.S. Supreme Court decision on the matter of transfer; the first decision in which the Supreme Court dealt with a juvenile court case.

labeling theory   The view that society creates the delinquent by labeling those who are apprehended as different from other youths when in reality they are different primarily because they have been tagged with a deviant label.

Law Enforcement Assistance Administration (LEAA)   A unit in the U.S. Department of Justice established by the Omnibus Crime Control and Safe Streets Act of 1968 to administer grants and provide guidance for crime-prevention projects. Until funding ended for LEAA in the late 1970s, its grants permitted the expansion of community-based programs throughout the nation.

learning disability (LD)   A disorder in one or more of the basic psychological processes involved in understanding or using spoken or written language.

least-restrictive model   A model based on the assumption that a juvenile's penetration into the justice system should be minimized as much as possible.

legislative waiver   A legislative action that narrows juvenile court jurisdiction, excluding from juvenile courts those youths charged with certain offenses.

life-course perspective   A sociological framework suggesting that four key factors determine the shape of the life course: location in time and place, linked lives, human agency, and timing of lives.

locura   A state of mind said to be desirable in a Mexican-American street gang; a type of craziness or wildness.

mandatory sentencing   The requirement that individuals who commit certain offenses be sentenced to a specified length of confinement if found guilty or adjudicated delinquent.

mandatory waiver   A provision that requires juvenile courts to waive cases under certain circumstances.

marijuana   The most frequently used illicit drug; usually smoked, it consists of dried hemp leaves and buds.

masculinity hypothesis   The idea that as girls become more boylike and acquire more masculine traits, they become more delinquent.

McKeiver v. Pennsylvania   A 1971 U.S. Supreme Court case that denied juveniles the right to trial by jury.

medical model   A correctional model whose proponents believe that delinquency is caused by factors that can be identified, isolated, treated, and cured—much like a disease.

minor   A person who is under the age of legal consent.

Miranda v. Arizona   The landmark 1966 U.S. Supreme Court ruling that suspects taken into police custody must, before any questioning can take place, be informed that they have the right to remain silent, that anything they say may be used against them, and that they have the right to legal counsel.

mother–son incest   Sexual activity that occurs between a mother and her son. Also refers to incest by stepmothers or the girlfriend(s) of the father.

neglect   A disregard for the physical, emotional, or moral needs of children. Child neglect involves the failure of the parent or caregiver to provide nutritious food, adequate clothing and sleeping arrangements, essential medical care, sufficient supervision, access to education, and normal experiences that produce feelings of being loved, wanted, secure, and worthy.

neutralization theory   A theory examining how youngsters attempt to justify or rationalize their responsibility for delinquent acts.

norms   The guidelines individuals follow in their relations with one another; shared standards of desirable behavior.

"nothing works"   The claim made by Robert Martinson and his colleagues in the mid-1970s that correctional treatment is ineffective in reducing recidivism of correctional clients.

offense against the family and children   A failure to provide support or neglect, desertion, or abuse of children or other family members.

Office of Juvenile Justice and Delinquency Prevention (OJJDP)   A federal agency established with the passage of the 1974 Juvenile Justice and Delinquency Prevention Act.

onset of delinquency   See *age of onset*.

opportunity theory   A perspective that holds that gang members turn to delinquency because of a sense of injustice about the lack of legitimate opportunities open to them.

orthomolecular imbalance   A chemical imbalance in the body, resulting from poor nutrition, allergies, and exposure to lead and certain other substances, which is said to lead to delinquency.

Outward Bound   A wilderness-type survival program that is popular in many states as an alternative to the institutionalization of juveniles.

parens patriae   A medieval English doctrine that sanctioned the right of the Crown to intervene in natural family relations whenever a child's welfare was threatened. The philosophy of the juvenile court is based on this legal concept.

peer group influence   The impact of the values and behaviors of fellow age-group members on teenagers' involvement in delinquency.

People   One of the two supergangs comprising the major Chicago street gangs.

petition   A document filed in juvenile court alleging that a juvenile is a delinquent and asking that the court assume jurisdiction over the juvenile or asking that an alleged delinquent be waived to criminal court for prosecution as an adult.

petitioner   In the juvenile justice system, an intake officer (prosecutor) who seeks court jurisdiction over a youthful offender.

placement facility type   The identification of a juvenile placement facility as publicly or privately owned/operated. Public facilities are those operated by state or local government agencies in which the employees working daily in the facilities and directly with the residents are state or local government employees. Private facilities are those operated by private nonprofit or for-profit corporations or organizations in which the employees working daily in the facilities and directly with the residents are employees of the private corporation or organization.

placement status   The identification categories of juveniles held in residential placement facilities. The status is usually based on one of the following: (1) committed (includes juveniles in placement in the facility as part of a court-ordered disposition); (2) detained (includes juveniles held while awaiting an adjudication hearing in juvenile court, juveniles held after adjudication while awaiting disposition or placement elsewhere, and juveniles awaiting transfer to or a hearing or trial in adult criminal court); and (3) diverted (includes juveniles sent to the facility in lieu of adjudication as part of a diversion agreement).

plea bargaining   A court process in which the defense counsel and the prosecution agree that the defendant will plead guilty, usually in exchange for a reduction of charges or a lessened sentence.

police discretion   A police officer's ability to choose from among a number of alternative dispositions when handling a situation.

police interrogation   The process of interviewing a person who has been arrested with the express purpose of obtaining a confession.

positive peer culture   A group treatment modality that (like its parent model, guided group interaction) aims to build a positive youth subculture. It encompasses a strategy that extends to all aspects of a youth's daily life.

Positive Youth Development (PYD)   A comprehensive way of thinking about adolescence that challenges the traditional deficit-based perspective by pointing out that youths can sometimes thrive even in the presence of multiple risk factors.

positivism   The view that just as laws operate in the medical, biological, and physical sciences, laws govern human behavior and these laws can be understood and used.

power-control thesis   The view that the relationship between gender and delinquency is linked to issues of power and control.

pretrial identification practices   The procedures such as fingerprinting, photographing, and placing juveniles in lineups for the purpose of identification prior to formal court appearance.

prevalence of delinquency   The percentage of the juvenile population who are involved in delinquent behavior.

primary deviation   According to labeling theory, the initial act of deviance that causes a person to be labeled a deviant.

primary prevention   The effort to reduce delinquency by modifying conditions in the physical and social environments that lead to juvenile crime.

private juvenile placement   A training school that operates under private auspices. The county or state generally pays the school a per diem rate for the care of youths committed to these facilities.

probation   A court-ordered nonpunitive juvenile disposition that emphasizes community-based services and treatment and close supervision by an officer of the court. Probation is essentially a sentence of confinement that is suspended so long as the probationer meets the conditions imposed by the court.

probation officer   An officer of the court who is expected to provide social history investigations, to supervise individuals who have been placed on probation, to maintain case files, to advise probationers on the conditions of their sentences, to perform any other probationary services that a judge may request, and to inform the court when persons on probation have violated the terms of that probation.

process of becoming deviant   In labeling theory, the concept that the process of acquiring a delinquent identity takes place in a number of steps.

Progressive era   The period from around 1890 to 1920, when a wave of optimism swept through American society and led to the acceptance of positivism.

prosecutor   The representative of the state in court proceedings. Also called *county's attorney*, *district attorney*, or *state attorney*.

psychoanalytic theory   A theory based on Sigmund Freud's insights, which have helped to shape the handling of juvenile delinquents. They include these axioms: (1) The personality is made up of three components—id, ego, and superego; (2) a normal child passes through three psychosexual stages of development—oral, anal, and phallic; and (3) a person's personality traits are developed in early childhood.

psychopath   An individual with a personality disorder, or a hard-core juvenile delinquent/adult criminal; also called a *sociopath*.

psychotherapy   A treatment method in which various adaptations of Freudian therapy are used by psychiatrists, clinical psychologists, and psychiatric social workers to encourage delinquents to talk about past conflicts that cause them to express emotional problems through aggressive or antisocial behavior.

radical criminology   A perspective that holds that the causes of crime are rooted in social conditions that empower the wealthy and the politically well organized but disenfranchise the less fortunate.

radical nonintervention   A policy toward delinquents that advises that authorities should "leave the kids alone whenever possible."

ranch   A public or private juvenile correctional institution that, like a forestry camp, is usually less secure than a training school and that has a more normal atmosphere.

rational emotive therapy   A cognitive restructuring strategy that seeks to identify delinquents' thinking errors (blaming others, trying to control or manipulate, failing to empathize, wanting to play the victim, etc.) and then to help young offenders "own" and control their behaviors.

reaction formation   The psychological strategy for dealing with frustration by becoming hostile toward an unattainable object.

reality therapy   A treatment modality developed by William Glasser and G. L. Harrington based on the principle that individuals must accept responsibility for their behavior.

reception and diagnostic center   A facility where juveniles who have been committed to correctional institutions frequently are first sent. This type of center diagnoses youths' problems and develops individualized treatment plans.

recidivism   The repetition of delinquent behavior by a youth who has been released from probation status or from training school.

referee   A juvenile justice worker who may or may not be a member of the bar. In many juvenile courts, referees assist judges in processing youths through the juvenile court system.

rehabilitation model   A correctional model whose goal is to change an offender's character, attitudes, or behavior so as to diminish his or her delinquent propensities. The medical, adjustment, and reintegration models are variants of this model because they are all committed to changing the offender.

reinforcement theory   A perspective that holds that behavior is governed by its consequences, especially rewards and punishments that follow from it.

reintegration model   A perspective that holds that offenders' problems must be solved in the community in which they occur and that community-based organizations can help offenders readjust to community life.

rejection by parents   The disapproval, repudiation, or other uncaring behavior directed by parents toward children.

reliability The extent to which a questionnaire or interview yields the same answers from the same juveniles when they are questioned two or more times.

remote location monitoring The use of electronic equipment to verify that an offender is at home or in a community correctional center during specified hours or to track his or her whereabouts; also called *electronic monitoring*.

representing The use by criminal street gangs of secret handshakes and special hand signs.

residential program A program conducted for the rehabilitation of youthful offenders within community-based and institutional settings.

residential social system The social hierarchy that is established by residents in an institution.

respondent The defense attorney in the juvenile court system.

restitution The court-ordered repayment to the victim; often used together with community service as a condition of juvenile probation.

reverse waiver A provision that permits a juvenile who is being prosecuted as an adult in criminal court to petition to have the case transferred to juvenile court for adjudication or disposition.

revocation of aftercare The cancellation of parole and return of the offender to an institution. It takes effect if a juvenile on aftercare commits another offense or violates the conditions of parole.

right to treatment The entitlement of a juvenile who has been committed to a training school to receive any needed services (e.g., therapy, education).

routine activities approach The contention that crime rate trends and cycles are related to the nature of everyday patterns of social interaction that characterize the society in which they occur.

running away The act of leaving the custody and home of parents or guardians without permission and failing to return within a reasonable length of time; a status offense.

school search The process of searching students and their lockers to determine whether drugs, weapons, or other contraband is present.

search and seizure The police procedure used in the investigation of crimes for the purpose of gathering evidence.

secondary deviation According to labeling theory, deviance that is a consequence of societal reaction to an initial delinquent act.

secondary prevention The intervention in the lives of juveniles or groups identified as being in circumstances that dispose them toward delinquency.

sedative A drug that is taken orally and affects the user by depressing the nervous system, causing drowsiness.

self-report study A study of juvenile crime based on surveys in which youths report on their own delinquent acts.

sentencing circle A form of restorative justice that incorporates principles of ancient, aboriginal tribal justice to address the harm suffered by crime victims and their families, the responsibilities of offenders, and the role of community.

sex-role socialization The process by which boys and girls internalize their culture's norms, sanctions, and expectations for members of their gender.

sexual abuse The intentional and wrongful physical contact with a person, with or without his or her consent, that entails a sexual purpose or component.

shelter care A facility that is used primarily to provide short-term care for status offenders and for dependent or neglected youths.

social capital theory James S. Coleman's perspective that holds that lower-class youths may become delinquent because they lack "social capital," or resources that reside in the social structure, including norms, networks, and relationships.

social contract An unstated or explicit agreement between a people and their government as to the rights and obligations of each.

social control theory A perspective that delinquent acts result when a juvenile's bond to society is weak or broken.

social development model A perspective based on the integration of social control and cultural learning theories that proposes that the development of attachments to parents will lead to attachments to school and a commitment to education as well as a belief in and commitment to conventional behavior and the law.

social disorganization theory An approach that posits that juvenile delinquency results when social control among the traditional primary groups, such as the family and the neighborhood, breaks down because of social disarray within the community.

social history report A written report of a juvenile's social background that probation officers prepare for a juvenile judge to assist the court in making a disposition of a youth who has been ruled delinquent.

social injustice According to many conflict-oriented criminologists, social injustice is found in apparent unfairness in the juvenile justice system arising from poor youths being disproportionately represented, female status offenders being subjected to sexist treatment, and racial minorities being dealt with more harshly than whites.

social interactionist theory A theoretical perspective that derives its explanatory power from the give-and-take that continuously occurs between social groups and between individuals and society.

socialization The process by which individuals come to internalize their culture; through this process, an individual learns the norms, sanctions, and expectations of being a member of a particular society.

social process theory A theoretical approach to delinquency that examines the interactions between individuals and their environments, especially those that might influence them to become involved in delinquent behavior.

social reaction theory A theory that focuses on the role that social and economic groups and institutions have in producing delinquent behavior.

social structure The relatively stable formal and informal arrangements that characterize a society, including its economic arrangements, social institutions, and values and norms.

sociobiology An expression of biological positivism that stresses the interaction between biological factors within an individual and the influence of the person's particular environment; also the systematic study of the biological basis of all social behavior.

sociopath See *psychopath*.

soft determinism The view that delinquents are neither wholly free nor wholly constrained in their choice of actions.

soft-line approach The lenient treatment of those youths who pose little threat to the social order.

specialization The repeated involvement of a juvenile in one type of delinquency during the course of his or her offending.

state training school   See *training school.*

station adjustment   One of several disposition options available to a police officer whereby a juvenile is taken to the police station following a complaint, the contact is recorded, and the juvenile is given an official reprimand and then released to his or her parents or guardians.

status frustration   The stress that individuals experience when they cannot attain their goals because of their socioeconomic class.

status offender   A juvenile who commits a minor act that is considered illegal only because he or she is underage.

status offense   A nondelinquent/noncriminal offense; an offense that is illegal for underage persons but not for adults. Status offenses include curfew violations, incorrigibility, running away, truancy, and underage drinking.

strain theory   A theory that proposes that the pressure the social structure exerts on youths who cannot attain cultural success goals will push them to engage in nonconforming behavior.

structural Marxists   A group that argues that the form taken by the legal system in a society can work to reinforce capitalist social relations.

supervision and discipline   The parental monitoring, guidance, and control of children's activities and behavior.

surveillance   The observation of probationers by probation officers, intended to ensure that probationers comply with the conditions of probation and that they do not break the law.

symbolic interactionist theory   A perspective in social psychology that analyzes the process of interaction among human beings at the symbolic level and that has influenced the development of several social process theories of delinquent behavior.

taking into custody   The process of arresting a juvenile for socially unacceptable or unlawful behavior.

teaching family group model   A community-based residential program that has had some success with delinquent youths.

teen court   A voluntary nonjudicial forum that keeps minor offenders out of the formal justice system; also known as *youth court.*

tertiary prevention   A program directed at the prevention of recidivism among youthful offenders.

theory of differential oppression   The view that in the United States, authority is unjustly used against children, who must adapt to adults' ideas of what constitutes "good children."

training school   A correctional facility for long-term placement of juvenile delinquents; may be public (run by a state department of corrections or youth commission) or private.

training school for girls   A correctional facility for long-term placement of adjudicated female juvenile delinquents.

trait-based personality model   A theory that attributes delinquent behavior to an individual's basic inborn characteristics.

transactional analysis (TA)   A therapy, based on interpreting and evaluating personal relationships, that has proved to be of immediate value to many delinquents. Using catchy language, TA promises delinquents who feel "not OK" that several easy steps can be taken to make them "OK."

transfer   The process of certifying a youth over to adult criminal court. It takes place by judicial waiver and legislative waiver.

truancy   A violation of a compulsory school attendance law; a status offense.

turning point   A gradual or dramatic change in the trajectory of an individual's life course.

underage drinking   The possession, use, or consumption of alcohol by a minor; a status offense.

Uniform Crime Reporting (UCR) Program   The Federal Bureau of Investigation's program for compiling annual data about crimes committed in the United States.

Uniform Crime Reports   The Federal Bureau of Investigation's annual statistical report of crimes committed in the United States.

upper age of juvenile court jurisdiction   The oldest age at which a juvenile court has original jurisdiction over an individual for law-violating behavior. It must be noted that in most states there are exceptions to the age criteria that place or permit youth at or below the state's upper age of jurisdiction to be under the original jurisdiction of the adult criminal court. For example, in most states if a youth of a certain age is charged with one of a defined list of what are commonly labeled "excluded offenses," the case must originate in the adult criminal court; in addition, in a number of states, the district attorney is given the discretion of filing certain cases either in the juvenile court or in the criminal court. Therefore, while the upper age of jurisdiction is commonly recognized in all states, there are numerous exceptions to age criteria.

utilitarianism   A doctrine that holds that the useful is the good and that the aim of social or political action should be the greatest good for the greatest number.

validity   The extent to which a research instrument measures what it says it measures.

vandalism   The act of destroying or damaging, or attempting to destroy or damage, the property of another without the owner's consent or destroying or damaging public property (except by burning).

victimization study   An ongoing survey of crime victims in the United States conducted by the Bureau of Justice Statistics to determine the extent of crime.

violence   A forceful physical assault with or without weapons. It includes many kinds of fighting, rape, other attacks, gang warfare, and so on.

volunteer program   The use of unpaid adult community members to assist probation officers in a variety of ways.

youth population at risk   For delinquency and status offense matters, this is the number of children from age 10 years old through the upper age of juvenile court jurisdiction. In all states, the upper age of jurisdiction is defined by statute (in most states, individuals are considered adults when they reach the age of 18 years old). Therefore, for these states, the delinquency and status offense youth population at risk would be the number of children who are 10 to 17 years of age living within the geographic area served by the court.

youth service bureau (YSB)   An agency outside the juvenile justice system that was designed to divert children and youths from the justice system by (1) mobilizing community resources to solve youth problems, (2) strengthening existing youth resources and developing new ones, and (3) promoting positive programs to remedy delinquency-generating conditions in the environment.

youth shelter   See *shelter care.*

Notes

CHAPTER 1

1. Kristen A. Graham, "Teen Sentenced for Terror Plot," *Philadelphia Inquirer*, October 7, 2006; "Media Information," Camden County Prosecutor's Office, August 10, 2006; Robert Strauss, "In Winslow, the Specter of Columbine," *New York Times*, April 23, 2006.

2. "Cops: Boy Scout Killed Parents, 2 Brothers," CBS News, February 4, 2008.

3. "Rapper Juvenile 4-Year-Old Daughter Murdered." www.top-socialite.com, 2007.

4. Robert Mitchum, "Family Friends Mourn Teen Accidentally Killed with Shotgun." chicagotribune.com.

5. Michael Wilson, "A 9-Year-Old Suspect in Court, 'Traumatized,' Her Lawyer Says," *New York Times*, June 3, 2005.

6. For an examination of the crises and strategies of adolescence, see David A. Wolfe, Peter G. Jaffe, and Claire V. Crooks, *Adolescence Risk Behaviors: Why Teens Experiment and Strategies to Keep Them Safe* (New Haven, Conn.: Yale University Press, 2006).

7. The concept of childhood is usually identified as beginning in the early decades of the twentieth century. For a good discussion of the social construction of adolescence, see Barry C. Feld, *Bad Kids: Race and the Transformation of the Juvenile Court* (New York: Oxford University Press, 1999), pp. 19–31.

8. Lloyd de Mause, ed., *The History of Childhood* (New York: Psycho-History Press), 1974, p. 1.

9. One of the exciting new areas of research is in relating adolescence to the life-course cycle or theory. See Silvia Bonimo, Elena Cattelino, and Silvia Ciairano, *Adolescent and Risk, Behavior, Functions, and Protective Factors* (New York: Springer-Verlag Italia), pp. 1–33.

10. Erik H. Erikson and Huey P. Newton, *In Seach of Common Ground* (New York: W. W. Norton, 1973), p. 52.

11. Joy G. Dryfoos, *Adolescents at Risk: Prevalence and Prevention* (New York: Oxford University Press, 1990), p. 25.

12. Christopher R. Edginton, Christophere L. Kowalski, and Steven W. Randall, *Youth Work: Emerging Perspectives in Youth Development* (Champaign, Ill.: Sagamore Publishing, 2005).

13. See David Kupelian, "Why Today's Youth Culture Has Gone Insane," *WorldNew Daily Exclusive Commentary,* January 16, 2004.

14. See "In the Heart of Freedom, in Chains," *City Journal,* 2007. http://city-journal.org/html/173black.america.html.

15. Federal Intragency Forum on Child and Family Statistics, *America's Children: Key National Indicators of Well-Being, 2008* (Washington, D.C.: U.S. Government Printing Office, 2008).

16. Ibid.

17. Howard N. Snyder and Melissa Sickmund, *Juvenile Offenders and Victims: 2006 National Report* (Washington, D.C.: National Center for Juvenile Justice and Office of Justice Programs).

18. Federal Intragency Forum on Child and Family Statistics, *America's Children.*

19. Ibid.

20. Nanette J. Davis, *Youth Crisis: Growing Up in the High-Risk Society* (Westport, Conn.: Praeger, 1999), p. 3.

21. Ibid.

22. Ibid., p. iii.

23. Children's Defense Fund's Mission Statement at www.childrensdefense.org.

24. Ibid.

25. Children's Defense Fund, *The State of America's Children 2008: Highlights.* www.childrendefense.org.

26. Danice K. Eaton et al., "Youth Risk Behavior Surveillance: United States, 2007," *MMWR Surveillance Summaries* 57 (2008), pp. 1–131.

27. Michael A. Gusseri, Teena Willoughby, and Heather Chalmers, "A Rationale and Method for Examining Reasons for Linkages among Adolescent Risk Behaviors," *Youth Adolescence* 36 (2007), pp. 279–289.

28. Ibid.

29. Eaton et al., "Youth Risk Behavior Surveillance."

30. David Huizinga, Rolf Loeber, Terence P. Thornberry, and Lynn Cothern, *Co-Occurrence of Delinquency and Other Problem Behaviors* (Washington, D.C.: Office of Juvenile Justice and Delinquency Prevention, 2000), p. 1. For an examination of the prevalence and patterns of co-occurring mental health problem symptoms, substance use, and delinquent conduct in a sample of multiple-problem and detained youths, see Cathryn C. Potter and Jeffrey M. Jenson, "Cluster Profiles of Multiple Problem Youth: Mental Health Problem Symptoms, Substance Use, and Delinquent Conduct," *Criminal Justice and Behavior* 30 (April 2003), pp. 230–250.

31. Carl McCurley and Howard N. Snyder, *Co-Occurrence of Substance Use Behaviors in Youth* (Washington, D.C.: U.S. Department of Justice, 2008).

32. Richard Jessor and S. L. Jessor, *Problem Behavior and Psychosocial Development: A Longitudinal Study of Youth* (New York: Academic Press, 1977). See also Richard Jessor, John E. Donovan, and Francis M. Costa, *Beyond Adolescence: Problem Behavior and Young Adult Development* (New York: Cambridge University Press, 1991); Michael Gottfredson and Travis Hirschi, *A General Theory of Crime* (Stanford, Calif.: Stanford University Press, 1990); and L. Zhang, J. W. Welte, and W. F. Wieczorek, "Underlying Common Factors of Adolescent Problem Behaviors," *Criminal Justice Behavior* 29 (2002), pp. 161–182.

33. John E. Donovan and Richard Jessor, "Structure of Problem Behavior in Adolescence and Young Adulthood," *Journal of Consulting and Clinical Psychology* 53 (1985), pp. 890–904. See also D. Wayne Osgood, Lloyd D. Johnston, Patrick M. O'Malley, and Jerald G. Bachman, "The Generality of Deviance in Late Adolescence and Early Adulthood," *American Sociological Review* 53 (1988), pp. 81–93.

34. Travis Hirschi, "A Brief Commentary on Akers' 'Delinquent Behavior, Drugs and Alcohol: What Is the Relationship?'" *Today's Delinquent* 3 (1984), pp. 49–52.

35. Gottfredson and Hirschi, *A General Theory of Crime.*

36. Helene Raskin White, "Early Problem Behavior and Later Drug Problems," *Journal of Research in Crime and Delinquency* 29 (November 1992), p. 414.

37. For this position, see also D. Wayne Osgood, "Covariation among Adolescent Problem Behaviors," paper presented at the Annual Meeting of the American Society of Criminology, Baltimore, Maryland, November 1990; and Helene R. White, "The Drug Use–Delinquency Connection in Adolescence," in *Drugs, Crime and the Criminal Justice System,* edited by Ralph Weisheit (Cincinnati, Ohio: Anderson, 1990), pp. 215–256.

38. See also Delbert S. Elliott, David Huizinga, and Scott Menard, *Multiple Problem Youth: Delinquency, Substance Use and Mental Health Problems* (New York: Springer-Verlag, 1989).

39. White, "Early Problem Behavior and Later Drug Problems." p. 412.

40. Ibid, p. 412. See also Jeffrey Fagan, Joseph G. Weis, Y.-T. Cheng, and John K. Watters, *Drug and Alcohol Use, Violent Delinquency and Social Bonding: Implications for Theory and Intervention* (San Francisco: URSA Institute, 1987).

41. See also Elliott, Huizinga, and Menard, *Multiple Problem Youth;* and Denise B. Kandel, Ora Simcha-Fagan, and Mark Davies, "Risk Factors for Delinquency and Illicit Drug Use from Adolescence to Young Adulthood," *Journal of Drug Issues* 16 (1986), pp. 67–90.

42. Federal Bureau of Investigation, *Crime in the United States 2007.* www.fbi.gov/ucr/05cius/index.html.

43. Jeffrey A. Butts, *Beyond the Tunnel Problem: Addressing Cross Cutting Issues That Impact Vulnerable Youth* (Washington, D.C.: Youth Transition Funders Group, 2008), p. 4.

44. *In re Poff,* 135 F. Supp. 224 (C.C.C. 1955).

45. Barry Krisberg and James Austin, *The Children of Ishmael: Critical Perspectives on Juvenile Justice* (Palo Alto, Calif.: Mayfield Publishing, 1978), p. 60.

46. Carol J. DeFrances, *Juveniles Prosecuted in State Criminal Courts* (Washington, D.C.: Office of Juvenile Justice and Delinquency Prevention, U.S. Department of Justice, 1997).

47. These interviews were conducted in two phases: as part of the juvenile victimization study in the 1970s and the follow-up of this study in 1989. In addition, Linda Dippold Bartollas interviewed parents, probation officers, juvenile court judges, and public school teachers in Illinois, Iowa, and Minnesota during the late 1980s and 1990s.

48. Meda Chesney-Lind and Lisa J. Pasko, *The Female Offender: Girls, Women, and Crime,* 2nd ed. (Thousand Oaks, Calif.: Sage, 2004).

49. See Chesney-Lind on the feminist theory of delinquency in Chapter 7.

50. Maynard L. Erickson, "Some Empirical Questions Concerning the Current Revolution in Juvenile Justice," in *The Future of Childhood and Juvenile Justice,* edited by LaMar Empey (Charlottesville: University of Virginia Press, 1979), pp. 277–311.

51. Solomon Kobrin, Frank R. Hellum, and John W. Peterson, "Offense Patterns of Status Offenders," in *Critical Issues in Juvenile Delinquency,* edited by David Shichor and Delos H. Kelley (Lexington, Mass.: D. C. Heath, 1980), pp. 203–235.

52. Ibid.

53. Ibid.

54. J. G. Weis, Karleen Sakumoto, John Sederstrom, and Carol Zeiss, *Jurisdiction and the Elusive Status Offender: A Comparison of Involvement in Delinquent Behavior and Status Offenses* (Washington, D.C.: U.S. Government Printing Office, 1980).

55. Joseph H. Rankin and L. Edward Wells, "From Status to Delinquent Offense Escalation," *Journal of Criminal Justice* 13 (1985), pp. 171–180.

56. Randall G. Shelden, John A. Horvath, and Sharon Tracy, "Do Status Offenders Get Worse? Some Clarifications on the Question of Escalation," *Crime and Delinquency* 35 (April 1989), pp. 214–215.

57. Ibid.

58. Thomas Kelley, "Status Offenders Can Be Different: A Comparative Study of Delinquent Careers," *Crime and Delinquency* 29 (1983), pp. 365–380.

59. Shelden, Horvath, and Tracy, "Do Status Offenders Get Worse?"

60. See Chris E. Marshall, Ineke Haen Marshall, and Charles W. Thomas, "The Implementation of Formal Procedures in Juvenile Court Processing of Status Offenders," *Journal of Criminal Justice* 11 (1983), pp. 195–211.

61. See Clemens Bartollas, Stuart J. Miller, and Simon Dinitz, *Juvenile Victimization: The Institutional Paradox* (New York: Halsted Press, 1976).

62. U.S. Congress, Senate, Committee on the Judiciary Subcommittee to Investigate Juvenile Delinquency, 1973, Juvenile Justice and Delinquency Prevention Act, S.3148 and S.821. 92d Cong., 2d Sess.; 93d Cong., 1st Sess.

63. Federal Advisory Committee on Juvenile Justice, *Annual Report 2008* (Washington, D.C.: Office of Juvenile Justice and Delinquency Prevention, 2008).

64. Ibid.

65. Ibid.

66. Thomas, "Are Status Offenders Really So Different?" pp. 440–442.

67. Ibid.

68. Martin Rouse, "The Diversion of Status Offenders, Criminalization, and the New York Family Court," revised paper presented at the Annual Meeting of the American Society of Criminology, Reno, Nevada, November 1989.

69. Bary Feld, *Bad Kids.*

70. Ibid.

71. Thomas J. Bernard, *The Cycle of Juvenile Justice* (New York: Oxford University Press, 1992).

72. George Santayana, *The Life of Reason* (London: Constable, 1905), p. 284.

73. David J. Rothman, *The Discovery of the Asylum* (Boston: Little, Brown, 1971).

74. Ibid.

75. Bradford Kinney Peirce, *A Half Century with Juvenile Delinquents* (Montclair, N.J.: Patterson Smith, 1969 [1869]), p. 41.

76. Roscoe Pound, "The Juvenile Court and the Law," *National Probation and Parole Association Yearbook* 1 (1944), p. 4.

77. *Kent v. United States,* 383 U.S. 541, 86 S.Ct. 1045, 16 L.Ed.2d 84 (1966); *In re Gault,* 387 U.S. 1, 18 L.Ed. 368 (1970); *McKeiver v. Pennsylvania,* 403 U.S. 528, 535 (1971); *In re Winship,* 397 U.S. 358, 90 S.Ct. 1928, 25

L.Ed.2d 368 (1970); and *Breed* v. *Jones*, 421 U.S. 519, 95 S.Ct. 1779 (1975).

78. *In re Gault.*

79. U.S. Congress, Juvenile Justice and Delinquency Prevention Act.

80. Ira M. Schwartz, *(In)justice for Juveniles: Rethinking the Best Interests of the Child* (Lexington, Mass.: Lexington Books, 1989).

81. National Advisory Committee for Juvenile Justice and Delinquency Prevention, *Serious Juvenile Crime: A Redirected Federal Effort* (Washington, D.C.: U.S. Department of Justice, 1984).

82. R. B. Coates, A. D. Miller, and L. E. Ohlin, *Diversity in a Youth Correctional System: Handling Delinquents in Massachusetts* (Cambridge, Mass.: Ballinger Publishing, 1978), p. 190.

83. Barry Krisberg et al., "The Watershed of Juvenile Justice Reform," *Crime and Delinquency* 32 (January 1986), pp. 5–38.

84. Alfred S. Regnery, "A Federal Perspective on Juvenile Justice Reform," *Crime and Delinquency* 32 (January 1986), p. 40. For an extensive examination of crime control in the 1980s, see Ted Gest, *Crime and Politics: Big Government's Erratic Campaign for Law and Order* (New York: Oxford University Press, 2001), pp. 41–62.

85. National Advisory Committee (NAC) for Juvenile Justice and Delinquency Prevention, *Serious Juvenile Crime,* p. 9.

86. Ibid., pp. 9, 11.

87. Ibid., p. 11.

88. Krisberg et al., "Watershed of Juvenile Justice Reform."

89. Schwartz, *(In)justice for Juveniles.*

90. Krisberg et al., "Watershed of Juvenile Justice Reform"; Barry C. Feld, "Legislative Policies toward the Serious Juvenile Offender," *Crime and Delinquency* 27 (October 1981), pp. 497–521.

91. Edward Cimler and Lee Roy Bearch, "Factors Involved in Juvenile Decisions about Crime," *Criminal Justice and Behavior* 8 (September 1981), pp. 275–286.

92. For the development of these trends, see the interview with Alfred Blumstein in *Law Enforcement News* 21 (April 30, 1995), pp. 1–2 and 11–12.

93. National Criminal Justice Association, *Juvenile Justice Reform Initiatives in the States: 1994–1996* (Washington, D.C.: Office of Juvenile Justice and Delinquency Prevention, 1997).

94. David McDowall, Colin Loftin, and Brian Wiersema, "The Impact of Youth Curfew Laws on Juvenile Crime Rates," *Crime and Delinquency* 46 (January 2000), pp. 76–91.

95. U.S. Conference of Mayors, *A Status Report on Youth Curfews in America's Cities: A 347-City Survey.* www.usmayors.org/uscm/news/publications/curfew.htm.

96. Howard N. Snyder, *Juvenile Arrests 1999: Juvenile Justice Bulletin* (Washington, D.C.: Office of Juvenile Justice and Delinquency Prevention, 2000).

97. National Criminal Justice Association, *Juvenile Justice Reform Initiatives in the States,* p. 13.

98. Andra Bannister, David Carter, and Joseph Schafer, "A National Police Survey on the Use of Juvenile Curfews, *Journal of Criminal Justice* 29 (2001), pp. 233–240.

99. Maike Males and Dan Macallair, *The Impact of Juvenile Curfews in California* (San Francisco: Justice Policy Institute, 1998).

100. Ibid.

101. Susan Pollet, "Responses to Juvenile Crime Consider the Extent of Parents' Responsibility for Children's Acts," *New York State Bar Journal* (July–August 2004), pp. 26–30.

102. See Mike Carlie, *Into the Abyss: A Personal Journey into the World of Street Gangs.* www.faculty.missouristate.edu/m/mko096f/.

103. National Criminal Justice Association, *Juvenile Justice Reform Initiatives in the States,* p. 27.

104. Doris Layton MacKenzie, David B. Wilson, Gaylene Styve Armstrong, and Angela R. Gover, "The Impact of Boot Camps and Traditional Institutions on Juvenile Residents: Perceptions, Adjustment, and Change," *Journal of Research in Crime and Delinquency* 38 (August 2000), pp. 279–313.

105. National Criminal Justice Association, *Juvenile Justice Reform Initiatives in the States.*

106. Ibid.

107. Donna Lyons, "National Conference of State Legislatures, State Legislature Report," *Juvenile Crime and Justice State Enactments* 9 (November 1995), pp. 13–14.

108. National Criminal Justice Association, *Juvenile Justice Reform Initiatives in the States,* p. 46.

109. Bernard, *The Cycle of Juvenile Justice.*

110. Andrew Abbott, "Of Time and Space: The Contemporary Relevance of the Chicago School," *Social Forces* 75 (1997), pp. 1149–1182. Quoted in James F. Short Jr., "The Level of Explanation Problem Revisited—The American Society of Criminology 1997 Presidential Address," *Criminology* 36 (1998), p. 6.

111. Abbott, "Of Time and Space," p. 1152.

112. Bernard, *The Cycle of Juvenile Justice.*

113. Glen H. Elder Jr., Monica Kirkpatrick Johnson, and Robert Crosnoe, "The Emergence and Development of Life Course Theory," in *Handbook of the Life Course,* edited by Jeylan T. Mortimer and Michael J. Shanahan (New York: Kluwer Academic/Plenum Publishers, 2003), pp. 3–19.

114. See G. H. Elder Jr., *Children of the Great Depression: Social Change in Life Experience, 25th Anniversary Edition* (Boulder, Colo.: Westview Press, 1999); G. H. Elder Jr. and E. D. Conger, *Children of the Land: Adversity and Success in Rural America* (Chicago: University of Chicago Press, 2000); and Glen H. Elder Jr., "Time, Human Agency, and Social Change: Perspectives on the Life Course," *Social Psychology Quarterly* 57 (1994), pp. 4–15.

115. The two most influential studies of the life course of the many that are cited in this text are Robert J. Sampson and John H. Laub, *Crime in the Making: Pathways and Turning Points through Life* (Cambridge, Mass.: Harvard University Press, 1993); and John H. Laub and Robert J. Sampson, *Shared Beginnings, Divergent Lives: Delinquent Boys to Age 70* (Cambridge, Mass.: Harvard University Press, 2003).

116. David P. Farrington, "Introduction to Integrated Developmental and Life-Course Theories of Offending," in *Integrated Developmental & Life-Course theories of Offending,* edited by David P. Farrington (New Brunswick and London: Transaction Publishers, 2005), pp. 1–14.

117. Elder, "Time, Human Agency, and Social Change." For an excellent review of agency, see Mustafas Emirbayer and Ann Mische, "What Is Agency?" *American Journal of Sociology* 103 (January 1998), pp. 962–1023.

118. Janet Z. Giele and Glen H. Elder Jr., "Life Course Research: Development of a Field," in *Methods of Life Course Research: Qualitative and Quantitative Approaches,* edited by Janet Z. Giele and Glen H. Elder Jr. (Thousand Oaks, Calif.: Sage, 1998), pp. 5–27.

119. John H. Laub, "Edwin H. Sutherland and the Michael-Adler Report: Searching for the Soul of Criminology Seventy Years Later," *Criminology* 44 (May 2006), p. 241.

120. Ibid., pp. 242–246. Reprinted with permission from the American Society of Criminology.

121. Children's Defense Fund, *The State of America's Children 2008.*

122. Clemens Bartollas and Stuart J. Miller, *Juvenile Justice in America,* 5th ed. (Upper Saddle River, N.J.: Prentice-Hall, 2008), p. 85.

CHAPTER 2

1. Robert Hanley, "Boy Sentenced to 18 Years for Murder of a 3-Year-Old," *New York Times,* December 13, 2003; "No Blame Assigned to Agency in Case of Boy Charged in Killing," *New York Times,* April 6, 2003; and Sue Chan, "10-Year-Old Boy Charged with Murder," Associated Press, March 29, 2003.

2. Donald J. Shoemaker, *Theories of Delinquency: An Examination of Explanations of Delinquent Behavior,* 5th ed. (New York: Oxford University Press, 2005).

3. Federal Bureau of Investigation, *Crime in the United States 2008.* www.fbi.gov/ucr/08cius/index.html.

4. Ibid.

5. Marie Simonetti Rosen, "A LEN Interview with Professor Alfred Blumstein," *Law Enforcement News* 21 (John Jay College of Criminal Justice, New York City) (April 30, 1995), pp. 10–13.

6. Ibid.

7. John J. DiIulio Jr., "Arresting Ideas: Tough Law Enforcement Is Driving Down Urban Crime," *Policy Review 74* (Fall 1995), pp. 1–5.

8. Rosen, "A LEN Interview with Alfred Blumstein, James Allen Fox, *Trends in Juvenile Violence: A Report to the United States Attorney General on Current and Future Rates of Juvenile Offending* (Bureau of Justice Statistics: Washington, D.C., 1996); and DiIulio, "Arresting Ideas."

9. Franklin E. Zimring, presentation given at the Annual Meeting of the National Criminal Justice Association, Chicago, Ill., May 30, 1996.

10. Franklin E. Zimring, "Crying Wolf over Teen Demons," *L.A. Times,* August 19, 1996, p. A17.

11. Philip J. Cook and John Laub, "The Unprecedented Epidemic in Youth Violence," in *Crime and Justice,* edited by Mark H. Moore and Michael Tonry (Chicago: University of Chicago Press, 1998), pp. 101–138.

12. Ibid.

13. I. R. Perlman, "Juvenile Court Statistics," *Juvenile Court Judges Journal* 16 (1965), pp. 1–3.

14. Charles Puzzanchera and Melissa Sickmund, *Juvenile Court Statistics 2005* (Pittsburgh, Penn.: National Center for Juvenile Justice, 2008), pp. 6–7.

15. Ibid.

16. Stephen A. Cernkovich, Peggy C. Giordano, and Meredith D. Pugh, "Chronic Offenders: The Missing Cases in Self-Report Delinquency," *Journal of Criminal Law and Criminology* 76 (1985), pp. 705–732.

17. Cynthia Jakob-Chien provided this information on the National Youth Survey.

18. Charles Puzzanchera, Anne L. Stahl, Terrence A. Finnegan, Nancy Tierney, and Howard N. Snyder, *Juvenile Court Statistics, 1999* (Pittsburgh, Penn.: National Center for Juvenile Justice, 2003).

19. Michael J. Hindelang, Travis Hirschi, and Joseph G. Weis, *Measuring Delinquency* (Beverly Hills, Calif.: Sage, 1981), p. 22.

20. Ibid.

21. James F. Short Jr. and F. Ivan Nye, "Reported Behavior as a Criterion of Deviant Behavior," *Social Problems 5* (Winter 1957–1958), p. 211.

22. Hindelang et al., *Measuring Delinquency.*

23. Cernkovich et al., "Chronic Offenders," p. 706. For other efforts to include frequent and serious offenders, see Ross Matsueda, Rosemary Gartner, Irving Piliavin, and Michael Polakowski, "The Prestige of Criminal and Conventional Occupations: A Subcultural Model of Criminal Activity," *American Sociological Review* 57 (1992), pp. 752–770; and James Inciardi, Ruth Horowitz, and Anne Pottieger, *Street Kids, Street Drugs, Street Crime: An Examination of Drug Use and Serious Delinquency in Miami* (Belmont, Calif.: Wadsworth, 1993).

24. Hindelang et al., *Measuring Delinquency,* p. 126. For the reliability of self-report studies, see also David H. Huizinga and Delbert S. Elliot, *A Longitudinal Study of Drug Use and Delinquency in a National Sample of Youth: An Assessment of Causal Order,* A Report of the National Youth Survey (Boulder, Colo.: Behavioral Research Institute, 1981); and Beatrice A. Rouse, Nicholas J. Kozel, and Louise G. Richards, eds., *Self-Report Methods of Estimating Drug Use: Meeting Current Challenges to Validity,* NIDA Research Monograph 57 (Rockville, Md.: National Institute on Drug Abuse, 1985).

25. Austin L. Porterfield, "Delinquency and Its Outcome in Court and College," *American Journal of Sociology* 49 (November 1943), pp. 199–208.

26. James F. Short Jr., "A Report on the Incidence of Criminal Behavior, Arrests, and Convictions in Selected Groups," *Research Studies of the State College of Washington* 22 (June 1954), pp. 110–118.

27. James F. Short Jr. and F. Ivan Nye, "Extent of Unrecorded Juvenile Delinquency: Tentative Conclusions," *Journal of Criminal Law, Criminology, and Police Science* 49 (November–December 1958), pp. 296–302.

28. Short and Nye, "Reported Behavior as a Criterion of Deviant Behavior."

29. David H. Huizinga and Delbert S. Elliott, "Juvenile Offenders: Prevalence, Offender Incidence, and Arrest Rates by Race," *Crime and Delinquency* 33 (April 1987), pp. 206–223.

30. Franklyn W. Dunford and Delbert S. Elliott, "Identifying Career Offenders Using Self-Reported Data," *Journal of Research in Crime and Delinquency* 21 (February 1984), pp. 57–82.

31. Ibid.

32. David H. Huizinga, Rolf Loeber, and Terence P. Thornberry, *Urban Delinquency and Substance Abuse: Initial Findings* (Washington, D.C.: U.S. Department of Justice, Office of Juvenile Justice and Delinquency Prevention, 1994).

33. *Guide for Implementing the Comprehensive Strategy for Serious, Violent, and Chronic Juvenile Offenders* (Washington, D.C.: Office of Juvenile Justice and Delinquency Prevention, 1995).

34. David S. Kirk, "Examining the Divergence across Self-Report and Official Data Sources on Inferences about the Adolescent Life-Course of Crime," *Journal of Quantitative Criminology* 22 (2006), pp. 107–129.

35. Andre B. Rosay, Stacy Skroban Najaska, and Denise C. Herz, "Differences in the Validity of Self-Reported Drug Use across Five Factors: Gender, Race, Age, Type of Drug, and Offense Seriousness," *Journal of Quantitative Criminology* 23 (2007), pp. 41–58.

36. Jerald G. Bachman and Patrick M. O'Malley, *A Continuing Study of American Youth (12th-Grade Survey, 1996)* (Ann Arbor, Mich.: Institute for Social Research, 1998).

37. Centers for Disease Control and Prevention, *Youth Risk Behavior Surveillance—United States* (Washington, D.C.: Centers for Disease Control and Prevention, 2004).

38. Michael Rand, *Criminal Victimization, 2006* (Washington, D.C.: Bureau of Justice Statistics, 2006).

39. See Summary page of the 2007 National Crime Victimization Survey.

40. Shannon M. Catalano, *Criminal Victimization, 2006* (Washington, D.C.: Bureau of Justice Statistics, 2007).

41. Ibid.

42. Ibid.

43. Ibid.

44. Ibid.

45. FBI, *Crime in the United States, 2008* (Washington, D.C.: U.S. Government Printing Office, 2009).

46. Howard N. Snyder, *Juvenile Arrests, 1999* (Washington, D.C.: Juvenile Justice Bulletin; Government Printing Office, 2000).

47. Peter E. Tracy, Marvin E. Wolfgang, and Robert M. Figlio, *Delinquency in Two Birth Cohorts: Executive Summary* (Washington, D.C.: U.S. Department of Justice, 1985).

48. Meda Chesney-Lind and Randall G. Shelden, *Girls, Delinquency, and Juvenile Justice*, 3rd ed. (Belmont, Calif.: Wadsworth/Thompson, 2004).

49. For a review of these studies, see Chesney-Lind and Shelden, *Girls*, pp. 19–23.

50. David C. Rowe, Alexander T. Vazsonyi, and Daniel J. Flannery, "Sex Differences in Crime: Do Means and Within-Sex Variation Have Similar Causes?" *Journal of Research in Crime and Delinquency* 32 (February 1995), pp. 84–100.

51. Hee-Soon Juon, Elaine Eggleston Doherty, and Margaret E. Ensminger, "Prospective Study of African Americans, *Journal of Quantitative Criminology* 22 (2006), pp. 193–214.

52. Chesney-Lind and Shelden, *Girls*.

53. Meda Chesney-Lind and Lisa Pasko, *The Female Offender: Girls, Women, and Crime* (Thousand Oaks, Calif.: Sage, 2004), p. 4.

54. Cited in Chesney-Lind and Shelden, *Girls*.

55. David P. Farrington, Rolf Loeber, Magda Stouthamer-Loeber, Welmoet B. Van Kammen, and Laura Schmidt, "Self-Reported Delinquency and a Combined Delinquency Seriousness Scale Based on Boys, Mothers, and Teachers: Concurrent and Predict Validity for African Americans and Caucasians," *Criminology* 34 (November 1996), pp. 493–517.

56. Jay R. Williams and Martin Gold, "From Delinquent Behavior to Official Delinquency," *Social Problems* 20 (1972), pp. 169–183; and Martin Gold and David J. Reimer, "Changing Patterns of Delinquent Behavior among Americans 13 through 16 Years Old: 1967–1972," *Crime and Delinquency Literature* 7 (1975), pp. 483–517.

57. Suzanne S. Ageton and Delbert S. Elliott, *The Incidence of Delinquent Behavior in a National Probability Sample of Adolescents* (Boulder, Colo.: Behavioral Research Institute, 1978).

58. Thomas L. McNulty and Paul E. Bellair, "Explaining Racial and Ethnic Differences in Serious Adolescent Violent Behavior," *Criminology* 41 (August 2003), pp. 709–746.

59. Alex R. Piquero and Robert W. Brame, "Assessing the Race-Crime and Ethnicity-Crime Relationship in a Sample of Serious Adolescent Delinquents," *Crime and Delinquency* 20 (2008), pp. 1–33.

60. Richard B. Felson, Glenn Deane, and David P. Armstrong, "Do Theories of Crime or Violence Explain Race Differences in Delinquency?" *Social Science Research* 37 (2008), pp. 623–641.

61. Joanne M. Kaufman, "Explaining the Race/Ethnicity-Violence Relationship: Neighborhood Context and Psychological Processes," *Justice Quarterly* 22 (June 2005), pp. 224–251.

62. Chesney-Lind and Shelden, *Girls*.

63. Charles Tittle, Wayne Villemez, and Douglas Smith, "The Myth of Social Class and Criminality: An Empirical Assessment of the Empirical Evidence," *American Sociological Review* 43 (1978), pp. 643–656.

64. Suzanne S. Ageton and Delbert S. Elliott, *The Incidence of Delinquent Behavior in a National Probability Sample of Adolescents* (Boulder, Colo.: Behavioral Research Institute, 1978).

65. Delbert Elliott and David Huizinga, "Social Class and Delinquent Behavior in a National Youth Panel," *Criminology* 21 (May 1983), pp. 149–177. For a discussion about whether different definitions of class are likely to produce different results on social class and delinquency, see Margaret Farnworth, Terence P. Thornberry, Alan J. Lizotte, and Marvin D. Krohn, *Social Background and the Early Onset of Delinquency: Exploring the Utility of Various Indicators of Social Class Background* (Albany, N.Y.: Rochester Youth Development Study, June 1990).

66. Margaret Farnworth, Terence P. Thornberry, Marvin D. Krohn, and Alan J. Lizotte, "Measurement in the Study of Class and Delinquency: Integrating Theory and Research," *Journal of Research in Crime and Delinquency* 31 (1994), p. 32.

67. Ibid.

68. Bradley R. Wright, Avshalom Caspi, Terrie Moffitt, Richard A. Miech, and Phil A. Silva, "Reconsidering the Relationship between SES and Delinquency: Causation but Not Correlation," *Criminology* 37 (February 1999), pp. 175, 190.

69. For a listing of some of this longitudinal research, see David P. Farrington, *Integrated Developmental Life-Course Theories of Offending: Advances in Criminological Theory* (New Brunswick and London: Transaction Publishers, 2005), pp. 3–4.

70. David P. Farrington, "Developmental and Life-Course Criminology: Key Theoretical and Empirical Issues: The 2002 Sutherland Award Address," *Criminology* 41 (May 2003), pp. 221–225. See also Farrington, *Integrated Developmental Life-Course Theories of Offending.*

71. Lila Kazemian and David P. Farrington, "Comparing the Validity of Prospective, Retrospective, and Official Onset for Different Offending Categories," *Journal of Quantitative Criminology* 21 (June 2005), pp. 224–251.

72. Alfred Blumstein, David P. Farrington, and Soumyo Moitra, "Delinquency Careers, Innocents, Desisters, and Persisters," in *Crime and Justice: An Annual Review*, 6th ed., edited by Michael Tonry and Norval Morris (Chicago: University of Chicago Press, 1985), pp. 187–220.

73. David P. Farrington, "Offending from 10 to 25 Years of Age," in *Prospective Studies of Crime and Delinquency,* edited by K. T. Van Dusen and S. A. Mednick (Boston: Kluwer-Nijhoff, 1983), pp. 17–37.

74. Cited in Barry Krisberg, *Guide for Implementing the Comprehensive Strategy for Serious, Violent, and Chronic Juvenile Offenders* (Washington, D.C.: Office of Juvenile Justice and Delinquency Prevention, 1995).

75. Ibid. For a comparison of prospective self-reports, retrospective self-reports, and official records in terms of onset of minor and serious forms of delinquency, see Kazemian and Farrington, "Comparing the Validity of Prospective, Retrospective, and Official Onset for Different Offending Categories," pp. 127–147.

76. David P. Farrington, Darrick Jolliffe, J. David Hawkins, Richard F. Catalano, Karl G. Hill, and Rick Kosterman, "Comparing Delinquency Careers in Court Records and Self-Reports," *Criminology* 41 (2003), pp. 933–942.

77. Kevin W. Alltucker, Michael Bullis, Daniel Close, and Paul Yovanoff, "Different Pathways to Juvenile Delinquency: Characteristics of Early and Late Starters in a Sample of Previously Incarcerated Youth," *Journal of Child and Family Studies* 15 (August 2006), pp. 479–492.

78. Rolf Loeber, Magda Stouthamer-Loeber, Welmoet Van Kammen, and David P. Farrington, "Initiation, Escalation and Desistance in Juvenile Offending and Their Correlates," *Journal of Criminal Law and Criminology* 82 (1991), pp. 36–82.

79. Rolf Loeber, Phen Wung, Kate Keenan, Bruce Giroux, Magda Stouthamer-Loeber, and Welmoet B. Van Kammen, "Developmental Pathways in Disruptive Child Behavior," *Development and Psychopathology* 5 (Winter–Spring, 1993), pp. 103–133.

80. See Barbara Tatem Kelley, Rolf Loeber, Kate Keenan, and Mary DeLamatre, *Developmental Pathways in Boys' Disruptive and Delinquent Behavior* (Washington, D.C.: Office of Juvenile Justice and Delinquency Prevention, 1997).

81. T. E. Moffitt, "Adolescent-Limited and Life-Course Persistent Antisocial Behavior: A Developmental Taxonomy," *Psychological Review* 100 (1993), pp. 674–701. For one of the studies that is highly supportive of Moffitt's taxonomy of offending behavior, see Paul Mazerolle, Robert Brame, Ray Paternoster, Alex Piquero, and Charles Dean, "Onset Age, Persistence, and Offending Versatility: Comparisons across Gender," *Criminology* 38 (November 2000), pp. 1143–1172.

82. Alex R. Piquero, Leah E. Daigle, Chris Gibson, Nicole Leeper Piquero, and Stephen G. Tibbetts, "Are Life-Course-Persistent Offenders at Risk for Adverse Health Outcomes?" *Journal of Research in Crime and Delinquency* 44 (May 2007), pp. 186–207.

83. Mazerolle et al., "Onset Age, Persistence, and Offending Versatility."

84. Glenn Deanne, David P. Armstrong, and Richard B. Felson, "An Examination of Offense Specialization Using Marginal Logit Models," *Criminology* 43 (November 2005), pp. 955–988.

85. D. Wayne Osgood and Christopher J. Schreck, "A New Method of Studying the Extent, Stability, and Predictors of Individual Specialization in Violence," *Criminology* 45 (2007), pp. 273–312.

86. For an investigation of gang involvement in crack cocaine sales, see Malcolm W. Klein, Cheryl L. Maxson, and Lea C. Cunningham, "'Crack,' Street Gangs, and Violence," *Criminology* 29 (1991), pp. 623–650.

87. Information based on interviews and interactions with these youths in 1990–1991.

88. Blumstein, Farrington, and Moitra, "Delinquency Careers."

89. David P. Farrington and J. David Hawkins, "Predicting Participation, Early Onset and Later Persistence in Officially Recorded Offending," *Criminal Behaviour and Mental Health* 1 (1991), p. 1.

90. Kimberly L. Kempf, "Crime Severity and Criminal Career Progression," *Journal of Criminal Law and Criminology* (1988), p. 537.

91. Peter Greenwood, *Selective Incapacitation* (Santa Monica, Calif.: RAND, 1982); Tracy, Wolfgang, and Figlio, *Delinquency in Two Birth Cohorts*; and Blumstein, Farrington, and Moitra, "Delinquent Careers."

92. Greenwood, *Selective Incapacitation.*

93. See Scott H. Decker and Barbara Salert, "Predicting the Career Criminal: An Empirical Test of the Greenwood Scale," *Journal of Criminal Law and Criminology* 77 (1986), p. 219.

94. Lila Kazemian and David P. Farrington, "Exploring Residual Career Length and Residual Number of Offenses for Two Generations of Repeat Offenders," *Journal of Research in Crime and Delinquency* 47 (February 2006), pp. 89–113.

95. Katherine S. Ratcliff and Lee N. Robins, "Risk Factors in the Continuation of Childhood Antisocial Behaviors into Adulthood," *International Journal of Mental Health* 7 (1979), pp. 96–116.

96. Nadine Lanctot, Stephen A. Cernkovich, and Peggy C. Giordano, "Delinquent Behavior, Official Delinquency, and Gender: Consequences for Adulthood Functioning and Well-Being," *Criminology* 45 (2007), pp. 191–222. See also Michael Massoglia, "Desistance or Displacement? The Changing Patterns of Offending from Adolescence to Young Adulthood," *Journal of Quantitative Criminology* 22 (2006), pp. 215–229.

97. Michael Gottfredson and Travis Hirschi, *A General Theory of Crime* (Palo Alto, Calif.: Stanford University Press, 1990), p. 107.

98. James Q. Wilson and Richard Herrnstein, *Crime and Human Nature* (New York: Simon and Schuster, 1985), p. 209.

99. Daniel S. Nagin and Raymond Paternoster, "On the Relationship of Past to Future Participation in Delinquency," *Criminology* 29 (May 1991), pp. 561–586.

100. Ibid., p. 163.

101. Ibid.

102. Ibid.

103. Robert J. Sampson and John H. Laub, *Crime in the Making: Pathways and Turning Points through Life* (Cambridge, Mass.: Harvard University Press, 1993). For further support of life-course theory, see Ronald L. Simons, Christine Johnson, Rand D. Conger, and Glen Elder Jr., "A Test of Latent Trait versus Life-Course Perspectives on the Stability of Adolescent Antisocial Behavior," *Criminology* 36 (May 1998), pp. 217–243.

104. John H. Laub and Robert J. Sampson, "Turning Points in the Life Course: Why Change Matters to the Study of Crime," *Criminology* 31 (August 1993), pp. 301–320.

105. Brian Francis, Keith Soohill, and Alex R. Piquero, "Estimation Issues and Generational Changes in Modeling Criminal Career Length, *Crime and Delinquency* 53 (January 2007), pp. 84–107. See also Michael E. Ezell, "Examining the Overall and Offense-Specific Criminal Career Lengths of a Sample of Serious Offenders," *Crime and Delinquency* 53 (January 2007), pp. 3–37; Rudy Haapanen, Lee Britton, and Tim Croisdale, "Persistent Criminality and Career Length," *Crime and Delinquency* 53 (January 2007), pp. 133–155; and Lili Kazemian and Marc Le Blanc, "Differential Cost Avoidance and Successful Criminal Careers: Random or Rational?" *Crime and Delinquency* 53 (January 2007), pp. 38–63.

106. A. Piquero, R. Brame, and D. Lynam, "Studying Criminal Career Length through Early Adulthood among Serious Offenders," *Crime and Delinquency* 50 (2004), pp. 412–435.

107. Ezell, "Examining the Overall and Offense-Specific Criminal Career Lengths of a Sample of Serious Offenders."

108. For more discussion on these issues, see David P. Farrington, "Introduction to Integrated Developmental and Life-Course Theories of Offending," in *Integrated Developmental Life-Course Theories of Offending*, pp. 1–14.

109. Alan J. Lizotte, Marvin D. Krohn, James C. Howell, Kimberly Tobin, and Gregory J. Howard, "Factors Influencing Gun Carrying among Young Urban Males over the Adolescent–Young Adult Life Course," *Criminology* 38 (2000), pp. 811–834; Philip J. Cook and Jens Ludwig, "Does Gun Prevalence Affect Teen Gun Carrying after All?" *Criminology* 42 (2004), pp. 27–54; and Anthony A. Braga, "Serious Youth Gun Offenders and the Epidemic of Youth Violence in Boston," *Journal of Quantitative Criminology* 19 (March 2003), pp. 33–54.

110. Ibid.

111. David M. Kennedy, Anthony A. Braga, and Anne M. Piehl, *Reducing Gun Violence: The Boston Gun Project's Operation Ceasefire* (Washington, D.C.: National Institute of Justice, 2001).

112. Office of Juvenile Justice and Delinquency Prevention, *Partnership to Reduce Juvenile Gun Violence Program* (Washington, D.C.: U.S. Department of Justice, 2008).

CHAPTER 3

1. David E. Kalist and Daniel Y. Lee, "First Names and Crime: Does Unpopularity Spell Trouble?" *Social Science Quarterly*, Vol. 90, No. 1 (2009), pp. 39–49.

2. Ibid., p. 40.

3. Ronald V. Clarke and Derek B. Cornish, "Modeling Offenders' Decisions: A Framework for Research and Policy," in *Crime and Justice*, 6th ed., edited by Michael Tonry and Norval Morris (Chicago: University of Chicago Press, 1985), pp. 147–185

4. Montesquieu, *On the Spirit of the Laws*, translated by Thomas Nugent, edited by David W. Carithers (Berkeley: University of California Press, 1977), originally published as *L'Esprit des Lois* (1747); Cesare Bonesana Beccaria, *On Crimes and Punishments*, translated by H. Paolucci (1764; reprint ed., Indianapolis: Bobbs-Merrill, 1963); Jeremy Bentham, *An Introduction to the Principles of Morals and Legislation* (1823; reprint ed., New York: Hafner Publishing, 1948).

5. Montesquieu, *On the Spirit of the Laws*, p. 158.

6. Ibid.

7. Beccaria, *On Crimes and Punishments*.

8. Ysabel Rennie, *The Search for Criminal Man: A Conceptual History of the Dangerous Offender* (Lexington, Mass.: Lexington Books, 1978), p. 15.

9. Beccaria, *On Crimes and Punishments*, p. 179.

10. Rennie, *The Search for Criminal Man*, p. 22.

11. Edward Cimler and Lee Roy Bearch, "Factors Involved in Juvenile Decisions about Crime," *Criminal Justice and Behavior* 8 (September 1981), pp. 275–286.

12. Anne Campbell, *Girl Delinquents* (New York: St. Martin's Press, 1981), p. 149.

13. Paul J. Brantingham and Patricia L. Brantingham, "The Spatial Patterning of Burglary," *Howard Journal of Penology and Crime Prevention* 14 (1975), pp. 11–24.

14. Clarke and Cornish, "Modeling Offenders' Decisions."

15. Derek B. Cornish and Ronald V. Clarke, eds., *The Reasoning Criminal: Rational Choice Perspectives on Offending* (New York: Springer, 1986); Kirk R. Williams and Richard Hawkins, "The Meaning of Arrest for Wife Assault," *Criminology* 27 (1989), pp. 163–181; Irving Piliavin, Craig Thornton, Rosemary Gartner, and Ross L. Matsueda, "Crime, Deterrence, and Rational Choice," *American Sociological Review* 51 (1986), pp. 101–119; Raymond Paternoster, "Decisions to Participate in and Desist from Four Types of Common Delinquency: Deterrence and the Rational Choice Perspective," *Law and Society Review* 23 (1989), pp. 7–40; Raymond Paternoster, "Absolute and Restrictive Deterrence in a Panel of Youth: Explaining the Onset, Persistence/Desistance, and Frequency of Delinquent Offending," *Social Problems* 36 (1989), pp. 289–309; Marcus Felson, "Predatory and Dispute-Related Violence: A Social-Interactionist Approach," in *Routine Activity and Rational Choice: Advances in Criminological Theory*, Vol. 5, edited by R. V. Clarke and M. Felson (New Brunswick, N.J.: Transaction Publishers, 1993); Marcus Felson, *Crime and Everyday Life: Insight and Implications for Society* (Thousand Oaks, Calif.: Pine Forge Press, 1994).

16. Ronald L. Akers, "Rational Choice, Deterrence, and Social Learning Theory in Criminology: The Path Not Taken," *Journal of Criminal Law and Criminology* 81 (Fall 1990), pp. 653–676.

17. Paternoster, "Absolute and Restrictive Deterrence in a Panel of Youth" and "Decisions to Participate in and Desist from Four Types of Common Delinquency."

18. Lawrence E. Cohen and Marcus Felson, "Social Change and Crime Rate Trends: A Routine Activity Approach," *American Sociological Review* (August 1979), pp. 588–609. For more recent expressions of the routine activities approach, see Felson, *Crime and Everyday Life.*

19. Steven F. Messner and Kenneth Tardiff, "The Social Ecology of Urban Homicides: An Application of the 'Routine Activities' Approach," *Criminology* 23 (1985), pp. 241–267.

20. D. Wayne Osgood, Janet K. Wilson, Patrick M. O'Malley, Jerald G. Bachman, and Lloyd D. Johnson, "Routine Activities and Individual Deviant Behavior," *American Sociological Review* 61 (1996), pp. 635–655.

21. Ibid., p. 635.

22. Timothy Brezina, "Delinquent Problem-Solving: An Interpretive Framework," *Journal of Research in Crime and Delinquency* (2000), pp. 3–30.

23. D. F. Greenberg, "Delinquency and the Age Structure of Society," *Contemporary Crisis* 1 (1977), pp. 189–223; Gordon B. Trasler, "Delinquency, Recidivism, and Desistance," *British Journal of Criminology* 19 (1979), pp. 314–322.

24. Marvin E. Wolfgang, Terence P. Thornberry, and Robert M. Figlio, *From Boy to Man: From Delinquency to Crime* (Chicago: University of Chicago Press, 1987). See also James F. Short Jr. and Fred L. Strodtbeck, *Group Process and Gang Delinquency* (Chicago: University of Chicago Press, 1965), pp. 248–265; and Charles W. Thomas and Donna M. Bishop, "The Effect of Formal and Informal Sanctions on Delinquency: A Longitudinal Comparison of Labeling and Deterrence Theories," *Journal of Criminal Law and Criminology* 75 (1984), p. 1244.

25. David Matza, *Delinquency and Drift* (New York: Wiley, 1964), p. 27. See also Silvan S. Tomkins, *Affect, Imagery, Consciousness: The Positive Affects* (New York: Springer, 1962), pp. 108–109.

26. Robert Agnew, "Determinism, Indeterminism, and Crime: An Empirical Exploration," *Criminology* 33 (1995), pp. 83–109.

27. This section on the Progressive era and the influence of positivism is based on David J. Rothman, *Conscience and Convenience: The Asylum and Its Alternatives in Progressive America* (Boston: Little, Brown, 1980). See p. 32.

28. Ibid. See pp. 43–60.

29. Matza, *Delinquency and Drift.*

30. Donald C. Gibbons, "Differential Treatment of Delinquents and Interpersonal Maturity Level: A Critique," *Social Services Review* 44 (1970), pp. 22–33.

31. James Q. Wilson and Richard J. Herrnstein, *Crime and Human Nature* (New York: Simon and Schuster, 1985).

32. Ian Taylor, Paul Walton, and Jock Young, *The New Criminology: For a Social Theory of Deviance* (New York: Harper and Row, 1973).

33. Ibid.

34. John Slawson, *The Delinquent Boys* (Boston: Budget Press, 1926).

35. Edwin Sutherland, "Mental Deficiency and Crime," in *Social Attitudes*, edited by Kimball Young (New York: Henry Holt, 1931), pp. 357–375.

36. William Sheldon, *Varieties of Delinquent Youth* (New York: Harper and Row, 1949).

37. Ibid.

38. Sheldon Glueck and Eleanor Glueck, *Physique and Delinquency* (New York: Harper and Row, 1956), p. 9.

39. Juan B. Cortes with Florence M. Gatti, *Delinquency and Crime: A Biopsychosocial Approach: Empirical, Theoretical, and Practical Aspects of Criminal Behavior* (New York: Seminar Press, 1972); Saleem A. Shahn and Loren H. Roth, "Biological and Psychophysiological Factors in Criminality," in *Handbook of Criminology*, edited by Daniel Glaser (Chicago: Rand McNally, 1974), pp. 101–173.

40. Shahn and Roth, "Biological and Psychophysiological Factors in Criminality."

41. Karl O. Christiansen, "A Preliminary Study of Criminality among Twins," in *Biosocial Bases of Criminal Behavior*, edited by S. A. Mednick and K. O. Christiansen (New York: Gardner, 1977), pp. 89–108; D. R. Cloninger et al., "Predisposition to Petty Criminality: II. Cross-Fostering Analysis of Gene–Environment Interaction," *Archives of General Psychiatry* 39 (November 1982), pp. 1242–1247; R. Crowe, "An Adoptive Study of Psychopathy: Preliminary Results from Arrest Records and Psychiatric Hospital Records," in *Genetic Research in Psychiatry*, edited by R. Fieve et al. (Baltimore: Johns Hopkins University Press, 1975); William F. Gabrielli and Sarnoff A. Mednick, "Urban Environment, Genetics, and Crime," *Criminology* 22 (November 1984), pp. 645–652; S. Sigvardsson et al., "Predisposition to Petty Criminality in Swedish Adoptees: III. Sex Differences and Validation of Male Typology," *Archives of General Psychiatry* 39 (November 1982), pp. 1248–1253.

42. Donald J. Shoemaker, *Theories of Delinquency: An Examination of Explanations of Delinquent Behavior*, 5th ed. (New York: Oxford University Press, 2005).

43. Christiansen, "A Preliminary Study of Criminality among Twins."

44. Thomas Bouchard Jr., "Genes, Environment, and Personality," *Science* 264 (1994), pp. 1700–1701.

45. Ibid., p. 1701.

46. Robert Plomin, Michael Owen, and Peter McGuffin, "The Genetic Basis of Complex Behaviors," *Science* 264 (1994), pp. 1733–1739.

47. M. J. H. Rietveld, J. J. Hudziak, M. Bartels, C. E. M. van Beijsterveldt, and D. I. Boomsma, "Heritability of Attention Problems in Children: Cross-Sectional Results from a Study of Twins, Age 3 to 12," *Neuropsychiatric Genetics* 1176 (2003), pp. 102–113.

48. The above discussion on recent studies of twins is based on John Paul Wright and Kevin M. Beaver, "Do Parents Matter in Creating Self-Control in Their Children? A Genetically Informed Test of Gottfredson and Hirschi's Theory of Low Self-Control," *Criminology* 43 (November 2005), pp. 1169–1202.

49. Minnestoa Twin Family Study. www.psych.umn.edu/psylabs/mtfs/specialhtm (accessed April 16, 2009).

50. Christiansen, "A Preliminary Study of Criminality among Twins."

51. Edwin H. Sutherland and Donald R. Cressey, *Criminology*, 10th ed. (New York: Lippincott, 1978).

52. D. J. West and D. P. Farrington, *Who Becomes Delinquent?* (London: Heinemann, 1973).

53. Lis Kirkegaard-Sorensen and Sarnoff A. Mednick, "A Prospective Study of Predictors of Criminality: Intelligence," in *Biosocial Basis of Criminal Behavior*, edited by Sarnoff A. Mednick and Karl O. Christiansen (New York: Gardner Press, 1977), pp. 255–266.

54. Robert A. Gordon, "Prevalence: The Rare Datum in Delinquency Measurement and Its Implications for the Theory of Delinquency," in *The Juvenile Justice System*, edited by Malcolm Klein (Beverly Hills, Calif.: Sage, 1976), pp. 201–284.

55. Robert A. Gordon, "IQ—Commensurability of Black–White Differences in Crime and Delinquency," paper presented at the Annual Meeting of the American Psychological Association, Washington, D.C., August 1986, p. 1.

56. Travis Hirschi and Michael Hindelang, "Intelligence and Delinquency: A Revisionist Review," *American Sociological Review* 42 (1977), pp. 471–486.

57. Ibid.

58. Wilson and Herrnstein, *Crime and Human Nature*, pp. 166–167.

59. For a study that supported the school performance model over the IQ/LD connection, see David A. Ward and Charles R. Tittle, "IQ and Delinquency: A Test of Two Competing Explanations," *Journal of Quantitative Criminology* 10 (1994), pp. 189–200.

60. Hans Eysenck, "The Technology of Consent," *New Scientist* 26 (June 1969), p. 689. For two papers that tested Eysenck's contributions, see Coleta van Dam, Eric E. J. De Bruyn, and Jan M. A. A. Janssens, "Personality, Delinquency, and Criminal Recidivism," *Adolescence* 42 (Winter 2007), pp. 763–776; and Penelope A. Hasking, "Reinforcement, Sensitivity, Coping, and Delinquent Behaviour in Adolescents," *Journal of Adolescence* 30 (2007), pp. 739–749.

61. Diana H. Fishbein and Robert W. Thatcher, "New Diagnostic Methods in Criminology: Assessing Organic Sources of Behavioral Disorders," *Journal of Research in Crime and Delinquency* 23 (August 1986), pp. 353–376.

62. Ibid.

63. F. A. Elliott, "Neurological Aspects of Antisocial Behavior," in *The Psychopath*, edited by W. H. Reid (New York: Bruner/Mazel, 1978), pp. 139–151; V. E. Krynicki, "Cerebral Dysfunction in Repetitively Assaultive Adolescents," *Journal of Nervous and Mental Disease* 166 (1978), pp. 59–67; F. Spellacy, "Neuropsychological Differences between Violent and Nonviolent Adolescents," *Journal of Clinical Psychology* 33 (1977), pp. 966–969; F. Spellacy, "Neuropsychological Discrimination between Violent and Nonviolent Men," *Journal of Clinical Psychology* 34 (1978), pp. 49–52.

64. Elizabeth Kandel and Sarnoff A. Mednick, "Perinatal Complications Predict Violent Offending," *Criminology* 29 (1991), p. 519.

65. S. Litt, "Perinatal Complications and Criminality," in Proceedings, 80th Annual Convention of the American Psychological Association in Washington, D.C., 1972; D. Mungas, "An Empirical Analysis of Specific Syndromes of Violent Behavior," *Journal of Nervous and Mental Disease* 17 (1983), pp. 354–361.

66. Kandel and Mednick, "Perinatal Complications Predict Violent Offending," p. 519.

67. Curt R. Bartol and Anne M. Bartol, *Delinquency and Justice: A Psychosocial Approach*, 2nd ed. (Upper Saddle River, N.J.: Prentice-Hall, 1998). For reading disability in delinquent youths, see John Shelley-Tremblay, Natalie O'Brien, and Jennifer Langhinrichsen-Rohling, "Reading Disability in Adjudicated Youth: Prevalence Rates, Current Models, Traditional and Innovative Treatments," *Aggression and Violent Behavior* 12 (2007), pp. 376–392.

68. Attention deficit disorder (ADD) webpage. www.dg58.dupage.kl2il.usx/counselors/add.htm (accessed July 15, 2004).

69. MTA Cooperative Group, "A 14-Month Randomized Clinical Trial of Treatment Strategies for Attention Deficit Hyperactivity Disorder," *Archives of General Psychiatry* 56 (1999), pp. 1088–1096.

70. Karen Stern, "A Treatment Study of Children with Attention Deficit Hyperactivity Disorder," *OJJDP Fact Sheet #20* (May 2001).

71. Karen V. Unger, "Learning Disability and Juvenile Delinquency," *Journal of Juvenile and Family Courts* 29 (1978), pp. 25–30.

72. Sharyn Neuwirth, *Learning Disabilities* (Washington, D.C.: National Institute of Mental Health, 1993), p. 3.

73. Ibid.

74. Donald Shoemaker, *Theories of Delinquency*, 5th ed. (New York: Oxford University Press, 2005).

75. Shah and Roth, "Biological and Psychophysiological Factors in Delinquency."

76. Among the research supporting the link between LD and delinquency is A. Berman, "Delinquents Are Disabled: An Innovative Approach to the Prevention and Treatment of Juvenile Delinquency," final report from the Neuropsychology Diagnostic Laboratory at the Rhode Island Training School, December 1974. One of the studies that does not show this link is that of Paul K. Broader et al., "Further Observations on the Link between Learning Disabilities and Juvenile Delinquency," *Journal of Educational Psychology* 73 (1981).

77. Abraham Hoffer was one of the early pioneers in this area. See Abraham Hoffer, "The Relation of Crime to Nutrition," *Humanist in Canada* 8 (1975), pp. 3–9.

78. S. Schoenthaler and I. Bier, "The Effect of Vitamin—Mineral Supplementation on Juvenile Delinquency among American Schoolchildren: A Randomized Double-Blind Placebo-Controlled Trial," *Journal of Alternative and Complementary Medicine: Research on Paradigm, Practice and Policy* 6 (2000), pp. 7–18.

79. Herbert Needleman, Julie Riess, Michael Tobin, Gretchen Biesecker, and Joel Greenhouse, "Bone Lead Level and Delinquent Behavior," *The Journal of the American Medical Association* 275 (1996), pp. 363–369.

80. Paul Stretesky and Michael Lynch, "The Relationship between Lead Exposure and Homicide," *Archives of Pediatric Adolescent Medicine* 155 (2001), pp. 579–582.

81. Sigmund Freud, *An Outline of Psychoanalysis*, translated by James Strachey (1940; reprint ed., New York: W. W. Norton, 1963).

82. Ibid.

83. Ibid.

84. LaMar T. Empey, *American Delinquency: Its Meaning and Construction* (Homewood, Ill.: Dorsey Press, 1982).

85. Hervey Cleckley, *The Mask of Sanity*, 3rd ed. (St. Louis, Mo.: Mosby, 1955).

86. See Kathleen M. Heide, "Parents Who Get Killed and the Children Who Kill Them," *Journal of Interpersonal Violence* 8 (December 1993), pp. 531–544.

87. William Healy, *Twenty-Five Years of Child Guidance: Studies from the Institute of Juvenile Research, Series C, no. 256* (Chicago: Illinois Department of Public Welfare, 1934).

88. August Aichhorn, *Wayward Youth* (New York: Viking Press, 1963).

89. Kate Friedlander, *The Psychoanalytic Approach to Juvenile Delinquency* (London: Routledge and Kegan Paul, 1947).

90. Marvin Zuckerman, *Sensation Seeking beyond the Optimal Level of Arousal* (Hillsdale, N.J.: Lawrence Erlbaum, 1979), p. 10.

91. Ibid.

92. Frederick Thrasher, *The Gang* (Chicago: University of Chicago Press, 1936); Henry D. McKay, "The Neighborhood and Child Conduct," *Annals of the American Academy of Political and Social Science* 261 (1949), pp. 32–41; P. Tappan, *Juvenile Delinquency* (New York: McGraw-Hill, 1949); A. Cohen, "The Delinquent Subculture," in *The Sociology of Crime and Delinquency*, 2nd ed., edited by M. Wolfgang, L. Savitz and N. Johnston (New York: Wiley, 1970), pp. 127–140; J. J. Tobias, "The Affluent Suburban Male Delinquent," *Crime and Delinquency* 16 (1970), pp. 273–279; and M. J. Hindelang, "The Relationship of Self-Reported Delinquency to Scales of the CPI and MMPI," *Journal of Criminal Law, Criminology and Police Science* 63 (1972), pp. 75–81.

93. Helene Raskin White, Erich W. Labouvie, and Marsha E. Bates, "The Relationship between Sensation Seeking and Delinquency: A Longitudinal Analysis," *Journal of Research in Crime and Delinquency* 22 (August 1985), pp. 195–211.

94. Walter R. Gove, "Why We Do What We Do: A Biopsychosocial Theory of Human Motivation," *Social Forces* 73 (1994), pp. 363–394.

95. Jack Katz, *Seductions of Crime: Moral and Sensual Attractions in Doing Evil* (New York: Basic Books, 1988).

96. Bill McCarthy, "Not Just 'For the Thrill of It': An Instrumentalist Elaboration of Katz's Explanation of Sneaky Thrill Property Crimes," *Criminology* 33 (November 1995). For other studies that have identified the importance of sensual experiences, see S. Lyng, "Edgework: A Social Psychological Analysis of Voluntary Risk Taking," *American Journal of Sociology* 95 (1990), pp. 851–856; and William J. Miller, "Edgework: A Model for Understanding Juvenile Delinquency," paper presented at the Annual Meeting of the Academy of Criminal Justice Sciences, Albuquerque, New Mexico, March 1998.

97. Wilson and Herrnstein, *Crime and Human Nature*.

98. Ibid.

99. Edgar Z. Friedenberg, "Solving Crime," *Readings: A Journal of Reviews and Commentary in Mental Health* (March 1986), p. 21.

100. Avshalom Caspi, Terrie E. Moffitt, Phil A. Silva, Magda Stouthamer-Loeber, Robert F. Krueger, and Pamela S. Schmutte, "Are Some People Crime-Prone? Replications of the Personality–Crime Relationships across Countries, Genders, Races, and Methods," *Criminology* 32 (1994), pp. 175–182. See also Douglas T. Kenrick and David C. Funder, "Profiting from Controversy: Lessons from the Person–Situation Debate," *American Psychologist* 43 (1988), pp. 23–34.

101. Caspi et al., "Are Some People Crime-Prone?"

102. Sheldon Glueck and Eleanor Glueck, *Unraveling Juvenile Delinquency* (Cambridge, Mass.: Harvard University Press for the Commonwealth Fund, 1950).

103. J. J. Conger and W. C. Miller, *Personality, Social Class, and Delinquency* (New York: Wiley, 1966).

104. Ibid.

105. Ibid.

106. Joshua D. Miller and Donald Lynam, "Structural Models of Personality and Their Relation to Antisocial Behavior: A Meta-Analytic Review," *Criminology* 39 (2001), pp. 765–798.

107. Richard L. Jenkins, "Delinquency and a Treatment Philosophy," in *Crime, Law and Corrections*, edited by Ralph Slovenko (Springfield, Ill.: Charles C. Thomas, 1966), pp. 131–145.

108. See Cleckley, *The Mask of Sanity*, pp. 382–417.

109. See R. Hare, "Psychopathy: A Clinical Construct Whose Time Has Come," *Criminal Justice and Behavior* 23 (1996), pp 25–54.

110. L. N. Robins, *Deviant Children Grown Up: A Sociological and Psychiatric Study of Sociopathic Personality* (Baltimore: Williams and Wilkins, 1966).

111. L. N. Robins et al., "The Adult Psychiatric Status of Black Schoolboys," *Archives of General Psychiatry* 24 (1971), pp. 338–345.

112. Linda Mealey, "The Sociobiology of Sociopathy: An Integrated Evolutionary Model," *Behavioral and Brain Sciences* 18 (1995), pp. 523–540.

113. Daniel C. Murrie, Dewey G. Cornell, Sebastian Kaplan, David McConville, and Andrea Levy-Elkon, "Psychopathy Scores and Violence among Juvenile Offenders: A Multi-Measure Study," *Behavioral Sciences and the Law* 22 (2004), pp. 49–67.

114. Raymond R. Corrado, Gina M. Vincent, Stephen D. Hart, and Irwin M. Cohen, "Predictive Validity of the Psychopathy Checklist: Youth Version for General and Violent Recidivism," *Behavioral Sciences and the Law* 22 (2004), pp. 5–22.

115. Rolf Holmqvist, "Psychopathy and Affect Consciousness in Young Criminal Offenders," *Journal of Interpersonal Violence* 23 (February 2008), pp. 209–224.

116. Ibid.

117. en.Wikipedia.org/wiki/Theory_of_cognitive development.

118. www.gse.harvard.edu/news/features/larry10012000_page2.html.

119. students.usm.maine.edu/bmcpha41/Kohlberg_stages_of_morality.htm.

120. www.aosy.edu/oconnort/crim/crimtheory06.htm.

121. Ibid.

122. Aaron T. Beck, *Prisoners of Hate: The Cognitive Basis of Anger, Hostility, and Violence* (New York: HarperCollins Publishers, 1999)

123. For a study that concluded it was impossible to determine significant differences between criminal and noncriminal personalities, see Karl Schuessler and Donald Cressey,

"Personality Characteristics of Criminals," *American Journal of Sociology* 55 (1955), pp. 476–484. For an investigation that found statistical differences in 81% of the studies, see Gordon Waldo and Simon Dinitz, "Personality Attributes of the Criminal: An Analysis of Research Studies 1950–1965," *Journal of Research in Crime and Delinquency* 4 (1967), pp. 185–201. The latter study does warn that these studies are full of methodological weaknesses. For a study that replicated Waldo and Dinitz's study and found that between the years 1966 and 1975, 80% of personality tests showed significant differences between criminals and noncriminals, see David J. Tennenbaum, "Personality and Criminality: A Summary and Implications of the Literature," *Journal of Criminal Justice* 5 (1977), pp. 225–235.

124. See citations for these studies in Chapter 2.

125. Terrie E. Moffitt, Donald R. Lynam, and Phil A. Silva, "Neuropsychological Tests Predicting Persistent Male Delinquency," *Criminology* 32 (May 1994), p. 277

126. Terrie E. Moffitt, "Adolescent-Limited and Life-Course-Persistent Antisocial Behavior: A Developmental Taxonomy," *Psychological Review* 100 (1993), pp. 674–701.

127. Terrie E. Moffitt, "The Neuropsychology of Conduct Disorder," *Development and Psychopathology* 5 (1993), pp. 135–151; and Terrie E. Moffitt, Avshalom Caspi, N. Dickson, Phil A. Silva, and W. Stanton, "Childhood-Onset versus Adolescent-Onset Antisocial Conduct Problems in Males: Natural History from Ages 3 to 18," *Development and Psychopathology* 8 (1996), pp. 399–424.

128. Ibid. For research that tested Moffitt's model of adolescence-limited delinquency, see Alex R. Piquero and Timothy Brezina, "Testing Moffitt's Account of Adolescence-Limited Delinquency," *Criminology* 39 (May 2001), pp. 353–410. These researchers found from their data from the Youth-in-Transition survey that adolescence-limited delinquency is characterized by rebellious delinquency rather than aggressive delinquency. Andrea G. Donker, Wilma H. Smeenk, Peter H. van der Laan, and Frank C. Verhulst, using data from the South-Holland Study, found support for Moffitt's prediction on the stability of longitudinal antisocial behavior. See Donker, Smeenk, van der Laan, and Verhulst, "Individual Stability of Antisocial Behavior from Childhood to Adulthood: Testing the Stability Postulate of Moffitt's Developmental Theory," *Criminology* 41 (August 2003), pp. 593–609.

129. Richard E. Tremblay, Frank Vitaro, Daniel Nagin et al., "The Montreal Longitudinal and Experimental Study: Rediscovering the Power of Descriptions," in *Taking Stock of Delinquency: An Overview of Findings from Contemporary Longitudinal Studies*, edited by Terence P. Thornberry and Marvin D. Krohn (New York: Kluwer Academic/Plenum Publishers, 2003), pp. 205–254.

130. Ibid.

131. Ibid.

132. Ibid., p. 243.

133. David P. Farrington, "Key Results from the First Forty Years of the Cambridge Study in Delinquent Development," in *Taking Stock of Delinquency*, edited by Terence P. Thornberry and Marvin D. Krohn (New York: Kluwer Academic/Plenum Publishers), pp. 137–183.

134. Ibid.

135. Ibid.

136. Ibid., p. 174.

137. Richard Dembo, Jennifer Wareham, Norman Poythress, Kathleen Meyers, and James Schmeider, "Psychosocial Functioning Problems over Time among High-Risk Youths: A Latent Class Transition Analysis," *Crime and Delinquency* 54 (2008), pp. 664–670.

138. Akers, "Rational Choice, Deterrence, and Social Learning Theory in Criminology."

139. Ibid.

140. Farrington, "Age and Crime." This chapter's section on desistance and crime is adapted in part from Robert J. Sampson and John H. Laub, "Understanding Desistance from Crime," in *Crime and Justice*, Vol. 28, edited by Michael Tonry (Chicago: University of Chicago Press, 2001), pp. 1–69.

141. Farrington, "Age and Crime."

142. Robert J. Sampson and John H. Laub, "A General Age-Graded Theory of Crime: Lessons Learned and the Future of Life-Course Criminology," in *Integrated Developmental and Life Course Theories of Offending: Advances in Criminological Theory*, edited by David P. Farrington (New Brunswick, 2005), pp. 165–181.

143. Ibid. For another study that found incarceration to be negatively associated with marriage and employment, see Beth M. Huebner, "The Effect of Incarceration on Marriage and Work over the Life Course," *Justice Quarterly* 22 (September 2005), pp. 281–303.

144. Ibid., p. 11.

145. Jeffrey A. Butts, *Beyond the Tunnel Problem: Addressing Cross-Cutting Issues That Impact Vulnerable Youth* (Chicago: University of Chicago, Chapin Hall Center for Children, 2008).

146. White House Task Force for Disadvantaged Youth, *Final Report,* October 2003.

147. Melvin Delgado, *New Frontiers for Youth Development in the Twenty-First Century* (New York: Columbia University Press, 2002), p. 164. Reprinted with permission of the publisher.

148. Howard N. Snyder and Melissa Sickmund, *Juvenile Justice and Victims 2006 National Report* (Washington, D.C.: U.S. Department of Justice Programs, Office of Juvenile Justice and Delinquency Prevention, 2006).

CHAPTER 4

1. "Murder Sentence," *The Villager*, November 22–28, 2006; "Teens Sentenced in Murder of Student," *Washington Square News*, October 4, 2006; Anemona Hartocollis, "No Release for Teenagers," *New York Times*, April 18, 2006.

2. For an article that lent support to Anderson's "code of the street" thesis, see Eric A. Stewart and Ronald L. Simons, "Structure and Culture in African American Adolescent Violence: A Partial Test of the 'Code of the Street' Thesis," *Justice Quarterly* 23 (March 2006), p. 1.

3. Robert J. Sampson and W. B. Groves, "Community Structure and Crime: Testing Social-Disorganization Theory," *American Journal of Sociology* 94 (1989), pp. 774–802.

4. Robert J. Sampson and William Julius Wilson, "Toward a Theory of Race, Crime, and Urban Equality," in *Crime and Inequality*, edited by John Hagan and Ruth D. Peterson (Stanford, Calif.: Stanford University Press, 1995), pp. 37–54.

5. See Emile Durkheim, *Suicide*, translated by John A. Spaulding and George Simpson (New York: Free Press of Glencoe, 1893).

6. There is a cultural deviance component to Shaw and McKay's perspective, but Ruth Rosner Kornhauser claims it is an unnecessary aspect of their social disorganization theory. See Ruth Rosner Kornhauser, *Social Sources of Delinquency: An Appraisal of Analytic Models* (Chicago: University of Chicago Press, 1978), p. 79.

7. Albert J. Reiss Jr., "Settling the Frontiers of a Pioneer in American Criminology: Henry McKay," in *Delinquency, Crime and Society,* edited by James F. Short Jr. (Chicago: University of Chicago Press, 1976), pp. 64–86.

8. Harold Finestone, *Victims of Change: Juvenile Delinquents in American Society* (Westport, Conn.: Greenwood Press, 1976).

9. George B. Vold and Thomas J. Bernard, *Theoretical Criminology,* 3rd ed. (New York: Oxford University Press, 1986).

10. Clifford R. Shaw, *Delinquency Areas* (Chicago: University of Chicago Press, 1929).

11. Clifford R. Shaw and Henry D. McKay, *Juvenile Delinquency and Urban Areas* (Chicago: University of Chicago Press, 1941).

12. Ysabel Rennie, *The Search for Criminal Man* (Lexington, Mass.: Lexington Books, 1978).

13. Finestone, *Victims of Change.*

14. Ibid.

15. Ibid.

16. Shaw and McKay, *Juvenile Delinquency and Urban Areas.*

17. John Laub, *Criminology in the Making: An Oral History* (Boston: Northeastern University Press, 1983).

18. Robert J. Bursik Jr., "Social Disorganization and Theories of Crime and Delinquency: Problems and Prospects," *Criminology* 26 (November 1988), pp. 519–551. See also Justice W. Patchin, Beth M. Huebner, John D. McCluskey, Sean P. Varano, and Timothy S. Bynum, "Exposure to Community Violence and Childhood Delinquency," *Crime and Delinquency* 52 (April 2006), pp. 307–332; and Amie L. Nielsen, Matthew T. Lee, and Ramiro Martinez Jr., "Integrating Race, Place and Motive in Social Disorganization Theory: Lessons from a Comparison of Black and Latino Homicide Types in Two Immigrant Destination Cities," *Criminology* 43 (August 2005), pp. 837–871.

19. Bursik, "Social Disorganization and Theories of Crime and Delinquency"; James M. Byrne and Robert J. Sampson, eds., *The Social Ecology of Crime* (New York: Springer-Verlag, 1986); Albert J. Reiss and Michael Tonry, eds., *Communities and Crime,* Vol. 8 (Chicago: University of Chicago Press, 1986); and Rodney Stark, "Deviant Places: A Theory of the Ecology of Crime," *Criminology* 25 (1987), pp. 893–909.

20. Bursik, "Social Disorganization and Theories of Crime and Delinquency." See also Charis E. Kubrin and Eric A. Stewart, "Predicting Who Reoffends: The Neglected Role of Neighborhood Context in Recidivism Studies," *Criminology* 44 (February 1, 2006), p. 165; and Barbara D. Warner, "The Role of Attenuated Culture in Social Disorganization Theory," *Criminology* 41 (2006), pp. 73–98.

21. Bursik, "Social Disorganization and Theories of Crime and Delinquency"; and Stacy DeCoster, Karen Heimer, and Stacy Wittrock, "Neighborhood Disadvantage, Social Capital, Street Context, and Youth Violence," *Sociological Quarterly* 47 (2006), pp. 723–753. For the relationship between social disorganization and drug trafficking, see Ramino Martinez Jr., Richard Rosenfeld, and Dennis Mares, "Social Disorganization, Drug Market Activity, and Neighborhood Violent Crime," *Urban Affairs Review* 43 (July 2008), pp. 846–874.

22. Stark, "Deviant Places."

23. Robert J. Bursik Jr., "Ecological Stability and the Dynamics of Delinquency," in *Communities and Crime,* edited by Reiss and Tonry, p. 36.

24. Kornhauser, *Social Sources of Delinquency,* p. 25. For a review of the decline of cultural deviance theory, see J. Mitchell Miller, Albert K. Cohen, and Kevin M. Bryant, "On the Demise and Morrow of Subculture Theories of Crime and Delinquency," *Journal of Crime and Justice* 20 (1997), pp. 167–178.

25. Walter B. Miller, "Lower-Class Culture as a Generation Milieu of Gang Delinquency," *Journal of Social Issues* 14 (1958), pp. 9–10.

26. Ibid.

27. Marvin E. Wolfgang and Franco Ferracuti, *The Subculture of Violence* (London: Tavistock, 1957). For a study that challenges the black subculture of violence thesis, see Liqun Cao, Anthony Adams, and Vickie J. Jensen, "A Test of the Black Subculture of Violence Thesis: A Research Note," *Criminology* 35 (May 1997), pp. 367–379.

28. Richard A. Cloward and Lloyd E. Ohlin, *Delinquency and Opportunity: A Theory of Delinquent Boys: The Culture of the Gang* (Glencoe, Ill.: Free Press, 1955).

29. This section's analysis of social structure and anomie is based on Robert K. Merton, *Social Theory and Social Structure,* 2nd ed. (New York: Free Press, 1957), pp. 131–132.

30. Ibid., p. 131.

31. Ibid.

32. Morton Deutsch and Robert M. Krauss, *Theories in Social Psychology* (New York: Basic Books, 1965), p. 198.

33. Merton, *Social Theory and Social Structure.*

34. Cloward and Ohlin, *Delinquency and Opportunity.*

35. Merton, *Social Theory and Social Structure,* p. 151.

36. Ibid., p. 155.

37. Ibid.

38. For Merton's recent thoughts about the emergence and present status of strain theory, see Robert K. Merton, "Opportunity Structure: The Emergence, Diffusion, and Differentiation of a Sociological Concept, 1930s–1950s," in *The Legacy of Anomie Theory: Advances in Criminological Theory,* Vol. 6, edited by Freda Adler and William S. Laufer (New Brunswick, N.J.: Transaction Publishers, 1995), pp. 3–78.

39. Velmer S. Burton Jr. and Francis T. Cullen "The Empirical Status of Strain Theory," *Journal of Crime and Justice* 15 (1992), pp. 1–30.

40. Steven F. Messner and Richard Rosenfeld, *Crime and the American Dream* (Belmont, Calif.: Wadsworth Publishing Company, 1994).

41. Jukka Savolainen, "Inequality, Welfare State, and Homicide: Further Support for the Institutional Anomie Theory," *Criminology* 38 (November 2000), pp. 617–663.

42. Velmer S. Burton Jr. and Francis T. Cullen, "The Empirical Status of Strain Theory," *Journal of Crime and Justice* 15 (1992), p. 5.

43. Marshall B. Clinard, "The Theoretical Implications of Anomie and Deviant Behavior," in *Anomie and Deviant Behavior*, edited by Marshall B. Clinard (New York: Free Press, 1964), p. 10.

44. Cloward and Ohlin, *Delinquency and Opportunity*; and Albert K. Cohen, *Delinquent Boys: The Culture of the Gang* (Glencoe, Ill.: Free Press, 1955).

45. Burton and Cullen, "The Empirical Status of Strain Theory," pp. 2–3.

46. Travis Hirschi, *Causes of Crime* (Berkeley: University of California Press, 1969); and Kornhauser, *Social Sources of Delinquency*.

47. Robert Agnew, "Foundations for a General Strain Theory of Crime and Delinquency," *Criminology* 30 (February 1992), pp. 47–87.

48. Thomas J. Bernard, "Control Criticisms of Strain Theory: An Assessment of Theoretical and Empirical Adequacy," *Journal of Research in Crime and Delinquency* 21 (1984), pp. 353–372; and Thomas J. Bernard, "Testing Structural Strain Theories," *Journal of Research in Crime and Delinquency* 24 (1987), pp. 262–280.

49. Robert Agnew, "A Revised Strain Theory of Delinquency," *Social Forces* 64 (1985), pp. 151–167.

50. Ibid., p. 151.

51. Robert Agnew, "The Contribution of 'Mainstream' Theories of the Explanation of Female Delinquency," in *The Delinquent Girl*, edited by Margaret A. Zahn (Philadelphia: Temple University Press, 2009), p. 8.

52. Ibid., pp. 7–29.

53. Agnew, "Foundations for a General Theory of Crime and Delinquency." See also Robert Agnew, "Building on the Foundation for a General Strain Theory," paper presented at the Annual Meeting of the American Society of Criminology in Washington, D.C., November 1998; and John P. Hoffman and Alan S. Miller, "A Latent Variable Analysis of General Strain Theory," *Journal of Quantitative Criminology* 14 (1998), pp. 83–110.

54. Agnew, "Foundations for a General Theory of Crime and Delinquency." See also Agnew, "Building on the Foundation for a General Strain Theory," and Hoffman and Miller, "A Latent Variable Analysis of General Strain Theory"; Stephen W. Baron, "Street Youth, Unemployment, and Crime: Is It That Simple? Using General Strain Theory to Untangle the Relationship," *Canadian Journal of Criminology and Criminal Justice* 50 (2008), pp. 399–434; Deanna M. Penez, Wesley G. Jennings, and Angela R. Gover, "Specifiying General Strain Theory: An Ethnically Relevant Approach," *Deviant Behavior* 29 (2008), pp. 544–578; and Byongoof Moon, David Blurton, and John D. McCluskey, "General Strain Theory and Delinquency: Focusing on the Influences of Key Strain Characteristics on Delinquency," *Crime and Delinquency* 54 (2008), pp. 582–613.

55. Cohen, *Delinquent Boys*.

56. Ibid.

57. Ibid., p. 87.

58. Ibid., pp. 113–114.

59. Ibid.

60. Ibid.

61. Ibid.

62. Ibid.

63. Ibid.

64. Albert K. Cohen, "The Sociology of the Deviant Act: Anomie Theory and Beyond," *American Sociological Review* 30 (1965), pp. 5–14.

65. Hirschi, *Causes of Delinquency*.

66. Vold and Bernard, *Theoretical Criminology*, p. 197.

67. Cloward and Ohlin, *Delinquency and Opportunity*, p. 97.

68. Ibid.

69. Ibid.

70. Ibid.

71. Ibid., p. 25.

72. Ibid.

73. Delbert S. Elliott and Harwin L. Voss, *Delinquency and Dropout* (Lexington, Mass.: Lexington Books, 1974).

74. Gwynn Nettler, *Explaining Crime*, 3rd ed. (New York: McGraw-Hill, 1984).

75. Kornhauser, *Social Sources of Delinquency*.

76. Merton, "Social Structure and Anomie," and Cloward and Ohlin, *Delinquency and Opportunity*.

77. For articles that examine children's poverty, see Greg J. Duncan, "Has Children's Poverty Become More Persistent?" *American Sociological Review* 56 (August 1991), pp. 538–550; and David J. Eggebeen and Daniel T. Lichter, "Race, Family Structure, and Changing Poverty among American Children," *American Sociological Review* 56 (December 1991), pp. 801–817.

78. G. Roger Jarjoura, Ruth A. Triplett, and Gregory P. Brinker, "Growing Up Poor: Examining the Link between Persistent Poverty and Delinquency," *Journal of Quantitative Criminology* 18 (June 2002), pp. 159–187.

79. Stephen W. Baron, "Street Youth, Unemployment and Crime: Is It That Simple? Using General Strain Theory to Untangle the Relationship," *Canadian Journal of Criminology and Criminal Justice* 50 (2008), pp. 399–434; Stephen W. Baron, "Street Youth, Gender, Financial Strain, and Crime: Exploring Broidy and Agnew's Extension to General Strain Theory," *Deviant Behavior* 28 (2007), pp. 273–302.

80. Robert Gillespie, "Economic Factors in Crime and Delinquency: A Critical Review of the Empirical Evidence," Hearings, Subcommittee on Crime of the Committee of the Judiciary, House of Representatives, 95th Congress, Serial 47 (Washington, D.C.: U.S. Government Printing Office, 1978), pp. 601–625.

81. Stephen W. Baron and Timothy F. Hartnagel, "Attributions, Affect, and Crime: Street Youths' Reactions to Unemployment," *Criminology* 35 (August 1997), pp. 409–434. However, another study challenges this relationship between employment and reduced rates of delinquency; see Matthew Ploeger, "Youth Employment and Delinquency: Reconsidering a Problematic Relationship," *Criminology* 35 (November 1997), pp. 659–675.

82. Steven F. Messner, Lawrence E. Raffalovich, and Richard McMillan, "Economic Deprivation and Changes in Homicide Arrest Rates for White and Black Youths, 1967–1998: A National Time-Series Analysis," *Criminology* 39 (August 2001), pp. 591–613.

83. Mary E. Pattillo, "Sweet Mothers and Gangbangers: Managing Crime in a Black Middle-Class Neighborhood," *Social Forces* (March 1998), pp. 747–774.

84. Thomas J. Bernard, "Angry Aggression among the 'Truly Disadvantaged,'" *Criminology* 28 (1990), pp. 73–96. See also William Julius Wilson, *The Truly Disadvantaged* (Chicago: University of Chicago Press, 1987).

85. Bernard, "Angry Aggression among the 'Truly Disadvantaged,'" pp. 73–96.

86. Ramiro Martinez Jr., Richard Rosenfeld, and Dennis Mares, "Social Disorganization, Drug Market Activity, and Neighborhood Violent Crime," *Urban Affairs Review* 43 (2008), pp. 846–874.

87. Robert J. Sampson, Jeffrey D. Morenoff, and Felton Earls, "Beyond Social Capital: Spatial Dynamics of Collective Efficacy for Children," *American Sociological Review* 64 (1999), pp. 633–660.

88. Margaret S. Archer, *Culture and Agency: The Place of Culture in Social Theory* (Cambridge, England: Cambridge University Press, 1988), p. ix.

89. George C. Homans, "Bringing Men Back In," *American Sociological Review* 29 (1964), pp. 809–818.

90. James S. Coleman, *Foundations of Social Theory* (Cambridge, Mass.: Harvard University Press, 1990).

91. John H. Laub and Robert J. Sampson, *Shared Beginnings, Divergent Lives: Delinquent Boys to Age 70* (Cambridge, Mass.: Harvard University Press, 2003), p. 145.

92. Ibid. See Chapters 6 and 7.

93. Akiva Liberman, *Adolescents, Neighborhoods and Violence: Recent Findings from the Project on Human Development in Chicago Neighborhoods* (Washington, D.C.: National Institute of Justice, 2007), pp. 4–5, from which some of the wording in this section is taken.

94. From www.icpsr.umich.edu/PHDCN. For more information on collective efficacy, see Robert J. Sampson, "The Embeddedness of Child and Adolescent Development: A COMMUNITY-Level Perspective on Urban Violence," in *Childhood Violence in the Inner City,* edited by Joan McCord (New York: Cambridge, 1997); Robert J. Sampson, Jeffrey Morenoff, and Felton Earls, "Beyond Social Capital: Spatial Dynamics of Collective Efficacy for Children," *American Sociological Review* 64 (1999); and Robert J. Sampson, Stephen W. Raudenbush, and Felton Earls, "Neighborhoods and Violent Crime: A Multilevel Study of Collective Efficacy," *Science* 277 (1997), pp. 918–924.

95. Robert J. Sampson, Jeffrey Morenoff, and Felton Earls, "Beyond Social Capital: Spatial Dynamics of Collective Efficacy for Children," *American Sociological Review* 64 (1999); and Robert J. Sampson, Stephen W. Raudenbush, and Felton Earls, "Neighborhoods and Violent Crime: A Multilevel Study of Collective Efficacy," *Science* 277 (1997), pp. 918–924.

96. Ibid.

97. From www.icpsr.umich.edu/PHDCN. For more information on collective efficacy, see Robert J. Sampson, "The Embeddedness of Child and Adolescent Development: A Community-Level Perspective on Urban Violence," in *Childhood Violence in the Inner City,* edited by Joan McCord (New York: Cambridge, 1997); Sampson, Morenoff, and Earls, "Beyond Social Capital," pp. 663–660; and Robert J. Sampson, Stephen W. Raudenbush, and Felton Earls, "Neighborhoods and Violent Crime: A Multilevel Study of Collective Efficacy," *Science* 277 (1997), pp. 918–924.

CHAPTER 5

1. Fox Butterfield, "Father Steals Best: Crime in an American Family," *New York Times*, August 21, 2002; Charles Laurence, "Liars, Cheats and Thieves All: Pa Would Have Been So Proud," *Daily Telegraph*, August 25, 2002; John Ritter, "A Town Wonders: Does Crime Run in Families?" *USA Today*, September 4, 2002.

2. For this symbolic interactionist perspective, see Charles H. Cooley, *Human Nature and the Social Order* (1902; reprint ed., New York: Schocken Books, 1964); George H. Mead, *Mind, Self and Society* (Chicago: University of Chicago Press, 1934).

3. Edwin H. Sutherland, "A Statement of the Theory," in *The Sutherland Papers,* edited by Albert Cohen, Alfred Lindesmith, and Karl Schuessler (Bloomington: Indiana University Press, 1956), pp. 7–29.

4. Edwin H. Sutherland, *Principles of Criminology* (Philadelphia: J. B. Lippincott, 1947).

5. Ross L. Matsueda, "The Current State of Differential Association Theory," *Crime and Delinquency* 34 (July 1988), pp. 277–306.

6. Harold Finestone, *Victims of Change: Juvenile Delinquents in American Society* (Westport, Conn.: Greenwood Press, 1976).

7. Matsueda, "The Current State of Differential Association Theory."

8. Daniel Glaser, "Differential Association and Criminological Prediction," *Social Problems* 8 (1960), p. 6.

9. Robert J. Burgess Jr. and Ronald L. Akers, "A Differential Association–Reinforcement Theory of Criminal Behavior," *Social Problems* 14 (1966), p. 128. See also Ronald L. Akers, *Deviant Behavior: A Social Learning Approach,* 3rd ed. (Belmont, Calif.: Wadsworth, 1985), p. 41.

10. Marvin D. Krohn et al., "Social Learning Try and Adolescent Cigarette Smoking: A Longitudinal Study," *Social Problems* 32 (June 1985), pp. 455–474.

11. For those who see little value in a theory such as differential association that cannot be tested, see Jack P. Gibbs, "The State of Criminology Theory," *Criminology* 25 (1987), pp. 821–840; Sheldon Glueck, "Theory and Fact in Criminology," *British Journal of Criminology* 7 (1956), pp. 92–109; and Travis Hirschi, *Causes of Delinquency* (Berkeley: University of California Press, 1969). For a defense of the testability of differential association theory, see James D. Orcutt, "Differential Association and Marijuana Use: A Closer Look at Sutherland (with a Little Help from Becker)," *Criminology* 25 (1987), pp. 341–358.

12. Ronald L. Akers, "Is Differential Association/Social Learning Cultural Deviance Theory?" *Criminology* 34 (1996), pp. 229–247.

13. Ibid.

14. Steven Box, *Deviance, Reality and Society* (New York: Holt, Rinehart and Winston, 1971).

15. C. R. Jeffery, "An Integrated Theory of Crime and Criminal Behavior," *Journal of Criminal Law, Criminology and Police Science* 49 (1959), pp. 533–552.

16. Matsueda, "The Current State of Differential Association Theory," p. 295.

17. David Matza, *Delinquency and Drift* (New York: Wiley, 1964), p. 28.

18. Ibid.

19. Gresham M. Sykes and David Matza, "Techniques of Neutralization: A Theory of Delinquency," *American Sociological Review* 22 (December 1957), pp. 644–670.

20. Ibid.

21. David Matza, *Delinquency and Drift* (New York: Wiley, 1964), p. 156.

22. Matza, *Delinquency and Drift.*

23. Ibid.

24. Ibid.

25. Ibid., p. 185.

26. Ibid.

27. Matza, *Delinquency and Drift.* See also Robert Agnew, "Determinism, Interdeterminism, and Crime: An Empirical Exploration," *Criminology* 33 (February 1995), p. 83.

28. Travis Hirschi, "On the Compatibility of Rational Choice and Social Control Theories of Crime," in *The Reasoning Criminal,* edited by Derek B. Cornish and Ronald V. Clarke (New York: Springer-Verlag, 1986), pp. 105–118; Michael R. Gottfredson and Travis Hirschi, eds., *Positive Criminology* (Newbury Park, Calif.: Sage, 1987); and Michael R. Gottfredson and Travis Hirschi, *A General Theory of Crime* (Palo Alto, Calif.: Stanford University Press, 1990).

29. See John S. Goldkamp, "Rational Choice and Determinism," in *Positive Criminology,* (Thousand Oaks, Calif.: Sage, 1987), pp. 125–137.

30. Ronald L. Akers, "Rational Choice, Deterrence, and Social Learning in Criminology: The Path Not Taken," *Journal of Criminal Law and Criminology* 81 (1990), pp. 653–676.

31. Ian Taylor, Paul Walton, and Jock Young, *The New Criminology* (New York: Harper and Row, 1973).

32. Robert Regoli and Eric Poole, "The Commitment of Delinquents to Their Misdeeds: A Reexamination," *Journal of Criminal Justice* 6 (1978), pp. 261–269; Michael J. Hindelang, "The Commitment of Delinquents to Their Misdeeds: Do Delinquents Drift?" *Social Problems* 17 (1970), pp. 50–59; and Michael J. Hindelang, "Moral Evaluation of Illegal Behaviors," *Social Problems* 21 (1974), pp. 370–385.

33. John Hagan, "Destiny and Drift: Subcultural Preferences, Status Attainments, and the Risks and Rewards of Youth," *American Sociological Review* 56 (1991), p. 567.

34. Donald J. Shoemaker, *Theories of Delinquency: An Examination of Explanations of Delinquent Behavior,* 5th ed. (New York: Oxford University Press, 2005).

35. Albert J. Reiss Jr., "Delinquency as the Failure of Personal and Social Controls," *American Sociological Review* 16 (1951), pp. 196–207.

36. F. Ivan Nye, *Family Relationships and Delinquent Behavior* (New York: John Wiley, 1958).

37. The principles of containment theory draw on Walter C. Reckless, "A New Theory of Delinquency and Crime," *Federal Probation* 24 (December 1961), pp. 42–46.

38. E. D. Lively, Simon Dinitz, and Walter C. Reckless, "Self-Concept as a Prediction of Juvenile Delinquency," *American Journal of Orthopsychiatry* 32 (1962), pp. 159–168; Gary F. Jensen, "Inner Containment and Delinquency," *Criminology* 64 (1973), pp. 464–470; and Franco Ferracuti, Simon Dinitz, and E. Acosta de Brenes, *Delinquents and Nondelinquents in the Puerto Rican Slum Culture* (Columbus: Ohio State University Press, 1975).

39. Timothy J. Owens, "Two Dimensions of Self-Esteem: Reciprocal Effects of Positive Self-Worth and Self-Deprecations on Adolescent Problems," *American Sociological Review* 59 (1994), pp. 391, 405; L. Edward Wells and Joseph H. Rankin, "Self-Concept as a Mediating Factor in Delinquency," *Social Psychology Quarterly* 46 (1983), p. 19; John D. McCarthy and Dean R. Hoge, "The Dynamics of Self-Esteem and Delinquency," *American Journal of Sociology* 90 (1984), p. 396; and W. E. Thompson and R. A. Dodder, "Juvenile Delinquency Explained? A Test of Containment Theory," *Youth and Society* 15 (December 1983), pp. 171–194.

40. Florence R. Rosenberg and Morris Rosenberg, "Self-Esteem and Delinquency," *Journal of Youth and Adolescence* 7 (1978), p. 280.

41. H. B. Kaplan, *Deviant Behavior in Defense of Self* (New York: Academic Press, 1980); and Rosenberg and Rosenberg, "Self-Esteem and Delinquency." See also Morris Rosenberg, Carmi Schooler, and Carrie Schoenbach, "Self-Esteem and Adolescent Problems," *American Sociological Review* 54 (1989), pp. 1004–1018.

42. Simon Dinitz and Betty A. Pfau-Vicent, "Self-Concept and Juvenile Delinquency: An Update," *Youth Society* 14 (December 1982), pp. 133–158.

43. Michael Schwartz and Sandra S. Tangri, "A Note on 'Self-Concept as an Insulator against Delinquency,'" *American Sociological Review* 30 (1965), pp. 922–926.

44. Hirschi, *Causes of Delinquency,* p. 16.

45. Ibid., p. 31.

46. Ibid., p. 34.

47. Ibid.

48. Ibid.

49. Ibid.

50. Ibid., p. 86.

51. Ibid.

52. Ibid., p. 22.

53. Ibid.

54. Ibid., p. 200.

55. Ibid.

56. Ibid.

57. Ibid., p. 135.

58. Ibid.

59. Ibid.

60. Barbara J. Costello and Paul R. Vowell, "Testing Control Theory and Differential Association: A Reanalysis of the Richmond Youth Project Data," *Criminology* 37 (November 1999), pp. 479–514; and Charles R. Tittle, *Control Balance: Toward a General Theory of Deviance* (Boulder, Colo.: Westview, 1995). For a recent attempt to test Tittle's control balance theory, see Alex R. Piquero and Matthew Hickman, "An Empirical Test of Tittle's Control Balance Theory," *Criminology* 37 (May 1999), pp. 319–341. See also Steven A. Cernkovich, "Evaluating Two Models of Delinquency Causation: Structural Theory and Control Theory," *Criminology* 25 (1987), pp. 335–352; Raymond A. Eve, "A Study of the Efficacy and Interactions of Several Theories for Explaining Rebelliousness among High School Students," *Journal of Criminal Law and Criminology* 69 (1978), pp. 115–125; Marvin D. Krohn and James L. Massey, "Social Control and Delinquent Behavior: An Examination of the Elements of the Social

Bond," *Sociological Quarterly* 21 (August 1980), p. 542; Elliott et al., *Explaining Delinquency and Drug Use*; Joseph H. Rankin, "Investigating the Interrelations among Social Control Variables and Conformity," *Journal of Criminal Law and Criminology* 67 (1977), pp. 470–480; Robert Agnew, "Social Control Theory and Delinquency: A Longitudinal Test," *Criminology* 23 (1985), pp. 47–61; Randy L. LaGrange and Helene Raskin White, "Age Differences in Delinquency: A Test of Theory," *Criminology* 23 (1985), pp. 19–45; Kimberly Kempf Leonard and Scott H. Decker, "Theory of Social Control: Does It Apply to the Very Young?" *Journal of Criminal Justice* 22 (1994), pp. 89–105; Robert L. Gardner and Donald J. Shoemaker, "Social Bonding and Delinquency: A Comparative Analysis," *Sociological Quarterly* 39 (1989), pp. 481–500; and Eric A. Stewart, "School Social Bonds, Social Climate, and School Misbehavior: A Multilevel Analysis," *Justice Quarterly* 20 (September 2003), pp. 575–604.

61. Shoemaker, *Theories of Delinquency.*

62. Leonard and Decker, "Theory of Social Control."

63. Among the growing number of works citing the advantages of integrated theory are Richard Johnson, *Juvenile Delinquency and Its Origins: An Integrated Theoretical Approach* (New York: Cambridge University Press, 1979); Elliott et al., *Explaining Delinquency and Drug Use;* Steven Messner, Marvin Krohn, and Allen Liska, eds., *Theoretical Integration in the Study of Deviance and Crime: Problems and Prospects* (Albany: State University of New York at Albany Press, 1989); and John Hagan and Bill McCarthy, *Mean Streets: Youth Crime and Homelessness* (New York: Cambridge University Press, 1997).

64. Shoemaker, *Theories of Delinquency.*

65. Ibid.

66. Ibid.

67. Ibid.

68. For other integrated theories, see James Q. Wilson and Richard J. Herrnstein, *Crime and Human Nature* (New York: Simon and Schuster, 1985), which is discussed in Chapter 3; Robert J. Sampson and John H. Laub, *Crime in the Making: Pathways and Turning Points through Life* (Cambridge, Mass.: Harvard University Press, 1993), which is discussed in Chapter 2; and Colvin and Pauly, "A Critique of Criminology," pp. 513–551, which is discussed in Chapter 6; John Hagan, A. R. Gillis, and John Simpson, "The Class Structure of Gender and Delinquency: Toward a Power-Control Theory of Common Delinquent Behavior," *American Journal of Sociology* 90 (1985), pp. 1151–1178.

69. Michael R. Gottfredson and Travis Hirschi, *A General Theory of Crime* (Palo Alto, Calif.: Stanford University Press, 1990); Elliott et al., *Explaining Delinquency and Drug Use;* Delbert S. Elliott, Suzanne S. Ageton, and Rachelle J. Canter, "An Integrated Theoretical Perspective on Delinquent Behavior," *Journal of Research in Crime and Delinquency* 16 (1979), pp. 3–27; Terence P. Thornberry, "Toward an Interactional Theory of Delinquency," *Criminology* 25 (1987), pp. 862–891; Terence P. Thornberry, Alan J. Lizotte, Marvin D. Krohn, Margaret Farnworth, and Sung Joon Jang, "Testing Interactional Theory: An Examination of Reciprocal Causal Relationships among Family, School, and Delinquency," *Journal of Criminal Law and*

Criminology 82 (1991), pp. 3–35; and J. David Hawkins and Joseph G. Weis, "The Social Development Model: An Integrated Approach to Delinquency Prevention," *Journal of Primary Prevention* 6 (Winter 1985), pp. 73–97.

70. Gottfredson and Hirschi, *A General Theory of Crime.*

71. Ibid., pp. 90–91.

72. Ibid., p. 87.

73. Ibid.

74. For a review of these studies, see T. David Evans, Francis T. Cullen, Velmer S. Burton Jr., R. Gregory Dunaway, and Michael L. Benson, "The Social Consequences of Self-Control: Testing the General Theory of Crime," *Criminology* 35 (1997), pp. 476–477. See also Ryan Charles Meldrum, "Beyond Parenting: An Examination of the Etiology of Self-Control," *Journal of Criminal Justice* 36 (2008), pp. 244–251; Alexander T. Vazsonyi and Rudi Klanjsek, "A Test of Self-Control Theory across Different Socioeconomic Strata," *Justice Quarterly* 25 (March 2008), pp. 101–131; and Stacey Nofziger, "The 'Cause' of Low Self-Control: The Influence of Maternal Self-Control," *Journal of Research in Crime and Delinquency* 45 (2008), pp. 191–224.

75. Harold G. Grasmick, Charles R. Tittle, Robert J. Bursik Jr., and Bruce J. Arneklev, "Testing the Core Empirical Implications of Gottfredson and Hirschi's General Theory of Crime," *Journal of Research in Crime and Delinquency* 30 (February 1993), pp. 47–54.

76. See Ronald L. Akers, "Self-Control as a General Theory of Crime," *Journal of Quantitative Criminology* 7 (1991), pp. 201–211.

77. Shoemaker, *Theories of Delinquency.*

78. Dennis M. Giever, Dana C. Lynskey, and Danette S. Monnet, "Gottfredson and Hirschi's General Theory of Crime and Youth Gangs: An Empirical Test on a Sample of Middle-School Students," unpublished paper sent to the authors, 1998. See also Meldrum, "Beyond Parenting"; Vazsonyi and Klanjsek, "A Test of Self-Control Theory across different Socioeconomic Strata; and Nofziger, "The 'Cause' of Low Self-Control."

79. Callie Harbin Burt, Ronald L. Simons, and Leslie G. Simons, "A Longitudinal Test of the Effects of Parenting and the Stability of Self-Control: Negative Evidence for the General Theory of Crime," *Criminology* 44 (2006), pp. 353–396.

80. Ibid, p. 353.

81. Delbert S. Elliott, Suzanne S. Ageton, and Rachelle J. Canter, "An Integrated Theoretical Perspective on Delinquent Behavior," *Journal of Research in Crime and Delinquency* 16 (1979), pp. 3–27.

82. Ibid.

83. Cynthia Jacob Chien, "Testing the Effect of the Key Theoretical Variable of Theories of Strain, Social Control and Social Learning on Types of Delinquency," paper presented at the Annual Meeting of the American Society of Criminology, Baltimore, November 1990.

84. Thornberry, "Toward an Interactional Theory of Delinquency."

85. Ibid.

86. Shoemaker, *Theories of Delinquency.*

87. Ibid.

88. Ibid.

89. Hawkins and Weis, "The Social Development Model."

90. Hirschi, *Causes of Delinquency.*

91. Clifford R. Shaw, *Delinquent Areas* (Chicago: University of Chicago Press, 1929); and Clifford Shaw and Henry D. McKay, *Juvenile Delinquency in Urban Areas* (Chicago: University of Chicago Press, 1942).

92. Hawkins et al., *Typology of Cause-Focused Strategies*.

93. John A. Claussen, *American Lives: Looking Back at the Children of the Great Depression* (New York: Free Press, 1993).

94. Ibid., p. viii.

95. Ibid.

96. Marvin D. Krohn, Terence P. Thornberry, Craig Rivera, and Marc Le Blanc, "Later Delinquency Careers," in *Child Development*, edited by Rolf Loeber and David P. Farrington (Thousand Oaks, Calif.: Sage, 2001), pp. 67–93.

97. Terence P. Thornberry, Marvin D. Krohn, Alan J. Lizotte, Carolyn A. Smith, and Kimberly Tobin, *Gangs and Delinquency in Developmental Perspective* (Cambridge, England: Cambridge University Press, 2003).

98. John H. Laub and Robert J. Sampson, *Shared Beginnings, Divergent Lives: Delinquent Boys to Age 70* (Cambridge, Mass.: Harvard University Press, 2003). See also Robert J. Sampson and John H. Laub, "A Life-Course Theory of Cumulative Disadvantage and the Stability of Delinquency," in *Developmental Theories of Crime and Delinquency*, edited by Terence P. Thornberry (New Brunswick, N.J.: Transaction Publishers, 1997), pp. 133–161.

99. Robert J. Sampson and John H. Laub, *Crime in the Making: Pathways and Turning Points through Life* (Cambridge, Mass.: Harvard University Press, 1993).

100. Laub and Sampson, *Shared Beginnings, Divergent Lives*; see especially Chapters 3 and 6.

101. Ibid., p. 149.

102. Shadd Maruna, *Making Good: How Ex-Convicts Reform and Rebuild Their Lives* (Washington, D.C.: American Psychological Association, 2001).

103. Peggy C. Giordano, Stephen A. Cernkovich, and Jennifer L. Rudolph, "Gender, Crime, and Delinquency: Toward a Theory of Cognitive Transformation," *American Journal of Sociology* 107 (January 2002), pp. 990–1064.

CHAPTER 6

1. Kevin Wack, "Teen Arsonist to Get Help at Long Creek," *Portland Press Herald*, July 1, 2004; Fox Butterfield, "New Look at Boy's Sentence in Boatyard Fire," *New York Times*, March 29, 2004; and Fox Butterfield, "A Federal Case for a Teenager: Family Sees Tie to Ex-President," *New York Times*, December 23, 2003.

2. Lening Zhang and Steven F. Messner, "The Severity of Official Punishment for Delinquency and Change in Interpersonal Relations in Chinese Society," *Journal of Research in Crime and Delinquency* 31 (November 1994), pp. 416–433.

3. Frederick M. Thrasher, *The Gang* (Chicago: University of Chicago Press, 1927).

4. Frank Tannenbaum, *Crime and the Community* (New York: Columbia University Press, 1938), pp. 19–20.

5. Ibid.

6. Edwin M. Lemert, *Social Pathology* (New York: McGraw-Hill, 1951).

7. Harold Finestone, *Victims of Change: Juvenile Delinquents in American Society* (Westport, Conn.: Greenwood Press, 1976).

8. Ibid., p. 198. For a discussion concerning the complexity of this process of moving from primary to secondary deviance, see Daniel L. Dotter and Julian B. Roebuck, "The Labeling Approach Re-Examined: Interactionism and the Components of Deviance," *Deviant Behavior* 9 (1988), pp. 19–32.

9. Finestone, *Victims of Change*.

10. Howard S. Becker, *Outsiders* (New York: Free Press, 1963), pp. 8–9.

11. Ibid.

12. Finestone, *Victims of Change*.

13. Edwin Schur, *Radical Nonintervention* (Englewood Cliffs, N.J.: Prentice-Hall, 1973), p. 155.

14. Zhang and Messner, "The Severity of Official Punishment for Delinquency and Change in Interpersonal Relations in Chinese Society," p. 418.

15. Francis Polymeria, Francis T. Cullen, and Joanne C. Gersten, "The Effects of Police and Mental Health Intervention on Juvenile Delinquency: Specifying Contingencies in the Impact of Formal Reaction," *Journal of Health and Social Behavior* 27 (1986), pp. 90–105.

16. Anthony Matarazzo, Peter J. Carrington, and Robert D. Hiscott, "The Effect of Prior Youth Court Dispositions on Current Disposition: An Application of Societal-Reaction Theory," *Theory of Quantitative Criminology* 17 (2001), pp. 169–200.

17. Jack P. Gibbs, "Conceptions of Deviant Behavior: The Old and the New," *Pacific Sociological Review* 9 (1966), pp. 9–14; Walter R. Gove, "Labeling and Mental Illness: A Critique," in *The Labeling of Deviance: Evaluating a Perspective*, 2nd ed., edited by Walter R. Gove (Beverly Hills, Calif.: Sage, 1980), pp. 53–59; John Hagan, "Extra-Legal Attitudes and Criminal Sanctioning: An Assessment and a Sociological Viewpoint," *Law and Society Review* 8 (1974), pp. 357–383; Travis Hirschi, "Labeling Theory and Juvenile Delinquency: An Assessment of the Evidence," in *The Labeling of Deviance: Evaluating a Perspective*, 2nd ed., edited by Walter R. Gove (Beverly Hills, Calif.: Sage, 1980), pp. 271–293; Charles R. Tittle, "Deterrence of Labeling?" *Social Forces* 53 (1975), pp. 399–410; and Charles F. Wellford, "Labeling Theory and Criminology: An Assessment," *Social Problems* 22 (1975), pp. 332–345.

18. Zhang and Messner, "The Severity of Official Punishment for Delinquency and Change in Interpersonal Relations in Chinese Society," p. 419. See also Tittle, "Deterrence of Labeling?" and Gove, "Labeling and Mental Illness."

19. Raymond Paternoster and Leeann Iovanni, "The Labeling Perspective and Delinquency: An Elaboration of the Theory and an Assessment of the Evidence," *Justice Quarterly* 6 (1989), p. 359.

20. Zhang and Messner, "The Severity of Official Punishment for Delinquency and Change in Interpersonal Relations in Chinese Society."

21. Ruth A. Triplett and G. Roger Jarjoura, "Theoretical and Empirical Specification of a Model of Informal Labeling," *Journal of Quantitative Criminology* 10 (1994), p. 243.

22. Raymond Paternoster and Ruth A. Triplett, "Disaggregating Self-Reported Delinquency and Its Implications for Theory," *Criminology* 26 (1988), p. 6. See also Lening Zhang, "Informal Reactions and Delinquency," *Criminal Justice and Behavior* 24 (March 1997), pp. 129–150.

23. John Braithwaite, *Crime, Shame and Reintegration* (Cambridge, England: Cambridge University Press, 1989).

See also Toni Makkai and John Braithwaite, "Reintegrative Shaming and Compliance with Regulatory Standards," *Criminology* 32 (August 1994), pp. 361–385.

24. Triplett and Jarjoura, "Theoretical and Empirical Specification of a Model of Informal Labeling."

25. Ruth Ann Triplett, "Labeling and Differential Association: The Effects on Delinquent Behavior," Ph.D. dissertation, University of Maryland, 1990. For a model of informal labeling, see Triplett and Jarjoura, "Theoretical and Empirical Specification of a Model of Informal Labeling," pp. 241–276.

26. J. D. Orcutt, "Societal Reaction and the Response to Deviation in Small Groups," *Social Forces* 52 (1973), pp. 259–267.

27. Robert J. Sampson and John H. Laub, "A Life-Course Theory of Cumulative Disadvantage and the Stability of Delinquency," in *Developmental Theories of Crime and Delinquency*, edited by Terence P. Thornberry (New Brunswick, N.J.: Transaction Publishers, 1997), pp. 133–161.

28. Jon Gunnar Bernburg and Marvin D. Krohn, "Labeling, Life Chances, and Adult Crime: The Direct and Indirect Effects of Official Intervention in Adolescence on Crime in Early Adulthood," *Criminology* 41 (November 2003), pp. 1287–1313.

29. Jon Gunnar Bernberg, Marvin D. Krohn, and Craig J. Rivera, "Official Labeling, Criminal Embeddedness, and Subsequent Delinquency: A Longitudinal Test of Labeling Theory," *Journal of Research in Crime and Delinquency* 43 (February 2006), pp. 67–88.

30. G. Nettler, *Explaining Crime*, 3rd ed. (New York: McGraw-Hill, 1984).

31. Donald J. Shoemaker, *Theories of Delinquency: An Examination of Explanations of Delinquency Behavior*, 5th ed. (New York: Oxford University Press, 2005).

32. Ross L. Matsueda, "Reflected Appraisals, Parental Labeling, and Delinquency: Specifying a Symbolic Interactional Theory," *American Journal of Sociology* 97 (1992), pp. 1577–1611; Karen Heimer and Ross L. Matsueda, "Role-Taking, Role Commitment, and Delinquency: A Theory of Differential Social Control," *American Sociological Review* 59 (1994), pp. 365–390; Karen Heimer, "Gender, Race, and the Pathways to Delinquency," in *Crime and Inequality*, edited by John Hagan and Ruth D. Peterson (Stanford, Calif.: Stanford University Press, 1995), pp. 140–173; Karen Heimer and Ross L. Matsueda, "A Symbolic Interactionist Theory of Motivation and Deviance: Interpreting Psychological Research," in *Motivation and Delinquency*, Vol. 44 of the Nebraska Symposium on Motivation, edited by D. Wayne Osgood (Lincoln, Neb.: University of Nebraska Press, 1997), pp. 223–276; and Ross L. Matsueda and Karen Heimer, "A Symbolic Interactionist Theory of Role-Transitions, Role Commitments, and Delinquency," in *Advances in Criminological Theory*, edited by T. P. Thornberry (New Brunswick, N.J.: Transaction Publishers, 1997), pp. 163–213.

33. Matsueda, "Reflected Appraisals, Parental Labeling, and Delinquency."

34. Ibid.

35. Ibid.

36. Heimer, "Gender, Race, and Delinquency," p. 141.

37. Matsueda and Heimer, "A Symbolic Interactionist Theory of Role-Transitions, Role Commitments, and Delinquency."

38. Ibid.

39. Ibid.

40. The following discussion is based on ibid., pp. 1580–1581.

41. George H. Mead, *Mind, Self and Society* (Chicago: University of Chicago Press, 1934).

42. Matsueda, "Reflected Appraisals, Parental Labeling, and Delinquency," p. 1580. See also Mead, *Mind, Self and Society*, and Herbert Blumer, *Symbolic Interactionism: Perspective and Method* (Englewood Cliffs, N.J.: Prentice-Hall, 1969).

43. Matsueda, "Reflected Appraisals, Parental Labeling, and Delinquency," p. 1581.

44. Scott Briar and Irving Piliavin, "Delinquency, Situational Inducements, and Commitment to Conformity," *Social Problems* 13 (1965), pp. 35–45.

45. James F. Short Jr. and Fred L. Strodtbeck, *Group Process and Gang Delinquency* (Chicago: University of Chicago Press, 1965).

46. Donald Gibbons, "Observations on the Study of Crime Causation," *American Journal of Sociology* 77 (1971), pp. 262–278.

47. Matsueda, "Reflected Appraisals, Parental Labeling, and Delinquency."

48. Charles H. Cooley, *Human Nature and the Social Order*, rev. ed. (New York: Scribners, 1922).

49. Mead, *Mind, Self, and Society.*

50. Matsueda, "Reflected Appraisals, Parental Labeling, and Delinquency."

51. Ibid.

52. Ibid., p. 1602.

53. Ibid.

54. Ibid.

55. Heimer, "Gender, Race, and Delinquency," p. 145.

56. Ibid.

57. Ibid., p. 146.

58. Heimer and Matsueda, "Role-Taking, Role Commitment, and Delinquency."

59. Bartusch and Matsueda, "Gender, Reflected Appraisals, and Labeling"; Heimer, "Gender, Interaction, and Delinquency"; Heimer, "Gender, Race, and the Pathways to Delinquency"; and Stacy De Coster and Karen Heimer, "The Relationship between Law Violation and Depression: An Interactionist Analysis," *Criminology* 39 (November 2001), pp. 799–836.

60. David Shichor, "The New Criminology: Some Critical Issues," *British Journal of Criminology* 20 (1980), pp. 29–48.

61. Viktor Afanasyer, *Marxist Philosophy* (Moscow: Foreign Language Publishing House, n.d.).

62. This interpretation of Hegel's "thesis–antithesis–synthesis" paradigm is frequently questioned. See Ron E. Roberts and Robert Marsh Kloss, *Social Movements: Between the Balcony and the Barricade*, 2nd ed. (St. Louis, Mo.: C. V. Mosby, 1979), p. 16.

63. Stephen Spitzer, "Toward a Marxian Theory of Deviance," *Social Problems* 22 (1975), pp. 638–651.

64. Georg Simmel, *Conflict*, translated by Kurt H. Wolf (Glencoe, Ill.: Free Press, 1955), p. 15.

65. Ralf Dahrendorf, "Out of Utopia: Toward a Reorientation of Sociological Analysis," *American Journal of Sociology* 64 (1958), pp. 115–127.

66. Richard Quinney, *Critique of Legal Order: Crime Control in Capitalist Society* (Boston: Little, Brown, 1974), p. 16.

67. William Bonger, *Criminality and Economic Conditions*, abridged ed. (Bloomington: Indiana University Press, 1969), p. 24.

68. See Larry Tifft and Dennis Sullivan, *Crime, Criminology, and Anarchism: The Struggle to Be Human* (Sanday, Orkney

Islands, Scotland: Cienfuegos Press, 1980); Raymond J. Michalowski, *Order, Law, and Crime: An Introduction to Criminology* (New York: Random House, 1985); and Harold E. Pepinsky, "A Sociology of Justice," *Annual Review of Sociology* 12 (1986), pp. 93–108.

69. Tifft and Sullivan, *Crime, Criminology, and Anarchism*, and Michalowski, *Order, Law, and Crime.*

70. Pepinsky, "A Sociology of Justice."

71. Jonathan H. Turner, *The Structure of Sociological Theory* (Homewood, Ill.: Dorsey Press, 1978), p. 124.

72. Karl Marx and Frederick Engels, *The Communist Manifesto* (1848; reprint ed., New York: International Publishers, 1979).

73. Ibid., p. 9.

74. Ibid.

75. Ibid.

76. Mark Colvin and John Pauly, "A Critique of Criminology: Toward an Integrated Structural–Marxist Theory of Delinquency Production," *American Journal of Sociology* 89 (November 1983), pp. 513–551.

77. Ibid.

78. Ibid.

79. Herman Schwendinger and Julia S. Schwendinger, "Marginal Youth and Social Policy," *Social Problems* 24 (December 1976), pp. 84–91.

80. Herman Schwendinger and Julia Siegel Schwendinger, *Adolescent Subcultures and Delinquency* (New York: Praeger, 1985), p. 3.

81. Schwendinger and Schwendinger, "Marginal Youth and Social Policy," pp. 84–91.

82. Ibid.

83. David O. Friedrichs, "Victimology: A Consideration of the Radical Critique," *Crime and Delinquency* 29 (1983), pp. 283–294.

84. This interview took place in February 1984, and the information is used with permission.

85. Max Weber, "Class, Status, Party," in *Class, Status and Power,* edited by Richard Bendix and S. M. Lipset (New York: Macmillan, 1953), pp. 63–75.

86. Ralf Dahrendorf, *Class and Class Conflict in Industrial Society* (Palo Alto, Calif.: Stanford University Press, 1959).

87. A. T. Turk, "Class, Conflict, and Criminalization," *Sociological Focus* 10 (August 1977), pp. 209–220.

88. Ian Taylor, Paul Walton, and Jock Young, *The New Criminology: For a Social Theory of Deviance* (Boston: Routledge and Kegan Paul, 1973).

89. John Hagan, A. R. Gillis, and John Simpson, "The Class Structure of Gender and Delinquency: Toward a Power-Control Theory of Common Delinquent Behavior," *American Journal of Sociology* 90 (1985) pp. 1151–1178; John Hagan, John Simpson, and A. R. Gillis, "The Sexual Stratification of Social Control: A Gender-Based Perspective on Crime and Delinquency," *British Journal of Sociology* 30 (1979), pp. 25–38; John Hagan, John Simpson, and A. R. Gillis, "Class in the Household: A Power-Control Theory of Gender and Delinquency," *American Journal of Sociology* 92 (January 1987), pp. 788–816; John Hagan, A. R. Gillis, and John Simpson, "Clarifying and Extending Power-Control Theory," *American Journal of Sociology* 95 (1990), pp. 1024–1037; and John Hagan, *Structural Criminology* (New Brunswick, N.J.: Rutgers University Press, 1989).

90. Robert M. Regoli and John D. Hewitt, *Delinquency in Society*, 8th ed. (Boston: Jones and Bartlett, 2010).

91. Beverly Kingston, Robert Regoli, and John D. Hewitt, "The Theory of Differential Oppression: A Developmental-Ecological Explanation of Adolescent Problem Behavior," *Critical Criminology* 11 (2003), pp. 237–260.

92. Regoli and Hewitt, *Delinquency in Society.*

93. In *Social Sources of Delinquency*, Ruth Rosner Kornhauser includes the discussion of Sellin under cultural deviance theory.

94. Thorsten Sellin, *Culture, Conflict, and Crime* (New York: Social Science Research Council, 1938).

95. Ibid.

96. Ibid., p. 29.

97. Ibid.

98. Ibid.

99. Ibid., p. 21.

100. Ibid.

101. George B. Vold, *Theoretical Criminology*, 2nd ed., prepared by Thomas J. Bernard (New York: Oxford University Press, 1979), p. 283. For a more up-to-date analysis of Vold, see Thomas J. Bernard and Jeffrey B. Snipes, *Theoretical Criminology*, 4th ed. (New York: Oxford University Press, 1998), pp. 236–238.

102. Ibid.

103. Friedrichs, "Radical Criminology in the United States."

104. For a review of radical humanism, see Kevin Anderson, "Humanism and Anti-Humanism in Radical Criminological Theory," in *Perspectives on Social Problems* 3 (1991), pp. 19–38; and Kevin Anderson, "Radical Criminology and the Overcoming of Alienation: Perspectives from Marxian and Gandhian Humanism," in *Criminology as Peacemaking*, edited by Harold E. Pepinsky and Richard Quinney (Bloomington: Indiana University Press, 1991), pp. 14–29.

105. Kay Pranis, "Face to Face: Spaces for Reflective Community Dialog," *VOMA Connection* (Summer 2000).

106. Ibid.

107. Kay Pranis, "Empathy Development in Youth through Restorative Practices," *Public Service Psychology* 25 (Spring 2000), pp. 17–21.

108. Ibid.

109. Ibid.

110. S. Stuart, "Restorative Processes: Mediation, Conferencing, and Circles." www.restorativejustice.org.

111. L. Parker, "Circles." www.restorativejustice.org.

112. G. Bazemore and M. Umbreit, *A Comparison of Four Restorative Conferencing Models* (Washington, D.C.: U.S. Department of Justice, Office of Juvenile Justice and Delinquency Prevention, and U.S. Department of Justice, National Institute of Corrections, 2001).

113. Lorenn Walker, Ted Sakai, and Kat Brady, "Restorative Circles—A Reentry Process for Hawaii Inmates," *Federal Probation* 70 (2006), pp. 33–37, 86.

114. Ibid. See also P. McCold, "Overview of Mediation, Conferencing and Circles," paper presented at the 10th United Nations Congress on Crime Prevention and Treatment of Offenders, International Institute for Restorative Practices, Vienna, Austria, April 10–17, 1998.

115. Nancy Rodriguez, "Restorative Justice at Work: Examining the Impact of Restorative Justice Resolutions on Juvenile Recidivism," *Crime and Delinquency* 53 (2007), pp. 355–378.

116. Kathleen J. Bergseth and Jeffrey A. Bouffard, "The Long-Term Impact of Restorative Justice Programming for Juvenile Offenders," *Journal of Criminal Justice* 35 (2007), pp. 433–451.

117. Gwen Robinson and Joanna Shapland, "Reducing Recidivism: A Task for Restorative Justice," *British Journal of Criminology* 48 (2008), pp. 337–358.

118. See Nan S. Park, Boom S. Lee, John M. Bolland, Alexander T. Vazsonyi, and Fei Sun, "Early Adolescent Pathways of Antisocial Behaviors in Poor, Inner-City Neighborhoods," *Journal of Early Adolescence* 28 (May 2008), pp. 185–205; and Robert Agnew, Shelley Keith Matthews, Jacob Bucher, Adria N. Welcher, and Corey Keyes, "Socioeconomic Status, Economic Problems, and Delinquency," *Youth & Society* 40 (2008), pp. 159–181.

119. Ibid., p. 159.

120. Some groups perceive greater injustice than others. See Kevin Buckler and James D. Unnever, "Racial and Ethnic Perceptions of Injustice: Testing the Core Hypotheses of Comparative Conflict Theory," *Journal of Criminal Justice* 36 (2008), pp. 270–278.

CHAPTER 7

1. Evelyn Larruba, "Girls Convicted as Adults Serve Time in Solitary," *Los Angeles Times*, January 3, 2002; Matt Olsen, "Kids in the Hole," *The Progressive*, August 1, 2003; and "Faith in Action: Getting Children Out of Jails in Los Angeles," from *No Turning Back: Promising Approaches to Reducing Racial and Ethnic Disparities Affecting Youth of Color in the Justice System* (Washington, D.C.: Building Blocks for Youth Initiative, 2005).

2. Meda Chesney-Lind, "Girls, Crime and Women's Place," *Crime and Delinquency* 35 (1988), pp. 5–29. See also Kathleen Daly and Meda Chesney-Lind, "Feminism and Criminology," *Justice Quarterly* 5 (1988), pp. 497–538.

3. Carol Smart, *Women, Crime, and Criminology: A Feminist Critique* (Boston: Routledge and Kegan Paul, 1976).

4. Dorie Klein, "Afterword: Twenty Years Ago . . . Today," in *The Criminal Justice System and Women: Offenders, Victims, and Workers* (New York: McGraw-Hill, 1995), pp. 47–53.

5. Ibid., p. 48.

6. Daly and Chesney-Lind, "Feminism and Criminology," p. 498.

7. Office of Juvenile Justice and Delinquency Prevention, "Addressing Female Development in Treatment," in *Juvenile Female Offenders: A Status of the States Report* (Washington, D.C.: U.S. Department of Justice, 1998).

8. Paul Mazerolle, "Gender, General Strain, and Delinquency: An Empirical Examination," *Justice Quarterly* 15 (March 1998), pp. 65–91.

9. Karen Heimer, "Gender, Race, and the Pathways to Delinquency: An Interactionist Perspective," in *Crime and Inequality*, edited by J. Hagan and R. Peterson (Stanford, Calif.: Stanford University Press, 1994), pp. 140–173.

10. Jody Miller, *One of the Guys* (New York: Oxford University Press, 2001).

11. Kathleen Daly, "Looking Back, Looking Forward: The Promise of Feminist Transformation," in *The Criminal Justice System and Women*, pp. 443–457.

12. Josephina Figueira-McDonough and Elaine Selo, "A Reformulation of the 'Equal Opportunity' Explanation of Female Delinquency," *Crime and Delinquency* 26 (1980),

pp. 333–343; John Hagan, A. R. Gillis, and John Simpson, "The Class Structure of Gender and Delinquency: Toward a Power-Control Theory of Common Delinquent Behavior," *American Journal of Sociology* 90 (1985), pp. 1151–1178; and Douglas A. Smith and Raymond Paternoster, "The Gender Gap in Theories of Deviance: Issues and Evidence," *Journal of Research in Crime and Delinquency* 24 (1987), pp. 140–172.

13. Eileen Leonard, "Theoretical Criminology and Gender," in *The Criminal Justice System and Women*, pp. 55–70.

14. Chesney-Lind, "Girls, Crime and Women's Place." For an update of this article, see Meda Chesney-Lind, "Girls, Delinquency, and Juvenile Justice: Toward a Feminist Theory of Young Women's Crime," in *The Criminal Justice System and Women*, pp. 71–88.

15. Leonard, "Theoretical Criminology and Gender."

16. Elizabeth V. Spelman, *Inessential Woman: Problems of Exclusion in Feminist Thought* (Boston: Beacon Press, 1989).

17. Meda Chesney-Lind, *The Female Offender: Girls, Women, and Crime* (Thousand Oaks, Calif.: Sage, 1974), p. 4.

18. Darrell Steffensmeier and Emilie Allen, "Gender and Crime: Toward a Gendered Theory of Female Delinquency," *Annual Review of Sociology* 22 (1996), pp. 459–487.

19. Kathleen Daly, "Gender, Crime, and Criminology," in *The Handbook of Crime and Punishment*, edited by Michael Tonry (New York: Oxford University Press, 1998), p. 100.

20. P. C. Giordano, J. A. Deines, and S. A. Cernkovich, "In and Out of Crime: A Life Course Perspective on Girls' Delinquency," in *Gender and Crime: Patterns in Victimization and Offending*, edited by Karen Heimer and Candace Kruttschnitt (New York: New York University Press, 2006), p. 18.

21. Ibid.

22. Ibid.

23. Daly and Chesney-Lind, "Feminism and Criminology."

24. Jody Miller and Christopher W. Mullins, "Taking Stock: The Status of Feminist Theories in Criminology," in *The Status of Criminological Theory: Advances in Criminological Theory*, Vol. 15, edited by F. Cullen, J. P. Wright, with K. Blevins, F. Adler, and W. Laufer (series eds.) (New Brunswick, N.J.: Transaction, 2006), pp. 206–230.

25. D. Steffensmeier and J. Schwartz, "Trends in Female Criminality: Is Crime Still a Man's World?" in *The Criminal Justice System and Women: Offenders, Prisoners, Victims and Workers*, 3rd ed., edited by B. R. Price and N. J. Sokoloff (New York: McGraw-Hill, 2004), pp. 95–111.

26. Miller and Mullins, "Taking Stock."

27. Karen Heimer, Stazcy Wittrock, and Unal Haline, "The Crimes of Poverty: Economic Marginalization and the Gender Gap in Crime," in *Gender and Crime: Patterns in Victimization and Offending*, p. 115.

28. Ibid., p. 121.

29. Ibid.

30. Daly, "Gender, Crime, and Criminology."

31. Barrie Thorne, *Gender Play: Girls and Boys in School* (New Brunswick, N.J.: Rutgers University Press, 1993), p. 2.

32. American Association of University Women (AAUW), *How Schools Are Shortchanging Girls* (Washington, D.C.: AAUW Educational Foundation, 1992).

33. P. Orenstein, *Schoolgirls* (New York: Doubleday, 1994).
34. Torme, *Gender Play.*
35. Ibid., p. 157.
36. Marty Beyer, "Delinquent Girls: A Developmental Perspective," *Kentucky Children's Rights Journal* 9 (Spring 2001), p. 17.
37. Ibid.
38. Ibid.
39. For most of the studies in this paragraph, see Jean Bottcher, "Social Practices of Gender: How Gender Relates to Delinquency in the Everyday Lives of High-Risk Youths," *Criminology* 39 (November 2001), p. 899.
40. Anne Campbell, "Female Participation in Gangs," in *The Modern Gang Reader*, edited by Malcolm W. Klein, Cheryl L. Maxson, and Jody Miller (Los Angeles: Roxbury, 1995), pp. 83–92.
41. John M. Hagedorn, *People and Folks,* 2nd ed. (Chicago: Lake View Press, 1998).
42. Jody Miller and Scott H. Decker, "Young Women and Gang Violence: Gender, Street Offending, and Violent Victimization in Gangs," *Justice Quarterly* 18 (March 2001), pp. 116–139.
43. Claire M. Renzetti and Daniel J. Curran, *Women, Men, and Society,* 2nd ed. (Boston: Allyn and Bacon, 1992).
44. C. S. Lederman, G. A. Dakof, M. A. Larreal, and L. Hua, "Characteristics of Adolescent Females in Juvenile Detention," *International Journal of Law and Psychiatry* 27 (2004), pp. 321–327; and M. Zahn, "The Causes of Girls' Delinquency and Their Program Implications," *Family Court Review* 45 (2007), pp. 456–465.
45. Lederman, Dakof, Larreal, and Hua, "Characteristics of Adolescent Females in Juvenile Detention."
46. B. Bloom and S. Covington, "Effective Gender-Responsive Interventions in Juvenile Justice: Addressing the Lives of Delinquent Girls," paper presented at the Annual Meeting of the American Society of Criminology, Atlanta, Georgia, 2001.
47. National Juvenile Justice Networking Forum, *Girls' Study Group* (Washington, D.C.: Research Triangle Institute, 2007). http://girlsstudygroup.rti.org/docs/GSG_NJJNC_Nune_2007.pdf.
48. Bloom and Covington, "Effective Gender-Responsive Interventions in Juvenile Justice."
49. Marty Beyer, "Delinquent Girls: A Developmental Perspective," *Kentucky Children's Rights Journal* (Spring 2001), p. 18.
50. Stephanie J. Funk, "Risk Assessment for Juveniles on Probation," *Criminal Justice and Behavior* 26 (March 1999), pp. 44–68. For the importance of peer relationships with girls, see also Daniel P. Mears, Matthew Ploeger, and Mark Warr, "Explaining the Gender Gap in Delinquency: Peer Influence and Moral Evaluations of Behavior," *Journal of Research in Crime and Delinquency* 35 (August 1998), pp. 251–266.
51. Joanne Belknap and Karen Holsinger, "An Overview of Delinquent Girls: How Theory and Practice Failed and the Need for Innovative Changes," in *Female Offenders: Critical Perspectives and Effective Interventions*, edited by R. T. Zaplin (Gaithersburg, Md.: Aspen Publishers, 1998), p. 1.
52. Leslie Acoca and K. Dedel, *No Place to Hide: Understanding and Meeting the Needs of Girls in the California Juvenile Justice System* (San Francisco: National Council on Crime and Delinquency, 1998).
53. Ibid.
54. Leslie Acoca, "Investing in Girls: A 21st Century Strategy," *Juvenile Justice* (October 1999), pp. 3–13.
55. Ibid.
56. W. R. Downs, T. Capshew, and B. Rindels, "Relationships between Adult Men's Alcohol Problems and Their Childhood Experiences of Parental Violence and Psychological Aggression," *Journal of Studies on Alcohol* (2004), pp. 336–345; National Center on Addiction and Substance Abuse at Columbia University (CASA), "Reducing Teen Smoking Can Cut Marijuana Use Significantly." www.casacolumbia.org/newsletter1457 (accessed November 2003).
57. Paul Mazerolle, "Gender, General Strain, and Delinquency: An Empirical Examination," *Justice Quarterly*, vol. 15, no. 65 (1998), pp. 65–91.
58. Cesare Lombroso, *The Female Offender* (New York: Appleton, 1920).
59. T. C. N. Gibbens, "Female Offenders," *British Journal of Hospital Medicine* 6 (1971), pp. 279–286.
60. J. Cowie, B. Cowie, and E. Slater, *Delinquency in Girls* (London: Heinemann, 1968).
61. Ibid.
62. Diana Fishbein, Shari Miller, Donna Marie Winn, and Gayle Dakof, "Biopsychological Factors, Gender, and Delinquency," in *The Delinquent Girl*, edited by Margaret A. Zahn (Philadelphia: Temple University Press, 2008), pp. 84–106.
63. Ibid.
64. W. I. Thomas, *Sex and Society* (Boston: Little, Brown, 1907).
65. Sigmund Freud, *New Introductory Lectures on Psychoanalysis* (New York: Norton, 1933).
66. Peter Bols, "Preoedipal Factors in the Etiology of Female Delinquency," *Psychoanalytic Study of the Child* 12 (1957), p. 232.
67. Peter Bols, "Three Typical Constellations in Female Delinquency," in *Family Dynamics and Female Sexual Delinquency,* edited by Otto Pollak (Palo Alto, Calif.: Science and Behavior Books, 1969), pp. 99–110.
68. Otto Pollak, *The Criminality of Women* (Philadelphia: University of Pennsylvania Press, 1950).
69. Gisela Konopka, *The Adolescent Girl in Conflict* (Englewood Cliffs, N.J.: Prentice-Hall, 1966).
70. These key factors from Konopka's *The Adolescent Girl in Conflict* are listed in Peter C. Kratcoski and John E. Kratcoski, "Changing Patterns in the Delinquent Activities of Boys and Girls: A Self-Reported Delinquency Analysis," *Adolescence* 18 (Spring 1975), pp. 83–91.
71. O. Miazad, *Human Rights Brief 10*, Washington College of Law. www.wel.american.edu/hrbrief/10-gender.cfm (accessed October 2007).
72. Robert Agnew, "The Contribution of 'Mainstream' Theories to the Explanation of Female Delinquency," in *The Delinquent Girl*, pp. 7–29.
73. Ibid.
74. Talcott Parsons, "Age and Sex in the Social Structure of the United States," *American Sociological Review* 7 (October 1942), pp. 614–616.; James S. Coleman, *The Adolescent Society* (New York: Free Press, 1961); and Ruth Rittenhouse, "A Theory and Comparison of Male

and Female Delinquency," Ph.D. dissertation, University of Michigan, Ann Arbor, 1963.

75. Susan K. Datesman, Frank R. Scarpitti, and Richard M. Stephenson, "Female Delinquency: An Application of Self and Opportunity Theories," *Journal of Research in Crime and Delinquency* 12 (1975), pp. 107–123; Jeffery O. Segrave and Douglas N. Hastad, "Evaluating Three Models of Delinquency Causation for Males and Females: Strain Theory, Subculture Theory, and Control Theory," *Sociological Focus* 18 (January 1985), pp. 1–17; and Stephen A. Cernkovich and Peggy C. Giordano, "Delinquency, Opportunity, and Gender," *Journal of Criminal Law and Criminology* 70 (1979), pp. 145–151.

76. Agnew, "The Contribution of 'Mainstream' Theories to the Explanation of Female Delinquency."

77. Travis Hirschi, *Causes of Delinquency* (Berkeley: University of California Press, 1969).

78. William E. Thornton Jr., Jennifer James, and William G. Doerner, *Delinquency and Justice* (Glenview, Ill.: Scott Foresman, 1982).

79. Agnew, "The Contribution of 'Mainstream' Theories to the Explanation of Female Delinquency."

80. Karen Heimer and Stacy De Coster, "The Gendering of Violent Behavior," *Criminology* 37 (1999), pp. 277–318.

81. Freda Adler, *Sisters in Crime* (New York: McGraw-Hill, 1975).

82. F. T. Cullen, K. M. Golden, and J. B. Cullen, "Sex and Delinquency: A Partial Test of the Masculinity Hypothesis," *Criminology* 15 (1977), pp. 87–104.

83. William E. Thornton and Jennifer James, "Masculinity and Delinquency Revisited," *British Journal of Criminology* 19 (July 1979), pp. 225–241.

84. John Hagan, John Simpson, and A. R. Gillis, "Class in the Household: A Power-Control Theory of Gender and Delinquency," *American Journal of Sociology* 92 (January 1987), pp. 788–816; and Hagan, Gillis, and Simpson, "The Class Structure of Gender and Delinquency."

85. Hagan, Simpson and Gillis, "Class in the Household."

86. Ibid., p. 793.

87. Ibid.

88. Agnew, "The Contribution of 'Mainstream' Theories to the Explanation of Female Delinquency."

89. Dawn Jeglum Bartusch and Ross L. Matsueda, "Gender, Reflected Appraisals, and Labeling: A Cross-Group Test of an Interactionist Theory of Delinquency," *Social Forces* 75 (September 1996), p. 145.

90. Ibid.

91. Karen Heimer, "Gender, Interaction, and Delinquency: Testing a Theory of Differential Social Control," *Social Psychology Quarterly* 59 (1996), p. 57.

92. Agnew, "The Contribution of 'Mainstream' Theories to the Explanation of Female Delinquency"; and J. Hagan and B. McCarthy, *Mean Streets and Homelessness* (Cambridge, Mass.: Cambridge University Press, 1997).

93. Ibid.

94. Giordano and Cernkovich, "Changing Patterns of Female Delinquency."

95. Chesney-Lind, "Girl's Crime and Woman's Place."

96. Sally S. Simpson, "Feminist Theory, Crime, and Justice," *Criminology* 27 (November 1989), pp. 605–631.

97. Kristine Olson Rogers, "For Her Own Protection: Conditions of Incarceration for Female Juvenile Offenders in the State of Connecticut," *Law and Society Review* 7 (1973), pp. 223–246.

98. Piers Beirne and James W. Messerschmidt, *Criminology*, 4th ed. (New York: Oxford University Press, 2007).

99. Sheila Balkan, Ronald Berger, and Janet Schmidt, *Crime and Deviance in America: A Critical Approach* (Monterey, Calif.: Wadsworth, 1980).

100. Beirne and Messerschmidt, *Criminology*.

101. A. M. Jaggar and P. Rothenberg, eds., *Feminist Framework* (New York: McGraw-Hill, 1984).

102. Beirne and Messerschmidt, *Criminology*.

103. B. R. Price and N. J. Sokoloff, eds., *The Criminal Justice System and Women: Offenders, Victims, and Workers*, 3rd ed. (New York: McGraw-Hill, 2005).

104. Joan H. Rollins, *Women's Minds, Women's Bodies: The Psychology of Women in a Biosocial Context* (Upper Saddle River, NJ: Prentice-Hall, 1996).

105. Smart, *Women, Crime, and Criminology*, p. 10.

106. P. H. Collins, *Black Feminist Thought* (New York: Routledge, Chapman, Hall, 1998).

107. Chesney-Lind, "Girl's Crime and Woman's Place."

108. Ibid.

109. Mimi Silbert and Ayala M. Pines, "Entrance into Prostitution," *Youth and Society* 13 (1982), pp. 471–500.

110. Cited in Chesney-Lind, "Girl's Crime and Woman's Place."

111. Spelman, *Inessential Woman*.

112. Ibid.

113. Etta A. Anderson, "The 'Chivalrous' Treatment of the Female Offender in the Arms of the Criminal Justice System: A Review of the Literature," *Social Problems* 23 (1976), pp. 350–357. See also Meda Chesney-Lind, "Judicial Enforcement of the Female Sex Role: The Family Court and Female Delinquency," *Issues in Criminology* 8 (1973), pp. 57–59; Kristine Olson Rogers, "For Her Own Protection: Conditions of Incarceration for Female Juvenile Offenders in the State of Connecticut," *Law and Society Review* 7 (1973), pp. 223–246; and John M. MacDonald and Meda Chesney-Lind, "Gender Bias and the Juvenile Justice Revisited: A Multiyear Analysis," *Crime and Delinquency* 47 (2001), pp. 173–198.

114. Marvin D. Krohn, James P. Curry, and Shirley Nelson-Kilger, "Is Chivalry Dead?" *Criminology* 21 (1983), pp. 417–439.

115. Christy A. Visher, "Gender, Police Arrest Decisions, and Notions of Chivalry," *Criminology* 21 (1983), pp. 5–28; and Chesney-Lind, "Judicial Enforcement of the Female Sex Role."

116. Jean Strauss, "To Be Minor and Female: The Legal Rights of Women under Twenty-One, *Ms.* 1 (1972), pp. 70–75; Yona Cohn, "Criteria for Probation Officers' Recommendations to Juvenile Court," *Crime and Delinquency* 1 (1963), pp. 272–275; Rogers, "For Her Own Protection;" Chesney-Lind, "Judicial Enforcement of the Female Sex Role;" and Laurie Schaffner, "Female Juvenile Delinquency: Sexual Solutions and Gender Bias in Juvenile Justice," paper presented at the Annual Meeting of the American Society of Criminology in Washington, D.C., November 1998.

117. Rosemary C. Sarri, "Juvenile Law: How It Penalizes Females," in *The Female Offender*, edited by Laura Crites, pp. 67–85 (Lexington, Mass.: D. C. Heath and Co., 1977).

118. Ibid., p. 76.

119. Randall G. Shelden and John Horvath, "Processing Offenders in a Juvenile Court: A Comparison of Males and Females," paper presented at the Annual Meeting of the Western Society of Criminology, Newport Beach, California, February–March, 1986, cited in Coramae Richey Mann, *Female Crime and Delinquency* (Tuscaloosa: University of Alabama Press, 1984); Meda Chesney-Lind, "Girls and Status Offenses: Is Juvenile Justice Still Sexist?" *Criminal Justice Abstracts* 20 (March 1988), pp. 144–165; Randall R. Beger and Harry Hoffman, "The Role of Gender in Detention Dispositioning of Juvenile Probation Violaters," *Journal of Crime and Justice* 21 (1998), pp. 173–186; Robert Terry, "Discrimination in the Police Handling of Juvenile Offenders by Social Control Agencies," *Journal of Research in Crime and Delinquency* 14 (1967), pp. 218–230; Rogers, "For Her Own Protection;" and Clemens Bartollas and Christopher M. Sieverdes, "Games Juveniles Play: How They Get Their Way," unpublished report, 1985.

120. Anne Rankin Mahoney and Carol Fenster, "Family Delinquents in a Suburban Court," in *Judge, Lawyer, Victim, Thief: Woman, Gender Roles and Criminal Justice*, edited by Nicole Hahn and Elizabeth Anne Stanko (Boston: Northeastern University Press, 1982), pp. 22–54.

121. Donna M. Bishop and Charles E. Frazier, "Gender Bias in Juvenile Justice Processing: Implications of the JJDP Act," *Journal of Criminal Law and Criminology* 82 (1992), pp. 1132–1152; and Carla P. Davis, "At Risk Girls and Delinquency Career Pathway," *Crime and Delinquency* 53 (July 2007), pp. 408–435.

122. Ibid.

123. Ibid.

124. Chesney-Lind, *The Female Offender*.

125. Ibid.

126. Lee Bowker and Malcolm Klein, "The Etiology of Female Juvenile Delinquency and Gang Membership: A Test of Psychological and Social Structural Explanations," *Adolescence* 13 (1983), pp. 750–751.

127. For many of these findings, see Joy G. Dryfoos, *Adolescents at Risk: Prevalence and Prevention* (New York: Oxford University Press, 1990).

128. Michele R. Decker, Anita Raj, and Jay G. Silverman, "Sexual Violence against Girls: Influences of Immigration and Acculturation," *Violence against Women* (May 2007), pp. 498–513.

129. Signithia Fordham, "'Those Loud Black Girls': (Black) Women, Silence and Gender 'Passing' in the Academy," in *Beyond Black and White: New Faces and Voices in U.S. Schools*, edited by Maxine Seller and Lois Weis (Albany: University of New York Press, 1997), pp. 81–111. See also Rod K. Bronson and Eric A. Stewart, "Young African American Women, the Street Code, and Violence: An Exploratory Analysis," *Journal of Crime and Justice* (2006), pp. 1–19.

130. Chesney-Lind, *The Female Offender*.

131. Finn-Aage Esbensen and L. Thomas Winfree, "Race and Gender Differences between Gang and Nongang Youths: Results from a Multisite Survey," *Justice Quarterly* 15 (September 1998), pp. 505–526.

132. H. C. Covey, Scott Menard, and R. Franzese, *Juvenile Gangs*, 2nd ed. (Springfield, Ill.: Charles C. Thomas, 1997), p. 240.

133. Chesney-Lind, *The Female Offender*, p. 23.

134. Spelman, *Inessential Woman*.

135. Diane K. Lewis, "A Response to Inequality: Black Women, Racism, and Sexism," *Signs: Journal of Women in Culture and Society* 3 (1977), p. 339. For this discussion on African-American women, I am indebted to Kathleen Daly, "Class–Race–Gender: Sloganeering in Search of Meaning," *Social Justice* 20 (1993), p. 58.

136. Lewis, "A Response to Inequality," p. 339.

137. "The Combahee River Collective Statement," in *Capitalist Patriarchy and the Case for Socialist Feminism*, edited by Zilah Eisenstein (New York: Monthly Review Press, 1979), pp. 362–372.

138. Daly, "Class–Race–Gender," p. 58.

139. Spelman, *Inessential Woman*, p. 123.

140. Ibid.

141. Jean Bottcher, "Social Practices of Gender: How Gender Relates to Delinquency in the Everyday Lives of High-Risk Youths," *Criminology* 39 (2001), pp. 905–925.

142. Bottcher, "Social Practices of Gender."

143. Amy V. D'Unger, Kenneth C. Land, and Patricia L. McCall, "Sex Differences in Age Patterns of Delinquent/Criminal Careers: Results from Poisson Latent Class Analyses of the Philadelphia Cohort Study," *Journal of Quantitative Criminology* 18 (December 2002), pp. 349–375.

144. Rebecca S. Katz, "Explaining Girls' and Women's Crime and Desistance in the Context of Their Victimization Experiences," *Violence against Women* 6 (June 2000), pp. 633–660.

145. Alex R. Piquero, Robert Brame, and Terrie E. Moffitt, "Extending the Study of Continuity and Change: Gender Differences in the Linkage between Adolescent and Adult Offending," *Journal of Quantitative Criminology* 21 (June 2005), pp. 219–243.

146. I. Sommers, D. R. Baskin, and J. Fagan, "Getting Out of the Life: Crime Desistance by Female Street Offenders," *Deviant Behavior* 15 (1994), pp. 125–149.

147. I. Sommers and D. R. Baskin, "Situational or Generalized Violence in Drug Dealing Networks," *Journal of Drug Issues* 27 (1997), pp. 833–849.

148. Peggy C. Giordano, Stephen A. Cernkovich, and Jennifer L. Rudolph, "Gender, Crime, and Desistance: Toward a Theory of Cognitive Transformation," *American Journal of Sociology* 107 (January 2002), p. 1038.

149. B. Bloom, B. Owen, and S Covington, "Women Offenders and the Gendered Effects of Public Policy," *Review of Policy Research* 21 (2004), pp. 31–48.

150. Ibid.

151. Ibid.

CHAPTER 8

1. Steve Barnes, "Mother of Heroin Seller Charged," *New York Times*, Friday, January 9, 2004; "Police Say 11-Year-Old Girl Sold Heroin on the Street," Associated Press, January 7, 2004; and "11-Year-Old Girl, Dressed in School Uniform, Sold Heroin on the Street for Mother," *Atlanta Journal Constitution*, January 4, 2007.

2. Marvin D. Krohn, Susan B. Stern, Terence P. Thornberry, and Sung Joon Jang, "The Measurement of Family Process Variables: The Effect of Adolescent and Parent Perceptions of Family Life on Delinquent Behavior," *Journal of*

Quantitative Criminology 8 (1992), p. 287. For these theories of delinquency, see Travis Hirschi, *Causes of Delinquency* (Berkeley: University of California Press, 1969); Marvin Krohn, "The Web of Conformity: A Network Approach to the Explanation of Delinquent Behavior," *Social Problems* 33 (1986), pp. 81–93; Gerald Patterson, *Coercive Family Process* (Eugene, Ore.: Castilia Press, 1982); and Terence Thornberry, "Toward an Interactional Theory of Delinquency," *Criminology* 25 (1987), pp. 863–892.

3. Kristin Y. Mack, Michael J. Lieber, Richard A. Featherstone, and Maria A. Monserud, "Reassessing the Family-Delinquency Association: Do Family Types, Family Processes, and Economic Factors Make a Difference?" *Journal of Criminal Justice* 35 (2007), pp. 51–67.

4. Krohn et al., "The Measurement of Family Process Variables." For studies supporting the proposition that family relationships and parenting skills are related to delinquency, see D. Elliott, D. Huizinga, and S. Ageton, *Explaining Delinquency and Drug Use* (Beverly Hills, Calif.: Sage, 1985); Walter R. Gove and R. Crutchfield, "The Family and Juvenile Delinquency," *Sociological Quarterly* 23 (1982), pp. 301–319; M. Krohn and J. Massey, "Social Control and Delinquent Behavior: An Examination of the Elements of the Social Bond," *Sociological Quarterly* 21 (1980), pp. 337–349; J. Laub and R. Sampson, "Unraveling Families and Delinquency: A Reanalysis of the Gluecks' Data," *Criminology* 26 (1988), pp. 355–380; R. Loeber and M. Stouthamer-Loeber, "Family Factors as Correlates and Predictors of Juvenile Conduct Problems and Delinquency," in *Crime and Justice: An Annual Review of Research,* edited by M. Tonry and N. Morris (Chicago: University of Chicago Press, 1986), pp. 29–149; W. J. McCord, J. McCord, and Irving Zola, *The Origins of Crime* (New York: Columbia University Press, 1959); F. I. Nye, *Family Relationships and Delinquency Behavior* (New York: John Wiley, 1958); G. R. Patterson and T. J. Dishion, "Contributions of Families and Peers to Delinquency," *Criminology* 23 (1985), pp. 63–79; and M. D. Wiatrowski, D. B. Griswold, and M. K. Roberts, "Social Control and Delinquency," *American Sociological Review* 46 (1981), pp. 524–541.

5. Lawrence Rosen, "Family and Delinquency: Structure or Function," *Criminology* 23 (1985), pp. 553–573.

6. Judith R. Harris, "Where Is the Child's Environment? A Group Socialization Theory of Development," *Psychological Review* 102 (1995), pp. 458–489; Judith R. Harris, *The Nurture Assumption: Why Children Turn Out the Way They Do* (New York: Free Press, 1998); and Judith R. Harris, *No Two Alike: Human Nature and Human Individuality* (New York: Norton, 2006).

7. Kevin M. Beaver and John Paul Wright, "A Child Effects Explanation for the Association between Family Risk and Involvement in an Antisocial Lifestyle," *Journal of Adolescent Research* 22 (2007), pp. 640–664.

8. Ibid.

9. W. D. Morrison, *Juvenile Offenders* (London: T. Fisher Unwin, 1896); Sophonisba P. Breckenridge and Edith Abbott, *The Delinquent Child and the Home* (New York: Russell Sage Foundation, 1912); William Healy, *The Individual Delinquent* (Boston: Little, Brown, 1915); William Healy and Augusta Bronner, *Delinquents and Criminals: Their Making and Unmaking* (New York: Macmillan, 1926); and Ernest H. Shideler, "Family Disintegration and the Delinquent Boy in the United States," *Journal of Criminal Law and Criminology* 8 (January 1918), pp. 709–732.

10. F. I. Nye, *Family Relationships and Delinquent Behavior* (New York: John Wiley, 1958); and R. A. Dentler and L. J. Monroe, "Social Correlates of Early Adolescent Theft," *American Sociological Review* 28 (1961), pp. 733–743.

11. Richard S. Sterne, *Delinquent Conduct and Broken Homes* (New Haven, Conn.: College and University Press, 1964); J. Toby, "The Differential Impact of Family Disorganization," *American Sociological Review* 22 (1957), pp. 505–512; T. P. Monahan, "Family Status and the Delinquent Child: A Reappraisal and Some New Findings," *Social Forces* 35 (1957), pp. 250–258; and T. P. Monahan, "Broken Homes by Age of Delinquent Children," *Journal of Social Psychology* 51 (1960), pp. 387–397.

12. Ross L. Matsueda and Karen Heimer, "Race, Family Structure, and Delinquency: A Test of Differential Association and Social Control Theories," *American Sociological Review* 52 (1987), pp. 826–840.

13. Marvin D. Free Jr., "Clarifying the Relationship between the Broken Home and Juvenile Delinquency: A Critique of the Current Literature," *Deviant Behavior* 12 (1991), pp. 109–167.

14. L. Edward Wells and Joseph H. Rankin, "Families and Delinquency: A Meta-Analysis of the Impact of Broken Homes," *Social Problems* 38 (February 1991), pp. 87–88.

15. Sheldon Glueck and Eleanor Glueck *Unraveling Juvenile Delinquency* (Cambridge, Mass.: Harvard University Press for the Commonwealth Fund, 1950); Nye, *Family Relationships and Delinquent Behavior*; and W. J. McCord, J. McCord, and Irving Zola, *The Origins of Crime* (New York: Columbia University Press, 1959).

16. Linda J. Waite and Lee A. Lillard, "Children and Marriage Disruption," *American Journal of Sociology* 96 (January 1991), p. 930.

17. Travis Hirschi, *Causes of Delinquency* (Berkeley: University of California Press, 1969).

18. R. Loeber and M. Stouthamer-Loeber, "Family Factors as Correlates and Predictors of Juvenile Conduct Problems and Delinquency," in *Crime and Justice: An Annual Review of Research,* edited by M. Tonry and N. Morris (Chicago: University of Chicago Press, 1986), pp. 29–149.

19. Glueck and Glueck, *Unraveling Juvenile Delinquency.*

20. Joan McCord, "Crime in Moral and Social Contexts," The American Society of Criminology 1989 Presidential Address, *Criminology* 28 (1990), pp. 1–26; David P. Farrington, and Barry J. Knight, "Stealing from a 'Lost' Letter: Effects of Victim Characteristics," *Criminal Justice and Behavior* 7 (1980), pp. 423–436; and Jenet L. Lauritsen, "Sibling Resemblance in Juvenile Delinquency: Findings from the National Youth Survey," *Criminology* 31 (August 1993), pp. 387–410.

21. Nye, *Family Relationships and Delinquent Behavior*; Glueck and Glueck, *Unraveling Juvenile Delinquency*; McCord, McCord, and Zola, *The Origins of Crime*; R. C. Audry, *Delinquency and Parental Pathology* (London: Methuen, 1960); Randy L. Lagrange and Helen R. White, "Age Differences in Delinquency: A Test of Theory," *Criminology* 23 (1985), pp. 19–45; Paul Howes and Howard

J. Markman, "Marital Quality and Child Functioning: A Longitudinal Investigation," *Child Development* 60 (1989), pp. 1044–1051; and Joan McCord, "Family Relationships, Juvenile Delinquency, and Adult Criminality," *Criminology* 29 (August 1991), pp. 11–23.

22. Loeber and Stouthamer-Loeber, "Family Factors as Correlates and Predictors of Juvenile Conduct Problems and Delinquency."

23. Nye, *Family Relationships and Delinquent Behavior*.

24. John Bowlby, *Maternal Care and Mental Health* (Geneva: World Health Organization, 1951); Hirschi, *Causes of Delinquency*; M. J. Hindelang, "Causes of Delinquency: A Partial Replication," *Social Problems* 21 (Spring 1973), pp. 471–487; and R. L. Austin, "Race, Father-Absence, and Female Delinquency," *Criminology* 15 (February 1978), pp. 484–504.

25. McCord, McCord, and Zola, *The Origins of Crime*; Glueck and Glueck, *Unraveling Juvenile Delinquency*; R. G. Audry, "Faulty Parental and Maternal Child Relationships, Affection, and Delinquency," *British Journal of Delinquency* 8 (1958), pp. 34–38; W. L. Slocum and C. L. Stone, "Family Culture Patterns and Delinquent-Type Behavior," *Marriage and Family Living* 25 (1963), pp. 202–208; Richard E. Johnson, "Attachments to Mother and Father as Distinct Factors in Female and Male Delinquent Behavior," paper presented at the Annual Meeting of the American Society of Criminology Toronto, Canada, November 1982; Rosen, "Family and Delinquency"; Joseph H. Rankin and Roger Kern, "Parental Attachments and Delinquency," *Criminology* 32 (November 1994), pp. 495–515; Mack, Lieber, Featherstone, and Monserud, "Reassessing the Family-Delinquency Association"; and Jennifer Stuart, Mark Fondacaro, Scott A. Miller, Veda Brown, and Eve M. Brank, "Procedural Justice in Family Conflict Resolution and Deviant Peer Group Involvement among Adolescents: The Mediating Influence of Peer Conflict," *Journal of Youth Adolescence* 37 (2008), pp. 674–684.

26. Hirschi, *Causes of Delinquency*.

27. Nye, *Family Relationships and Delinquent Behavior*; and G. F. Jensen and Raymond Eve, "Sex Differences in Delinquency: An Examination of Popular Sociological Explanations," *Criminology* 12 (1976), pp. 427–448.

28. Loeber and Stouthamer-Loeber, "Family Factors as Correlates and Predictors of Juvenile Conduct Problems and Delinquency," p. 43.

29. John Paul Wright and Francis T. Cullen, "Parental Efficacy and Delinquent Behavior: Do Control and Support Matter?" *Criminology* 39 (2001), pp. 677–705.

30. Ronald L. Simons, Leslie Gordon Simons, Callie Harbin Burt, Gene H. Brody, and Carolyn Cutrona, "Collective Efficacy, Authoritative Parenting and Delinquency: A Longitudinal Test of a Model Integrating Community- and Family-Level Processes," *Criminology* (November 2005), pp. 989–1029.

31. Glueck and Glueck, *Unraveling Juvenile Delinquency*.

32. J. Laub and R. Sampson, "Unraveling Families and Delinquency: A Reanalysis of the Gluecks' Data," *Criminology* 26 (1988), pp. 355–380; and Robert J. Sampson and John H. Laub, *Crime in the Making: Pathways and Turning Points through Life* (Cambridge, Mass.: Harvard University Press, 1993).

33. Loeber and Stouthamer-Loeber, "Family Factors as Correlates and Predictors of Juvenile Conduct Problems and Delinquency."

34. See Glueck and Glueck, *Unraveling Juvenile Delinquency*, pp. 91–92.

35. *America's Children in Brief: Key National Indicators of Well-Being 2008* (Washington, D.C.: Federal Interagency Forum on Child and Family Statistics, 2008).

36. Terence P. Thornberry, Carolyn A. Smith, Craig Rivera, David Huizinga, and Magda Stouthamer-Loeber, "Family Disruption and Delinquency," *Juvenile Justice Bulletin* (September 1999).

37. Ibid.

38. *America's Children in Brief: Key National Indicators of Well-Being 2004* (Washington, D.C.: Federal Interagency Forum on Child and Family Statistics, 2004).

39. Ibid.

40. Ibid.

41. National Coalition for the Homeless, *Homeless Youth: NCH Fact Sheet #13* (Washington, D.C.: National Coalition for the Homeless, 2006).

42. U.S. Department of Labor, Bureau of Labor Statistics. www.bls.gov.

43. Ibid.

44. Federal Bureau of Investigation, *Crime in the United States 2007* (Washington, DC: U.S. Department of Justice, 2008).

45. Michael Hershorn and Alan Rosenbaum, "Children of Marital Violence: A Closer Look at the Unintended Victims," *American Journal of Orthopsychiatry* 55 (April 1985), pp. 169–184. See also R. L. McNeely and Gloria Robinson-Simpson, "The Truth about Domestic Violence: A Falsely Framed Issue," *Social Work* 32 (November–December 1997), pp. 485–490.

46. Karen Heimer, "Socioeconomic Status: Subcultural Definitions and Violent Delinquency," *Social Forces* 75 (1997), pp. 799–833.

47. Comments made by Mike Carlie in the *Into the Abyss: A Personal Journey into the World of Street Gangs*, Chapter 12. See www.faculty.missouristate.edu/M/MichaelCarlie/what_I_learned_about/media.htm.

48. This is the general consensus of the vast amount of research done on this topic.

49. See Walter B. Miller, *The Growth of Youth Gang Problems in the United States: 1970–98* (Washington, D.C.: U.S. Department of Justice, Office of Juvenile Justice and Delinquency Prevention, 2001).

50. Ibid.

51. *Experts Debate Effects of Violent Video Games*, September 26, 2005. See http://homepage.mac.com/iajukes/blogwavestudio/LH20050626175144/ LHA2005092622.

52. Ibid.

53. Ibid.

54. Ibid.

55. CATTA, *Protecting Our Children against Internet Perpetrators* (Sonoma State University: California Institute on Human Services, 2006).

56. Wikipedia, *Gangsta rap*. http://en.wikipedia.org/wiki/Gangsta_rap.

57. Ibid.

58. Ibid.

59. Matthew T. Zingraff and Michael J. Belyea, "Child Abuse and Violent Crime," in *The Dilemmas of Punishment*,

edited by Kenneth C. Haas and Geoffrey P. Alpert (Prospect Heights, Ill.: Waveland Press, 1986), pp. 49–53.

60. Kathleen M. Heide, "Evidence of Child Maltreatment among Adolescent Parricide Offenders," *International Journal of Offender Therapy and Comparative Criminology* 38 (1994), pp. 151–162.

61. Ibid.

62. Barbara Tatem Kelley, Terence P. Thornberry, and Carolyn A. Smith, "In the Wake of Childhood Maltreatment," *Juvenile Justice Bulletin* (Washington, D.C.: U.S. Department of Justice, Office of Juvenile Justice and Delinquency Prevention, 1997).

63. Adapted from Janis Wolak, David Finkelhor, and Kimberly J. Mitchell, *Child-Pornography Possessors Arrested in Internet-Related Crimes: Findings from the National Juvenile Online Victimization Study* (Washington, D.C.: National Center for Missing and Exploited Children), pp. vii–viii; and Janis Wolak, David Finkelhor, and Kimberly J. Mitchell, "Internet-Initiated Sex Crimes against Minors: Implications for Prevention Based on Findings from a National Study," *Journal of Adolescent Health* 35 (2004), p. 424.

64. Joan McCord, "A Forty Year Perspective on Effects of Child Abuse and Neglect," *Child Abuse and Neglect* 7 (1983), pp. 265–270.

65. Cathy Spatz Widom, "Child Abuse, Neglect, and Violent Criminal Behavior," *Criminology* 27 (1989), pp. 251–271. See also Cathy Spatz Widom, *The Cycle of Violence* (Washington, D.C.: National Institute of Justice, 1992), p. 3.

66. Cathy S. Widom and Michael G. Maxfield, "An Update on the 'Cycle of Violence'," *Research in Brief* (Washington, D.C.: National Institute of Justice, 2001).

67. Ibid. For other support for the relationship between abuse and neglect and later violent behavior, see Carlos E. Climent and Frank R. Erwin, "Historical Data on the Evaluation of Violent Subjects: A Hypothesis-Generating Study," *American Journal of Psychiatry* 27 (1972), pp. 621–624; Dorothy O. Lewis, Shelly S. Shanok, Jonathan H. Pincus, and Gilbert H. Glaser, "Violent Juvenile Delinquents: Psychiatric, Neurological, Psychological and Abuse Factors," *Journal of the American Academy of Child Psychiatry* 18 (1979), pp. 307–319; and Mark Monane, "Physical Abuse in Psychiatrically Hospitalized Children and Adolescents," *Journal of the American Academy of Child Psychiatry* 23 (1984), pp. 653–658.

68. Terence Thornberry, "Violent Families and Youth Violence," *OJJDP Fact Sheet* (Washington, D.C.: Office of Juvenile Justice and Delinquency Prevention, 1994).

69. Matthew T. Zingraff, Jeffrey Leiter, Kristen A. Myers, and Matthew C. Johnson, "Child Maltreatment and Youthful Problem Behaviors," *Criminology* 31 (1993), p. 173.

70. Ibid.

71. C. Henry Kempe et al., "The Battered-Child Syndrome," *Journal of the American Medical Association* 181 (July 1962), pp. 17–24.

72. Children's Bureau, *Child Maltreatment 2007* (Washington, D.C.: U.S. Department of Health and Human Services, 2007), p. xii. See also Catalina M. Arata, Jennifer Langhinrichsen-Rohling, David Bowers, and Natalie O'Brien, "Differential Correlates of Multi-Type Maltreatment among Urban Youth," *Child Abuse and Neglect* 32 (2007), pp. 393–415.

73. Ibid.

74. Ibid.

75. Ibid.

76. Ibid.

77. *In the Interest of Children: A Century of Progress* (Denver: American Humane Association, Children's Division, 1966).

78. Norman A. Polansky, Christine Deaix, and Shlomo A. Sharlin, *Child Neglect: Understanding and Reaching the Parent* (New York: Welfare League of America, 1972), pp. 21–52. See also Cynthia Crosson-Tower, *Understanding Child Abuse and Neglect* (Boston: Allyn and Bacon, 1999).

79. Crosson-Tower, *Understanding Child Abuse and Neglect*.

80. Ibid.

81. Norman A. Polansky et al., *Damaged Parents: An Anatomy of Child Neglect* (Chicago: University of Chicago Press, 1981). See also Nico Trocme, "Development and Preliminary Evaluation of the Ontario Child Neglect Index," *Child Maltreatment* 1 (1996), pp. 145–155.

82. Richard J. Gelles and Claire Pedrick Cornell, *Intimate Violence in Families,* 2nd ed. (Newbury Park, Calif.: Sage, 1985), p. 42.

83. Ibid.

84. Murray A. Straus, "Discipline and Deviance: Physical Punishment of Children and Violence and Other Crime in Adulthood," *Social Problems* 38 (May 1991), pp. 103–123.

85. James Garbarino and Gwen Gilliam, *Understanding Abusive Families* (Lexington, Mass.: D. C. Heath, 1980).

86. Interviewed in May 1981.

87. Stephanie Amedeo and John Gartrell, "An Empirical Examination of Five Theories of Physical Child Abuse," paper presented at the Annual Meeting of the American Society of Criminology, Reno, Nevada, November 1989.

88. Blair Justice and Rita Justice, *The Abusive Family* (New York: Human Services Press, 1976).

89. The National Incidence Study, *Third National Study of Child Abuse and Neglect* (Washington, D.C.: Child Welfare Information Gateway, 1996), pp. 1–10.

90. David G. Gil, *Violence against Children: Physical Abuse in the United States* (Cambridge, Mass.: Harvard University Press, 1970).

91. Kempe et al., "Battered Child Syndrome"; B. Fontana, *Somewhere a Child Is Crying: Maltreatment—Causes and Prevention* (New York: Macmillan, 1973); and R. Galdston, "Observations of Children Who Have Been Physically Abused by Their Parents," *American Journal of Psychiatry* 122 (1965), pp. 440–443.

92. Leontine Young, *Wednesday's Children: A Study of Child Neglect and Abuse* (New York: McGraw-Hill, 1964).

93. Blair Justice and Rita Justice, *The Broken Taboo: Sex in the Family* (New York: Human Sciences Press, 1979).

94. Ibid., p. 27.

95. Linda Gordon, "Incest and Resistance Patterns of Father–Daughter Incest, 1880–1930," *Social Problems* 33 (April 1986), pp. 253–267.

96. David Finkelhor and Lisa M. Jones, *Explanations for the Decline in Child Sexual Abuse Cases* (Washington, D.C.: Office of Juvenile Justice and Delinquency Prevention, 2004).

97. Ibid.

98. For a more extensive discussion of the four types of incest possible within a family unit, see Crosson-Tower, *Understanding Child Abuse and Neglect*, pp. 155–162.

99. Angela Browne and David Finkelhor, "Impact of Child Abuse: A Review of the Research," *Psychological Bulletin* 99 (1986), pp. 66–77.

100. K. C. Meiselman, *Incest: A Psychological Study of Causes and Effects with Treatment Recommendations* (San Francisco: Jossey-Bass, 1978); and Christine A. Curtois, *Adult Survivors of Child Sexual Abuse* (Milwaukee, Wis.: Families International, 1993).

101. Interviewed as part of a court case with which the author was involved.

102. Justice and Justice, *The Broken Taboo*.

103. A. Nicholas Groth, "Patterns of Sexual Assault against Children and Adolescents," in Ann Wolbert Burgess, A. Nicholas Groth, Lynda Lytle Holmstrom, and Suzanne M. Sgroi (eds.), *Sexual Assault of Children and Adolescents* (Lexington, Mass.: D. C. Heath, 1978).

104. Justice and Justice, *The Broken Taboo*.

105. Ibid.

106. Office on Child Abuse and Neglect, *Child Sexual Abuse*.

107. Justice and Justice, *The Broken Taboo*.

108. Eli H. Newberger and Richard Bourne, "The Medicalization and Legalization of Child Abuse," *American Journal of Orthopsychiatry* 48 (October 1977), pp. 593–607; and Straus, Gelles, and Steinmetz, *Behind Closed Doors*.

109. Garbarino and Gilliam, *Understanding Abusive Families*.

110. Angela R. Gover and Doris Layton MacKenzie, "Child Maltreatment and Adjustment to Juvenile Correctional Institutions," *Criminal Justice and Behavior* 30 (2003), pp. 374–396. See also Angela R. Gover, "Native American Ethnicity and Childhood Maltreatment as Variables in Perceptions and Adjustment to Boot Camps v. Traditional Correctional Settings," in *Rehabilitation Issues: Problems and Prospects in Boot Camps* (New York: Haworth Press, 2005), pp. 177–198; and Kimberly J. Mitchell, Michele Ybara, and David Finkelhor, "The Relative Importance of Online Victimization in Understanding Depression, Delinquency, and Substance Abuse," *Child Maltreatment* 12 (2007), pp. 314–324.

111. Meda Chesney-Lind, "Girls' Crime and Women's Place: Toward a Feminist Model of Juvenile Delinquency," paper presented at the Annual Meeting of the American Society of Criminology, Montreal, Canada, 1987; M. Geller and L. Ford-Somma, *Caring for Delinquent Girls: An Examination of New Jersey's Correctional System* (Trenton: New Jersey Law Enforcement Planning Academy, 1989).

112. *Incest: If You Think the Word Is Ugly, Take a Look at Its Effects* (Minneapolis: Christopher Street, 1979), p. 10.

113. For a review of these studies, see Diane D. Broadhurst, "The Effect of Child Abuse and Neglect in the School-Aged Child," in *The Maltreatment of the School-Aged Child,* edited by Richard Volpe, Margot Breton, and Judith Mitton (Lexington, Mass.: D. C. Heath, 1980), pp. 19–41.

114. R. S. Kempe and C. H. Kempe, *Child Abuse* (Cambridge, Mass.: Harvard University Press, 1978), p. 125.

115. Florance Blager and H. P. Martin, "Speech and Language of Abused Children," in *The Abused Child: A Multidisciplinary Approach in Development Issues and Psychological Problems,* edited by H. P. Martin (Cambridge, Mass.: Ballinger, 1976).

116. D. F. Kline and J. Christiansen, *Educational and Psychological Problems of Abused Children* (Logan: Utah State University Department of Special Education, 1975).

117. Martin, "Neurological Status of Abused Children," in H. P. Martin, *The Abused Child* (Cambridge, Mass.: Ballinger, 1976), pp. 67–82.

118. Ibid.

119. M. Halperin, *Helping Maltreated Children* (St. Louis, Mo.: C. V. Mosby, 1979).

120. Kline and Christiansen, *Educational and Psychological Problems.*

121. T. Houten and M. Golembiewski, *A Study of Runaway Youth and Their Families* (Washington, D.C.: Youth Alternatives Project, 1976); J. Streit, "A Test and Procedure to Identify Secondary School Children Who Have a High Probability of Drug Abuse," *Dissertation Abstracts International* 34 (1974), pp. 10–13; and Glaser and Frosh, *Child Sexual Abuse.*

122. Widom, "Child Abuse, Neglect, and Violent Criminal Behavior." See also Bergsmann, "The Forgotten Few: Juvenile Female Offenders," p. 74.

123. S. D. Peters, "The Relationship between Childhood Sexual Victimization and Adult Depression among Afro-American and White Women," unpublished doctoral dissertation, University of California, Los Angeles, 1984.

124. Richard Dembo, Max Dertke, Lawrence La Voie, Scott Borders, Mark Washburn, and James Schmeidler, "Physical Abuse, Sexual Victimization and Illicit Drug Use: A Structural Analysis among High Risk Adolescents," *Journal of Adolescence* 10 (1987), pp. 13–34; and Rosie Teague, Paul Mazerolle, Margot Legosz, and Jennifer Sanderson, "Linking Childhood Exposure to Physical Abuse and Adult Offending: Examining Mediating Factors and Gendered Relationships," *Justice Quarterly* 25 (2008), pp. 313–348.

125. Ibid., pp. 11–12.

126. Sarah Nordgren, "Experts Find Links between Teen Mothers, Sexual Abuse," *Waterloo Courier*, September 11, 1995.

127. David Finkelhor, *Sexually Victimized Children* (New York: Free Press, 1979).

128. J. James and J. Meyerding, "Early Sexual Experiences as a Factor in Prostitution," *Archives in Sexual Behavior* 7 (1977), pp. 31–42.

129. Justice and Justice, *The Broken Taboo*.

130. See *Incest: If You Think the Word Is Ugly*, p. 13.

131. Star Goodkind, Irene Nq, and Rosemary C. Sari, "The Impact of Sexual Abuse in the Lives of Young Women Involved or at Risk of Involvement with the Juvenile Justice System," *Violence against Women* 12 (May 2006), pp. 456–477. See also Melissa Jonson-Reid and Ineke Way, "Adolescent Sexual Offenders: Incidence of Childhood Maltreatment, Serious Emotional Disturbance, and Prior Offenses," *American Journal of Orthopsychiatry* 71 (January 2001), pp. 120–130.

132. Widom, "Child Abuse, Neglect, and Violent Criminal Behavior." See also Todd I. Herrenkohl, Cynthia Souse, Emiko A. Tajima, Roy C. Herrenkohl, and Carrie A. Moylan, *Trauma Violence Abuse* 9 (2008), pp. 84–99.

133. Richard J. Gelles, "Violence in the Family: A Review of Research in the Seventies," *Journal of Marriage and the Family* (November 1980), pp. 467–479.

134. Terence P. Thornberry, *Violent Families and Youth Violence* (Washington, D.C.: U.S. Department of Justice, 1994).

135. Timothy O. Ireland, Carolyn A. Smith, and Terence P. Thornberry, "Developmental Issues in the Impact of Child Maltreatment on Later Delinquency and Drug Use." *Criminology* 40 (May 2002), pp. 359–401.

136. Peggy C. Giordano, Stephen A. Cernkovich, and Jennifer L. Rudolph, "Gender, Crime, and Delinquency: Toward a Theory of Cognitive Transformation," *American Journal of Sociology* 107 (January 2002), pp. 1000–1003.

137. The first part of the following section is modified from Howard N. Snyder and Melissa Sickmund, *Juvenile Offenders and Victims: 1999 National Report* (Washington, D.C.: Office of Juvenile Justice and Delinquency Prevention, 1999), pp. 43–44. See also David Finkelhor, Theodore P. Cross, and Elise N. Cantor, "How the Justice System Responds to Juvenile Victims: A Comprehensive Model, *Juvenile Justice Bulletin* (December 2005).

138. Finkelhor, Cross, and Cantor, "How the Justice System Responds to Juvenile Victims."

139. U.S. Department of Health and Human Services, Administration on Children, Youth, and Families, *Child Maltreatment 2002: Reports from the States to the National Child Abuse and Neglect Data System* (Washington, D.C.: U.S. Government Printing Office, 2004).

140. Children's Bureau, *The Adoption and Foster Care Analysis Reporting System Preliminary Report* (Washington, D.C.: U.S. Department of Health and Human Services, Administration on Children, Youth, and Families, 2001).

141. Timothy O. Ireland, Carolyn A. Smith, and Terence P. Thornberry, "Developmental Issues in the Impact of Child Maltreatment on Later Delinquency and Drug Use," *Criminology* 40 (May 2002), pp. 360–363. See also Robert J. Sampson and John H. Laub, "Crime and Deviance in the Life Course," in *Life-Course Criminology,* edited by Alex Piquero and Paul Mazerolle (Belmont, Calif.: Wadsworth/Thompson Learning, 2001), pp. 21–42.

142. Michael R. Gottfredson and Travis Hirschi, *A General Theory of Crime* (Stanford, Calif.: Stanford University Press, 1990).

143. Carter Hay, "Parenting, Self-Control, and Delinquency: A Test of Self-Control Theory," *Criminology* 39 (August 2001), pp. 707–736.

144. Ronald L. Simons, Chyi-In Wu, Kuei-Hsui Lin, Leslie Gordon, and Rand D. Conger, "A Cross-Cultural Examination of the Link between Corporal Punishment and Adolescent Antisocial Behavior," *Criminology* 38 (January 2000), pp. 47–79.

145. Karen Heimer, "Socioeconomic Status, Subcultural Definitions, and Violent Delinquency," *Social Forces* 75 (1997), pp. 799–833.

146. Shannon E. Cavanagh, "Family Structure History and Adolescent Adjustment," *Journal of Family Issues* 29 (2008), pp. 944–980.

147. Jennifer E. Lansford, Shari Miller-Johnson, Lisa J. Berlin, Kenneth A. Dodge, John E. Bates, and Gregory S. Pettit, "Early Physical Abuse and Later Violent Delinquency: A Prospective Longitudinal Study," *Child Maltreatment* 12 (2007), pp. 233–245.

148. Robert J. Sampson, John H. Laub, and Christopher Wimer, "Does Marriage Reduce Crime? A Counterfactual Approach to Within Individual Casual Effects," *Criminology* 44 (2006), p. 20.

149. Children's Bureau, *Child Maltreatment 2004* (Washington, D.C.: U.S. Department of Health and Human Services, 2004).

150. Widom, "Child Victims."

CHAPTER 9

1. "Shooter Obsessed With Violence," Associated Press, March 23, 2005.

2. For one attempt to explain the homicides in school, see Shirley R. Holmes, "Homicide in School: A Preliminary Discussion," *Journal of Gang Research* 7 (Summer 2000), pp. 29–36. Editorials attempting to explain school homicides have included Patrick O'Neill, "Experts: Inner Chaos Fuels Kids Who Kill," *The Oregonian*, January 22, 1999; Gordon Witkin, Mike Tharp, Joanne M. Schrof, Thomas Toch, and Christy Scattarella, "Again in Springfield, a Familiar School Scene: Bloody Kids, Grieving Parents, a Teen Accused of Murder," *U.S. News On Line*, January 6, 1998; and Margaret Warner, "A Deadly Trend," *The NewsHour with Jim Lehrer On Line Focus*, May 22, 1998.

3. Janet Cristopulos, the aunt of Chris Geschke, provided this story.

4. John F. Feldhusen, John R. Thurston, and James J. Benning, "A Longitudinal Study of Delinquency and Other Aspects of Children's Behavior," *International Journal of Criminology and Penology* 1 (1973), pp. 341–351.

5. Delbert S. Elliott and Harwin Voss, *Delinquency and Dropout* (Lexington, Mass.: Lexington Books, 1974).

6. Arthur L. Stinchcombe, *Rebellion in a High School* (Chicago: Quadrangle Press, 1964).

7. Eugene Maguin and Rolf Loeber, "Academic Performance and Delinquency," in *Crime and Justice: A Review of Research*, edited by Michael Tonry (Chicago and London: University of Chicago Press, 1996), p. 145.

8. Joel H. Spring, *Education and the Rise of the Corporate State* (Boston: Beacon Press, 1972), p. 62.

9. Joan Newman and Graeme Newman, "Crime and Punishment in the Schooling Process: A Historical Analysis," in *Violence and Crime in the Schools,* edited by Keith Baker and Robert J. Rubel (Lexington, Mass.: Lexington Books, 1980), pp. 729–768

10. Horace Mann and the Reverend M. H. Smith, *Sequel to the So-Called Correspondence between the Rev. M. H. Smith and Horace Mann* (Boston: W. B. Fowle, 1847).

11. John Dewey, "My Pedagogic Creed" (1897), reprinted in *Teaching in American Culture*, edited by K. Gezi and J. Meyers (New York: Holt, Rinehart, and Winston, 1968), pp. 408–411.

12. *Brown v. Board of Education of Topeka, Kansas* (1954), 347 U.S. 483.

13. John Goodlad, *A Place Called School* (New York: McGraw-Hill, 1984), p. 1.

14. Julius Menacker, Ward Weldon, and Emanuel Hurwitz, "Community Influences on School Crime and Violence," *Urban Education* 25 (1990), pp. 68–80.

15. Mihaly Csikszentmihalyi, Reed Larson, and Suzanne Prescott, "The Ecology of Adolescent Activities and Experience," *Journal of Youth and Adolescence* 6 (1977), pp. 281–294.

16. Martin Gold, "School Experiences, Self-Esteem, and Delinquent Behavior: A Theory for Alternative Schools," *Crime and Delinquency* 24 (1978), pp. 322–335.

17. Urie Bronfenbrenner, "The Origins of Alienation," *Scientific American* 231 (1973), p. 53.

18. Kathryn A. Buckner, "School Drug Tests: A Fourth Amendment Perspective," *University of Illinois Law Review* 5 (1987), pp. 275–310.

19. For a discussion of school disorder, see Wayne N. Welsh, "Effects of Student and School Factors on Five Measures of School Disorder," *Justice Quarterly* 18 (December 2001), pp. 911–947.

20. This finding is from J. P. DeVoe, K. Kaufman, P. Ruddy, S. A. Miller, A. K. Planty, M. Snyder, T. D. Duhart, and M. R. Rand, *Indicators of School Crime and Safety: 2002* (Washington, D.C.: U.S. Departments of Education and Justice, 2002). For a discussion of students' fear, see Lynn A. Addington, "Students' Fear after Columbine: Findings from a Randomized Experiment," *Journal of Quantitative Criminology* 19 (December 2003), pp. 367–387.

21. For a discussion of weapons in school, see Pamela Wilcox and Richard R. Clayton, "A Multilevel Analysis of School-Based Weapons Possession," *Justice Quarterly* 18 (September 2001), pp. 510–539.

22. Ron Banks, *Bullying in Schools, ERIC Digest.* www.ericddigests.org/1997–4bullying/bullying.htm.

23. Norman A. White and Rolf Loeber, "Bullying and Special Education as Predictors of Serious Delinquency," *Journal of Research in Crime and Delinquency* 45 (2008), pp. 380–397.

24. Gianluca Gini and Tiziana Pozzoli, "Association between Bullying and Psychosomatic Problems: A Meta-Analysis," *Pediatrics* 123 (2009), pp. 1059–1065.

25. David B. Estell, Thomas W. Farmjer, Matthew J. Irvin, Amity Crowther, Patrick Akos, and Daniel J. Boudah, "Students with Exceptionalities and the Peer Group Context of Bullying and Victimization in Late Elementary School," *Journal of Child Family Studies* 18 (2009), pp. 136–150.

26. Anne L. Sawyer, Catherine P. Bradshaw, and Lindsey M. O'Brennan, "Examining Ethnic, Gender, and Developmental Differences in the Way Children Report Being a Victim of 'Bullying' on Self-Report Measures," *Journal of Adolescent Health* 43 (2008), pp. 106–114.

27. LaMar T. Empey and S. G. Lubeck, *Explaining Delinquency* (Lexington, Mass.: Lexington Books, 1971); M. Gold, *Status Forces in Delinquent Boys* (Ann Arbor: Institute for Social Research, University of Michigan, 1963); Martin Gold and D. W. Mann, "Delinquency as Defense," *American Journal of Orthopsychiatry* 42 (1972), pp. 463–479; T. Hirschi, *Causes of Delinquency* (Berkeley: University of California Press, 1969); H. B. Kaplan, "Sequel of Self-Derogation: Predicting from a General Theory of Deviant Behavior," *Youth and Society* 7 (1975), pp. 171–197; and A. L. Rhodes and A. J. Reiss Jr., "Apathy, Truancy, and Delinquency as Adaptations to School Failure," *Social Forces* 48 (1969), pp. 12–22.

28. Hirschi, *Causes of Delinquency.*

29. M. L. Erickson, M. L. Scott, and L. T. Empey, *School Experience and Delinquency* (Provo, Utah: Brigham Young University, 1964); R. J. Havighurst et al., *Growing Up in River City* (New York: John Wiley and Sons, 1962); W. Healy and A. F. Bronner, *New Light on Delinquency and Its Treatment* (New Haven, Conn.: Yale University Press, 1963); and W. C. Kvaraceus, *Juvenile Delinquency and the School* (New York: World Book Company, 1945).

30. J. David Hawkins and Denise M. Lishner, "Schooling and Delinquency," in *Handbook on Crime and Delinquency Prevention* (Westport, Conn.: Greenwood Press, 1987), pp. 23–54.

31. Maguin and Loeber, "Academic Performance and Delinquency," p. 145.

32. Ann Arnett Ferguson, *Bad Boys: Public Schools in the Making of Black Masculinity* (Ann Arbor: University of Michigan Press, 2000). For other accounts with similar findings, see John D. Hull, "Do Teachers Punish According to Race?" *Time*, April 4, 1994, pp. 30–31; Minnesota Department of Children, Families, and Learning, *Student Suspension and Expulsion: Report to the Legislature* (St. Paul: Minnesota Department of Children, Families, and Learning, 1996); Commission for Positive Change in the Oakland Public Schools, *Keeping Children in Schools: Sounding the Alarm on Suspensions* (Oakland, Calif.: Commission for Positive Change in the Oakland Public Schools, 1992).

33. Richard B. Felson and Jeremy Staff, "Explaining the Academic Performance and Delinquency Relationship," *Criminology* 44 (2006), pp. 299–320.

34. Albert K. Cohen, *Delinquent Boys: The Culture of the Gang* (Glencoe, Ill.: Free Press, 1955).

35. Jackson Toby, "Orientation to Education as a Factor in the School Maladjustment of Lower-Class Children," *Social Forces* 35 (1957), pp. 259–266.

36. John C. Phillips, "The Creation of Deviant Behavior in American High Schools," in *Violence and Crime in the Schools,* edited by Keith Baker and Robert J. Rubal (Lexington, Mass.: Lexington Books, 1980), pp. 115–127.

37. Kenneth Polk and F. Lynn Richmond, "Those Who Fail," in *Schools and Delinquency* (Englewood Cliffs, N.J.: Prentice-Hall, 1972), pp. 59–69.

38. For this discussion, see LaMar T. Empey, Mark C. Stafford, and Carter H. Hay, *American Delinquency: Its Meaning and Construction* (Belmont, Calif.: Wadsworth, 1999), p. 195.

39. Cohen, *Delinquent Boys.*

40. Walter B. Miller, "Lower-Class Culture as a Generating Milieu of Gang Delinquency," *Journal of Social Issues* 14 (1958), pp. 5–19.

41. Hirschi, *Causes of Delinquency.* See Kevin M. Beaver, John Paul Wright, and Michael O. Maumem, "The Effects of School Classroom Characteristics on Low Self-Control: A Multilevel Analysis," *Journal of Criminal Justice* 36 (2008), pp. 174–181.

42. Edwin M. Lemert, *Social Pathology* (New York: McGraw-Hill, 1951).

43. Mark Colvin and John Pauly, "A Critique of Criminology: Toward an Integrated Structural-Marxist Theory of Delinquency Production," *American Journal of Sociology* 89 (November 1983), pp. 513–551.

44. Michael R. Gottfredson and Travis Hirschi, *A General Theory of Crime* (Palo Alto, Calif.: Stanford University Press, 1990).

45. Terence P. Thornberry, "Toward an Interactional Theory of Delinquency," *Criminology* 25 (1987), pp. 862–891.

46. Wayne N. Welsh, Jack R. Greene, and Patricia H. Jenkins, "School Disorder: The Influence of Individual, Institutional, and Community Factors," *Criminology* 37 (February 1999), pp. 73–116.

47. Stephen Goldstein, "The Scope and Sources of School Board Authority to Regulate Student Conduct and Status: A Non-constitutional Analysis," 117 U. Pa. L. Rev. 373, 1969.

48. E. Edmund Reutter Jr., *Legal Aspects of Control of Student Activities by Public School Authorities* (Topeka, Kan.: National Organization on Legal Problems of Education, 1970).

49. *Hanson v. Broothby*, 318 F. Supp. 1183 (D. Mass., 1970).

50. *Burnside v. Byars*, 363 F.2d 744 (5th Cir. 1966).

51. This section on the rights of students is derived in part from Robert J. Rubel and Arthur H. Goldsmith, "Reflections on the Rights of Students and the Rise of School Violence," in *Violence and Crime in the Schools*, pp. 73–77.

52. *Dixon v. Alabama State Board of Education*, 294 F.2d 150, 158 (5th Cir. 1961; cert. denied, 368 U.S. 930).

53. *Tinker v. Des Moines Independent School District*, 383 U.S. 503.

54. *Bethel School District No. 403 v. Fraser*, 478 U.S. 675, 106 S.Ct. 3159, 92 L.Ed.2d 549 (1986).

55. *Hazelwood School District v. Kuhlmeier*, 488 U.S. 260, 108 S.Ct. 562, 98 L.Ed.2d 592 (1988).

56. *Goss v. Lopez*, 419 U.S. 565.

57. *Wood v. Strickland*, 420 U.S. 308.

58. *Baker v. Owen*, 423 U.S. 907, affirming 395 F. Supp. 294 (1975); and *Ingraham v. Wright*, 430 U.S. 651 (1975).

59. 423 U.S. 907, affirming 395 F. Supp. 294 (1975).

60. *West Virginia State Board of Education v. Barnette*, 319 U.S. 624.

61. *Tinker v. Des Moines Independent School District*.

62. *Yoo v. Moynihan*, 20 Conn. Supp. 375 (1969).

63. *Richards v. Thurston*, 424 F.2d 1281 (1st Cir. 1970).

64. *Crossen v. Fatsi*, 309 F. Supp. 114 (1970).

65. *Scott v. Board of Education, U.F. School District #17, Hicksville*, 61 Misc. 2d 333, 305 N.Y.S.2d 601 (1969).

66. *Bannister v. Paradix*, 316 F. Supp. 185 (1970).

67. *Richards v. Thurston*.

68. Ronald D. Stephens, "School-Based Interventions: Safety and Security," *The Gang Intervention Handbook*, edited by Arnold P. Goldstein and C. Ronald Huff (Champaign, Ill.: Research Press, 1993), pp. 257–300.

69. *New Jersey v. T.L.O.*, 469 U.S. (1985).

70. Ibid.

71. Ibid.

72. For an extensive discussion of the relevant issues and court decisions related to the police in the schools, see Samuel M. Davis, *Rights of Juveniles: The Juvenile Justice System* (St. Paul, Minn.: Thompson Publishing, 2003), Sections 3–19 to 3–34.3.

73. J. M. Sanchez, "Expelling the Fourth Amendment from American Schools: Students' Rights Six Years after T.L.O.," *Law and Education Journal* 21 (1992), pp. 381–413.

74. *Veronia School District 47J v. Action*, 115 S.Ct. 2394 (1995).

75. *Board of Education of Independent School District No. 92 of Pottawatomie County et al. v. Earls*, 536 U.S. 822 (2002).

76. Rubel and Goldsmith, "Reflections on the Rights of Students."

77. Sheila Heavihide, *Violence and Discipline Problems in U.S. Public Schools 1996–1997* (Washington, D.C.: U.S. Department of Education, 1998).

78. Ibid.

79. Ibid.

80. Ibid.

81. Ibid.

82. Zeng-yin Chen and Howard B. Kaplan, "School Failure in Early Adolescence and Status Attainment in Middle Adulthood: A Longitudinal Study, *Sociology of Education* 76 (April 2003), pp. 110–127.

83. Christopher B. Swanson, *Who Graduates? Who Doesn't? A Statistical Portrait of Public High School Graduation, Class of 2001* (Washington, D.C.: Urban Institute, 2004).

84. Wendy Schwartz, *After-School and Community Technology Programs for Low-Income Families* (Washington, D.C.: Educational Resource Information Center [ERIC] Clearinghouse on Urban Education, 2003).

85. Robert Sampson and John Laub, *Crime in the Making: Pathways and Turning Points through Life* (Cambridge, Mass.: Harvard University Press, 1993).

86. Richard Arum and Irenee R. Beattie, "High School Experience and the Risk of Adult Incarceration," *Criminology* 37 (August 1999), pp. 515–539.

87. Ibid.

88. *Mentoring in America 2005: A Snapshot of the Current State of Mentoring* (2005). www.mentoring.org/program_staff/evaluation/2005_national_poll.php.

89. National Mentoring Center, *School-Based Mentoring*. www.nerel.org/mentoring/topic_school.html.

90. Carla Herrera, *School-Based Mentoring: A Closer Look* (Philadelphia: Public/Private Ventures, 2004).

91. *Mentoring in America 2005*.

92. *Public Alternative Schools for At-Risk Students*, Indicators 27 (2003). http://165.224.221.98/programs/coe/2003/section4/indicator27.asp.

93. Ibid.

94. Ibid.

95. Stanley Cohen, *Visions of Social Control: Crime, Punishment and Classification* (Cambridge, England: Polity Press, 1985), pp. 80–81.

96. Jacqueline R. Scherer, "School–Community Relations Network Strategies," in *Violence and Crime in the Schools* (New York: Lexington, 1980), pp. 61–70.

97. J. H. Price and S. A. Everett, "A National Assessment of Secondary School Principals' Perceptions of Violence in the Schools," *Health Education and Behavior* 24 (1997), pp. 218–229.

98. Delbert S. Elliott, Beatrix A. Hamburg, and Kirk R. Williams, *Violence in American Schools: A New Perspective* (New York: Cambridge University Press, 1998), p. 1.

99. Ibid.

CHAPTER 10

1. Walter Simon, e-mail to Topix website, August 28, 2008; Henry K. Lee, "S. F. Man Involved in Fatal Shootout Is Charged," *San Francisco Chronicle*, June 1, 2007; Jaxon Van Derbeken, "3 Tenderloin Slayings Are Called Drug-Related," *San Francisco Chronicle*, April 26, 2007; Jaxon

Van Derbeken, "Suspects Held in S. F. Slayings Faced Weapons Charges in '06," *San Francisco Chronicle*, April 17, 2007; and Jaxon Van Derbeken, "Former Gang Member Explains Street Reality to Community Leaders," *San Francisco Chronicle*, June 17, 2006.

2. Robert Walker, "Mara Salvatrucha MS-13, *Gangs OR Us*. www.gangsorus.com/marasalvatrucha13.html (accessed September 10, 2006).

3. Ibid.

4. Robert J. Bursik Jr., "Social Disorganization and Theories of Crime and Delinquency: Problems and Prospects," *Criminology* 26 (November 1988), pp. 519–551.

5. See Mark Warr and Mark Stafford, "The Influence of Delinquent Peers: What They Think or What They Do," *Criminology* 29 (November 1991), pp. 851–866; Robert Agnew, "The Interactive Effects of Peer Variables on Delinquency," *Criminology* 29 (February 1991), pp. 47–72; Mark Warr, "Age, Peers, and Delinquency," *Criminology* 31 (February 1993), pp. 17–40; and Terence P. Thornberry, Alan J. Lizotte, Marvin D. Krohn, Margaret Farnworth, and Sung Joon Jang, "Delinquent Peers, Beliefs, and Delinquent Behavior: A Longitudinal Test of Interactional Theory," *Criminology* 32 (February 1994), pp. 47–83.

6. S. P. Breckinridge and Edith Abbott, *The Delinquent Child and the Home* (New York: Russell Sage Foundation, 1917); and Clifford R. Shaw and Henry D. McKay, "The Juvenile Delinquent," in *Illinois Crime Survey* (Chicago: Illinois Associations for Criminal Justice, 1931).

7. Maynard L. Erickson and Gary F. Jensen, "Delinquency Is Still Group Behavior: Toward Revitalizing the Group Premise in the Sociology of Deviance," *Journal of Criminal Law and Criminology* 68 (1977), pp. 388–395.

8. M. M. Craig and L. A. Budd, "The Juvenile Offender: Recidivism and Companions," *Crime and Delinquency* 13 (1967), pp. 344–351; and Michael J. Hindelang, "With a Little Help from Their Friends: Group Participation in Reported Delinquent Behavior," *British Journal of Criminology* 16 (1976), pp. 109–125.

9. Elizabeth S. Piper, "Violent Offenders: Lone Wolf or Wolf-pack?" paper presented at the Annual Meeting of the American Society of Criminology, San Diego, California, November 1985.

10. Travis Hirschi, *Causes of Delinquency* (Berkeley: University of California Press, 1969), p. 141.

11. Interview with Peggy Giordano conducted in 1984.

12. Warr, "Age, Peers, and Delinquency," pp. 17, 25.

13. Ross L. Matsueda and Kathleen Anderson, "The Dynamics of Delinquent Peers and Delinquent Behavior," *Criminology* 36 (1998), p. 270.

14. Agnew, "The Interactive Effects of Peer Variables on Delinquency."

15. Dana L. Haynie and D. Wayne Osgood, "Reconsidering Peers and Delinquency: How Do Peers Matter? *Social Forces* 84 (December 2005), pp. 1109–1130. For other factors related to peer influence, see Peter J. Carrington, "Co-Offending and the Development of the Delinquent Career," *Criminology* 47 (November 2009), pp. 1295–1329 and Jean Marie McGloin, "Delinquency Balance: Revisiting Peer Influence," *Criminology* 47 (May 2009), pp. 439–478.

16. Merry Morash, "Gender, Peer Group Experiences, and Seriousness of Delinquency," *Journal of Research in Crime and Delinquency* 25 (1986), pp. 43–67.

17. Joan McCord and Kevin P. Conway, "Co-Offending and Patterns of Juvenile Crime," *NIJ: Research in Brief* (Washington, D.C.: National Institute of Justice, Office of Justice Programs, 2005).

18. See Giordano's interview in Clemens Bartollas, *Juvenile Delinquency* (New York: Macmillan Publishing Co., 1985), pp. 352–354.

19. Carl S. Taylor, *Dangerous Society* (East Lansing: Michigan State University Press, 1990).

20. Luc Sante, *Low Life: Lures and Snares of Old New York* (New York: Vintage Books, 1991).

21. Robert Redfield, *Folk Culture of Yucatán* (Chicago: University of Chicago Press, 1941).

22. James C. Howell, *Youth Gangs: An Overview* (Washington, D.C.: Office of Justice Programs, Office of Juvenile Justice and Delinquency Prevention, 1998); and Sante, *Low Life*.

23. Frederick Thrasher, *The Gang: A Study of 1,313 Gangs in Chicago* (Chicago: University of Chicago Press, 1927).

24. Ibid.

25. See Walter B. Miller, "The Impact of a Total Community Delinquency Control Project," *Social Problems* 10 (Fall 1962), pp. 168–191.

26. H. Craig Collins, "Youth Gangs of the 70s: An Urban Plague," *Police Chief* 42 (September 1975), pp. 50–54.

27. Ibid., p. 50.

28. Interview with student in March 1974.

29. John C. Quicker and Akil S. Batani-Khalfani, "Clique Succession among South Los Angeles Street Gangs: The Case of the Crips," paper presented to the Annual Meeting of the American Society of Criminology, Reno, Nevada, November 1989.

30. See David Dawley, *A Nation of Lords: The Autobiography of the Vice Lords* (Garden City, N.Y.: Anchor Books, 1973).

31. James Jacobs, *Stateville: The Penitentiary in Mass Society* (Chicago: University of Chicago Press, 1977).

32. Ibid.

33. Paul Weingarten, "Mean Streets," *Chicago Tribune Magazine* 19 (September 1982), p. 12.

34. Malcolm K. Klein, *Studies on Crime and Crime Prevention* (Stockholm, Sweden: Scandinavian University Press, 1993), p. 88.

35. Arlen Egley Jr. and Christina E. Ritz, *Highlights of the 2005 National Youth Gang Survey* (Washington, D.C.: Office of Juvenile Justice and Delinquency Prevention, 2008).

36. Finn-Aage Esbensen, *Preventing Adolescent Gang Involvement: Juvenile Justice Bulletin* (Washington, D.C.: Office of Juvenile Justice and Delinquency Prevention, 2000).

37. Thrasher, *The Gang*, p. 57.

38. W. B. Miller, "Gangs, Groups, and Serious Youth Crime," in *Critical Issues in Juvenile Delinquency*, edited by D. Schichor and D. H. Kelly (Lexington, Mass.: D.C. Heath), p. 121.

39. Esbensen, *Preventing Adolescent Gang Involvement*.

40. James C. Howell, *OJJDP Fact Sheet* (Washington, D.C.: Office of Juvenile Justice and Delinquency Prevention, 1997).

41. Arlen Egley Jr., James C. Howell, and Aline K. Major, *National Youth Gang Survey 1999–2001* (Washington, D.C.: Office of Juvenile Justice and Delinquency Prevention, U.S. Government Printing Office, 2006).

42. For the role behavior of juveniles in gangs, see Mike Carlie, *Into the Abyss: A Personal Journal into the World of Street Gangs.* www.faculty.missouristate.edu/m/mkc096f/.

43. Howell, *Youth Gangs.* See also Scott H. Decker and B. Van Winkle, *Life in the Gang: Family, Friends, and Violence* (New York: Cambridge University Press, 1996).

44. J. D. Vigil, "Cholos and Gangs: Culture Change and Street Youths in Los Angeles," in *Gangs in America*, edited by C. Ronald Huff (Newbury Park, Calif.: Sage, 1990), pp. 146–152.

45. J. D. Vigil and J. M. Long, "Emic and Etic Perspectives on Gang Culture: The Chicano Case," in *Gangs in America*, pp. 55–68.

46. Discussion of Vigil and Long's typology is based on Randall G. Shelden, Sharon K. Tracy, and William B. Brown, *Youth Gangs in American Society* (Belmont, Calif.: Wadsworth, 1997), pp. 69–70.

47. Ira Reiner, *Gangs, Crime and Violence in Los Angeles: Findings and Proposals from the District Attorney's Office* (Arlington, Va.: National Youth Gang Information Center, 1992).

48. Adapted from Shelden, Tracy, and Brown, *Youth Gangs in American Society*, pp. 70–71.

49. Interview in 1982 at the Iowa State Penitentiary at Fort Madison, Iowa.

50. Richard A. Cloward and Lloyd E. Ohlin, *Delinquency and Opportunity: A Theory of Delinquent Gangs* (New York: Free Press, 1960).

51. Lewis Yablonsky, *The Violent Gang* (New York: Macmillan, 1962).

52. Taylor, *Dangerous Society.*

53. C. Ronald Huff, "Youth Gangs and Public Policy," *Crime and Delinquency* 35 (October 1989), pp. 524–537.

54. Jeffrey Fagan, "The Social Organization of Drug Use and Drug Dealing among Urban Gangs," *Criminology* 27 (1989), pp. 633–664.

55. Malcolm W. Klein and Cheryl L. Maxson, *Gang Structure, Crime Patterns, and Police Responses.* Final Report to the National Institute of Justice (Washington, D.C.: Office of Juvenile Justice and Delinquency Prevention, 1996).

56. Taylor, *Dangerous Society.*

57. Ibid.

58. Carl S. Taylor, "Gang Imperialism," in *Gangs in America*, p. 113.

59. Huff, "Youth Gangs and Public Policy."

60. Fagan, "The Social Organization of Drug Use and Drug Dealing among Gangs," *Criminology* 27 (1989), pp. 251–271.

61. Klein and Maxson, *Gang Structure, Crime Patterns, and Police Responses.*

62. Ibid.

63. See L. J. Bobrowski, *Collecting, Organizing and Reporting Street Crime* (Chicago: Chicago Police Department, Special Function Group, 1988).

64. In a 1998 conversation, Willie Johnson, the leader of the Vice Lord Nation, reported that there are now 11 divisions of the Vice Lord Nation.

65. G. David Curry, Scott H. Decker, and Arlen Egley Jr., "Gang Involvement and Delinquency in a Middle School Population," *Justice Quarterly* 19 (June 2002), pp. 275–292.

66. C. Ronald Huff and K. S. Trump, "Youth Violence and Gangs: School Safety Initiatives in Urban and Suburban School Districts," *Education and Urban Safety* 28 (1996), pp. 4492–4503. For the violence of youth gangs in schools, see also George W. Knox, *An Introduction to Gangs* (Berrien Springs, Mich.: Vande Vere Publishing, 1993); I. A. Spergel, G. D. Curry, R. A. Ross, and R. Chance, *Survey of Youth Gang Problems and Programs in 45 Cities and 6 Sites* (Chicago: University of Chicago, School of Social Service Administration, 1989); and Huff, "Youth Gangs and Public Policy."

67. George W. Knox, David Laske, and Edward Tromanhauser, "Chicago Schools Revisited," *Bulletin of the Illinois Public Education Association* 16 (Spring 1992). For the relationship between gangs and weapons, see also Edward Tromanhauser, "The Relationship between Street Gang Membership and the Possession and Use of Firearms," paper presented at the Annual Meeting of the American Society of Criminology, Boston, Massachusetts, November 1994.

68. Joseph F. Sheley and James D. Wright, "Gun Acquisition and Possession in Selected Juvenile Samples," *Research in Brief* (Washington, D.C.: National Institute of Justice, 1993).

69. Charles M. Callahan and Ira Rivara, "Urban High School Youth and Handguns: A School-Based Survey," *Journal of the American Medical Association* (June 1992), pp. 3038–3042.

70. Comment made in 1995 to one of the authors. For a study that reveals gang members report higher levels of victimization, see Chris Melde, Terrence J. Taylor, and Finn-Aage Esbensen, "'I Got Your Back': An Examination of the Protective Function of Gang Membership in Adolescence," *Criminology* 47 (May 2009), pp. 565–594.

71. For more information on drive-by shootings, see William B. Sanders, *Gangbangs and Drive-Bys: Grounded Culture and Juvenile Gang Violence* (New York: Aldine de Gruyter, 1994).

72. Ronald D. Stephens, "School-Based Interventions: Safety and Security," in *The Gang Intervention Handbook*, edited by Arnold P. Goldstein and C. Ronald Huff (Champaign, Ill.: Research Press, 1993), pp. 222–223.

73. Fagan, "The Social Organization of Drug Use and Drug Dealing among Urban Gangs," pp. 663–664.

74. Elizabeth Huffmaster McConnell and Elizabeth Peltz, "An Examination of Youth Gang Problems at Alpha High School," unpublished paper, 1989.

75. See "Dope Fiend Teaches Algebra at Austin High," *Austin Voice* 9 (March 1 and March 8, 1994).

76. Daniel J. Monti, *Wannabe: Gangs in Suburbs and Schools* (Cambridge, England: Blackwell, 1994).

77. Patricia Wen, "Boston Gangs: A Hard World," *Boston Globe*, Tuesday, May 10, 1988. For a description of the various roles within gang drug trafficking, see Felix M. Padilla, *The Gang as an American Enterprise* (New Brunswick, N.J.: Rutgers University Press, 1992).

78. Martin Sanchez Janowski, *Islands in the Street: Gangs and American Urban Society* (Berkeley: University of California Press, 1991). For a more up-to-date article by Sanchez-Jankowski, see "Gangs and Social Change," *Theoretical Criminology* 7 (2003), pp. 191–216.

79. Ibid.

80. Joan Moore, Diego Vigil, and Robert Garcia, "Residence and Territoriality in Chicano Gangs," *Social Problems* 31 (December 1985), pp. 182–194.

81. Jankowski, *Islands in the Street.*

82. Elaine S. Knapp, *Embattled Youth: Kids, Gangs, and Drugs* (Chicago: Council of State Governments, 1988), p. 13.

83. Interview with gang leader in 1995.

84. Carlie, *Into the Abyss.*

85. Ibid.

86. John M. Hagedorn, *People and Folks: Gangs, Crime and the Underclass in a Rustbelt City*, 2nd ed. (Chicago: Lake View Press, 1988); Huff, "Youth Gangs and Public Policy"; and Dennis P. Rosenbaum and Jane A. Grant, *Gangs and Youth Problems in Evanston* (Chicago: Northwestern University, Center for Urban Affairs, 1983).

87. Cheryl Maxson, Malcolm W. Klein, and Lea C. Cunningham, *Street Gangs and Drug Sales*, National Institute of Justice Report (Washington, D.C.: National Institute of Justice, 1993). See also Cheryl L. Maxson, "Gang Members on the Move," *Juvenile Justice Bulletin* (Washington, D.C.: Office of Justice Programs, Office of Juvenile Justice and Delinquency Prevention, 1998).

88. See Reiner, *Gangs, Crime and Violence in Los Angeles.*

89. Jeffrey Fagan, "Social Processes of Delinquency and Drug Use among Urban Gangs," in *Gangs in America,* pp. 182–219. See also Fagan, "The Social Organization of Drug Use and Drug Dealing among Urban Gangs."

90. *2005 National Gang Threat Assessment* (Washington, D.C.: Bureau of Justice Statistics, 2005).

91. Ibid.

92. Ibid.

93. Terence P. Thornberry, "Membership in Youth Gangs and Involvement in Serious and Violent Offending," in *Serious and Violent Juvenile Offenders: Risk Factors and Successful Interventions,* edited by R. Loeber and D. P. Farrington (Thousand Oaks, Calif.: Sage, 1998), pp. 147–166.

94. Huff, *Criminal Behavior of Gang Members and At-Risk Youths.*

95. Arlen Egley Jr. and Christina E. Ritz, *Highlights of the 2004 National Youth Gang Survey* (Washington, D.C.: Office of Juvenile Justice and Delinquency Prevention, 2006), p. 1. For 1996, 1997, and 1998 gang homicides, see G. David Curry, Cheryl L. Maxson, and James C. Howell, "Youth Gang Homicides in the 1990s," *OJJDP Fact Sheet* (Washington, D.C.: Office of Juvenile Justice and Delinquency Prevention, 2001), p. 1. A real problem with homicide statistics is that it is difficult to know whether a given killing is gang motivated, gang affiliated, or nongang related. See Richard Rosenfeld, Timothy M. Bray, and Arlen Egley Jr., "Facilitating Violence: A Comparison of Gang-Motivated, Gang-Affiliated, and Nongang Youth Homicides," *Journal of Quantitative Criminology* 15 (1999), pp. 495–516.

96. Scott H. Decker, Tim Bynum, and Deborah Weisel, "A Tale of Two Cities: Gangs as Organized Crime Groups," *Justice Quarterly* 15 (September 1998), pp. 395–425.

97. Thrasher, *The Gang.*

98. Curry et al., "National Assessment of Law Enforcement Anti-Gang Information Resources."

99. This seven-stage development scheme was developed from conversations with a variety of individuals, ranging from gang leaders and gang members to police administrators, school officials, and newspaper reporters, across the nation.

100. Gang youths were very reluctant to talk about the percentage.

101. Interview with youth in August 1990.

102. Interview with adolescent in February 1991.

103. Interview with gang member in October 1989.

104. Comment made by a teacher to the author following a gang seminar he presented in March 1990.

105. *2005 National Gang Threat Assessment.*

106. For an examination of Chicano gangs, see James Diego Vigil, *Barrio Gangs: Street Life and Identity in Southern California* (Austin: University of Texas Press, 1988); and Joan Moore, *Home Boys: Gangs, Drugs, and Prison in the Barrios of Los Angeles* (Philadelphia: Temple University Press, 1978).

107. See Ko-Lin Chin, "Chinese Gangs and Extortion," in *Gangs in America*, pp. 129–145.

108. James Diego Vigil and Steve Chong Yun, "Vietnamese Youth Gangs in Southern California," in *Gangs in America,* pp. 146–162.

109. Reiner, *Gangs, Crime and Violence in Los Angeles.*

110. Howell, *Youth Gangs.*

111. Finn-Aage Esbensen and D. W. Osgood, *National Evaluation of G.R.E.A.T.: Research in Brief* (Washington, D.C.: Office of Justice Programs, National Institute of Justice, 1997).

112. For an examination of the seriousness of the problem of Satanism among American youths, see Philip Jenkins and Daniel Maier-Katkin, "Satanism: Myth and Reality in a Contemporary Moral Panic," revised paper presented at the American Society of Criminology, Baltimore, Maryland, November 1990.

113. See Pete Simi, Lowell Smith, and Ann M. S. Reiser, "From Punk Kids to Public Enemy Number One," *Deviant Behavior* 29 (2009), pp. 753–774.

114. See Eric Henderson, Stephen J. Kunitz, and Jerrold E. Levy, "The Origins of Navajo Youth Gangs," *American Indian Culture and Research Journal* 23 (1999), pp. 243–264.

115. Ibid.

116. See Freda Adler, *Sisters in Crime: The Rise of the New Female Criminal* (New York: McGraw-Hill, 1975); W. B. Miller, "The Molls," *Society* 11 (1973), pp. 32–35; E. Ackley and B. Fliegel, "A Social Work Approach to Street Corner Girls," *Social Work* 5 (1960), pp. 29–31; and Peggy C. Giordano, "Girls, Guys and Gangs: The Changing Social Context of Female Delinquency," *Journal of Criminal Law and Criminology* 69 (1978), p. 130.

117. Lee Bowker and M. W. Klein, "Female Participation in Delinquent Gang Motivation," *Adolescence* 15 (1980), pp. 508–519; J. C. Quicker, *Home Girls: Characterizing Chicano Gangs* (San Pedro, Calif.: International University Press, 1983).

118. J. C. Quicker, *Home Girls: Characterizing Chicano Gangs.*

119. Finn-Aage Esbensen, Elizabeth Piper Deschenes, and L. Thomas Winfree Jr., "Differences between Gang Girls and Gang Boys: Results from a Multisite Survey," *Youth Society* 31 (1999), pp. 27–53.

120. Carl S. Taylor, *Girls, Gangs, Women and Drugs* (East Lansing: Michigan State University Press, 1993).

121. Beth Bjerregaard and Carolyn Smith, "Gender Differences in Gang Participation, Delinquency, and Substance Abuse," *Journal of Quantitative Criminology* 9 (1993), pp. 329–355.

122. Joan Moore and John Hagedorn, "Female Gangs: A Focus on Research," *Juvenile Justice Bulletin* (Washington, D.C.: Office of Juvenile Justice and Delinquency Prevention, 2001).

123. Esbensen, Deschenes, and Winfree Jr., "Differences between Gang Girls and Gang Boys: Results from a Multi-Site Survey."

124. Jody Miller, "Gender and Victimization Risk among Young Women in Gangs," *Journal of Research in Crime and Delinquency* 35 (November 1998), pp. 429–453; Jody Miller and Rod K. Brunson, "Gender Dynamics in Youth Gangs: A Comparison of Males' and Females' Accounts," *Justice Quarterly* 17 (September 2000), pp. 420–447; Jody Miller and Scott Decker, "Young Women and Gang Violence: Gender, Street Offending, and Violent Victimization in Gangs," *Justice Quarterly* 18 (March 2001), pp. 115–139; and Jody Miller, *One of the Guys: Girls, Gangs, and Gender* (New York: Oxford University Press, 2001).

125. Miller and Brunson, "Gender Dynamics in Youth Gangs."

126. Miller, "Gender and Victimization Risk among Young Women in Gangs"; and Miller, *One of the Guys*.

127. Karen Joe and Meda Chesney-Lind, "Just Every Mother's Angel: An Analysis of Gender and Ethnic Variations in Youth Gang Membership," paper presented at the Annual Meeting of the American Society of Criminology, Phoenix, Arizona, November 1993.

128. Ibid.

129. H. A. Bloch and A. Niederhoffer, *The Gang: A Study in Adolescent Behavior* (New York: Philosophical Library, 1958).

130. Cloward and Ohlin, *Delinquency and Opportunity*.

131. Albert K. Cohen, *Delinquent Boys: The Culture of the Gang* (Glencoe, Ill.: Free Presss, 1955).

132. Walter B. Miller, "Lower-Class Culture as a Generating Milieu of Gang Delinquency," *Journal of Social Issues* 14 (1958), pp. 5–19.

133. Yablonsky, *The Violent Gang*.

134. Bjerregaard and Smith, "Gender Differences in Gang Participation, Delinquency, and Substance Use."

135. See Patrick G. Jackson, "Theories and Findings about Youth Gangs," *Criminal Justice Abstracts* (June 1989), pp. 322–323.

136. See Gerald D. Suttles, *The Social Order of the Slum: Ethnicity and Territory in the Inner City* (Chicago: University of Chicago Press, 1968); and Thrasher, *The Gang*.

137. Jankowski, *Islands in the Street*.

138. See William Julius Wilson, *The Truly Disadvantaged: The Inner City, the Underclass, and Public Policy* (Chicago: University of Chicago Press, 1987).

139. G. David Curry and Irving A. Spergel, "Gang Homicide, Delinquency, and Community," *Criminology* (1988), pp. 381–405.

140. J. E. Fagan, "Gangs, Drugs, and Neighborhood Change," in *Gangs in America*, pp. 39–74.

141. Hagedorn, *People and Folks*.

142. Vigil, *Barrio Gangs*, p. 101.

143. Jankowski, *Islands in the Street*, p. 139.

144. Ibid.

145. Decker and Van Winkle, *Life in the Gang*.

146. Correspondence from Michael F. de Vries. See also R. E. Johnson, A. C. Marcos, and S. J. Bahr, "The Role of Peers in the Complex Etiology of Adolescent Drug Use," *Criminology* 25 (1987), pp. 323–340.

147. Terence P. Thornberry, Marvin D. Krohn, Alan J. Lizotte, and Carolyn A. Smith, *Gangs and Delinquency in Developmental Perspective* (Cambridge, England: Cambridge Press, 2003).

148. Ibid.

149. Ibid., p. 3.

150. See Huff, "Youth Gangs and Public Policy."

151. James Short Jr., "Gangs, Neighborhood, and Youth Crime." *Criminal Justice Bulletin* 5 (Washington, D.C.: Department of Justice, 1965), pp. 1–11. See also Terence J. Taylor, Dana Peterson, Finn-Aage Esbensen, and Adrienne Freng, "Gang Membership as a Risk Factor for Adolescent Violent Victimization," *Journal of Research in Crime and Delinquency* 44 (2007), pp. 251–380.

152. I. A. Spergel, G. D. Curry, R. A. Ross, and R. Chance, *Survey of Youth Gang Problems and Programs in 45 Cities and 6 Sites*, Tech. Report No. 2, National Youth Gang Suppression and Intervention Project (Chicago: University of Chicago, School of Social Service Administration, 1989).

153. Ibid.

154. Ibid.

155. Ibid., p. 218.

156. Ibid.

157. Howell, "Youth Gangs."

158. Ibid.

159. Terence P. Thornberry and James H. Burch II, "Gang Members and Delinquent Behavior," *Juvenile Justice Bulletin* (Washington, D.C.: Office of Justice Programs, Office of Juvenile Justice and Delinquency Prevention, 1997).

CHAPTER 11

1. Steven Kurutz, "Unmerry Prankster," *New York Times*, May 22, 2005; and Nicole Gelinas, "Criminal Mischief," *City Journal*, May 24, 2005.

2. Matthew G. Muters and Christina Bethke were extremely helpful in doing the literature review and in drafting materials for this chapter.

3. Rand Drug Policy Research Center, *Newsletter* (June 1995).

4. Howard Abadinsky, *Drugs: An Introduction*, 4th ed. (Belmont, Calif.: Wadsworth/Thompson Learning, 2001).

5. In 1990, the U.S. Supreme Court ruled 6–3 in an Oregon case that states can prohibit the use of peyote by members of the Native American church [*Employment Division, Department of Human Resources of Oregon* v. *Smith*, 494 U.S. 872 (1990)]. But Congress enacted a statute providing a defense for those who use the substance "with good faith practice of a religious belief."

6. Abadinsky, *Drugs*.

7. *Juveniles and Drugs* (Washington, D.C.: Office of National Drug Control Policy, 2004).

8. L. D. Johnston, P. M. O'Malley, J. G. Bachman, and J. E. Schulenberg, *Monitoring the Future National Results on Adolescent Drug Use: Overview of Key Findings 2008* (Bethesda, Md.: National Institute on Drug Abuse, 2009).

9. Centers for Disease Control and Prevention, *Youth Risk Behavior Surveillance—United States* (Washington, D.C.: Centers for Disease Control and Prevention, 2004).

10. U.S. Department of Health and Human Services, *2002 National Household Survey on Drug Abuse* (Washington, D. C.: U.S. Department of Health and Human Services, 2003).

11. Ibid.

12. U.S. Department of Health and Human Services, *2002 National Household Survey on Drug Abuse*.

13. James A. Inciardi, *The War on Drugs, II* (Mountain View, Calif.: Mayfield, 1992), p. 62.

14. Public Health Service, *Healthy People 2000: National Health Promotion and Disease Prevention Objectives—Full*

Report with Commentary (Washington, D.C.: DHHS Publication, 1991).

15. Johnston, O'Malley, Bachman, and Schulenberg, *Monitoring the Future National Results on Adolescent Drug Use.*

16. Ibid.

17. Ali H. Mokdad, James S. Marks, Donna F. Stroup, and Julie L. Gerberding, "Actual Causes of Death in the United States, 2000," *Journal of the American Medical Association*, Vol. 291, No. 10 (March 10, 2004), pp. 1238–1245.

18. For many other names, see Inciardi, *The War on Drugs II.*

19. For a review of these studies, see Joseph M. Rey, Andres Martin, and Peter Krabman, "Is the Party Over? Cannabis and Juvenile Psychiatric Disorder: The Past Ten Years," *Journal of the American Academy of Child and Adolescent Psychiatry* 43 (October 2004), pp. 1194–1208.

20. Inciardi, *The War on Drugs II.*

21. Gordon Witkin, "The Men Who Created Crack," *U.S. News & World Report* (August 29, 1991), pp. 44–53. See also Malcolm W. Klein, Cheryl L. Maxson, and Lea C. Cunningham, "'Crack,' Street Gangs, and Violence," *Criminology* 29 (November 1991), pp. 623–650.

22. Inciardi, *The War on Drugs II.*

23. Ibid.

24. Ibid.

25. "Cocaine Abuse," *NIDA Capsules* (November 1989).

26. James N. Hall, "Impact of Mother's Cocaine Use," *Street Pharmacologist* 11 (October 1987).

27. U.S. Department of Health and Human Services, *2004 National Household Survey on Drug Abuse* (Washington, D.C.: Department of Health and Human Services, 2005).

28. T. M. McSherry, "Program Experiences with the Solvent Abuser in Philadelphia," in *Epidemiology of Inhalant Abuse: An Update,* edited by R. A. Crider and B. A. Rouse (Washington, D.C.: National Institute on Drug Abuse Research Monograph 85, 1989), pp. 106–120.

29. U.S. Food and Drug Administration, *Frequently Asked Questions.* www.fed.gov/oc/buyonline/faqs.html.

30. Inciardi, *The War on Drugs II.*

31. Abadinsky, *Drugs.*

32. Bureau of Justice Statistics, *Drug Enforcement Report* (Washington, D.C.: U.S. Department of Justice, January 3, 1990).

33. Substance Abuse Health Service Administration, *Preliminary Estimates from the 1997 National Household Survey on Drug Abuse.*

34. University of Michigan News and Information Services, January 24, 1991.

35. National Institute on Drug Abuse, *Infofax: Steroids* (Anabolic-Androgenic, 1999).

36. Ibid.

37. National Institute on Drug Abuse, *Monitoring the Future: National Results on Adolescent Drug Use: Overview of Key Findings,* 2006.

38. National Institute on Drug Abuse, *Research Report: Anabolic Steroid Abuse* (Washington, D.C.: U.S. Department of Justice, April 2000).

39. Ibid.

40. Inciardi, *The War on Drugs II.*

41. For an overview of medical complications associated with heroin addiction, see Jerome J. Platt, *Heroin Addiction:*

Theory, Research, and Treatment (Malabar, Fla.: Robert E. Krieger, 1986), pp. 80–102.

42. National Institute on Drug Abuse, *Data from the Drug Abuse Warning Network: Annual Trend Data, 2007* (Washington, D.C.: Bureau of Justice Statistics, 2008).

43. Joy G. Dryfoos, *Adolescents at Risk: Prevalence and Prevention* (New York: Oxford University Press, 1990), pp. 48–49.

44. David M. Altschuler and Paul J. Brounstein, "Patterns of Drug Use, Drug Trafficking, and Other Delinquency among Inner-City Adolescent Males in Washington, D.C.," *Criminology* 29 (1991), p. 590.

45. Lloyd D. Johnson et al., "Drugs and Delinquency: A Search for Causal Connections," in *Longitudinal Research on Drug Use: Empirical Finds and Methodological Issues,* edited by Denise B. Kandel, Ronald C. Kessler, and Rebecca Z. Margulies (Washington, D.C.: Hemisphere, 1978), pp. 137–156; J. C. Friedman and A. S. Friedman, "Drug Use and Delinquency among Lower Class, Court Adjudicated Adolescent Boys," in *Drug Use in America* 1 (Washington, D.C.: National Commission on Marijuana and Drug Abuse: Government Printing Office, 1973); J. A. Inciardi, "Heroin Use and Street Crime," *Crime and Delinquency* 25 (1979), pp. 335–346; and L. N. Robins and G. E. Murphy, "Drug Use in a Normal Population of Young Negro Men," *American Journal of Public Health* 57 (1967), pp. 1580–1596.

46. Altschuler and Brounstein, "Patterns of Drug Use, Drug Trafficking, and Other Delinquency among Inner-City Adolescent Males in Washington, D.C."; Richard Jessor and Shirley L. Jessor, *Problem Behavior and Psychosocial Development: A Longitudinal Study of Youth* (New York: Academic Press, 1977); R. L. Akers, "Delinquent Behavior, Drugs and Alcohol: What Is the Relationship?" *Today's Delinquent* 3 (1984), pp. 19–47; D. S. Elliott and D. Huizinga, *The Relationship between Delinquent Behavior and ADM Problems* (Boulder, Colo.: Behavior Research Institute, 1985); and Delbert S. Elliott, David Huizinga, and Scott Menard, *Multiple Problem Youth: Delinquency, Substance Use, and Mental Health Problems* (New York: Springer-Verlag, 1989). See also Richard Felson, Jukka Savolainer, Mikko Aaltonen, and Heta Moustgaard, "Is the Association between Alcohol Use and Delinquency—Causal or Spurious?" *Criminology* 46 (2008), pp. 786–808.

47. See Marc Le Blanc and Nathalie Kaspy, "Trajectories of Delinquency and Problem Behavior: Comparison of Social and Personal Control Characteristics of Adjudicated Boys on Synchronous and Nonsynchronous Paths," *Journal of Quantitative Criminology* 14 (1998), pp. 181–214; and Helene Raskin White, "Marijuana Use and Delinquency: A Test of the 'Independent Cause' Hypothesis," *Journal of Drug Issues* (1991), pp. 231–256.

48. Jessor and Jessor, *Problem Behavior and Psychosocial Development;* Denise B. Kandel, "Epidemiological and Psychosocial Perspectives on Adolescent Drug Use," *Journal of American Academic Clinical Psychiatry* 21 (1982), pp. 328–347; and Lee N. Robins and Katherine S. Ratcliff, "Risk Factors in the Continuation of Childhood Antisocial Behavior into Adulthood," *Internal Journal of Mental Health* 7 (1979), pp. 96–116.

49. John M. Wallace Jr. and Jerald G. Bachman, "Explaining Racial/Ethnic Differences in Adolescent Drug Use: The

Impact of Background and Lifestyle," *Social Problems* 38 (August 1991), p. 334. See also Jessor and Jessor, *Problem Behavior and Psychosocial Development*; and Richard Jessor, "Problem Behavior Theory, Psychosocial Development, and Adolescent Problem Drinking," *British Journal of Addiction* 82 (1987), pp. 331–342.

50. David Huizinga, Rolf Loeber, and Terence Thornberry, *Urban Delinquency and Substance Abuse Initial Findings: Research Summary* (Washington, D.C.: U.S. Department of Justice; Office of Juvenile Justice and Delinquency Prevention, 1994).

51. Peter W. Greenwood, "Substance Abuse Problems among High-Risk Youth and Potential Interventions," *Crime and Delinquency* 38 (October 1992), pp. 444–458.

52. Quoted in Greenwood, "Substance Abuse Problems among High-Risk Youth," p. 447.

53. Wallace and Bachman, "Explaining Racial/Ethnic Differences in Adolescent Drug Use."

54. Elliott, Huizinga, and Menard, *Multiple Problem Youth*.

55. Wallace and Bachman, "Explaining Racial/Ethnic Differences in Adolescent Drug Use."

56. Bureau of Justice Statistics, *Drugs, Crime, and the Justice System* (Washington, D.C.: Government Printing Office, 1993).

57. Kandel, Kessler, and Margulies, *Longitudinal Research on Drug Use*.

58. J. David Hawkins, Richard F. Catalano, and Devon D. Brewer, "Preventing Serious, Violent, and Chronic Juvenile Offending," in *A Sourcebook: Serious, Violent and Chronic Juvenile Offenders*, edited by James C. Howell, Barry Krisberg, J. David Hawkins, and John J. Wilson (Thousand Oaks, Calif.: Sage, 1995).

59. Delbert S. Elliott, David Huizinga, and Suzanne S. Ageton, *Explaining Delinquency and Drug Use* (Beverly Hills, Calif.: Sage, 1985).

60. D. S. Elliott and D. Huizinga, "The Relationship between Delinquent Behavior and ADM Problem Behaviors," paper prepared for the ADAMHA/OJJDP State of the Art Research Conference on Juvenile Offenders with Serious Drug/Alcohol and Mental Health Problems, Bethesda, Maryland, April 17–18, 1984.

61. J. Fagan, J. Weis, and Y. Cheng, "Delinquency and Substance Use among Inner-City Students." *The Journal of Drug Abuse* (1990), pp. 351–402.

62. Altschuler and Brounstein, "Patterns of Drug Use, Drug Trafficking and Other Delinquency among Inner-City Adolescent Males in Washington, D.C."

63. Klein, Maxson, and Cunningham, "'Crack,' Street Gangs, and Violence."

64. Based on an interview in April 1995.

65. Felix M. Padilla, *The Gang as an American Enterprise* (New Brunswick, N.J.: Rutgers University Press, 1992).

66. Daniel J. Monti, *Wannabe Gangs in Suburbs and Schools* (Cambridge, England: Blackwell, 1994).

67. Padilla, *The Gang as an American Enterprise*.

68. Monti, *Wannabe Gangs in Suburbs and Schools*.

69. Ibid., p. 55.

70. R. L. Simons, R. D. Conger, and L. B. Whitbeck, "A Multistage Social Learning Model of the Influence of Family and Peers upon Adolescent Substance Abuse," *Journal of Drug Issues* 18 (1988), p. 293.

71. John Petraitis, Brian R. Flay, and Todd Q. Miller, "Reviewing Theories of Adolescent Substance Use: Organizing Pieces in the Puzzle," *Psychological Bulletin* 117 (1995), pp. 67–86. See also W. Alex Mason, Julia E. Hitchings, Robert J. McMahon, and Richard L. Spoth, "A Test of Three Alternative Hypotheses Regarding the Effects of Early Delinquency on Adolescent Psychosocial Functioning and Substance Involvement," *Journal of Abnormal Child Psychology* 35 (2007), pp. 831–843; and David B. Henry and Kimberly Kobus, "Early Adolescent Social Networks and Substance Use," *Journal of Early Adolescence* 27 (2007), pp. 346–362.

72. Ibid.

73. I. Ajken and M. Fishbein, *Understanding Attitudes and Predicting Social Behavior* (Englewood Cliffs, N.J.: Prentice-Hall, 1980).

74. Isidor Chein, Donald L. Gerard, Robert S. Lee, and Eva Rosenfeld, *The Road to H: Narcotics, Juvenile Delinquency and Social Policy* (New York: Basic Books, 1964), p. 14.

75. Philippe Bourgois, "Just Another Night on Crack Street," *New York Times*, November 12, 1989, pp. 52–53, 60–65, 94.

76. For the positive relationship between peers and drug use, see T. J. Dishion and R. Loeber, "Adolescent Marijuana and Alcohol Use: The Role of Parents and Peers Revisited," *American Journal of Drug and Alcohol Abuse* 11 (1985), pp. 11–25; Elliott, Huizinga, and Ageton, *Explaining Delinquency and Drug Use*; Terence P. Thornberry, Margaret Farnworth, Marvin D. Krohn, and Alan J. Lizotte, "Peer Influence and Initiation to Drug Use," Working Paper No. 2 (National Department of Justice, n.d.); and D. B. Kandel, "Adolescent Marijuana Use: Role of Parents and Peers," *Science* 181 (1973), pp. 1067–1081; and Jonathan R. Brauer, "Testing Social Learning Theory Using Reinforcement's Residue: A Multilevel Analysis of Self–Reported Theft and Marijuana Use in the National Youth Survey," *Criminology* 47 (August 2009), pp. 929–970. However, for research that found no predominant effects of peer pressure on substance use, see Mark D. Reed and Pamela Wilcox Roundtree, "Peer Pressure and Adolescent Substance Use," *Journal of Quantitative Criminology* 13 (1997), pp. 143–180.

77. Petraitis, Flay, and Miller, "Reviewing Theories of Adolescent Substance Use." See also Joan L. Neff and Dennis E. Waite, "Male versus Female Substance Abuse Patterns among Incarcerated Juvenile Offenders: Comparing Strain and Social Learning Variables," *Justice Quarterly* 24 (March 2007), pp. 106–132.

78. Travis Hirschi, *Causes of Delinquency* (Berkeley: University of California Press, 1969); J. D. Hawkins and J. G. Weis, "The Social Development Model: An Integrated Approach to Delinquency Prevention," *Journal of Primary Prevention* 6 (1985), pp. 73–97; Jayne A. Fulkerson, Keryn E. Pasch, Cheryl L. Perry, and Kelli Konro, "Relationships between Alcohol-Related Informal Social Control, Parental Monitoring and Adolescent Problem Behaviors among Racially Diverse Urban Youth," *Journal of Community Health* 33 (2008), pp. 425–433.

79. Hirschi, *Causes of Delinquency*.

80. J. D. Hawkins, R. F. Catalano, and J. Y. Miller, "Risk and Protective Factors for Alcohol and Other Drug Problems in Adolescence and Early Adulthood," *Psychological Bulletin* 112 (1992), pp. 64–105.

81. Radical theorists have made this a theme of their research on poor adolescents, especially minority ones. See Chapter 6.

82. Elliott, Huizinga, and Ageton, *Explaining Delinquency and Drug Use.*

83. D. S. Elliott, D. Huizinga, and S. Menard, *Multiple Problem Youth: Delinquency, Substance Abuse Mental Health Problems* (New York: Springer-Verlag, 1989).

84. Ibid.

85. Simons, Conger, and Whitbeck, "A Multistage Social Learning Model of the Influence of Family and Peers upon Adolescent Substance Abuse," pp. 101–125.

86. Ibid.

87. Greenwood, "Substance Abuse Problems among High-Risk Youth." For the reciprocal relationships that interactional theory posits among drug use, association with drug-using peers, and beliefs about drug use, see Marvin D. Krohn, Alan J. Lizotte, Terence P. Thornberry, Carolyn Smith, and David McDowall, "Reciprocal Causal Relationships among Drug Use, Peers, and Beliefs: A Five-Wave Panel Model," *Journal of Drug Issues* 26 (1996), pp. 405–428.

88. Marcia Chaiken and Bruce Johnson, *Characteristics of Different Types of Drug-Involved Youth* (Washington, D.C.: National Institute of Justice, 1988).

89. Marvin S. Krohn, Alan J. Lizotte, and Cynthia M. Perez, "The Interrelationships between Substance Use and Precocious Transitions to Adult Status," *Journal of Health and Social Behavior* 38 (March 1997), pp. 87–101.

90. Ibid.

91. Glen H. Elder Jr., "Time, Human Agency, and Social Change: Perspectives on the Life Course," *Social Psychology Quarterly* 57 (1994), pp. 4–15.

92. Krohn, Lizotte, and Perez, "The Interrelationships between Substance Use and Precocious Transitions to Adult Status."

93. Gary M. McClelland, Linda A. Teplin, and Karen M. Abram, *Detention and Prevalence of Substance Use among Juvenile Detainees* (Washington, D.C.: Office of Juvenile Justice and Delinquency Prevention, 2004); see the report for the citations supporting each generalization.

94. The author has interviewed a number of adult former drug addicts and staff of therapeutic communities, and these explanations were typically given for why a drug addict went straight and stayed clean.

95. See D. B. Kandel and J. A. Logan, "Patterns of Drug Use from Adolescence to Young Adulthood: Periods of Risk for Initiation, Continued Use, and Discontinuation," *American Public Health* 74 (1984), pp. 660–666.

96. L. A. Goodman and W. H. Kruskal, *Measures of Association for Cross Classification* (New York: Springer-Verlag, 1979).

97. L. Thomas Winfree Jr., Christine S. Sellers, and Dennis L. Clason, "Social Learning and Adolescent Deviance Abstention: Toward Understanding the Reasons for Initiating, Quitting, and Avoiding Drugs," *Journal of Quantitative Criminology* 9 (1993), pp. 101–125.

98. Ryan D. Schroeder, Peggy C. Giordano, and Stephen A. Cernkovich, "Drug Use and Processes," *Criminology* 45 (2007), pp. 192–222.

99. Sharon Mihalic, Katherine Irwin, Abigail Fagan, Diane Ballard, and Delbert Elliott, *Blueprint for Violence Prevention* (Washington, D.C.: Office of Juvenile Justice and Delinquency Prevention, 2004).

100. G. Botvin, S. Mihalic, and J. K. Grotpeter, "Life Skills Training," in *Blueprint for Violence Prevention: Book 5*, edited by D. S. Elliott (Boulder: University of Colorado, Institute of Behavioral Sciences, Center for the Study and Prevention of Violence, 1998).

101. Mihalic, Irwin, Fagan, Ballard, and Elliott, *Blueprint for Violence Prevention.*

102. Ibid.

103. Ibid.

104. National Institute of Justice, *The D.A.R.E. Program: A Review of Prevalence, User Satisfaction, and Effectiveness* (Washington, D.C.: U.S. Department of Justice, 1994).

105. William DeJong, *Arresting the Demand for Drugs: Police and School Partnership to Prevent Drug Abuse* (Washington, D.C.: National Institute of Justice, 1987).

106. Phyllis Ellickson, Robert Bell, and K. McGuigan, "Preventing Adolescent Drug Use: Long-Term Results of a Junior High Program," *American Journal of Public Health* 83 (1993), pp. 856–861.

107. Deanna Atkinson, an administrator in the Élan program, suggested this list of noteworthy programs in a September 1995 telephone conversation.

108. For information on Élan, see its web page: www.elanschool.com.

109. Ibid. There are also several statements from former residents testifying to the brutal methods used at Élan and Élan's negative effects on them.

110. *Drug Courts: The Second Decade* (Washington, D.C.: National Institute of Justice, 2006).

111. Gordon Bazemore and Lode Walgrave, "Restorative Juvenile Justice: In Search of Fundamentals and an Outline for Systemic Reform," in *Restorative Juvenile Justice: Repairing the Harm of Youth Crime*, edited by Gordon Bazemore and Lode Walgrave (Monsey, N.Y.: Criminal Justice Press, 1999), pp. 45–74.

112. Ibid.

113. Thomas J. Dishion, Deborah Capaldi, Kathleen M. Spracklen, and Li Fuzhong, "Peer Ecology of Adolescent Drug Use," *Development and Psychopathology* 7 (1995), pp. 803–824.

CHAPTER 12

1. Stanley Cohen, *Visions of Social Control: Crime, Punishment and Classification* (Cambridge, England: Policy Press, 1985), p. 236.

2. J. David Hawkins et al., *Reports of the National Juvenile Justice Assessment Centers: A Typology of Cause-Focused Strategies of Delinquency Prevention* (Washington, D.C.: U.S. Government Printing Office, 1980).

3. For development of these levels of prevention, see Steven P. Lab, *Crime Prevention: Approaches, Practices and Evaluations* (Cincinnati, Ohio: Anderson, 2000), pp. 19–22.

4. James O. Finckenauer, *Scared Straight! and the Panacea Phenomenon* (Englewood Cliffs, N.J.: Prentice-Hall, 1982).

5. U.S. Congress, House, Subcommittee on Human Resources of the Committee on Education and Labor, Hearings, Oversight on Scared Straight! 96th Cong. 1st Sess. (June 4, 1979), p. 305.

6. Finckenauer, *Scared Straight!*

7. Joan McCord, "A Thirty-Year Follow-Up of Treatment Efforts," *American Psychologist* 33 (1978), p. 284. See also Joan McCord, "Crime in Moral and Social Contexts— The American Society of Criminology, 1989 Presidential Address," *Criminology* 28 (1990), pp. 1–25.

8. Richard J. Lundman, *Prevention and Control of Juvenile Delinquency* (New York: Oxford Unviersity Press, 1984).

9. Ibid.

10. Walter B. Miller, "The Impact of a Total Community Delinquency Control Project," *Social Problems* 10 (Fall 1962), pp. 168–191.

11. Walter C. Reckless and Simon Dinitz, *The Prevention of Juvenile Delinquency: An Experiment* (Columbus: Ohio State University Press, 1972).

12. Cited in Finckenauer, *Scared Straight!* p. 35.

13. Richard J. Lundman, Paul T. McFarlane, and Frank R. Scarpitti, "Delinquency Prevention: A Description and Assessment of Projects Reported in the Professional Literature," *Crime and Delinquency* 22 (July 1976), p. 307.

14. Richard J. Lundman and Frank R. Scarpitti, "Delinquency Prevention: Recommendations for Future Projects," *Crime and Delinquency* 24 (April 1978), p. 207.

15. Ibid.

16. Richard J. Lundman, *Prevention and Control of Juvenile Delinquency,* 3rd ed. (New York: Oxford University Press, 2001).

17. Gail Wasserman, Laurie S. Miller, and Lynn Cothern, "Prevention of Serious and Violent Juvenile Offending," *Juvenile Justice Bulletin* (April 2000).

18. Office of Juvenile Justice and Delinquency Prevention, *Guide for Implementing the Comprehensive Strategy for Serious, Violent, and Chronic Juvenile Offenders* (Washington, D.C.: U.S. Department of Justice, 1995).

19. *OJJDP Model Programs Guide,* p. 1. www/dsgonline. com/mpg2.5/prevention.htm.

20. Ibid.

21. B. Bernard, *Fostering Resiliency in Kids: Protective Facts in the Family, School, and Community* (Portland, Ore.: Northwest Regional Educational Laboratory, 1991); and P. Benson, *All Kids Are Our Kids: What Communities Must Do to Raise Caring and Responsible Children and Adolescents,* 2nd ed. (Hoboken, N.J.: Jossey-Bass, 2006).

22. J. Pollard, J. D. Hawkins, and M. Arthur, "Risk and Protection: Are Both Necessary to Understand Diverse Behavioral Outcomes in Adolescence?" *Social Work Research* 23 (1999), pp. 145–158.

23. Sharon Mihalic, Katherine Irwin, Abigail Fagan, Diane Ballard, and Delbert Elliott, *Successful Implementation: Lessons from Blueprints* (Washington, D.C.: Office of Juvenile Justice and Delinquency Prevention, 2004), p. 1.

24. Sharon Mihalic, Katherine Irwin, Abigail Fagan, Diane Ballard, and Delbert Elliott, *Blueprints for Violence Prevention* (Washington, D.C.: Office of Juvenile Justice and Delinquency Prevention, 2004), p. 55.

25. D. E. McGill, S. Mihalic, and J. K. Grotpeter, "Big Brothers Big Sisters of America," in *Blueprints for Violence Prevention: Book 2,* edited by D. S. Elliott (Boulder: University of Colorado, Institute of Behavioral Science, Center for the Study and Prevention of Violence, 1997), p. 55.

26. Mihalic, Irwin, Fagan, Ballard, and Elliott, *Blueprints for Violence Prevention,* pp. 30–31.

27. M. A. Pentz, S. Mihalic, and J. K. Grotpeter, "The Midwestern Prevention Project," in *Blueprints for Violence Prevention: Book 1,* edited by D. S. Elliott (Boulder: University of Colorado, Institute of Behavioral Science, Center for the Study and Prevention of Violence, 1997), pp. 30–31.

28. Mihalic, Irwin, Fagan, Ballard, and Elliott, *Blueprints for Violence Prevention,* pp. 26–27.

29. J. F. Alexander et al., "Functional Family Therapy," in *Blueprints for Violence Prevention: Book 3,* edited by D. S. Elliott (Boulder: University of Colorado, Institute of Behavioral Science, Center for the Study and Prevention of Violence, 2000), pp. 26–27.

30. Mihalic, Irwin, Fagan, Ballard, and Elliott, *Blueprints for Violence Prevention,* pp. 22–23.

31. C. Webster-Stratton et al., "The Incredible Years: Parent, Teacher and Child Training Series," in *Blueprints for Violence Prevention: Book 11,* edited by D. S. Elliott (Boulder: University of Colorado, Institute of Behavioral Science, Center for the Study and Prevention of Violence, 2001), pp. 22–23.

32. Mihalic, Irwin, Fagan, Ballard, and Elliott, *Blueprints for Violence Prevention,* p. 47.

33. G. Botvin, S. Mihalic, and J. K. Grotpeter, "Life Skills Training," in *Blueprints for Violence Prevention: Book 5,* edited by D. S. Elliott (Boulder: University of Colorado, Institute of Behavioral Science, Center for the Study and Prevention of Violence, 1998), p. 47.

34. Mihalic, Irwin, Fagan, Ballard, and Elliott, *Blueprints for Violence Prevention,* pp. 31–33.

35. Pentz, Mihalic, and Grotpeter, "The Midwestern Prevention Project," pp. 31–33.

36. Mihalic, Irwin, Fagan, Ballard, and Elliott, *Blueprints for Violence Prevention,* pp. 56–58.

37. P. Chamberlain and S. Mihalic, "Multidimensional Treatment Foster Care," in *Blueprints for Violence Prevention: Book 8,* edited by D. S. Elliott (Boulder: University of Colorado, Institute of Behavioral Science, Center for the Study and Prevention of Violence, 1998), pp. 56–58.

38. Mihalic, Irwin, Fagan, Ballard, and Elliott, *Blueprints for Violence Prevention,* pp. 27–28.

39. S. W. Henggeler et al., "Multisystemic Therapy," in *Blueprints for Violence Prevention: Book 6,* edited by D. S. Elliott (Boulder: University of Colorado, Institute of Behavioral Science, Center for the Study and Prevention of Violence, 2001), pp. 27–28.

40. Mihalic, Irwin, Fagan, Ballard, and Elliott, *Blueprints for Violence Prevention,* pp. 18–20.

41. D. Olds et al., "Prenatal and Infancy Home Visitation by Nurses," in *Blueprints for Violence Prevention: Book 7,* edited by D. S. Elliott (Boulder: University of Colorado, Institute of Behavioral Science, Center for the Study and Prevention of Violence, 1998), pp. 18–20.

42. Mihalic, Irwin, Fagan, Ballard, and Elliott, *Blueprints for Violence Prevention,* pp. 17–18.

43. Ibid.

44. Ibid.

45. M. Greenberg, M. Kusche, and S. Mihalic, "Promoting Alternative Thinking Strategies," in *Blueprints for Violence Prevention: Book 2.*

46. Carlos A. Cuevas, David Finkelhor, Heather A. Turner, and Richard K. Ormrod, "Juvenile Delinquency and

Victimization: A Theoretical Typology," *Journal of Interpersonal Violence* 22 (2007), pp. 1581–1602.

47. Ibid.

48. Ibid. Another typology of victimization can be found in Clemens Bartollas, Stuart J. Miller, and Simon Dinitz, *Juvenile Victimization: The Institutional Paradox* (New York: John Wiley and Company, 1976).

49. Joy G. Dryfoos, *Adolescents at Risk: Prevalence and Prevention* (New York: Oxford University Press, 1990).

50. James C. Howell, ed., *Guide for Implementing the Comprehensive Strategy for Serious, Violent, and Chronic Juvenile Offenders* (Washington, D.C.: Office of Juvenile Justice and Delinquency Prevention, 1995).

51. Ibid.

52. Ibid.

53. Ibid.

54. Ibid.

55. Ibid.

56. Kathleen Coolbaugh and Cynthia J. Hansel, "The Comprehensive Strategy: Lessons Learned from the Pilot Sites," *Juvenile Justice Bulletin* (2000).

57. Ibid.

58. These results are consistently found in the professional literature of delinquency.

59. Joy G. Dryfoos, *Adolescents at Risk: Prevalence and Prevention* (New York: Oxford University Press, 1990).

60. Joseph G. Weis and John Sederstrom, *The Prevention of Serious Delinquency: What to Do* (Washington, D.C.: National Institute for Juvenile Justice and Delinquency Prevention, 1981).

CHAPTER 13

1. "Lionel Tate Gets 10 Years in Robbery Plea Deal," CBS News, February 19, 2008; "Lionel Tate Pleads Guilty to Pizza Robbery," Fox News, March 1, 2006; and Abby Goodnough, "Youngster Given Life Term for Killing Gets New Trial," *New York Times*, December 11, 2003.

2. Elizabeth S. Scott and Thomas Grisso, "The Evolution of Adolescence: A Developmental Perspective on Juvenile Justice Reform," *Journal of Criminal Law & Criminology* 88 (1997), pp. 137–189.

3. Anthony M. Platt, *The Child Savers,* 2nd ed. (Chicago: University of Chicago Press, 1977), p. 3.

4. Ibid. For interpretations similar to Platt's, see also Sanford J. Fox, "Juvenile Justice Reform: An Historic Perspective," *Stanford Law Review* 22 (1970), p. 1187; and Douglas Rendleman, *"Parens Patriae:* From Chancery to the Juvenile Court," *South Carolina Law Review* 28 (1971), p. 205.

5. David Shichor, "Historical and Current Trends in American Juvenile Justice," *Juvenile and Family Court Journal* 34 (August 1983), pp. 61–75.

6. John Augustus, *First Probation Officer* (Montclair, N.J.: Patterson-Smith Company, 1972).

7. David J. Rothman, *The Discovery of the Asylum* (Boston: Little, Brown, 1971).

8. Steven Schlossman, "Delinquent Children: The Juvenile Reform School," in *The Oxford History of the Prison,* edited by Norval Morris and David J. Rothman (New York: Oxford University Press, 1995), pp. 325–349.

9. Rothman, *The Discovery of the Asylum.*

10. Schlossman, "Delinquent Children."

11. See Howard Polsky, *Cottage Six: The Social System of Delinquent Boys in Residential Treatment* (New York: Russell Sage Foundation, 1963); Clemens Bartollas, Stuart J. Miller, and Simon Dinitz, *Juvenile Victimization: The Institutional Paradox* (New York: Halsted Press, 1976); Barry C. Feld, *Neutralizing Inmate Violence: The Juvenile Offender in Institutions* (Cambridge, Mass.: Ballinger, 1977); and Kenneth Wooden, *Weeping in the Playtime of Others: America's Incarcerated Children* (New York: McGraw-Hill, 1976).

12. Scott B. Peterson and Jill Beres, *Report to the Nation 1993 to 2008: The Global Youth Justice Movement, 15 Year Update on Youth Courts and Teen Courts* (Global Issues Resource Center Cuyahoga Community College, 2008).

13. Ibid.

14. Ibid.

15. T. M. Godwin, *Peer Justice and Youth Empowerment: An Implementation Guide for Teen Court Programs* (Lexington, Ky.: American Probation and Parole Association, 1998).

16. Marilyn Roberts, Jennifer Brophy, and Caroline Cooper, *The Juvenile Drug Court Movement* (Washington, D.C.: Office of the Juvenile Justice and Delinquency Prevention, 1997).

17. Ibid.

18. Ibid.

19. Andrew Rutherford and Robert McDermott, *National Evaluation Program Phase Report: Juvenile Diversion* (Washington, D.C.: U.S. Government Printing Office, 1976).

20. Ibid.

21. For specific numbers of staff in juvenile corrections, see Timothy J. Flanagan and Kathleen Maguire, *Sourcebook of Criminal Justice Statistics—1999* (Washington, D.C.: U.S. Government Printing Office, 2000).

22. Ibid.

23. Howard N. Snyder and Melissa Sickmund, *Juvenile Offenders and Victims: 1999 National Report* (Washington, D.C.: Office of Juvenile Justice and Delinquency Prevention, 1999).

24. John H. Laub and Robert J. Sampson, *Shared Beginnings, Divergent Lives: Delinquent Boys to Age 70* (Cambridge, Mass.: Harvard University Press, 2003).

25. Barry Krisberg, James Austin, and Patrick Steele, *Unlocking Juvenile Corrections: Evaluating the Massachusetts Department of Youth Services* (San Francisco: National Council on Crime and Delinquency, 1989).

26. Minnesota Legislative Auditor, *Residential Facilities for Juvenile Offenders* (St. Paul: State of Minnesota, 1995).

27. Peter Greenwood and Franklin Zimring, *One More Chance: The Pursuit of Promising Intervention Strategies for Chronic Juvenile Offenders* (Santa Monica, Calif.: RAND, 1985), p. 40.

28. William P. Evans, Randall Brown, and Eric Killian, "Decision Making and Perceived Postdetention Success among Incarcerated Youth," *Crime and Delinquency* 48 (October 2002), pp. 553–567.

29. Andrew von Hirsch, *Doing Justice: The Choice of Punishments* (New York: Hill & Wang, 1976).

30. President's Commission on Law Enforcement and Administration of Justice, *Task Force Report: Corrections* (Washington, D.C.: U.S. Government Printing Office, 1967).

31. Fogel, *"We Are the Living Proof": The Justice Model for Corrections* (Cincinnati, Ohio: Anderson, 1975); von

Hirsch, *Doing Justice*; and Twentieth Century Fund Task Force on Sentencing Policy toward Young Offenders, *Confronting Youth Crime* (New York: Holmes and Meier, 1978).

32. Fogel, *"We Are the Living Proof."*

33. Daniel W. Van Ness, "Justice That Restores: From Impersonal to Personal Justice," *Criminal Justice: Retribution vs. Restoration*, edited by Burt Galaway and Joe Hudson (Binghamton, N.Y.: Hayworth Press, 2004), pp. 93–109; H. Zehr, *Retributive Justice, Restorative Justice* (Akron, Penn.: Mennonite Central Committee, 1985); and H. Zehr, *Changing Lenses* (Scottsdale, Penn.: Herald Press, 1990).

34. G. Bazemore, "What's 'New' about the Balanced Approach?" *Juvenile and Family Court Journal* (1997), pp. 53–73.

35. Ibid.

36. See James Q. Wilson, *Thinking about Crime,* rev. ed. (New York: Basic Books, 1983); and Ernest van den Haag, *Punishing Criminals: Concerning a Very Old and Painful Question* (New York: Hill and Wang, 1976).

37. Snyder and Sickmund, *Juvenile Offenders and Victims*.

38. Ibid., p. 89.

39. Ibid.

40. Donna M. Bishop, "The Role of Race and Ethnicity in Juvenile Justice Processing," in *Our Children, Their Children: Confronting Racial and Ethnic Differences in American Juvenile Justice,*" edited by Darnell F. Hawkins and Kimberly Kempf-Leonard (Chicago: University of Chicago Press, 2005), p. 23.

41. Ibid.

42. Janet L. Lauritsen, "Racial and Ethnic Differences in Judicial Offending," in *Our Children, Their Children,* pp. 91–95.

43. Ibid.

44. Bishop, "The Role of Race and Ethnicity in Juvenile Justice Processing."

45. Carl E. Pope and William Feyerherm, *Minorities and the Juvenile Justice System* (Washington, D.C.: Office of Juvenile Justice and Delinquency Prevention, 1995), pp. 2–3.

46. Ibid. See also Donna M. Bishop and Charles E. Frazier, *A Study of Race and Juvenile Processing in Florida,* report submitted to the Florida Supreme Court Racial and Ethnic Bias Study Commission, 1990; and Carl E. Pope, Rick Ovell, and Heidi M. Hsia, *Disproportionate Minority Confinement: A Review of the Research Literature from 1989 through 2001* (Washington, D.C.: Office of Juvenile Justice and Delinquency Prevention, 2002).

47. Snyder and Sickmund, *Juvenile Offenders and Victims*.

48. Michael J. Leiber, *The Contexts of Juvenile Justice Decision Making* (Albany: State University of New York, 2003).

49. Marvin E. Wolfgang, Robert M. Figlio, and Thorsten Sellin, *Delinquency in a Birth Cohort* (Chicago: University of Chicago Press, 1972).

50. Lyle W. Shannon, *Assessing the Relationships of Adult Criminal Careers to Juvenile Careers: A Summary* (Washington, D.C.: U.S. Government Printing Office, 1982).

51. Donna Martin Hamparian et al., *The Violent Few: A Study of Dangerous Juvenile Offenders* (Lexington, Mass.: Lexington Books, 1980).

52. Christopher Murray, Chris Baird, Ned Loughran, Fred Mills, and John Platt, *Safety and Welfare Plan: Implementing Reform in California* (Sacramento: California Department of Corrections and Rehabilitation, 2006), p. 1.

53. David W. Springer, *Transforming Juvenile Justice in Texas: A Framework for Action* (Austin, Tex.: Blue Ribbon Task Force Report, 2007).

54. M. Coates, R. Coates, and B. Vos, "The Impact of Victim–Offender Mediation—Two Decades of Research," *Federal Probation* 65 (2001), pp. 29–36.

55. Katherine van Wormer and Clemens Bartollas, *Women and the Criminal Justice System*, 3rd ed. (Upper Saddle River: Prentice-Hall, 2011).

56. Lawrence W. Sherman, David P. Farrington, and Brandon Welsh, *Understanding and Implementing Correctional Options That Work* (Harrisburg: Pennsylvania Department of Corrections, 2003).

57. Ibid.

CHAPTER 14

1. Interviewed in 1999 by author.

2. Robert Portune, *Changing Adolescent Attitudes toward Police* (Cincinnati, Ohio: Anderson, 1971).

3. L. Thomas Winfree Jr. and Curt T. Griffiths, "Adolescents' Attitudes toward the Police: A Survey of High School Students," in *Juvenile Delinquency: Little Brother Grows Up* (Beverly Hills, Calif.: Sage, 1977), pp. 79–99.

4. William T. Rusinko, W. Johnson Knowlton, and Carlton A. Hornung, "The Importance of Police Contact in the Formulation of Youths' Attitudes toward Police," *Journal of Criminal Justice* 6 (1978), pp. 53–76; J. P. Clark and E. P. Wenninger, "The Attitudes of Juveniles toward the Legal Institution," *Journal of Criminal Law, Criminology, and Police Science* 55 (1964), pp. 482–489; D. C. Gibbons, *Delinquent Behavior* (Englewood Cliffs, N.J.: Prentice-Hall, 1976); and V. I. Cizanckas and C. W. Purviance, "Changing Attitudes of Black Youths," *Police Chief* 40 (1973), pp. 42–45.

5. Scott H. Decker, "Citizen Attitudes toward the Police: A Review of Past Findings and Suggestions for Future Policy," *Journal of Police Science and Administration* 9 (1981), pp. 80–87.

6. Komanduri S. Murty, Julian B. Roebuck, and Joann D. Smith, "The Image of Police in Black Atlanta Communities," *Journal of Police Science and Administration* 17 (1990), pp. 250–257.

7. Michael J. Leiber, Mahesh K. Nalla, and Margaret Farnworth, "Explaining Juveniles' Attitudes toward the Police," *Justice Quarterly* 15 (March 1998), pp. 151–174.

8. Data for 2001 are from Lloyd D. Johnston, Jerald G. Bachman, and Patrick M. O'Malley, *Monitoring the Future Project Questionnaires Responses: High School Seniors* (Ann Arbor: Institute for Social Research, Survey Research Center, University of Michigan).

9. James Q. Wilson, "Dilemmas of Police Administration," *Police Administration Review* 28 (September–October 1968), pp. 407–417.

10. Stephanie M. Myers, *Police Encounters with Juvenile Suspects: Explaining the Use of Authority and Provision of Support* (Washington, D.C.: National Institute of Justice, 2004).

11. Donald J. Black and Albert J. Reiss Jr., "Police Control of Juveniles," *American Sociological Review* 35 (February 1979), pp. 63–77.

12. Robert M. Terry, "Discrimination in the Handling of Juvenile Offenders by Social Control Agencies," *Journal of Research in Crime and Delinquency* 4 (July 1967), pp. 218–230; Nathan Goldman, *The Differential Selection of Juvenile Offenders for Court Appearance* (New York: National Council on Crime and Delinquency 1963); Black and Reiss, "Police Control of Juveniles"; and Irving Piliavin and Scott Briar, "Police Encounters with Juveniles," *American Journal of Sociology* 70 (September 1964), pp. 206–214.

13. Terry, "Discrimination in the Handling of Juvenile Offenders"; Black and Weiss, "Police Control of Juveniles"; and Robert M. Emerson, *Judging Delinquents: Context and Process in Juvenile Court* (Chicago: Aldine, 1969).

14. Gail Armstrong, "Females under the Law—Protected but Unequal," *Crime and Delinquency* 23 (April 1977), pp. 109–120; Meda Chesney-Lind, "Judicial Paternalism and the Female Status Offender," *Crime and Delinquency* 23 (April 1977), pp. 121–130; and Meda Chesney-Lind, "Girls and Status Offenses: Is Juvenile Justice Still Sexist?" *Criminal Justice Abstracts* (March 1988), pp. 144–165.

15. Meda Chesney-Lind, "Juvenile Delinquency: The Sexualization of Female Crime," *Psychology Today* 8 (July 1974), pp. 43–46; and I. Richard Perleman, "Antisocial Behavior of the Minor in the United States," in *Society, Delinquency, and Delinquent Behavior*, edited by Harwin L. Voss (Boston: Little, Brown, 1970), pp. 35–43.

16. Theodore N. Ferdinand and Elmer C. Luchterhand, "Inner-City Youths, the Police, the Juvenile Court, and Justice," *Social Problems* 17 (Spring 1970), pp. 510–527; Goldman, *The Differential Selection of Juvenile Offenders for Court Appearance*; and Piliavin and Briar, "Police Encounters with Juveniles."

17. Marvin E. Wolfgang, Robert M. Figlio, and Thorsten Sellin, *Delinquency in a Birth Cohort* (Chicago: University of Chicago Press, 1972).

18. Philip W. Harris, "Race and Juvenile Justice: Examining the Impact of Structural and Policy Changes on Racial Disproportionality," paper presented at the 39th Annual Meeting of the American Society of Criminology, Montreal, Quebec, Canada, November 13, 1987.

19. James T. Carey et al., *The Handling of Juveniles from Offense to Disposition* (Washington, D.C.: U.S. Government Printing Office, 1976); A. W. McEachern and Riva Bauzer, "Factors Related to Disposition in Juvenile–Police Contacts," in *Juvenile Gangs in Context*, edited by Malcolm W. Klein (Englewood Cliffs, N.J.: Prentice-Hall, 1967), pp. 148–160; Thorsten Sellin and Marvin E. Wolfgang, *The Measurement of Delinquency* (New York: John Wiley & Sons, 1964); and Ferdinand and Luchterhand, "Inner-City Youths."

20. Merry Morash, "Establishment of Juvenile Police Record," *Criminology* 22 (February 1984), pp. 97–111.

21. Interview with an assistant police chief in August 1980.

22. Irving Piliavin and Scott Briar, "Police Encounters with Juveniles," *American Journal of Sociology* 70 (September 1964), pp. 206–214.

23. Carl Werthman and Irving Piliavin, "Gang Members and Police," in *The Police*, edited by David Jo. Bordua (New York: Wiley, 1967), pp. 56–98.

24. Richard J. Lundman, Richard E. Sykes, and John P. Clark, "Police Control of Juveniles: A Replication," *Journal of Research in Crime and Delinquency* 15 (January 1978), pp. 74–91.

25. David A. Klinger, "Demeanor or Crime? Why 'Hostile' Citizens Are More Likely to Be Arrested," *Criminology* 32 (1994), pp. 475–493; and David A. Klinger, "More on Demeanor and Arrest in Dade County," *Criminology* 34 (1996), pp. 61–82.

26. Robert E. Worden and Robin L. Shepard, "Demeanor, Crime, and Police Behavior: A Reexamination of the Police Services Study Data," *Criminology* 34 (1996), pp. 83–105.

27. Goldman, *The Differential Selection of Juvenile Offenders for Court Appearance*.

28. Wilson, "Dilemmas of Police Administration."

29. Howard N. Snyder and Melissa Sickmund, *Juvenile Offenders and Victims: 1999 National Report* (Washington, D.C.: National Center for Juvenile Justice, 1999).

30. Ibid.

31. Ibid.

32. A. Stahl, T. Finnegan, and W. Kang, *Easy Access to Juvenile Court Statistics: 1995–2000* (Washington, D.C.: National Center for Juvenile Justice, 2002).

33. The following section is based on H. Ted Rubin, *Juvenile Justice: Police Practice and Law* (Santa Monica, Calif.: Goodyear, 1979), pp. 75–82.

34. *Mapp v. Ohio*, 367 U.S. 643 (1961).

35. *State v. Lowry*, 230 A.2d 907 (1967).

36. *In re Two Brothers and a Case of Liquor,* Juvenile Court of the District of Columbia, 1966, reported in *Washington Law Reporter* 95 (1967), p. 113.

37. Ronald D. Stephens, "School-Based Interventions: Safety and Security," *The Gang Intervention Handbook*, edited by Arnold P. Goldstein and C. Ronald Huff (Champaign, Ill.: Research Press, 1993), p. 221.

38. *Haley v. Ohio*, 332 U.S. 596 (1948).

39. *Brown v. Mississippi*, 399 F.2d 467 (5th Cir. 1968).

40. Samuel M. Davis, *Rights of Juveniles: The Juvenile Justice System*, 2nd ed. (New York: Thompson, 2005), Sections 3–45.

41. *Miranda v. Arizona*, 384 U.S. 436 (1966).

42. *In re Gault*, 387 U.S. (1967).

43. *Fare v. Michael C.*, 442 U.S. 23, 99 S.Ct. 2560 (1979).

44. T. Grisso, *Juveniles' Waiver of Rights: Legal and Psychological Competence* (New York: Plenum Press, 1981).

45. *People v. Lara*, 62 Cal. Rptr. 586 (1967); cert. denied, 392 U.S. 945 (1968).

46. *In re Mellot*, 217 S.E. 2d 745 (C.A.N. Ca. 1975).

47. *In re Dennis P. Fletcher*, 248 A.2d. 364 (Md. 1968); cert. denied, 396 U.S. 852 (1969).

48. *Commonwealth v. Guyton*, 405 Mass. 497 (1989).

49. *Commonwealth v. McNeil*, 399 Mass. 71 (1987).

50. Gisli H. Gudjonsson, Jon Fridrik Sigurdsson, Inga Dora Sigfusdottir, and Bryndis Bjork Asgeirsdottir, "False Confession and Individual Differences: The Importance of Victimization among Youth," *Personality and Individual Differences* 45 (2008), pp. 801–805.

51. Elyce Z. Ferster and Thomas F. Courtless, "The Beginning of Juvenile Justice, Police Practices, and the Juvenile Offender," *Vanderbilt Law Review* 22 (April 1969), pp. 598–601.

52. Snyder and Sickmund, *Juvenile Offenders and Victims: 1999*.

53. *United States v. Wade*, 388 U.S. 218, 87 S.Ct. 1926 (1967).

54. *Kirby v. Illinois*, 406 U.S. 682, 92 S.Ct. 1877 (1972).

55. *In re Holley*, 107 R.I. 615, 268 A.2d 723 (1970).

56. Snyder and Sickmund, *Juvenile Offenders and Victims: 1999.*

57. *In re Carl T.*, 81 Cal. Rptr. 655 (2d C.A., 1969).

58. Gorden Bazemore and Scott Senjo, "Police Encounters with Juveniles Revisited," *International Journal of Police Strategies and Management* 20 (1997), pp. 60–82.

59. U.S. Department of Justice, "Community Policing," *National Institute of Justice Journal* 225 (1992), pp. 1–32.

60. Interview with Ann Miller in September 2001.

61. Office of Justice Programs, *America's Missing: Broadcast Emergency Response: Frequently Asked Questions on AMBER Alert.* www.amberalert.gov/faqs.html.

62. Snyder and Sickmund, *Juvenile Offenders and Victims: 1999.*

63. Howard N. Snyder and Melissa Sickmund, *Juvenile Offenders and Victims: 2006 National Report* (Washington, D.C.: National Center for Juvenile Justice, Office of Juvenile Justice and Delinquency Prevention, 2006).

64. See Mark S. Hamm, *American Skinheads: The Criminology and Control of Hate Crime* (Westport, Conn.: Praeger, 1993).

65. Snyder and Sickmund, *Juvenile Offenders and Victims: 2006 National Report.*

66. Finn-Aage Esbensen and D. Wayne Osgood, *National Evaluation of G.R.E.A.T.* (Washington, D.C.: National Institute of Justice, Office of Justice Programs, 1997).

67. Ibid.

68. Finn-Aage Esbensen and D. Wayne Osgood, "Gang Resistance Education and Training (G.R.E.A.T.): Results from the National Evaluation," *Journal of Research in Crime and Delinquency* 36 (1999), pp. 194–225.

69. Norman D. Wright, "From Risk to Resiliency: The Role of Law-Related Education," Institute on Law and Civil Education pamphlet (Des Moines, Iowa, June 20–21, 1995).

70. Carole L. Hahn, "The Status of the Social Studies in Public School in the United States: Another Look," *Social Education* 49 (1985), pp. 220–223.

71. Judith Warrent Little and Frances Haley, *Implementing Effective LRE Programs* (Boulder, Colo.: Social Science Education Consortium, 1982).

72. William DeJong, *Arresting the Demand for Drugs: Police and School Partnership to Prevent Drug Abuse* (Washington, D.C.: National Institute of Justice, 1987).

73. *COPS in Schools: The COPS Commitment to School Safety* (Washington, D.C.: Office of Community-Oriented Policing Services, n.d.). For how police resource officers spend their time, see Richard Lawrence, "The Role of Police–School Liaison Officers in School Crime Prevention," paper presented at the Annual Meeting of the Academy of Criminal Justice Sciences, Albuquerque, New Mexico, March 11, 1998.

74. Ronald D. Stephens, "School-Based Interventions: Safety and Security," in Arnold P. Goldstein and Ronald C. Huff, (eds.) *The Gang Intervention Handbook* (Champaign, IL: Research Press, 1993), pp. 219–256.

75. Jerome A. Needle and William Vaughn Stapleton, "Police Handling of Youth Gangs," in *Reports of the National Juvenile Justice Assessment Centers* (Washington, D.C.: U.S. Department of Justice, 1983).

76. Ibid.

77. National Institute of Justice, *The D.A.R.E. Program: A Review of Prevalence, User Satisfaction, and Effectiveness* (Washington, D.C.: U.S. Department of Justice, 1994).

78. Dennis P. Rosenbaum, "Just Say No to D.A.R.E.," *Crime and Public Policy* 6 (2007), pp. 815–824.

79. Ibid.

80. Ibid.

CHAPTER 15

1. David Stout, "Supreme Court Bars Death Penalty for Juvenile Killers," *New York Times*, March 1, 2005; Richard Willing, "Teen Killers' Executions Weighed," *USA Today*, October 11, 2004; and "Christopher Simmons," International Justice Project, March 1, 2005.

2. Gustav L. Schramm, "The Judge Meets the Boy and His Family," *National Probation Association 1945 Yearbook*, p. 182.

3. G. Larry Mays, "Transferring Juveniles to Adult Courts: Legal Guidelines and Constraints," paper presented at the Annual Meeting of the American Society of Criminology, Reno, Nevada, November 1989.

4. Barry Krisberg, *The Juvenile Court: Reclaiming the Vision* (San Francisco: National Council on Crime and Delinquency, 1988); Arnold Binder, "The Juvenile Court: The U.S. Constitution, and When the Twain Shall Meet," *Journal of Criminal Justice* 12 (1982), pp. 355–366; and Charles E. Springer, *Justice for Children* (Washington, D.C.: U.S. Department of Justice, 1986).

5. Lisa Aversa Richette, *The Throwaway Children* (New York: Lippincott, 1969); Patrick Murphy, *Our Kindly Parent— The State* (New York: Viking Press, 1974); Howard James, *Children in Trouble: A National Scandal* (New York: Pocket Books, 1971); and William Ayers, *A Kind and Just Parent* (Boston: Beacon Press, 1997).

6. Leonard P. Edwards, "The Juvenile Court and the Role of the Juvenile Court Judge," *National Council of Juvenile and Family Court Judges* 43 (1992), p. 4.

7. Ibid.

8. Ibid.

9. Cited in Edwards, "The Juvenile Court and the Role of the Juvenile Court Judge," p. 4.

10. Dean J. Champion, "Teenage Felons and Waiver Hearings: Some Recent Trends, 1980–1988," *Crime and Delinquency* 35 (October 1985), pp. 439–479.

11. Barry C. Feld, "The Transformation of the Juvenile Court," *Minnesota Law Review* 75 (February 1991), p. 711.

12. Drafted by the American Legislative Exchange Council and Rose Institute of State and Local Government at Claremont McKenna College, Claremont, California.

13. For an extensive discussion of these sweeping changes in Minnesota's juvenile code, see Barry C. Feld, "Violent Youth and Public Policy: A Case Study of Juvenile Justice Law Reform," *Minnesota Law Review* 79 (May 1995), pp. 965–1128.

14. See Feld, "The Transformation of the Juvenile Court," pp. 691–725; Barry C. Feld, "Criminalizing Juvenile Justice: Rules of Procedure for Juvenile Court," *Minnesota Law Review* 69 (1984), pp. 141–164; and Janet E. Ainsworth, "Re-Imagining Childhood and Reconstructing the Legal Order: The Case for Abolishing the Juvenile Court," in *Child, Parent, and State*, edited by S. Randall Humm, Beate Anna Ort, Martin Mazen Anbari, Wendy S. Lader, and William Scott Biel (Philadelphia: Temple University Press, 1994), pp. 561–595.

15. Jeffrey A. Butts and Adele V. Harrell, *Delinquents or Criminals: Policy Options for Young Offenders* (Washington, D.C.: Urban Institute, 1998).

16. Barry C. Feld, *Bad Kids: Race and the Transformation of Juvenile Court* (New York: Oxford University Press, 1999).

17. Ibid., p. 317.

18. Ibid.

19. Ibid.

20. For a biting criticism of this proposal to abolish the juvenile court, see Mark I. Soler, "Re-Imagining the Juvenile Court," in *Child, Parent, and State*, pp. 596–624.

21. Anthony M. Platt, *The Child Saver*, 2nd ed. (Chicago: University of Chicago Press, 1977), p. 144.

22. Ibid.

23. Frederic L. Faust and Paul J. Brantingham, eds., *Juvenile Justice Philosophy* (St. Paul, Minn.: West, 1974).

24. Ibid.

25. Ibid.

26. *Kent v. United States*, 383 U.S. 541, 86 S.Ct. 1045, 16 L.Ed.2d 84 (1966).

27. Ibid.

28. *In re Gault*, 387 U.S. 1, 18 L.Ed.2d 527, 87 S.Ct. 1428 (1967).

29. Ibid.

30. *Haley v. Ohio*, 332 U.S. 596 (1948); and *Gallegos v. Colorado*, 370 U.S. 49, 82 S.Ct. 1209 (1962).

31. *In re Winship*, 397 U.S. 358, 90 S.Ct. 1968, 25 L.Ed.2d 368 (1970).

32. *McKeiver v. Pennsylvania*, 403 U.S. 528, 535 (1971); *In re Barbara Burrus*, 275 N.C. 517, 169 S.E.2d 879 (1969); and *In re Terry*, 438 Pa., 339, 265A.2d 350 (1970).

33. *McKeiver v. Pennsylvania*.

34. Feld, "Violent Youth and Public Policy."

35. *Breed v. Jones*, 421 U.S. 519, 95 S.Ct. 1779 (1975).

36. H. Ted Rubin, *Juvenile Justice: Policy, Practice, and Law* (Santa Monica, Calif.: Goodyear Publishing, 1979).

37. See Charles Thomas and Ineke Marshall, "The Effect of Legal Representation on Juvenile Court Disposition," paper presented at the Southern Sociological Society in Louisville, April 8–11, 1981. Also see S. H. Clarke and G. G. Koch, "Juvenile Court: Therapy or Crime Control and Do Lawyers Make a Difference?" *Law and Society Review* 14 (1980), pp. 263–308.

38. Thomas and Marshall, "The Effect of Legal Representation on Juvenile Court Disposition."

39. Charles Puzzanchera and Melissa Sickmund, *Juvenile Court Statistics 2005* (Pittsburgh, Penn.: National Center for Juvenile Justice, 2008).

40. Brenda R. McCarthy, "An Analysis of Detention," *Juvenile and Family Court Journal* 36 (1985), pp. 43–59. For other discussions of detention, see Lydia Rosner, "Juvenile Secure Detention," *Journal of Offender Counseling, Services, and Rehabilitation* 12 (1988), pp. 77–93; and Charles E. Frazier and Donna M. Bishop, "The Pretrial Detention of Juveniles and Its Impact on Case Disposition," *Journal of Criminal Law and Criminology* 76 (1985), pp. 1132–1152.

41. Puzzanchera and Sickmund, *Juvenile Court Statistics 2005*.

42. *Creek v. Stone*, 379 F.2d 106 (D.C. Cir. 1967).

43. *Schall v. Martin* (1984), *United States Law Review* 52 (47), pp. 4681–4696.

44. Ibid., p. 4681.

45. Ibid.

46. Feld, "Criminalizing Juvenile Justice."

47. Duran Bell Jr. and Kevin Lang, "The Intake Dispositions of Juvenile Offenders," *Journal of Research on Crime and Delinquency* 22 (1985), pp. 309–328. See also Randall G. Sheldon and John A. Horvath, "Intake Processing in a Juvenile Court: A Comparison of Legal and Nonlegal Variables," *Juvenile and Family Court Journal* 38 (1987), pp. 13–19.

48. Bell and Lang, "The Intake Dispositions of Juvenile Offenders."

49. Puzzanchera and Sickmund, *Juvenile Court Statistics 2005*.

50. Emily Gaarder and Joanne Belknap, "Tenuous Borders: Girls Transferred to Adult Court," *Criminology* (August 2002), pp. 481–517.

51. Charles W. Thomas and Shay Bilchik, "Prosecuting Juveniles in Criminal Courts: A legal and Empirical Analysis," *Journal of Criminal Law and Criminology* 76 (Summer 1985), pp. 439–479.

52. Barry C. Feld, "The Juvenile Court Meets the Principle of the Offense: Legislative Changes in Juvenile Waiver Statutes," *Journal of Criminal Law and Criminology* 78 (1987), pp. 471–503.

53. Barry C. Feld, "Legislative Policies toward the Serious Juvenile Offender," *Crime and Delinquency* 27 (October 1981), pp. 497–521.

54. Ibid.

55. Samuel M. Davis, *Rights of Juveniles: The Juvenile Justice System*, 2nd ed. (New York: Clark Boardman Company, 1986), Section 4-2. See also Melissa Sickmund, *How Juveniles Get to Juvenile Court* (Washington, D.C.: Juvenile Justice Bulletin, 1994).

56. Davis, *Rights of Juveniles*.

57. Donna Bishop, Charles E. Frazier, and John C. Henretta, "Prosecutorial Waiver: Case Study of a Questionable Reform," *Crime and Delinquency* 35 (1989), pp. 179–201.

58. Marcy R. Podkopacz and Barry C. Feld, "The End of the Line: An Empirical Study of Judicial Waiver," *Journal of Criminal Law and Criminology* 86 (1996), pp. 449–492.

59. Lee Ann Osburn and Peter A. Rose, "Prosecuting Juveniles as Adults: The Question for 'Objective' Decisions," *Criminology* 22 (1984), pp. 187–202.

60. Donna M. Bishop, Charles E. Frazier, Lonn Lanza-Kaduce, and Lawrence Winner, "The Transfer of Juveniles to Criminal Court: Does It Make a Difference?" *Crime and Delinquency* 42 (1996), pp. 171–191.

61. Howard N. Snyder and Melissa Sickmund, *Juvenile Offenders and Victims: 2006 National Report* (Washington, D.C.: Department of Justice, Office of Justice Programs, 2006).

62. For example, in the laws of Pennsylvania, Act No. 333 (Section 18a) requires a hearing date within 10 days after the filing of a petition.

63. Rubin, *Juvenile Justice*.

64. Terence P. Thornberry, "Sentencing Disparities in the Juvenile Justice System," *Journal of Criminal Law and Criminology* 70 (Summer 1979), pp. 164–171.

65. M. A. Bortner, *Inside a Juvenile Court: The Tarnished Idea of Individualized Justice* (New York: New York University Press, 1982).

66. Lawrence Cohen, "Delinquency Dispositions: An Empirical Analysis of Processing Decisions in Three Juvenile Courts,"

Analytic Report 9 (Washington, D.C.: U.S. Government Printing Office, 1975), p. 51.

67. Rubin, *Juvenile Justice*. See also Joseph B. Sanborn, "Factors Perceived to Affect Delinquent Dispositions in Juvenile Court: Putting the Sentencing Decision into Context," *Crime and Delinquency* 42 (January 1996), pp. 99–113.

68. Ruth D. Peterson, "Youthful Offender Designations and Sentencing in the New York Criminal Courts," *Social Problems* 35 (April 1988), pp. 111–130. See also Christina De Jong and Kenneth C. Jackson, "Putting Race into Context: Race, Juvenile Justice Processing, and Urbanization, *Justice Quarterly* 15 (September 1998), pp. 487–504; and Barry C. Feld, "Social Structure, Race, and the Transformation of the Juvenile Court," paper presented at the Annual Meeting of the American Society of Criminology, Washington, D.C., November 1998.

69. Davis, *Rights of Juveniles*.

70. Ibid.

71. Feld, *Bad Kids*.

72. Martin L. Forst, Bruce A. Fisher, and Robert B. Coates, "Indeterminate and Determinate Sentencing of Juvenile Delinquents: A National Survey of Approaches to Commitment and Release Decision-Making," *Juvenile and Family Court Journal* 36 (Summer 1985), pp. 1–12.

73. Daniel P. Mears and Samuel H. Field, "Theorizing Sanctioning in a Criminalized Juvenile Court," *Criminology* 38 (November 2000), pp. 983–1020.

74. Ibid.

75. Barry Feld, "Violent Youth and Public Policy: Minnesota Juvenile Justice Task Force and 1994 Legislative Reform," paper presented at the Annual Meeting of the American Society of Criminology, Miami, Florida, 1994. See also Feld, "Violent Youth and Public Policy."

76. Barry Krisberg et al., *Guide for Implementing the Comprehensive Strategy for Serious, Violent, and Chronic Juvenile Offenders* (Washington, D.C.: Office of Juvenile Justice and Delinquency Prevention, 1995).

77. John J. Wilson and James C. Howell, *Serious and Chronic Juvenile Offenders: A Comprehensive Strategy,* Fact Sheet #4 (Washington, D.C.: U.S. Department of Justice, August 1993).

78. Ibid.

79. Ibid.

80. Shelley Zavlek, *Planning Community-Based Facilities for Violent Juvenile Offenders as Part of a System of Graduated Sanctions* (Washington, D.C.: Office of Juvenile Justice and Delinquency Prevention, 2005), p. 5.

81. Ibid.

82. Richard Redding, "Juvenile Transfer Laws: An Effective Deterrent to Delinquency?" *Juvenile Justice Bulletin* (Washington, D.C.: OJJDP, U.S. Department of Justice, 2008).

83. L. Lanza-Kaduce, F. Lane, D. M. Bishop, and C. E. Frazier, "Juvenile Offenders and Adult Felony Recidivism: The Impact of Transfer," *Journal of Crime and Justice* 28 (2005), pp. 59–77.

84. Ibid.

85. Redding, "Juvenile Transfer Laws: An Effective Deterrent to Delinquency?"

86. Clemens Bartollas, Stuart J. Miller, and Simon Dinitz, unpublished manuscript.

87. "Death in Prison Sentences for 13- and 14–Year–Olds." http://www.cji.org/eji/childrenprison/deathinprison.

88. Associated Press, "High Court Looks at Life in Prison for Juveniles," http://www.msnbc.msn.com/id/33789880/ns/politics-more_politics/?gt1=43001; accessed January 2, 2010.

89. National Council of Juvenile and Family Court Judges, *Juvenile Delinquency Guidelines: Improving Court Practice in Juvenile Delinquency Cases* (Reno, Nevada: National Council of Juvenile and Family Court Judges, 2005).

90. Ibid.

CHAPTER 16

1. Christopher Murray, Chris Baird, Ned Loughran, Fred Mills, and John Platt, *Safety and Welfare Plan: Implementing Reform in California* (Sacramento, Calfiornia: California Department of Corrections and Rehabilitation, Division of Juvenile Justice, 2006).

2. David W. Springer, *Transforming Juvenile Justice in Texas: A Framework for Action* (Austin: Blue Ribbon Task Force Report, 2007).

3. "Juvenile School Would Grow," *Hartford Courant*, February 10, 2008; Alison Leigh Cowan, "New Connecticut Law May Save a Troubled Prison for Juveniles," *New York Times*, July 30, 2007; Christine Stuart, "Juvenile Injustice," *CT News Junkie*, July 19, 2006; and Nan Shnitzler, "Connecticut Juvenile Training School to Close," *New England Psychologist*, October 2005, http://www.masspsy.com/leading/0510_ne_CT.html.

4. Holbrook Mohr, "18 Cruelty and Death in Juvenile Detention Centers," Associated Press, March 2, 2008.

5. Ibid.

6. Patrick Griffin and Patricia Torbet, eds., *Desktop Guide to Good Juvenile Probation Practice* (Washington, D.C.: National Center for Juvenile Justice, 2002), p. 2.

7. Ibid.

8. Ibid.

9. Ibid.

10. Larry Grubb, juvenile probation officer in Sangamon County, Illinois, was extremely helpful in shaping this section on the functions of probation.

11. OJJDP Model Program Guide, *Restitution/Community Service*. www.dsgonline.com/mpg_non_flash/restitution?community?service.htm.

12. Griffin and Torbet, *Desktop Guide to Good Juvenile Probation Practice*.

13. Ibid.

14. Information gained during an on-site visit and updated in a phone call to a staff member in September 2001.

15. See James Byrne, Arthur Lurigio, and Joan Petersilia, "Smart Sentencing: The Emergence of Intermediate Sanctions," *Federal Probation* 50 (1986), pp. 166–181; and Emily Walker, "The Community Intensive Treatment for Youth Program: A Specialized Community-Based Program for High-Risk Youth in Alabama," *Law and Psychology Review* 13 (1989), pp. 175–199.

16. Cecil Marshall and Keith Snyder, "Intensive and Aftercare Probation Services in Pennsylvania," paper presented at the Annual Meeting of the American Society of Criminology, Baltimore, Maryland, November 7, 1990.

17. Ted Palmer, *The Re-Emergence of Correctional Intervention* (Newbury Park, Calif.: Sage, 1992), p. 82.

18. Barry Krisberg et al., *Juvenile Intensive Planning Guide* (Washington, D.C.: Office of Juvenile Justice and Delinquency Prevention, 1994).

19. Richard A. Ball, Ronald Huff, and J. Robert Lilly, *House Arrest and Correctional Policy: Doing Time at Home* (Newbury Park, Calif.: Sage, 1988).

20. Griffin and Torbet, *Desktop Guide to Good Juvenile Probation Practice.*

21. TDCJ-Community Justice Assistance Division, *Electronic Monitoring: Agency Brief* (Austin: Texas Department of Criminal Justice, 1997).

22. Joseph B. Vaughn, "A Survey of Juvenile Electronic Monitoring and Home Confinement Program," *Juvenile and Family Court Journal* 40 (1989), pp. 1–36.

23. TDCJ-Community Justice Assistance Division, *Electronic Monitoring.*

24. Ibid.

25. Oliver J. Keller Jr. and Benedict S. Alper, *Halfway Houses: Community-Centered Correction and Treatment* (Lexington, Mass.: D. C. Heath, 1970).

26. D. L. Fixsen, E. L. Philllips, and M. M. Wolf, "The Teaching Family Model of Group Home Treatment," in *Closing Correctional Institutions,* edited by Yitzak Bakal (Lexington, Mass.: D. C. Heath, 1973), pp. 107–116.

27. Ronald H. Bailey, "Florida," *Corrections Magazine* 1 (September 1974), p. 66.

28. Information from Dynamic Action Resistance Enterprise (DARE), Jamaica Plain, Massachusetts.

29. Information on Associated Marine Institutes supplied in a phone conversation with Ms. Magie Valdès in 1996.

30. Ibid. See also Ronald H. Bailey, "Can Delinquents Be Saved by the Sea?" *Corrections Magazine* 1 (September 1974), pp. 77–84.

31. Refer to Joshua L. Miner and Joe Boldt, *Outward Bound USA: Learning through Experience* (New York: William Morrow, 1981). For other examinations of Outward Bound–type programs, see Steven Flagg Scott, "Outward Bound: An Adjunct to the Treatment of Juvenile Delinquents: Florida's STEP Program," *New England Journal on Criminal and Civil Confinement* 11 (1985), pp. 420–436; and Thomas C. Castellano and Irina R. Soderstrom, "Wilderness Challenges and Recidivism: A Program Evaluation," paper presented at the Annual Meeting of the American Society of Criminology, Baltimore, Maryland, November 1990.

32. *Outward Bound USA.* www.outwardbound.org/outreach.html.

33. Howard N. Snyder and Melissa Sickmund, *Juvenile Offenders and Victims: 2006 National Report* (Washington, D.C.: National Center for Juvenile Justice, Office of Justice Programs, 2006).

34. Ibid.

35. Ibid.

36. Ibid.

37. Ibid.

38. Murray, Baird, Loughran, Mills, and Platt, *Safety and Welfare Plan.*

39. Jean Bottcher, "Evaluating the Youth Authority's Boot Camp: The First Five Months," paper presented at the Western Society of Criminology, Monterey, California, February 1993; and Institute for Criminological Research and American Institute for Research, *Boot Camp for Juvenile Offenders: Constructive Intervention and Early Support—Implementation Evaluation Final Report* (New Brunswick, N.J.: Rutgers University, 1992).

40. Roberta C. Cronin, *Boot Camps for Adult and Juvenile Offenders: Overview and Update.* Final Summary Report Presented to the National Institute of Justice (1994), p. 37.

41. Anthony W. Salerno, "Boot Camps: A Critique and a Proposed Alternative," *Journal of Offender Rehabilitation* 20 (1994), pp. 147–158.

42. Ibid.

43. Doris Layton MacKenzie, David B. Wilson, Gaylene Styve Armstrong, and Angela R. Gover, "The Impact of Boot Camps and Traditional Institutions on Juvenile Residents: Perceptions, Adjustment, and Change," *Journal of Research in Crime and Delinquency* 38 (August 2000), pp. 279–313.

44. Ibid. See also Gaylene Styve Armstrong and Doris Layton MacKenzie, "Private versus Public Juvenile Correctional Facilities: Do Differences in Environmental Quality Exist?" *Crime and Delinquency* 49 (October 2003), pp. 542–563.

45. MacKenzie et al., "The Impact of Boot Camps and Traditional Institutions on Juvenile Residents."

46. Alexandra Marks, "States Fall Out of (Tough) Love with Boot Camps," *Christian Science Monitor*, December 27, 1999, p. 1.

47. Associated Press, "Teen Dies at Boot Camp for Troubled Kids," *Milwaukee Times*, July 4, 2001. For an article that suggests that what takes place at boot camps may be considered cruel and unusual and give rise to costly inmate litigation, see Faith E. Lutze and David C. Brody, "Mental Abuse as Cruel and Unusual Punishment: Do Boot Camp Prisons Violate the Eighth Amendment?" *Crime and Delinquency* 45 (April 1999), pp. 242–255.

48. Marks, "States Fall Out of (Tough) Love with Boot Camps."

49. Steve Lerner, *Bodily Harm: The Pattern of Fear and Violence at the California Youth Authority* (Bolinas, Calif.: Common Knowledge Press, 1986). For other studies of gangs in training schools, see L. Thomas Winfree Jr. and G. Larry Mays, "Family and Peer Influences on Gang Involvement: A Comparison of Institutionalized and Free-World Youths in a Southeastern State," paper presented at the Annual Meeting of the American Society of Criminology, Boston, Massachusetts, November 1994; L. Thomas Winfree Jr., G. Larry Mays, and Teresa Vigil-Backstrom, "Youth Gangs and Incarcerated Delinquents: Exploring the Ties between Gang Membership, Delinquency and Social Learning Theory," *Justice Quarterly* 11 (June 1994), pp. 229–256; Task Force Report of the National Gang Crime Research Center, "The Economics of Gang Life," paper presented at the Annual Meeting of the Academy of Criminal Justice Sciences, Boston, Massachusetts, March 1995; Task Force Report of the National Gang Crime Research Center, "The Economics of Gang Life," paper presented at the Annual Meeting of the Academy of Criminal Justice Sciences, Boston, Massachusetts, March 1995; and M. A. Bortner and Linda M. Williams, *Youth in Prison: We the People of Unit Four* (New York: Routledge, 1997).

50. For the diverse forms of state juvenile institutionalization, see Kelly Dedel, "National Profile of the Organization of Juvenile Correctional Systems," *Crime and Delinquency* 44 (1998), pp. 507–525.

51. Bradford Smith, "Children in Custody: 20-Year Trends in Juvenile Detention, Correctional, and Shelter Facilities," *Crime and Delinquency* 44 (October 1998), pp. 526–543.

52. Bartollas has conducted research of juvenile institutions in Illinois, Iowa, Minnesota, North Carolina, Ohio, and South Carolina.

53. Ibid.

54. Mark W. Lipsey, David B. Wilson, and Lynn Cothern, *Effective Intervention for Serious Juvenile Offenders: Juvenile Justice Bulletin* (Washington, D.C.: Office of Juvenile Justice and Delinquency Prevention, 2000).

55. Randall G. Sheldon and Sharon Tracey, "Violent Female Juvenile Offenders: An Ignored Minority with the Juvenile Justice System," *Juvenile and Family Court Journal* 43 (1992), pp. 33–40.

56. Bartollas's examination of training schools in six states led him to these conclusions. Also, he worked in one Ohio training school for four years.

57. Ibid.

58. Peter W. Greenwood, Susan Turner, and Kathy Rosenblatt, *Evaluation of Paint Creek Youth Center: Preliminary Results* (Santa Monica, Calif.: RAND, 1989).

59. Ibid.

60. For an examination of recommendations for positive leadership of juvenile facilities, see Joseph Heinz, Theresa Wise, and Clemens Bartollas, *Successful Management of Juvenile Residential Facilities: A Performance-Based Approach* (Alexandria, Virginia: American Correctional Association, 2010).

61. David Shichor and Clemens Bartollas, "Private and Public Placements: Is There a Difference?" *Crime and Delinquency* 36 (April 1990), pp. 289–299.

62. Gordon E. Barker and W. Thomas Adams, "The Social Structure of a Correctional Institution," *Journal of Criminal Law, Criminology and Police Science* 49 (1959), pp. 417–499.

63. Howard Polsky, *Cottage Six: The Social System of Delinquent Boys in Residential Treatment* (New York: Russell Sage Foundation, 1963), pp. 69–88.

64. Sethard Fisher, "Social Organization in a Correction Residence," *Pacific Sociological Review* 5 (Fall 1961), p. 89.

65. Ibid., pp. 89–90.

66. Clemens Bartollas, Stuart J. Miller, and Simon Dinitz, *Juvenile Victimization: the Institutional Paradox* (New York: Halsted Press, 1976), pp. 131–150.

67. Stuart J. Miller, Clemens Bartollas, and Simon Dinitz, "Juvenile Victimization Revisited: A Fifteen-Year Follow-Up at TICO" (unpublished manuscript, 1989).

68. M. Forst, J. Fagan, and T. S. Vivona, "Youth in Prisons and Training Schools: Perceptions and Consequences of the Treatment-Custody Dichotomy," *Juvenile and Family Court Journal* 40 (1989), pp. 1–14.

69. A. Sedlack, "Sexual Assault of Youth in Residential Placement," presentation at Bureau of Justice Statistics Workshop, Washington, D.C., January 18, 2005.

70. A. J. Beck and T. A. Hugher, *Sexual Violence Reported by Correctional Authorities 2004* (Washington, D.C.: Bureau of Justice Statistics, 2005).

71. Richard Tewsbury, "What We Know about Sexual Violence in Juvenile Corrections," paper presented at the 2007 Winter Conference, Grapevine, Texas.

72. Ibid.

73. Rose Giallombardo, *The Social World of Imprisoned Girls: A Comparative Study of Institutions for Juvenile Delinquents* (New York: John Wiley & Sons, 1974).

74. Ibid.

75. Alice Propper, *Prison Homosexuality: Myth and Reality* (Lexington, Mass.: D. C. Heath, 1981).

76. Christopher M. Sieverdes and Clemens Bartollas, "Institutional Adjustment among Female Delinquents," in *Administrative Issues in Criminal Justice,* edited by Alvin W. Cohn and Ben Ward (Beverly Hills, Calif.: Sage, 1981), pp. 91–103.

77. Ibid.

78. Clemens Bartollas and Christopher M. Sieverdes, "The Victimized White in a Juvenile Correctional System," *Crime and Delinquency* 34 (October 1981), pp. 534–543.

79. Ibid.

80. *White v. Reid*, 125 F. Supp. (D. D. C. 1954); *Inmates of the Boys' Training School v. Affeck*, 346 F. Supp. 1354 and (D. R. I. 1972); and *Nelson v. Heyne*, 355 F. Supp. 451 (N. D. Ind. 1973).

81. *Morales v. Turman*, 364 F. Supp. 166 (E. D. Tex. 1973); *Morales v. Turman*, No. 74-3436, U.S. Court of Appeals for the Fifth Circuit, 562 F.2d 993; 1977 U.S. App. LEXIS 10794, November 11, 1977. As corrected, Petition for Rehearing and Rearing En Banc; denied December 16, 1977; *Morales v. Turman*, Civil Action No. 1948, United States District Court for the Eastern District of Texas, Sherman Division, 569 F. Supp. 332; 1983 U.S. Dist. LEXIS 15935; and 37 Fed. R. Serv. 2d (Callaghan) 1294, June 28, 1983.

82. Ibid.

83. Adrienne Volnik, "Right to Treatment: Case Development in Juvenile Law," *Justice System Journal* 3 (Spring 1973), pp. 303–304.

84. *Pena v. New York State Division for Youth*, 419 F. Supp. 203 (S. D. N. Y. 1976); *Morales v. Turman* and *Morgan v. Sproat*, 432 F. Supp. 1130 (S. D. Miss. 1977); and *State v. Werner*, 242 S.E.2d 907 (W. Va. 1978).

85. See *Lollis v. New York State Dept. of Social Services*, 322 F. Supp. 473 (S. D. N. Y. 1970); and *U.S. ex. rel. Stewart v. Coughlin*, No. C. 1793 (N. D. 111, November 22, 1971).

86. *Alexander v. Boys and South Carolina Department of Juvenile Justice*, 876 F. Supp. 773 (1995).

87. *Morgan v. Sproat*, 432 F. Supp. 1130, 1136 (S.D. Miss. 1997).

88. *Germany v. Vance*, 868 F.2d 9 (1st Cir. 1989).

89. *John L. v. Adams*, 969 F.2d 228 (6th Cir. 1992).

90. Patricia Puritz and Mary Ann Scali, *Beyond the Walls: Improving Conditions of Confinement for Youth in Custody: Report* (Washington, D.C.: Office of Juvenile Justice and Delinquency Prevention, 1998).

91. Kristin Parsons Winokur, Alisa Smith, Stephanie R. Bontranger, and Julia L. Blankenship, "Juvenile Recidivism and Length of Stay," *Journal of Criminal Justice* 36 (2008), pp. 126–137.

92. Patricia McFall Torbet, *Organization and Administration of Juvenile Services: Probation, Aftercare, and State Delinquent Institutions* (Pittsburgh, Penn.: National Center for Juvenile Justice, 1988).

93. D. M. Altschuler and T. L. Armstrong, *Intensive Aftercare for High-Risk Juveniles: A Community Care Model* (Washington, D.C.: Office of Juvenile Justice and Delinquency Prevention, 1994).

94. Palmer, *The Re-Emergence of Correctional Intervention.*

95. David M. Altschuler and Troy L. Armstrong, *Intensive Aftercare for High-Risk Juveniles: Policies and Procedures* (Washington, D.C.: Office of Juvenile Justice and Delinquency Prevention, 1994).

96. For more extensive examination of these intensive aftercare programs, see Betsie McNulty, Richard Wiebush, and Thao Le, "Intensive Aftercare Programs for Serious Juvenile Offenders: Preliminary Results of Process and Outcome Evaluation," paper presented at the Annual Meeting of the American Society of Criminology, Washington, D.C., November 1998.

97. Richard G. Wiebush, Betsie McNulty, and Thao Le, *Implementation of the Intensive Community-Based Aftercare Program* (Washington, D.C.: Office of Juvenile Justice and Delinquency Prevention, 2000).

98. For an example of a house detention component of an aftercare program, see W. H. Barton and Jeffrey A. Butts, "Visible Options: Intensive Supervision Program for Juvenile Delinquents," *Crime and Delinquency* (1990), pp. 238–256.

99. Melissa Sickmund, *Juveniles in Corrections: National Report Series Bulletin* (Washington, D.C.: Office of Juvenile Justice and Delinquency Prevention, 2004).

100. Donna Hamparian et al., "Youth in Adult Court: Between Two Worlds," *Major Issues in Juvenile Justice Information and Training* (Columbus, Ohio: Academy for Contemporary Problems, 1981).

101. Vic Rychaert, "15 Youths Doing Time with State's Meanest," *Indianapolis Star,* April 30, 2001.

102. Snyder and Sickmund, *Juvenile Offenders and Victims.*

103. Dedel, "National Profile of the Organization of State Juvenile Corrections Systems."

104. For a list of these studies, see Winokur, Smith, Bontranger, and Blankenship, "Juvenile Recidivism and Length of Stay," p. 127.

105. Ashley G. Blackgurn, Janet L. Mullings, James W. Marquart, and Chad R. Trulson, "Toward an Understanding of Violent Institutionalized Delinquents," *Youth Violence and Juvenile Justice* (January 2007), pp. 35–56.

106. Ibid., p. 1.

107. Ibid.

108. Winokur, Smith, Bontranger, and Blankenship, "Juvenile Recidivism and Length of Stay."

109. J. Myner, J. Sandman, G. Cappelletty, and B. Perimutter, "Variables Related to Recidivism among Juvenile Offenders," *International Journal of Offender Therapy and Comparative Criminology* 42 (1998), pp. 65–80.

110. P. Buderi, *Secrecy Shrouds Decisions about Release of Juvenile Major Offenders: Far Ranging Negative Ramifications Likely* (Richmond: Mental Health Association of Virginia Public Policy and Advocacy, 1999).

111. D. Gottfredson and W. H. Barton, "Deinstitutionalization of Juvenile Offenders," *Criminology* 31 (1993), pp. 591–610.

112. Ibid.

113. Winokur, Smith, Bontranger, and Blankenship, "Juvenile Recidivism and Length of Stay."

114. Sedlack, *Sexual Assault of Youth in Residential Placement.*

115. See *Criminal Justice Newsletter* (Letter Publications, 2008).

Photo Credits

Subject Index